Dimensions of Tolerance

DIMENSIONS

OF

TOLERANCE

What Americans Believe about Civil Liberties

Herbert McClosky

and

Alida Brill

Russell Sage Foundation / New York

The Russell Sage Foundation

The Russell Sage Foundation, one of the oldest of America's general purpose foundations, was established in 1907 by Mrs. Margaret Olivia Sage for "the improvement of social and living conditions in the United States." The Foundation seeks to fulfill this mandate by fostering the development and dissemination of knowledge about the political, social, and economic problems of America. It conducts research in the social sciences and public policy, and publishes books and pamphlets that derive from this research.

The Foundation provides support for individual scholars and collaborates with other granting agencies and academic institutions in studies of social problems. It maintains a professional staff of social scientists who engage in their own research as well as advise on Foundation programs and projects. The Foundation also conducts a Visiting Scholar Program, under which established scholars working in areas of current interest to the Foundation join the staff for a year to consult and to continue their own research and writing. Finally, a Postdoctoral Fellowship Program enables promising young scholars to devote full time to their research while in residence for a year at the Foundation.

The Board of Trustees is responsible for the general policies and oversight of the Foundation, while the immediate administrative direction of the program and staff is vested in the President, assisted by the officers and staff. The President bears final responsibility for the decision to publish a manuscript as a Russell Sage Foundation book. In reaching a judgment on the competence, accuracy, and objectivity of each study, the President is advised by the staff and a panel of special readers.

The conclusions and interpretations in Russell Sage Foundation publications are those of the authors and not of the Foundation, its Trustees, or its staff. Publication by the Foundation, therefore, does not imply endorsement of the contents of the study. It does signify that the manuscript has been reviewed by competent scholars in the field and that the Foundation finds it worthy of public consideration.

Library of Congress Catalog Number: 82-72959
ISBN: 0-87154-591-8
10 9 8 7 6 5 4 3 2 1

Contents

3 2 3. 4
M 1 3 2 c

v

Contents

Acknowledgments

ALTHOUGH the practice of thanking others who have helped in the conduct of research and the preparation of a book has become something of a ritual, the thanks we wish to express here are meant to be anything but ritualistic.

A project as extensive as the civil liberties study on which this book reports is bound to owe a great many debts to a great many people. Its completion could never have been accomplished by the authors alone, but required the able and generous assistance of many colleagues, staff members, and friends, to whom we wish to express our sincerest gratitude.

The research for this book and the preparation of the manuscript were made possible by a grant from the Russell Sage Foundation. Colleagues at the foundation offered numerous helpful suggestions for the design of the study and critical comments on the drafts of the manuscript. We greatly benefited from the support of the foundation's officers and board of trustees. Hugh (Tony) Cline, former president of the Russell Sage Foundation, warmly encouraged the development of the proposal which led to the funding of the research. Marshall A. Robinson, the current president of the foundation, was patient and helpful during the final stages of the writing and editing of the manuscript.

Professor Stanton Wheeler offered valuable advice which clarified our ideas on the legal aspects of civil liberties, and his friendship and loyalty helped us through difficult days during the later stages of the project.

We are also indebted to David B. Truman for his professional and personal commitment to the project, for his wise counsel, and for the intellectual and spiritual refueling he offered at every detour we encountered in the course of our efforts.

We are deeply grateful to Mr. Arthur Keiser and the Gallup Organization for their assistance in distributing our questionnaire to a na-

Acknowledgments

tional cross-section sample of the general population and in selecting our sample of opinion leaders in some three hundred communities across the nation. Without their bountiful cooperation, counsel, and help, this study might never have been possible.

The Survey Research Center at the University of California, Berkeley, was the home base for this project, and we were greatly dependent upon its staff and facilities for the administration of the project. Under the expert direction of Selma Monsky's Field Survey Services department, the countless tasks involved in converting raw questionnaire responses into research findings were handled as painlessly as possible. We are especially grateful to Sheila Leary, who supervised the coding of the questionnaire responses; to Heidi Nebel, who had major responsibility for data reduction and the preparation and "cleaning" of computer tapes; and to Cynthia Warias, for her cooperative and efficient handling of administrative and budgetary matters.

We were fortunate to have at the Center a superbly qualified and devoted research and support staff. Among our research assistants, Charles A. Bann, Dennis Chong, and Barbara Geddes not only took charge of much of the computing required by the project, but contributed greatly to the intellectual product through their excellent research memoranda and their penetrating and invaluable criticisms and suggestions on all aspects of the research and writing. A colleague, Professor Christopher Achen, made available to us his superb skills as a research methodologist, and we found more than one occasion to avail ourselves of his keen insights and judicious advice.

We also wish to thank Don Chisholm, Scott Thompson, and Eileen Zimkind, who assisted the project during its initial stages. E. Deborah Jay and Russell Neuman played a vital role at the data collection stage of the Opinions and Values Survey (OVS), from which we have drawn some of the findings reported in the present volume. John Zaller, also a research assistant on the OVS project, offered valuable advice and criticisms for the Civil Liberties Survey.

The help and cooperation we received from the support staff of the project was extraordinary. Their contribution to the day-to-day operation of the project was both indispensable and extremely gratifying. A group of ever-patient secretaries and clerical staff assisted with the collection of data, maintained our extensive records and files, helped to prepare the code book and other essential documentation, and turned our scribbles into readable prose. We wish to express our heartfelt thanks to Kirsten Hydorn, Rebecca Klatch, Nancy Schremp, Lois Schwartz, Sharon Sample, Alice Roberts, Hetty de Sterke, and Madeline Spitaleri. Thanks are also due to Carol McKevitt, who, in exemplary fashion, prepared and maintained the vital records of the project during the past few years, handled our library affairs, organized and typed many of the tables, and assisted in the typing of parts of the manuscript.

In New York, the heaviest responsibility for typing a seemingly endless number of research memoranda, tables, and draft chapters of the manuscript fell to John Brennan, while in Berkeley similar responsibilities were assumed by Roberta Friedman. We are enormously grateful to both of them for the care, efficiency, and intelligence they exhibited in performing tasks which, though indispensable to the completion of this book, were often tedious and made the most severe demands on their patience, accuracy, alertness, and good will.

We owe a special debt to a group of (former) graduating seniors from the School of Law, University of California, Berkeley, who, at our request and under the supervision of Gary L. Bostwick, prepared an excellent set of highly instructive memoranda summarizing the state of the law in the various domains of civil liberties, which provided us with vital background material for chapters 2 to 5. The law students, and the domains of civil liberties law they summarized, were Brent Appel (due process), Gary Bostwick (privacy, lifestyle), Evelyn Christine Cooper (freedom of speech, press, and the First Amendment), Richard A. Cowart (restrictions and qualifications on due process), Henry Lerner (the rights of criminal defendants), Wendy Morgan (lifestyle), Jessica Pers (academic freedom), and Arnold Wagner (freedom of assembly and religion). Professor Alan Westin and Professor Howard Latin advised us on the various concepts and legal issues raised in our discussion of privacy in chapter 5.

We were also fortunate in having the manuscript reviewed by an unusually qualified group of editors, including Jean C. Yoder and Herbert Morton, who offered insightful comments. Priscilla Lewis, publications director at the Russell Sage Foundation, guided the manuscript through each stage of production with skill and nurturance. Sylvia Newman edited the manuscript and greatly improved it by her exceptional editorial judgment. Fred Haynes prepared the numerous figures, bringing patient and meticulous attention to their variety and detail. Jane Isay, copublisher of Basic Books, represents the best of what a publisher and editor should be—wise, critical, loyal, demanding, and untiring.

The civil liberties project was inspired by a conversation with Professor J. Merrill Shanks, then director of the Survey Research Center,

Acknowledgments

Berkeley. It was he who first emphasized the desirability of undertaking at the Center a new, updated study of the attitudes of Americans toward civil liberties, and he followed that suggestion with unwavering support for every phase of the project from its earliest days to its completion as a manuscript. Without his initial inspiration, and continued backing and assistance, it is doubtful that the civil liberties project would ever have come into existence.

Perhaps our most invaluable critic was Robert K. Merton, without whose continuing assistance and illuminating observations and suggestions this project might have remained only an interesting data set. Professor Merton read the manuscript with extraordinary care and attention to detail as well as reasoning, noting every intellectual snare and pitfall along the way and taking the trouble to suggest alternative routes that were more firmly grounded. His comments led us to rethink, and to revise many parts of the manuscript. Any flaws in reasoning or interpretation that remain can be traced to our failure to take full advantage of his sagacious advice.

We wish, finally, to express our great debt to the thousands of respondents across the country who agreed to participate in this study, selflessly completing lengthy (twenty-four-page) questionnaires and answering hundreds of questions on dozens of vexing issues. That so many people were willing to labor so long, with no gain to themselves but only for the sake of enhancing knowledge, was extremely gratifying.

The caveat exonerating all others for errors of fact or interpretation is a familiar one, but no less valid here on that account. We have been fortunate to have the advice and assistance of a splendid group of associates, but we alone are responsible for any misstatements, misinterpretations, or other failings that remain.

Alida Brill   Herbert McClosky
New York City, 1983   *Berkeley, California, 1983*

Dimensions of Tolerance

CHAPTER 1

An Introduction to the Nature of Freedom and Tolerance

WHEN, in 1762, Rousseau opened his classic treatise *The Social Contract* with the thundering pronouncement that "Man is born free [yet] everywhere he is in chains" and asked how this curious condition might be legitimated, he was, in effect, raising the moral question that underlies all forms of social control: namely, by what right does one person gain the authority to rule another? If, as Rousseau believed, human beings are free by nature and therefore it violates the "natural order to alienate [their] liberty," how can anyone legitimately curtail their freedom, censor their opinions and conduct, and compel them to obey rules which they dislike and would prefer to renounce?

The question posed by Rousseau is among the most fundamental in political philosophy. It seeks to discover and to establish the grounds by which some individuals acquire the moral authority to command others, even to the point of requiring them to obey—indeed, to obey willingly—decisions they may despise.

While we hope in the course of this book to illuminate some of the moral issues surrounding freedom and control, the overarching question on which we shall focus is not, however, Rousseau's moral dilemma about the legitimacy of authority. It is the question of what influences prompt some men and women to honor and protect civil liberties, while others give priority to obedience and conformity. Because our primary emphasis will be empirical rather than moral or philosophical, we intend to address, through the analysis of the data we have collected in the studies on which we shall report, such conflicting but interrelated questions as: Why are some people led to honor and protect the liberties even of those they despise? Why are others led to repress the liberties of fellow citizens—to choose to censor those who hold unconventional beliefs? In this volume, thus, we shall pay more attention to the "causal" why than to the "moral" or "normative" why.

We also depart from Rousseau in his conviction, common to Enlightenment philosophers of the eighteenth century, that freedom is part of the "natural" order. Enlightenment philosophers believed that human beings yearn *by nature* to be free and are in chains not because they take naturally to bondage but because autocrats and their confederates, through usurpations of powers that rightfully belong to the governed, have enveloped their subjects in a web of large and small tyrannies.

While we share the Enlightenment view that people rarely *choose* to be slaves, we are not convinced that the craving for freedom is inborn, much less that tolerance of others and the notion of reciprocity of rights are inclinations natural to everyone. Although freedom has emerged in some parts of the world as a preferred condition, the desire for it scarcely represents the manifestation of an innate human trait. Of the many social practices invented to accommodate differences among people, none is more remarkable than freedom. In our view, what makes political freedom so extraordinary is precisely that it gives evidence of being, if anything, "unnatural." Data from studies of psychological and group behavior (see, for example, the Asch, Sherif, Festinger, and numerous other group-conformity experiments) suggest that it is probably contrary to human impulse to endure, much less to encourage, deviant opinions or behaviors on the part of others, especially if their opinions and conduct are perceived as threatening to one's own interests and values, or, equally distressing, potentially hazardous to the social order and its cherished creeds and symbols.

Far more common, and probably more natural in the absence of appropriate social learning, is the urge to restrain or otherwise coerce nonconformists and dissenters, especially if their beliefs or conduct depart sharply from community norms and are perceived as unusually objectionable. As we shall see in the report of our findings, some people are so powerfully motivated by the urge to suppress unorthodox forms of speech and behavior that they are unable to countenance departures from conventionality even when they live in a society which glorifies tolerance as the dominant or "official" norm, a *sine qua non* of democracy itself, proclaimed and praised in countless speeches and published documents by the nation's recognized spokesmen. Even in a country in which freedom is, verbally at least, among the most prized of all values, its existence and survival, like its denial, still taxes human understanding. That freedom is an extraordinary human invention and a precarious notion by no means intrinsic to human society was recognized by Ortega y Gasset in *The Revolt of the Masses* (1932). In a notable passage, he writes that liberalism (by which he meant liberty) is

> that principle of political right, according to which the public authority, in spite of being all-powerful, limits itself and attempts, even at its own expense, to leave room in the State over which it rules for those to live who neither think or feel as it does. . . . [Freedom] is the supreme form of generosity; it is the right which the majority concedes to minorities and hence it is the noblest cry that has ever resounded in this planet. It announces the determination to share existence with the enemy; more than that, with an enemy which is weak. It was incredible that the human species should have arrived at so noble an attitude, so paradoxical, so refined, so acrobatic, so anti-natural. Hence it is not to be wondered at that this same humanity should soon appear anxious to get rid of it. It is a discipline too difficult and too complex to take firm root on earth. (p. 83)

We share Ortega's view that honoring other people's claims to freedom imposes an inordinate demand on the human conscience. One is asked not only to tolerate but to protect the right of others to express opinions or engage in conduct one may regard as distasteful, dangerous, or otherwise egregious. Seen from this perspective, the wonder is not that the world has so often been led by tyrants and populated by slavish conformists, but that the right to think, speak, and act freely has been sufficiently accepted in some societies to have attained institutional sanction and to be given official protection.

That a government should forbear from using its awesome power against dissenters, revolutionaries, or suspected criminals and should instead protect these individuals from arbitrary arrest, unauthorized searches and seizures, or the admission in a criminal trial of illegally gathered evidence is surely among the most extraordinary developments in human history. The same holds for the majority's willingness to permit opponents to challenge or impugn their most cherished values and symbols. Most of us have been so frequently exposed to the shibboleths about the sanctity of freedom that we fail to comprehend fully how remarkable it is for a political system and its constituents to permit individuals or groups to engage in assaults on the community's moral and political sensibilities and its prevailing social norms. How many Americans, one wonders, have come to this view because they understand and embrace John Stuart Mill's principle that the mass of citizens must desist from "interfering with the liberty of action of any of their number," except for "self-protection" or "to prevent harm to others"? (*On Liberty*, pp. 8–9.) As we shall see, the weight of evidence is against this assumption. The extent to which the mass public grasps the fine points of the arguments for tolerance is far less than one might wish for.

The historical and contemporary record further illustrates the difficulty in both the concept and the reality of liberty. Comparatively few societies have honored liberty, even to the degree to which we in America have become accustomed. Until the modern era, with the exception of brief periods in a few classical Greek and Roman city-states, notably Athens, liberty and tolerance had been virtually unknown throughout the course of history. If one were to draw a line representing the level of human freedom and tolerance that stretched throughout the eons of human history, from primeval times down to the present, a detectable measure of freedom would not even appear on the line until nearly the very end. One could identify along the line isolated incidents of struggles for liberty, such as the rebellion in 1215 of certain English peers who demanded and received from King John a charter of rights and political liberties, the Magna Carta. Such incidents, however, are infrequent, narrow in scope, and largely evanescent in their impact. Even the Magna Carta did not bring an end to absolute monarchy in England or significantly extend liberty to large numbers of people, much less to the average man and woman. The few modest concessions to freedom and tolerance made during the Middle Ages and the Renaissance were directed not to the general population, but to the already privileged.

With occasional exceptions, such as the handful of quasi-democratic New England colonial settlements, a measure of religious toleration in Holland, and the circumscribed liberties granted in response to the Glorious Revolution and the Petition of Rights in 1689, freedom was notable more for its absence than for its influence. If conditions remained oppressive even in England and America, where one could at least detect signs of the gradual attenuation of tyranny, the levels of political repression and despotism were more severe on the continent and still harsher elsewhere in the world. While it might overstate the case slightly to claim that tolerance and political freedom did not substantially take hold until the eighteenth century, it would distort the facts more to contend that political freedom and religious toleration flourished to any significant extent in any of the world's political systems that preceded that century. (Cf. Jordan 1965.)

Even today, two centuries after the American and French Revolutions, those convulsive upheavals that were enthusiastically hailed by their defenders as the turning point in human liberation, the world's multitudes continue to live under political regimes that are scarcely less oppressive than the absolutisms of the past. Except for the inhabitants of a few genuinely democratic states, most of the human race appear not to have rid themselves of the bonds that had for centuries restrained their ancestors. They have moved from the uniformity and conformity of primitive societies to the cruel imperial despotisms of, say, Russia under the tsars, only to find themselves in the twentieth century still fettered by autocratic governments which deny freedom as a sign of the weakness and decadence of democracy. Two of the most powerful nations in the world—the Soviet Union and Communist China—have between them subjugated almost a third of the earth's entire population, crushing individual liberty and dissent and engaging in what may well be the world's most ambitious experiments to convert millions who might otherwise wish to be free. Moreover, these countries have satellite and client states, some of which had previously enjoyed at least a measure of freedom. Now, they are subject nations, in which liberty and tolerance have become alien concepts, risky even to contemplate, as the Czechoslovakian and Polish flirtations with freedom illustrate so dramatically.

This portrait of the status of freedom in the world is a somber one. Not only do vast numbers of people live under despotic government, but the levels of oppression and cruelty that prevail in many countries are almost unimaginable to those of us accustomed to democratic rule. While variations occur from year to year in the governance of nations, as regimes change and dictatorships arise or are overthrown, the overall condition of human rights throughout the world remains grim. This is no private opinion. In 1975, for example, the International Press Institute announced that more than half the world was without a free press. Nations such as India, which had once enjoyed freedom of publication, had experienced a dramatic switch from a free press to a controlled press—a shift encountered with growing frequency as nations that were once touched by democracy fell under the sway of military juntas or other forms of dictatorship.

Amnesty International, an organization established for the express purpose of monitoring the growth and decline of freedom throughout the world, commented by way of summary in its 1978 report of developments in 111 countries

> give[s] a depressing picture of systematic violations of basic human rights in most of the countries of the world. People are imprisoned because of their opinions, prisoners are tortured and even executed.
>
> In some Latin American and African countries terrorist acts have been given authorization by governments. Kidnapping, torture, and killing have been developed into a systematic method of wiping out opposition....
>
> In several Asian countries the rulers make use of emergency laws to "legalize" the preventive detention of political opponents: by this technique, governments detain people without trial for long periods....
>
> Besides these new tendencies, old-type violations continue in many countries. [This] Report gives a horrifying account of how the leaders of too many nations continue to condone or instigate terrorist methods against their own citizens.

Furthermore, as Ortega observed long before, "Nothing indicates more clearly the characteristics of the day than the fact that there are so few countries *where an opposition exists*" (Ortega 1932, pp. 83–84; authors' italics). While he attributed this condition to the rise of the multitude, to their "deadly hatred of all that is not itself," and to their consequent tendency to crush "and annihilate every opposing group," the practice of denying the right of political opposition and silencing its advocates is widespread and existed long before the rise of so-called mass society. Indeed, the history of government is predominantly a history of one-party systems (or their equivalent). The reluctance of oligarchies to legitimate the rights of organized political opposition and to share power with them is only one more sign of the general intolerance toward dissenters, critics, or political rivals which one can readily discern from even a cursory reading of political history.

Although it is not the purpose of this book to provide a detailed historical account of the course of liberty in America, a short description will aid in illustrating our point. Even in the United States, freedom and tolerance have been historically compelled to struggle for recognition and survival. The road to the current level of acceptance of civil liberties has been, from the beginning, far rockier than most Americans realize or care to admit. Colonial America, so vividly identified in the public mind with the emancipation of an entire continent from European forms of tyranny, was, in many respects, a congeries of petty despotisms. As one student of American colonialism has observed:

> The persistent image of colonial America as a society that cherished freedom of expression is a sentimental hallucination that ignores history. The evidence provides little support for the notion that the colonies hospitably received advocates of obnoxious or detestable ideas on matters that counted. Nor is there reason to believe that rambunctious unorthodoxies suffered only from Puritan bigots and tyrannous royal judges. The American people and their representatives simply did not understand that freedom of thought and expression means equal freedom for the other fellow, particularly the fellow with the hated ideas. (Levy 1963, p. xxix)

This assessment of freedom is shared by other scholars of early American history. They are inclined to agree that the apparent diversity in politics and religion remarked by some historians "was a consequence not of tolerance and mutual respect—an overall ideology of freedom—but of the existence of many communities within the society each with its own canons of orthodoxy." The existence of many small "closed enclaves" made it possible for an individual to search out and "settle in with his co-believers in safety and comfort," from which vantage point "he could help [to impose] group beliefs on all within reach" (Roche 1958, pp. 8, 11). Levy (1963) observes that each community outside the big cities "tended to be a tight little island clutching to its own orthodoxy and willing to banish unwelcome dissidence or punish it extralegally" (p. xxx).

In general, there was little need for active suppression, mainly because groups were inclined to segregate themselves in order to escape the hatred of other groups.

> Wise Unitarians avoided the Anglican or Puritan establishments; Puritans, unless they were seeking expulsion, steered clear of the Anglican colonies, and devout Anglicans reciprocated; Anabaptists, Quakers, and other sectarians were well advised to confine their proselytizing to Pennsylvania and Rhode Island. Catholics, who were associated in the public mind with the international French conspiracy, had the most difficult time of all. Only in Pennsylvania, where William Penn had established such minimal religious standards as belief in one God and Jesus Christ, was the

> door consistently open, or perhaps ajar, to those of the Roman faith. Indeed, at the close of the colonial period, the only place where the public exercise of Catholic rites was permitted was Pennsylvania, and this was over the protest of the last governor.   (Roche 1958, pp. 9–10)

Thus, Roche concludes, individual freedom in early, rural America "depended not on a national principle of fair play, but rather on the ability of an individual to find a community where his views would not engender wrath and its inevitable fellows: the tarpot, lash, and noose" (Roche 1958, pp. 20–21).

The condition of civil liberties did not improve dramatically with the War of Independence and its aftermath. The Sons of Liberty and other partisans of the colonial cause denounced the suggestion that the principle of freedom could be extended to include the expression of pro-British sentiments. They ran cartoons depicting, in the name of liberty, "the tarring and feathering" of British Tories, called for punishments (such as boycotts) against merchants who refused "to cooperate in the nonimportation movement of the early 1770s," and made frequent use of the common law of seditious libel to deter or suppress nonconformist opinions (Levy 1963, pp. xxx, xlviii; Roche 1958, pp. 12–13). Although one might be inclined to discount some of these responses as the temporary aberrations of oppressed colonials struggling for freedom and independence, signs of other intolerant beliefs and conduct continued to crop up in the decades that followed the revolutionary era.

For some years after the Constitution was adopted, various states continued to deny large numbers of people the right to vote because of race, color, religion, sex, nationality, and property qualifications. Universal manhood suffrage was not legally established until 1870, with the adoption of the Fifteenth Amendment, which prohibited restrictions on voting based on race, color, or previous condition of servitude. (Despite this clear constitutional prohibition, blacks in reality were prevented from voting in many southern states by a variety of subterfuges, such as literacy tests, the "Grandfather clause," and the "white primary"—a practice that was not fully corrected until the adoption of the federal Voting Rights Act of 1965.) Equally astonishing in a nation that prided itself on its democracy and freedom, suffrage for women was not entirely secured until the ratification of the Nineteenth Amendment in 1920.

Prior to the adoption of the Constitution, almost every colony had instituted an established religion, and at least two states, Massachusetts and Connecticut, retained an established church for several decades after the adoption of a federal constitutional provision that explicitly required the separation of church and state. The Alien and Sedition Acts adopted in 1798 represented an even more blatant flouting of libertarian principles by providing for the deportation of aliens whose "radical" ideas the President considered dangerous to the Republic and the arrest of American citizens who, in speech or writing, defamed or otherwise maligned the President or members of Congress. Thus, the mere exercise of freedom of speech, a right guaranteed in the First Amendment, was sufficient to send men to prison or into exile; and this contingency, in turn, was sufficient to intimidate countless editors into silence on vital issues.

Of all the violations of civil liberties, since colonial times, the suppression, cruelty, and discrimination against racial and ethnic minorities—blacks, Orientals, Indians, and Mexicans—were by far the most severe. And of the several forms of racial suppression and denial of elementary rights, slavery was, of course, the most egregious. American slavery is too familiar to require much discussion here. It is enough to observe that slavery was sanctioned not only in practice but in law; slaves suffered a *complete* loss not only of *civil rights* (which refer mainly to equality), but of *civil liberties* (which refer mainly to freedom). The institution of slavery also affected the civil liberties of countless citizens who were not slaves, especially the abolitionists.

The mere advocacy of abolition was regarded by many who sympathized with slavery as "inflammatory, dangerous, and mischievous," and since one "cannot speak, write, or act in such a manner as to endanger the moral well-being of society," they thought it entirely appropriate to deny freedom of the press to those who were the authors of such "mischief" (Richmond, Virginia, *Enquirer*, February 4, 1832; quoted in Nye 1949, p. 125). Wherever slaveholders and their supporters had the power, they were often prepared not only to suppress abolitionist editors, but to bar discussions of slavery in southern colleges and schools, to ban abolitionist literature from the mails, and to intimidate both blacks and whites through mob violence and assaults on individuals. (Nye 1949, pp. 23, 73.) In the period following the Civil War, some of the proslavery groups grew into terrorist organizations such as the Ku Klux Klan.

The formal abolition of slavery did not afford slaves and other blacks full stature as citizens. Despite gradual and significant improvements in their treatment and the liberties available to them, blacks continued to suffer the many forms of discrimination and abuse that societies stratified along caste lines reserved for persons who occupy the lowest and most reviled ranks. The forms of racial subjugation are more subtle and less severe now than they were in the past, but it is obvious that they have not been completely eradicated.

Only in our recent past have legislative and judicial decisions succeeded in outlawing such demeaning forms of discrimination as segregated eating places and drinking fountains, living and hotel accommodations, schools and public conveyances, and even churches—to say nothing of discrimination in access to preferred jobs. As we have suggested, many forms of segregation fall more appropriately under the rubric of civil rights than of civil liberties, but in every case they impose severe limitations on the exercise of freedom as well.

Much of what follows in succeeding chapters of this book will be directed to questions that bear on the present status of civil liberties in America. It would be premature at this point to consider whether tolerance appears over the years to have grown stronger, weaker, or to have remained at a fairly constant level. Perhaps it is sufficient for the moment to observe that violations of civil liberties have not been uncommon in the present century and have at times even assumed forms that many would regard as grotesque. One need only recall the deportation and internment in prison camps of thousands of Japanese-American citizens during World War II; or the assaults against civil liberties and indignities against human rights and sensibilities unleashed by Senator Joseph McCarthy in the early 1950s, as well as the legislative abuses of civil liberties contained in the Smith Act and the McCarran Act.

It is not our purpose, however, to compile an inventory of injustices committed against the American people in the course of the nation's history, nor to present a list of the violations against constitutional liberties. We have no reason to think that the American record on this score is worse than that of other nations and many reasons to think it is considerably better. Our intention, rather, has been to note the infrequency of liberty and the frequency of its suppression throughout history even to the present day; to take heed of its precarious standing in those parts of the world in which it has only recently begun to take hold; and to observe how labile and vulnerable its existence can be even among people who have known freedom for centuries and consider themselves devoted to its principles and practices. The record, in short, shows that liberty is a frail and tenuous reed, slow to take root, rare, and often short-lived.

What, then, in light of so bleak a record, is one to make of the claim that freedom is innate in the human soul, that tolerance of divergent opinions and dissent is "natural," and that all human beings sooner or later learn the mutual benefits of reciprocity associated with tolerance and the sharing of freedom? Certainly the evidence on this issue suggests a stronger case for Ortega's pessimism than for the optimism of Rousseau and the Encyclopedists.

Why Freedom and Tolerance Are So Rare and So Difficult to Maintain

The ubiquity of slavery and oppression throughout human history leads one to wonder whether intolerance rather than tolerance may be the easier and more natural posture for most people to assume. Perhaps the impulse to strike out against opponents or ideas that one finds frightening or hateful is a survival mechanism, a product of the evolutionary process. Most creatures survive by recognizing their enemies and learning how to cope with them. If one has sufficient strength and cunning to repel the enemy, one is inclined to do so unless one has discovered that, for some reason, another type of response is legally or socially required, or preferred. As we shall see, this response is a learned one and the ability to learn it is often limited.

Many people, it seems, fear what is different because they distrust what they do not understand or cannot control. As John Stuart Mill observed:

> The practical principle which guides people to their opinions on the regulation of human conduct is the feeling in each person's mind that everybody should be required to act as he, and those with whom he sympathizes, would like them to act. No one, indeed, acknowledges to himself that his standard of judgment is his own liking; but an opinion on a point of conduct.... [T]o an ordinary man, however, his own preference, thus supported, is not only a perfectly satisfactory reason but the only one he generally has for any of his notions of morality, taste or propriety, which are not expressly written in his religious creed, and his chief guide in the interpretation even of that. (p. 64)

For psychological and sociological reasons too complex to be considered fully here, human beings exhibit a powerful tendency to discover or settle upon social norms—that is, a range of acceptable rules of conduct, standards of right and wrong—to which one can refer without having to debate every issue as though for the first time. Through such standards people avoid the psychological pain of continuous conflict and disagreement. Norms supply, in effect, settled opinions and therefore provide conditions for stability and predictability in everyday life as well as in public affairs. Human beings require stability, order, and structure in their lives in order to go about their daily tasks and to feel safe against the terrors of the unknown, they tend to converge around opinions, values, and standards of conduct that are familiar to them and that bear the stamp of social approval.

Because the established standards tend to be accepted as the correct standards, those who flout them are often seen as thoughtless, ignorant, or wicked. To choose to be different in one's attitude toward venerated objects and symbols—religion, the nation, the flag, the family, the Deity—is seen as a sign of depravity. Why should one permit, much less safeguard or encourage, recalcitrance, error, malicious scorn for objects and values that right-minded people know to be correct or even sacred?

This inclination to fix upon standards and invest them with infallibility is strengthened by the tendency of the average person to distrust or fear whatever is unfamiliar or beyond comprehension. As Mill observes:

> The general average of mankind are not only moderate in intellect, but also moderate in inclination; they have no tastes or wishes strong enough to incline them to do anything unusual, and they consequently do not understand those who have, and class all such with the wild and intemperate whom they are accustomed to look down upon. (p. 134)

Mill thus recognizes an elementary and often neglected truth—namely, that the danger to freedom and individual autonomy arises not only from political despots or heedless, arbitrary governments, but from one's fellow citizens as well. For many purposes, in fact, the tyranny of friends, neighbors, or fellow citizens is far greater than the oppression of organized government. Public opinion, it should be noted, is often far behind political officials in its attitudes toward conventional behavior and in its readiness to permit variations and diversity in human conduct. Survey and poll data show that the general public is often more severe and punitive in its attitudes than are political leaders, more restrictive and inclined to demand conformity with traditional community standards (Stouffer 1955). To some extent these findings reflect the lesser familiarity of the public with the specifics of the behavior to which they are responding and their greater indifference to the nuances and subtleties of key questions being debated in the legislatures and the courts. They also reflect to some extent, a greater ignorance of the law and the "rules of the game."

We do not mean to suggest that the public is an invariable enemy of tolerance, or that governments as such have a greater propensity for abiding departures from established norms than do its citizens. We do mean to suggest, however, that on many questions which are close to the surface of everyday human existence and thereby arouse fear and anger, the public is often less tolerant than the officials who are charged with making and enforcing law on these matters.

We also mean to suggest—a point of vital concern for the significance of this book—that the attitudes and beliefs of the American public on questions of tolerance, freedom, and control are often as important to know, sometimes more important, in fact, than the opinions of governing officials. We mean, finally, to emphasize that many forms of intimidation and human oppression occur not only at the level of political decision and enforcement but at the level of the neighborhood, the community, and the reference group. Men and women often pay more attention to the opinions of their peers and neighbors than they do to the attitudes or potential actions of their rulers.

Support for tolerance and civil liberties becomes still more remarkable when we consider how much social learning is needed before people will not only permit but also *protect* ideas and conduct they consider morally or socially unacceptable. The impulse to strike down a threatening enemy seems to require little learning or knowledge. More information and greater sophistication are needed to grasp the difficult philosophical principles that underlie the defense of tolerance. Tolerance also requires an ability, less common than one might wish, to understand the rules of the democratic game. It is no simple matter to learn the arguments for freedom and tolerance formulated and debated by such notable minds as John Stuart Mill, Judge Learned Hand, Alexander Meiklejohn, Justices Cardozo, Brandeis, Black, and other justices of the Supreme Court. Much of their reasoning is subtle, complex, and esoteric. Rarely are the answers self-evident.

The notion of tolerance itself is a thorny one. Granting liberty to one person implies a principle of reciprocity—a notion that appears to be simple enough but is difficult for many people to grasp. Those who believe they know the "truth" on a particular issue, and, in addition, enjoy the right to expound it, may find it difficult to understand why they have an obligation to permit someone with a contrary (and hence obviously false) view to enjoy an equal opportunity for freedom of expression. If one knows that the Nazis preach doctrines that are both hateful and wrong, by what moral obligation is one bound to permit them to publish their views or to assemble and proselytize in an effort to persuade others? One may find it hard to understand why the false and virulent opinions held by such extremists should enjoy the same right to be expressed as the opinions held by people "known" to have balanced and benign views. Many are unable to digest the idea that silencing revolutionaries and extremists violates a fundamental principle of freedom, since freedom depends on a mutual obligation to grant to others what one claims for oneself.

Decisions involving such cases of reciprocity are not as farfetched as they may seem at first. Indeed, they are fairly common. Instances in which those on one side of a political or intellectual dispute challenge the right of their opponents to publicize their heinous views while insisting on the right to express their own correct and benevolent views turn up in countless public disputes over controversial issues. Does one have the same right to demonstrate in favor of war as in favor of peace? Does the First Amendment guarantee the right to preach race hatred as well as love? Does one have a right to rant against God that is equal to the right to praise Him? Does one have the same right to publish artistic photographs or copies of museum paintings as to publish prurient or "filthy" pictures?

During the 1960s many missed the irony in their conduct and rhetoric and saw no violation of the reciprocity principle in their actions. Student and faculty activists, for example, staged protest demonstrations designed to prevent speakers from presenting favorable views on the Vietnam War or on aspects of the student movement. Various members of the "establishment" as well as prowar forces squelched assemblies and demonstrations in the name of patriotism. We believe there is almost no instance of suppression of opinion which does not to some degree violate the canons of reciprocity. The problem is exacerbated when zeal and a passionate desire for change (whether for reform or its opposite) are involved. Though perhaps admirable in certain contexts, zeal is itself one of the major forces leading to censorship and suppression. Social reformers, high minded, impassioned, and convinced of the nobility of their cause are sometimes led to try to silence opponents whose beliefs, in their view, can only be motivated by malice, selfishness, ignorance, or some other evil intention. As Mill observed: "The spirit of improvement is not always a spirit of liberty, for it may aim at forcing improvements on an unwilling people. . . . [The] only unfailing and permanent source of improvement is liberty, since by it there are as many independent centers of improvement as there are individuals" (p. 136).

Neither the radicals on the right nor the radicals on the left are much impressed with the virtues of reciprocity. Both feel they *possess* the truth, know unequivocally who the enemies are, how malevolent their motivations are, and what distorted opinions they are likely to advocate. How shortsighted, then, to assist them by offering a platform from which to launch their malicious lies. How naive to be bound by a mere *abstract* principle such as reciprocity, one that can result only in promoting the cause of the enemy.

How can one persuade political or religious zealots that their own liberty, and that of the nation itself, is jeopardized by denying liberty to others? Or that politics and civility depend upon mutual obligations, compromise, trade-offs, give-and-take, the willingness to impose limits on one's own impulses and to refrain from striking down unorthodoxies and the (perhaps) misguided people who advocate them? Although groups on the political extremes are (in the United States at least) obviously in the minority, they are the champions of their own forms of orthodoxy. They have little patience with diversity and seek, instead, uniformity in opinion and lifestyle. They do not hold with Mill that different persons "require different conditions for their spiritual development" (p. 133). We need to remember, however, that what we have said of zealots and "true believers" at the far ends of the ideological distribution is in varying, although lesser, degree true of some people at all points on the political spectrum.

No leap of the imagination or perception of fine distinctions is needed to strike out against hated or feared ideas and their advocates, or to demand adherence to orthodoxy. Intolerance places little burden upon us to search for and locate the fine line between the permissible and the impermissible, to understand the grounds for distinguishing acceptable from unacceptable conduct. Tolerance, by contrast, tends more often to be the product of deliberation: it requires the weighing of alternatives and attention to the consequences of choosing one

17

course over another. Tolerance is more likely to take into account questions about the conditions under which certain actions may or may not be allowed. Under what circumstances, for example, should a community permit a group to hold an "agitational" meeting in a civic auditorium? When should a police officer be allowed to search an automobile for concealed weapons after having stopped the vehicle for a traffic violation?

To uphold the tolerant (or civil libertarian) attitude toward conduct, one needs to wrestle with numerous difficult questions of this kind, as the courts and the legislatures have so often had to do. Most of the issues one has to confront in deciding whether to permit "deviant" opinions or conduct are vexing. Plausible arguments can often be found to support both sides of the issue. When a community is legally or even nominally committed to libertarian values, it must frequently weigh the benefits of freedom against the possible danger to the community of permitting the expression of certain unorthodox opinions and actions.

Decisions to suppress or censor feared or distasteful behavior, however, usually require less reflection. A film that explicitly depicts erotic acts may simply be confiscated; a campus speaker who defends an unpopular war may be shouted down and silenced by student demonstrators; a book that contains seditious or obscene materials may be removed from the school library. The people who engage in such censorship will probably feel little need to explore the moral and philosophical issues their actions raise or to concern themselves with the possibility that they may, by their acts of suppression, be violating the Constitution, the laws, or the nation's civil libertarian norms.

We are not suggesting that all expressions of intolerance are mindless or ignorant, for it sometimes happens that thoughtful people, after careful deliberation, come down on the side of prohibiting certain forms of lawful conduct. This was the case, for example, among many of the people who, although usually identified with the cause of civil liberties, urged the authorities to deny the American Nazi party a permit to march through a section of Skokie, Illinois, populated by many Jews who had survived the Holocaust. (See Gibson and Bingham 1979.) To them, the right of the Nazis to assemble (or to parade) had to be subordinated to the moral claims of Jewish refugees to be protected against a reminder of Nazi terror. Skokie, however, was an exceptional case; in most cases, defending the civil liberties of outcasts, dissenters, criminals, or other marginal members of society ordinarily entails a more difficult and complex decision process than is involved in suppressing them.

As the foregoing suggests, the adoption of a positive orientation toward civil liberties is made difficult by the fact that tolerance is often more costly than intolerance. Having to protect the rights of people whose ideas or conduct one despises often exacts a high psychological price. Even the most dedicated civil libertarian can scarcely avoid feeling conflicted (and therefore pained) when called upon not only to recognize but also to *protect* the constitutional rights and civil liberties of terrorists, racists, leaders of organized crime, and other individuals who stand at the far edge of society's boundaries.

Support for civil liberties also exacts social costs. Freedom is in some respects distributive: expanding the rights of one group may reduce the power of others. An increase in the rights of the servant narrows the authority and prerogatives of the master. Greater freedom for women, blacks, students, children, indigents, prisoners, or other groups heretofore treated as "subordinate" limits the power of the people who formerly enjoyed command or superiority over them. While granting liberties to groups previously oppressed may in the long run enlarge everyone's freedom, it may in the short run beget severe countermeasures among those who feel themselves victimized by the change. Often the result is to heighten conflict and to intensify efforts to diminish the rights of one's antagonists. The interplay of freedom and control, and the competition of claims is, to be sure, not always a zero-sum game, but it would be naive to suppose that it is a game in which all the players benefit equally. So long as this is the case, the distribution of individual liberties is bound to remain an important source of conflict in society. One, of course, encounters cases—the outlawing of segregation is an example—in which the balance of costs and benefits (at least in a democratic society) is clear. In other instances, however, such as the banning of textbooks that offend community sensibilities or the lightening of sentences for convicted felons, the balance may be unclear and subject to vigorous dispute.

Although we frequently speak of freedom and control as though they were polarities, freedom cannot function effectively in the absence of controls. Controversies over the magnitude of the controls needed to ensure the optimal enforcement of civil liberties are intrinsic features of every democratic society. Not every law that is intended to extend civil liberties will actually increase the freedom available to the citizenry as a whole. If a law that was designed to protect the rights of loiterers merely served to increase the number of "muggers" and criminal marauders in a community, the effect might be to inhibit rather than to increase the ability of most citizens to travel freely and safely on the public streets. It might even lead to demands for curfews and other limitations on freedom of travel. So long as freedom and control remain simultaneously antagonistic and interdependent, tensions concerning the appropriate boundaries between them are, in a free society, inescapable.

These examples serve to remind us that the exercise of liberty is continually bedeviled by the need to strike a proper balance between freedom and control. No democratic society can avoid having to wrestle with questions about the optimal "adjustment between individual independence and social control" (Mill, pp. 63–4), or the degree of tolerance that ought to prevail in the various domains of human conduct. Not only are laws necessary to the enjoyment of freedom, but each of those laws represents, in effect, a limitation on the exercise of freedom itself. Many civil libertarians are reluctant to think of limiting freedom in any way, especially freedom of speech, although they would doubtless concede the familiar observation that (to take the extreme instance) granting total freedom to any individual could, in theory at least, result in the restriction of freedom for everyone else.

In practice, the problems faced by democratic governments in balancing liberty and control involve such questions as the value of wiretapping for effective law enforcement versus the invasion of privacy; or the rights of teachers to use textbooks that teach evolution versus the rights of fundamentalist parents to raise their children to believe in the literal interpretation of Genesis. A more dramatic example of the unceasing war between freedom and control is represented by the conflict between the government and the press over the question of a newspaper's right to print a detailed manual of the procedures necessary to construct a hydrogen bomb. How much weight ought one to assign to the rights guaranteed in the First Amendment when confronted with the possibility that "terrorists armed with small nuclear weapons [could hold] entire communities hostage on the threat of catastrophe"? (editorial, San Francisco *Chronicle*, September 23, 1979).

Issues such as these serve to point up the risks in treating freedom and tolerance as absolute values. Freedom, however desirable on balance, is not invariably a social good. Tolerance does not oblige us to consider every opinion, or every instance of protected conduct, as legally inviolable. Ascertaining the point at which liberties cease to be protected because they are troublesome beyond a community's capacity to tolerate is among the most vexing problems faced by any modern democratic government, especially in light of what has been described as the "rights explosion."

This is not the place to consider at length the elusive and difficult issue of whether changes in the status of tolerance, civil liberties, and other rights have generally proved more beneficial than harmful. It might be useful by way of introduction, however, to call attention to the existence of the controversy and to cite a few examples of the problem and events it brings to the surface.

American society has witnessed a number of freedom-related changes that can be described without hyperbole as dramatic. Without attempting at the moment to sort them out according to the direction of their impact, we can cite as having significance for civil liberties such events as Watergate, revelations about wiretapping, the Ellsberg publication of classified information and the events it triggered, judicial pressures to compel journalists to reveal their sources, invasions of privacy by intelligence agencies in the name of national security, and assaults on academic freedom by students, the public, and even faculty members.

Standards have been shifting with respect to attitudes toward patriotism, "treason," the prerogatives of "national defense," the flag, and other insignia of political allegiance. Great changes can be discerned in patterns of parental authority, the rights of women, ethnic minorities, children, students, and others hitherto assigned subordinate roles. Recent years have also witnessed striking shifts in what many have come to regard as legitimate forms of political participation, including mass protests, sit-ins, symbolic speech, and certain types of civil disobedience.

Changes, often startling in their rapidity, can be observed in both the public and official attitudes toward "crimes" to which the participating parties have consented. Striking shifts have occurred in the standards of permissible conduct governing dress, sexual habits, and styles of cohabitation. Increasing informality in manners, conventions of language, and changing standards regarding pornography, obscenity, and nudity are discernible in the media and in everyday personal and official conduct. Changes in the field of law enforcement have been equally noteworthy. The right to be apprised of one's legal rights and to be represented by attorneys has become part of the established law. The courts are now more likely to question the use of evidence extracted by confession. More emphasis is being given to the selection of "representative" juries, and persons accused of crimes can more effectively challenge adverse verdicts on grounds of procedural errors. Persons convicted of crimes are now less often punished by incarceration, and, among those imprisoned, opportunities for the redress of grievances have expanded.

These and related developments have led some observers to speak of a rights explosion, though not always with unqualified approval. (See *U.S. News & World Report,* October 23, 1978.) Groups which were once silenced or unorganized—the aged, homosexuals, prisoners, the physically and mentally handicapped—have found their voice and have entered the political arena to claim their share not only of the national wealth, but also of the freedom and equality that are presumed to be the legacies left by the Founders to every American.

The growing demands for the expression of rights, however, have not been universally welcomed. Some Americans are concerned that in their heedless rush to claim their alleged inheritance, the multitudes have mainly succeeded in trampling upon the nation's most cherished values, traditions, and institutions—the family; religion; the law; respect for authority; and standards of excellence, achievement, and self-discipline. Still others are concerned that time-honored liberties, such as freedom of religion, are being exploited to protect highly deviant cults such as the People's Temple, which culminated in the Jonestown mass suicides and executions.

It should be clear, even from these examples, that the expanding claims for freedom and tolerance have led to resistance and a distrust of civil liberties among those who feel they are being harmed by the changes. Today they are being asked to tolerate groups, opinions, and activities that were not even discussed a short time ago, such as the right of homosexuals to cohabit openly or the right of women to have elective abortions. The proliferation of liberties, thus, has understandably heightened public concern about the consequences of extending rights further.

As we have progressed through this chapter, it has become increasingly plain that while we often speak of tolerance and intolerance, or freedom and control, as though they were simple and self-evident ideas, they are, conceptually and in practice, complex notions that need continually to be qualified and observed from more than one perspective in order to appreciate their meaning.

22

An Introduction to the Nature of Freedom and Tolerance

Several other caveats and qualifications need to be added (or highlighted) before we turn to the examination of our research findings. Although obvious, it is still worth noting that not every decision to limit certain types of (presumably protected) speech or action deserves to be labeled "intolerant." No right, however deeply cherished, is or ought to be absolute. Even liberty, the most prized of all rights, has limits, and a wise society will enforce them. As interpreted by the courts, liberty does not include, for example, permission to make an agitational speech which incites a riot or, in the famous example employed by Justice Holmes, falsely to shout "fire" in a crowded theater. The justices of the U.S. Supreme Court, who are generally well disposed toward freedom, are called upon in dozens of cases every year to decide where the line should be drawn between honoring or prohibiting the exercise of a particular form of liberty.

The line between tolerance and intolerance is rarely fixed. What one person considers tolerance, another considers treason, as we observed in the conflicting responses to certain Americans who, during the Vietnam War, demonstrated in favor of a Vietcong victory. In their own eyes they were exercising a protected right; in the eyes of their critics, however, they were giving aid and comfort to a wartime enemy. In short, in analyzing freedom and tolerance, we would be oversimplifying matters greatly if we were to assume that every form of permissiveness is an example of tolerance and every form of restraint an instance of intolerance.

If we define freedom as merely the absence of restraint, we oversimplify the concept and we overlook its many dimensions. Freedom involves not only the removal of restraints, but a weighing and balancing of utilities, in which the absence of restraint is only one element. One needs to take into account, for example, the impact of freedom on other values, such as equality; the various forms that freedom takes and the conditions under which it might be exercised. For example, some people wish to expand freedom in matters of speech but to narrow it in matters of worship so as to eliminate exotic cults that call themselves religions. Some people want more protection for the accused in a criminal trial but greater restraints on newspapers, whose reports might bias judges and juries.

Tolerance is not a universal condition or principle that retains the same appearance in all circumstances. Conduct easily tolerated in peacetime may be considered unacceptable in wartime. The desecration of the flag by undergraduates as a prank takes on a different meaning than the same action instigated by partisans of a foreign power with whom we are at war. Whether a community decides to permit or suppress an act depends in significant measure on who commits the act, for what purpose, and under what conditions. This does not mean that rules governing these matters do not exist or that general rules for granting or withholding tolerance cannot be developed. General principles covering such matters *have* been developed by legislatures and enforced in the courts. What *is* being said, however, is that the enforcement of those principles is subject to qualifications of "time, place, and manner." A mass demonstration held in a public park might receive police protection, but might be dispersed if held at the city's busiest intersection. A cross burning by the Ku Klux Klan might more easily be tolerated in a field outside of a southern town than in Harlem.

Even in a country with democratic norms, tolerance is a complex issue. The constraints of language compel us to speak of it as though it had a single dimension and could be treated as a universal construct. We could not begin to speak of it at all were we required in every instance to specify all the conditions and qualifications under which it functions or ought to function. That the realities of communication prevent us from doing so should not, however, blind us to the fact that such conditions and qualifications exist.

Preface to
Research Findings

Before beginning the presentation and discussion of our research findings bearing on these issues and concepts we will briefly describe the study and some of the procedures we employed. The data reported in this volume have been drawn mainly from two national studies we conducted in 1978–1979 and in 1976–1977. Both included large cross-section area-probability samples of the general population, drawn for us by the Gallup Organization, which also distributed our questionnaires to respondents. Both studies also included samples of special (that is, opinion elite) populations.

The study on which we primarily rely for the research evidence reported in this book is the Civil Liberties Survey (CLS), conducted in 1978–1979. This study utilized a national cross-section random sample of 1,993 adult Americans as well as a sample of 1,891 community leaders and activists engaged in various vocations and playing various roles. The community elite sample contained officials and opinion leaders from government, colleges and universities, the press, the clergy, the law (lawyers and judges), the police, school administrators and teachers, voluntary organizations (business, fraternal, and civic), trade unions, and the like. Both the community leader and mass population samples were selected from the same 300 geographic locations (that is, sampling units) across the country.* The survey questionnaire employed in this study contains numerous questions on virtually every major aspect of civil liberties, as well as a large number of other questions that might help to explain a respondent's tolerance or intolerance.

The second major study from which we report data is the Opinion and Values Survey (OVS), conducted in 1976–1977 on a national cross-section sample of 938 respondents. Additional samples of opinion elites were drawn randomly from the membership lists of twenty-three national organizations, together with two randomly drawn special sub-samples from *Who's Who* and the *Black Who's Who* (yielding a total of 2,987 elite respondents). While five of the elite groups were nonpartisan, the remaining groups represented all the major segments across the political spectrum, with the exception of the far left, whose member organizations were unwilling to participate.

A further word about the questionnaires used in the two studies: In each study the elite and mass samples filled out identical questionnaires, so that the elite-mass comparisons reported for each study represent findings on respondents who have addressed and answered the same questions. With a few exceptions, the questions in the CLS differed from those in the OVS. Each survey was tailored to its major purpose—the measurement and study of political ideologies (OVS) or the study of attitudes toward civil liberties (CLS). Despite their differences, however, both studies contained various items that reflected opinions in the several domains of civil liberties—freedom of speech, press, assembly, association, religion, dissent, due process, privacy, lifestyle, and the like. Other items reflected constructs or variables useful in explaining orientation toward civil liberties, such as conformity, conventionality, patriotism, anomie, misanthropy and social responsibility.

It will be evident from the items in the tables that both studies employ a new format that resembles in some ways a sentence-completion question. In each case the respondent is offered a choice of two alternative responses that will complete the thought contained in the stem. We have striven, wherever possible, to provide alternatives that are fundamental and divergent, but that are equally plausible and so-

---

*We are greatly indebted to the Gallup Organization for selecting the national cross-section sample and delivering our questionnaire to the respondents. Gallup interviewers also selected the respondents in our community leader sample, in accordance with our instructions.

cially acceptable. They are also moderate in flavor and language (rather than stereotypical or inflammatory), and they are sufficiently encompassing in their reach so as to permit most respondents to select one of the alternatives without seriously misrepresenting their views. We have also included Neither and Undecided alternatives for respondents who might not be satisfied by either of the substantive alternatives presented.

The advantages of this format, in our opinion, rest not only in its effort to avoid overly colorful and tendentious language, but in its elimination of the problem of acquiescent response set (that is, the tendency to agree with items regardless of their content) and its ability to confront a respondent with meaningful alternatives which exact a cost for choosing one answer rather than the other. Most of the items compel the respondent to reflect upon the answers, which are often subtle and complicated enough to require thoughtful deliberation—thereby reducing to some extent the "nonattitude" problem. (See Converse 1970.) In addition, each item, despite the amount of information sometimes crowded into the content, is brief and to the point, simple to score, and lends itself nicely to the construction of scales and other cumulative indicators. Some 265 questions of this type were included in the Opinions and Values Survey and 327 in the Civil Liberties Survey. The questionnaires include, in addition, 82 opinion questions in other formats. (See Appendix A for the full CLS questionnaire.) The items were scrambled and presented to the respondents in random order, but can easily be reassembled into indexes or scales, as the investigators choose. To date, our experience with this format has shown it to be unusually powerful in enabling us to range respondents on a number of attitude dimensions and to clearly discriminate those who score at different levels of each dimension.

The reader will observe that we have also, from time to time, reported data from other studies that bear on the questions we are addressing. Chief among these is the study of Political Affiliations and Belief (PAB), conducted by the senior author in 1958 to assess (among other things) differences in the political attitudes of political leaders and the mass public. The samples responding to the survey on which the PAB study was based included a national, cross-section sample of 1,484 adult respondents,* and a sample of 3,020 political leaders or influentials—men and women who had served as delegates or alter-

---

* This sample was also drawn by the Gallup Organization, whose interviewers, in addition, delivered the lengthy self-administered questionnaire to the respondents.

nates to the 1956 Democratic and Republican conventions. Included in the leader sample were officials and other participants from all levels and branches of government and party activity.

While the PAB study was designed to explore a large number of political attitudes, it also contained some items and scales that bear on civil liberties and other democratic rights (see McClosky 1964). Although these measures are less well developed than those employed in our more recent studies, they are useful for purposes of comparison. The findings from the PAB study also throw light on some of the issues which have been more fully illuminated in the CLS and OVS studies.

For a more complete description of the sampling and follow-up procedures employed in the research, as well as a discussion of some methodological issues, the reader is directed to Appendix B.

One further set of comments is in order before we discuss our research findings. At various points in the course of the analysis we refer to "social learning" as a key process by which civil libertarian and other social norms are acquired. As we have indicated, the tendency to support civil liberties is learned, but since many of these liberties are highly complex and recondite, learning to support them is often difficult. A number of elements are involved in the process of effective social learning, and various hurdles have to be cleared.

The term "social learning," as we employ it in this book, refers to a process by which individuals acquire their values, standards, and views about public affairs through their interaction with particular subcultures and social environments which reward or "reenforce" them for beliefs and conduct approved by society and punish them for beliefs and conduct not approved by society (or significant segments of it). A fair amount of social learning regarding public issues also occurs, of course, through encountering ideas and norms that are disseminated by such institutions as the schools, the media, voluntary associations, and the churches. In addition, one is likely to learn about society's norms through observing the consequences of other people's actions and through modeling one's behavior on the behavior of those who are perceived as providing cues to approved conduct.

Although the process of social learning is highly complicated for any given individual, it can be conceived, essentially, as involving three stages: the *exposure* to a given set of norms (in this case civil libertarian norms), the *comprehension* of those norms, and their *acceptance* or internalization.

Exposure. The members of a large and complex society obviously vary greatly in their exposure to the norms of civil liberties. Those who function at the center (or centers) of the political culture—who serve as the political, economic, cultural, and intellectual leaders of opinion—are far more likely than those who function at the periphery to have encountered the norms and to have discovered which beliefs or values are considered "definitive" or "legitimate" and which are not. By virtue of their social location, their greater education, their more frequent involvement in community activities, their participation in the public colloquy on questions of the day, and their affiliation with social networks whose members often discuss and hold informed views on vital public issues, they are often exposed to the ideas and principles which constitute the society's creed. As one moves from the centers of public involvement toward the periphery, exposure to the constituent values of the political culture declines. As exposure declines, there is an attendant decline in the social learning of the norms by which the political culture presumes to be governed.

Comprehension. To be effectively learned civil libertarian norms must not only be encountered, but *comprehended.* As the members of the public vary greatly in their access to the norms, so do they also differ markedly in their training and ability to comprehend them. Many individuals, though somewhat exposed to the norms, fail nevertheless to learn them—or learn them only in vague or distorted form. Often they lack the knowledge to distinguish between beliefs or conduct that are consonant with constitutional principles and those that violate them.

Many members of the society, especially those at the periphery, find questions about civil liberties and other public affairs of little interest. Not only do their concerns lie elsewhere, but they rarely engage in the kinds of activities or associate with groups that are likely to stimulate their interest in public questions or motivate them to acquire knowledge and understanding about matters that seem to them remote, arcane, and difficult to decipher. While they may find it easy to endorse *abstract* statements of support for the more familiar civil liberties, they find it far more difficult to grasp (and hence to embrace) the more specific or applied versions of those liberties, especially when the social or psychological cost for supporting them is high. (They may believe, for example, that permitting certain liberties will lead to disorder, to an increase in crime, or to the exposure of young people to morally debasing ideas.) They may resist learning other libertarian norms that are "unclear," in the sense that the opinion leaders of society remain somewhat divided in their views of those norms. Still other libertarian norms may strike them as offensive to conventional standards of morals and conduct and likely to undermine cherished social institutions such as the nation, the family, or religion. Nor are they likely to be receptive to civil libertarian norms that are not yet "settled," but that are still fairly new or in the process of "emerging" (for example, homosexual freedom or the right to choose abortion).

A great many people, in other words, lack the experience, interest, or intellectual capacity to understand and come to grips with norms that are specific (rather than abstract), unconventional, still being contested, or not yet fully crystallized. Some individuals, in addition, may be hindered from comprehending the norms by social or psychological impediments such as personality disturbances which interfere with the learning process or mental characteristics which make it difficult for them to entertain fine distinctions or to handle complex or subtle ideas. Still others may shy away from acquiring certain values because they fear disapproval by friends or neighbors.

Acceptance. Some people in the society may encounter, and even comprehend, the norms of civil liberties without accepting or internalizing them. For example, they may disapprove of certain norms, regarding them as dangerous, repugnant, or otherwise offensive. (The civil liberties associated with the right to preach atheism, to advocate revolution, or to publish sexually explicit materials may strike them as socially so destructive as to be insupportable.) Other individuals may try to withhold certain civil liberties from groups they despise. Still others may be wedded to values, doctrines, or ideologies that are uncongenial to civil liberties. For example, to many radical extremists of the left or right, tolerance is a benighted and sentimental notion that prevents the realization of the social order they desire. Other individuals, though not necessarily antagonistic to certain civil liberties in principle, may refuse to embrace them fully because they see them as conflicting with values they regard more highly, such as law and order, religious orthodoxy, patriotism, national defense, or the preservation of traditional family values.

Thus, although some individuals, owing to lack of exposure or comprehension, will fail almost entirely to learn many of the libertarian norms of the society, others, for reasons such as we have just indicated, will learn them only imperfectly or incompletely. In general, however, the norms of the political culture (including libertarian norms) are likely to be most effectively learned by people who, by reason of social location and personal endowment, have been most exposed to the norms and best able to comprehend them.

We should also add a brief word about the use of the term "elite" in this volume and about the variations in terminology we have employed when referring to our so-called elite samples.*

It will become clear in the following chapters that we employ the term "elite" to signify any of a number of different categories of people who, because of their social role, vocation, or involvement in public affairs, are in a favorable position to exert above-average influence on public opinion or decisions.

When we speak of elites we do not have in mind a privileged or governing class or a class of people who have power to control others. Some of the people we have included among the elites are public officials or party activists; some are officers of community organizations or are engaged in other activities (for example, newspaper editors, clergymen) that qualify them as "opinion leaders"; some have achieved higher status, influence, or prestige through their professional or public activities and might be described as "influentials" or "notables." In the present volume, we have used these terms interchangeably with the term elite, so that no special significance should be assigned to the latter term (when encountered in the text or tables) as distinguished from such terms as opinion leaders or influentials.

* For a fuller discussion of the terms "elite" and "mass," as used in this book, see chapter 6, pp. 236–43.

CHAPTER 2

The First Amendment: Freedom of Speech and Press

> Congress shall make no law respecting an establishment of religion, or prohibiting the free exercise thereof; or abridging the freedom of speech, or of the press, or the right of the people to assemble, and to petition the government for a redress of grievances.　　—First Amendment, U.S. Constitution

ALTHOUGH it contains only forty-four words and was not ratified until two years after the adoption of the main body of the Constitution itself, the first of the ten amendments that compose the Bill of Rights is considered by many legal scholars to be the cornerstone of American liberties. Despite the general and somewhat imprecise nature of its language, the First Amendment has served to set the democratic tone of American political life. No other provision of the Constitution has exerted greater influence in establishing and defending the conditions of free expression on which democracy rests. Nor has any other constitutional provision done more to set limits on arbitrary political authority or helped to safeguard citizens against the potentially unlimited power of government. For at least the past half century, its provisions have been interpreted by the Supreme Court to apply not only to the federal government but to the states as well, as its key terms have by extension been incorporated into the Fourteenth Amendment.

Owing to its place at the center of the democratic process, and the importance of its promise of individual freedom, the First Amendment has probably generated more debate among jurists and legal commentators during the present century than any other provision of the Constitution. The Amendment, by its very nature, was bound to arouse controversy, as it functions to protect the rights of every citizen to express opinions and engage in conduct which inevitably antagonize other citizens and strain the patience of governing officials. Because of the many variations in the forms and conditions under which freedom of expression might be exercised, it is virtually impossible, or so it appears, to set down interpretative rules that will effectively cover every contingency—unless one is prepared to argue that the right of free expression is absolute and subject to no limitations.

In the course of its evolution, the Amendment has spawned numerous new issues and rights. Its phrases have been extended, shaped, and reshaped, as the nation has confronted changing circumstances and new challenges (Shapiro 1966). The meaning of such terms as speech, press, and assembly have been broadened to encompass such forms of conduct as picketing, parading, demonstrating, and protesting. Court cases involving the First Amendment have been provoked by controversies over academic freedom, public disturbances relating to the exercise of free speech, and the uses of public facilities for assembly and advocacy.

The First Amendment has been called upon to protect the right to remain silent as well as the right to be heard, the right to withhold government secrets as well as the right of access to government files under "freedom of information" acts. It has been extended to the issue of "fairness" in the balancing of opinions expressed on radio and television and to the censoring of films. Freedom of speech and press under the Amendment now have reference not only to the spoken or written word, but to symbolic speech and other forms of expression that incorporate conduct. Included among these are such diverse matters as the burning of draft cards; the refusal to disclose to a congressional committee the names of political confederates, to salute the flag, or to take a loyalty oath; and the desecration of the flag or other national insignia.

Questions have also been raised under the First Amendment about the content of advertisements, prior restraints on the publication of "obscene" or "seditious" books and magazines, the operation of a theater that displays nudity, the content and posting of signs, and the distribution of leaflets that litter the streets or that contain lewd, defamatory, or seditious materials. The Amendment has played a vital role in cases involving the uses and presumed privacy of the mails, the issuance of passports to travel abroad, as well as the more obvious issues of press censorship, such as the banning from public libraries of books deemed dangerous, and the uses of speech and press to advocate violent revolution. Other cases have raised questions about the libeling of public officials and celebrities and the freedom to disseminate offensive opinions or false accusations in the course of an election campaign.*

The right to assemble and to petition for the redress of grievances has raised questions about the authority of government to grant or withhold permits to parade, demonstrate, or conduct meetings in certain public places. These rights have also been broadened to incorporate freedom of association, a liberty nowhere mentioned in the Constitution but one that nevertheless grants individuals the right to join with others to promote public policies they mutually favor. Freedom of association, in turn, includes the right to form organizations that advocate or oppose government measures, to organize trade unions that engage in collective bargaining, to form political parties (including parties that oppose the incumbent administration or even the government itself), and to establish various other alliances for the advancement of group interests and goals.

The preceding list is meant to be illustrative rather than exhaustive. Some of the rights mentioned (freedom of the press or freedom of worship serve as notable examples) are considered by many judges and legal commentators as largely "settled" and as virtually absolute. Others, such as the right to parade or the right to hold public meetings, are generally accepted as valid but are subject to qualifications and restrictions that reflect the conditions under which they are exercised. Still others (for example, obscenity, public nudity, profanity, libel, the desecration of national insignia) remain highly controversial and enjoy only minimal and uncertain protection under the First Amendment. All, however, are subject to limitations affecting the "time, place, and

---

*For a summary of the legal status of First Amendment Protection, we are greatly indebted to Evelyn Christine Cooper, who prepared a memorandum at our request in 1977.

34

manner" in which they are exercised. Even the freedom to express one's opinions, which eminent justices such as Black and Douglas have held to be virtually beyond restriction or regulation, is thought by equally eminent and ardent partisans of the First Amendment, such as Alexander Meiklejohn or Justice Holmes, to be limited by the "facts" surrounding its exercise. Free speech, Meiklejohn observed, does not grant anyone the right to shout into a hospital room and disturb the patients, nor does it permit one to speak out of turn or on an irrelevant topic at a town meeting called to discuss a particular issue (Meiklejohn 1948, pp. 55–60).

Justice Holmes in his famous opinion in *Schenck* v. *U.S.* (249 U.S. 47, 1919)—a case in which a socialist leader was charged with unlawfully distributing a circular urging resistance to the draft during World War I—argued for a conviction on the ground that

> the character of every act depends upon the circumstances in which it was done. The most stringent protection of free speech would not protect a man in falsely shouting fire in a theater, and causing a panic. . . . The question in every case is whether the words are used in such circumstances and are of such a nature as to create a clear and present danger that they will bring about the substantive evils that Congress has a right to prevent. It is a question of proximity and degree.

Holmes argues, in effect, that many utterances that are constitutionally protected in peacetime would enjoy no protection in wartime. In short, the rights listed under the First Amendment, like all other rights, can be stated only as statements of general principle; they are not self-defining, but acquire their meaning after they have been interpreted (usually by the courts) in light of the facts to which they are being applied.

In the domain of academic freedom, which represents in some degree an application of First Amendment rights to secondary schools and colleges, the Court has upheld, as a form of symbolic speech, the right of students and teachers to wear black armbands in order to protest the nation's participation in a war.* In the case of *Healy* v. *James* (408 U.S. 169, 1972), the Court also acknowledged the right of students to organize themselves into chapters of the Students for a Democratic Society (SDS), a radical organization. The Court reasoned in these cases that "First Amendment rights . . . are available to teachers and stu-

---

* For a summary of the legal status of academic freedom, we are greatly indebted to Jessica Pers, who prepared a memorandum at our request in 1977.

dents. It can hardly be argued that either teachers or students shed their constitutional right to freedom of speech or expression at the schoolhouse gate." It is not sufficient that school authorities fear a disturbance, since "undifferentiated fear or apprehension of disturbance is not enough to overcome the right to freedom of expression." The need to risk possible disturbance "is the basis of our national strength." In the *Healy* case, the Court went on to emphasize that "state colleges and universities are not enclaves immune to the sweep of the First Amendment. . . . While the freedom of association is not explicitly set out in the First Amendment, it has long been implicit in the freedom of speech, assembly, and petition." Denial of official recognition of a student organization abridges the right of association (*Healy* v. *James*; excerpted in Haiman 1976, p. 84).

The opinions expressed by the Court's majority in the *Healy* case do not represent a unanimous view on this aspect of the Amendment. The most telling presentation of a dissenting view was made by Justice Black in the *Tinker* case (393 U.S. 503, 1969), in which the Court upheld the rights of students to protest the Vietnam War by wearing black armbands, despite orders from the school officials to remove them. Addressing the subject of student protests and defiance of school authority, Black observed that if the time has come "when pupils of state supported schools . . . can defy and flout orders of school officials to keep their minds on their own school work, it is the beginning of a new revolutionary era of permissiveness in this country fostered by the judiciary. [A state's] public schools . . . are operated to give students opportunity to learn, not to talk politics by actual speech, or by 'symbolic' speech." Students all over the land, Black observed, are already engaged in sit-ins and break-ins and are "apparently confident that they know far more about how to operate public school systems than do their parents, teachers, and elected school officials." Soon they will believe "it is their right to control the schools rather than the right of the State that collects taxes to hire the teachers for the benefit of the pupils" (excerpted in Haiman 1976, pp. 82–83).

Despite the majority decision in *Tinker*, in practice it has been Black's view which has often prevailed, as the Court has on various occasions refused to interfere with school regulations affecting student dress, the wearing of insignia, and the circulation of militant newspapers. But both federal and state courts have repeatedly struck down regulations that restrict the right of college students to choose and hear controversial visiting speakers on the grounds that this is a form of speech protected under the First Amendment. (Cf. Dorsen 1970, p. 576.)

While some uncertainties attend the question of a professor's right to express in the classroom any view he or she chooses, the courts are not likely to permit arbitrary restrictions to be imposed on academic inquiries or to restrict a teacher's "classroom references" (Dorsen 1970, p. 556). It appears from the present state of constitutional opinion that a teacher cannot be required, on the one side, to endorse community orthodoxies or, on the other, to refrain from mentioning or teaching a body of "respected human thought" (*Epperson* v. *Arkansas*, 393 U.S. 97, 1968). Freedom of expression in the classroom, however, is by no means unrestricted. Among other qualifications, a professor must present his or her material with appropriate moderation (as distinguished from a propaganda harangue), with concern for factual accuracy, and with an unbiased selection of evidence designed to educate rather than to proselytize. In general, however, secondary school teachers and, to a greater degree, university professors have gained increasing freedom from loyalty oaths, bans on membership in certain political groups, and termination for private behavior (Dorsen 1970, p. 548).

As the discussion of our research findings will bear out, there are large discrepancies between the judicial standing of the right of free speech and the public's response to concrete applications of that First Amendment right. One is obliged, however, to observe that the principles embodied in the First Amendment have not always enjoyed the lofty standing in American constitutional law that they hold today. Like the other provisions of the Bill of Rights, the First Amendment was not included in the original Constitution of 1787 but, along with those provisions, was adopted under pressure from Madison, Jefferson, and other democrats of the day who were concerned to protect citizens against the danger that the national government might one day grow overly powerful or even despotic. Oppression by highhanded centralized governments was, after all, a condition familiar to the colonists, who had only recently succeeded in throwing off the fetters of what many of them had regarded as tyranny.

Nevertheless, freedom of speech and press, though predominantly favored (in the words of the Continental Congress of 1774) as essential to "the advancement of truth, science, arts, and morality in general," was a much less robust right than it was later to become (Levy 1963, p. xix). Although John Peter Zenger had been acquitted in a landmark case in 1735 on a charge of publishing material critical of government, his acquittal rested not on the principle of unrestricted freedom of the press, but on the narrower grounds that the allegations he had published were shown to be factually true. Had they been proven false, Zenger would presumably have been convicted of "seditious libel"—a crime virtually equivalent to treason.

Even among the advocates of free speech and press the notion that one could freely criticize the government was by no means universally acknowledged. Those who championed freedom of the press at the time were not so much concerned with eliminating the concept of seditious libel itself as with modifying it to eliminate the "truth" test, thus making it legally possible to publish dissenting material even if it turned out to be inaccurate. They also hoped to eradicate any vestiges of the ancient practice of prior restraint on publication (Shapiro 1966), a practice against which John Milton had especially inveighed in *Areopagitica*.

At the time of the American Revolution and during the decades that followed, a person could still be arrested and criminally prosecuted for utterances or published writings that criticized officials, praised the British king or parliament, or contained "malicious falsehoods," "licentious opinions," or defamatory criticisms (Levy 1963, p. xlix). It should occasion little surprise that as late as 1798, a Congress dominated by the Federalists could adopt a set of laws restricting popular liberties, the most significant of which was the Sedition Act. The Act aimed to silence any publication that could be shown to have been maliciously motivated, "libelous" (both legally and factually) in its criticisms of governing officials, and false in its assertions. Its unstated objective, apparently, was to silence or at least to discourage criticism of the Federalists by their opponents.

So draconian a measure was bound to affront prevailing sensibilities. The passage of the Sedition Act proved a turning point by arousing the Republican and other libertarian forces against Federalist efforts to suppress freedom of speech and press. Jefferson, upon becoming President in 1800, pardoned the editors and other publicists who had been convicted under the Act. The Act itself ran out in 1801 and was not renewed by the newly elected Congress. Philosophies of freedom that had been circulating in England (through, for example, the writings of Cato,* Locke, and other libertarians) were now more

---

*Cato was the joint pseudonym of two Whig political journalists whose writings were, in Clinton Rossiter's view, "the most popular, quotable, esteemed source of political ideas in the colonial period," more influential (in his opinion) than those of John Locke (Levy 1963, xxxiii).

widely disseminated than ever among American intellectuals. The essential thrust of the views represented in these libertarian philosophies was that freedom of thought, speech, and publication were *natural rights* which extended even to the criticism of government and its officials.

The argument advanced in the early nineteenth century for freedom of the press rested not only on its status as a natural right, but on its utility for popular, democratic government. Along with other First Amendment rights, it came to be viewed by the libertarians of the day as indispensable to a republican form of government. John Thompson, a noted writer of the period, reiterated in eloquent language that government exists by popular consent and cannot, therefore, tell citizens what they can or cannot think about certain subjects. Nor can a citizen be guilty of seditious writing, since "the concept of seditiousness" implies a relationship of inferiority in which the citizens are subjects bound to a master, rather than the reverse.*

To these arguments one can add the democratic belief that freedom of expression is obviously essential for registering popular consent and holding rulers accountable. To be genuine, consent must be freely given; and to be freely given, it must be the product of unhindered communication. At a minimum, all citizens must have the opportunity to obtain the information they need to evaluate their rulers fairly. They must be free to exchange opinions, to persuade others by facts and argument, and to be persuaded in turn. Effective consent and accountability presuppose the unhampered opportunity for citizens to test the truth or falsity of government claims; to evaluate the government, its policies, and its officeholders; and to participate (via speech, press, assembly, and association) in efforts to achieve peaceful and orderly change.

Thompson and other champions of freedom of the press had little patience with the arguments that suppression was sometimes justified because newspapers "teemed with misrepresentations or with undeserved abuse of private or public character." Does it follow, he asked, "that we ought to be deprived of Liberty because it may be, or has been, abused? Will Justice not rather say, let misrepresentation be exposed by the force of truth? . . . *In no case whatever use coercive measures.*

---

* *An Inquiry, Concerning the Liberty and Licentiousness of the Press and the Uncontrollable Nature of the Human Mind* (cited by Levy 1963). Thompson's view of the impossibility of seditious libel in a democracy was greatly elaborated more than 150 years later by such authorities on the First Amendment as Harry Kalven. See his article on the *New York Times* decision, in Kurland 1975, pp. 84–114.

Truth is at all times sufficiently powerful. Coercion may *silence*, but it can never convince."* Thompson, like so many other civil libertarians before and since, took it as axiomatic that in a fair and open contest of contending opinions, truth would invariably prevail over falsehood; and that the only appropriate corrective for error was a free exchange of ideas from which the truth was bound to emerge.

Another libertarian publicist of the day, George Hay, went beyond the conventional arguments of that period to maintain that freedom of the press cannot justifiably be regulated or restricted. Anticipating arguments that were later to be made by Justice Black, Hay observed:

> The word "freedom" has meaning. It is either absolute, that is, exempt from all law, or it is qualified, that is, regulated by law. If it be exempt from the control of law, the Sedition Bill which controls the "freedom of the press" is unconstitutional. But if it is to be regulated by law, the [First] Amendment which declared that Congress shall make no law to abridge the freedom of the press, which freedom however may be regulated by law, is the grossest absurdity that ever was conceived by the human mind.
> (Hay; in Levy 1963, pp. 190–91)

Noteworthy for their freshness and acuity are the views advanced by Tunis Wortman, a New York lawyer and writer—"an outstanding democratic theorist of his time" (Levy 1963, p. 229). His fundamental postulate was that the human intellect is by its very nature inquisitive, searching, and imaginative and therefore beyond external control. The mind seeks "to extend its researches into every subject." Its thoughts "spring spontaneously" from every situation and event that confronts us. "When once the intellectual train commences, its direction is not to be diverted, its force not to be subdued; . . . to prescribe bounds to the empire of thought, would of all tasks be the most herculean."†

Why, Wortman asks, were human beings furnished with "the sublime attribute of reason"? Was it intended that their "most exalted and distinguished powers should be chained into a state of dormant quiescence and inactivity"? Given the nature of the human mind,

> A liberty of investigation into every subject of thought is . . . indisposable to the progression and happiness of mankind . . . of all the rights which

---

*Text contained in Levy 1963, p. 316. The argument, of course, was by no means new. John Milton had, two centuries earlier, made essentially the same point in *Areopagitica*: "If truth is in the field, we do injury to misdoubt her strength. Let [Truth] and falsehood grapple; who ever knew truth put to the worse in a free and open encounter?"

†"A Treatise Concerning Political Enquiry, and the Liberty of the Press"; in Levy 1963, p. 231.

can be attributed to man, that of communicating his sentiments is the most sacred and inestimable. It is impossible that the imagination should conceive a more horrible and pernicious tyranny than that which would restrain the Intercourse of Thought. Who is not aware that much of the happiness of intelligent and social Beings consists in the pleasure of unrestrained conversation . . . and the sublime delight of communicating their ideas with a confidence unmingled with terror?

(Wortman; in Levy 1963, pp. 242–43)

As Wortman argues, government has no proper authority to coerce thought or interfere with the free play of the human imagination. A government dedicated to justice, therefore, has "nothing to apprehend. Tyranny alone should tremble at the sternly inquisitive glance of enlightened investigation" (in Levy 1963, pp. 233–34). The genuine object of government is "superintendence" and the suppression of crime.

The views expressed by Wortman, Hay, and Thompson (as well as such congressmen as Albert Gallatin, John Nicholas, and Edward Livingston) did not, of course, represent the prevailing opinions of all of the leading statesmen and commentators at the end of the eighteenth century. Hamilton and the other Federalists held a much more restrictive view of the liberties embodied in the First Amendment. For example, a majority report of Congress, considering the repeal of the Sedition Act, maintained that the liberty of the press does not give anyone a license to publish whatever he or she pleases without punishment for injury to others, but only grants permission to publish without prior restraint.*

Even Jefferson wavered at various stages on such questions as prosecution for seditious libel or for making false assertions in the press. Jefferson, who seems to have been especially incensed by what he considered the vulgarity and mendacity of the press, was not only severe in his criticisms of journalistic excesses, but was apparently prepared at certain points in his career to prosecute editors for seditious utterances and the printing of falsehoods. In his first Inaugural Address in 1800, however, he reasserted his belief in the right of any individual to advocate the dissolution of the Union or to abolish the republican form of government. He was convinced that such "error of opinion may be tolerated where reason is left free to combat it." The later Jefferson, though still dispirited by the abuses of the press, had

---

*"Majority and Minority Reports on the Repeal of the Sedition Act, February 25, 1799"; text reprinted in Levy 1963, pp. 173–74.

nevertheless become resigned to the necessity for granting the press the fullest measure of freedom.

Madison's view of the First Amendment and freedom of speech and press was more radical. He believed "that the Sedition Act was unconstitutional; that the United States possessed no jurisdiction over common-law crimes (and thus, presumably, over such alleged crimes as seditious libel); and that a popular or free republican government cannot be libeled. Madison further believed that the First Amendment was intended to supersede the common law on speech and press; and that the freedom guaranteed by the Amendment was absolute, so far as the federal government was concerned, because it could not be abridged by any authority of the United States" (Levy 1960, p. 273). In short, Madison's views appear to have anticipated the interpretations of the First Amendment advanced by most civil libertarian judges and commentators of the last fifty years.

Apart from certain restraints on the publication of obscenity,* defamation, and, for a time, seditious libel, the press (and in particular the print media) has, since the early eighteenth century, enjoyed a virtually unrestricted right to report the news and publish its opinions. Certain forms of speech and publication were at one point in the Supreme Court's history deemed unworthy of First Amendment protection. According to Justice Murphy in *Chaplinsky* v. *New Hampshire* (315 U.S. 568, 1942), these included the

> lewd and obscene, the profane, the libelous, and the insulting or "fighting words"—those which by their very utterance inflict injury or tend to incite an immediate breach of the peace. It has been well observed that such utterances are no essential part of any exposition of ideas, and are of such slight social value as a step to truth that any benefit that may be derived from them is clearly outweighed by the social interest in order and morality.

Nevertheless, the Court has in various cases (both before and after Chaplinsky) produced opinions that have effectively diminished the impact of these restraints. In *Near* v. *Minnesota* (283 U.S. 679, 1931), and, more recently, in refusing to enjoin the *New York Times* from publishing the Pentagon Papers (obtained illegally by an employee of the Department of Defense), the Court has reiterated its stand against prior restraint on the press. It has insisted in such cases as *Lewis* v. *New*

---

*Obscenity will be dealt with in chapter 5 on attitudes toward lifestyle. Speech and publication bearing on sedition will be treated later in the present chapter.

Orleans (415 U.S. 130, 1974) that statutes which seek to prohibit "fighting words" must be narrowly drawn and highly specific.

In the famous case of the *New York Times* v. *Sullivan* (376 U.S. 254, 1964), the Court refused damages for defamation in a libel suit brought by an Alabama police official who claimed that an advertisement in the *Times* had falsely accused the southern police of mishandling racial disturbances. Unless "actual malice" can be demonstrated, the Court held, the publication of a false (and even damaging) statement against an individual or a group cannot be considered libelous. According to Kalven, in this case the Court effectively eliminated "seditious libel" as a possible crime (in Kurland 1975, pp. 84–114). Kalven also concluded that the Court had at last rejected the principle that only true criticisms are protected and that false ones are not. The Constitution, he observed, does not distinguish between the true and the false. The Court recognized that "erroneous statement is inevitable in free debate, and . . . must be protected if the freedoms of expression are to have the 'breathing space' that they need . . . to survive." In the absense of such protection, people would be afraid to speak or sell books and would censor themselves in order to avoid punishment. A truth test would have a "chilling effect" on free speech and publication.

Kalven interpreted the *New York Times* case as holding, in essence, that "no matter how speech is classified, there must still be First Amendment consideration and review. No category of speech is any longer beneath the protection of the First Amendment." The central meaning of that Amendment is that citizens may, with impunity, criticize the stewardship of their governors and the government itself. As Justice Brennan put the matter in his majority opinion, "neither factual error nor defamatory content suffices to remove the Constitutional shield from criticism of official conduct." The Sedition Act of 1798 was at last declared unconstitutional (in Kurland 1975, pp. 110–11).

The *New York Times* rule was subsequently extended by the courts to "public figures" who are not governing officials—to individuals, for example, who are active in community and social affairs. The assumption here is that public figures invite attention and comment by their activities and have access to channels in the media through which they can reply to alleged defamation (*Gertz* v. *Robert Welch, Inc.* 94 S. Ct. 2997, 1974). (Cf. Cooper 1977.) Like governing officials, they achieve fame or notoriety which makes it difficult or impossible for them to recover damages for libel or defamation. Discriminatory though this may appear to the person libeled, it is a measure of the extraordinarily broad range of freedom that has been accorded the press under the Court's reading of the First Amendment.

The Supreme Court, however, has not been wholly consistent in its application of First Amendment principles or in its criteria for deciding what may or may not be prohibited. While the general tendency of the Court over the past two centuries has been to broaden the interpretation of the liberties included in the First Amendment, the Court has frequently wavered in its reading of particular rights. Forms of speech and publication permitted in one decade have been denied in the next, and the reverse. To some extent this reflects changes in the Court's personnel, in the political climate of the country, and in the standards by which certain forms of expression are judged. Some justices have held First Amendment liberties to be absolute; others have accorded them a "preferred position"; while still others have assigned them equal weight with other provisions of the Constitution.

Different tests have been applied by the Court at different stages in deciding what forms of expression may or may not be prohibited. In some cases, the Court has concentrated mainly on the "clear and present danger" test. Yet, some justices, and many legal commentators, have found this test inappropriate in many circumstances. Some students of the First Amendment believe that the test allows the government to cut off expression as soon as it comes close to being effective (Emerson 1970, pp. 14–16). For a time, the "clear and present danger" doctrine was replaced by the "bad tendencies" test, in which speech or publications that were not considered dangerous in themselves might nevertheless be prohibited because their indirect consequences might be "bad" (Gitlow v. New York, 268 U.S. 652, 1925). According to this doctrine, the government has the authority to halt danger to the state at its incipience, and need not wait until danger is imminent. This test has also been found wanting by many judges and constitutional lawyers, since many forms of speech and press, innocuous in themselves, might be outlawed on the vague ground that they might subsequently lead to damaging outcomes.

In more recent years, the Court has frequently employed a "balancing test," in which the benefits associated with a given instance of free expression are weighed against the potential risks to other interests of society, such as national security or internal order (Shapiro 1966). Many constitutional authorities believe this test to be *ad hoc*, arbitrary, and so lacking in recognizable principle as scarcely to be a test at all (Emerson 1970). The test most often used by the Court at present in deciding which forms of expression should be permitted or proscribed might be loosely described as a combination of the principle of clear and present danger plus *direct* incitement of prohibited conduct. That is to say, speech or publication which directly provokes an audience to engage in some form of dangerous conduct (for example, violent demonstrations, riots, attempts to seize power by force, physical harm to others) may be prohibited or punished after the fact, but the connection between the utterance or publication and the ensuing consequence must be clear, direct, and specific.

A series of Supreme Court rulings on revolutionary advocacy and action illustrate the status of the right of free speech and press (as well as association) under current American law. In the Smith Act, adopted in 1940, Congress explicitly prohibited advocacy of violence to overthrow the government and made it a crime to be a member of an organization dedicated to such a purpose. In 1950, in the McCarran Act, Congress required all Communist "action" or "front" organizations to register with the Department of Justice and to publish their membership lists.

The constitutionality of the Smith Act was upheld in *Dennis* v. *U.S.* (341 U.S. 494, 1951), in which the Court decided that Congress has the power to prevent attempts to overthrow the government by force and can regulate or prohibit speech or writing that has both the intention and the "tendency" to incite such action. Although the Court in a later case, *Yates* v. *U.S.* (354 U.S. 298, 1957), distinguished between the teaching of abstract revolutionary doctrines and advocacy of revolutionary *action* (a distinction that effectively put an end to prosecution under the Smith Act), it nevertheless remained illegal to engage in "advocacy directed at promoting . . . concrete action for the forcible overthrow of the Government."

Four years later, in *Scales* v. *U.S.* (376 U.S. 290, 1961), the Court dealt with the "guilt by association" aspects of the Smith and McCarran Acts by holding that one could not be punished for membership in a revolutionary organization, and for its advocacy of revolutionary ideas, unless one was an "active" member possessing full knowledge of the organization's aims and having the specific intention of carrying them out.

In general, the protection offered by the First Amendment has been interpreted by the courts as applying mainly to the area of *expression* and does not extend to *actions* against the government, such as treason, rebellion, espionage, and sabotage. Protesting against the nation's foreign and defense policies is, for the most part, now considered by the Court as a legitimate exercise of free speech or press. If, however, such dissent deliberately aims to produce a direct and specific result (for example, incitement to participate in actions that impede a war effort), the Court may regard it as "speech plus" (speech plus action) and withhold constitutional protection (Cooper 1977).

In the matter of extending the freedom to publish, and even to advocate, controversial ideas without fear of legal punishment, the aforementioned case of *New York Times* v. *Sullivan* has particular relevance. Not only did the Court decide that a particular news story or advertisement enjoyed First Amendment protection even if it were not factually accurate, but it established (in the opinion of Kalven and other constitutional authorities) that government officials and, *a fortiori*, the government itself could not be defamed by the writings of critics or opponents. Those who criticize their government, however virulent the accusations, are not committing treason but merely exercising their First Amendment rights and duties as citizens.

Thus, the Court has said, in effect, that a democracy must tolerate even those opinions which attack democratic institutions. Emerson sums up the arguments for this view: opinions must remain open to challenge if they are not to become dead dogmas; even groups hostile to democracy hold some ideas that are "valid, or partially valid"; suppression "imperils the process by which freedom of expression promotes unity and achieves consent throughout society"; suppression drives the opposition underground and encourages solution by force rather than by reason; it also unleashes hatred, prejudice, and fear, curtailing the freedom not only of those who are suppressed but of others as well (Emerson 1970, pp. 51–53).

For many of the Founders, as for some contemporary writers, the liberties embodied in the First Amendment were (and are) thought to be "natural rights" and hence inviolable—an interpretation derived in part from such English philosophers and publicists as John Locke, Richard Hooker, and (later) Thomas Paine. (Cf. Rothman 1976.) When Jefferson and his colleagues asserted in the Declaration that it was self-evident that all men are "endowed by their Creator with certain inalienable Rights," they were echoing the belief that these rights are natural and ineradicable. Individuals possess them by virtue of being human, and therefore creatures of dignity and worth. No government can justifiably deprive them of their liberties and other natural rights, as these are essential aspects of their humanity. Furthermore, since people cannot rightly be governed except by their own consent, no person would voluntarily relinquish to an external authority the power to dispose of that which is already his or hers by natural right. The exercise of consent, in turn, presupposes freedom of exchange, and hence freedom of speech, press, assembly, and conscience.

The early proponents of the First Amendment, thus, based their defense of it not primarily on the utility of freedom (though they were cognizant of this as well) but on its hallowed status as a property with which every human being is innately endowed.

Today, those who defend freedom of speech and press are less likely to rest their case on the doctrine of natural rights—although the sanctity with which they invest these liberties is virtually the equivalent of a natural rights justification. They continue, in other words, to perceive these rights as *inherent* and inseparable from the person (whereas critics of libertarianism are more likely to view them *as benefits or privileges to be earned*). (Cf. Berns 1957.) Free speech, press, assembly, and other First Amendment rights may be subject to regulations governing the "time, place, and manner" of their exercise, but they are conceived, in their essential nature, as inextinguishable. Emerson, for example, asserts (among other arguments) that such rights as freedom of publication belong to a person "purely in his capacity as an individual. [They derive] from the widely accepted purpose of western thought that the proper end of man is the realization of his character and potentialities as a human being . . . " (Emerson 1963; excerpted in Haiman 1976, p. 203).

Other commentators (Alexander Meiklejohn is perhaps the leading exemplar) trace the authority of the First Amendment not to the sanctity of the individual or to any updated notion of natural rights, but to the principle of self-government. The vital point, says Meiklejohn,

is that no suggestion of policy shall be denied a hearing because it is on one side of the issue rather than another. And this means that though citizens may, on other grounds, be barred from speaking, they may not be barred because their views are thought to be false or dangerous. No plan of action shall be outlawed because someone in control thinks it unwise, unfair, un-American. No speaker may be declared "out of order" because we disagree with what he intends to say. And the reason for this equality of status in the fields of ideas lies deep in the very foundations of the self-governing process. When men govern themselves, it is they—and no one else—who must pass judgment upon unwisdom and unfairness and danger. And that means that unwise ideas must have a hearing as well as wise ones, unfair as well as fair, dangerous as well as safe, un-American as well as American. (1948, pp. 26–27)

To these arguments Meiklejohn adds that we must give a hearing even to those "who hate and despise freedom," to those who, if they had the power, would destroy our institutions. "Our action must be guided, not by their principles, but by ours. We listen, not because they desire to speak, but because we need to hear. . . . The attempt to know has a unique status . . . to which all other activities are subordinated. This is one reason why the First Amendment recognizes that freedom of public discussion can never be abridged" (Meiklejohn 1948a, p. 205).

The right of free speech and publication is, of course, frequently abused. Speakers and writers often mislead audiences by withholding essential facts or presenting themselves and their cause in a false light. However unprincipled and intemperate the presentation, however seriously it misrepresents facts, there are no universally accepted criteria that can be applied in practice to enable us to distinguish advocates who are honorable from those who are unscrupulous, no certain standards that would authorize us to esteem the former and censor the latter. In this as in so many other matters that characterize imperfect conduct in an imperfect society, one has no choice in a democracy but to risk the possibility that error may for a time prevail. One permits falsehoods to be uttered and disseminated so that truths will enjoy at least an equal opportunity to be heard.

Findings on Freedom of Speech

When stated in their most general or abstract form, the liberties contained in the First Amendment are so widely endorsed by both the general public and opinion leaders as to suggest that freedom of expression may very well be the most cherished of all American rights. Public opinion surveys dating back to the 1930s indicate that Americans have routinely expressed overwhelming approval of the general right of individuals to think and speak as they choose. The data reported in figure 2.1 are by no means unusual. As reported earlier

(McClosky 1964), 89 percent of the respondents in our PAB survey (1958) professed to believe in "free speech for all no matter what their views might be." Over 80 percent agreed with the statement that "people who hate our way of life should still have a chance to talk and be heard"; 86 percent of the American public (and 92 percent of their political leaders) subscribed to the claim advanced by John Stuart Mill that "unless there is freedom for many points of view to be presented, there is little chance that the truth can ever be known." In a national poll conducted in the 1940s, 97 percent of the American public replied affirmatively when asked simply "Do you believe in freedom of speech?" (Erskine 1970).

While evidence of this kind testifies to the importance of free speech as an American ideal, it should not be taken at face value. As soon as one moves from questions about freedom of speech in the abstract to questions about the exercise of speech in particular situations, the level of support drops off sharply. As reported in table 2.1 even the honorific value of freedom of thought and speech has various limitations assigned to it by many of the same people who endorse the right in the abstract.

For example, fewer than 60 percent of the mass public in our sample would grant freedom of speech to people who are intolerant of the opinions of others, while about the same number believe it is wrong "to keep people from expressing unpopular opinions." Only 49 percent would uphold the right of individuals to express certain opinions if the majority voted to ban those opinions. (Cf. McClosky 1949.) Even fewer (41 percent) would permit foreigners who criticize our government to visit or study here. Approximately half the general population would require loyalty oaths for all government employees; the same number would forbid government authorities from opening the mail of persons "suspected of being in contact with fugitives." Less than half (49 percent) believe that one has a right to protect one's diary—the most intimate form of personal expression—from being made public in the course of a court trial.

When we turn to the OVS items in table 2.1, which involve highly unpopular or unconventional opinions, the level of public tolerance for freedom of expression is again (with two exceptions) moderate or low. Only 18 percent would permit the American Nazi party to use the town hall to hold a public meeting, and only 23 percent would grant a group's request to use a public building to denounce the government. Even such vague behavior as free speech for "extremists" or the utter-

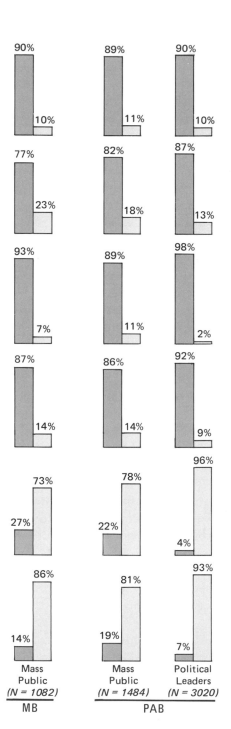

I believe in free speech for all no matter what their views might be.

People who hate our way of life should still have a chance to talk and be heard.

We could never be free if we gave up the right to criticize our government.

Unless there is freedom for many points of view to be presented, there is little chance that the truth can ever be known.

In a properly organized society, everyone would hold the same beliefs and there would be no cause for conflict.

The idea that everyone has a right to his own opinions is being carried too far these days.

Agree   Disagree

| Mass Public (N = 1082) MB | Mass Public (N = 1484) | Political Leaders (N = 3020) PAB |

FIGURE 2.1
Support for Freedom of Speech in the Abstract
(CLS/MB/PAB)

When countries like Chile, Russia, or Uganda clearly violate the human rights of their citizens, which of these policies should the U.S. follow:

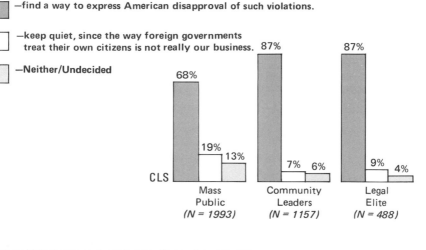

When making decisions about public affairs, the majority:

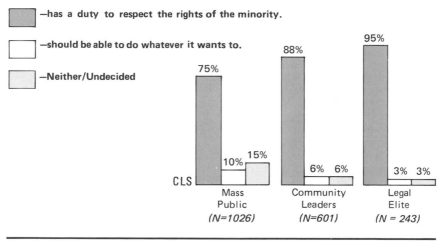

Notes: Because percentages have been rounded off, occasionally there will be disparities in totals (columns will not add up to 100 percent).

See the Preface to Research Findings in Chapter 1 and Appendix B for an analysis of the components of various categories used in the PAB, CLS, and OVS studies: that is "Political Leaders," "Legal Elite," and so forth.

The CLS was conducted in 1978-1979; the OVS in 1976-1977; and the PAB in 1958.

The Marginal Believers (MB) Survey consists of a cross-section sample of 1082 Minnesota respondents, administered in 1955 by special arrangement with the Minnesota Poll.

TABLE 2.1
Attitudes Toward Free Speech Under Various Conditions

	CLS		
	Mass Public	Community Leaders	Legal Elite
	(N = 1993)	(N = 1157)	(N = 488)
Free speech should be granted:			
—to everyone regardless of how intolerant they are of other people's opinions.	58%	76%	87%
—only to people who are willing to grant the same rights of free speech to everyone else.	27	19	9
—Neither/Undecided	15	6	4
Should foreigners who dislike our government and criticize it be allowed to visit or study here?			
—Yes.	41	69	81
—No.	47	24	15
—Neither/Undecided	12	7	4
If the majority votes in a referendum to ban the public expression of certain opinions, should the majority opinion be followed?			
—No, because free speech is a more fundamental right than majority rule.	49	67	86
—Yes, because no group has a greater right than the majority to decide which opinions can or cannot be expressed.	23	15	6
—Neither/Undecided	28	17	8
A person's diary should be considered:			
—so personal and private a document that no one, not even a judge and jury, is entitled to see it without the person's consent.	49	53	38
—legal evidence if that person is on trial for a serious crime.	33	32	47
—Neither/Undecided	18	15	16
Should government authorities be allowed to open the mail of people suspected of being in contact with fugitives?			
—No, it would violate a person's right to correspond with his friends.	50	55	57
—Yes, as it may help the police catch criminals they have been looking for.	31	28	22
—Neither/Undecided	20	17	21
Loyalty oaths for all government employees:*			
—are unnecessary, since most government employees are loyal Americans anyway.	23	34	44
—should be required, to be sure that only patriotic people work for the government.	50	35	29
—Neither/Undecided	27	31	28

	OVS	
	Mass Public	Opinion Leaders
	(N = 938)	(N = 845)
When it comes to free speech, extremists:		
—should have the same rights as everyone else.	60%	86%
—should not be allowed to spread their propaganda.	19	3
—Neither/Undecided	21	11

	OVS	
	Mass Public	**Opinion Leaders**
	(N = 938)	**(N = 845)**
"Crackpot" ideas:		
—have as much right to be heard as sensible ideas.	50%	81%
—sometimes have to be censored for the public good.	32	10
—Neither/Undecided	18	9
Should a community allow the American Nazi party to use its town hall to hold a public meeting?		
—Yes.	18	41
—No.	66	41
—Neither/Undecided	16	18
If a speaker at a public meeting begins to make racial slurs, the audience should:		
—let him have his say and then answer him.	74	84
—stop him from speaking.	14	6
—Neither/Undecided	12	10
If a group asks to use a public building to hold a meeting denouncing the government, their request should be:		
—granted.	23	51
—denied.	57	26
—Neither/Undecided	20	23
For children to be properly educated:		
—they should be free to discuss all ideas and subjects, no matter what.	70	85
—they should be protected against ideas the community considers wrong or dangerous.	15	3
—Neither/Undecided	15	12
Meetings urging America to make war against an enemy nation:		
—have as much right to be held as meetings that support peace.	53	80
—are so inhumane that we should not allow them to be held.	18	4
—Neither/Undecided	28	16

	PAB	
	Mass Public	**Political Leaders**
	(N = 1484)	**(N = 3020)**
It's wrong to keep people from expressing unpopular opinions.		
Agree	61%	72%
Disagree	39	28

NOTES: Because percentages have been rounded off, occasionally there will be disparities in totals (columns will not add up to 100 percent).

See the Preface to Research Findings (p. 25) and Appendix B for a description of the leader and mass public samples of various categories used in the PAB, CLS, and OVS studies: that is "Political Leaders," "Legal Elite," and so forth.

The CLS was conducted in 1978–1979; the OVS in 1976–1977; and the PAB study in 1958.

*This item was included in Form A of the CLS questionnaire (see Appendix A). For the Mass Public, N = 1026; for Community Leaders, N = 601; for Legal Elite, N = 243.

ance of "crackpot" ideas would be permitted by only 60 and 50 percent, respectively, of our general population samples.

These figures suggest that freedom of speech is, in the public mind, a more tenuous right than one might infer from the nearly universal endorsement it receives when stated in its abstract forms. Its fragility becomes even more apparent when we turn to academic freedom. A number of items relating to various aspects of academic freedom have been set out in table 2.2, and the scores registered on these items bear witness to the low regard held by the public for the academic rights of teachers, students, and the professoriate in general.

Although academic and research freedom have been esteemed by academics as necessary conditions for intellectual freedom, this view is not shared by a majority of Americans. On some items, such as the right of high school teachers to express opinions that are in conflict with the views of the community, scarcely 25 percent of the general public are willing to acknowledge this as a right. Between one half and two thirds of the general population would refuse to hire a professor if he or she held unusual or extreme views on politics or racial differences. One of the most extraordinary sets of responses concerns professors who are "suspected of spreading false ideas" in their classes: only 4 percent of the mass public believe that a professor should not be interfered with, and 77 percent of the population would "send someone into his classes to check on him." Since this item goes to the heart of the principle of academic freedom, the responses to it (not only by the public but by the community leaders and the legal elite as well) tell us a great deal about the views of nonacademicians toward rights that are taken for granted within the academy.

The First Amendment rights of students do not fare well either. Only 41 percent of the public would permit college students to choose their own guest speakers, while 45 percent want speakers to be screened beforehand to eliminate those who might "advocate dangerous or extreme ideas." As for the rights of student protesters, an issue about which the public has frequently expressed its disapproval and alarm, one third of the national sample would pay serious attention to student demands, but approximately the same number would simply suspend or expel them from school.

Although a majority claim to believe that "the goal of science is to discover truth, whatever it may be," only 10 percent are willing to entrust the conduct of government-financed university research to the research investigators themselves and would permit them to work

TABLE 2.2
Free Speech and Academic Freedom

	CLS		
	Mass Public	**Community Leaders**	**Legal Elite**
	(N = 1993)	**(N = 1157)**	**(N = 488)**
On issues of religion, morals, and politics, high school teachers have the right to express their opinions in class:			
—even if they go against the community's most precious values and beliefs.	25%	38%	46%
—only if those opinions do not offend the community's beliefs.	30	21	16
—Neither/Undecided	44	42	38
When a community pays a teacher's salary, it:			
—doesn't buy the right to censor the opinions she expresses in the classroom.	29	39	48
—has the right to keep her from teaching ideas that go against the community's standards.	53	45	37
—Neither/Undecided	18	16	15
If a professor is suspected of spreading false ideas in his classes, college officials:			
—should not interfere since it would violate his rights.	4	10	17
—should send someone into his classes to check on him.	77	61	57
—Neither/Undecided	20	30	26
Refusing to hire a professor because of his unusual political beliefs:			
—is never justified.	18	19	25
—may be necessary if his views are really extreme.	66	66	58
—Neither/Undecided	16	15	17
Refusing to hire a professor because he believes certain races are inferior:			
—cannot be justified.	29	33	37
—may be necessary if his views are really extreme.	52	50	41
—Neither/Undecided	19	17	22
Scientific research that might show women or minorities in a bad light:			
—should be allowed because the goal of science is to discover truth, whatever it may be.	59	80	90
—should be banned because the results might damage their self-respect.	13	5	0
—Neither/Undecided	28	16	10
Regulation or control of government-financed research carried on at universities is:			
—unjustified because government has no right to meddle in university affairs.	10	10	12
—justified because some of the research may be dangerous.	60	63	55
—Neither/ Undecided	30	27	32

TABLE 2.2 (continued)
Free Speech and Academic Freedom

	CLS		
	Mass Public	**Community Leaders**	**Legal Elite**
	(N = 1993)	**(N = 1157)**	**(N = 488)**
Government regulation of scientific experiments done on human beings:			
—interferes with a scientist's freedom to decide what research would benefit mankind most.	6%	4%	6%
—is necessary to assure that people won't be harmed by the experiments.	72	83	83
—Neither/Undecided	21	14	11
When inviting guest speakers to a college campus:			
—students should be free to invite anyone they want to hear.	41	60	80
—the speakers should be screened beforehand to be sure they don't advocate dangerous or extreme ideas.	45	26	12
—Neither/Undecided	14	14	9
Mass student protest demonstrations:			
—should be allowed by college officials as long as they are nonviolent.	68	82	88
—have no place on a college campus and the participating students should be punished.	21	13	9
—Neither/Undecided	12	5	3
If it is discovered that an elementary school teacher is a lesbian:			
—she should be able to go on teaching because sexual preference should not be a ground for dismissal.	44	51	59
—she should not be allowed to continue teaching.	35	28	22
—Neither/Undecided	21	21	18

	OVS	
	Mass Public	**Opinion Leaders**
	(N = 938)	**(N = 845)**
On issues of religion, morals, and politics, high school teachers have the right to express their opinions in class:		
—even if they go against the community's standards.	28%	46%
—only if those opinions are acceptable to the community.	32	12
—Neither/Undecided	40	42
The best way to handle campus protesters is to:		
—pay serious attention to their demands.	33	57
—suspend or expel them from school.	35	37
—Neither/Undecided	32	36

without government regulation. An even smaller number (6 percent) would leave scientists free from government regulation in conducting scientific experiments on human beings. While they are solicitous of the welfare of human subjects, they are unwilling to permit scientists "to decide what research would benefit mankind most."

The low levels of support for academic freedom among the general public and the elites (although the latter do score higher) testify to the difficulty of incorporating some of the more subtle or esoteric civil liberties norms. Popular support for various applied forms of free speech tends not to be overwhelming in any sphere, but the public is especially sensitive to questions concerning the exercise of freedom in the educational realm, perhaps because it involves the development of ideas and conduct among the young. The American people appear never to have conclusively decided that the education of the young should be the exclusive province of educators. Especially at the primary and secondary levels of schooling they are inclined to look upon teachers as public servants, who serve at the bidding of the community. Educators are perceived as narrowly limited in the authority they should exert over the minds of students and as answerable to the community both for their personal conduct and for the manner in which they perform their roles. As the data illustrate, the belief that educators should enjoy First Amendment rights in carrying out their educational duties is by no means universally acknowledged. For many Americans, these rights have little standing when set against the awesome responsibility that teachers bear in helping to train the young.

Teaching may be a respected profession as compared with most other vocations, but apparently its members are not among those whose social and political opinions are widely valued or trusted. Often they are perceived as bookish, naive intellectuals who lack experience of the world. Even if the populace were to concede in the abstract that educators have a right to their own opinions, most do not extend this right to the context of the classroom or the research laboratory. The public's attitude toward a teacher's right to express unorthodox opinions *outside* the classroom remains a bit uncertain, but it is plain from the data that many people regard the exercise of that freedom within the classroom as legally and morally questionable, and in any event as socially undesirable. A large segment of the population, including many who score high on libertarianism, do not accept the argument made by educators that freedom of expression within the classroom is essential to the discovery of truth and the proper education of the young.

Findings on Freedom of the Press

Although the Court's decisions on freedom of the press do not grant to newspapers or other media the absolute right to publish, broadcast, or portray any and all opinions on any and all subjects, the decisions tend to uphold standards of freedom of publication that are far broader than the standards one encounters among the general public. Here, as in other domains of civil liberties, the norms set out in the Bill of Rights and gradually elaborated by the legislatures, the courts, and legal commentators filter down to the public slowly and imperfectly. Whereas the courts have edged increasingly toward the view that the media ought to be as free of regulation as possible, the mass public tends to express the belief that all the media, including newspapers and books, are potentially dangerous to society and damaging to public morals. They ought, therefore, to be more closely regulated.

The data in figure 2.2 indicate that large sections of the population perceive certain topics as inherently inappropriate for discussion in the media. Some subjects, such as obscenity, pornography, or matters affecting sexual conduct, may be regarded by some as suitable for private communication but offensive when they enter the public domain. The possible reasons for this response are beyond our present concerns, but as we can see from the items presented in figure 2.2, rarely do more than one third of the mass public take a civil libertarian stand on the issues reflected in the items. By contrast, over half the population favor the censoring of "obscene" books (though the exact nature of the obscenity is not specified). The majority would also ban television programs which show people "actually making love" and would oppose the sale of "pornographic" films, books, and magazines because they lower the community's moral standards and lead disturbed people to commit "violent sex crimes." Nearly half would prohibit films which use foul language or display nudity or sexual conduct; and the same proportion would remove from the high school libraries books "that describe explicit sexual acts." Some 45 percent would also authorize the

Postmaster General to prohibit the mailing of "obscene" books or magazines.

That social learning is involved in the nature of these responses may be inferred from the scores registered by the elite groups included in figure 2.2. In every case the opinions leaders, the community leaders, and legal elite (lawyers and judges) select the libertarian alternative more often than does the general public. In a few cases—for example, the censoring of obscene books or predictions about the effects of pornographic films—the more "tolerant" response is chosen by the legal elites at least twice as often. However, this is not to say that the elites are uniformly libertarian in their attitudes toward the publication of allegedly obscene or pornographic materials. As one can observe in figure 2.2, the use of the media for the portrayal of sexual conduct is resisted even among the more knowledgeable and sophisticated members of the population. In this as in most other matters involving the expression of presumably questionable material, the legal elites register, by a significant margin, the most tolerant scores. Whatever their private feelings about the publication of erotic or other sexual materials, they have adopted stands that are much more in keeping with the principles of free expression that the courts have tended to maintain. Although one can assume that the elites do not significantly differ from the general population in their inner anxieties and discomforts about the public displays of sexual matters, they have acquired standards about the right to publish that lead them to overcome to a greater degree any personal reservations they may have about the public parading of sexually provocative materials.

When we turn to the beliefs held about radicals and other dissenters or politically "deviant" minorities, we discover once again that the public often lags far behind the courts and other constitutional authorities in its tolerance toward freedom of the press. In figure 2.3 we have included items from both the CLS and the OVS studies that bear to some extent on the public's attitudes toward censorship of the media. A majority of the public in both studies (55 percent) believe that "to protect its moral values, a society sometimes has to forbid certain things from being published." Presumably they would support prior restraints on the publication of materials they considered morally damaging.

The public's willingness to censor the press under certain conditions is expressed in even more extreme form when more than 80 percent say they would permit a newspaper to publish its opinions "only

Novels that describe explicit sex acts:

- —should be permitted in the library if they are worthwhile literature.
- —have no place in a high school library and should be banned.
- —Neither/Undecided

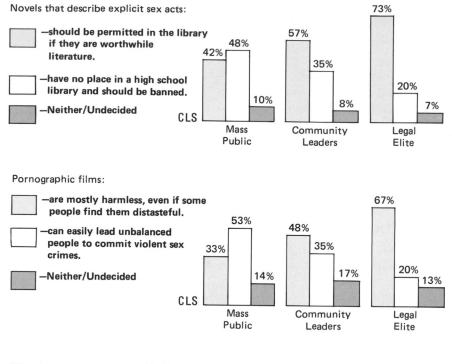

CLS

| | Mass Public | Community Leaders | Legal Elite |
| | 42% 48% 10% | 57% 35% 8% | 73% 20% 7% |

Pornographic films:

- —are mostly harmless, even if some people find them distasteful.
- —can easily lead unbalanced people to commit violent sex crimes.
- —Neither/Undecided

CLS

| | Mass Public | Community Leaders | Legal Elite |
| | 33% 53% 14% | 48% 35% 17% | 67% 20% 13% |

When it comes to pornographic films about sex:

- —people should be allowed to see anything they want to, no matter how "filthy" it is.
- —The community should set the standards for what people are allowed to see.
- —Neither/Undecided

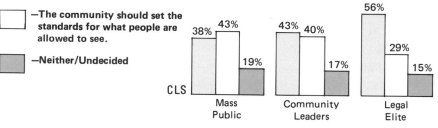

CLS

| | Mass Public | Community Leaders | Legal Elite |
| | 38% 43% 19% | 43% 40% 17% | 56% 29% 15% |

The Postmaster General should have:

- —no right to decide what kind of books or magazines can be sent through the mails.
- —the right to prohibit the mailing of obscene books or magazines.
- —Neither/Undecided

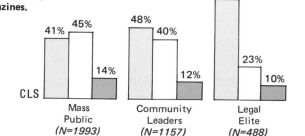

CLS

| | Mass Public (N=1993) | Community Leaders (N=1157) | Legal Elite (N=488) |
| | 41% 45% 14% | 48% 40% 12% | 68% 23% 10% |

FIGURE 2.2
Freedom of Publication and the Tolerance of Obscenity
(CLS/OVS)

Television programs that show people actually making love:

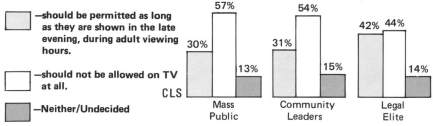

- —should be permitted as long as they are shown in the late evening, during adult viewing hours.
- —should not be allowed on TV at all.
- —Neither/Undecided

CLS

	Mass Public	Community Leaders	Legal Elite

Mass Public: 30% 57% 13%
Community Leaders: 31% 54% 15%
Legal Elite: 42% 44% 14%

Selling pornographic films, books, and magazines:

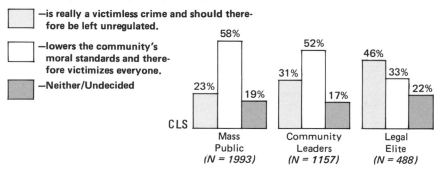

- —is really a victimless crime and should therefore be left unregulated.
- —lowers the community's moral standards and therefore victimizes everyone.
- —Neither/Undecided

CLS

Mass Public (N = 1993): 23% 58% 19%
Community Leaders (N = 1157): 31% 52% 17%
Legal Elite (N = 488): 46% 33% 22%

Censoring obscene books:

- —is an old-fashioned idea that no longer makes sense.
- —is necessary to protect community standards.
- —Neither/Undecided

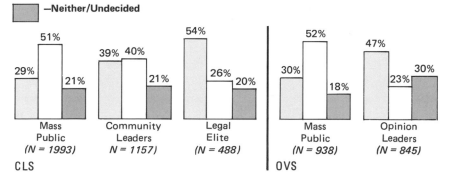

Mass Public (N = 1993): 29% 51% 21%
Community Leaders (N = 1157): 39% 40% 21%
Legal Elite (N = 488): 54% 26% 20%

Mass Public (N = 938): 30% 52% 18%
Opinion Leaders (N = 845): 47% 23% 30%

CLS   OVS

How do you feel about movies that use foul language or show nudity and sexual acts on the screen?

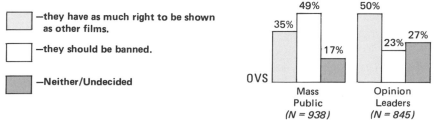

- —they have as much right to be shown as other films.
- —they should be banned.
- —Neither/Undecided

OVS

Mass Public (N = 938): 35% 49% 17%
Opinion Leaders (N = 845): 50% 23% 27%

Giving a federal board of censors the power to decide which TV programs can or cannot be shown:

 —violates the public's right to watch what it pleases.

☐ —is necessary to protect the public against violent or obscene shows.

 —Neither/Undecided

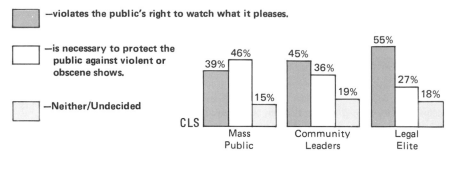

CLS

| Mass Public | Community Leaders | Legal Elite |

The movie industry:

 —should be free to make movies on any subject it chooses.

☐ —should not be permitted to make movies that offend certain minorities or religious groups.

 —Neither/Undecided

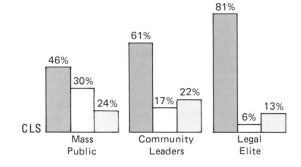

CLS

| Mass Public | Community Leaders | Legal Elite |

If a news photographer takes pictures of a famous person entering a house of prostitution, publishing the photos should be:

 —permitted under the guarantees of a free press.

☐ —forbidden as an invasion of privacy.

 —Neither/Undecided

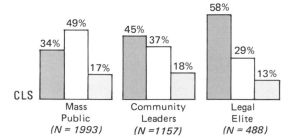

CLS

| Mass Public (N = 1993) | Community Leaders (N = 1157) | Legal Elite (N = 488) |

FIGURE 2.3
Free Press and Censorship
(CLS/OVS)

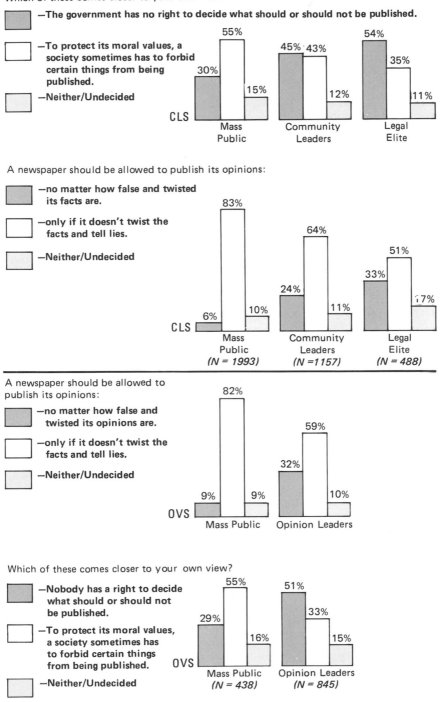

Which of these comes closer to your own view?

—The government has no right to decide what should or should not be published.

—To protect its moral values, a society sometimes has to forbid certain things from being published.

—Neither/Undecided

CLS

	Mass Public	Community Leaders	Legal Elite
	30% / 55% / 15%	45% / 43% / 12%	54% / 35% / 11%

A newspaper should be allowed to publish its opinions:

—no matter how false and twisted its facts are.

—only if it doesn't twist the facts and tell lies.

—Neither/Undecided

CLS

	Mass Public (N = 1993)	Community Leaders (N = 1157)	Legal Elite (N = 488)
	6% / 83% / 10%	24% / 64% / 11%	33% / 51% / 17%

A newspaper should be allowed to publish its opinions:

—no matter how false and twisted its opinions are.

—only if it doesn't twist the facts and tell lies.

—Neither/Undecided

OVS

	Mass Public	Opinion Leaders
	9% / 82% / 9%	32% / 59% / 10%

Which of these comes closer to your own view?

—Nobody has a right to decide what should or should not be published.

—To protect its moral values, a society sometimes has to forbid certain things from being published.

—Neither/Undecided

OVS

	Mass Public (N = 438)	Opinion Leaders (N = 845)
	29% / 55% / 16%	51% / 33% / 15%

if it doesn't twist the facts and tell lies." Notwithstanding the Court's rulings in such cases as *Sullivan* and the present state of the law, a vast majority of the public say in essence that they want to qualify the right to publish by applying a truth test to the content of published materials. Only 6 percent of the mass public in the CLS sample and 9 percent in the OVS sample would set no restrictions on the freedom to publish. Even if one conceded that many respondents did not answer this challenging and provocative question with a full sense of its import, the findings nevertheless testify to the failure, on the part of most of the population, to grasp certain critical notions which define the principle of a free press.

Even the majority of respondents in the elite samples have not fully absorbed the rules which have led the Court to refuse to censor newspapers, books, magazines, or other media that distort the news or disseminate false information. Only one fourth of the community leaders and one third of the opinion and legal elites acknowledge a newspaper's right to publish even if it twists the facts and tells lies. Obviously, this is a difficult principle to accept, as one can further infer from the finding that only 38 percent of the respondents in our ACLU sample subscribe to it. Indeed, of the many elite groups included in our surveys, only the members of the Conference of Editorial Writers endorse (by a majority of 82 percent) the principle of free press involved here.

Figure 2.3 also contains items which provide a less severe test of tolerance toward the rights of the media, such as the censoring of TV programs, the freedom of the movie industry to make films on any subject it chooses, and the right to publish embarrassing photographs of celebrities. Among the mass public, support for the libertarian responses to these items ranges from 34 percent to 46 percent. In each case, the elites, especially the lawyers and judges, respond in a way that suggests their greater agreement with prevailing constitutional standards. These and our other findings which show the community leaders to be more tolerant than the general public are consistent with the results turned up in the national surveys conducted by Stouffer in 1954 and by Nunn and his colleagues, who replicated the Stouffer study, in 1978.

One of the areas of social conflict affecting freedom of the press and the rights of newspaper reporters concerns press coverage of public trials and the alleged inviolability of a reporter's news sources. The issues that bear on this clash are of particular interest because they represent a classic conflict between competing rights—free press versus fair trial, and the right of the public to know versus the right to privacy.

Journalists often feel that the first obligation of a newspaper is to furnish information to the public, including information about crimes and criminal trials, as well as other matters affecting the public interest. They also feel that unless reporters can protect the privacy of their sources and guarantee confidentiality, they will lose their access to the people who supply information to them, a contingency they regard as fatal to the conduct of a free press. Hence, journalists argue, reporters occupy a protected position in society by virtue of their special mission as emissaries of the public.

Those who take issue with the press on these matters, such as judges, prosecutors, and defense attorneys, argue that a journalist is a citizen like any other, that journalists should enjoy no special prerogatives and should be bound by the same laws and procedures governing privacy and the conduct of trials to which all citizens are subject. Nothing in the First Amendment grants immunity against testifying or revealing the grounds for the information one publishes. According to this view, the First Amendment does not create two classes of citizens—one subject to subpoena and other legal obligations and the other sheltered from the legal process. Insofar as press coverage of a crime or a criminal trial may bias public opinion and affect the judgments of potential jurors, the exercise of a free press infringes on another guaranteed liberty—a defendant's right to a fair trial. Out of respect for a defendant's rights, therefore, the court has sometimes felt it had no alternative except to bar the press from a trial or to compel reporters to provide information about their sources.

In figure 2.4, we present the results from several questions bearing on these issues. The responses to these items indicate that except for believing that reporters ought not to be jailed for refusing to reveal their news sources, the public is sharply divided on such issues as banning the press from a trial, preventing the press from giving heavy publicity to sensational crimes, or forcing reporters to testify before a grand jury. The community leaders and the lawyers and judges tend to come down more often on the side of the right of the press to cover criminal trials and to print stories about dramatic or sensational crimes. Most members of the legal elite, however, do not believe that reporters have a right to refuse to disclose their news sources during the course of a trial—an issue on which the courts and the press are currently

Should a judge ever be allowed to ban the press from covering a criminal trial?

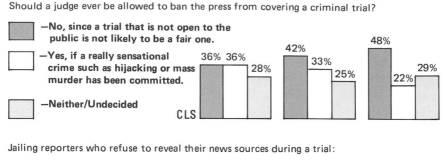

—No, since a trial that is not open to the public is not likely to be a fair one.

—Yes, if a really sensational crime such as hijacking or mass murder has been committed.

—Neither/Undecided

Jailing reporters who refuse to reveal their news sources during a trial:

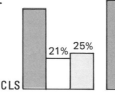

—is wrong because people with important information will then be afraid to tell the truth to reporters.

—is justified when the names of the sources are necessary for a fair trial.

—Neither/Undecided

Heavy press coverage of dramatic crimes like murders or terrorist incidents:

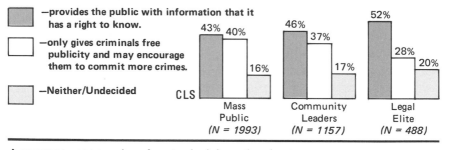

—provides the public with information that it has a right to know.

—only gives criminals free publicity and may encourage them to commit more crimes.

—Neither/Undecided

Mass Public (N = 1993)   Community Leaders (N = 1157)   Legal Elite (N = 488)

A newspaper reporter who refuses to give information about a possible crime to a grand jury or congressional committee should be:

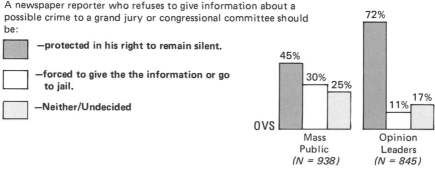

—protected in his right to remain silent.

—forced to give the the information or go to jail.

—Neither/Undecided

Mass Public (N = 938)   Opinion Leaders (N = 845)

FIGURE 2.4
Free Press, Fair Trial, and the Rights of Journalists
(CLS/OVS)

locked in sharp conflict. Public opinion on these matters, thus, appears not to have crystallized as yet, and while the press is not without its defenders, neither does it lack for critics.

Lest it be thought that the moderate levels of support found among the general population for freedom of the press reflect a poor opinion of the media, it is worth noting that the public's attitude toward the press appears to be a positive one.* According to the data recorded in table 2.3, two thirds of the public believe that newspapers try to report the news honestly and fairly (only 21 percent express cynicism toward the integrity of the press), while three fourths of the respondents credit newspapers for trying to print what is newsworthy. Apparently, the impulse to control the press arises not from hostility toward the media as such, but from a failure to understand fully the nature of the right of free press which government is obliged to honor under the conditions of the First Amendment. Except for segments of the elite samples, the public supports freedom of the media in the same way it supports freedom in general--as an abstract value to be cher-

TABLE 2.3
Public Attitudes Toward the Press

	CLS		
	Mass Public	**Community Leaders**	**Legal Elite**
	(N=1993)	**(N=1157)**	**(N=488)**
On the whole, the newspapers:			
—try to do a fair and honest job of reporting the news.	66%	69%	59%
—are mainly interested in selling papers and don't care how accurately they report the news.	21	19	28
—Neither/Undecided	13	12	13

	OVS	
	Mass Public	**Opinion Leaders**
	(N=938)	**(N=845)**
Most newspapers in this country mainly print:		
—the views of the wealthy businessmen who own them.	9%	7%
—whatever they think is newsworthy.	77	81
—Neither/Undecided	15	13

* For a discussion of support by the American people for a free press, as well as a desire for fairness in the presentation of news (for example, presenting both sides of issues, equal coverage for opposing candidates, and so forth), see Immerwahr et al. 1980.

ished, but only as long as it is not being challenged by a conflicting value or claim.

In few instances do we find the right of free press more readily subordinated than when it clashes with fears about national security and the dissemination of unorthodox or extreme political views. (See figure 2.5.) While the public exhibits a fair amount of support for the right of radicals and other people with "extreme political views" to work in the media, one encounters much greater resistance to the use of the media for the promotion of radical views or causes. Only 32 percent of the mass public would permit libraries to distribute books that "preach the overthrow of the government," whereas 50 percent would ban such books. In the earlier PAB study approximately half the population subscribed to the vague statement that a book that contains "wrong political views" should not be published. As we saw in figure 2.3, a majority of the public believe that a society must "sometimes . . . forbid certain things from being published" in order to safeguard its moral standards.

Radicals of the right are feared as well as radicals of the left: for example, only 29 percent of the public would permit American Nazis and the Ku Klux Klan to state their views on television. Even fewer would permit a group to buy advertising space in a newspaper to advocate war against another country. Over one third of the population would close down a newspaper that preaches "race hatred." But 57 percent would not try to discourage the printing and distribution of a humor magazine that "ridicules or makes fun of blacks, women, or other minority groups"; an even larger number (67 percent) believe that a television station has a right to recommend "the use of military action against demonstrators"—a score that appears to be elevated by the public's animosity (confirmed in our surveys) against political protesters and demonstrators in general.

We again observe that, except for a single item in figure 2.5, the elite samples score substantially more tolerant than the general public. On most items involving internal security and the publication of politically unorthodox views, the proportion selecting the civil libertarian response is at least twice as high among the legal elites as among the mass public. One should not conclude, however, that the elites are uniformly tolerant and that the general public is invariably intolerant. As we have observed in previous tables, a majority of the general public seem willing to acknowledge the First Amendment rights of "extremists," "crackpots," publishers of racist materials, and producers of controversial movies. Elites, on the other hand, are unwilling to support the rights of newspapers to publish illegally acquired government documents or to print stories that "distort the facts and tell lies." About half of the elites surveyed would also ban from the libraries books "that could show terrorists how to build bombs." (See figure 2.6.)

Thus, while a majority of the general public and nearly all of the elite groups will tolerate the opinions of "crackpots" and tasteless humorists, they perceive the utterances of Nazis, Klansmen, revolutionaries, and other opponents of the system as more threatening to the social order and hence more difficult to tolerate. The publication of stolen national security secrets and the distribution of "how-to" manuals for the construction of bombs pose so palpable a threat to national security that even the highly civil libertarian members of the elite samples are prepared to support prohibitions against their dissemination.

Since elites (see discussion in chapter 6) are more frequently and intimately exposed to the prevailing official and legal norms of the society, and are often more favorably oriented toward civil libertarian values, how is it that in response to items such as those listed in figure 2.6 they fail to endorse the principle of free press? Part of the answer, as we have suggested, lies in the especially challenging nature of the issues being posed. Moreover, these items involve issues on which clear norms have not been established, or on which they have begun to emerge only recently.

Consider the issue of publications that jeopardize national security secrets or help terrorists build bombs. A case involving both of these possibilities arose in 1979 when the magazine *The Progressive* announced that it intended to publish an article entitled "The H-Bomb Secret—How We Got It and Why We're Telling It." Persuaded that publication of the article might enable certain nations and technically sophisticated terrorists to build a nuclear bomb, a federal district judge reluctantly granted a government request for a temporary injunction restraining *The Progressive* from going to press with its article. "You can't speak freely when you're dead," the judge explained (*New York Times*, March 1, 1979).

Although *The Progressive* case ended without a definitive court ruling (the injunction was lifted when a similar article on the same subject was published by another newspaper), the controversy generated by the issue was notable on several counts. One was a widespread fear among champions of the First Amendment that if the case reached the Supreme Court, the initial prior restraint injunction might be upheld

People with extreme political ideas who want to work as newspaper or TV reporters:

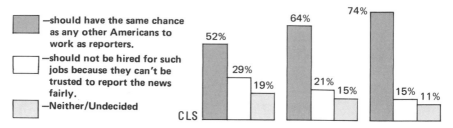

Should groups like the Nazis and Ku Klux Klan be allowed to appear on public television to state their views?

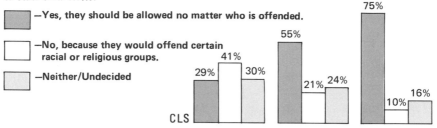

A humor magazine which ridicules or makes fun of blacks, women, or other minority groups:

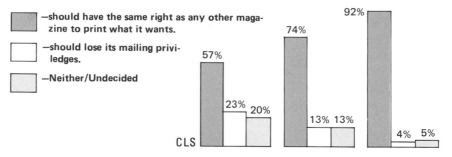

If the majority in a referendum votes to stop publication of newspapers that preach race hatred:

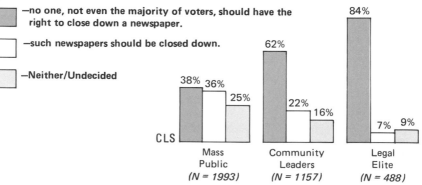

FIGURE 2.5
Free Press and the Advocacy of Radical or Unorthodox Ideas
(CLS/OVS)

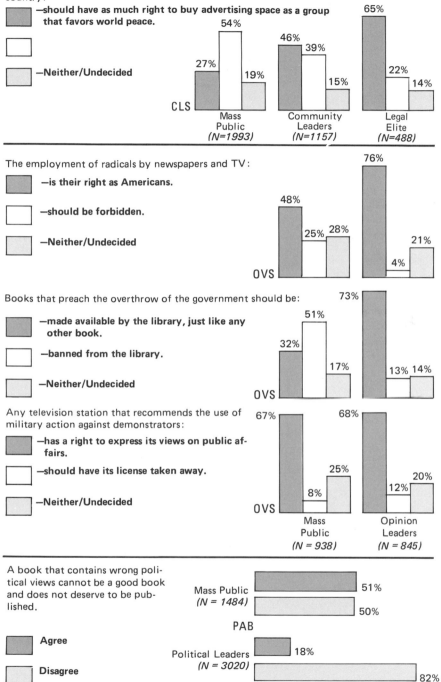

A group that wants to buy advertising space in a newspaper to advocate war against another country:

- —should have as much right to buy advertising space as a group that favors world peace.
- —Neither/Undecided

CLS

	Mass Public (N=1993)	Community Leaders (N=1157)	Legal Elite (N=488)
	27% / 54% / 19%	46% / 39% / 15%	65% / 22% / 14%

The employment of radicals by newspapers and TV:

- —is their right as Americans.
- —should be forbidden.
- —Neither/Undecided

OVS — 48% / 25% / 28% — 76% / 4% / 21%

Books that preach the overthrow of the government should be:

- —made available by the library, just like any other book.
- —banned from the library.
- —Neither/Undecided

OVS — 32% / 51% / 17% — 73% / 13% / 14%

Any television station that recommends the use of military action against demonstrators:

- —has a right to express its views on public affairs.
- —should have its license taken away.
- —Neither/Undecided

OVS

	Mass Public (N = 938)	Opinion Leaders (N = 845)
	67% / 8% / 25%	68% / 12% / 20%

A book that contains wrong political views cannot be a good book and does not deserve to be published.

- Agree
- Disagree

PAB

Mass Public (N = 1484): 51% / 50%

Political Leaders (N = 3020): 18% / 82%

Books that could show terrorists how to build bombs should be:

 —available in the library like any other book.

—banned from public libraries.

—Neither/Undecided

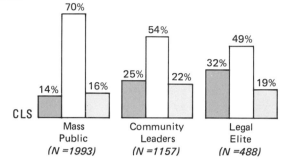

When a TV station reports secret information illegally taken from a government office:

 —it's just doing its job of informing the public.

—the station owners should be
fined or punished.

—Neither/Undecided

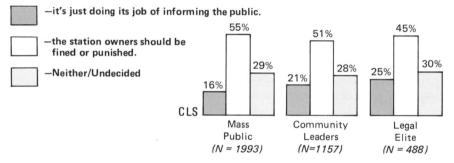

FIGURE 2.6
Free Press and the Publication of "Dangerous" Materials
(CLS)

and made permanent, thereby jeopardizing a vital principle of freedom of the press. Another was a serious split on the issue within the press community itself. The *Washington Post* called the affair a "real First Amendment loser," and even the American Society of Newspaper Editors was torn on whether or not to take a stand on the issue ("Editors Debate Support for Magazine on Bomb Article," *New York Times*, May 3, 1979).

The publication of the Pentagon Papers was perceived as less threatening than the publication of instructions for the building of a nuclear bomb, but it also generated a great deal of controversy. Journalists were divided on the question of whether national security documents stolen by a government employee should be disseminated to the public via the press. A series of public opinion polls conducted at the time (1971) by different polling agencies (Gallup, Harris, the Minnesota Poll) indicated that the public, though preponderantly supporting the right of the *New York Times* to publish the documents, was nevertheless split on the issue. The public was also uncertain about the ground rules which ought to govern the issue. While a plurality felt it was necessary for the American public to be told "the truth about Vietnam," a substantial majority (70 percent) thought the documents should not be published "if there is any doubt about violating the national security" (Erskine 1971–72).

These examples illustrate the indecision surrounding First Amendment issues which are emerging and around which norms have not yet crystallized, either in the courts or among opinion leaders. Given the sharp differences among the elites about the right to publish materials which might threaten national security, one would scarcely expect to find agreement and strong support among the mass public on issues of this kind. Where clear norms have not already established themselves among national elites, there appears to be little chance that the public will support those liberties with much frequency or consistency. Among the mass public, one can also detect in the data a pattern of support for at least some of the rights of groups that are considered "obnoxious," but not for those that are perceived as "dangerous." In contrast, elite opinion tends to be more consistent with the principles outlined by the Supreme Court.

Radicalism, Nonconformity, and Civil Liberties

The reluctance of the majority to acknowledge that radicals have the same right to express their views as any other groups reflects the distaste, as well as the fear and antagonism, that most of the mass public feel toward political malcontents. As one can observe in figure 2.7, at least half the population regard left-wing radicals as a serious threat to our national security (only 16 percent regard them as "a small, harmless minority"). Over one fourth of the public also believe the United States has been "drifting to the left, toward communism." While not all radical organizations (of the left or right) advocate force to bring about social change, they are associated in the public mind with the use of violence, a characteristic, whether real or imagined, of which the public overwhelmingly disapproves. While the elites share with the general public its abhorrence of violence as a tactic to correct injustice, far fewer opinion leaders (18 percent) regard left-wing radicals as a serious threat to our national security. They are also less inclined to believe that the country is drifting toward communism.

Both direct and indirect evidence suggests that support for freedom of speech and press is affected not only by one's general orientation toward "deviant" or unorthodox views, but also by the specific political coloration of those views. Hostility toward left-wing ideologies, especially communism, and a desire to prohibit the dissemination of revolutionary opinions have been typical of the American public's response for as long as we have been able to measure that response through opinion polling. To cite a few examples from the dozens that are available: Stouffer found in 1954 that only 27 percent of the general public would permit an admitted Communist to speak in their community, and a minuscule 6 percent would allow him or her to keep a job as a college teacher. Nearly three fourths would remove books written by a Communist from the public libraries. Some 77 percent would take away the citizenship of an admitted Communist, 51 percent would actually put him or her in jail, and 64 percent would favor the tapping of private telephones to gather evidence against Communists. Some 73 percent thought it a good idea to report to the FBI "any neighbors or acquaintances" they suspected of being Communists (Stouffer 1955).

While the Stouffer study was conducted during the so-called McCarthyism period, data from other surveys, before and after, reveal the same tendency to deny various civil liberties to Communists, radicals,

Using violence to achieve political goals:

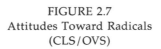 —is sometimes the only way to get injustices corrected.

—is wrong because there are many peaceful ways for people to get their views across.

—Neither/Undecided

86%   83%   75%

CLS   6%   7%   11%   7%   16%   10%

| | Mass Public *(N = 1993)* | Community Leaders *(N = 1157)* | Legal Elite *(N = 488)* |

Left-wing radicals within our borders:

—are really a small, harmless minority.

—are more of a threat to our national security than many people think.

—Neither/Undecided

50%   45%   37%

OVS   16%   34%   18%

In recent years the American system has been drifting:

—to the right, toward fascism.

—to the left, toward communism.

—Neither/Undecided

74%

63%

27%   16%

OVS   10%   11%

| | Mass Public *(N = 938)* | Opinion Leaders *(N = 845)* |

FIGURE 2.7
Attitudes Toward Radicals
(CLS/OVS)

or other groups suspected of seditious conduct. In 1948, Gallup found that 63 percent of the public favored passage of the Mundt-Nixon bill, "which required members of the Communist party to register with the Justice Department" (Simon 1974). When Gallup asked in 1948 and 1950 whether Communist party members should be forced to register, some 67 percent to 80 percent of the public responded affirmatively. During the debate on the Taft-Hartley bill in the mid-1940s, over 80 percent of the public, according to Gallup, approved of a law that would require labor leaders to take a loyalty oath before they could participate in labor negotiations before the National Labor Relations Board (Simon 1974). Gallup reported in 1949 that three fourths of the population would deny Communists the right to teach in colleges and universities, and 70 percent would require all university teachers to swear that they are not Communists. In six different surveys conducted by the National Opinion Research Center (NORC) in the 1950s and 1960s, only 14 percent to 19 percent of the electorate expressed a willingness to permit Communists to speak on the radio. Although 96 percent of the public said they believed in freedom of speech, data from surveys conducted by Gallup and Roper in 1938 and 1941 show 38 percent and 22 percent, respectively, as willing to allow radicals to "hold meetings and express their views in the community" (Simon 1974).

Hyman and Sheatsley (1953) also cite Gallup reports for 1938 and 1942 in which 58 percent to 64 percent maintained that radicals should not be allowed to hold meetings and express their views. In a survey in 1936, Gallup reported that almost half the population contended that the press should not have the right to say anything it wants about public officials. And some 38 percent in 1940 (according to an Office of Public Opinion Research poll) would forbid people who oppose our form of government from expressing their views in public (Simon 1974). Similarly, a NORC survey in 1943 revealed that almost one third of the public subscribed to the view that, even in peacetime, newspapers should not be allowed to criticize our form of government (Hyman and Sheatsley 1953).

Although the passing of the McCarthy era and the weakening of the Cold War have somewhat diminished the fear of domestic communism, many Americans are still reluctant to honor the civil liberties of those who express highly unconventional political values. Prothro and Grigg reported in 1960 that while 95 percent of their survey sample expressed agreement with the abstract statement of democratic rights included in the study, only 44 percent would allow Communists to speak, and almost 60 percent would bar Communists from becoming candidates for public office. A Harris poll conducted in 1970 found that 73 percent of the electorate agreed that "a citizen has the right to print any point of view he wants," but 52 percent of the respondents would nevertheless "ban newspapers which preach revolution" (Erskine and Siegel 1975).*

Although Nunn et al. (1978) and Davis (1975) (both of whom have replicated the Stouffer study) report a considerable increase in tolerance toward nonconformists and Communists in the twenty-year period between the Stouffer study and their own surveys, opposition to the enjoyment of civil liberties by admitted Communists remains fairly substantial. Nunn et al. report that only 53 percent of the general population would permit a Communist to make a speech in their community, 54 percent would allow a book written by a Communist to remain in the public library, and 30 percent would uphold the right of a Communist teacher to keep his or her job. The figures reported by Davis. based on a NORC survey in 1974, roughly approximate the figures yielded by the Nunn survey.

As we have observed in the data reported, the elites tend to express far greater tolerance than the mass public toward the exercise of First Amendment rights—a finding also substantiated in Stouffer's data and reconfirmed by the findings of Nunn and NORC. These and other data underscore the observation, suggested earlier by our own findings, that in the matter of acknowledging the First Amendment rights of political nonconformists, the mass public lags behind the courts, the legislatures, opinion leaders, and influentials.

The general electorate, however, does not regard itself as hostile or lukewarm in its attitudes toward freedom and tolerance. In table 2.4, the vast majority of the American public express their pride in the degree of freedom enjoyed by Americans, and they applaud the United States for granting more freedom of speech than other countries. They also seem to approve the underlying principles of tolerance, stating, for example, that it is a mark of maturity rather than weakness to be "understanding of people with whom one disagrees." The American self-image appears to be one of a free people, proud of their independence and diversity, open to new ideas, aware of the benefits of public

---

* For further illustration of these trends, see also Minnesota Poll, 1962; Chandler 1972; Wilson 1975.

TABLE 2.4
Americans' View of Themselves Regarding Tolerance and Freedom (OVS)

	Mass Public	Opinion Leaders
	(N=938)	(N=845)
Compared to other countries, the United States has:		
—less freedom of speech.	0%	0%
—more freedom of speech.	95	93
—Neither/Undecided	4	7
Future generations will remember the United States chiefly for:		
—its cruelty and disregard for human rights.	2	1
—its freedom and generosity.	78	76
—Neither/Undecided	20	23
The way this country is run:		
—freedom is a myth, more imaginary than real.	11	5
—most people enjoy quite a bit of freedom.	82	91
—Neither/Undecided	7	4
Being "understanding" toward people with whom you disagree is a sign of:		
—maturity.	91	98
—weakness.	3	0
—Neither/Undecided	7	2
Most important questions:		
—can usually be answered in more than one way.	75	89
—have a right answer and a wrong answer.	17	6
—Neither/Undecided	8	5
For children to be properly educated:		
—they should be free to discuss all ideas and subjects, no matter what.	70	85
—they should be protected against ideas the community considers wrong or dangerous.	15	3
—Neither/Undecided	15	12

colloquy, and prepared to permit the expression and discussion of divergent opinions and creeds. This self-portrait might be considered valid if one were to focus exclusively on the public's readiness to endorse freedom of speech and press in the abstract. Although we have stressed the difficulty of learning civil libertarian norms, that difficulty is not nearly so great when one has reference only to abstract statements about liberty. One has little reason to be surprised that over 90 percent of the American people profess to believe in the rights of free speech and free press. Stated in their most general form, these notions are by now commonplace; as abstract concepts free of the complexities and contingencies that mark the realities of everyday life, they are accessible to almost every school child. One can endorse them at virtually no cost.

Learning the nature and contours of these liberties in their numerous concrete applications, however, is a far more formidable task. It is no simple matter to comprehend their special meaning and value as they compete with other cherished goals—such as stable government and national security. It is one thing to say that every individual has a right to form and express his or her own opinions but quite another to extend that right to the publishing of opinions that are insulting or harmful to one's country, faith, race, or deepest moral convictions.

Discrepancies between the verbal endorsement of an abstract idea and its application in practice does not necessarily signify logical inconsistency. Rather, it may reflect responses to what are perceived as different sets of stimuli. Asking people to approve the notion of "free speech for all" is not the same as asking them to grant use of the community's forum to those who advocate the overthrow of the government by violence, the confiscation of Jewish-owned property, or guerrilla warfare against the police. Many people who feel these actions are too egregious to contemplate do not regard their advocacy as the mere exercise of free speech, but as assaults on revered objects or groups.

Whereas the more resolute civil libertarians in a democratic society are inclined to believe that the ultimate test of one's commitment to free speech and press is the ability to tolerate the utterance of alien opinions that arouse fear and loathing, those less committed to civil liberties tend to separate the preaching of such opinions from the principle of free speech. For them, freedom of speech and press seems to mean the right to disagree about approved subjects or, perhaps more accurately, the right to hold different opinions so long as they are socially acceptable.

Although the members of such organizations as the American Civil Liberties Union are likely to see that the abstract principles embodied in the First Amendment protect the rights of *all* groups to make outrageous proposals, people who are relatively uninstructed about civil liberties are likely to respond less to legal or philosophical considerations abut the right of free expression than to the content of the proposals themselves. Hence, they see no contradiction in avowing their belief in freedom of speech on the one side, and their willingness, on the other, to suppress Klan members who advocate discrimination against blacks or radicals who teach that violence is necessary to overthrow capitalism. By their standards, these groups have exceeded their claims to constitutional protection.

To many patriots, the right of free expression does not grant American Communists the right to pledge their loyalty to the Soviet Union. Similarly, many who say they support freedom of worship do not believe that it includes the right of a religious cult to "brainwash" naive adolescents and convert them into disciples. In these and many parallel cases, the respondents seem to allot the "preferred position" not to the First Amendment, but to some other value which turns out to conflict with the First Amendment. Doubtless, many of these respondents do not mean to disavow freedom of speech and press, which they endorse in the abstract; instead, they are drawn more strongly to some competing value, which they endorse in the concrete instance.

The problem of achieving consistency in the responses to a civil liberties issue is further complicated by the *context* in which a given group (whether approved or despised) proposes to exercise its rights. Respondents who agree that radicals or atheists have the same general right to speak as other Americans may nevertheless be unwilling to allow them to address a school assembly or to hold a public meeting in the town hall. In these cases, respondents may feel that they are being asked not merely to *tolerate* the expression of opinions by unpopular groups, but to *abet* them by granting them access to a public forum.

The readiness to deny freedom of speech and press in specific contexts can be traced in part to the fact that the exercise of liberties in these circumstances is perceived as an increased threat. Whereas granting an abstract right to speak and publish exacts little or no cost, permitting Nazis to sell anti-Semitic newspapers in Jewish communities or atheists to speak at school assemblies can be socially and psychologically costly. Such uses of speech or press may represent painful assaults on cherished convictions. Or the activities may lead to physical assaults, violent confrontations, or riots. Although many Supreme Court justices, the American Civil Liberties Union, and other defenders of the First Amendment may regard these possible outcomes as unavoidable risks attached to the protected liberties, the offended groups may not share that perception. As we will see more fully from the data reported, increases in the perceived harmfulness of groups greatly decreases the levels of tolerance that respondents accord them. It occasions no surprise that groups perceived as dangerous are less tolerated than groups perceived as benign—especially among the more unsophisticated respondents, who may lack the background to understand that the First Amendment, as interpreted by the Courts, grants the same rights to hated or feared groups as to benign ones.

For reasons related to the foregoing, it is often difficult to predict, from individuals' abstract statements about freedom of speech and press, how they will act when (or if) faced with the decision of supporting or opposing these rights. The expressed attitude, as Zellman (1975) observes, interacts with the situation, so that an individual's conduct in recognizing the rights of others will often vary as the situation varies. Both the assertion of civil libertarian values and the conduct toward these values will also vary according to the *Zeitgeist*. When, as sometimes happens in the history of societies, the *Zeitgeist* becomes especially uncongenial to the utterance of unorthodox political beliefs, the difficulty of acting upon libertarian values may be greatly increased.

One should also keep in mind that while freedom is, in the abstract, among the most venerated of all American values, not all manifestations of freedom are thought to be desirable. When a majority of the public say that individuals should be free to say or publish whatever they please, they do not mean that individuals should be free to publish slander, obscenity, bigotry, or attacks on the authority of government. (Cf. Hyman and Sheatsley 1954.) Although the *Chaplinsky* dictum (315 U.S. 568, 1942) that certain forms of speech are bad and hence unprotected by the First Amendment has been softened and qualified by subsequent Supreme Court decisions, it is still strongly endorsed by a majority of the public.

It would be surprising if no discrepancies were to turn up between abstract and particular expressions of freedom of speech and press. Even the most civil libertarian justices of the Supreme Court are disinclined to regard these liberties as absolute and have set limits on the time, place, and manner of their exercise. Nor are they likely to regard as legitimate the use of speech and press for the purpose of harming others or infringing on their rights. Even the most revered rights do not function in a vacuum, but continually come up against competing values. The rights of press and speech, although highly esteemed, are not the only values that are prized; and in the minds of many people, under certain conditions they need to give way to other values that are also highly prized by their proponents—the equality of women and minorities, the elimination of bigotry, the avoidance of war, and the protection of privacy. A strong belief in the liberties of the First Amendment does not blot out all other concerns. In light of these competing commitments, it would be unrealistic to expect that an abstract belief in freedom of expression will invariably be translated into support for any and all forms of free speech and press.

In focusing on the discrepancies between the abstract and the applied forms of freedom of expression, we are not suggesting that the endorsement of freedom in the abstract is meaningless. Even though support for the right of free speech as a general principle does not always carry over to its application in concrete situations, it may still matter whether one endorses or opposes the general principle itself. There are individuals, groups, and even entire nations (for example, Soviet Russia, Libya, Argentina) among whom the rights of freedom of speech and press are not even approved in the abstract, but are explicitly repudiated as damaging or unnecessary. For those who at least acknowledge the principle, freedom is the *norm*, limited in its applications perhaps, but a valued goal to be upheld wherever possible. For the others, intolerance is the norm, and the freedom to speak and publish as one chooses is likely to be regarded as an invitation to public disorder and dangerous to established authority.

As we have argued, a great deal of social learning is required in order to appreciate the relation between such rights as freedom of speech and press and the many complex issues with which these liberties must come to grips. This necessitates a fair measure of education as well as political knowledge and sophistication. It is greatly helped by familiarity with the vital public documents and events that have shaped the history of freedom and by exposure to discourse among informed people for whom questions about the boundaries of freedom and control are salient. In short, access to essential information about freedom and the ability and motivation to comprehend it are required for adequate social learning. The number of people in a large complex society who can meet these criteria is likely to be rather small, even when the society is relatively well educated, highly urbanized, fairly cosmopolitan, and served by a variety of print and broadcast media. Part of the difficulty stems from one's location in the social structure; many are simply too far removed from the main intellectual currents that transmit the principal ideas and values which evolve into civil libertarian norms.

Part of the difficulty, however, is inherent in the differences between concepts as stated in highly generalized, imprecise forms, and concepts encountered in the context of the practical exigencies of daily existence. Learning complex norms concerning the application of freedom and control demands a larger capacity for subtlety and a greater ability to make fine distinctions about public decisions than most people possess. It requires an ability to assess costs and benefits, as well as a willingness to entertain alternative explanations and weigh alternative outcomes. These characteristics tend not to be abundant among the mass public. Nor, as one can infer from their scores on the application of First Amendment rights, do they flourish universally among the opinion elites. These characteristics are, however, more frequent at the higher levels of public involvement and intellectual activity than at the lower.

Although we have said that some people reject specific civil liberties because they prize certain competing values even more highly, many members of the society reject them out of ignorance or cognitive incapacity. Some lack the background or intellectual foundation to understand the case for freedom of speech and press. Others are unable to follow the logic of the arguments which lead the more informed and more sophisticated members of the society to embrace the norms. Since these norms are, as we have said, complex and subtle, they are most readily learned by the society's elites, who are better placed and better trained to learn them. As we observed in an earlier publication (McClosky 1964), political and opinion leaders have far greater opportunity to learn the arguments for freedom and other democratic values; they are active and articulate participants in the public forum; they are better educated and better informed; they play strategic roles in the conduct of social and political affairs; and they share more directly in the formulation of public policy. Although it may not always be to their interest to support libertarian norms, they are nevertheless far more able than the mass public to *learn* them and to *understand* the arguments for supporting them. For example, they can grasp more readily the principle of reciprocity on which basic rights depend so heavily, and they can relate such rights as freedom of speech and press to the other concerns of the society.

In tables 2.5 and 2.6 some of these relationships can be observed even within the mass public. In table 2.3 we have focused on support for free speech among respondents in the general population who score high, compared with those who score low, on three measures which reflect levels of sophistication and cosmopolitanism. One of the measures we have used for this purpose is a political sophistication quiz, a ten-item achievement test that simultaneously assesses respondents' political knowledge and their understanding of the political process.* As table 2.5 bears out, the relationship is a strong one, with 44 percent of the politically sophisticated respondents scoring high on our six-item index of support for free speech compared with only 15 percent of the politically unsophisticated. The relationship between education and support for free speech is at least equally strong and perhaps a bit stronger: 54 percent of those who have attended graduate school score high on the index of free speech compared with 14 percent of those who have not gone beyond grade school—a ratio of five

TABLE 2.5

Sophistication and Support for Free Speech Among the Mass Public (CLS)

		Political Sophistication		
		Low	Middle	High
		(N=599)	(N=616)	(N=777)
Support for Free Speech	% Low	41	31	18
	% Middle	44	40	37
	% High	15	29	44

		Education					
		Grade School	High School	Some College	College	Graduate School	Professional School
		(N=186)	(N=896)	(N=439)	(N=245)	(N=162)	(N=60)
Support for Free Speech	% Low	54	35	22	17	9	22
	% Middle	33	45	38	35	36	35
	% High	14	19	40	49	54	43

		Community Size				
		Rural −2500	Town Small City	Suburb	Medium City	Large City
		(N=664)	(N=501)	(N=199)	(N=280)	(N=343)
Support for Free Speech	% Low	39	28	23	30	23
	% Middle	31	29	28	29	34
	% High	30	43	49	41	43

*This test was included in the questionnaire through the insertion into the item pool of a variety of knowledge questions cast in our standard question format. For details, see Appendix C.

to one. The relationship between community size (an indirect and much weaker measure of sophistication) produces (as expected) weaker results, though in the same direction.

Table 2.6 parallels table 2.5, except that it assesses support for freedom of the *press* (as measured by a ten-item scale) rather than *speech*. The relationships are similar. The greater the sophistication (whether measured by the political sophistication quiz, education, or size of community), the greater is the support for freedom of the press.

It will be recalled that marked differences in tolerance between the civic elites and the mass public were reported by Stouffer (1955) and Nunn et al. (1978). In our PAB survey of political leaders and the mass public, the leaders scored higher than the general population on

TABLE 2.6
Sophistication and Support for Free Press
Among the Mass Public (CLS)

		Political Sophistication		
		Low	Middle	High
		(N=599)	(N=616)	(N=777)
Support	% Low	43	39	32
for Free	% Middle	34	30	23
Press	% High	23	30	45

		Education					
		Grade School	High School	Some College	College	Graduate School	Professional School
		(N=186)	(N=896)	(N=439)	(N=245)	(N=162)	(N=60)
Support	% Low	58	43	30	23	23	38
for Free	% Middle	27	31	30	28	22	17
Press	% High	15	26	39	49	54	45

		Community Size				
		Rural −2500	Town Small City	Suburb	Medium City	Large City
		(N=664)	(N=501)	(N=199)	(N=280)	(N=343)
Support	% Low	42	25	26	25	23
for Free	% Middle	36	40	31	41	40
Press	% High	22	35	43	34	37

85

virtually every item that reflected support for freedom of speech and press. And, as one will recall from the many item scores reported in the preceding figures and tables in this chapter, the opinion and community elites in the OVS and CLS studies exhibit consistently stronger support for freedom of speech and press than does the mass public. These differences show up even more impressively when the items are cumulated into scales or indices. For example, whereas 32 percent of the mass public in the CLS score high on our ten-item scale that measures support for freedom of the press, the percentage high for the community leaders is 56 percent; for the legal elite it is greater still: 71 percent. With regard to freedom of speech, the comparable percentages for the three samples are 33, 68, and 87, respectively.

To assess more systematically the relation between knowledge of civil liberties and *support* for civil liberties, we have constructed a Civil Liberties Quiz (in effect, a ten-item achievement test) which assesses one's knowledge of the present state of constitutional law and practice affecting a variety of civil liberties issues. The relations between respondents' scores on the Civil Liberties Quiz and their support for freedom of speech and press are shown in table 2.7.

The findings resemble and tend to confirm the findings reported for political sophistication: the more respondents know about the laws and legal practices governing civil liberties issues, the stronger their support for freedom of speech and press. For example, among the members of the mass public who have little knowledge of civil liberties, only 18 percent score high on the scale measuring support for freedom of speech, whereas 48 percent of those who are better informed strongly support the right to exercise free speech.

Essentially the same relationships hold for the community and legal elites: even among these better informed and relatively sophisticated groups, support for freedom of speech (and press) increases as knowledge of civil liberties increases. Indeed, the combination of elite status *plus* knowledge of civil liberties strengthens support for freedom of speech and press even further. Thus, whereas 48 percent of the better informed among the general public score high on freedom of speech, the comparable figure for the community leaders is 73 percent, and for the lawyers and judges an extraordinary 85 percent. The same pattern recurs on the scale measuring support for freedom of the press, where the parallel scores are 51 percent for the general population, 65 percent for the community leaders, and 76 percent for the legal elites.

The data in table 2.7 also shed additional light on our earlier analy-

TABLE 2.7

Knowledge of Civil Liberties Law and Support for Free Speech and Press

		Mass Public			**Community Leaders**			**Legal Elite**		
		Low	Middle	High	Low	Middle	High	Low*	Middle	High
		(N=764)	(N=731)	(N=497)	(N=177)	(N=398)	(N=581)	(N=19)	(N=133)	(N=339)
Support for Free Speech	% Low	40	28	15	24	16	6	—	5	2
	% Middle	42	40	37	35	28	22	—	16	12
	% High	18	32	48	41	57	73	—	80	85
Support for Free Press	% Low	45	37	26	35	21	15	—	8	7
	% Middle	32	29	24	26	29	20	—	21	17
	% HIgh	23	34	51	38	50	65	—	71	76

* N is too small to calculate for this column.

NOTE: Knowledge of civil liberties is measured by scores on the Civil Liberties Quiz. The cutting points for low, middle, and high on the Civil Liberties Quiz were determined by dividing the distribution of scores for the mass public into thirds. To ensure comparability, the same cutting points are used for the community and legal elite samples as for the mass public sample.

sis of the apparent discrepancies between abstract and concrete support for freedom of speech and press. Since, as we observed, endorsement of these rights in the abstract is uniformly high for both the mass public and the elites, the data, based as they are on responses to scale items measuring specific applications of freedom of speech and press, confirm our theoretical expectation that the greatest discrepancies between abstract and particular responses to the rights of free speech and press will be found chiefly among those who have the least knowledge of the norms governing these rights. Ignorance of the norms, in short, increases inconsistency in their application—that is to say, as individuals become more informed about civil libertarian norms, they become more consistent in relating their stands on specific civil liberties issues to their endorsement of civil liberties values in the abstract. The more intimate people's knowledge of the constitutional rules governing such complex domains as freedom of speech and press, the greater is the probability that they will have learned how to connect the general principle to the concrete instance and will be able to thread their way from one to the other.

The differences between the mass public and the legal elite in their scores on measures of freedom of speech and press are especially striking. Except for their scores on certain items referring to liberties that complicate or impede the work of the courts in administering justice, the legal elite exhibits the strongest support for freedom of speech and press of all groups in the CLS. In table 2.8 we have listed, in summary form, items from the CLS study that relate to free speech and free press, and we have shown (in rank order) the percentage differences in the civil libertarian scores of the mass public and the legal elites. Apart from the last few items, which refer mainly to liberties affecting the administration of justice (for example, reporters who refuse to reveal their news sources during a trial), the legal elites score the items in a libertarian direction far more often than does the mass public: on half the items, for example, the lawyers and judges score between 25 percent and 50 percent higher than the general public.

As can be seen in table 2.8, the largest differences between the general public's responses and those of the lawyers and judges turn up on such matters as the right of all groups, whatever their views, to associate freely, to hold nonconformist religious opinions, to enjoy equal access to the media, and to choose and hear speakers of all shades of opinion. Large differences occur on the right to advocate any cause one chooses and on the right to publish books or broadcast materials

TABLE 2.8

Percentage Differences between Mass Public and
Elites in Support for Free Speech and Press

Item Summaries	% **Difference Between Mass Public and Legal Elite**	% **Difference Between Mass Public and Community Leaders**
Allow students to form campus Nazi club?	+51	+20
Allow atheists to make fun of God in public?	+49	+27
Allow Nazis and KKK to appear on TV?	+46	+26
Allow foreigners who dislike or criticize U.S. to visit here?	+40	+28
Screen speakers on college campuses for extreme ideas?	+39	+19
Prohibit protesters from mocking President at public speeches?	+38	+22
Groups have right to buy news space to advocate war?	+38	+20
Prohibit movie industry from making films which offend minorities?	+36	+16
Should magazine which ridicules women and blacks lose mailing privileges?	+35	+17
Outlaw use of obscene gestures against public officials (or is it a form of free speech)?	+32	+13
Ban research that shows women and minorities in bad light?	+32	+21
Remove novels with explicit sex acts from high school libraries?	+31	+15
Can Postmaster General prohibit mailing of obscene books?	+27	+ 7
Can newspaper print opinions, even if it twists facts?	+27	+18
Should government censor the press?	+25	+15
Hire political extremists to work on newspaper or TV?	+22	+12
High school teacher can/can't express opinion on religion, morals, politics?	+21	+12
Can community censor teacher in classroom?	+20	+10
Should porno films be banned?	+18	+ 5
Ban books on how to build bombs?	+18	+11
Allow lesbian to teach school?	+15	+ 7

TABLE 2.8 (continued)
Percentage Differences between Mass Public and
Elites in Support for Free Speech and Press

Item Summaries	% Difference Between Mass Public and Legal Elite	% Difference Between Mass Public and Community Leaders
Should officials check on professor suspected of spreading false ideas in class?	+14	+ 6
Should lovemaking on TV be permitted or not?	+12	+ 1
TV reporting of secret government information: fine station, or are they informing the public rightfully?	+ 9	+ 5
Can one justify refusing to hire a racist professor?	+ 8	+ 4
Should government be allowed to open mail of suspected criminals?	+ 7	+ 1
Should government regulate science experiments, or is scientist free to decide on research?	0	− 3
Is a person's diary legal evidence or a personal, private document?	−11	+ 4
Jail reporters who refuse to reveal news sources during a trial?	−16	+ 7

NOTE: A minus (−) sign in the percentage differences indicates that a larger proportion of the mass public takes a civil libertarian stand on the item than the legal elite (or, in the second column, the community leaders). A plus (+) sign indicates that the legal elite (or community leaders) has scored more libertarian, by the number of percentage points shown, than the mass public. All data are from the CLS.

that present unpopular opinions even if they offend certain groups or deal with sensitive subjects. All these are well grounded in constitutional law. The legal elite also reacts far more tolerantly to such forms of symbolic speech as the right to mock the President by wearing a death mask as he speaks or the right to desecrate the flag as a symbolic gesture of protest (see chapter 3).

The differences between the mass public and the legal elite, however, tend to be smaller on issues that have emerged on the political scene more recently and are still being debated among legal authorities and other elites. Many of the issues on which the differences are smaller tend also to be more vexing and inherently controversial, such as the right of the media to publish or broadcast secret information stolen from government sources; the requirement that radio and television present "balanced political views" (which seems fair on the one hand, but represents a form of censorship on the other); and the right of the press to give special publicity to sensational crimes (which some believe only serves to inspire further crimes and may also prevent the conduct of a fair trial). Also included in this list are such unsettled issues as the right of homosexuals to teach in the public schools; the right of research scientists to experiment freely; the right of government to invade the privacy of the mails in some circumstances; and the right of a television station to run programs showing explicit sexual conduct.

For the most part, however, lawyers and judges exhibit substantially more tolerance than the mass public (or the community elites) in matters affecting freedom of speech and press. In addition to a college education, lawyers and judges have had training in the principles of constitutional law, and many of them are compelled by the nature of their daily work to confront and weigh the arguments for and against granting or withholding human rights. They are also forced by their vocation to make careful distinctions about the appropriate applications of various liberties. Although many work in legal fields which seem remote from the application of civil liberties (such as corporation or tax law), they are, as a class, far more familiar than the general public or community elites with the principles elaborated by the courts concerning such matters as freedom of speech and press. In short, by training and experience, this group is unusually familiar with the ideas, principles, laws, and judicial decisions that make up the body of civil libertarian norms.

In addition, by the nature of their profession, lawyers and judges are predisposed to abide by (and to incorporate into their own body of beliefs) the prevailing legal standards affecting civil liberties. Perhaps more than any other vocational group in society, they pay attention to the decisions of the Supreme Court, the reasoning that led to the decisions, and the boundaries of freedom and control which the Court has established. This can be inferred not only from anecdotal and intuitive observation, but from the data just reported which show that the legal elites achieved the highest scores of all of our samples on the Civil Liberties Quiz, confirming their superior knowledge of the law governing speech, press, and other civil liberties.

The finding that greater support for First Amendment rights is found among lawyers, judges, community elites, opinion leaders, and the nation's governing officials and political leaders does not signify that they are by nature more sympathetic or generous than the average person. It suggests, rather, that they enjoy greater opportunities for learning constitutional norms and thus are better prepared than most members of the mass public to decipher highly vexing and elusive questions about the application of civil libertarian rights.

If one judges by the responses of the mass public to survey questions, one has little reason to expect that the population as a whole will display a sensitive understanding of the constitutional norms that govern the free exercise of speech and publication. Awareness of these matters seems severely diminished by deficiencies in levels of social learning. Only a minority of the mass public fully appreciate why freedom of speech and press should be granted to dissenters and to others who challenge conventional opinion. Few appear to understand that the measure of one's commitment to the liberty one proclaims in the abstract must, in a free society, rest on one's willingness to make freedom available to those who conform least to expected standards. Insofar as these matters are better understood and more firmly believed by those who, in one role or another, help to govern the society, one is tempted to conclude that, owing to the vagaries of the social process, the protection of First Amendment rights rests principally on the very groups the Amendment was mainly designed to control—the courts, the legislature, political leaders, and the opinion elites of the society.

CHAPTER 3

The First Amendment: Symbolic Speech, Conduct, Assembly, and Religion

FREEDOM OF SPEECH, as we have observed, enjoys unusual protection under the Constitution and, except for regulations governing the time, place, and manner of its exercise, is treated by the courts as virtually inviolable. Forms of conduct intended to express beliefs, however, enjoy much less protection. You may advocate a revolution, but starting one is a crime. Nothing in the First Amendment acknowledges the right of militants to assemble their followers into paramilitary cadres and distribute arms for the purpose of intimidating the government or inciting revolution. You may publicly recommend complete freeedom of sexual conduct, but (in principle at least) you can be arrested for practicing it.

The distinction between speech and conduct in these particular examples may seem clear enough, but the clarity is not always so evident. The Court has on numerous occasions grappled with the question of whether certain forms of speech might more appropriately be considered action (for example, producing panic by falsely shouting "fire" in a crowded theater); or whether certain forms of action might more appropriately be considered speech (for example, wearing black armbands at school to protest a war). Often, too, the courts have had to confront the question of where speech leaves off and conduct begins—

as in the case of pickets who shout slogans and block passageways or speakers at a mass meeting who, by their inflammatory remarks, transform their audience into an angry mob.

Although analytically defensible, the distinction between speech and conduct cannot always be sustained in practice. Some forms of "expression" are themselves overt and inseparable from "conduct." Picketing and parading, although undeniably forms of conduct, are also forms of expression and are sometimes treated as such under the First Amendment. So, too, are certain forms of civil disobedience, such as lying down to stop traffic in order to protest political policies, or refusing, on grounds of conscience, to register for the draft. Alexander Bickel (1975) challenges the attempts to draw a sharp distinction between conduct and such forms of speech as obscenity. "What," he asks, "is a live sex show—communication or conduct?" Walter Berns (1957), going even further in the argument against unlimited freedom of expression, contends that the distinction between free speech or conscience on the one side and speech that gives rise to unlawful action on the other is in reality a spurious one.

As one might assume, incidents of "speech plus" which present themselves as permissible forms of expression under the First Amendment receive protection from the courts less consistently than "pure" speech. Nevertheless, despite the ambiguities, the courts, along with many leading commentators on the Constitution, have repeatedly tried to maintain the distinction between expression and conduct, sanctioning the one and limiting the other. In the *Whitney* case (274 U.S. 357, 1927), for example, Brandeis argued that even advocacy which urges the violation of laws "is not justification for denying free speech where the advocacy falls short of incitement . . . the wide difference between advocacy and incitement, between preparation and attempt, . . . must be borne in mind." In the *Dennis* case (341 U.S. 494, 1951), Justice Douglas, arguing against conviction, observed that the case involved no *overt acts* of violence against the system, but only *speech*. That it might have been the motive or purpose of the plaintiffs to bring about a violent revolution is irrelevant, since one cannot, under the First Amendment, probe people's minds and punish them for what they *think*, rather than for what they *do*.

Why is conduct usually considered less tolerable than speech? And why, under the First Amendment, does it enjoy less protection than speech? The reason, we suppose, is that conduct seems intuitively to have a greater potential for inflicting injury. Words may sting, but a physical blow may tear the flesh and draw blood. The principle is recognized in the childhood jingle: "Sticks and stones may break my bones, but words will never harm me."

Because speech is regarded as primarily the expression of conscience or opinion (although it may also be abusive or defamatory), it seems less threatening than action. We believe we can ignore speech if we choose, but not a physical blow. Actions represent a far greater danger to order, stability, safety, or national security. As long as exchanges among people (or nations) are conducted at the level of words, offenders can be mollified, fended off, or even disregarded, but action contains a potential for physical assault that is far more frightening than even the most insulting and provocative language. Even if one were to concede, as Justice Powell argued in *Rosenfeld* v. *New Jersey* (408 U.S. 901, 1972), that "the shock and sense of affront, and sometimes the injury to mind and spirit, can be as great from words as from some physical attacks," it is nevertheless rare that speech has a power to injure equal to that of action.

As the data illustrate, the exercise of the right of assembly is feared far more than expression alone. By bringing people together at the same location and subjecting them to a common set of influences, an assembly has a particular capacity for inducing mass action and possibly violence. The threat of organized action is obviously more ominous than the mere speaking or publication of words. As Justice Jackson commented in *Kunz* v. *New York* (340 U.S. 290, 1951):

> The impact of publishing on public order has no similarity with that of a street meeting. . . . Few are the riots caused by publication alone, few are the mobs that have not their immediate origin in harangue.

Because assemblies have usually been perceived by lawmakers and the courts as more volatile and potentially more dangerous, the right to assemble has usually been subjected to more severe controls than the right to express oneself in speech or writing. (Cf. *Hague* v. *CIO*, 307 U.S. 496, 1939.) Closer regulation is thought to be required whenever people gather to picket, parade, demonstrate, or hear the words of speakers who may inflame the crowd.

DIMENSIONS OF TOLERANCE

Symbolic Speech

In recent years the court has tried to deal with certain forms of action that are closely intermingled with expression by increasingly designating them as symbolic speech. So recognized, they enjoy greater constitutional protection than they would if they were regarded as action and somewhat less protection than they would if they were regarded as pure speech. This form of speech, it is assumed, takes the guise of conduct not for the sake of action, but for the purpose of dramatically communicating opinion. Symbolic speech usually represents an effort to persuade others by calling attention to a particular cause through gesture, theatrics, movement, or other forms of conduct. Picketing and parading, as we have observed, are forms of action, but they are often employed to express a point of view. So, too, are such forms of conduct as burning flags, mutilating draft cards, or wearing black armbands to protest the nation's participation in a war. All intermingle overt action and the expression of opinion. So long as these forms of symbolic speech do not immediately endanger or incite public disorder, the Court has tended to uphold their legality.*

The right to speak, it should be noted, also includes the right *not* to speak, or, if one prefers, the right to express one's views by choosing to remain silent—in reality a form of conduct. In a case involving the refusal of Jehovah's Witnesses to compel their children to pledge allegiance to the flag, Justice Jackson, in a landmark opinion, observed that the issue before the Court involved a conflict "between authority and the rights of the individual." The flag salute, he argued, is a symbolic form of utterance, "a primitive but effective way of communicating ideas. . . . To sustain the compulsory flag salute we are required to say that a Bill of Rights which guards the individual's right to speak his own mind, left it open to public authorities to compel him to utter what is not in his mind" (*West Virginia State Board of Education* v. *Barnette*, 319 U.S. 624, 1943).

The First Amendment, in short, forbids government from forcing dissenters to agree with the consensus, no matter how desirable the goal of social unity may be in any given circumstance. Under the Constitution, adherence to socially approved belief must be won through persuasion; it cannot be forced.

---

*See especially *Spence* v. *Washington*, 418 U.S. 405, 1974; *Tinker* v. *Des Moines School District*; *Russo* v. *Central School District*, 469 F. 2d 623, 1972; *James* v. *Board of Education*, 461 F. 2d 566, 1972.

Nevertheless, on past occasions (especially during the 1940s and 1950s), the government has attempted to coerce loyalty by forcing individuals, especially government employees, to declare their allegiance by disavowing their support for subversive or "alien" doctrines (cf. Haiman 1976). These "loyalty oaths" were required by federal and state statutes in a number of contexts: for the issuance of a passport, for the opportunity to participate in labor negotiations under the National Labor Relations Act, for membership in the bar, for getting one's name placed on an election ballot, and for the right to hold academic employment. As fear of Communist subversion declined in the 1960s, the courts began to find such oaths vague and in violation of the First Amendment in that they punished nonsigners for their beliefs and for their possible membership in organizations to which they were legally entitled to belong.*

Freedom of Assembly and Association

The freedom to express opinions in a public forum—more familiarly known as the right of assembly—is protected by the First Amendment along with freedom of speech, press, and the right to petition for the redress of grievances. As the Supreme Court has observed, the inclusion of these seemingly distinct rights in the same amendment was not by "accident or coincidence." On the contrary, they are "cognate rights" and "inseparable" (*Thomas* v. *Collins*, 323 U.S. 516, 1945). The right of assembly also provides the legal foundation for the right to engage in mass protests which are intended to sway public opinion and/or influence official conduct. Protest meetings enjoy protection so long as they do not seek to violate the law. They are, says Kalven (1967), a claim "of privilege in the exercise of basic rights."

Speech without assembly, without the opportunity to meet with others in order to exchange ideas and to persuade them, would so severely diminish the potency of the right of free speech as to render it virtually meaningless. Nor can one hope to petition the government effectively without the opportunity to associate oneself with others in

*Cf. *Baggett* v. *Bullitt*, 377 U.S. 360, 1964; *Elfbrandt* v. *Russell*, 384 U.S. 11, 1966; *Keyishian* v. *New York*, 385 U.S. 589, 1967; *Communist Party of Indiana* v. *Whitcomb*, 414 U.S. 441, 1974.

the joint presentation of grievances. Like freedom of the press, freedom of assembly is an essential vehicle by which free speech is made vital.

So, too, is the right of freedom of association essential. The twin rights of assembly and association, in turn, provide the constitutional foundations for the right to form political organizations such as political parties. In combination with freedom of speech and press, these rights provide for the claim to organize opposition parties or other alliances that dissent from the rule of the incumbents. In essence, freedom of association represents the transformation of an assembly into an organized unit, enabling a group to act more effectively for the redress of grievances and the pursuit of common goals.

While the Constitution makes no direct reference to freedom of association, the right to form groups for the purposes previously stated largely derives from the right of assembly and the right to petition the government. In his observations of American life, de Tocqueville considered the right of association a right of the highest order, essential to democracy, as it provided an effective means to deter rulers from abusing their power.

> The most natural privilege of man, next to the right of acting for himself, is that of combining his exertions with those of his fellow creatures and of acting in common with them. The right of association therefore appears to me almost as inalienable in its nature as the right of personal liberty.
> (Quoted in Fellman 1975, p. 26)

Constitutional scholars and the courts now consider the freedom to unite with others for common purposes essentially a First Amendment right. Despite some restrictions, the right to associate has been clearly recognized by the Court as an indispensable feature of a free government, in which citizens must be allowed to organize and consult in order to advance their common purposes and to hold government accountable. (Cf. *U.S.* v. *Cruikshank*, 92 U.S. 542, 1876.) The courts have upheld the right to form political parties that compete for political office (as a right guaranteed by the First Amendment) and, in effect, have recognized the right to form and belong to any organization not engaged in sedition or other criminal activities. The laws once governing registration of members of radical organizations are no longer operative; and in a set of cases involving the NAACP, the Court struck down parallel laws on the ground that requiring an organization to disclose the names of its members would have a chilling effect on its recruitment and activities and would therefore amount to an unconstitutional restraint on freedom of association. (Cf. *NAACP* v. *Alabama*, 357 U.S. 499, 1958; *Bates* v. *City of Little Rock*, 361 U.S. 516, 1960.)

Although it is an old and familiar right, the freedom to assemble continually gives rise to questions about where, when, by whom, and under what conditions the right may be exercised. The reasons are not difficult to comprehend. Holding a meeting in a public place—especially in the streets or in a public park—may bring a group into conflict with others who wish to occupy the same facilities or who fear that the meeting will in some way harm them. One must not assume, of course, that all public assemblages turn into "mobs" or result in riots. The vast majority are benign and peaceful meetings of individuals who have come together to exchange opinions or to plan actions the community deems worthy.

Nevertheless, assemblies do have a greater potential for creating a public nuisance than do most other forms of liberty. Frequently, they are accompanied by the distribution of handbills that are forced upon passers-by or that litter the streets. Many employ loudspeakers that assault the ears of neighbors and bystanders. Often they are held at locations that block vehicular or pedestrian traffic. When an assembly takes the form of a picket line or protest demonstration, passageways are frequently blocked so that others cannot enter or leave the premises. Protest marches may aim to intimidate opponents and spectators by assuming menacing postures or by employing signs, banners, or slogans designed as much to strike fear among onlookers as to register opinions. The rhetoric employed at meetings of militants and zealots may so inflame the audience as to lead to mob action and violence. Groups such as the American Nazi party, the Ku Klux Klan, or the Communist party are viewed in some communities as so outrageous that their very act of holding a public meeting is perceived as a provocation and as a willful breach of the peace.

Although the right of assembly often incorporates the right of free speech and is an essential feature of freedom of expression, it is unequivocally a form of conduct and therefore usually poses greater risks for the peace and good order of the community than do most other civil liberties. It is also more likely to be perceived as threatening, especially when it takes the form of picketing, mass marches, demonstrations, vigils outside courthouses or prisons, or sit-ins at lunch counters, factories, or university buildings. All such activities, though peaceful in themselves, contain the seeds of disorder and may provoke clashes with the police. Partly for these reasons, freedom of assembly has become one of the most confusing and difficult rights for people (and even for the courts) to comprehend. It is a right that is highly likely to invite regulation and to inspire a fair measure of intolerance.

Despite such reservations, the courts have tended in most cases to uphold the right to parade; to hold peaceful outdoor meetings or demonstrations; to distribute leaflets; to picket, solicit, or canvass in public places. At times, however, the courts have set restrictions on these activities by withholding permits or by issuing injunctions in an effort to balance the public interest in peace and order against the individual's interest in expressing his or her views.* Policy considerations "which may justify reasonable and impartial regulation of speech in public places are: keeping the streets and sidewalks open and safe for traffic, keeping them free from litter, preserving peace and order, and limiting, to an extent, the amount of noise and inconvenience which may be caused by public exercise of free speech" (Wagner 1977). The courts have also on some occasions imposed limits on the exercise of speech on private property, since activity of this kind may clash with laws against trespass and, to some degree, with laws protecting privacy (Wagner). On many occasions, however, the Court has insisted that the general public put up with some inconvenience in order to assure others the right to assemble and to make speeches in public byways and forums. (Cf. *Lovell* v. *Griffin* 303 U.S. 444, 1938; *Hague* v. *CIO* 307 U.S. 496, 1939.)

The ideological or doctrinal persuasion of the speeches or pickets or demonstrations is a matter to which the law is indifferent. No one (not even a Nazi) can be prevented from speaking solely because his or her views are considered obnoxious or provocative. A community, said Justice Breitel in the New York case of *Rockwell* v. *Morris* (211 N.Y.S. 2d 25, 1960), "need not wait to be subverted by street riots and stormtroopers; but, also, it cannot . . . suppress a speaker, *in prior restraint,* on the basis of news reports, hysteria, or inference that what he did yesterday, he will do today" (our italics). Speakers may be punished if they incite "others to immediate unlawful action," but they cannot be barred "for the unpopularity of their views, their shocking quality, their obnoxiousness, and even their alarming impact." For speakers to be denied the right to address an assembly it must be shown beyond doubt that they are actually speaking criminally or are about to do so.

---

*For a summary of the legal status of freedom of assembly and religion, we are greatly indebted to Arnold Wagner, who prepared a memorandum at our request in 1977.

Otherwise their right to address an audience in a public place must be protected, no matter how offensive.

Marches, pickets, public demonstrations, and other forms of organized mass protest present problems that are even more vexing than those arising from simple public gatherings. Exercising the right of assembly by means of these activities brings into sharp focus the competing interests of free expression and public order. In each of them the specter of violence arises: large and potentially hostile masses of people face each other in an emotionally volatile atmosphere, and experience has shown that beatings, riots, and even murders can occur. Hence, such forms of protest are considered legitimate objects of state regulation. (Cf. Cooper 1977.; *Walker v. Birmingham*, 388 U.S. 307, 1967; *Cox v. New Hampshire*, 312 U.S. 569, 1941.) The courts have insisted, however, that the regulation of such activities must be reasonable and nondiscriminatory, and that any system of permits or licenses cannot discriminate against any group because of its views (Cooper 1977). (Cf. *Kunz v. New York*, 340 U.S. 290, 1951).

In keeping with the government's power to regulate the time, place, and manner in which speech is exercised, the courts and legislatures have on various occasions restricted the places in which assemblies or picketing may occur. As the Court has frequently observed, "the First Amendment does not grant the right to say whatever one pleases, wherever one pleases, whenever one pleases" (Haiman 1976, p. 47). Mass demonstrations to protest political meetings, conventions, or speeches, for example, offer a troublesome set of problems for law enforcement authorities. While such demonstrations, when peaceful, are also lawful, the police and other legal officials have some discretion in deciding when and where they can be held. In the case of a political convention, for example, the police can restrict picketing or mass assemblies to certain parts of the city, somewhat removed from the convention center, providing such restrictions are essential to the maintenance of order and the peaceful conduct of the meeting (Haiman 1976, p. 47). In many states, protest demonstrations cannot be held in front of a courthouse, on the assumption that such activities would interfere with the progress of a "fair trial" (*Cox v. Louisiana*, 379, U.S. 536, 1965; see also, Haiman, p. 47). Similar restrictions have been upheld against picketing on jailhouse grounds. On the other hand, quiet sit-ins (a type of symbolic speech) in libraries, at lunch counters, and even in airports and terminals have sometimes been upheld as appropriate nonverbal forms of speech, providing, or course, they remain peaceful (*Brown* v. *Louisiana*, 383 U.S. 131, 1966).

Public speech which stirs an audience to violence proves even more difficult to define conclusively. Certain forms of provocative speech uttered in the course of a meeting are not protected by the First Amendment. A speech that directly incites a riot, or otherwise "breaches the peace," cannot be defended under the free speech or religion clauses of the First Amendment. The question of what constitutes exaggerated or abusive speech, which is ordinarily protected, and what constitutes "fighting words" or inflammatory language beyond the boundaries of the First Amendment is neither a simple matter nor objectively measurable. Statutes or regulations that seek to prohibit speech, however, "must be highly specific and narrowly drawn" (*Lewis* v. *New Orleans*, 94 S. Ct. 970, 1974; cf. Cooper 1977).

The justices of the Supreme Court have often disagreed about where to drawn the boundaries of inflammatory speech or "fighting words." In the well-known case of *Terminello* v. *City of Chicago* (337 U.S. 1, 1949), a speech was delivered in an auditorium by Father Terminello, which, by its content, provoked a riot. The Court, with Justice Douglas delivering the majority opinion, overturned a lower court's conviction of Terminello in part on the grounds that

> a function of free speech under our system of government is to invite disputes. It may indeed best serve its high purpose when it induces a condition of unrest, creates dissatisfaction with conditions as they are, or even stirs people to anger. Speech is often provocative and challenging. . . . That is why freedom of speech, though not absolute, . . . is nevertheless protected against censorship or punishment, unless shown likely to produce a clear and present danger of a serious substantive evil that arises far above public inconvenience, annoyance, or unrest.

The thrust of this argument provoked Justice Jackson to dissent on grounds that the Terminello speech had, in fact, resulted in a riot. The Court's majority, he said, has proceeded as though one "must forego order to achieve liberty. . . . Rioting is a substantive evil, which . . . the State and City have the right and the duty to prevent and punish." (Cf. Haiman 1976.)

Justice Jackson's admonitions did not go unheeded. Two years later the Court ruled against a soapbox orator who was arrested for stirring his audience to threats of violence (*Feiner* v. *New York*, 340 U.S. 315,

1951). The *Feiner* case was not to revolve the issue either, for in subsequent cases the Court wavered or was divided on the issue of speech that is not only opprobrious but profane, "filthy," indecent, and "calculated to offend the sensibilities of an unwilling audience." The nation's courts have in some cases punished such speech and in other cases defended it.

Freedom of Religion

Although tolerance is in all spheres difficult to achieve, it has been particularly difficult to achieve in the sphere of religion. Of the several rights included in the First Amendment and in the Bill of Rights, freedom of religion is named first. It is not by chance, for no other form of intolerance has been as ubiquitous as religious persecution. In the eighteenth century, as in preceding centuries, the efforts to gain religious liberty were central to the struggles for freedom of belief, paving the way, by argument and physical resistance, for the later struggles for democratic rights in general.

Most advocates of religious freedom were not champions of democracy or advocates of civil liberties as such. Many, upon gaining a measure of security for themselves, were inclined to turn oppressor and persecute the disciples of other religions. (Cf. Pfeffer 1977.) The tendency for the faithful of one religion to display intolerance toward the followers of another arises, in part, out of the nature of religion itself, which is usually based on some form of "revealed" truth. As the product of revelation, it is distinguished from more inductively derived scientific or secular "truths." Whereas the latter are, in principle, "open" and subject to challenge, refutation, and proof, a revealed truth, by its very nature, can be neither refuted nor confirmed—and its devotees are unreceptive to challenge or disagreement.

Despite the impulse toward orthodoxy and absolutism inherent in numerous religions of the eighteenth century, many of the faithful, especially among Protestants, found it useful to make "common cause" with the more secular-minded (Morgan 1977). Partly because they feared the "reestablishment" of the Anglican or Catholic churches, they joined the campaign to separate church and state. By the time of the American Revolution, the doctrines of the European Enlightenment, profoundly secular in their thrust, had come to enjoy a considerable vogue among American intellectuals (Morgan, 1977)—and especially among such statesmen as Jefferson, Madison, Paine, and Mason.

As democratic values become stronger, an ideology of tolerance began to take hold, even among many of the faithful. With this development and the proliferation of religious denominations, which prevented any single religion from becoming strong enough to dominate the others, certain norms of the Reformation were also strengthened. These norms held religion to be a matter of private conscience, an accommodation between the individual and God, through which each person was to find his or her own path to salvation. Hence, many different forms of religious belief were possible. Religion became more and more a matter of private conscience and conviction rather than a set of theological dogmas enforced by civil authorities. It became increasingly plain that no government could be permitted to enforce its own "official" religion or to prohibit its constituents from exercising their religious conscience in whatever fashion they chose.

The guarantee of freedom of worship in the First Amendment consists, in effect, of two guarantees. One provides that "Congress shall make no law respecting an establishment of religion," and the other forbids Congress from prohibiting "the free exercise" of religion. While both clauses are meant to advance religious freedom, the presence of one complicates the other. Determining the scope of these twin mandates "has proved a troublesome task, compounded by the inherent potential for conflict between them: a state's friendliness to religion may violate the establishment clause, whereas unfriendliness may run afoul of the free exercise clause" (Wagner 1977). Both the "establishment" and "free exercise" clauses have surfaced in a number of contexts. Their most frequent application and conflict has come in the field of education, where Congress, the state legislatures, and the courts have had to wrestle with problems affecting financial aid to the schools and "the intrusion of religion into public schools" (Wagner 1977).

In *Everson* v. *Board of Education* (330 U.S. 1, 1947), the first important Supreme Court case dealing with the religious aspects of government subsidies to parochial schools, the Court held that a state could subsidize the bus fares of students, whether they attended public or sectarian schools. Since the subsidy was paid directly to parents and was primarily designed not to promote religion but to help children get to school safely and expeditiously, the state subsidy was thought to have no bearing on the issue of religion.*

The *Everson* opinion also made a special attempt to interpret the meaning of the prohibition in the First Amendment against laws respecting "an establishment of religion." According to Black, this clause means that

> neither a state nor the Federal Government can set up a church. Neither can pass laws which aid one religion over another. Neither can force nor influence a person to go or to remain away from a church against his will or force him to profess a belief in any religion. No person can be punished for entertaining or professing religious beliefs, for church attendance or nonattendance. No tax in any amount—can be levied to support any religious activities or institutions.

The clause banning the establishment of religion, Black concluded, was meant to erect, in Jefferson's words, "a wall of separation between church and state." This phrase, widely quoted though controversial, has become the guiding principle for public politics affecting the use of civil institutions for religious purposes.†

In a series of cases, beginning with *Engel* v. *Vitale* (370 U.S. 421, 1962), the Court decided that the government could not require a public school to provide opportunities for school prayers or even to use a nondenominational prayer prepared by state officials. The test of the legality of any program of school prayers or Bible-reading in the public schools was whether its purpose or effect was to promote religion. In the important case of *Abington School District* v. *Schempp* (374 U.S. 203, 1963), the Court further decided that a state violated the establishment clause of the First Amendment by "requiring the selection and reading at the opening of the school day of verses from the Holy Bible and the recitation of the Lord's Prayer by the students in unison." It now appears that "religion is barred from entering the public school: prayer, Bible-reading and in-class religious instruction are all forbidden" (Wagner 1977).

---

*The thrust of this finding, however, was later reversed when the Court decided that the state of Missouri could provide bus transportation for public school students but not for private school students (*Luetkemeyer* v. *Kaufman*, 419 U.S. 888, 1974).

†While the First Amendment forbade the establishment by *Congress* of a state religion at the federal level, some of the states continued for several decades to maintain an established church. Connecticut, for example, did not abolish its established religion until 1818. (Cf. Roche, 1958.) With the adoption of the Fourteenth Amendment, of course, all the prohibitions against federal actions contained in the Bill of Rights were applied to the states as well.

Far less settled, however, is the question of government aid to private schools, which breaches to some extent the separation between church and state. In one case the state of New York was permitted to lend textbooks, free of charge, to all students in certain grades, even if they were attending private schools. In another case, the Court in a close decision held that it was valid for federal aid to be given to church-related institutions of higher learning for the purpose of constructing academic facilities that would be used for secular purposes for the first twenty years. However, the Court has also ruled on various occasions against government regulations or programs that provided aid to parochial schools. In *Lemon* v. *Kurtzman* (403 U.S. 602, 1971), for example, the Court held that government could not, under the First Amendment, provide a salary supplement to private (that is, parochial) school teachers. In the *Nyquist* case, the Court held that New York could not give financial aid to private schools in low-income areas for the maintenance and repair of their buildings. As evidence of the uncertainty that characterizes the law in this area, the Court in *Meek* v. *Pittinger* (421 U.S. 349, 1975) approved the state loan of textbooks to private schools, but forbade the loan of other instructional materials.

The issue of separating church and state has also surfaced in areas other than education. The Court has on various occasions upheld the Sunday closing laws adopted by some states. Such laws, the justices decided, had no bearing on the establishment of religion, but were "intended simply to provide a uniform day of rest—a secular and hence permissible goal" (Wagner 1977).

In another series of cases involving compulsory medical treatment for people whose religion forbade such treatment (for example, Christian Scientists), the Court has proceeded more pragmatically. It ruled in favor of such compulsory treatment when, as in an epidemic, the health of the community is at stake; when the patient is a child and hence unable to decide such questions; or when the medical risk is serious and medical treatment is vital. Even these ground rules, however, have not been uniformly followed. One can find decisions on both sides of almost every issue involving a clash between religious conscience and the compulsory ordering of medical care. Claims for draft exemptions on religious grounds have proved equally vexing. In general, the courts will now grant an exemption from military service to anyone with sincerely held conscientious objections, whether explicitly religious in origin or not. Each case, however, has to be determined on its individual merits, except perhaps for those cases in which one is a member of a religion (for example, the Quakers) which has a long-established and widely recognized stand against military service.

The same respect for freedom of religious conscience was shown in the well-known flag salute case, *West Virginia State Board of Education* v. *Barnette* (319 U.S. 624, 1943), in which the Court held unconstitutional a state law which required public school children to salute the flag despite their religious objections (derived from Exodus) against bowing down before "any graven image." The Court also held a Wisconsin school attendance law unconstitutional insofar as it required the child of an Amish family to continue in school beyond the eighth grade. Recognition of the importance of religious belief was also evident in court decisions granting a conditional exemption to a citizen who refused, on religious grounds, to serve as a juror ("judge not lest ye be judged"). A California statute prohibiting the use of peyote was held to be unconstitutional insofar as the state attempted to apply it to Native American religious ceremonies. And the Court also held that a Seventh Day Adventist, fired from her job for refusing to work on Saturday, could not be denied employment compensation benefits under a South Carolina law which appeared to disqualify her for failing "to accept available suitable work when offered" (Wagner 1977).

In other cases, however, clashes between religious belief and the secular interests of society have been resolved in favor of society's standards. Thus, the Court has held that polygamy among Mormons is unconstitutional. It has also held that the state cannot prohibit the teaching of evolution in the public schools. Nor will all forms of religious belief qualify one for an exemption from military service. Nevertheless, as even this brief review makes plain, freedom of religion is a highly respected (and highly sensitive) provision of the First Amendment. Insofar as it applies to belief alone, it is virtually absolute. Constitutional complications arise when the followers of certain religions attempt to translate their beliefs into conduct that clashes with existing government regulations. As we observed in the discussion of freedom of speech, press, and assembly, no type or amount of religious conviction can overcome legal prohibitions against harming others, committing crimes, or inciting violence.

Findings on Symbolic Speech

Despite the growing tendency of the courts to accept certain actions as symbolic forms of speech and therefore entitled to protection, the majority of Americans do not hold attitudes which reflect this legal trend. As can be seen in table 3.1, only a small minority of the general public (about one in four) are willing to endorse the right to make political statements by means of dramatic or shocking actions. Even actions which appear to be relatively harmless are not widely tolerated. Despite such eloquent defenses as Justice Jackson's on the right to remain silent and to refuse to salute the flag, 47 percent of those who responded to the question would suspend or dismiss a school teacher who tried to exercise this right. Only one third of the population would allow someone to engage in so vague a form of conduct as showing "disrespect for the flag," while the number who would permit the desecration of the flag is even smaller (18 percent). Only 22 percent regard the use of obscene gestures to express one's anger against public officials as a constitutionally protected right.

The level of support for libertarian responses declines even further when symbolic speech blends into civil disobedience. As one can easily discern in table 3.2, the proportion of the general population who are prepared to tolerate outright disobedience of the law—whether to serve one's conscience or to correct injustice—is extremely small. Only 9 percent of the mass public in the OVS sample would permit a person to disobey a law he or she feels to be morally wrong. In the CLS sample, only 10 percent feel there is merit in calling attention to an unjust law by refusing to obey it.

It should not be surprising that large portions of the American public are unsympathetic to the exercise of most forms of symbolic speech. The recognition and acceptance of certain forms of symbolic speech by the courts is a relatively recent development, and the norms that have been emerging around such forms of expression are not widely familiar either to the elites or to the mass public. Additionally, most forms of symbolic speech tend to go beyond either literal interpretations of the law, or, equally important, well-established standards of conduct and decorum. Learning to tolerate symbolic forms of speech is even more difficult than learning to tolerate the more conventional types of speech. For many people, symbolic speech (speech plus) seems less an instance of expression than of conduct, and a form of conduct

TABLE 3.1
Support for Symbolic Speech

	CLS		
	Mass Public	**Community Leaders**	**Legal Elite**
	(N=1993)	**(N=1157)**	**(N=488)**
A person who publicly burns or spits on the flag:			
—may be behaving badly but should not be punished for it by law.	18%	29%	43%
—should be fined or punished in some way.	72	61	50
—Neither/Undecided	10	10	7
The use of obscene gestures to express anger against a public official:			
—should be considered a constitutionally protected form of free speech.	22	35	54
—is so rude it should be outlawed.	45	34	21
—Neither/Undecided	33	31	25
Protesters who mock the President by wearing death masks at one of his public speeches:			
—should have the right to appear in any kind of costume they want.	32	54	70
—should be removed from the audience by the police.	51	30	15
—Neither/Undecided	17	16	15

	OVS		
	Mass Public	**Opinion Leaders**	**ACLU**
	(N=938)	**(N=845)**	**(N=352)**
A teacher who refuses to salute the flag at a school assembly:			
—should be allowed to refuse and follow his or her conscience.	32%	58%	87%
—should be suspended or dismissed.	47	17	5
—Neither/Undecided	20	25	9
Any American who shows disrespect for the flag:			
—has the right to think what he pleases.	33	55	85
—should be turned over to patriots to be taught a lesson.	23	3	0
—Neither/Undecided	44	42	15
When a young man doesn't believe in war:			
—it's his right to believe whatever he likes.	40	63	87
—it's his patriotic duty to serve no matter how he feels.	41	20	5
—Neither/Undecided	19	17	9

NOTES: Because percentages have been rounded off, occasionally there will be disparities in totals (columns will not add up to 100 percent).

See the Preface to Research Findings (p. 25) and Appendix B for description of the leader and mass public samples of various categories used in the PAB, CLS, and OVS studies: that is "Political Leaders," "Legal Elite," and so forth.

The CLS was conducted in 1978–1979; The OVS in 1976–77; and the PAB in 1958.

TABLE 3.2
Support for Civil Disobedience

	CLS		
	Mass Public	**Community Leaders**	**Legal Elite**
	(N=1993)	**(N=1157)**	**(N=488)**
When a law goes against a person's conscience, he should:			
—be allowed to disobey it so long as he has good reason and doesn't hurt anyone else.	18%	23%	20%
—be required nevertheless to obey it, or else all law will lose its meaning.	60	58	63
—Neither/Undecided	22	19	17
People who demonstrate against laws they consider unjust by lying down in the streets and blocking traffic:			
—deserve credit for being willing to act on their ideals.	20	27	28
—are just lawbreakers and should be treated as such.	57	49	47
—Neither/Undecided	23	24	25
When a law is particularly unjust, one possible way to change it is:			
—to call it to the world's attention by refusing to obey it.	10	20	28
—to obey it strictly, but try to persuade the lawmakers to change it in the standard way.	74	67	59
—Neither/Undecided	15	13	13
Citizens who refuse to pay their income tax in protest against the use of money to pay for abortions:			
—should not be forced to pay for something they believe to be morally wrong.	19	8	3
—should be subject to the same penalties as other tax evaders.	65	84	88
—Neither/Undecided	16	8	9
Which of these comes closer to what you believe?			
—Although law is necessary for an orderly society, some laws are so unjust that people should simply refuse to obey them.	17	27	30
—In an orderly country, laws must be obeyed by everyone, even if they are sometimes wrong.	58	54	53
—Neither/Undecided	25	19	17
A person who is willing to risk going to jail for breaking the law in the hope of correcting some serious injustice:			
—is acting heroically and is more likely to gain his objectives than by obeying the law.	20	34	31
—is acting foolishly, since he could probably get further by working within the law.	60	49	49
—Neither/Undecided	20	17	21

	OVS		
	Mass Public	**Opinion Leaders**	**ACLU**
	(N=938)	(N=845)	(N=352)
A person who feels strongly that a law is morally wrong and goes against his conscience:			
—should be allowed to disobey it without being punished.	9%	9%	16%
—should be required to obey the law no matter what he believes.	54	39	22
—Neither/Undecided	37	53	62
In order to get the government to act:			
—breaking the law is sometimes necessary.	17	36	60
—breaking the law is never justified.	61	41	24
—Neither/Undecided	22	24	16

that is at best willful and at worst dangerous. Many Americans doubtless find it extremely bewildering that in a nation governed by an orderly legislative process, some people find it necessary to lie down and block traffic in order to get a law changed. On the other hand, the citizen who has a substantial investment in the libertarian norms of the society is more inclined to interpret such forms of conduct not as crimes but as expressions of conscience, however repugnant their manifestation.

The data on symbolic speech from table 3.1 further validate our findings that the community leaders are significantly more tolerant of freedom of speech and press than the mass public and that the legal elites are more tolerant still. (The percentage scoring high on our scale of symbolic speech was 36 percent for the mass public, 55 percent for the community leaders, and 72 percent for the lawyers and judges.) The difference between the mass public and the legal elites on such items as dishonoring the flag, using obscene gestures against officials, and mocking the President are fairly large, ranging from 26 percent to 39 percent.

There is no reason to suppose that the elites relish this type of behavior any more than the mass public does. Their greater willingness to abide it reflects their greater understanding of the reasons for tolerance in a democratic society. Support for our belief that knowledge of civil liberties has a substantial bearing on the endorsement of symbolic speech as a First Amendment right can be inferred from the scores registered by the members of the American Civil Liberties Union in table 3.1 Approximately 87 percent of the ACLU members chose the tolerant response on both the flag salute and the disrespect-for-the-flag items, and only a small percentage opted for the antilibertarian response.

Evidence of a more direct nature can be found in table 3.3, which shows that those who score high on the Civil Liberties Quiz are substantially more tolerant of symbolic speech than those who are relatively uninformed about the prevailing civil libertarian norms. Moreover, the differences remain just as large when one turns from the mass population sample to the community elite sample. In the mass population, 50 percent of those who are well informed about civil liberties score high, as opposed to 23 percent of those who are poorly informed, a difference of 27 percent. In the community leader sample, the comparable figures are 63 percent and 31 percent, a difference of 32 percent. It seems fair to say that despite the somewhat abstruse nature of symbolic speech as a subcategory of civil liberties (or perhaps because of its abstruse nature) tolerance of the various types of symbolic speech is strongly influenced by the degree to which respondents are sophisticated about civil liberties in general. Although symbolic speech usually contains an element of unpopular conduct as well as speech, and therefore tends to receive less public favor than the more conventional forms of free speech and press, support for symbolic speech increases markedly as knowledge and understanding of civil libertarian norms increase.

As previously noted, the public levels of tolerance are greatly lowered when we turn to those forms of symbolic speech that shade into civil disobedience. As Kalven (1967) has pointed out, civil disobedience, in its classic form, represents "a deliberate violation of the law for the sake of protest and as a matter of individual conscience," but it does not claim "immunity from punishment." As we saw in table 3.2, few members of the public are prepared to allow anyone to violate the law without being punished for it, no matter how moral the purpose. The number of people selecting the libertarian response for each of the eight items in the table range from 6 percent to 20 percent, with the average falling around 15 percent. In every case, a substantial majority chose the response that demands adherence to the law, regardless of conscience or the unfairness of the law in question.

It is worth noting that although the elites tend to have a greater appreciation for the case for civil disobedience than does the mass public, the differences are slight. The elites are scarcely more sympathetic than the general population to civil disobedience as a form of political expression. For example, whereas 32 percent of the mass public score high on a seven-item scale designed to measure support for civil disobedience, the percentage scoring high among the elite samples is not much larger—40 percent for the community leaders and 41 percent for the legal elites. In addition, controlling for knowledge of civil liberties (as we have done in table 3.4) has little effect on the civil disobedience scores of the mass public, although it does have some effect on the scores of the elites.

Questions of civil disobedience are particularly troublesome in that they generally involve conflicting values. As de Toqueville long ago observed, and as we can detect from our data and from intuitive observation, Americans greatly respect individuality and adherence to conscience. In their fantasy life at any rate, Americans revere folk heroes such as Thoreau who go their own way and live by their principles. The hero typified by the western "loner" who stands apart from the mob and refuses to bend to unjust authority is one of the familiar and recurring themes of American folklore. Catchwords such as individualism, independence, self-determination, and personal autonomy are, in the abstract at least, highly valued by most Americans. However, all the items in table 3.4 involve some form of lawbreaking; and despite the stereotype that portrays Americans as a "lawless" people, a concern for obeying the law is deeply etched into the American consciousness. Hence, when citizens are asked to choose between a policy that reflects conscience and one that requires them to sanction the deliberate breaking of a law, not many are willing to approve the latter. (The norms that have developed around issues of civil disobedience are predominantly hostile to lawbreaking.) Even elites, who exhibit a stronger inclination than the mass public to strike out against "unjust" laws, cannot bring themselves to say in any great number that these objectives warrant violating the law. They share with the mass public the belief that adequate opportunities exist for bringing about change without having to violate the law.

In general, both the community leaders and the legal elites exhibit, in the matter of symbolic speech as in other First Amendment rights, greater tolerance than the mass public. When the expression of opinion involves actions which, though provocative or offensive, are nevertheless harmless or without immediate or direct consequences, the elites tend (though only by pluralities or small majorities) to uphold them as legitimate forms of expression. When, however, symbolic speech in-

113

TABLE 3.3
Knowledge of Civil Liberties and Support for Symbolic Speech
(percentage down)

		Mass Public				Community Leaders				Legal Elite		
		Low	Middle	High	Total	Low	Middle	High	Total	Low*	Middle	High	Total
		(N = 664)	(N = 667)	(N = 662)	(N = 1993)	(N = 139)	(N = 322)	(N = 696)	(N = 1157)	(N = 8)	(N = 61)	(N = 419)	(N = 488)
Support for Symbolic Speech	% Low	41	26	17	28	34	19	11	16	—	5	6	6
	% Middle	37	39	33	36	35	34	27	30	—	26	22	22
	% High	23	35	50	36	31	47	63	55	—	69	72	72

*N is too small to calculate percentages for this column.

TABLE 3.4
Knowledge of Civil Liberties and Support for Civil Disobedience as a Form of "Expression"
(percentage down)

		Mass Public				Community Leaders				Legal Elite		
		Low	Middle	High	Total	Low	Middle	High	Total	Low*	Middle	High	Total
		(N = 664)	(N = 667)	(N = 662)	(N = 1993)	(N = 139)	(N = 322)	(N = 696)	(N = 1157)	(N = 8)	(N = 61)	(N = 419)	(N = 488)
Support for Civil Disobedience	% Low	26	29	29	28	41	35	30	33	—	31	29	30
	% Middle	43	40	37	40	35	31	23	27	—	33	30	30
	% High	31	31	34	32	25	34	46	40	—	36	42	41

*N is too small to calculate percentages for this column.

volves the blocking of roadways, deliberate violations of the law, or the use of political violence, only a small minority of the elites are willing to extend First Amendment protection.

The data also support the observation that elite opinion on these matters tends to conform more closely than popular opinion to the principles enunciated by the courts. This holds especially for the legal elites, who possess the most intimate knowledge of judicial opinion and are most strongly disposed to follow it. While they are more inclined by education, training, and daily experience to acquire the norms that protect civil liberties, they tend also to be highly sensitive to conduct that deliberately flouts the law or impedes the work of the courts. Hence, though they are drawn to honor the liberties specified or implied by the First Amendment, they are also more likely to be conscious of the limitations on the exercise of liberties that have been written into the laws by the legislatures and the courts.

Neither the mass public nor the elites believe that people who decide, for reasons of conscience, to disobey a cruel or unjust law are wicked and acting disloyally. Witness, for example, their responses to the following item:

	Mass Public	Community Leaders	Legal Elite
	(N = 1993)	(N = 1157)	(N = 485)
People who disobey a law they believe to be particularly cruel or unjust:			
—often love America deeply and want it to live up to its ideals.	57%	70%	75%
—are disloyal Americans who want to harm this country.	8	3	3
—Neither/Undecided	35	27	23

Thus, almost three fourths of the community and legal elites, and a majority of the general public, accept the stated motivations of those who engage in civil disobedience, taking them to be loyal Americans who are seeking to persuade the nation to live up to its professed ideals. In light of the American glorification of the individualist hero who stands up for conscience and defies unjust authority, they may even admire such dissidents. Nevertheless, when forced to choose, they reject the notion that a high-minded cause entitles one to break the law. Even members of the ACLU do not believe that a person has a right to disobey a law he or she considers morally wrong, although a majority acknowledge in principle that breaking the law may sometimes be necessary to spur government to act.

In the matter of symbolic speech that takes the form of civil disobedience, neither the courts nor the elites accept the libertarian stance as the accepted norm. Although lawyers, judges, and other members of the elite (as well as half the members of the mass public) seem to understand why an individual might feel impelled to disobey an unjust law as an act of conscience, they nevertheless believe that obedience to the law is essential to an orderly society, especially in a democracy which provides institutionalized opportunities for correcting injustice and bringing about change.

Findings on the Right of Assembly and Association

Popular and elite attitudes toward the right of assembly reflect the complex nature of this right, as well as the uncertainty the courts themselves have exhibited toward its exercise. The public, in keeping with the pattern of its responses to other First Amendment rights, lags far behind the Court and, on many issues, well behind the elites in its readiness to adhere to prevailing constitutional norms regarding assembly. Even within these limits, however, the public's response to the right of assembly varies, depending on the kind of group that wishes to exercise the right.

In figure 3.1 we see that despite the widespread popular distaste for campus demonstrations, two thirds of the mass public would not punish students for participating in them as long as the demonstrations were *peaceful*. Similarly, although the "freedom-riders" of the civil rights movement were scarcely popular at the height of their activity during the early 1960s, most Americans (70 percent) now agree that their actions "helped bring about needed reforms that gave blacks their just rights."

While these figures indicate that there is a reservoir of popular acceptance of the right of the politically disaffected to express their feelings through public assemblies, the level of support begins to drop as soon as there is any suggestion that their meetings might become violent. Thus, only 50 percent of the mass public would permit a demonstration to continue if there were reason to believe that it might turn violent—and then only if it were carefully monitored by the police. Even fewer (26 percent) would grant police protection to a group with a reputation for violence if it were picketing the White House.

Popular support for freedom of assembly tends to be strained even further when the assembly becomes a mass protest. Only 41 percent of the public are willing to endorse, even in the abstract, the right to hold a mass protest march that most people in the community oppose. (See figure 3.2.) The percentage supporting the exercise of that right in various specific contexts is even lower. Only one third of the mass public would permit protesters to hold a meeting outside the city jail. One fourth of the respondents want the government to keep a list of people who take part in protest demonstrations. Only 6 percent of the general population would grant a permit to a political group that wanted to hold a parade that blocked traffic in a midtown area for two hours. (Thus, the argument advanced by many constitutional authorities—including Justice Roberts in *Hague* v. *CIO*—that the use of the public streets "has, from ancient times, been a part of privileges, immunities, rights, and liberties of citizens" receives little sympathy from the public when the exercise of that right temporarily interferes with the flow of traffic.) However, the public's lack of sympathy for protest meetings or parades goes beyond the mere inconvenience they may cause: witness the finding that, by a ratio of four to one, respondents believe that the government has been "too easy" rather than "too tough" in its handling of protesters.

The public's response to the exercise of the right of assembly is also affected by the ideological character of the group wishing to exercise that right. In figure 3.3 we see that only 18 percent of the public would supply police protection for marches and rallies held by the Nazis and other "extreme groups" (the very groups, as a practical matter, which are most likely to require such protection). As we saw in chapter 2, approximately two thirds would deny the American Nazi party the opportunity to use the town hall to hold a public meeting, and only 23 percent would permit a group to hold a meeting in a public building for the purpose of denouncing the government. At the same time, a majority of the public believe that a group has as much right to hold a meeting to advocate war against an enemy nation as to advocate peace.

In order to achieve a better sense of the joint effects of group popularity and ideology on one's recognition of the right of assembly, we asked respondents in the CLS whether groups of varying character

Mass student protest demonstrations:

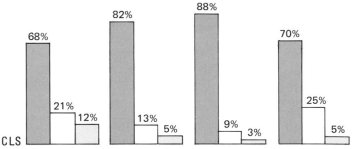

—should be allowed by college officials as long as they are nonviolent.

—have no place on a college campus and the participating students should be punished.

—Neither/Undecided

The nonviolent marches, boycotts, and sit-ins of black people in the South during the early 1960s:

—helped bring about needed reforms that gave blacks their just rights.

—merely caused trouble and probably did more harm than good in the long run.

—Neither/Undecided

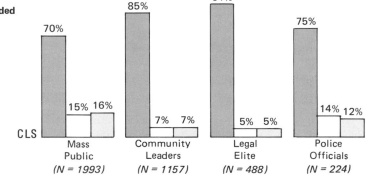

| | Mass Public (N = 1993) | Community Leaders (N = 1157) | Legal Elite (N = 488) | Police Officials (N = 224) |

Notes: Because percentages have been rounded off, occasionally there will be disparities in totals (columns will not add up to 100 percent).

See the Preface to Research Findings in Chapter 1 and Appendix B for an analysis of the components

FIGURE 3.1
Violence and the Right of Assembly
(CLS)

When authorities have reason to believe that a political demonstration will become violent, they should:

—**keep an eye on the demonstration but allow it to be held.**

—**seek a court order to stop the demonstration.**

—**Neither/Undecided**

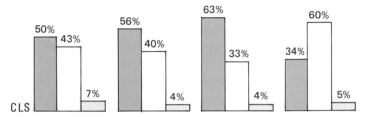

If a political group known for its violent activities wants to picket the White House:

—**it should be granted police protection like any other group.**

—**it should be prevented from doing so because it might endanger the President.**

—**Neither/Undecided**

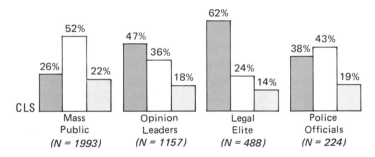

| | Mass Public (N = 1993) | Opinion Leaders (N = 1157) | Legal Elite (N = 488) | Police Officials (N = 224) |

of various categories used in the PAB, CLS, and OVS studies: that is "Political Leaders," "Legal Elite," and so forth.

The CLS was conducted in 1978-1979; the OVS in 1976-1977; and the PAB in 1958.

Should demonstrators be allowed to hold a mass protest for some unpopular cause?

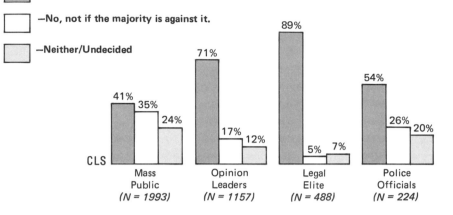

Should a political protest group be granted a permit to hold a parade that blocks midtown traffic for two hours?

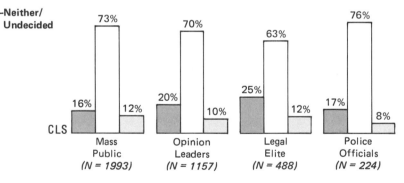

FIGURE 3.2
Assembly and the Right to Protest
(CLS/OVS)

If a group wanted to hold a protest demonstration in front of the city jail, would city officials be justified in banning it?

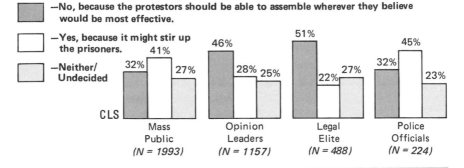

—No, because the protestors should be able to assemble wherever they believe would be most effective.

—Yes, because it might stir up the prisoners.

—Neither/Undecided

CLS

| Mass Public (N = 1993) | Opinion Leaders (N = 1157) | Legal Elite (N = 488) | Police Officials (N = 224) |

Is it a good idea, or a bad idea for the government to keep a list of people who take part in protest demonstrations?

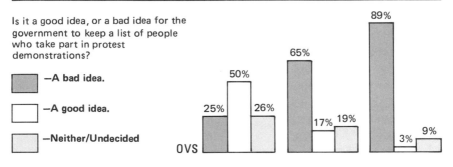

—A bad idea.

—A good idea.

—Neither/Undecided

OVS

In handling protest demonstrations, the government has usually been:

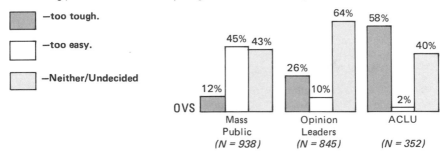

—too tough.

—too easy.

—Neither/Undecided

OVS

| Mass Public (N = 938) | Opinion Leaders (N = 845) | ACLU (N = 352) |

When groups like the Nazis or other extreme groups require police protection at their rallies and marches, the community should:

 —supply and pay for whatever police protection is needed.

☐ —prohibit such groups from holding rallies because of the costs and dangers involved.

☐ —Neither/Undecided

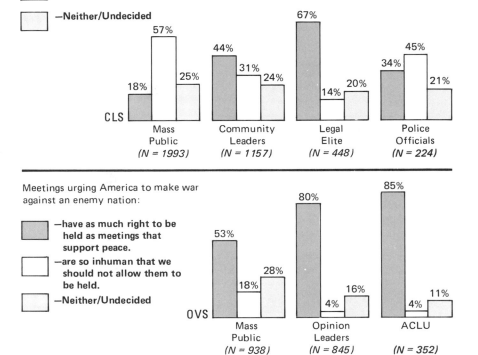

FIGURE 3.3
"Extremists" and the Right of Assembly
(CLS/OVS)

and political coloration should be allowed to use the civic auditorium to express their views. The results are presented in table 3.5, and they offer a dramatic demonstration of the degree to which attitudes vary as the popularity of the group and its cause varies. The questions in this table represent a more severe test of tolerance than some of the other questions we have used because they ask respondents not merely whether they believe that certain groups have certain rights, but whether they favor or oppose the use of their community's civic auditorium by the groups listed and for the purposes stated. In other words, respondents are placed under a particular strain in answering these questions; if they say "yes" to a group, they appear to be saying, in effect, that they are willing to see their tax dollars used to promote the cause of that group.

Although every group listed, no matter how controversial, is equally entitled under the First Amendment to hold meetings in the civic auditorium and to express the views indicated, public support ranges from 69 percent for Protestant groups who want to hold a revival meeting to 5 percent for revolutionary groups who advocate the violent overthrow of the government. Of the thirteen groups listed, only four—Protestants, right-to-life groups, conservationists, and ERA supporters—manage to gain majority support for the use of the auditorium. The proportion drops dramatically to 26 percent for gay liberation groups and declines steadily as one proceeds downward in the table from atheistic groups to revolutionaries. In eight of the thirteen cases, fewer than 20 percent (from 18 percent to 5 percent) are willing to allow a controversial group to meet.

We have no way of telling whether the denial or the approval of the right of assembly represents a response mainly to the group named or to the cause it hopes to advance. Both variables are clearly at work. Some groups (for example, Protestants), whether liked or disliked, are clearly less objectionable to the general public than others (for example, atheists); while some purposes (for example, the holding of a revival meeting) are clearly less offensive to the mass public than others (for example, the advocacy of war).

These findings indicate that the public has failed to learn that the First Amendment guarantees all citizens, regardless of ideological persuasion or political objectives, an equal claim to the community's facilities. Even if one grants that in practice these claims have not always been recognized by community officials (including the judiciary), and that they have sometimes discriminated against certain groups the pub-

TABLE 3.5
The Right of Assembly:
What Activities Should a Community Allow?

Should a community allow its civic auditorium to be used by:		Mass Public (N=1993)	Community Leaders (N=1157)	Legal Elite (N=488)	Police Officials (N=224)
Protestant groups who want to hold a revival meeting?	Yes	69%	72%	74%	71%
	No	16	16	17	16
	It depends/ Undecided	16	13	9	13
right-to-life groups to preach against abortion?	Yes	65	73	81	67
	No	18	14	10	18
	It depends/ Undecided	17	14	8	15
conservationists to protest the construction of a nuclear power plant?	Yes	60	75	87	64
	No	19	12	7	21
	It depends/ Undecided	21	13	7	14
feminists to organize a march for the Equal Rights Amendment (ERA)?	Yes	53	75	87	58
	No	24	13	8	21
	It depends/ Undecided	23	12	6	21
gay liberation movements to organize for homosexual rights?	Yes	26	46	65	21
	No	59	40	26	63
	It depends/ Undecided	15	15	8	17
atheists who want to preach against God and religion?	Yes	18	41	66	17
	No	71	44	24	73
	It depends/ Undecided	12	15	9	10
student protesters who call for a sit-in at city hall to shut down the city's offices?	Yes	15	30	44	11
	No	66	53	43	76
	It depends/ Undecided	19	17	13	13
patriotic groups to advocate war against some foreign country?	Yes	13	27	52	14
	No	67	51	30	66
	It depends/ Undecided	20	22	18	20
the Jewish Defense League (JDL) to advocate a war against certain Arab countries?	Yes	9	22	42	6
	No	76	62	42	84
	It depends/ Undecided	15	16	17	10

Should a community allow its civic auditorium to be used by:		Mass Public (N=1993)	Community Leaders (N=1157)	Legal Elite (N=488)	Police Officials (N=224)
foreign radicals who	Yes	6%	17%	32%	4%
want to express their	No	87	72	52	92
hatred of America?	It depends/				
	Undecided	7	11	16	5
the Palestine Liberation	Yes	6	16	33	5
Organization (PLO) to	No	87	74	53	89
attack Jews and call for	It depends/				
the destruction of Israel?	Undecided	7	10	14	6
the American Nazi party	Yes	6	18	37	3
to preach race hatred	No	89	74	51	92
against Jews and other	It depends/				
minorities?	Undecided	5	8	13	5
revolutionaries who	Yes	5	11	21	2
advocate the violent	No	89	81	68	96
overthrow of the	It depends/				
American government?	Undecided	6	8	11	2

NOTE: Items are rank ordered, high to low, by responses of the mass public.

lic fears or perceives as unorthodox, the principle of equal treatment has become one of our established norms. Under existing constitutional law, it is difficult (if not impossible) to make a persuasive legal case for denying to unconventional political groups the use of a public auditorium while permitting its use by conventional groups. Although the principle seems plain enough, many citizens have failed to comprehend why people with unorthodox or offensive opinions are entitled to use the community's tax-supported facilities to express their views.

The data showing that a large majority of the population would deny to unpopular groups the use of the community's facilities to express unpopular opinions suggest that most Americans have only a crude sense of the meaning of a "right" as that concept has evolved in the American experience. They apparently fail to appreciate that a right is a claim enjoyed by *every* citizen in the nation and that its exercise does not depend upon society's approval of disapproval. Although the notion of a right may at first glance appear self-evident, it is in reality an elusive and mysterious concept. To comprehend it one must believe that every individual born into a society possesses an inherent set of claims or entitlements which the government and society (as well as one's fellow citizens) are legally and morally required to honor.

All people, by the simple fact of their existence, are protected in the enjoyment of their rights by an invisible shield which places them (in the matters encompassed by those rights) beyond the reach of the awesome power of rulers. Equally remarkable, they enjoy this extraordinary immunity whether or not they have done anything to earn it. One individual's claim to protection in the enjoyment of rights is equal to that of everyone else's, no matter how virtuous or wicked or deserving the person may be.

In a culture which strongly emphasizes achievement and reward, the notion that one enjoys an ineradicable and inviolable claim which one has done nothing to earn is difficult to grasp. It is far easier to grasp the idea that a right is a *privilege*, a reward for proper conduct or conformity to community standards—and it is precisely in these terms that the concept of a right is often understood (or, more accurately perhaps, misunderstood). By this reasoning, those who behave disreputably or who endanger the society by their conduct or who fail to play the game by the rules should be denied the benefits enjoyed by more deserving citizens.

To be sure, many Americans have a "gut" feeling about their own rights and would be quick to object if they were violated. This, however, would not necessarily signify that they adequately understand the nature of a right under the American Constitution. They would object, in part, because they are unlikely to regard their own conduct as offensive or their own claims as unwarranted. It is mainly when they are asked about the rights or conduct of others that they can point to people who have abused their privilege to speak or assemble freely and are no longer "entitled" to enjoy certain rights. Even among people who glorify freedom and profess to admire nonconforming individualists, the notion of a right as essential to the enjoyment of liberty and as a shield for the protection of nonconformers is not always well understood—a testimony in part to the recondite nature of the concept.

Essentially the same pattern of elite-mass differences we observed in the data on free speech and press turns up for the right of assembly. On every item in figures 3.1–3.3 and table 3.5, the opinion leaders are more willing than the general population to permit public assemblies to be held by objectionable groups for objectionable purposes. In keeping with the now familiar pattern, the legal elites are even more willing than the opinion leaders to support the right of unpopular groups to meet for unpopular causes. Consider, for example, table 3.5. Whereas the public strongly supports the rights of Protestants to assemble for the propagation of their doctrines, it overwhelmingly opposes the granting of the same right to atheists. While many of the opinion leaders are inclined to discriminate against atheists as well, only one fourth of the lawyers and judges would deny their right to use the auditorium "to preach against God and religion," and two thirds would support it.

Nevertheless, even the legal elites do not uniformly endorse the exercise of the right of assembly by all groups. They tend to oppose the use of public facilities for meeting by such unpopular groups as foreign radicals, the PLO, the American Nazi party, and political revolutionaries. Despite their high levels of tolerance in general, their greater knowledge of civil liberties, and their grasp of constitutional requirements concerning such liberties, they are largely unwilling to extend this right to certain groups whose character or doctrines they find especially egregious. In these instances, they are less closely attuned to the Supreme Court's rulings on the right of assembly than one might expect. Their distaste for certain groups and causes overwhelms their apparent understanding of the constitutional principles involved. In figures 3.1–3.3 and table 3.5, we have also included the responses of police officials to the various forms of public assembly. Data on the police are of particular interest, since the exercise of the right of assembly frequently requires the cooperation of the police. Although in a later chapter we will consider in more detail the attitudes of the police toward civil liberties, it should be noted here that, despite their greater experience and familiarity with the laws governing public assemblies, the police differ only slightly from the mass public in their willingness to tolerate the exercise of the right of assembly by certain groups. In some cases they are slightly more tolerant than the general public, but in other cases they are not. Most of the differences, however, are so small as to be statistically insignificant.

In our view, the attitude of the police officials toward the right of assembly does not necessarily signify that they are as poorly informed about the norms as the mass public, but that their knowledge of the norms is colored by their experiences and the requirements of their role. The police are charged with the realization of certain objectives, such as the maintenance of public order, which does not always coincide with strict adherence to libertarian norms, but may, in fact, conflict with them. The responsibility for keeping the peace may thus lead the police to interpret the norms in a selective or biased fashion. A public meeting that turns into a brawl may present a vague threat to the community as a whole, but to the police it represents an immediate and palpable physical danger. The police are bound, therefore, to perceive some assemblies as "safe" (and therefore to be permitted) and others as "unsafe" or troublesome (and therefore to be closely regulated or prohibited, if possible). What the legal elites may regard primarily as a question of constitutional rights, the police may view as a set of events that might lead to riots and bloodshed.

In their response to the items in figures 3.1–3.3 and table 3.5, the police appear to be least tolerant of assemblies that interfere with the effective performance of their job or that might expose them to physical injury. Additionally, although the police do not embrace a single political ideology, they tend to converge around certain outlooks. By virtue of the subcultures from which they are self-selected, and the indoctrination to which they are subject as members of a closely knit vocational group, they are likely to develop a particular antipathy toward protesters, revolutionaries, and "troublemakers." They perceive many militant or "extremist" groups not only as "un-American" in spirit, but as enemies (sometimes declared enemies) of the police themselves.

The intolerance registered in the preceding tables toward the exercise of assembly by groups perceived as "offensive" tends to be carried over to the freedom of association. Despite the Court's decisions to the contrary, the mass public seems to have few qualms about interfering with the right of association—particularly when they view an organization as politically extreme. Evidence of this can be found in table 3.6. For example, over two thirds of the general population would prohibit college students from forming a Nazi organization on campus. The number of respondents who believe that radical organizations have the right to be protected against infiltration by police agents is also rather small, ranging from 6 percent to 24 percent on the three questions that address this issue. Approximately two thirds of the general population regard police surveillance of such associations as necessary for national security. Perhaps because the legal norms governing surveillance of groups considered dangerous have not been firmly formed or uniformly enforced, the responses of the influentials in our samples are not strikingly more tolerant than those of the mass public.

Despite the antilibertarian scores of many members of the mass public, a word of caution might be appropriate concerning their interpretation. Although the public's responses fail in many instances to

TABLE 3.6

The First Amendment and the Right of Association

	CLS			
	Mass Public	Community Leaders	Legal Elite	Police Officials
	(N=1993)	(N=1157)	(N=488)	(N=224)
If some students at a college want to form a "Campus Nazi Club":				
—they should be allowed to do so.	17%	37%	67%	24%
—college officials should ban such clubs from campus.	67	47	24	60
—Neither/Undecided	16	16	9	16
When undercover police agents secretly join far right or far left political groups to keep an eye on them:				
—they are violating the rights of the group's members.	8	11	14	0
—they are only doing what is necessary to protect our society.	76	75	69	92
—Neither/Undecided	17	14	18	8
The use of federal agents to spy on radical organizations:				
—is a waste of time and money since radicals in this country are too weak to do much harm anyway.	6	14	19	2
—is vital to national security and the fight against communism.	68	53	39	80
—Neither/Undecided	26	34	41	19

	OVS	
	Mass Public	Opinion Leaders
	(N=938)	(N=845)
The use of federal agents to spy on radical organizations:		
—violates their right to political freedom.	24%	47%
—is necessary for national security.	59	30
—Neither/Undecided	17	23

reflect the legal norms contained in the Constitution and enunciated by the Court, one need not assume that Americans are predominantly hostile to the rights of assembly or association as such. Blanket generalizations asserting that Americans support or oppose such rights as assembly may be misleading, for, as we have seen, the responses to the exercise of a right are strongly influenced by the character of the group that wishes to exercise the right and the nature of the proposals it intends to advance. The findings, however, do tell us something about the limits of support for freedom of assembly and association in America.

As expected, the data suggest that tolerance toward the exercise of the right of assembly or association is considerably higher when the groups that wish to assemble are perceived as honoring what are thought to be the acceptable rules. For example, few Americans would question the right of Democratic or Republican party members to assemble for the purpose of adopting organizational programs. Many respondents, however, would not hold out the same right to the Communist party or the Ku Klux Klan.

Findings on Freedom of Religion

Data from our own surveys and those of others indicate that while the mass public tends to endorse the free exercise of religion in general, and to this extent appears to have embraced the "official" norms, the level of support for religious freedom begins to decline markedly as one introduces qualifying considerations or issues of a more specific nature. The findings in figure 3.4 indicate that almost 70 percent of the mass public agree that freedom of worship applies to all religious groups, no matter how extreme their beliefs, while only 8 percent would deny the free exercise of religion to religions the community regards as "strange," "fanatical," or "weird." Among community leaders, support for the free expression of religion rises to 80 percent, and among the legal elite, to 85 percent.

Support among the elites for the free expression of religion remains strong even when they are asked about extending this right to atheists. Among the mass public, however, support declines significantly. Only 48 percent of the public would grant atheists the right to

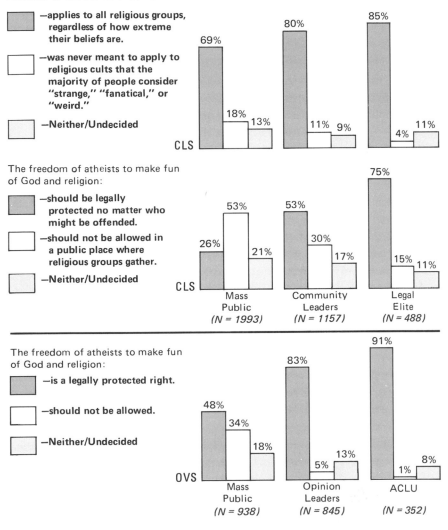

Freedom to worship as one pleases:

- —applies to all religious groups, regardless of how extreme their beliefs are.
- —was never meant to apply to religious cults that the majority of people consider "strange," "fanatical," or "weird."
- —Neither/Undecided

CLS

The freedom of atheists to make fun of God and religion:

- —should be legally protected no matter who might be offended.
- —should not be allowed in a public place where religious groups gather.
- —Neither/Undecided

CLS

Mass Public (N = 1993)   Community Leaders (N = 1157)   Legal Elite (N = 488)

The freedom of atheists to make fun of God and religion:

- —is a legally protected right.
- —should not be allowed.
- —Neither/Undecided

OVS

Mass Public (N = 938)   Opinion Leaders (N = 845)   ACLU (N = 352)

FIGURE 3.4
Freedom of Religion
(CLS/OVS)

"make fun of God and religion," apparently signifying that many who have learned to tolerate differences in religious orientation do not think this right extends to nonbelievers, and especially to people who deny the existence of God. Apparently atheism represents a greater threat to many of the faithful than does belief in some other religion. The psychological distance between a doctrine which proclaims the existence of God and one which denies it is perhaps greater than the distance between any two competing religions. Atheism not only questions the warranty of all claims about revelation, but challenges all religious cosmologies at their very foundations, and hence frightens many people who are able to hang on to their faith only by suspending doubt.

That the majority of elite members are willing to tolerate the dissemination of atheistic notions testifies to their learning of constitutional norms and the norms of a secular society which accords a high place to reason, skepticism, and the value of empirical evidence.

Among the general public, support for the right of atheists "to make fun of God and religion" declines even further (to 26 percent) when the question is one of exercising this right "in a public place where religious groups gather." Here, of course, the test of tolerance has become still more difficult, for now it is not merely the expression of atheistic views that is at issue but the danger that the devout will be directly exposed to ideas which violate their religious sensibilities. The public's willingness to recognize atheism as a protected form of religious freedom is lower still when (as we saw in table 3.5) the issue is one of granting atheists permission to use the community's civic auditorium "to preach against God and religion."* Elite tolerance of atheism also declines somewhat when it is put to these more severe tests, but their scores, though reduced, continue to remain fairly high.

---

* The absolute scores of tolerance for the rights of atheists appear to vary greatly depending upon the form and content of the question, whether the term "atheism" is used in asking the question, and the time at which it was asked. Stouffer, in 1954, found that only 37 percent were willing to allow a person "to make a speech . . . against churches and religion"; but in the early 1970s, NORC and Nunn et al. reported that this figure had risen to almost two thirds. NORC reported that only 40–42 percent were willing to allow such people to teach in a college or university, while 60–61 percent would oppose the removal from the library of a book written by such a person. Wilson (1975), analyzing findings from a survey conducted by the U.S. Commission on Obscenity and Pornography, reported that in 1970 only 32 percent of the sample responded "yes" to the question "Should people be allowed to make speeches against God?" None of these questions included the word "atheists," and none employed phrases such as "making fun of God and religion," or doing so "in a public place where religious groups gather"—in our opinion a much more severe set of tests.

One of the issues that has proved most troubling to both advocates and critics of religious freedom, as well as to the courts, concerns the right of young people (in defiance of their parents' wishes) to join such religious cults as the Unification Church (the so-called Moonies) or the disciples of Hare Krishna. At one level, this issue raises the question of the right of young people to worship as they please, and at another, the rights of parents, as legal guardians of their children, to supervise their behavior. The problem is further exacerbated when parents attempt to force their children to disaffiliate from religious cults by a "deprogramming" effort. A majority of the public reject the notion that young people should be free to practice any religion they please. Over 60 percent believe that parents have "the right and duty to protect their children from influences they consider harmful." The response pattern to this question among the community leaders is similar, while the lawyers and judges divide evenly on the question. The entire issue is one which has emerged only recently, and norms governing it are far from crystallized.

Of the several issues involving religious tolerance, the question of separation of church and state seems to be the most bewildering. As can be seen in this item from the OVS study, nowhere is the discrepancy between popular opinion and constitutional principles (as interpreted by the Court) as great as it is on this issue. Despite the Court's decisions to the contrary, 10 percent of the mass public are willing to forbid prayers in the public schools, while 80 percent would permit them. While the differences between elite and mass opinions on this question are substantial, the principle behind the separation of church and state insofar as it applies to prayers in the public schools has not been absorbed even by most opinion leaders (except for members of the ACLU).

	Mass Public (N=938)	Opinion Leaders (N=845)	ACLU (N=352)
Prayers in the public schools should be:			
—forbidden.	10%	34%	69%
—permitted.	80	48	17
—Neither/Undecided	10	18	14

While there can be little doubt that the vast majority of Americans are presently opposed to the establishment of an official state church, the question of maintaining "a wall of separation between church and state" has proved one of the most difficult for many Americans to grasp. Believing as they do in the value of both religion and the state, they do not see why the two ought to be kept entirely separate. This confusion may be heightened by the instances in which the principle is violated without much fuss. For example, the name of God is inveighed by civil authorities in the imprint on the nation's coins, in various inscriptions on public buildings (including the Supreme Court itself), in the use of prayers to open the meetings of Congress and other legislative bodies, and in the swearing in of various public officials as well as witnesses in court trials.

Another possibility to consider is that respondents may feel that the more tolerant view is to grant (rather than to forbid) assistance to religious groups by permitting school prayers, financial aid to parochial schools and so forth. To prohibit the public schools from conducting prayers strikes many as an expression of intolerance toward religion rather than the reverse. Withholding government funds from denominational schools or refusing to permit them to use publicly owned facilities (such as school buses or textbooks) may seem to some people discriminatory, reflecting a prejudice against religion. Not everyone is equally equipped to know and appreciate the kinds of arguments Jefferson and Madison made for keeping state and church as independent of each other as possible. Not everyone is equally sensitive to the arguments about the dangers, to religion as well as to civil society, in allowing government to insinuate its power into the internal affairs of religious organizations and, conversely, permitting the more powerful religions to gain government favor at the expense of weaker ones.

By making religion entirely a matter of private conscience, shielded in certain critical respects from government regulation or influence, the framers of the First Amendment intended to protect religious conscience rather than the reverse. By refusing to finance parochial schools, the state avoids the risk of becoming entangled in affairs which the American Constitution assigns to the domain of religion (that is, to private conscience). The government is thus removed from the temptation to assist certain religions and to punish others, to give preference or dominion to one creed over others.

Once again, the norms of equality and reciprocity implicit in the doctrine of separation, though difficult to comprehend, are not so recondite that they cannot be learned, so long as one has the opportunity, capacity, and motivation to learn them. Yet, as the data make plain, vast numbers of people have not learned them. The norms are maintained, nevertheless, by having been institutionalized through the First Amendment, court decisions, and related commentaries, and through the attention paid to such matters by those members of society who, by their concern and knowledge of civil liberties, serve as repositories and protectors of libertarian values, in matters affecting religious as well as secular belief and conduct.

CHAPTER 4

The Rights of Due Process

ALTHOUGH the First Amendment's guarantees of freedom are often acclaimed as the foundations of American democracy, their enforcement depends heavily upon rights contained in the Fifth and Fourteenth Amendments which provide that no person shall be deprived of "life, liberty, or property without due process of law."

The concept of due process is nowhere defined in the Constitution, but its general meaning is clear enough, and its more specific meanings have been fleshed out over the past two centuries by the courts, the legislatures, and various regulatory bodies. Due process is largely synonymous with "fundamental fairness." Its fundamental aim is to safeguard individuals against arbitrary treatment by officials. Under the limitations of the due process clause, government cannot deal with citizens in any way it pleases, even if the citizens have broken the law or committed crimes. Government cannot incarcerate citizens or take their property (much less their lives), without proceeding in a fair and orderly fashion as prescribed by the Constitution, statutes, court rulings, and administrative regulations. A citizen cannot be subjected to the caprice or malice of governing institutions or officials (Casper 1972). Nor, as the Court's interpretation of the Constitution would have it, can individuals be subjected to "cruel and unusual punishments" (Eighth Amendment).

The principles and practices of due process interest us here primarily for their effect on criminal justice and therefore on the rights of alleged lawbreakers. However, the rights of due process are vital for the safety of *every* resident of society. Individuals can not fully enjoy their rights as citizens of a democracy (including First Amendment rights) without the assurance of a substantial measure of security against arbitrary arrest or incarceration. A person who can be thrown into prison at the whim of the authorities, physically mistreated, and held for indeterminate periods without effective recourse is living not in a lawful democracy, but in a polity bordering on despotism.

Imprisonment, of course, represents the ultimate denial of liberty, exposing the victim to countless restraints and humiliations to which free men and women are rarely, if ever, subject. But the denial of due process also endangers, if indeed it does not nullify, many of the other rights promised in the Constitution. Such liberties as freedom of speech, press, and religion survive in part because they can be enforced through established legal procedures, impartially administered. If citizens can be arrested summarily or otherwise punished for what they say or publish, for worshipping as they choose, or for assembling with others to register their views, they are effectively deprived of their First Amendment rights. In the absence of due process deterrents, the rights associated with privacy could also be invaded.

Due process, thus, is indispensable to democratic government. Without it, an individual is largely defenseless against assaults upon his or her life, liberty, or possessions. In addition to providing criminal safeguards, however, the due process clauses of the Fifth and Fourteenth Amendments also offer administrative protections of a civil nature. Officials are required by law to hold hearings or establish other procedures for the protection of property rights; for the granting of benefits (such as welfare, disability payments, or pensions); for the loss of public employment to which one is entitled by tenure or contract; for permits authorizing the manufacture and sale of certain commodities; for permission to hold a parade on a public thoroughfare; and numerous other matters affecting the possible retention or loss of liberty or property. While administrative due process bears less significantly on civil liberties questions than does criminal due process, it is nevertheless vital to an orderly society ruled by law and committed to the notion of equal treatment for equal claimants* (Appel 1977 and Lerner 1977).

The importance of due process for free government was readily appreciated by the Founders. Given their knowledge of European absolutisms and their direct experience with the English and French monarchies, they were only too aware of the hazards to "life, liberty and property" associated with governments that enjoyed unlimited or arbitrary

---

*For a summary of the legal status of due process protection, we are indebted to Brent Appel and Henry Lerner, who prepared a memorandum at our request in 1977.

power. They knew of numerous incidents in which property had been unjustly confiscated or taxed. They had witnessed the imprisonment and execution of countless individuals on the whim of the sovereign power. The framers of the Constitution knew of the extraordinary cruelties practiced in the prisons and of the brutal treatment suffered by suspects or inmates who had little opportunity to appeal to law or to procedural protections. In short, justice, even under a government as advanced as Great Britain's, was often neither fair nor impartial.

It was the awareness of these injustices, in part, that led the authors of the Bill of Rights, and legislators and judges in subsequent decades, to formulate principles of due process by which fairness in criminal and other governmental proceedings might be assured to every citizen. As American politics grew more democratic, and as the rights named in the Constitution were broadened through judicial and legislative interpretation, due process protections also expanded. Numerous rules were elaborated affecting police and judicial procedure, the admissibility of evidence, the right to counsel, the treatment of prisoners, coerced confessions, restrictions on search and seizure, and dozens of other matters affecting procedural rights. The rights of due process although initially provided in the Constitution, take their form and character in significant measure from developments in the society itself, reflecting the status of its democratic and humanitarian values.

The due process guarantees, as stated in the Bill of Rights, or as subsequently developed, touch on almost every phase of the criminal justice system. Perhaps the most important guarantee (set forth in the Sixth Amendment) is the right of persons accused of a criminal offense to a fair, "speedy," and "public" trial in which their guilt or innocence is decided by an impartial jury of peers. The Sixth Amendment further provides that defendants shall be informed of the accusation and be able to confront the witnesses against them. They also have the right to subpoena witnesses in their favor and (in the federal courts) to be represented by counsel in their own defense. The presiding judge must also be impartial, which means that he or she can have no personal interest in the outcome of a case and no personal bias for or against a defendant (*Mayberry* v. *Pennsylvania*, 400 U.S. 455, 1970). These and most other rights of due process have, under the Fourteenth Amendment, now become available in state jurisdiction as well.

The guarantee of a "public" trial was a reaction to the gross abuses which had occurred in the secret proceedings of the English Star Chamber, the Spanish Inquisition, and the French Lettre de Cachet. Its purpose is not only to guard against judicial abuses, including perjury by witnesses, but to expose the plight of the defendant and thus allow persons with relevant evidence to come forward (Lerner 1977). With a few exceptions all trials must be open to the public. Failure to fulfill this requirement can lead to a reversal of the defendant's conviction.*

The right to a "fair trial" extends to the nature of the jury and its deliberations. Jurors are required to be impartial and are instructed not to convict a defendant unless the evidence confirms his guilt "beyond a reasonable doubt." A mere preponderance of evidence is not sufficient for conviction. (*In Re Winship*, 397 U.S. 358, 1970). The prosecution, moreover, must prove its case through actual *evidence*, not by prejudicial appeals to the jury or by defaming the defendant's character. The accused, for example, cannot be convicted because he has been portrayed as a "gangster," a "vagrant," a "habitual criminal," or a "lewd and lascivious" person (Lerner 1977). In most cases reference cannot be made in the presence of the jury to the defendant's previous crimes or prison record. Nor can he or she be required to wear prison garb or shackles at the trial. The accused must be able to understand the nature of the charges and the purposes of the proceedings against him and to assist counsel in the preparation of his own defense (Appel, citing *Dusky* v. *U.S.*, 362 U.S. 402, 1960). The statute the defendant is accused of violating must clearly describe the nature of the crime. While these and similar requirements of due process are doubtless violated in practice on occasion, they are among the rules that define a fair trial and that provide the grounds for overturning a conviction.

A number of due process requirements also apply to the context and manner in which the trial is conducted. The trial must be held in an atmosphere free of the influence of prejudicial publicity in order that an impartial jury can be selected and an unbiased verdict rendered. The defendant is entitled to know in advance the identity of the prosecution witnesses so that he (or his attorney) may confront them, subject them to effective cross-examination, impeach their testimony, and permit the jury to weigh their demeanor and credibility (Lerner 1977). The prosecution is also required to make available to the defendant all evidence it has uncovered in his favor, and it cannot suppress information that bears on his guilt or innocence (*Brady* v. *Maryland*, 373 U.S. 83, 1963). (Since the prosecution ordinarily enjoys far greater re-

---

* Although it happens only rarely, defendants themselves may be excluded from the courtroom if their behavior is so recalcitrant and disorderly as to impede the expeditious conduct of their trial (*Illinois* v. *Allen*, 397 U.S. 337, 1970).

sources than the defendant, the sharing of evidence—or so-called pre-trial discovery—is a vital due process protection.) Nor can the prosecution permit testimony to be given against the defendant which it knows to be false (Appel, citing *Napue* v. *Illinois*, 360 U.S. 246, 1959). The trial itself must be speedy so that the accused cannot be incarcerated for lengthy periods before (and during) the course of his trial. In *McNabb* v. *United States* (318 U.S. 332, 1943), the Supreme Court held that the mere fact of a protracted detention may be taken as a sign that the suspect has been subjected to violent and illegal police procedures (Amsterdam 1970).

Of the several due process guarantees enjoyed by the accused, few are more vital to their protection than the provision in the Fifth Amendment that "no person shall be compelled in any criminal case to be a witness against himself." This privilege against self-incrimination was earlier developed under English criminal practice and was designed to prevent the police and other law enforcement authorities from coercing suspects or witnesses into admissions that might result in criminal penalties. The most serious danger to accused persons, of course, is that they will be led against their will, through physical or psychological duress, to confess to crimes they have not committed.

The existence of such a right is puzzling to many citizens. What is the point of it and how can it be justified? Why should the job of law enforcement not be made easier rather than more difficult? Their concern is well summarized by Casper (1972):

> Why should those accused of crime not be asked questions about their guilt or innocence? Why should they not be required to give their version of the alleged crime and have their testimony subjected to cross-examination and available to the judge or jury in determining guilt or innocence? To many, it appears that the innocent have nothing to fear from such testimony, and that only the guilty will potentially suffer. (pp. 252–53)

Plausible as such questions may seem, they overlook considerations vital to a fair system of law enforcement. Coerced confessions are notoriously unreliable. Out of fear, psychological distress, or the hope of obtaining a better "deal," or out of a desire simply to terminate an unrelieved interrogation by police officers, defendants have been known to confess to crimes they could not possibly have committed. The Court has recognized this and, in such cases as *Brown* v. *Mississippi* (297 U.S. 278, 1936), overturned the conviction of a defendant who had been tortured into confession (Casper 1972).

The Court may throw out admissions by a defendant that result from procedures far less terrifying than torture. In *Spano* v. *New York* (260 U.S. 315, 1959), the Court held that law enforcement officials could not use "duress, promises, fraud, or trickery to obtain incriminating statements." Testimony so obtained is generally inadmissible (Appel 1977). Even vague or mild threats or the failure to permit a defendant to call or consult with his or her lawyer at the time of the investigation may be sufficient to violate due process and to exclude evidence resulting from the interrogation. (See *Escobedo* v. *Illinois*, 378, U.S. 478, 1964.)

Along with the assurances against self-incrimination, perhaps no other due process right is as essential to a defendant's protection against unfair treatment as the right to counsel. The importance of the right to a proper legal defense can scarcely be overestimated, since few defendants have an adequate idea of the protections they are entitled to, before, during, and after trial. Criminal proceedings invariably involve many technical points of law, as well as a number of rights which the accused may justifiably claim. The rules governing the quality and admissibility of evidence, disclosure, self-incrimination, appeals, the treatment of the accused at the time of arrest, at the police station, and at the trial often involve subtle and obscure points of law and criminal practice. In the absence of an attorney the accused is likely to be at the mercy of the police and prosecutorial forces whose interest (and job) it is to convict. Even an impartial judge, obliged to look out for the defendant's interest as well as the state's, cannot adequately substitute for a defense attorney whose concern is to protect the defendant's rights at every turn and, if possible, to win his or her acquittal.

Although the Sixth Amendment provides that "In all criminal prosecutions, the accused shall enjoy the right . . . to have the assistance of Counsel for his defense," this provision applied at first only to the federal government, and its specific applications to criminal procedure remained to be spelled out. It was finally extended to the states in 1963 in the landmark case of *Gideon* v. *Wainright* (372 U.S. 35, 1963), which also provided that the state must appoint competent counsel in the event the defendant is without funds.

This decision by no means resolved all of the issues surrounding the right to counsel. Key among these was the question of the scope of the right: at what stages of the criminal proceeding, for example, is counsel entitled to be present? In a series of cases bearing on this and related issues, the Court evolved the view that defendants are entitled to have an attorney present at every "critical stage" of the proceeding and that a critical stage is one in which "substantial rights of a criminal accused may be affected" (*Mempa* v. *Rhea,* 389 U.S. 128, 1967). In the important case of *Escobedo* v. *Illinois,* the Court held that the right to counsel extends to the station house and that evidence (such as a confession) obtained there in violation of the right to consult an attorney can be excluded from the trial (Amsterdam 1970).

In the celebrated case of *Miranda* v. *Arizona* (384 U.S. 436, 1966), the Court carried the right to counsel even further, holding not only that suspects must be informed of their right to remain silent (in keeping with their privilege against self-incrimination) at the time of their arrest and prior to questioning, but also that they have a right to have an attorney present at the time of questioning to advise them of their rights—an attorney appointed by the court in the event they lack the funds to retain private counsel. Even the appointment of an "incompetent" defense attorney may be taken as a denial of defendants' due process rights. Evidence obtained in violation of *Miranda* is not generally admissible, and if defendants are denied the services of counsel at the time they plead, at the trial, or at the time of sentencing, "reversal of the subsequent conviction is automatic" (Appel 1977).

The rights of due process also provide that, except for certain capital cases, the accused is entitled to be released on bail prior to trial and that bail shall not be "excessive." Under the Fifth Amendment a defendant once tried may not be tried again for the same crime. The purpose of this constitutional protection against "double jeopardy" is to spare the defendant the harassment, anxiety, and expense of multiple prosecutions (Lerner 1977).

If convicted, the defendant cannot, under the Eighth Amendment, be subjected to "cruel and unusual punishments." The death penalty has not been considered by the Court as a "cruel and unusual punishment," but its its enforcement has been hedged about with severe qualifications, including the provision that its infliction cannot be made mandatory but must depend upon the exercise of discretion by the jury, which is also required to consider mitigating circumstances. As a further protection, the offender, found guilty in a lower court, is entitled to an appellate review of his or her case by a higher court.

The due process rights we have summarized normally apply to the population as a whole. However, certain groups in the society such as aliens, mental patients, prisoners, felons, government employees, and military personnel enjoy these rights to a more limited extent. Aliens, for example, may be deported for mental defects, criminal conduct, poverty, drug use, or "moral turpitude"—characteristics which would not ordinarily lead to a denial of due process for an American citizen. While aliens whom the government wishes to deport are entitled to *procedural* due process, they are not entitled to a judicial review of the procedures by which they are excluded. Many mental patients also suffer a denial of due process whenever they are confined to institutions because of their personal characteristics rather than their actions. In most states, they are nominally entitled to a hearing and a court order, but in many instances they are confined without a hearing as "emergency" cases or on the mere certification of physicians that they are "dangerous" or in need of treatment. Their right to counsel is limited, and they enjoy no privilege against self-incrimination.

By comparison, prison inmates are able to make a stronger claim on their constitutional protections, although in practice their rights are also restricted in many ways.* Prevailing judicial opinion holds that prisoners retain all the rights of ordinary citizens except those expressly taken from them by law (Cowart 1977). They enjoy the right of *habeas corpus* and have access to counsel and to the courts. Their mail to and from their lawyers, the judiciary, and other officials cannot be censored unless prison authorities can show that it will endanger prison security or interfere with the rehabilitation program. They are also supposed to have access to legal materials and, in some states, even to a well-stocked law library. The same freedom and limitations hold for access to general reading materials and to the publication by prisoners of their own thoughts. In general, prisoners also enjoy freedom of religion, although prison officials have some discretion in recognizing what is and is not a "religion." Religious privileges cannot, however, be denied to any sect without a hearing concerning its beliefs and practices. Prisoners also have a right to medical care and to a "safe" environment. When prisoners are subject to disciplinary proceedings, they are entitled to written notice, the right to make a defense, and a written statement by the hearing committee setting forth the evidence and the reasons for the disciplinary actions taken (Cowart 1977, citing *Wolff* v. *McDonnell*, 418 U.S. 39, 1974).

The types of discipline suffered by inmates for violation of prison rules or for crimes committed in prison are in principle limited by the Eighth Amendment's ban on cruel and unusual punishment. They can,

---

* For a summary of the legal status of prisoners' rights, we are greatly indebted to Richard A. Cowart, who prepared a memorandum at our request in 1977.

however, be placed in solitary confinement for certain breaches of discipline, and they may be dealt with severely if they endanger prison safety. Prisoners are not protected against the Fourth Amendment's prohibition against unreasonable searches and seizures, and they enjoy only to a limited extent the Fifth Amendment's prohibition against compulsory self-incrimination. They or their quarters may be searched without warrant, such searches having been upheld in the courts unless they are clearly unreasonable, repetitive, or conducted in an unnecessarily degrading manner (*U.S.* v. *Edwards,* 415 U.S. 800, 1974). An inmate's confessions, even if illegally obtained, may be introduced into parole hearings or other prison disciplinary proceedings (Cowart 1977).

Under prevailing law, prison administrations cannot make retribution their dominant objective, but must emphasize instead the reformation and rehabilitation of offenders (Hirschkop 1970, citing *Williams* v. *New York,* 337 U.S. 241, 1949). Despite some reforms and advances, major abuses continue to characterize prison administration. Inmates have no recourse against the intermingling of prisoners of different degrees of criminality and no effective way of securing their own safety against sexual and other types of assaults by fellow inmates. Nor do they have effective recourse against arbitrary decisions and punitive actions by guards and prison officials. Although the courts increasingly recognize that prisoners have due process rights, it remains a reality of prison life, as Hirschkop observes, that prisoners are sometimes badly treated or severely punished, and that the courts are reluctant to monitor the internal affairs of the prison system.

Restrictions on the rights of due process also exist for felons after they have been released from prison. Felons cannot carry arms or serve in the military. They may be deprived of their "good character," which could severely jeopardize their opportunity to obtain licenses or employment. They lose the right to hold office, to serve on a jury, and, in some states, to vote. They cannot hold a position of trust, such as executor of a will or administrator of an estate, and they may be designated as morally unfit for many occupations. Restrictions against hiring felons are particularly severe in the public sector, where civil service or administrative regulations often prohibit the employment of persons convicted of a felony. In some states felons are disqualified from participating in pension funds and have difficulty obtaining automobile and other types of insurance, although they retain their legal capacity to sue and be sued or to enter into contracts (Cowart 1977). Although in a few states felons may apply to have their criminal records expunged and their rights restored, they have few due process opportunities to remove or escape from the various disabilities that result from their conviction as felons.

The condition of public employees is more complicated. As public employees, many enjoy, on the one side, the benefits of working under tenure or contract, which affords a propertied interest in continued employment and thus provides the protection of constitutional guarantees of due process. On the other side, public employees relinquish certain rights enjoyed by other citizens, such as the right to engage in partisan political activities (under the Hatch Act). Restrictions on due process are particularly severe for members of the military. The courts have traditionally held that certain of the rights provided in the Constitution do not apply to service personnel and that their personal rights are defined by Congress and executive order (Cowart 1977). Military commanders exert extraordinary power over their subordinates, can punish them for disobeying orders or violating discipline, and can bring them to trial through courts-martial over which commanders have considerable influence. Although the due process rights to which those in the service are entitled are rather restricted, they can appeal the verdict of a court-martial to the federal courts, and they have a right to complain to superior officers and to special branches of the military about living conditions, staff assignments, or unreasonable discipline.

As the foregoing attests, legal norms exist even for groups whose rights are restricted, but they are not always enforced. In the matter of criminal procedure, for example, "the vast majority of all defendants convicted in criminal cases plead guilty to the charges placed against them" (Casper 1972). Often they do so as part of a "plea bargain" arranged between the accused, the defense attorneys, the prosecutor, and the judge. A plea bargain is, in effect, a *trade,* in which the defendant agrees to plead guilty and forego a trial in return for some benefit, such as a reduced charge or a lighter sentence. The defense attorneys may press for such a bargain because they believe the client is guilty (or will be found guilty) and hope to get the best possible "deal." The prosecutor is often interested because it assures a conviction and saves the state the time, cost, and uncertainty of a court trial. The police, though less in favor of plea bargaining, are nevertheless able to record the crime as "solved" and to clear it from their register of unsolved crimes (Casper 1972). The judge, like the prosecutor, is also eager to save the court the time and expense of a lengthy trial.

Plea bargaining and the ready acceptance of guilty pleas affect due process in important ways. Vital issues of criminal procedure and practice, involving possible violations of due process, never get to the higher courts, much less to the Supreme Court (Amsterdam 1970). Issues that should be argued, thought through, and resolved by the highest court are thus suppressed or never surface. For all practical purposes the defendants relinquish the opportunity to avail themselves of the due process rights already in existence, and this failure to challenge the accusation or procedures used against them prevents other due process guarantees from being formulated.

Knowing that their practices are not likely to be challenged affords the police greater opportunity for abusing due process. At the level of the station house (far removed from the field of vision of the higher courts) the police can bend the rules, violating due process in such matters as booking, searches and seizures, line-up identification, entrapment, and confessions, or by ignoring the *Miranda* rules. The district attorney also exerts control over the grand jury and hence over the charges to be included in the indictment.

In light of these practices, some students of criminal procedure complain that, below the level of the Supreme Court, "the entire system of criminal justice is solidly massed against the criminal suspect." Even the critics, however, allow that Supreme Court decisions have "recently enhanced the ability of state criminal defendants . . . to claim the protection of constitutional guarantees" in certain procedural areas (Amsterdam 1970) and that the rules of due process have had at least some effect on actual practice. Such cases as *Gideon*, for example, have, in fact, extended the right to be represented by counsel to state (as well as federal) criminal proceedings; and the expansion of due process requirements by the courts has in a number of cases led to such practices as the actual exclusion of "illegal" evidence from criminal trials and the sharing of the prosecution's evidence with the defendant. Despite the distance between the Supreme Court and the station house, the judiciary has gradually been picking up on such abuses as coerced confessions, violations of the privilege against self-incrimination, failure to make counsel available at various stages of the proceedings, warrantless invasions of a suspect's privacy rights, and the like. It would be naive to suppose that a perfect correspondence can ever exist between the constitutional norms as stated by the higher courts and the actual practices at the level of enforcement. There are simply too many cases, too many arrests, too many conflicting interests, and too many variations in the types of crimes and criminals encountered by the police to achieve a perfect match between the stated principle and its application. But there are also forces, including defense attorneys and citizen groups such as the ACLU and the NAACP, which monitor the norms and practices of law enforcement and due process and which continually function to expand the latter and bring the former into line with announced legal standards.

Findings on Due Process

As we found with other civil liberties, the principles of due process tend to be supported by the public more often in the abstract than in their concrete application. In fact, the ambivalence which many Americans express in their attitudes toward civil liberties is especially evident in the area of due process. Support is greater for due process guarantees that are highly visible and familiar (for example, the right to a public trial, to an attorney, to trial by jury) than for those which are more subtle, less familiar, or legally more complex. The endorsement of general principles of due process clearly seems to be governed by a sense of "fairness." Procedures which strike the public as "fair" or "just" tend to be approved while those which seem to them "unfair," or "unjust," or "unreasonable" tend to be rejected.

The extent to which the public and the community and legal elites embrace the principles of fairness or justice in the abstract can be observed from the items in table 4. 1. When forced to choose, 60 percent of the general public, 79 percent of the community leaders, and 91 percent of the legal elites say they prefer that a guilty person go free than an innocent person be convicted. (Even the police strongly endorse this principle.) Few things, it seems, appear more unjust to most Americans than sending an innocent person to prison. Nor do Americans believe that enforcing the law entitles the government to violate the Constitution, "bend the rules," treat even an arrested gangster differently from anyone else, or deny a jury trial even to muggers who are caught red-handed in the act of robbing older people. On the contrary, citizens expect the government to set an example so that the law might be respected.

The commitment to the general principles of fairness and justice carries over to the public perception of actual law enforcement. (See

TABLE 4.1
Support for Due Process Principles in the Abstract

	CLS			
	Mass Public	**Community Leaders**	**Legal Elite**	**Police Officials**
	(N=1993)	**(N=1157)**	**(N=488)**	**(N=224)**
All systems of justice make mistakes, but which do you think is worse?				
—To convict an innocent person.	60%	79%	91%	77%
—To let a guilty person go free.	21	10	4	13
—Neither/Undecided	19	12	5	9
Suppose the President and Congress have to violate a constitutional principle to pass an important law the people wanted. Would you support them in this action?				
—No, because protecting the Constitution is more important to the national welfare than any law could possibly be.	49	67	81	59
—Yes, because the Constitution shouldn't be allowed to stand in the way of what the people need and want.	22	14	7	21
—Neither/Undecided	29	19	11	21
When police catch a violent gangster, they should:				
—treat him humanely, just as they should treat everyone they arrest.	78	90	96	92
—be allowed to be a bit rough with him if he refuses to give them the information they need to solve a crime.	15	6	3	6
—Neither/Undecided	7	3	1	2
If someone is caught red-handed beating and robbing an older person on the street:				
—the suspect should still be entitled to a jury trial and all the usual legal protections.	72	90	97	88
—it's just a waste of taxpayers' money to bother with the usual expensive trial.	16	6	2	8
—Neither/Undecided	13	4	1	5
In order for the government to effectively prosecute the leaders of organized crime:				
—it should stick strictly to the rules if the government wants other people to respect the law.	68	79	90	74
—it may sometimes have to bend the rules if there is no other way to convict them.	20	13	7	17
—Neither/Undecided	13	8	3	9

	OVS	
	Mass Public	**Opinion Leaders**
	(N=938)	(N=845)
In enforcing the law, the authorities:		
—should stick to the rules if they want other people to respect the law.	62%	80%
—sometimes have to break the rules in order to bring criminals to justice.	24	11
—Neither/Undecided	14	10
In dealing with crime the most important consideration is to:		
—protect the rights of the accused.	40	46
—stop crime even if we have to violate the rights of the accused.	23	9
—Neither/Undecided	37	45

NOTES: Because percentages have been rounded off, occasionally there will be disparities in totals (columns will not add up to 100 percent).

See the Preface to Research Findings (p. 25) and Appendix B for description of the leader and mass public samples of various categories used in the PAB, CLS, and OVS studies: that is "Political Leaders," "Legal Elite," and so forth.

The CLS was conducted in 1978–1979; the OVS in 1976–1977; and the PAB in 1958.

figure 4.1.) Americans (except for the police themselves) are inclined to believe (although not by large margins) that the police treat some groups unfairly; that without laws protecting the rights of the accused, the police would "push people around more than they do now"; and that, if brought to trial, a rich person will receive better treatment than a poor one. The feeling is plainly indicated that conduct by the police or the courts which discriminates against certain groups and favors others violates the American sense of fair play and equality before the law. And most people seem to feel that the police and the courts are somewhat more biased toward certain groups than toward others.

The weight of opinion begins to shift, however, when respondents are questioned about activities that involve actual crime and lawbreaking, providing fairness is not manifestly an issue. In table 4.2 the public strongly registers its view (by a margin of 76 percent to 2 percent) that the courts are too easy on people who break the law. Similarly, despite the suspicion of the police already noted, the public overwhelmingly favors increasing the power of the police "to deal with today's crime." By a ratio of almost seven to one, the general population considers security against crime in the streets as even more impor-

If there were no laws protecting the rights of accused lawbreakers, most policemen would probably:

 —push people around more than they do now.

☐ —treat people fairly anyway.

▨ —Neither/Undecided

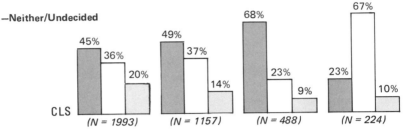

CLS

(N = 1993)   (N = 1157)   (N = 488)   (N = 224)

In the American court system:

▨ —a rich person usually gets treated better than a poor person.

☐ —almost every citizen can expect an equally fair trial.

▨ —Neither/Undecided

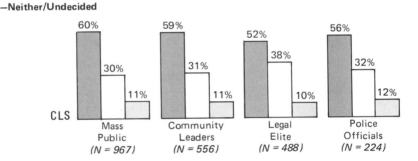

CLS

Mass Public	Community Leaders	Legal Elite	Police Officials
(N = 967)	(N = 556)	(N = 488)	(N = 224)

Notes: Because percentages have been rounded off, occasionally there will be disparities in totals (columns will not add up to 100 percent).

FIGURE 4.1
Perceptions of Unfair Treatment by the Police and Courts
(CLS/OVS)

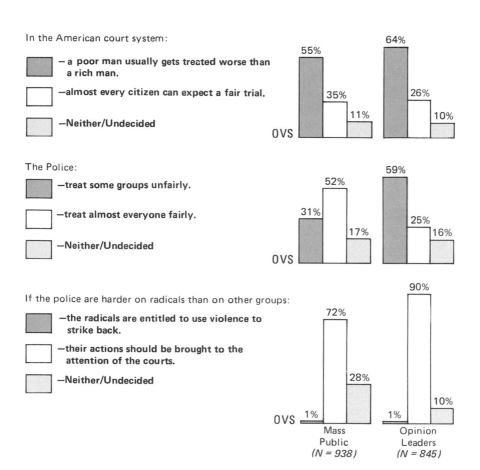

In the American court system:

- a poor man usually gets treated worse than a rich man.
- almost every citizen can expect a fair trial.
- Neither/Undecided

55% 35% 11%

64% 26% 10%

The Police:

- treat some groups unfairly.
- treat almost everyone fairly.
- Neither/Undecided

31% 52% 17%

59% 25% 16%

If the police are harder on radicals than on other groups:

- the radicals are entitled to use violence to strike back.
- their actions should be brought to the attention of the courts.
- Neither/Undecided

1% 72% 28%

1% 90% 10%

Mass Public (N = 938)

Opinion Leaders (N = 845)

See the Preface to Research Findings in Chapter 1 and Appendix B for an analysis of the components of various categories used in the PAB, CLS, and OVS studies: that is "Political Leaders," "Legal Elite," and so forth.

The CLS was conducted in 1978-1979; the OVS in 1976-1977; and the PAB in 1958.

TABLE 4.2
Due Process and Responses to Lawbreaking

	CLS				OVS	
	Mass Public	Community Leaders	Legal Elite	Police Officials	Mass Public	Opinion Leaders
	(N=1993)	(N=1157)	(N=488)	(N=224)	(N=938)	(N=845)
In dealing with muggings and other serious street crime, which is more important?						
—To protect the rights of suspects.	10%	18%	35%	17%		
—To stop such crimes and make the streets safe even if we sometimes have to violate the suspect's rights.	67	53	31	55		
—Neither/Undecided	23	29	34	28		
When riots break out, the police:						
—often use too much force and cause more violence than might otherwise have occurred.	27	31	35	7		
—are usually too easy on the rioters.	33	23	16	44		
—Neither/Undecided	40	46	48	49		
The death penalty is:						
—morally wrong, doesn't really prevent crime, and should be abolished.	15	32	35	3		
—a proper and necessary punishment for criminals who have committed horrible crimes, such as premeditated murder.	72	58	55	93		
—Neither/Undecided	13	10	11	4		
When two people are arrested, one a habitual criminal and the other a citizen never before in trouble with the law, would the police be justified in treating them differently when arresting and booking them?*						
—No, because everybody is entitled to the same treatment under the law no matter who they are.	54	60	59	66		
—Yes, because there is more chance the habitual criminal actually committed the crime, and he may also be dangerous.	36	30	29	22		
—Neither/Undecided	10	11	12	12		
In your opinion, are the courts too hard or too easy on people who break the law?						
—Too hard.					2%	2%
—Too easy.					76	50
—Neither/Undecided					22	48

The power of the police:		
—is too great and should be cut down.	7	7
—should be increased to deal with today's crime.	69	36
—Neither/Undecided	24	57
One important thing we might do to reduce crime is to:		
—abolish the prison system, which is cruel and breeds crime.	5	8
—hire more policemen.	44	31
—Neither/Undecided	50	61
When black militant groups use violence to achieve their goals:		
—they deserve our support considering the way blacks have been treated.	3	5
—they should be arrested.	84	75
—Neither/Undecided	13	20
When the country is at war, people suspected of disloyalty:		
—should be fully protected in their constitutional rights.	28	60
—should be watched closely or kept in custody.	54	22
—Neither/Undecided	18	18
For such crimes as killing a policeman or prison guard, the punishment should be:		
—life imprisonment.	24	36
—the death penalty.	58	35
—Neither/Undecided	18	29

	Chandler[†]
	(N=1136)
On the whole, do you feel that the *rulings* of the Supreme Court in recent years have given *too much* consideration to the rights of people suspected of crimes?	
—Yes	63%
—No	26
—Don't know/No answer	11

	NORC[‡]
Are we spending too much, too little, or about the right amount to halt the rising crime rate?	
—Too much	6%
—Too little	67
—About the right amount	26

* This item was included in Form B of the CLS questionnaire (see Appendix A). For the Mass Public, N=967; for Community Leaders, N=556; for Legal Elite, N=240; for Police Officials, N=122.
[†] Chandler 1972
[‡] NORC 1980; p. 21

tant than protecting the rights of the accused—a view strongly shared by the community elites and the police.*

In confronting the issue of police conduct during riots, neither the mass public nor the elites have strongly defined views. By a slight margin the mass public feels that the police are too easy on rioters, while the elites, especially the legal elites, are inclined to believe that the police often use excessive force in quelling riots. Support is overwhelming among all groups, however, for arresting militants who "use violence to achieve their goals." (This fits with the finding previously reported in which both the public and the elites registered strong support for obedience to law, even when one's conscience is violated.) The mass public is more disposed to disregard due process rights in wartime and is willing to place under close surveillance or in custody people who are suspected of disloyalty. In both our studies, the public is strongly in favor of the death penalty for persons who have killed a policeman or prison guard or committed some other "horrible" crime.

In the course of our earlier discussions on the constitutional and popular status of various civil liberties, we have observed that the norms governing certain liberties are especially difficult for the general public (and in some instances even for opinion leaders) to learn. Some due process requirements, such as those governing the rules of evidence, are poorly understood because their purposes are obscure, except to the legally initiated. Others are either misunderstood or rejected because they appear to *promote* crime rather than deter it—to favor the criminals at the expense of the victims. We should also keep in mind that apart from the inherently complex and elusive nature of certain due process rights, most Americans have little or no direct experience with them. Having never been arrested for a crime or required to follow a highly tangled and recondite set of legal procedures from the point of arrest to the point of sentencing or appeal, the public finds many of the guarantees that fall within the compass of due process remote and esoteric, rules which bear only indirectly, if at all, on their daily lives.

Accepting the due process rights of criminal defendants becomes even more difficult for the public because of its growing fear of crime and its increasing hostility toward lawbreakers. As we have just seen, many citizens feel that the courts are too easy on criminals and that

---

* This response, which is predominantly rejected by the judges and lawyers, appears to conflict with the responses to a related question presented in table 4.1, but that question required the respondent to repudiate a suspect's right to a jury trial—a due process right that few Americans are, in the abstract at least, willing to relinquish.

stronger law enforcement measures and tougher criminal laws are needed. Even when certain legal procedures, such as the reading of the *Miranda* rules to arrested suspects are repeatedly portrayed in police dramas on television, the reasons for such rules are not set forth and the justifications for them remain puzzling. Obviously, one may know of the existence of a right without understanding it, so that one "learns" the right only vaguely and incompletely. In the absence of an "internalized" or more thorough understanding, one is less likely to rise to the defense of a right or to extend it to a suspect as a matter of course. The reasons for certain due process protections are not intuitively obvious, especially to the relatively uninformed, Why, for example, should a suspect not be tried for a second time for a particular crime if new evidence is uncovered that convincingly proves his or her guilt? Why should important evidence not be admissible in a criminal trial even if it was "improperly" turned up in the course of a search for evidence bearing on another crime? And why should a defendant, once found guilty, be allowed more than a single appeal?

One of the due process protections that puzzles many is the "right" to bail.* No sooner are criminals apprehended (perhaps for a most heinous crime) than they are allowed, upon posting what may be a relatively modest sum, to go free until the actual commencement of their trials. Rather than removing them from the community while evidence is being gathered and the case prepared by the prosecution and the defense, they are (in the eyes of some critics) let loose and given the opportunity to commit further crimes—potential menaces to witnesses and to possible future victims. In figure 4.2 we see that only 16 percent of the general public would permit "a person suspected of serious crimes" to be let out on bail, while two thirds would keep the accused "safely in prison until the trial" (the latter view was publicly endorsed by Chief Justice Burger himself).† Some 57 percent believe that it is necessary to incarcerate suspects when they are dangerous. While more opinion leaders are favorably disposed toward pretrial release, the differences from the mass public on this issue are comparatively modest. A majority of the general public and 74 percent of the community leaders, however, indirectly indicate their support for the

---

*The Eighth Ammendment prohibits "excessive bail" and does not explicitly guarantee a "right" to bail. Judicial practice, however, has treated bail as a right except in certain capital cases.

†See his address to the American Bar Association, *New York Times*, February 9, 1981.

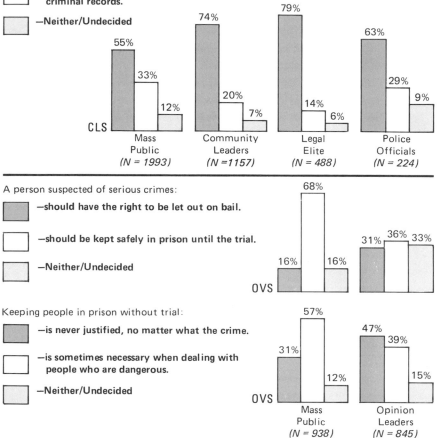

Keeping people in prison for long periods of time before bringing them to trial:

- ▇ —should not be allowed, no matter what the crime.
- ☐ —is sometimes necessary when dealing with people who have long and dangerous criminal records.
- ▨ —Neither/Undecided

CLS

Mass Public (N = 1993)	Community Leaders (N =1157)	Legal Elite (N = 488)	Police Officials (N = 224)
55% 33% 12%	74% 20% 7%	79% 14% 6%	63% 29% 9%

A person suspected of serious crimes:

- ▇ —should have the right to be let out on bail.
- ☐ —should be kept safely in prison until the trial.
- ▨ —Neither/Undecided

OVS

16% 68% 16%   31% 36% 33%

Keeping people in prison without trial:

- ▇ —is never justified, no matter what the crime.
- ☐ —is sometimes necessary when dealing with people who are dangerous.
- ▨ —Neither/Undecided

OVS

Mass Public (N = 938)	Opinion Leaders (N = 845)
31% 57% 12%	47% 39% 15%

If a person is suspected of a serious crime, do you think the police should be allowed to hold him in jail, until they can get enough evidence to officially charge him?

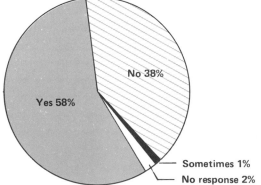

Yes 58%

No 38%

Sometimes 1%

No response 2%

(Chandler 1972, p. 9; N = 1136)

FIGURE 4.2
Pre-Trial Release and the Right to Bail
(CLS/OVS/Chandler)

constitutional guarantee of a speedy trial when they express the view that the state should not be allowed to keep suspects in prison for long periods of time before bringing them to trial, no matter what crime they are charged with committing. Even 63 percent of the police hold this view, as do 79 percent of the lawyers and judges. Although one might assume that the elites also fear crime, they appear to have absorbed the arguments for pretrial release to a greater extent than the mass public.

Among the mass public, only a plurality are inclined to endorse the principle against self-incrimination, and by a relatively small margin at that. All the items listed in table 4.3 raise questions in some form about the right of suspects to be safeguarded against forced confessions or the giving of testimony that might tend to incriminate them. The Fifth Amendment reads that no person "shall be compelled to be a witness against himself," and while a fair proportion of the general public seem to subscribe to this principle, it fails to gain majority support. Thus, 40 percent assert that forcing people to testify against themselves is "never justified," while 42 percent are unwilling to grant the authorities the power to "pressure" criminals into confessing crimes.

The right to refuse to bear witness against oneself is, as we have suggested, a protection based on complex and subtle considerations. One ought not to be surprised that support for it is modest. Many people cannot understand why suspected criminals should be permitted "to hide behind the law," especially since their alleged crimes have demonstrated disrespect for the law. They feel that the average person is already victimized by criminals, and that it is dangerously misguided to accord lawbreakers the further advantage of permitting them to remain beyond the reach of interrogation, testimony, and cross-examination. Without the defendants' testimony, and without being able to observe them on the witness stand, it is often impossible to convict them of crimes that they "obviously" have committed—or, for that matter, to acquit them if they are actually innocent. To many observers it seems clear that innocent defendants would be eager to testify in order to introduce evidence in their own defense; while guilty defendants would refuse to testify in order to conceal evidence that might convict them. If defendants have nothing to hide, why should they not be willing to answer questions put by the prosecutor and the judge? If they "take the Fifth," is it not *prima facie* evidence that they are hiding something and are indeed guilty?

These and related arguments, so often raised by critics of the Fifth

TABLE 4.3
Due Process Protection Against Self-Incrimination

	CLS			
	Mass Public	**Community Leaders**	**Legal Elite**	**Police Officials**
	(N=1993)	**(N=1157)**	**(N=488)**	**(N=224)**
Forcing people to testify against themselves in court:				
—is never justified, no matter how terrible the crime.	40%	67%	93%	68%
—may be necessary when they are accused of very brutal crimes.	35	18	3	21
—Neither/Undecided	26	15	3	11

	OVS	
	Mass Public	**Opinion Leaders**
	(N=938)	**(N=845)**
Laws protecting people accused of crime from testifying against themselves should be:		
—strengthened.	26%	37%
—weakened or abolished.	20	7
—Neither/Undecided	54	56
When a criminal refuses to confess his crimes, the authorities:		
—have no right to push him around, no matter what.	42	65
—are entitled to pressure him until he does.	22	5
—Neither/Undecided	36	31

	Chandler*
	(N=1136)
At their trials, do you think suspected criminals should have a right to refuse to answer questions if they feel their answers may be used against them?	
—Yes	54%
—No	42
—Sometimes	1
—No response	3

*Chandler 1972, p. 12.

Amendment's protection against self-incrimination, have a strong appeal for large segments of the population; and one wonders whether the arguments in defense of the principle would enjoy much acceptance were it not for the frequency with which the principle is enunciated in the media. Not surprisingly, as table 4.3 confirms, support for the principle is usually greater among the elites than among the mass public (an extraordinary 93 percent of the legal elites would not permit defendants to be forced to testify against themselves).

Closely related to the right to refuse to bear witness against oneself is the right to be informed, at the time of one's arrest, that one can choose to remain silent. According to the opinion delivered by Chief Justice Warren, in *Miranda*, a suspect

> must be warned prior to any questioning that he has the right to remain silent, that anything he says can be used against him in a court of law, that he has the right to the presence of an attorney, and that if he cannot afford an attorney one will be appointed for him prior to any questioning if he so desires. Opportunity to exercise these rights must be afforded to him throughout the interrogation.

While the individual may "knowingly and intelligently" waive these rights, no admissions obtained in the absence of warnings and waivers can be used as evidence against a defendant in the course of his or her trial.

The media, and particularly police dramas on television, have brought the *Miranda* principle of the right to remain silent to the attention of the mass public with greater frequency than any other of the due process rights. This is probably the reason that a majority of the public endorse a suspect's right to remain silent following arrest. Table 4.4 contains several items expressing alternative opinions about this right, and support for it is in each case substantially greater than opposition to it. Some 79 percent of the public subscribe to the general notion that the right to remain silent "is necessary to a fair system of law enforcement," while 82 percent rate it as an "important" or "extremely important" right. Some 58 percent say that it is necessary to protect suspects against the "third degree" and forced confessions, while only 26 percent claim that it gives criminals too much protection. Support for the principle is even greater among community leaders and the legal elite (89 percent of the lawyers and judges endorse it), while 70 percent of the police recognize it as a constitutional right. (As one would expect, however, the police are less inclined to view it as a

TABLE 4.4
Due Process and Miranda: The Right to Remain Silent

	CLS			
	Mass Public	**Community Leaders**	**Legal Elite**	**Police Officials**
	(N=1993)	(N=1157)	(N=488)	(N=224)
The "right to remain silent":				
—is needed to protect individuals from the "third degree" and forced confessions.	58%	74%	89%	50%
—has harmed the country by giving criminals too much protection.	26	15	6	32
—Neither/Undecided	16	11	5	19
Once an arrested person says he wishes to remain silent, the authorities:				
—should stop all further questioning at once.	52	58	89	70
—should keep asking questions to try to get the suspect to admit his crime.	22	22	6	17
—Neither/Undecided	26	21	5	13
How would you rate the right to remain silent if arrested?				
—Extremely important	46	52	70	38
—Important	36	33	20	32
—Somewhat important	10	9	5	13
—Less important	5	4	5	16
—Other	3	2	0	2

	OVS	
	Mass Public	**Opinion Leaders**
	(N=938)	(N=845)
Requiring policemen to tell a suspect that he has the right to remain silent:		
—is necessary to a fair system of law enforcement.	79%	89%
—prevents the police from doing their job properly.	11	4
—Neither/Undecided	10	8

needed protection against the "third degree" and forced confessions.) In assessing these responses, we are again faced with the question (for which unfortunately, no data are available) whether the popular response is a rote response, induced by media exposure, or whether it represents a genuine understanding and approval of the arguments that led the Court to the *Miranda* decision. Some of the same cautions raised in our discussion of the privilege against self-incrimination apply equally well here.

Support for the right of counsel is widespread among all groups, including the police. (See table 4.5.) In the CLS, 81 percent of the mass public and nearly 90 percent of the community and legal elites recognize this right and subscribe to the notion that the government itself should bear the expense of providing an attorney, if necessary.

Equally supported, by both the mass public and the elites, are the familiar principles of a "fair trial." We observe in table 4.6 that three fourths of the general public hold that the right to a fair trial should not depend on the nature of the crime, but should be available even to rapists, child molesters, and the perpetrators of other "inhuman" crimes. Approximately the same proportion endorse the right to a jury

TABLE 4.5
Due Process: The Right to Counsel

	CLS			
	Mass Public	**Community Leaders**	**Legal Elite**	**Police Officials**
	(N=1993)	**(N=1157)**	**(N=488)**	**(N=224)**
Giving everyone accused of a crime a qualified lawyer even if the government has to pay for it:				
—is absolutely necessary to protect individual rights.	81%	88%	89%	72%
—is wasteful and goes beyond the requirements of justice.	10	7	7	19
—Neither/Undecided	9	5	5	9

	OVS	
	Mass Public	**Opinion Leaders**
	(N=938)	**(N=845)**
Giving everyone accused of crime the best possible lawyer, even if the government has to pay the legal fees is:		
—necessary to protect individual rights.	59%	70%
—wasteful and goes beyond the requirement of justice.	23	15
—Neither/Undecided	19	15

TABLE 4.6
Due Process: The Right to a "Fair Trial"

	CLS			
	Mass Public	**Community Leaders**	**Legal Elite**	**Police Officials**
	(N=1993)	(N=1157)	(N=488)	(N=224)
Should rapists or child molesters be given the same sort of "fair trial" as other criminals?				
—Yes, because the right to a fair trial should not depend on the nature of the crime.	73%	91%	99%	94%
—No, because their crimes are so inhuman that they do not deserve the usual legal protections.	21	7	1	5
—Neither/Undecided	6	2	0	1
The right to trial by jury:				
—is still the best way for someone accused of a crime to receive a fair judgment.	79	87	86	83
—is overrated because juries can so often be swayed by a clever lawyer.	14	9	8	13
—Neither/Undecided	8	4	6	4
How would you rate the right to a public trial by jury?				
—Extremely important	79	87	86	82
—Important	17	12	11	15
—Somewhat important	2	1	3	3
—Less important	0	0	1	1
—Other	1	0	0	0

	Chandler*
	(N=1136)
In criminal cases, do you think the government should ever have the right to hold a secret trial?	
—Yes	20%
—No	75
—Sometimes	1
—No response	4
During court trials, do you think the government should ever be allowed to keep the identity of witnesses from the defendant?	
—Yes	40
—No	54
—Sometimes	2
—No response	4
In most criminal cases, the judge conducts the trial and a jury decides guilt or innocence. Instead of the jury, would it be better if the judge alone decided innocence or guilt?	
—Yes	14
—No	82
—Sometimes	1
—No response	3

*Chandler 1972.

trial as "the best way for someone accused of a crime to receive a fair judgment"—and elite support for both these rights is even higher. In the CBS polls conducted in 1970, a majority of the public registered their opposition to the use of secret trials or secret witnesses. Familiarity with the principles involved and a sense of fair play appear to be motivating the public response to most of these questions.

There are, however, some rules of trial procedure involving technical principles which are more difficult to grasp and which the public fails to support. In figure 4.3, for example, only 11 percent of the general population would acquit a defendant if the judge in the trial made a mistake in legal procedure; two thirds of the sample believe that setting a defendant free for such a reason "would be carrying legal technicalities too far." The community elites register similar scores on this question, but the police officials are even more hostile than the mass public to acquittals based on such legal technicalities. As we have come to expect, the lawyers and judges are more likely to say that the defendant ought to be set free, even if the judge's error was a small one. The mass public also resists the idea of setting defendants free if their guilt has been established by illegally gathered evidence, with the opinion leaders and the lawyers and judges once again more sympathetic to the legally established norm. As for "double jeopardy," which is explicitly prohibited by the Fifth Amendment, 58 percent of the mass public would subject a defendant, once found innocent, to a second trial for the same crime if new evidence were uncovered.

Each of the items in figure 4.3 involves a procedural right that is relatively "technical" and more remote from the everyday experience of the average citizen than, say, the right to a jury trial. The reluctance of most respondents to exonerate criminals because of technical violations in the conduct of their trials doubtless reflects the widespread fear of crime (cf. Nunn et al. 1978) and the overwhelming belief, reported in table 4.2, that the courts are too easy on people who break the law. Since (as one can infer from the internal evidence) most people have little understanding of the reasons for these technicalities, it does not strike them as "fair" that someone who has committed a frightful crime should be let off simply because an error was made in the trial procedure or because evidence was turned up at a later date or in an unorthodox fashion. According to this line of reasoning, if defendants have been notified of the charges against them, represented by counsel, tried publicly before a jury, permitted to challenge their accusers in open court, allowed to refuse to testify, and have enjoyed the other

If a person is acquitted of a crime because the judge made a mistake in legal procedure during the trial:

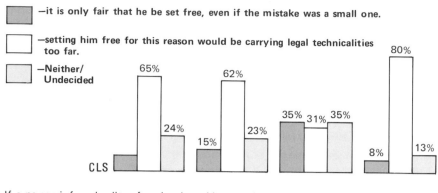

—it is only fair that he be set free, even if the mistake was a small one.

—setting him free for this reason would be carrying legal technicalities too far.

—Neither/ Undecided

If a person is found guilty of a crime by evidence gathered through illegal methods:

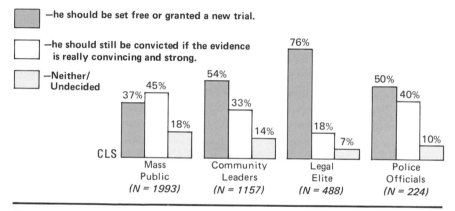

—he should be set free or granted a new trial.

—he should still be convicted if the evidence is really convincing and strong.

—Neither/ Undecided

CLS

| Mass Public (N = 1993) | Community Leaders (N = 1157) | Legal Elite (N = 488) | Police Officials (N = 224) |

If a person is found guilty of a crime by evidence gathered by illegal methods:

—he should be set free.

—he should be convicted no matter how the evidence was collected.

—Neither/Undecided

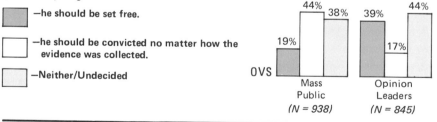

OVS

Mass Public (N = 938)   Opinion Leaders (N = 845)

If a man is found innocent of a serious crime but new evidence is uncovered later, do you think that he should be tried again for the same crime?

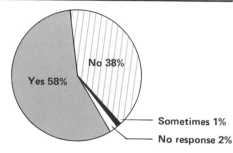

Yes 58%   No 38%   Sometimes 1%   No response 2%

(Chandler 1972; N = 1136)

FIGURE 4.3
Technical Violations of "Fair Trial"
(CLS/OVS/Chandler)

benefits of a "fair trial," why should the state go out of its way to free them on some fine point of procedure that does nothing to establish their innocence? Add these technicalities to such protections as the right against self-incrimination, and it becomes plain (as many ordinary citizens see it) that the scales of justice have been "rigged" in favor of lawbreakers and against their victims.

The public's attitude toward due process is also reflected, at least indirectly, in their views concerning the treatment of criminals and convicted felons. Data bearing on this issue are presented in table 4.7; and while they indicate that there is some *pro forma* support for the due process principle of prisoner rehabilitation, the preponderant sentiment is to treat criminals as "wrongdoers who must be punished." Nearly two thirds of the public in the CLS sample believe that we can better reduce crime by giving "longer and tougher prison sentences to hardened criminals" than by treating them "more humanely" (only 18 percent prefer the latter alternative). Even the lawyers and judges opt for more severe prison sentences (by a margin of over two to one), and the same opinion is held even more strongly by police officials (84 percent). Only one fourth of the mass public in our studies believe that "improving the treatment of prisoners would probably reduce crime." There is little sentiment also for the view that criminals should be treated as people who are sick and need help rather than as malefactors who deserve to be punished for their deeds.

It will come as no surprise that the police are especially unsympathetic to measures that appear to pamper criminals—people who are, after all, their "natural" enemies. Of all groups, the police take the hardest line toward the punishment of felons and express the least faith that any program of rehabilitation might convert them into upstanding citizens. Lawyers and judges are more sympathetic than the police to the rights of prisoners, but their views on these questions differ only slightly from those of the general population.

The public, as the data suggest, is divided on questions of how far the legal system should go to protect the due process rights of lawbreakers. Some believe that the highest priority is the maintenance of law and order. Others, however, though fearing crime and wanting to convict the guilty, are primarily concerned with the rights of the accused. In practice, this translates into favoring the adoption of measures which either help to convict persons guilty of a crime, or, conversely, ensure that no innocent persons are unwittingly punished. Clearly, there is often a trade-off between these two objectives. Since

TABLE 4.7
Due Process and the Treatment of Prisoners

	CLS			
	Mass Public	**Community Leaders**	**Legal Elite**	**Police Officials**
	(N=1993)	(N=1157)	(N=488)	(N=224)
Which of these policies do you think would be more effective in reducing crime?				
—Treating prisoners more humanely so they will gain self-respect and become law-abiding citizens.	18%	26%	24%	6%
—Giving longer and tougher prison sentences to hardened criminals.	64	54	52	84
—Neither/Undecided	18	21	25	10
Improving the treatment of prisoners:				
—would probably reduce crime.	27	34	39	11
—would probably increase crime.	24	15	10	32
—Neither/Undecided	49	51	51	57
In dealing with people imprisoned for crime, it is better to:				
—try to rehabilitate them and return them to normal life.	62	72	67	50
—punish them for the wrongs they have done.	25	16	19	40
—Neither/Undecided	14	13	14	10
Which do you believe?				
—All but the most hardened criminals could be rehabilitated if society would only make the effort.	41	47	41	23
—Very few criminals can be turned into good citizens no matter what we do.	35	25	33	59
—Neither/Undecided	24	28	26	18
The use of prisoners for medical experiments should be:				
—forbidden, because prisoners might feel they have to cooperate in order to be treated better.	16	13	17	12
—permitted, as long as the prisoners give their consent.	73	77	74	80
—Neither/Undecided	11	10	9	8

	OVS	
	Mass Public	**Opinion Leaders**
	(N=938)	(N=845)
Criminals should be treated as people who are:		
—sick and need help.	23%	22%
—wrongdoers who must be punished.	55	38
—Neither/Undecided	22	41

the premise of our system of criminal justice is that the accused are to be considered innocent unless their guilt is proven beyond a reasonable doubt, we try to set up legal roadblocks against the conviction of the innocent. At the same time, we aim to achieve a system of law enforcement that will not commit the contrary error of acquitting persons who are guilty of crimes.

Many of the legal reforms which have occurred in the recent past have been designed to reduce the likelihood of convicting the innocent, notwithstanding a sizable proportion of the general public who believe that the legal system is making it too easy for criminals to elude capture and conviction at the expense of their victims. We should also observe at the close of this chapter that people exhibit a fair amount of consistency in the stands they take across a variety of due process issues, which can be traced to their basic orientations toward law and order and their beliefs about protecting the rights of the accused. In order to show this, we have constructed short opinion scales for both our studies to ascertain whether a respondent places greater priority on controlling crime (and hence reducing the probability of permitting the guilty to go free) or on ensuring that the rights of the accused are protected (and hence reducing the probability that the innocent will be found guilty).* The views of those favoring law and order and those emphasizing the protection of the rights of the accused were then compared on a variety of specific due process issues covering a number of different subdomains.

These results, summarized in table 4.8, show rather convincingly that a deep-seated value conflict is pervasive across a variety of due process issues concerning a person's right to a jury trial, the right to remain silent, the admissibility of evidence collected in an illegal fashion, and so forth. In every instance, those who mainly favor protecting the rights of the accused are more likely, by differences often amounting to as much as 20 percent to 40 percent, to endorse the civil libertarian alternative than are those for whom law and order is the higher priority. Moreover, the differences between these ideal-types are even greater in the samples of opinion leaders, indicating once again that they display a more consistent and doctrinally determined set of beliefs

---

* The law and order scales in the CLS and OVS studies consist of five and three items, respectively. Two items which best illustrate the content of these scales are "In dealing with crime, the most important consideration is to: (a) protect the rights of the accused; or (b) stop crime even if we have to violate the rights of the accused," and "All systems of justice make mistakes, but which do you think is worse? (a) To convict an innocent person; or (b) to let a guilty person go free."

TABLE 4.8
Law and Order Versus the "Rights of the Accused": Responses to Selected Due Process Items (percentage down)*

	CLS			
	Mass Public		Community Leaders	
	For Rights of Accused	For Law and Order	For Rights of Accused	For Law and Order
Item Summaries	(N=781)	(N=581)	(N=770)	(N=142)
Police are too easy, or use too much force on rioters.				
Pro-CL	36%	18%	37%	10%
Anti-CL	23	44	16	51
Death penalty is proper or morally wrong.				
Pro-CL	25	5	40	6
Anti-CL	62	83	49	84
Police must be limited by law to protect accused.				
Pro-CL	55	34	55	33
Anti-CL	28	43	31	51
Support or oppose law which violates Constitution.				
Pro-CL	30	19	36	25
Anti-CL	8	15	7	9
Forcing people to testify against themselves may be necessary, or is never justified.				
Pro-CL	59	21	78	35
Anti-CL	20	52	11	44
Privacy of defendant's diary.				
Pro-CL	55	39	57	37
Anti-CL	29	40	29	43
The right to remain silent is needed, or has harmed the country.				
Pro-CL	75	39	83	44
Anti-CL	12	43	8	41
Should authorities respect, or ignore, the right to remain silent?				
Pro-CL	64	38	65	32
Anti-CL	16	30	17	43
Providing lawyer for accused is necessary or wasteful.				
Pro-CL	89	67	93	66
Anti-CL	5	17	4	19
Fair trial for rapists.				
Pro-CL	91	47	96	63
Anti-CL	7	42	3	30

Item Summaries	CLS			
	Mass Public		Community Leaders	
	For Rights of Accused	For Law and Order	For Rights of Accused	For Law and Order
	(N=781)	(N=581)	(N=770)	(N=142)
Right to trial by jury is overrated, or best way to achieve fairness.				
Pro-CL	43%	34%	46%	32%
Anti-CL	4	10	3	10
Should mistakes during trial be binding?				
Pro-CL	16	7	19	6
Anti-CL	57	70	56	81
Support or oppose illegal methods to prove guilt.				
Pro-CL	53	21	67	17
Anti-CL	29	61	22	66
Keeping people in prison without trial is never justified, or is sometimes necessary.				
Pro-CL	69	40	78	54
Anti-CL	21	46	16	40

Item Summaries	OVS			
	Mass Public		Opinion Leaders	
	For Rights of Accused	For Law and Order	For Rights of Accused	For Law and Order
	(N=332)	(N=380)	(N=530)	(N=140)
Courts are too hard, or too easy, on law-breakers.				
Pro-CL	4%	1%	2%	1%
Anti-CL	63	85	39	77
Police power should be cut or increased.				
Pro-CL	13	4	10	0
Anti-CL	53	82	24	72
To reduce crime, hire more policemen or abolish prison system.				
Pro-CL	9	3	11	1
Anti-CL	36	55	25	46
In war, protest or watch the disloyal.				
Pro-CL	43	16	71	34
Anti-CL	40	66	14	45

TABLE 4.8 *(continued)*

	OVS			
	Mass Public		**Opinion Leaders**	
	For Rights of Accused	**For Law and Order**	**For Rights of Accused**	**For Law and Order**
Item Summaries	(N=332)	(N=380)	(N=530)	(N=140)
For or against capital punishment.				
Pro-CL	31%	19%	43%	15%
Anti-CL	46	68	25	61
Strengthen or weaken Fifth Amendment.				
Pro-CL	30	20	44	19
Anti-CL	11	27	4	17
Support or oppose the right to remain silent.				
Pro-CL	90	66	93	66
Anti-CL	2	20	1	14
Providing lawyer for accused is necessary or wasteful.				
Pro-CL	70	45	75	48
Anti-CL	14	32	11	32
Allow or disallow legal evidence.				
Pro-CL	29	10	51	7
Anti-CL	24	61	8	43
Bail or prison for accused.				
Pro-CL	27	8	35	19
Anti-CL	53	77	30	53
Keeping people in prison without trial is never justified, or is sometimes necessary.				
Pro-CL	46	19	51	27
Anti-CL	42	68	34	57

*Those scoring Neither or Undecided on the items have been omitted from this table. We have also omitted, for purposes of simplifying the table, the middle category, that is, those who were neither clearly for the rights of the accused nor clearly for law and order.

than does the public as a whole. Both the mass public and the elites, however, tend not to respond to specific due process issues in an idiosyncratic or haphazard manner, but to judge them instead against more basic and, we suspect, deeply ingrained principles or feelings.

CHAPTER 5

The Rights of Privacy and Lifestyle

ALTHOUGH the Constitution makes no explicit reference to a right of privacy, it is among the most vital safeguards enjoyed by Americans against government infringements on personal autonomy. Privacy is not so much a single right as a broad class of immunities that Justice Brandeis, in *Olmstead* v. *United States* (277 U.S. 438, 1928), trenchantly characterized as "the right to be let alone." Actually, however, the right is broader than this, for it includes not only the inviolability of a person's thoughts against unwarranted probes, but protections against government interference with certain forms of conduct considered personal and beyond the reach of the state. It also includes the legal recognition that there are some spheres of opinion and conduct over which the individual has exclusive control.

As Justice Douglas observed in *Griswold* v. *Connecticut* (381 U.S. 479, 1965) privacy is, in effect, guaranteed by various provisions of the Bill of Rights, such as "the rights of association and expression protected by the First Amendment, the Third Amendment prohibition on the quartering of soldiers in private houses in times of peace, the Fourth Amendment's protection against unreasonable searches and seizures, and the Fifth Amendment's protection against self-incrimination." (Cf. Casper 1972.) Some of the rights that fall under privacy might also be classified under due process as well. Wiretapping without a warrant is an example, as are "unreasonable searches and seizures" of one's home or one's person. Permitting police to infiltrate or spy on criminal or radical organizations or to compile dossiers on individuals may invade not only privacy but also due process. Exerting duress on suspects to force them to reveal damaging information against themselves violates both their due process privilege against self-incrimination and the immunity they presumably enjoy against being forced to reveal their private thoughts or facts about their conduct which they might wish to keep confidential. The gathering (without a search warrant) of private information on individuals through various new electronic techniques of "bugging," surveillance, and computer storage of records not only subjects citizens to questionable investigatory procedures, but prevents them from determining for themselves "when, how, and to what extent information about them is communicated to others" (Westin 1967).

Questions about the nature and limits of privacy have also been raised in such diverse cases as a father's right to demand the withdrawal of life support systems used to keep alive a permanently brain-damaged and comatose daughter; the prohibition of sodomy between consenting adults; and the admissibility of evidence turned up by trained dogs sniffing for marijuana in luggage at airports. The rights of privacy have become an issue (sometimes unspoken) in defending the inviolability of beliefs in the conflict between religious conscience and a teacher's refusal to salute the flag; in the right of a woman to have an abortion; in the freedom of employees to dress in a fashion disapproved by their employers; and in the ability of individuals to seek damages against newspapers which publish embarrassing photographs of them taken without permission.

The intimate connection between the rights of privacy, due process, and such First Amendment guarantees as freedom of speech and association point up the importance of privacy as a constitutional right. Justice Brandeis, in his *Olmstead* dissent, described privacy as "the most comprehensive of rights and the right most valued by civilized men." One can scarcely maintain a sense of personal security if one must continually confront governing officials who are forever searching for damaging information and threatening to expose it. (Cf. Greenawalt 1970.) Put in the simplest terms, the right to be protected against the exposure of one's opinions or to engage safely in conduct that primarily concerns oneself rather than society is a right essential to civilized life and to the enjoyment of other vital civil liberties. Over the years its importance has, if anything, increased as the technology for electronic surveillance, information-gathering, and information storage (via computers) has advanced. An indication of the value placed on privacy may be gleaned from the fact that 76 percent of the public say, in response to a survey, that privacy should be added to "life, liberty, and the pursuit of happiness" as a right "fundamental for both the individual and a just society" (Harris and Westin 1979).

172

The importance assigned by the public to the right of privacy may also be inferred from the widespread fear that the right is increasingly being invaded or lost. Harris and Westin (1979) report that 64 percent of the general population they surveyed stated that they were "very" or "somewhat" concerned about threats to their personal privacy. Some 51 percent expressed the belief that in the next ten years "we will have lost much of our ability to keep important aspects of our lives private from the government," while approximately the same number said they were "worried" about how government and business will use the personal information they collect on private individuals.

In general, public concern about the erosion of privacy and the potential abuse of the personal information collected by government and business has been increasing (Harris and Westin 1979)—a reflection, one assumes, of the advances in technology for obtaining and storing data, the expansion of governmental activities, and the greater frequency with which members of the public seek services from government and business that require the divulging of personal information. Additionally, incidents have come to light in which government agencies, such as the FBI or the intelligence branches of the Army, appear to have overstepped their legal mandates and to have gathered unauthorized confidential information on individuals or political groups.

We must remind ourselves that the privacy which many people fear we are in danger of losing is, as we have noted, not a single monolithic right, but rather a class of liberties. Bostwick (1976) has developed a taxonomy of privacy in which he divides privacy rights into three subclasses: the privacy of *repose*, the privacy of *sanctuary*, and the privacy of *intimate decision*. Each of these so-called zones of privacy protects a different type of human transaction.

The zone of repose refers to freedom from external influences that disturb our comfort, sensibilities, peace of mind, or sense of well-being. It is a passive right that most closely embodies the freedom to be let alone. It includes, for example, the right not to be solicited for the sale of goods in a private residence; not to receive erotic or provocative mail if one has asked the post office to withhold such mail; and not to be disturbed by sound trucks and loudspeakers that advertise or play loud music. Bostwick maintains that the zone of repose does not enjoy genuine constitutional protection unless, as Justice Harlan has held, "substantial privacy interests are being invaded in an essentially intolerable manner." The privacy of repose often comes into conflict with the right of free expression, and it is up to the legislature and the courts to determine if the guarantees of the First Amendment have been employed in a manner so offensive that they wrongly undermine the right to be free of "intolerable" intrusions.

The zone of sanctuary primarily involves protections against the government's ability to uncover certain kinds of information about an individual. The right of sanctuary "allows an individual to keep some things private" by establishing a zone of privileges and immunities which prevents other persons from seeing, hearing, or knowing about them. The constitutional provision that lies at the heart of the zone of sanctuary (and hence of the right of privacy as such) is the Fourth Amendment's prohibition against unreasonable searches and seizures which protects the "right of the people to be secure in their persons, houses, papers, and effects." This prohibition is reinforced by the additional stipulation that no search warrants "shall issue but upon probable cause, supported by oath or affirmation, and particularily describing the place to be searched, and the persons or things to be seized." Government, thus, is allowed to search and even to seize contraband materials, but (with some exceptions) only if the search is not "unreasonable" and has been authorized by a valid warrant. A search warrant is not a "hunting license" to explore the premises as one pleases and without restriction. Rather, it must specify the area or persons to be searched, the scope of the search, and the persons or goods that can be searched and seized. Evidence gathered by enforcement authorities that fails to meet these standards will ordinarily be considered "illegal evidence" and excluded from the trial.*

Bostwick includes within the zone of sanctuary such privacy rights as a journalist's privilege not to reveal his sources, a lawyer's privilege not to disclose the confidence of his clients, security against wiretapping and other forms of electronic surveillance, the confidentiality of bank records or student files, and the safeguarding of private meetings

---

*Exceptions to these rules are usually permitted if the search is part of a lawful arrest or if the police are in "hot pursuit" of a dangerous suspect. A person arrested for some presumed criminal activity may be searched or "patted down" if the police have reason to believe he or she is armed. If the officers enter a house to make an arrest they may observe anything that is lying about in "plain view." They may also search areas in which the suspect may have concealed a weapon. Contrary to popular opinion, the police may also search an automobile they have stopped on the public highways if they have probable cause to believe it contains items subject to seizure. There are various other "exigent circumstances" in which the police may search without a warrant—for example, if they hear screams from a home, or need to take blood samples from a drunken driver involved in an accident, or if there is danger that evidence will be destroyed (Bostwick 1977; also Casper 1972).

against infiltration or espionage by the police—or for that matter by anyone else. In the legal discipline, the classification of "privilege" primarily refers to the broad subject of evidence. Material that is privileged cannot be introduced into trials or other judicial hearings, on the assumption that certain types of relationships are to be encouraged and protected so that the participants may, within limits, be assured that their confidential communications will not be revealed in court. One of the most familiar examples of privilege involves the confidential communications between client and attorney. Another involves the communications between clergyman and penitent—a privilege so strong that a clergyman may refuse to disclose it even if the penitent waives the privilege. Privilege also exists in the relationship between patient and physician or psychiatrist, although there are many exceptions to this rule (for example, malpractice or collaboration in a crime).

One of the best known and most protected forms of privilege involves the marriage relationship. In most jurisdictions a married person cannot be called as a witness against his or her spouse in a criminal trial—a privilege that continues to apply even if the marriage has been terminated. (The privilege does not apply, however, if the crime is committed against the spouse or one of their children; for example, child abuse or wife-beating.) Though the number of such privileges are few, they are strongly protected and essential to the principle of privacy. They confirm that certain forms of testimony cannot be compelled by the courts and that certain relationships or forms of conduct are indeed inviolate and beyond effective interference by the state.

One of the more controversial forms of privilege concerns the information gathered by journalists. The Supreme Court has explicitly stated that the Constitution does not bestow a privilege upon journalists that protects them from revealing their sources, and no federal "shield law" presently exists to protect journalistic privilege. Nevertheless, the courts have generally recognized that journalists have a limited or conditional privilege to protect their news sources. Usually, the courts have tried to balance the journalist's privilege to withhold information or news sources against the defendant's right to a fair trial, or against the government's interest in the vigorous pursuit of justice. The results of this conflict have been mixed. The same uncertainty is evident from the fact that about half the states have shield laws and the other half do not (Bostwick 1977).

The privacy of intimate decision differs from the privacy of repose and sanctuary in its emphasis upon individual autonomy. This zone prevents the state from learning about or interfering with those aspects of thought and conduct which are considered so personal that individuals should enjoy complete autonomy over them unless the state has a compelling interest in interfering with them.

The nature of intimate decision was spelled out in the Alaska case of *Ravin* v. *State* (537 P. 2d. 494, Alas. 1975), where it was held that "one aspect of a private matter is that it *is* private, that is, that it does not adversely affect persons beyond the actor, and hence is none of their business" (quoted in Bostwick 1976). Questions of intimate decision are not likely to have an adverse effect on anyone "other than the persons making the decision, and thus . . . it is none of anyone else's business" (Bostwick 1976). Even if such decisions take place in the public arena, they involve personal matters which, by virtue of their intimacy, are thought to be immune from the state's interference.

The zone of intimate decision protects various forms of conduct that might appropriately be listed under "freedom of lifestyle." In the case of *Griswold* v. *Connecticut* (381 U.S. 479, 1965), the Court ruled that "married persons are free to decide whether to use contraceptives without interference from the state." In *Roe* v. *Wade* (410 U.S. 113, 1973) and *Doe* v. *Bolton* (410 U.S. 179 1973), the Court held that "the right of privacy . . . is broad enough to encompass a woman's decision whether or not to terminate her pregnancy." In *Loving* v. *Virginia* (388 U.S. 1, 1967), the Court struck down a Virginia statute that prohibited racially mixed marriages. "Marriage," the Court ruled, "is one of the basic civil rights" of mankind, and since the state had no legitimate interest in preserving the "racial integrity of its citizens," it could not justifiably invade the zone of intimate decision and prohibit intermarriage between races (quoted in Bostwick 1976). Apart from the question of the private or public nature of our conduct, the relevant questions for the privacy of intimate decision are: What does the state have a legal claim to know about us? What may we think, say, and do without the rest of society having the right to demand that it should be made public?

Despite the dramatic changes in lifestyles involving sexual freedom and the growing view that decisions about sexual conduct are private, the legislatures and the courts dealing with these matters appear to reflect public opinion rather than to lead it in a more civil libertarian direction. For example, although the *Griswold* case placed severe limits on the state's authority to regulate married sexual activity, the courts have not been willing to say that married couples can engage in any type of sexual activity they please. In some states, for example, they are legally prohibited from engaging in sodomy. Often such acts are still considered "deviant sexual activity" or "crimes against nature." In 1976 a Virginia court held in *Doe* v. *Commonwealths Attorney* (403 F. Supp. 1199, E.D. Va. 1975) that a sodomy statute that prohibited homosexual acts (even in private) was constitutional, and the U.S. Supreme Court allowed the decision to stand. The number of statutes of this sort, however, has been declining, and so has their enforcement.

However, the sexual conduct of unmarried couples, or of homosexuals, is even less protected by the existing rules of privacy. As legal matters now stand, the claim that individuals in these categories, as consenting adults, should be allowed to conduct their sexual lives as they please has received little support in the courts. Nevertheless, although regulations against such sexual conduct as fornication and adultery have been upheld by the courts as constitutional, they are, when conducted in private, rarely enforced (as long as they do not involve minors, coercion, or money). In adopting this posture, the courts, and other law enforcement authorities, appear to be reflecting the ambivalence that characterizes these matters in the public mind.

Being gay, of course, is not in itself a crime, as no law can make it a crime to *be* anything. A homosexual charged with crime must be prosecuted for *conduct*, not for his or her sexual predilections or preferences (Bostwick 1977). Often the statutes employed to discourage homosexual practices do not address homosexuality as such, but focus instead on such "crimes" as sodomy or such euphemisms as loitering, indecent exposure, vagrancy, solicitation, or disorderly conduct. In some communities, and especially in the more cosmopolitan communities, such laws are rarely or only sporadically enforced. In other communities, they are regularly enforced. Much depends not only on the mores of the community, but on the attitudes and zeal of the law enforcement officials.

Although the major civil rights legislation which aims to protect racial minorities, women, or religious groups from discrimination in such matters as housing, jobs, and public accommodations has not been extended to homosexuals (gays are particularly subject to exclusion from sensitive or "public interest" occupations such as teaching or law), local governments have in some cases adopted fair housing, fair employment, or human rights ordinances that prohibit discrimination on the basis of sexual preferences.* Since 1976, the federal government

---

* For a summary of the legal status of the rights of homosexuals, we are greatly indebted to Wendy Morgan, who prepared a memorandum at our request in 1977.

has stated in its guidelines that "Court decisions require that persons not be disqualified from Federal employment solely on the basis of homosexual conduct" (quoted in Morgan 1977).

Gays, no less than other categories of persons, enjoy the legal right to express their ideas in a public forum, to demonstrate peacefully, to form student organizations, to publish newspapers, and to participate in any of the other forms of expression protected by the First Amendment. Gay organizations also have the right to incorporate, to acquire tax deductible status, and to receive federal, state, and local funds (Morgan *1977*). Many states, nevertheless, still have statutes condemning "any sexual intercourse which is unnatural, detestable, and abominable," under which homosexuals can be (and have been) discriminated against, or otherwise punished.

Limits have been enforced, although inconsistently, in such matters as admitting or deporting alien homosexuals from the United States. At the discretion of immigration authorities (with some possibility of appeal to the courts), alien homosexuals may be deported or denied entry into the United States for "sexual deviation," lack of "good moral character," or conviction for moral turpitude. Although homosexuals may own property jointly, and name each other as beneficiaries of life insurance or pension plans, they cannot enter into a legal marriage in any state and cannot enjoy the financial benefits of marriage, such as inheritance, community property, or recovery for wrongful death. As for custody of children, no uniform legal practices have evolved so far, although the Supreme Court ruled, in *Stanley* v. *State of Illinois* (405 U.S. 645, 1972), that "a homosexual parent cannot be conclusively presumed to be an unfit parent" (Morgan 1977). Perhaps the most severe legal restrictions against homosexuality exist in the military. The official military position is that gays "cannot be tolerated," that they are security risks and must be promptly separated from the service. In practice, however, homosexuals in the military are not often prosecuted, and recent court cases have even begun to challenge the principle of mandatory exclusion as irrational and capricious.

The abortion issue also involves the zone of intimate decision. Until 1973, abortion was generally considered illegal in the United States, although some states made allowance for abortions under exigent circumstances: for example, if they were necessary to save the life or mental health of the mother, to prevent the birth of a severely deformed or mentally incapacitated child, or to prevent births from rape or incest. After some years of lower court decisions which gradually liberalized the restrictions against abortion, the Supreme Court, in effect, legalized abortion on request by ruling that a woman, in consultation with her physician, was free to decide whether or not to have an abortion during the first trimester of pregnancy (*Roe* v. *Wade*, 410 U.S. 113, 1973; *Doe* v. *Bolton*, 410 U.S. 179, 1973). While the state (the Court argued) retains a legitimate interest in assuring the safety of patients under all medical procedures, the danger from modern abortion procedures is so slight during the early stages of pregnancy that the state's need to protect a woman against this procedure in the first trimester "has largely disappeared." The state's interest increases, however, as the period of pregnancy lengthens. In the second trimester, thus, the state could regulate abortion procedures in order to promote the health of the mother. In the last trimester, the state could regulate and even prohibit abortion when necessary to preserve the life or health of the mother.

Although the Constitution "does not explicitly mention any right of privacy," as Justice Blackmun observed in delivering the majority opinion in *Roe*, "the Court has recognized that a right of personal privacy, or a guarantee of certain areas or zones of privacy, does exist under the Constitution."

> This right of privacy . . . is broad enough to encompass a woman's decision whether or not to terminate her pregnancy. The detriment that the State would impose by denying this choice altogether is apparent. Specific and direct harm medically diagnosable even in early pregnancy may be involved. Maternity, or additional offspring, may force upon a woman a distressful life and future. Psychological harm may be imminent. Mental and physical health may be taxed by child care. There is also the distress, for all concerned, associated with the unwanted child, and there is the problem of bringing a child into a family already unable, psychologically and otherwise, to care for it. . . . We, therefore, conclude that the right of personal privacy includes the abortion decision, but that this right is not unqualified and must be considered against important state interests in regulation.

The *Roe* decision, as one might expect, proved highly controversial. Efforts have been made by several state governments, and by a number of hospitals and doctors, to circumvent the ruling or to prevent it from coming into effect. Both Congress and various state legislatures have acted to prohibit the use of Medicaid or of other public funds to pay for abortions for indigent mothers. Self-described "right-to-life" groups have campaigned intensively against abortion for *any* reason, and have gone so far as to seek a constitutional amendment prohibiting it. The defenders of abortion have argued, among other things, that proscriptions against abortion, like the earlier prohibitions against contraception outlawed by *Griswold*, violate private rights. In the case of abortion, such proscriptions are "an impermissible invasion of each woman's constitutional right to control the use of her body" (Lister 1970).

Questions of privacy and the right of intimate decision also arise in connection with some of the developments associated with the lifestyle of the so-called counterculture. Do individuals have the right to be protected in their conduct when they choose to defy conventional standards and adopt lifestyles outside the "established" culture?

The courts have said, for example, that it is not a crime to be a "hippie," and they have acted upon that premise. Thus, they ruled that food stamps cannot be denied to people who live with an unrelated person. They have also struck down a city ordinance that tried to bar hippies from standing on private property. And participants in the counterculture can claim all the same liberties that their fellow citizens enjoy. This does not mean, of course, that these people are not harassed by frequent (and often illegal) searches (usually for marijuana or other drugs), school or employment regulations against long hair or unconventional appearance, or discrimination in housing and employment arising from communal living. Rarely, however, is such harassment or discrimination explicitly authorized by law. Indeed, the counterculture (as distinguished from earlier communities of intellectuals) is a rather recent phenomenon, and legal norms and statutes bearing on countercultural lifestyles have had little time to develop.

Obscenity and pornography refer to conduct or expressions that people can see or hear rather than act out themselves. The legal principles regulating obscenity and pornography, and the decisions determining the kinds of materials that are protected from interference, are highly uncertain and confusing. Obscenity and pornography fall at the margins of the right of free press (censorship) and the claims of privacy.* This area of constitutional law is one of the most amorphous (Bostwick 1977). Obscenity and pornography, though forms of expression, enjoy no protection under the First Amendment, so that the state is free to suppress them. The power to suppress, however, is not unlimited, for much depends on whether certain rather vague conditions

---

* See our discussion of obscenity and pornogaphy in light of censorship and free press in chapter 2.

have or have not been satisfied. As matters now stand, especially since the attempt to censor the novel *Fanny Hill* (383 U.S. 413, 1966), a work is judged to be legally obscene if (a) an average person applying contemporary community standards would find that the material as a whole appeals to a prurient interest; (b) the work contains patently offensive depictions of sexual activities; and (c) the work is found to be "utterly without redeeming social value" (*Roth* v. *United States*, 354 U.S. 476, 1957; *Ginzburg* v. *United States*, 383 U.S. 463, 1966).

Although these tests are extremely vague,* the Supreme Court has tended to reverse the obscenity findings of the lower courts.† Only when sexual activity was explicitly depicted, or the distributor of the material was "pandering"—that is, advertising and promoting sexual materials in an "obscene" way—has the Court been inclined to censor a work or convict someone of a crime for distributing it. The Court has also ruled that while importing or mailing pornographic materials may be subject to criminal penalties, the state's power to regulate obscenity "does not extend to mere possession [of obscene materials] in the privacy of [one's] own home" (*Stanley* v. *Georgia*, 394 U.S. 557, 1969); (quoted in Bostwick 1976). Thus, under the rules governing privacy, people can possess any type of pornography in the home, but they are not free to import it or transport it across state lines. Pornographic material possessed in the home, however, must be for private rather than commercial use (Bostwick 1977; *Ravin* v. *State*).

Concern has frequently been voiced (or embodied in state statutes) that minors are especially vulnerable and might easily be incited by "obscene" books "to violent, depraved, or immoral acts." Obscene literature, the Court said in the *Roth* case, cannot enjoy constitutional protection because it is utterly without "redeeming social importance." (Cf. Worton 1975.) In his dissenting opinion, Justice Douglas observed that by making "the legality of a publication turn on the purity of thought which a book or tract instills in the mind of the reader . . . punishment is inflicted for thoughts provoked, not for overt acts nor antisocial conduct." He further noted that the "absence of dependable information on the effect of obscene literature on human conduct should make us wary. It should put us on the side of protecting soci-

---

*What, for example, is an "average person"? What is the nature and size of the community whose standards are to be applied? What does it mean for a work to be utterly without "redeeming social value"?

† For an extensive review of court cases referring to obscenity, see Haiman 1976, pp. 111–67; also Cooper 1977.

ety's interest in literature." The critics of book censorship have also complained that, by using young people as the standard for deciding what should be regarded as obscene, the adult population (in the words of Justice Frankfurter in *Butler* v. *Michigan*) is reduced "to reading only what is fit for children."

Films, unlike printed materials, were first considered purely as "entertainment" and did not enjoy freedom from prior censorship. Until the 1960s, in fact, films had to be approved and licensed by state licensing boards before they could be shown. These boards could also delete particular portions of a film considered morally offensive. FIlms, it was thought, did not enjoy the protection of the First Amendment.

This view of the unprotected status of motion pictures began to be modified in *Burstyn* v. *Wilson* (343 U.S. 495, 1952), a case that involved not only *obscenity* but *sacrilege*. The case arose when the New York State Board of Regents censored an Italian film, *The Miracle*, on the grounds that it was sacrilegious. The Court, upon reviewing the arguments, was led to conclude that motion pictures, as "a significant medium for the communication of ideas," did indeed fall under the protection of the First Amendment.

Henceforth, the Court by degrees began to permit films to be shown that had been denied licenses on the grounds that their sexual depictions were "immoral" or that they depicted crime or violence. In the celebrated case of *Kingsley International Pictures Corporation* v. *Regents of University of State of New York* (360 U.S. 684, 1959), involving the denial by the State of New York of a license to exhibit a film based on *Lady Chatterley's Lover*, the Court held that the film advocated an *idea* (that is, "that adultery under certain circumstances may be proper") and that it therefore enjoyed the protection of the First Amendment to advocate ideas. "To deny a license to a film because it portrays a relationship contrary to [prevailing] moral standards . . . misconceives what it is that the Constitution protects. . . . It protects advocacy of the opinion that adultery may sometimes be proper, no less than advocacy of socialism or the single tax."

In light of this opinion, an effort was made by plaintiffs in *Times Film Corporation*, v. *Chicago* (365 U.S. 43, 1961) to eliminate the licensing requirement entirely. Although the effort failed by a single vote, the case provided an opportunity for Chief Justice Warren, joined by Justices Black, Douglas, and Brennan, to press the issue further in a notable dissent. Warren observed that by granting city officials the power to withhold a license from any film they deemed unworthy, a licensing ordinance gives "formal sanction to censorship in its purest and most far-reaching form. . . . It officially unleashes the censor and permits him to roam at will." The rejection by the First Amendment of "prior censorship through licensing and previous restraint is an inherent and basic principle of freedom of speech and the press."

From these sentiments it was a short step to the opinion expressed in *Freeman* v. *Maryland* (380 U.S. 51, 1965), in which the Court for all practical purposes put an end to the licensing and prior censorship of films by ruling that the burden of proof is on the would-be censor to demonstrate promptly to a court that a given film ought not to be shown. The same principle was later applied to theatrical performances as well. (Cf. Haiman 1976; Worton 1975c.) The film industry, partly to forestall new efforts to impose government censorship, has now set up its own classification system in which films are rated according to their appropriateness for children.

Findings on Privacy and Lifestyle

We have observed in our review of the legal status of privacy that certain forms of communication or information are considered confidential or "privileged" and need not be divulged to the courts or any other branch of government. As is evident from figure 5.1, the public is generally sympathetic to privilege—at least as it pertains to journalists and the psychiatric relationship. Some 62 percent of the public in the Harris and Westin survey believe that journalists should not be required to reveal their unpublished notes and sources to the courts. Both the public and the elites in our CLS study also lean strongly toward the somewhat surprising view that a psychiatrist should report to the police a patient's expressed intention to commit a serious crime.

As we have had occasion to note in earlier chapters, approximately half the mass public and the community elites endorse the privilege against self-incrimination, which can be viewed not only as a due process right but as a privacy right that protects the individual from improper searches and seizures by the government. In *Boyd* v. *United States* (116 U.S. 616, 1886), a case described by Casper as a "milestone"

If a patient tells his psychiatrist that he is planning to commit a serious crime, the psychiatrist should:

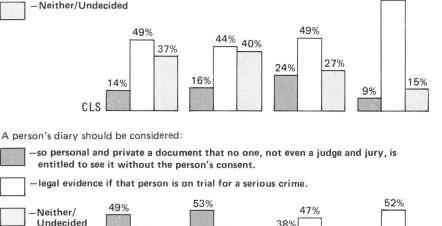

—remain silent because his first duty is to his patient.

—report it to the police.

—Neither/Undecided

CLS

A person's diary should be considered:

—so personal and private a document that no one, not even a judge and jury, is entitled to see it without the person's consent.

—legal evidence if that person is on trial for a serious crime.

—Neither/Undecided

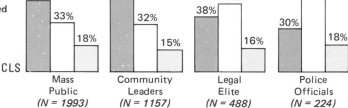

CLS

| Mass Public (N = 1993) | Community Leaders (N = 1157) | Legal Elite (N = 488) | Police Officials (N = 224) |

Should journalists be required to reveal their unpublished notes and sources to the courts? One view holds that the privacy of sources should be protected to ensure that people feel free to talk to the press. Others say that this is less important than providing the courts with all the evidence needed to reach fair decisions. Which is closest to the way you feel?

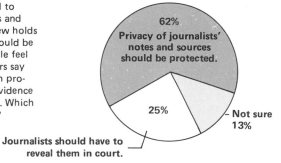

62%
Privacy of journalists' notes and sources should be protected.

25%

Not sure 13%

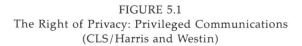

Journalists should have to reveal them in court.

(Adapted from Harris and Westin 1979; N = 1505)

FIGURE 5.1
The Right of Privacy: Privileged Communications
(CLS/Harris and Westin)

among search and seizure cases, the Court held that "the seizure of a man's private books and papers to be used against him is [not] substantially different from compelling him to be a witness against himself."

The public's responses to questions about search and seizure are presented in table 5.1. While the data indicate that most Americans are preponderantly opposed to searches without a court order, their attitudes are not entirely consistent. On the one hand, they are, by substantial margins, against any search of a person's home without a warrant. On the other hand, they believe (by a two-to-one margin) that police officers who stop a car for a traffic violation should also be allowed to search the car if they suspect it contains drugs or stolen goods—a view shared by the community elites and even more strongly by the police. The public clearly disregards the principle which prohibits a search without a warrant when they strongly endorse the use of dogs in airports "to help police locate dangerous narcotics in suitcases or lockers." Thus, in the application of the longstanding and familiar protections against searching a person's home without a court order, or accosting an innocent person to demand identification, Americans tend to uphold the right of privacy. Under the newer and less familiar applications of this right, however, the reverse is true.

As in the other cases we have examined, popular support for civil liberties tends to be greater when the norms are clear and well established and weaker or more uncertain when the norms are newly emerging, still unfamiliar to many members of the mass public, and not yet firmly fixed in the body of constitutional principles endorsed by the courts. In addition, although most respondents find it unjust for law enforcement officers to barge into someone's home and begin to search without legal authorization, many of them feel it necessary and appropriate for the authorities to take unusual measures to counteract the stealthy and clever maneuvers of drug importers and other dealers in dangerous narcotics.

The attitudes expressed toward wiretapping by the mass public and the elites, however, are again somewhat equivocal. As can be seen in table 5.2, much depends on the type of questions asked. Nunn et al. (1978) report that from the time of Stouffer's survey in 1954 to their own survey in 1973, the public's unwillingness to allow the phones of Communists to be tapped rose from 27 percent to 49 percent. Harris and Westin report data from their 1978 survey showing that 87 percent of adult Americans believe that the police should not be able to tap the telephones of the "members of an organization never convicted of

TABLE 5.1
The Right of Privacy: Attitudes Toward Search and Seizure

	CLS			
	Mass Public	**Community Leaders**	**Legal Elite**	**Police Officials**
	(N=1993)	**(N=1157)**	**(N=488)**	**(N=224)**
If a police officer stops a car for a traffic violation, he should be:				
—limited to dealing with the traffic violation and nothing else.	30%	30%	50%	20%
—allowed to search the car if he suspects it contains narcotics or stolen goods.	58	59	31	67
—Neither/Undecided	12	10	19	13
The use of dogs in airports to help police locate dangerous narcotics in suitcases or lockers:				
—violates a traveler's privacy.	5	4	9	0
—is justified in order to catch drug dealers.	89	91	84	99
—Neither/Undecided	5	5	7	1
How would you rate protection of your home against searches without a warrant?				
—Extremely important	74	78	82	64
—Important	20	18	14	23
—Somewhat important	4	3	3	8
—Less important	2	1	1	5
—Other	1	0	0	1

	OVS	
	Mass Public	**Opinion Leaders**
	(N=938)	**(N=845)**
Searching a person's home or car without a search warrant:		
—should never be allowed.	59%	72%
—is sometimes justified in order to solve a crime.	33	20
—Neither/Undecided	9	8

	Chandler* (N=1136)
If the police suspect that drugs, guns, or other criminal evidence is hidden in someone's house, should they be allowed to enter the house without first obtaining a search warrant?	
—Yes	32%
—No	66
—Sometimes	1
—No response	1

	Harris and Westin[†] (N=1511)
Do you think the police should have the right to stop anyone on the street and demand to see some identification even if the person is not doing anything illegal, or shouldn't they have this right?	
—should not have this right.	72%
—should have this right.	24
—Not sure.	4

NOTES: Because percentages have been rounded off, occasionally there will be disparities in totals (columns will not add up to 100 percent).

See the Preface to Research Findings (p. 25) and Appendix B for description of the leader and mass public samples of various categories used in the PAB, CLS, and OVS studies: that is "Political Leaders," "Legal Elite," and so forth.

The CLS was conducted in 1978–1979; the OVS in 1976–1977; and the PAB in 1958.

*Chandler 1972.

[†] Harris and Westin 1979.

crime . . . without obtaining a court order," even if the police believe "they might engage in illegal acts in the future." As for their own security, an overwhelming majority of respondents in the CLS study rate privacy in their own phone conversations as "important" or "extremely important."

Nevertheless, data from both the OVS and CLS studies (reported in table 5.2) indicate that considerable support exists for tapping the telephones of known criminals suspected of planning new crimes, providing the police have a legal warrant authorizing the wiretap. The

TABLE 5.2
The Right of Privacy: Attitudes Toward Wiretapping

	CLS			
	Mass Public	**Community Leaders**	**Legal Elite**	**Police Officials**
	(N=1993)	**(N=1157)**	**(N=488)**	**(N=224)**
Tapping telephones with a legal warrant:				
—still violates personal privacy and should be outlawed by Congress.	19%	17%	14%	2%
—can be justified when used against known criminals suspected of planning new crimes.	73	77	76	94
—Neither/Undecided	9	6	10	4
If the leaders of organized crime meet in a private home or office to discuss their criminal activities:				
—they should be free to hold such a meeting without interference.	15	18	20	5
—the police should be able to "bug" their meeting place to collect evidence against them.	61	61	54	81
—Neither/Undecided	24	21	26	14
How would you rate the right to privacy in your correspondence or phone conversations?				
—Extremely important	79	82	75	61
—Important	17	15	20	26
—Somewhat important	2	3	5	7
—Less important	1	1	0	5
—Other	0	0	1	1

	OVS	
	Mass Public	**Opinion Leaders**
	(N=938)	**(N=845)**
Tapping telephones of people suspected of planning crimes:		
—should be prohibited as an invasion of privacy.	36%	47%
—is necessary to reduce crime.	46	24
—Neither/Undecided	18	29

	Harris and Westin*
	(N=1513)
Can police tap the telephones of "members of an organization never convicted of a crime" but whom they believe "might engage in illegal acts in the future . . . without obtaining a court order"?	
—Should be able.	11%
—Should not be able.	87
—Not sure.	3

* Harris and Westin 1979.

public, the leaders, and even the lawyers and judges also exhibit few compunctions about "bugging" the meetings of the leaders of organized crime in order "to collect evidence against them." Thus, while government wiretapping of innocent (or unspecified) people as a general practice is apparently perceived as unfair by most Americans, they do not seem to regard it as improper to eavesdrop (especially under court order) on the activities or meetings of known criminals. Indeed, they are inclined to consider electronic surveillance in these instances as necessary to reduce crime. As one might expect, the police officials in our CLS study are even more strongly disposed than the mass public toward the use of wiretaps or "bugs" as devices for combating crime.

Police surveillance of criminal or radical organizations and their activities also takes the form of infiltrating them, keeping lists of members or of persons who attend meetings, and performing other undercover work. Surveillance activities that employ secret agents and informers occupy a somewhat "gray" area in the law. There are not many cases on which to base an assessment of the legal status of using such methods, and the few cases that have reached the Supreme Court have gone in favor of admitting evidence collected through covert police methods. Although the Court has suggested that the Fourth Amendment may have some bearing on the government's use of such methods of surveillance, it would be difficult to predict how the courts would come out on questions involving the use of secret agents and informers. (Cf. Greenawalt 1971.)

There can be little doubt, however, about the attitudes of the general public on this aspect of surveillance and privacy. As their responses in table 5.3 bear out, the great majority of Americans believe that the use of undercover police methods, informers, and secret agents is appropriate, or even necessary, to protect the nation against radicals and criminals. Hence, they endorse, usually by substantial margins, the use of police or federal agents to spy on radical organizations, to keep lists of people who engage in protest demonstrations, to infiltrate far left and far right organizations, and to keep a "steady watch" on possible criminals, terrorists, or hijackers. Only at the extreme suggestion of having patriots check the records of ordinary American citizens does the mass public come out on the side of the right of privacy. The results regarding elite attitudes in these matters are somewhat more equivocal. In the OVS study, the opinion leaders are far more critical of the use of undercover methods and secret agents to spy on radicals; they strongly oppose surveillance or incarceration of suspected "disloyals" in time of

TABLE 5.3
The Right of Privacy: Police Surveillance Against Radicals and Criminals

	CLS			
	Mass Public	Community Leaders	Legal Elite	Police Officials
	(N=1993)	(N=1157)	(N=488)	(N=224)
When undercover police agents secretly join far right or far left political groups to keep an eye on them:				
—they are violating the rights of the group's members.	8%	11%	13%	0%
—they are only doing what is necessary to protect our society.	76	75	69	92
—Neither/Undecided	17	14	18	8
Do you think the government should keep a steady watch on people it believes may commit serious crimes, terrorist acts, or hijackings?				
—No, because it would violate the privacy of the individuals who have not yet committed any crime.	12	15	19	6
—Yes, because it may prevent innocent people from being hurt or killed.	75	72	65	90
—Neither/Undecided	12	13	15	4

	OVS	
	Mass Public	Opinion Leaders
	(N=938)	(N=845)
Is it:		
—a bad idea for the government to keep a list of people who take part in protest demonstrations.	25%	65%
—a good idea.	50	17
—Neither/Undecided	26	19
An American citizen:		
—is entitled to have his privacy respected, no matter what he believes.	72	88
—shouldn't mind having his record checked by patriotic groups.	21	7
—Neither/Undecided	8	5

	Harris and Westin*
	(N=1513)
When the police believe that members of an organization never convicted of a crime might engage in illegal acts in the future, do you think they should or should not be able, without a court order, to keep their movements under surveillance? To put undercover agents into the organization?	
Keep movements under surveillance:	
—should be able.	55%
—should not be able.	42
—Not sure.	3
Put undercover agents into the organization:	
—should be able.	48
—should not be able.	45
—Not sure.	6

*Adapted from Harris and Westin 1979.

war. However, in the CLS study, the community leaders and legal elite tend on the whole to side with the mass public on these matters.* Police officials, of course, overwhelmingly favor the use of covert methods to maintain surveillance over groups they consider dangerous.

Since clear norms have not yet developed in matters affecting surveillance of groups considered dangerous, the public is likely to regard criminals, political extremists, and potential enemy sympathizers as "fair game." They are people whose claims to privacy are severely weakened because they appear to have rejected the nation's values. Those who favor the use of informers, and other covert methods against groups engaged in crime or radical politics, appear, from their responses, to regard such forms of surveillance as proper activities undertaken by a prudent nation in order to protect its citizens and its institutions. Respondents who elect these answers are not likely to regard secret surveillance as unfair or illegal, but as essential to a sensible defense of the social order. Those who reject these methods are likely to consider them primarily as invasions of privacy that violate individual rights to autonomy of belief and the sanctity of the person.

In matters affecting the privacy of confidential personal records, most of our respondents show great concern. (See table 5.4.) Although bank records, school files, prison records, service records, and even tax returns enjoy only minimal protection in practice, the public—and to a significantly greater extent the elites—appear to feel strongly that the privacy of individual records (with some exceptions) ought not to be invaded.

Apart from fears about the excessive amounts and possible misuse of personal information collected by the Census Bureau, the Internal Revenue Service, banks, and credit bureaus, the public seems to be especially concerned about the use of computers. Fear of the computer as a threat to personal privacy has risen (according to the Harris poll) from 38 percent in 1974 to 54 percent in 1978. Harris and Westin also report that 80 percent of the public feel that computers have made it much easier to obtain confidential personal information about individuals—a view shared by 78 percent of the business employers in their survey. And almost two thirds of the public say that the use of computers must be sharply restricted in the future if privacy is to be preserved.

Data concerning questions of access and inviolability of personal

---

* These differences, we believe, can be attributed in part to the differences in the composition of the OVS and CLS elite samples.

records and documents are presented in table 5.4. Although school districts, for example, make student records available to prospective employers, juvenile courts, local police, the health department, the CIA, and the FBI (among others), almost two thirds of the general population and an even larger proportion of the elites would not permit school officials to release students' high school and college records without their consent. They also believe that students should be able to inspect their own school files to make sure that the information in them is correct (an attitude consistent with current federal law on this matter).

Bank records are also accessible to government for many purposes, both in practice and by statute. Large transactions, in fact, must be reported to the Treasury Department. The Internal Revenue Service has access to bank records, as do other agencies, so that clients cannot reasonably expect privacy in their financial dealings (Bostwick 1977). The public, however, feels strongly that bank records ought to be confidential, although it is rather evenly divided on the issue of making a person's credit rating available to his or her creditors. It is also opposed to any violations of the privacy of the mail, even if the persons sending or receiving the mail are suspected of engaging in illegal activities. While the public divides on the question of potential risks to the privacy of citizens that would arise if the government were to maintain a centralized data bank stored in computers, 43 percent of the community elites and 49 percent of the legal elites perceive such a development as endangering both liberty and privacy and would forbid it by law.

The one instance in which both the mass public and the elites would clearly violate the privacy of individual files concerns the availability of prison records, which they strongly believe ought to be made known to potential employers for their own protection. The same general lack of sympathy toward prisoners which we noted earlier is extended beyond the period of their imprisonment to the period of their release.

In considering the right of privacy, a word should also be said about the "right" of the government to keep certain types of information secret from the public. Existing law provides that once a document has been classified by the executive branch, the public cannot claim access to it. The doctrine of executive privilege, moreover, gives the executive branch the power in certain cases to withhold information from Congress, the judiciary, and the public (Bostwick 1977). Under the Freedom of Information Act, however, many kinds of information are

TABLE 5.4
The Right of Privacy: The Confidentiality of Records

	CLS			
	Mass Public	**Community Leaders**	**Legal Elite**	**Police Officials**
	(N=1993)	**(N=1157)**	**(N=488)**	**(N=224)**
A student's high school and college records should be released by school officials:				
—only with the consent of the student.	63%	77%	83%	57%
—to any government agencies or potential employers who ask to see them.	29	19	12	39
—Neither/Undecided	8	4	5	4
Should students have the right to inspect all records and letters of recommendation in their school files?				
—Yes, to make sure the information in them is correct.	66	67	73	69
—No, because otherwise the people who write the letters may not say what they really think.	20	22	19	19
—Neither/Undecided	15	10	9	12
Should government authorities be allowed to open the mail of people suspected of being in contact with fugitives?				
—No, it would violate a person's right to correspond with his friends.	50	55	57	34
—Yes, as it may help the police catch criminals they have been looking for.	31	28	22	46
—Neither/Undecided	20	17	21	21
A person's credit rating:				
—should not be given to anyone without his consent.	44	47	46	38
—should be made available to his creditors, since they stand to lose if he fails to pay his debts.	50	50	47	59
—Neither/Undecided	6	4	6	3
The use of computers by the government to maintain central records on the health, employment, housing, and income of private citizens:				
—is dangerous to individual liberty and privacy and should be forbidden by law.	33	43	49	29
—would help the government fight organized crime and provide emergency assistance and other services to people who need them.	31	23	21	34
—Neither/Undecided	36	34	31	37

TABLE 5.4 *(continued)*

	CLS			
	Mass Public	**Community Leaders**	**Legal Elite**	**Police Officials**
	(N=1993)	(N=1157)	(N=488)	(N=224)
When applying for a job, a person's prison record:				
—should be kept confidential since the ex-convict deserves a chance to make a fresh start.	28%	19%	14%	10%
—should be made available to potential employers since they are taking a risk.	52	63	70	80
—Neither/Undecided	19	18	16	10

	Harris and Westin*
	(N=1513)
For some years now the law has allowed people access to federal government files about themselves. Some government agencies complain that answering these requests is time-consuming and expensive. Do you feel that people should have access to their records even if it is costly for the government to provide this, or shouldn't they?	
—Should have.	85%
—Should not have.	8
—Not sure.	6
Should police be allowed to open the mail of the members of an organization never convicted of a crime, but whom they believe might engage in illegal acts in the future, without obtaining a court order?	
—Should not be allowed.	92
—Should be allowed.	7
—Not sure.	2
Should police be able to look into the bank records of members of an organization never convicted of a crime, but whom they believe might engage in illegal acts in the future, without obtaining a court order?	
—Should not be able to look into bank records.	81
—Should be able.	15
—Not sure.	4

*Adapted from Harris and Westin 1979.

now available upon request. Since 1977, under the so-called Sunshine Act, most federal regulatory agencies must also open their meetings to the public.

There seems little question, from the data available, that the public supports the right of the government to keep certain types of information secret, and, as can be seen in figure 5.2, it is prepared to punish those who violate the confidentiality of classified government documents. Both the mass public and the elites would, by margins of over two to one, fine or punish offenders, a finding that is also borne out by the Harris and Westin survey. Public concern for the privacy of confidential documents, thus, extends beyond individual records to those of the government itself.

As the foregoing suggests, the legislature, the courts, and the public recognize that privacy is, to some extent, a constitutional right and a form of freedom to be protected. Despite the Fourth Amendment and other constitutional provisions, it is, however, an emerging right and support for it is uneven and uncertain. It is strongly respected in some domains of privacy, but only weakly in others. When compared with such rights as freedom of speech and press (with which it is often in conflict), the right of privacy is distinctly subordinate. Although newspapers have on occasion been sued for publishing information on individuals that is considered private but not "newsworthy," the courts have generally upheld the right of the press to publish such information. This has almost invariably been the outcome when the persons involved are famous or prominent.

As we have previously indicated, the zone of intimate decision emphasizes individual autonomy and encompasses questions affecting freedom of lifestyle and current standards of morality and personal conduct. Our findings illustrate that whatever the public may think about particular issues within this zone, there is a marked preference (in the abstract at least) for conventional values and traditional modes of conduct.

As one can see in table 5.5, the mass public, by a ratio of two to one, wants our laws "to enforce the community's standards of right and wrong" rather than to "protect a citizen's right to live by any moral standards he chooses." Some 62 percent of the public want the community to adopt laws "to stamp out 'sin'—such as prostitution, gambling, pornography." While the majority do not view changes in lifestyle (such as "divorce, men and women living together without being married, coed dormitories in college) as signs of "moral decay"

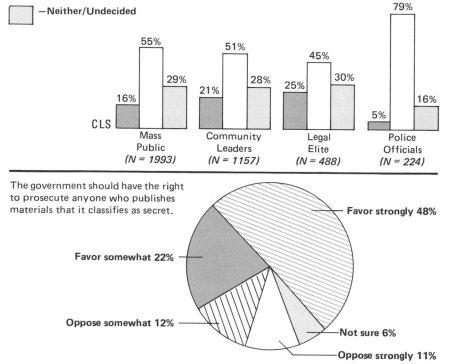

When a TV station reports secret information illegally taken from a government office:

▨ —it's just doing its job of informing the public.

☐ —the station owners should be fined or punished in some way for reporting such information.

▨ —Neither/Undecided

CLS

Mass Public
(N = 1993)
16% 55% 29%

Community Leaders
(N = 1157)
21% 51% 28%

Legal Elite
(N = 488)
25% 45% 30%

Police Officials
(N = 224)
5% 79% 16%

The government should have the right to prosecute anyone who publishes materials that it classifies as secret.

Favor strongly 48%

Favor somewhat 22%

Oppose somewhat 12%

Not sure 6%

Oppose strongly 11%

(Adapted from Harris and Westin, 1979; N = 1513)

FIGURE 5.2
The Privacy of Government Secrets
(CLS/Harris and Westin)

TABLE 5.5
The Right of Privacy: Attitudes Toward Prevailing Moral Standards

	CLS			
	Mass Public	**Community Leaders**	**Legal Elite**	**Police Officials**
	(N=1993)	(N=1157)	(N=488)	(N=224)
These days:				
—people have healthier and more relaxed ideas about sex.	42%	55%	63%	47%
—there is too much sexual freedom and loose living.	48	34	26	40
—Neither/Undecided	10	12	11	13
Would it be right for a community to adopt laws which try to stamp out "sin"—such as prostitution, gambling, pornography, etc?				
—Yes	62	48	31	62
—No	18	25	41	14
—It depends/Undecided	20	27	27	24

	OVS	
	Mass Public	**Opinion Leaders**
	(N=938)	(N=845)
Our laws should aim to:		
—protect a citizen's right to live by any moral standards he chooses.	23%	34%
—enforce the community's standards of right and wrong.	55	34
—Neither/Undecided	21	32

	Washington Post **Survey***
	(N=2505)
How do you feel about such changes in lifestyle as divorce, men and women living together without being married, coed dormitories in college, etc.? Generally speaking, are they a sign of increasing moral decay or that Americans are becoming more tolerant?	
—Americans becoming more tolerant	56%
—A sign of increasing moral decay	37
—Neither/Both	7

TABLE 5.5 (continued)

	Yankelovich, Skelly, and White[†]
Having to follow certain rules of behavior are really to the benefit of everyone.	
—Agree	72%
—Disagree	8
—No strong opinion	18
In recent years many of the traditional values toward such things as work, sexual morality and respect for authority have been questioned by those who think they no longer provide good guidelines on how to live and behave. Which statement about these traditional guidelines comes closest to your point of view?	
—Most are still useful	57
—Many are no longer useful	31
—Most are no longer useful	10

	Time/Yankelovich, Skelly, and White[‡]		
	Welcome	Reject	No Opinion
Many people feel we are undergoing a period of rapid social change and changes in people's values. Which of these changes would you welcome or reject?			
—More emphasis on traditional family ties	84%	4%	13%
—More emphasis on religious beliefs	67	9	24
—More acceptance of sexual freedom	21	46	23

* Adapted from _Washington Post_, November 1979.
† Adapted from Yankelovich, Skelly, and White 1978.
‡ Adapted from _Time_/Yankelovich, Skelly, and White, March 1978.

(56 percent say these changes show that Americans are becoming more tolerant), they nevertheless prefer traditional values as "guidelines on how to live and behave." Some 72 percent believe that "having to follow certain rules of behavior are really to the benefit of everyone," while 84 percent would welcome more emphasis on "traditional family ties" and 67 percent would like to see more emphasis on the value of religious beliefs. By contrast, only 21 percent would welcome "more acceptance of sexual freedom."

The data from the CLS study indicate that almost half the general population believe that at present "there is too much sexual freedom and loose living." The community leaders and the legal elites, being somewhat more cosmopolitan, are more inclined to believe that the ideas people have about sex today are "healthier and more relaxed." Note that these responses reflect *attitudes* toward shifting moral standards rather than a desire to either tolerate or suppress them. Nevertheless, they do provide some insights into the public's general orientation toward certain emerging liberties which affect lifestyles.

In keeping with the ambivalence exhibited by the courts and other government agencies, the public's attitudes toward sexual conduct and related matters (for example, nudity and topless dancing) reflect both tolerance and intolerance. In the abstract, as is evident in tables 5.6 and 5.7, a large majority (72 percent to 79 percent) of the American people now say that freedom of sexual conduct between adults (especially heterosexual conduct) should be left to the individuals themselves rather than regulated by law. A majority of 59 percent no longer regard premarital sex as wrong—a 36 percent rise in a period of nine years. Some 78 percent would regard it as an invasion of privacy to publish the details of "an extramarital affair that a public official is having with another person." Another 78 percent would consider it an invasion of privacy for the press to publish a photograph of "a well-known politician entering a pornographic book shop" (Harris and Westin 1979). Some 61 percent of the mass public, and an even higher proportion of the legal and community elite, believe that birth control devices should be available to teenagers "if they want them." And, surprisingly, over two thirds of American adults approve of sex education in the schools.

It seems clear that, in general, support for freedom of sexual conduct has been increasing and, depending upon the issue, often receives the majority's endorsement. Nevertheless, the public continues to feel that other forms of sexual conduct, disapproved of in the past, are still "morally wrong." Although premarital sex is rapidly gaining acceptance, extramarital sex continues to be considered wrong by 87 percent of the public. (See table 5.7.) Some 82 percent consider infidelity among married women to be wrong. The parallel figure for married men is 79 percent. Although the majority believe that birth control devices should be available to teenagers (table 5.6), some 66 percent regard sexual relations among teenagers as wrong.

If we turn to the responses to questions about some of the specific forms of sexual freedom, such as homosexuality, we find evidence of the same ambivalence we witnessed in the data on sexual freedom in general. Once again, the public's responses appear to reflect, in part at

TABLE 5.6
The Right of Privacy: Sexual Freedom

	CLS			
	Mass Public	**Community Leaders**	**Legal Elite**	**Police Officials**
	(N=1993)	(N=1157)	(N=488)	(N=224)
Birth control devices:				
—should be available to teenagers if they want them.	61%	68%	79%	63%
—should be kept from teenagers since they are too young to handle sexual matters sensibly.	20	13	8	14
—Neither/Undecided	19	19	13	23

	OVS	
	Mass Public	**Opinion Leaders**
	(N=938)	(N=845)
Freedom in sexual conduct between adults should be:		
—left up to the individuals.	72%	88%
—regulated by law.	14	4
—Neither/Undecided	14	8

	Harris and Westin*
	(N=1513)
How should heterosexual relations between unmarried adults be treated? Should they be:	
—left to the individual.	79%
—allowed but regulated by law.	3
—totally forbidden by law.	13
Not sure	5
Would you consider it an invasion of privacy or not for a newspaper or television to publish the details of an extramarital affair that a public official is having with another person?	
—Yes, an invasion of privacy	78
—No, not an invasion of privacy	19
—Not sure	3

	Nunn et al[+]
	(N=3454)
Do you approve or disapprove of teaching about sex in the schools?	
—Approve and would allow	67%
—Disapprove but would allow	5
—Disapprove but would allow with qualifications	8
—Disapprove and definitely would not allow	20

	Gallup Organization and NORC[‡]	
	Not Wrong	**Wrong**
If a man and a woman have sex relations before marriage, do you think it is always or sometimes wrong, or not wrong at all?		
—1978	59%	41%
—1972	51	49
—1969	23	77

*Adapted from Harris and Westin 1979.
[+] Computed from Nunn et al 1978, table 9.
[‡] Adapted from Gallup Organization 1969; NORC 1980, p. 28.

TABLE 5.7
The Right of Privacy: Attitudes Toward the Morality of Sexual Freedom

	CLS			
	Mass Public	**Community Leaders**	**Legal Elite**	**Police Officials**
	(N=1993)	(N=1157)	(N=488)	(N=224)
Television programs that show people actually making love:				
—should be permitted as long as they are shown in the late evening, during adult viewing hours.	30%	31%	42%	24%
—should not be allowed on TV at all.	57	54	44	61
—Neither/Undecided	13	15	14	15

	NORC*	
	Not Wrong	Wrong
What is your opinion about a *married* person having sexual relations with someone *other* than the marriage partner. Is it generally wrong or not wrong?		
—1977	13%	87%
—1976	15	84
—1974	13	86
—1973	16	84

	Yankelovich, Skelly, and White	
	Not a Moral Issue	Morally Wrong
Which of the following activities do you feel are morally wrong from your own personal point of view—and which do you feel are not a moral issue?[+]		
—Infidelity among married women	18%	82%
—Infidelity among married men	21	79
—Sexual relations among teenagers	34	66

	Acceptable	Unacceptable
Which of the following activities do you consider *acceptable* or *unacceptable*, at least for other people if not for yourself?[‡]		
—Nude bathing beaches	37%	63%
—Male nudity in movies	39	61
—Female nudity in movies	44	56
—Topless waitresses in nightclubs	47	53
—Open discussion of sex on television	56	44

* Adapted from NORC 1980.
+ Adapted from 1978 Study.
‡ Adapted from 1977 Study.

least, the current uncertainty of the legal and social norms concerning homosexuality. Doubtless the inconsistencies that turn up in the data on the tolerance of freedom for homosexuals reflect these uncertainties. The items in table 5.8 indicate that homosexuality, for the most

TABLE 5.8
The Public's Perception of Homosexuals

	CLS			
	Mass Public	**Community Leaders**	**Legal Elite**	**Police Officials**
	(N=1993)	(N=1157)	(N=488)	(N=224)
Homosexuals should be understood as people who:				
—have simply chosen a different sexual life style.	41%	44%	46%	29%
—are sick and need help.	42	37	31	52
—Neither/Undecided	16	19	23	19
Certain groups are considered harmful to the country, and others beneficial. How would you describe your own feelings about Gay Liberation (Homosexual) Groups? Do you believe they are mostly harmful or mostly beneficial to the country?				
—Mostly harmful	38	29	23	46
—Obnoxious but not harmful	44	49	47	48
—Mostly beneficial	7	14	17	2
—Undecided	11	8	14	4
When I see a homosexual couple embracing or walking hand in hand:				
—it doesn't really upset me.	21	23	29	13
—I must admit it bothers me.	68	69	65	83
—Neither/Undecided	11	8	7	4

	Time/Yankelovich, Skelly, and White*
How do you feel about homosexual relations between consenting adults?	
—Not a moral issue	42%
—Morally wrong	58

	NORC[†]
How do you feel about sexual relations between two adults of the same sex?	
—Not a moral issue	22%
—Morally wrong	78

* *Time*/Yankelovich, Skelly and White 1977–78.
[†] NORC 1980.

202

part, is still strongly disapproved and regarded as morally wrong (in one survey, by 78 percent of the population). Some 42 percent of the general public continue to regard homosexuals as "sick" rather than as people who have merely chosen an alternative sexual preference.

These evaluations carry over to the views many people hold on questions of civil liberties for gays (see figure 5.3). Half the population do not think that complete equality for homosexuals in teaching and other public jobs is a good idea. A surprisingly large number (58 percent) would deny to gay liberation movements the use of the community's auditorium to promote homosexual rights. (Once again, the elites, and specifically the legal elites, are more inclined to honor this First Amendment right.) Approximately half the general public would also prohibit homosexual bars, with the elites again more willing to permit such establishments. Only one third of the public would allow lesbian mothers to retain custody of their own children (a third would not permit it and the remainder are undecided). On the controversial, highly charged question of the legal right of gays to marry one another, the opinion among all groups is strongly negative.

Yet when the public is asked whether "homosexual relations in private between consenting adults" should be left to the individual or forbidden by law, they strongly express the view that they should be left to the individual and are beyond the majority's control. Thus, they are saying, in effect, that sexual preference is a private matter and ought not to be forbidden or regulated by the state, however "immoral" it may seem (figure 5.4). A majority of respondents also regard it as consistent with "the American ideal of human rights for all" to adopt local ordinances that assure gays equality in jobs and housing—a response, in our view, that expresses once again the general desire to be "fair" in the treatment of citizens. Elements of the same motivation may also be present in the willingness to allow a lesbian elementary school teacher to continue teaching "because sexual preference should not be a ground for dismissal"—this despite the belief that "complete equality" for homosexuals in teaching and other public service jobs is not considered a good idea.

In any event, homosexual rights offer another example of emerging (rather than settled) liberties, and hence give rise to a number of incongruities, if not outright inconsistencies, in both the legal standing and popular beliefs regarding homosexual conduct. From all appearances, we are witnessing substantial changes in the way homosexuality is legally and popularly perceived and, as a result, in the civil liberties

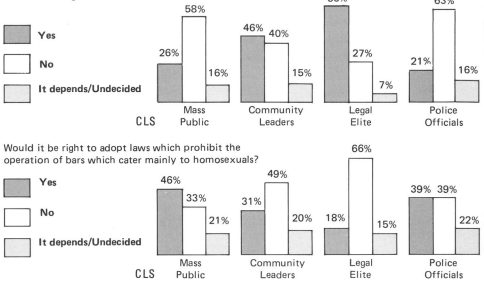

Should a community allow its auditorium to be used by gay liberation movements to organize for homosexual rights?

- Yes
- No
- It depends/Undecided

CLS

	Mass Public	Community Leaders	Legal Elite	Police Officials
Yes	26%	46%	66%	21%
No	58%	40%	27%	63%
It depends/Undecided	16%	15%	7%	16%

Would it be right to adopt laws which prohibit the operation of bars which cater mainly to homosexuals?

- Yes
- No
- It depends/Undecided

CLS

	Mass Public	Community Leaders	Legal Elite	Police Officials
Yes	46%	31%	18%	39%
No	33%	49%	66%	39%
It depends/Undecided	21%	20%	15%	22%

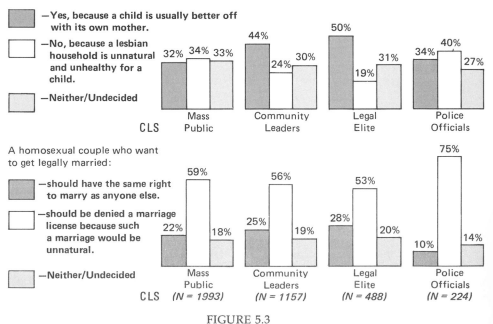

Should lesbian mothers be allowed to have custody of their own children?

- —Yes, because a child is usually better off with its own mother.
- —No, because a lesbian household is unnatural and unhealthy for a child.
- —Neither/Undecided

CLS

	Mass Public	Community Leaders	Legal Elite	Police Officials
Yes	32%	44%	50%	34%
No	34%	24%	19%	40%
Neither/Undecided	33%	30%	31%	27%

A homosexual couple who want to get legally married:

- —should have the same right to marry as anyone else.
- —should be denied a marriage license because such a marriage would be unnatural.
- —Neither/Undecided

CLS

	Mass Public (N = 1993)	Community Leaders (N = 1157)	Legal Elite (N = 488)	Police Officials (N = 224)
same right	22%	25%	28%	10%
denied	59%	56%	53%	75%
Neither/Undecided	18%	19%	20%	14%

FIGURE 5.3
Privacy and the Denial of Homosexual Rights
(CLS/*Time*/Yankelovich, Skelly, and White)

What would you do if a homosexual teacher was fired because of his or her sexual preference?

—Nothing, since I favor the action.

—Would not get involved since my actions wouldn't matter anyway.

—I would contribute money, write letters, have petitions signed.

—I would join an organization, protest march, attend rallies, etc.

—I'm undecided what I would do.

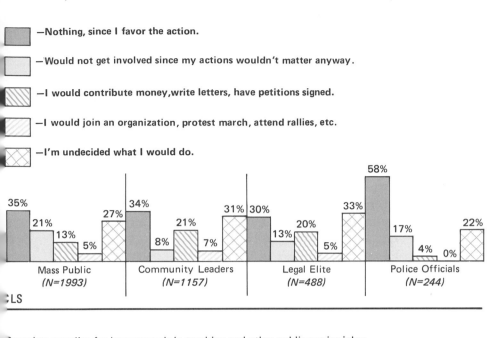

| Mass Public (N=1993) | Community Leaders (N=1157) | Legal Elite (N=488) | Police Officials (N=244) |

CLS

Complete equality for homosexuals in teaching and other public service jobs:

—should be protected by law.

—may sound fair but is not really a good idea.

—Neither/Undecided

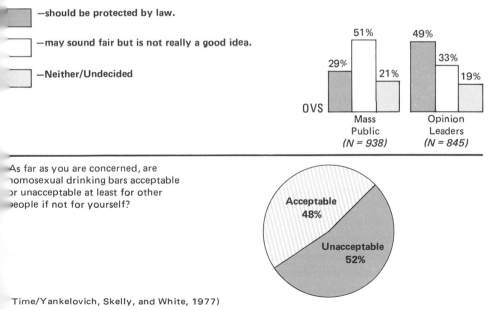

OVS

Mass Public (N = 938)   Opinion Leaders (N = 845)

As far as you are concerned, are homosexual drinking bars acceptable or unacceptable at least for other people if not for yourself?

Acceptable 48%

Unacceptable 52%

Time/Yankelovich, Skelly, and White, 1977)

For the most part, local ordinances that guarantee equal rights to homosexuals in such matters as jobs and housing:

- —uphold the American ideal of human rights for all.
- —damage American moral standards.
- —Neither/ Undecided

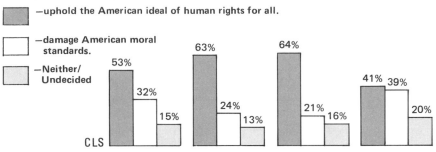

If it is discovered that an elementary school teacher is a lesbian:

- —she should be able to go on teaching because sexual preference should not be a ground for dismissal.
- —she should not be allowed to continue teaching.
- —Neither/ Undecided

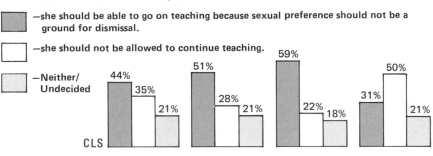

Suppose the majority gets a law passed making homosexuality a crime. Should homosexuals be fined or arrested?

- —No, because a person's sexual preference is a private matter beyond the majority's wishes.
- —Yes, because the majority has the right to decide the kind of society it wants.
- —Neither/ Undecided

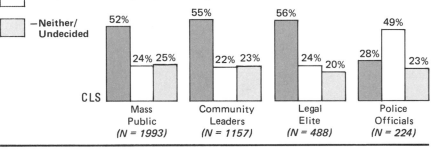

How should homosexual relations in private between consenting adults be treated? Should it be:

Allowed but regulated by law 5%

Totally forbidden by law 20%

Left to the individual 70%

Not sure 5%

(Adapted from Harris and Westin, 1979; *N = 1512*)

FIGURE 5.4
The Privacy of Homosexual Preferences
(CLS/Harris and Westin)

homosexuals enjoy. As usual, these changes appear to be developing most rapidly among opinion leaders and other elite groups, with the exception, as usual, of police officials, whose attitudes toward homosexual rights are, on the whole, even more critical than those of the mass public. In general, however, legislatures, courts, and the public appear to be moving toward the view that a person ought to have control of his or her own body and, in keeping with Mill's principle, that government should regulate the behavior of competent adults only if it demonstrably threatens "the rights, safety, or interests of others." (Cf. Lister 1970.)

If the public's attitudes toward homosexuality and freedom of sexual conduct are mixed, their views on such sexually related forms of expression as pornography and obscenity are preponderantly negative. Our findings concerning the freedom to possess, exhibit, or distribute pornographic materials reflect to some extent the uncertainty of the popular norms regarding this zone of intimate decision, as well as the antagonism predominant in the law toward obscenity and pornography. The data in table 5.9 indicate that a large part of the public consid-

TABLE 5.9

The Right of Privacy: The Distribution of Pornographic Materials

	CLS			
	Mass Public	**Community Leaders**	**Legal Elite**	**Police Officials**
	(N=1993)	**(N=1157)**	**(N=488)**	**(N=224)**
Selling pornographic films, books, and magazines:				
—is really a victimless crime and should therefore be left unregulated.	23%	31%	46%	14%
—lowers the community's moral standards and therefore victimizes everyone.	58	52	33	66
—Neither/Undecided	19	17	22	21
	NORC*			
Which of these statements comes closest to your feelings about pornography laws?				
—There should be laws against the distribution of pornography whatever the age.	43%			
—There should be laws against distribution to persons under 18.	49			
—There should be no laws against the distribution of pornography.	7			

* NORC 1980.

207

ers the selling of pornographic films, books, and magazines as clearly harmful to community standards, rather than as "victimless crimes" that ought not to be regulated by law. The public is joined in this view by the community leaders as well as the police. Many Americans find pornography so offensive that they would prohibit the distribution of pornographic material not only to the young, but to people of all ages.

Much the same antipathy to pornography is evident in the popular responses to the publication of books that are considered "obscene" or that describe explicit sexual conduct. (See table 5.10.) The response to these items demonstrate the public's concern for the protection of community standards, and the willingness of a large proportion of the American people (48 percent) to ban from high school libraries novels "that describe explicit sex acts." In the many cases that have been fought through the courts on the issue of book censorship, the would-

TABLE 5.10
The Right of Privacy: Censorship of Pornographic Publications

	CLS			
	Mass Public	**Community Leaders**	**Legal Elite**	**Police Officials**
	(N=1993)	(N=1157)	(N=488)	(N=224)
Censoring obscene books:				
—is an old-fashioned idea that no longer makes sense.	29%	39%	54%	21%
—is necessary to protect community standards.	50	40	26	61
—Neither/Undecided	21	21	20	18
Novels that describe explicit sex acts:				
—should be permitted in the library if they are worthwhile literature.	42	57	73	39
—have no place in a high school library and should be banned.	48	35	20	49
—Neither/Undecided	10	8	7	12
	Harris and Westin*			
	(N=1513)			
How should we treat the selling of pornographic books and magazines in bookstores?				
—Should be left to the individual	24%			
—Should be allowed but regulated by law	30			
—Should be totally forbidden by law	44			
—Not sure	2			

* Adapted from Harris and Westin 1979.

be censors as well as some judges have expressed their eagerness to protect the community, and especially the young, from material that appeals to "prurient interest"—defined in *Roth* v. *United States* (354 U.S. 476, 1957) as "a shameful or morbid interest in nudity, sex or excretion."

By way of further controlling the distribution of "obscene" books or magazines, 44 percent of the mass public endorse the authority of the Postmaster General to bar them from the mails. Power to restrict the circulation through the mails of literature and pictures that are "obscene, lewd, or lascivious," or "filthy" and "indecent," or designed to give information for "preventing conception or producing abortion"—was authorized in the Comstock Act of 1873 (Worton 1975c). With some modifications, the Comstock Act is still in effect, and the Postmaster General still retains the power to restrict the distribution of obscene or pornographic materials from the mails—subject, however, to judicial review.

The public also continues to harbor anxieties about the character of the films that are shown in movie theaters, as illustrated by the data in table 5.11. An individual's right to view a film containing pornographic materials is seen by 43 percent of the public as a matter to be determined by the community. Only 38 percent of the general population believe that "people should be allowed to see anything they want to, no matter how 'filthy' it is." Some two thirds regard pornography in movies as "morally wrong," and approximately half the population would ban such films entirely. Movies that portray open sexual relations are perceived as especially "unacceptable" and the showing of nudity is only somewhat less so. A majority of adult Americans would not allow X-rated movies to be shown at all, and they are unwilling to dismiss such films as merely distasteful and essentially harmless. Hence, although the courts have gradually (although only recently) declared their general, though qualified, opposition to the censoring of films, the public lags behind.

Despite the legal roadblocks set up by the Supreme Court against prior censorship, the possibility of censoring motion pictures has not been eliminated entirely, and there is still a certain amount of ambiguity attached to the right to portray on film various forms of conduct regarded as "obscene." Some of this uncertainty is evident in the data on film censorship, although the preponderant sentiment (except among the legal elites) remains critical of the notion that the films people choose to see are their own business. For large segments of the

TABLE 5.11
The Right of Privacy: Censorship of Pornographic Films

	CLS			
	Mass Public	**Community Leaders**	**Legal Elite**	**Police Officials**
	(N=1993)	**(N=1157)**	**(N=488)**	**(N=224)**
When it comes to pornographic films about sex:				
—people should be allowed to see anything they want to, no matter how "filthy" it is.	38%	43%	56%	29%
—the community should set the standards for what people are allowed to see.	43	40	29	54
—Neither/Undecided	18	17	15	17

	OVS	
	Mass Public	**Opinion Leaders**
	(N=938)	**(N=845)**
How do you feel about movies that use foul language or show nudity and sexual acts on the screen?		
—they have as much right to be shown as other films.	35%	50%
—they should be banned.	49	23
—Neither/Undecided	17	27

	Time/Yankelovich, Skelly, and White*	
	Acceptable	**Unacceptable**
As far as you are concerned, do you feel the following activities are acceptable or unacceptable, at least for other people even if not for yourself?		
—Pornographic movies as long as they are X-rated	43%	57%
—Open sexual relations in adult only movies	32	68
—Male nudity in movies	39	61
—Female nudity in movies	44	56
Do you feel that pornography in movies is morally wrong or not?		
—Not morally wrong	34%	
—Morally wrong	67	

	Nunn et al[†]
	(N=3371)
Do you approve or disapprove of showing X-rated movies?	
—Approve and would allow	27%
—Disapprove but would allow	10
—Disapprove but would allow with qualifications	6
—Disapprove and definitely would not allow	56

* Adapted from *Time*/Yankelovich et al. 1977.
† Computed from Nunn et al. 1978, Table 9.

population, the showing of a film is a public event with substantial public consequences for moral conduct. Hence, films are in their view a fit subject for regulation.

Although the public retains fairly severe attitudes toward freedom of sexual conduct and its depiction in the media, the prevailing attitude toward prostitution (ordinarily considered a crime in the United States)* is comparatively permissive. (See table 5.12.) By a margin of almost five to three, the mass public would prefer to license and regulate prostitution rather than arrest the people who engage in it. The majority of the general public also believe that the decision to engage in prostitution should be either left to the individual or allowed but regulated by law, and 37 percent would legally forbid it. Most people appear to believe that prostitution is essentially a private matter involving sexual activity between consenting adults rather than an activity heavily invested with public significance. In keeping with this view, approximately half the population also consider it an invasion of privacy to publish the names of men who have been arrested for soliciting prostitutes. And in a classic conflict between the rights of privacy and freedom of the press, approximately half the general population (though not the elites) would forbid, as "an invasion of privacy," the photographing of a famous person entering a house of prostitution.

It is not surprising that the public's predominant attitude toward prostitution is one of resigned acceptance, if not actual tolerance. Few respondents, we believe, would regard prostitution as a *right* or as a form of freedom that enjoys constitutional protection. Many, however, obviously view it as essentially a personal matter, at worst a "victimless crime," that ought to be left to private, individual decision. It is a matter in which a woman ought to be free to determine the use of her own body. To some extent, no doubt, this tendency to abide prostitution results from its familiarity and persistence as an institution. Although it is scarcely a socially approved form of conduct, neither does it strike the majority as especially dangerous. Most people seem inclined rather to treat it with a certain levity as a form of conduct best assigned to the zone of private decision.

The same levity and tendency to tolerate what is perceived as a benign form of human eccentricity is not so apparent in matters relating to privacy and the counterculture. Such data as we have collected on these matters tend to reflect the absence of clear norms. On some

---

*Only Nevada has legalized prostitution, and then only for certain counties. Some Arizona counties also permit prostitution.

TABLE 5.12
Prostitution and the Right of Privacy

	CLS			
	Mass Public	**Community Leaders**	**Legal Elite**	**Police Officials**
	(N=1993)	**(N=1157)**	**(N=488)**	**(N=224)**
In dealing with prostitution, the government should:				
—license and regulate it.	47%	49%	61%	49%
—arrest or fine the people who have anything to do with it.	30	25	15	34
—Neither/Undecided	23	26	23	17
If a news photographer takes pictures of a famous person entering a house of prostitution, publishing the photos should be:				
—permitted under the guarantees of a free press.	34	45	58	41
—forbidden as an invasion of privacy.	49	37	29	44
—Neither/Undecided	17	18	13	15

	Harris and Westin*
	(N=1512)
How should we treat engaging in prostitution? Should it be:	
—Left to the individual	35%
—Allowed but regulated by law	24
—Totally forbidden by law	37
—Not sure	4
How do you regard publication by a newspaper of the names of men who have been arrested for soliciting prostitutes?	
—An invasion of privacy	49
—Not an invasion of privacy	47
—Not sure	4

	Time/Yankelovich, Skelly, and White[†]
As far as you are concerned, is the use of massage parlors acceptable or unacceptable at least for other people if not for yourself?	
—Acceptable	36%
—Unacceptable	64

* Adapted from Harris and Westin 1979.
[†] Time/Yankelovich et al. 1977.

questions the public supports unconventional lifestyles and on others it does not. It is clear from table 5.13 that hippies are not popular with the mass public, which tends to view them as lazy and unwilling to work. It also believes that a community has a right to adopt laws that would prevent hippies from moving in. On the other hand, the majority of the public do not feel it is morally wrong for couples to live together without marriage, providing they do not have children who will remain illegitimate. And, surprisingly, neither the public nor the elites favor the dismissal of a school teacher who lives with a man to whom she is not married.

The use of marijuana, though now widely practiced, is still associated in the minds of many citizens with the counterculture. Whether so regarded or not, the growth, sale, possession, or smoking of marijuana continues to be prohibited by law in most communities in the United States. Like the laws against prostitution and pornography, however, the legal prohibitions against the use of marijuana are often only sporadically and halfheartedly enforced in many places, though a greater effort is made to prevent its growth and sale. In any event, there can be no question, given the data in table 5.14, that the use of marijuana is still widely disapproved by the mass public. The majority regard it as "unacceptable" or "morally wrong" and favor the adoption of laws which would fine or otherwise punish people who grow, sell, or smoke marijuana. As many as 69 percent continue to oppose its legalization. The norms, however, appear to be changing. The number of people who would legalize its use has increased steadily over the past decade (see table 5.14). Most respondents would leave it to the individual to decide whether or not to smoke marijuana in a private residence. To this extent, at least, the use of marijuana is regarded as a private matter, not to be regulated or forbidden by law. It seems a fair assumption that, as with alcohol, the use of marijuana will increasingly come to be perceived as a matter of personal choice and for all practical purposes a right protected under the constitutional laws of privacy. The same prediction seems appropriate for other matters of lifestyle, such as sexual freedom among unmarried consenting adults, cohabitation without marriage, homosexuality, and the publication of pornography. All these matters are so indifferently and erratically enforced (if indeed they are enforced at all) that eventually statutes and court decisions are bound to reflect reality and practice more closely and thus transform prohibited forms of behavior into protected forms of private conduct.

Some of the forms of "private" conduct we have considered, such

TABLE 5.13
Privacy and the Counterculture

	CLS			
	Mass Public	**Community Leaders**	**Legal Elite**	**Police Officials**
	(N=1993)	**(N=1157)**	**(N=488)**	**(N=224)**
Most young people who "drop out" or become "hippies":				
—are trying to tell us something important about what's wrong with our society.	23%	28%	21%	10%
—are lazy, spoiled, and don't want to work.	47	32	36	54
—Neither/Undecided	30	40	43	36
Would it be right to adopt laws which prevent "hippies" and "street people" from moving into the community?				
—Yes	44	30	19	39
—No	26	41	62	28
—It depends/Undecided	30	29	18	33
Would it be right to adopt laws which dismiss a school teacher who lives with a man to whom she is not married?				
—Yes	26	22	14	18
—No	56	60	71	58
—It depends/Undecided	19	18	14	24
	Time/**Yankelovich, Skelly, and White**			
Do you feel that it is, or is not, morally wrong for couples to live together who are not married? *				
—Not morally wrong	54%			
—Morally wrong	46			
Do you feel that it is, or is not, morally wrong for people to decide to have children even though they are not legally married and don't intend to be? [†]				
—Not morally wrong	32			
—Morally wrong	68			

* Adapted from 1977 study.
[†] Adapted from 1978 study.

TABLE 5.14
Privacy and the Use of Marijuana

	CLS			
	Mass Public	**Community Leaders**	**Legal Elite**	**Police Officials**
	(N=1993)	**(N=1157)**	**(N=488)**	**(N=224)**
Would it be right for a community to adopt laws which punish people severely for selling or growing marijuana?				
—Yes	52%	37%	23%	59%
—No	28	37	57	16
—It depends/Undecided	19	27	19	25
Would it be right for a community to adopt laws which impose fines for smoking marijuana?				
—Yes	53	43	43	74
—No	28	34	41	11
—It depends/Undecided	19	23	16	14

	Gallup Organization and NORC*	
	Yes, Legalize	**No, don't Legalize**
Do you think the use of marijuana should be made legal or not?		
—1978	31%	69%
—1975	21	79
—1973	18	82
—1969	13	88

	Time/Yankelovich, Skelly, and White[†]
Do you feel that it is, or is not, morally wrong to use marijuana?	
—Not morally wrong	46%
—Morally wrong	54
How do you feel about the use of marijuana—do you regard it as acceptable or unacceptable at least for other people even if not for yourself?	
—Acceptable	47
—Unacceptable	53

	Harris and Westin[‡]
	(N=1512)
How should we treat the smoking of marijuana in a private residence? Should it be	
—left to the individual	55%
—allowed but regulated by law	14
—totally forbidden by law	29
—Not sure	2

* Adapted from Gallup Organization 1969; NORC 1980.
[†] Adapted from *Time*/Yankelovich et al. 1977:
[‡] Adapted from Harris and Westin 1978.

as homosexuality, prostitution, and the use of marijuana, extend the zone of intimate decision to include the individual's right to control the use of his or her own body, providing one does not threaten or harm others. Two civil liberties issues that involve autonomy over the use of one's body have been emerging with increasing frequency: euthanasia and abortion. Euthanasia, though by no means a new idea, has only recently emerged as a legal and social question to be taken seriously. Does one have a "right to die" if one is afflicted with an agonizing terminal illness or has suffered an irreparable injury to the brain that has permanently destroyed consciousness? Does the victim in such cases have the right to have his or her physician or guardian stop treatment—in effect, to choose death rather than to prolong life for its own sake? There is surprisingly strong support (see table 5.15) among both the mass public and the elites for the right to withdraw life-prolonging treatment at the request of the victim or the victim's family, when the attending physicians see no chance of recovery. This opinion is in keeping with the major court decision on this question concerning Karen Quinlan, in which the New Jersey Supreme Court found that the father of an incurably comatose daughter had the right to order her life-support systems disconnected. Bills permitting euthanasia have

TABLE 5.15
Privacy and the Right to Die (CLS)

	Mass Public	Community Leaders	Legal Elite	Police Officials
	(N=1993)	(N=1157)	(N=488)	(N=224)
If an accident victim suffers hopeless brain damage and the doctors agree she can never again regain consciousness:				
—the victim's family should have the right to stop any treatment that helps keep her alive.	73%	83%	80%	77%
—treatment should be continued because human life is sacred and must be preserved as long as possible.	13	8	8	14
—Neither/Undecided	14	9	12	9
A person who has no chance whatever to recover from painful terminal illness:				
—should have the right to die when he or she chooses.	59	66	81	66
—unfortunately must wait until life naturally runs out.	30	26	12	28
—Neither/Undecided	11	8	8	7

been introduced in some state legislatures, but in most states euthanasia continues to be a crime, although very few doctors, in fact, have been prosecuted for covertly practicing it (Bostwick 1977). At any rate, the right of the victim to terminate a hopeless illness has come increasingly to be considered by legal scholars and civil libertarians as a privacy right, and we may assume that the New Jersey decision in the Quinlan case will eventually be extended to other states, especially in light of the public's view of this matter.

Although a woman's freedom to have an abortion has presumably been resolved by the Court, the right must still be considered an emerging one. Table 5.16 indicates that the majority of the general population, and an even larger proportion of the elites, believe that having an abortion is a matter for individual decision (in effect, a privacy right); that a woman should be free to have an abortion if she wishes; and that, unfortunate though it may be, it is sometimes "best for all concerned." On what is perhaps the most difficult question in the table, some 48 percent would leave the abortion decision entirely up to the woman herself, while 40 percent would prohibit abortion except in extreme cases such as rape or danger to the mother's life.

However, a few surveys have turned up findings in which the majority (though not a large one) would deny the right of an abortion even to a married woman who wants no more children, and an abortion for this reason is (in one survey) considered by 57 percent of the population as "morally wrong." (See table 5.17.) Furthermore, our own CLS study finds that despite the public's expressed belief that abortion should be left "entirely up to the woman," some 47 percent nevertheless say that the father should have a legal right to prevent the abortion if he wishes, since it is his child, too.

To what extent these variations in response reflect question wording and variations in the survey methods employed is impossible to say. Part of the inconsistency, no doubt, results from the historical recency of the abortion issue and its judicial resolution. Some of the uncertainty encountered in the data reflects the highly sensitive and still controversial nature of the abortion question as such, involving as it does powerful religious beliefs, disputes about the point at which an embryo should be considered a "person," and the moral and psychological uneasiness felt by some women about terminating an embryo to which their own bodies have given life. Although, as we have said, the preponderant opinion supports the Court's ruling upholding the right of abortion, sufficient time has not yet elapsed to permit a norm to

217

TABLE 5.16
Privacy and the Right to Abortion

	CLS			
	Mass Public	**Community Leaders**	**Legal Elite**	**Police Officials**
	(N=1993)	**(N=1157)**	**(N=488)**	**(N=224)**
Having an abortion for any reason is:				
—unfortunate, but sometimes best for all concerned.	65%	77%	79%	72%
—like murder, and should be legally prohibited.	23	13	10	16
—Neither/Undecided	13	10	12	12
Abortion during the early weeks of pregnancy should be:				
—left entirely up to the woman.	48	57	65	48
—prohibited except in such extreme cases as rape, the risk of a deformed child, or danger to the mother's life.	40	28	22	38
—Neither/Undecided	12	16	13	14
Birth control devices:				
—should be available to teenagers if they want them.	61	68	78	63
—should be kept from teenagers since they are too young to handle sexual matters sensibly.	20	13	8	14
—Neither/Undecided	19	19	13	23

	OVS	
	Mass Public	**Opinion Leaders**
	(N=938)	**(N=845)**
The right of a woman to have an abortion during the early weeks of pregnancy should be:		
—left entirely up to her.	67%	80%
—severely limited by law.	24	11
—Neither/Undecided	10	9

	Harris and Westin*
	(N=1513)
Having an abortion should be:	
—left to the individual.	59%
—allowed but regulated by law.	17
—totally forbidden by law.	21
—Not sure.	3

	NBC News/AP⁺	
	Yes	**No**
Do you believe that every woman who wants an abortion should be able to have one?		
—1979	56%	44%
—October 1978	59	41
—August 1978	59	41

* Adapted from Harris and Westin 1979.
⁺ Survey by NBC News/AP 1978–79.

TABLE 5.17
Resistance to the Right to Abortion

	CLS			
	Mass Public	**Community Leaders**	**Legal Elite**	**Police Officials**
	(N=1993)	**(N=1157)**	**(N=488)**	**(N=224)**
If a pregnant woman wants an abortion and the father of the child objects, should he have a legal right to prevent it?				
—No, the decision should be entirely the woman's.	31%	40%	43%	29%
—Yes, it's his child too, after all.	47	37	36	46
—Neither/Undecided	22	24	22	25
If a woman on welfare becomes pregnant and wants an abortion, should the government pay for it?				
—Yes she should not be penalized for being poor.	36	52	60	38
—No, it would be an improper use of our federal tax money.	45	33	29	44
—Neither/Undecided	19	15	11	18

	Gallup Organization and NORC [*]	
	Yes	**No**
Should abortion be legal if a woman is married and wants no more children?		
—1978	40%	60%
—1975	46	54
—1972	40	60
—1969	15	85

	***Time*/Yankelovich, Skelly, and White** [†]
In your opinion, is having an abortion because no more children are wanted morally wrong or not?	
—Not morally wrong	43%
—Morally wrong	57

[*] Adapted from Gallup Organization 1969; NORC 1980.
[†] *Time*/Yankelovich et al. 1978.

crystallize. Since the issues surrounding abortion (and especially abortion and the right of privacy) are complex, and the roots of moral and psychological resistance deep, a fair amount of social learning is required to embrace the idea of "abortion on demand." As our data make plain, the civil libertarian norms, in this as in so many instances, are most quickly and firmly learned by opinion leaders and other elites, who more often encounter and reflect upon the kinds of arguments that led the Court to its decision about abortion and privacy in the *Roe* case.

Lifestyle Liberties and the Status of Women

In the last decade or two, questions bearing upon lifestyle, the rights of privacy, and civil liberties in general have come increasingly to the fore with the rapid growth of the women's movement. An exploration into the reasons for the extraordinary rise in women's consciousness and their willingness to organize for the achievement of their rights is beyond the scope of this volume. This much, however, should be said: the turning point appears to have been World War II, when millions of women joined the work force, demonstrating their ability to serve in the military, in executive and managerial posts, in the professions, and even in such activities as manufacturing, shipbuilding, and heavy industry. Although the trend declined after the war, the movement out of the kitchen and into the work force altered not only women's visions of themselves and of their potential capacities, but the way in which they were perceived by men in general and by employers in particular.

The effort to free women from their traditional and subordinate roles was also inspired to some extent by the civil rights movement, which heightened group consciousness and developed many of the arguments and tactics for raising the status of groups suffering discrimination. Organizations for the liberation of women have also been imaginative and effective in achieving media coverage and gaining access to the articulate elites in government, the press, the professions, the universities, and, to some extent, industry and labor. The women's movement needs also to be seen as part of the "rights explosion," which has been evident not only in various domains of civil liberties, but in the expansion of civil rights and liberties for such minorities as blacks, Chicanos, homosexuals, senior citizens, children, criminal defendants, prisoners, the handicapped, and now even the terminally ill and dying. Once under way, the women's movement, like several other movements, has expanded at an increasingly accelerated rate, attracting adherents in sufficient number to certify its legitimacy and power and to launch fresh struggles for new and even more far-reaching goals.

The Civil Rights Act of 1964 made it unlawful for an employer to discriminate against an employee because of sex in such matters as hiring, dismissal, and the terms, conditions, or privileges of employment. The Equal Pay Act of 1963 provided that an employer may not pay men and women different wages for equal work on jobs requiring equal skill and responsibility, unless the different rates are based on criteria other than sex. The federal government itself is now forbidden by executive order from discriminating between men and women in any matters affecting employment, duties, wages, or benefits, and most of the state governments have adopted similar regulations. In addition, federal executive orders provide that any employer holding a contract with the federal government may not discriminate on the basis of sex. The 1964 Civil Rights Act failed to prohibit sexual discrimination in the use of public accommodations, but in the much publicized case of *Seidenburg* v. *McSorley's Old Ale House, Inc.* (317 F. Supp. 593, 1970), the court held that a public bar may not refuse to serve women. The question of sexual discrimination in employment or membership in bona fide *private* membership clubs, however, has not been resolved and remains an issue very much in dispute (Morgan 1977).

In general, the courts tend to find sexual discrimination if there is no rational basis for the discrimination. If a facility is public, rather than private, no rational grounds are likely to exist for denying women access. The same principle holds in many economic matters. Thus, in *Reed* v. *Reed* (404 U.S. 71, 1971), the Court struck down, as a violation of the equal protection clause of the Constitution, legislation which gave a mandatory preference to men over women in appointing administrators of an estate. In *Frontiero* v. *Richardson* (411 U.S. 677, 1973), the Court declared it illegal for an Air Force regulation to require female, but not male, members to prove the dependency of a spouse in order to obtain certain benefits.

Sexual discrimination, however, may be allowed to stand if gender is a "bona fide occupational qualification," reasonably necessary to the normal operation of the business or enterprise. Accordingly, sex becomes a rational criterion in choosing an actor or actress, a sorority "housemother," or the coach of a professional football team, for example. But under the Civil Rights Act, employment cannot be denied because of differences in the physical capability or endurance of men and women. Nor can an employer advertise in help wanted columns under male or female headings unless sex is a bona fide occupational qualification (Morgan 1977).

Equality, however, has not been achieved in various matters affecting legal transactions by women or a wife's legal status in the family. In many states, for example, a wife cannot retain her own name but must take her husband's name if she is to avoid certain penalties in employment, insurance, retirement pensions, and the like. In our data the public divides fairly evenly—43 percent versus 44 percent—on a woman's right to keep her own name after marriage. The elites, however, support her right by a ratio of approximately two to one. In Louisiana, men have complete management over the family property and income, and a wife does not even have control over her own earnings. In Idaho, the husband must sign a mortgage on his wife's separate property, but she does not sign on his. Women find it more difficult in many communities to arrange bank loans, to establish credit, or to obtain a mortgage for the purchase of a home. And despite laws requiring equal opportunity in hiring, promotions, and wages in employment, substantial differences between men and women continue to exist in many occupations in most parts of the country (Morgan 1977).

The public's response to the changing status of women has been favorable on the whole, and the trend has clearly been in the direction of increasing their civil liberties and civil rights. In the abstract, at least, a substantial majority of the American people and their opinion leaders rate "equal rights for women in all matters" as important or extremely important. (See table 5.18.) Such evidence as is available indicates, moreover, an increasing approval of the efforts to strengthen "women's status in society today." The figures rose from 42 percent approval in 1970 to 65 percent in 1979. Even by 1970, however, a majority (most of them men) favored the Equal Rights Amendment (Chandler 1972).

A distinction should be made, however, between the public's attitude toward expanding women's rights and its response to women's "liberation." Only 39 percent of the general public (though a much larger proportion of the opinion leaders) express approval of the women's liberation movement. And in a 1970 CBS news survey, some 55 percent expressed disapproval of the methods employed by the women's movement (Chandler 1972). Here, as one can so frequently observe in the public's response to organizational militancy, a movement's objectives—or many of them—may be favored, while its tactics in promoting the objectives are not. Whereas the objectives may be viewed as fair and reasonable, their militant advocates are often perceived as extreme and unrealistic in their demands. Thus, although a substantial

TABLE 5.18
Response to Women's Rights in the Abstract

	CLS			
	Mass Public	**Community Leaders**	**Legal Elite**	**Police Officials**
	(N=1993)	(N=1157)	(N=488)	(N=224)
How would you rate equal rights for women in all matters?				
—Extremely important	32%	46%	44%	24%
—Important	34	35	33	47
—Somewhat important	19	12	14	19
—Less important	12	7	8	9
—Undecided	4	1	1	1
Certain groups are considered harmful to the country, and others beneficial. How would you describe your own feelings about Women's Liberation (Feminist) Groups? Do you believe that they are mostly harmful or mostly beneficial to the country?				
—Mostly harmful	13	9	5	11
—Obnoxious but not harmful	40	39	35	53
—Mostly beneficial	33	45	49	22
—Undecided	14	8	10	14

	OVS	
	Mass Public	**Opinion Leaders**
	(N=938)	(N=845)
In general, do you approve or disapprove of the women's liberation movement:		
—Approve.	39%	75%
—Disapprove.	39	12
—Neither/Undecided	22	14

	Harris and ABC News/Harris*		
	Favor	**Oppose**	**Not Sure**
There has been much talk recently about changing women's status in society today. On the whole, do you favor or oppose most of the efforts to strengthen and change women's status in society today?			
—1979	65%	28%	7%
—1978	64	25	11
—1977	64	27	9
—1975	59	28	13
—1971	48	36	16
—1970	42	41	17

	Chandler†		
	(N=1136)		
	Total Sample	**Men**	**Women**
The Equal Rights Amendment would guarantee that women would have all of the rights that men have. Do you favor or oppose adding such an amendment to the Constitution?			
—Favor the amendment	56%	66%	47%
—Oppose the amendment	37	28	44
—No response	7	7	8

* Louis Harris and Associates 1978; ABC News/Louis Harris, February 1977.
† Chandler 1972.

majority favor the efforts to achieve equality and improve the status of women, 40 percent of the respondents in our CLS mass public sample regard the women's liberation movement as "obnoxious" and 13 percent consider it "mostly harmful."

The crucial problem around which most questions of women's rights revolve has to do with women's role in society, especially their place in the home or as workers outside the home. Despite the many significant changes we have witnessed in the rights and status of women, a surprising number of adult Americans would prefer to have women stay home and have families rather than seek careers. In table 5.19, we find that only one fourth of the mass public and one third of the elites believe we would be better off if women "were encouraged to have careers of their own." Surveys conducted over a six-year period—from 1973 to 1978—indicate that half the population still believe it makes sense to say that "women's place is in the home." The proportion is even greater if young children are involved: 57 percent believe, and another 20 percent "partially believe," that women with young children should not work outside the home "unless it is financially necessary." Some 40 percent (1977) and 48 percent (1970) of both sexes also believe that working women make worse mothers than women who don't work outside the home. And the women themselves appear to give higher priority to their husband's career than to their own: some 90 percent say they would give up their career and relocate if it were essential to their husband's career; but only 22 percent believe their husband would do the same for them.

One must be careful, however, not to take these responses too literally or to overinterpret their meaning. To some extent the responses are influenced by the kinds of questions that are asked. Thus, we see in table 5.20 that two thirds of the general public disagree when the question asks in sweeping and somewhat hyperbolic fashion whether women "should take care of running their homes and leave running the country to men." If the question asks whether the respondent approves or disapproves of a married woman earning money in business or industry if she has a husband capable of supporting her, 72 percent say that they approve (a rise from 60 percent in 1970). Also worth noting is that 80 percent of the population said, in 1978, that if their party nominated a qualified woman for president, they would vote for her (an increase of 30 percent in a thirty-year period). Under some circumstances, thus, in response to certain questions, a large proportion of the general public appear to endorse careers for women outside the

TABLE 5.19
Perception of Women's Role: Home versus Career

	CLS			
	Mass Public	**Community Leaders**	**Legal Elite**	**Police Officials**
	(N=1993)	**(N=1157)**	**(N=488)**	**(N=224)**
Everyone would be better off if more women:				
—were encouraged to have careers of their own.	25%	31%	33%	18%
—were satisfied to stay home and have families.	34	20	19	31
—Neither/Undecided	42	49	48	51

	Yankelovich, Skelly, and White*		
	Disagree	**Agree**	**No Strong Opinion**
Do you agree or disagree that while there are some exceptions, the statement that "woman's place is in the home" still makes sense?			
—1978	30%	47%	21%
—1975	32	51	17
—1974	31	49	20
—1973	28	49	23

	Time/Yankelovich, Skelly, and White[†]
How do you feel about the opinion that a woman with young children should not work at a job outside the home unless it is financially necessary?	
—No longer believe it	23%
—Partially believe it	20
—Believe it	57

	CBS News/*New York Times*[‡]	
	1977	**1970**
Would you say that working women generally seem to make better, or worse, mothers than women who don't work outside the home?		
—Better mothers	24%	23%
—Worse mothers	40	48
—No difference	24	16
—No opinion	12	13

	Gallup Organization[§]	
	Disagree	**Agree**
If it were essential to my husband's career I would give up my career and relocate.	10%	90%
If it were essential to my career that we move, my husband would give up his job and look for another.	78	22

* Adapted from Yankelovich et al. 1978.
[†] Adapted from *Time*/Yankelovich et al. 1978.
[‡] CBS News/*New York Times* 1977.
[§] Gallup Organization 1977; asked of younger married women working outside the home.

TABLE 5.20
Support for Women's Role Outside the Home

	Gallup, Roper, and NORC*	
	Approve	**Disapprove**
Do you approve or disapprove of a married woman earning money in business or industry if she has a husband capable of supporting her?		
—1978	72%	26%
—1975	70	28
—1972	64	34
—1970	60	35
—1945	24	60
	NORC[†]	
	Disagree	**Agree**
Do you agree or disagree with this statement: Women should take care of running their homes and leave running the country to men?		
—1978	68%	32%
—1977	62	38
—1975	64	36
—1974	65	35
	Gallup Organization[‡]	
	Yes	**No**
If your party nominated a woman for president, would you vote for her if she were qualified for the job?		
—1978	80%	20%
—1975	76	24
—1971	69	31
—1969	58	42
—1967	59	41
—1963	57	43
—1958	55	45
—1955	54	46
—1949	50	50

* 1980 studies.
[†] NORC 1980.
[‡] Gallup Organization 1949–78.

home, and the available data suggest that this attitude is becoming more prevalent.

That the public wants employed women to be treated fairly may be inferred from the responses in table 5.21. Some 60 percent of the general public and an even larger proportion of the elites reject as an

TABLE 5.21
Employment and the Rights of Women

	CLS			
	Mass Public	Community Leaders	Legal Elite	Police Officials
	(N=1993)	(N=1157)	(N=488)	(N=224)
When women aren't given the same chance as men in job hiring, it is usually because:				
—the employers still have old-fashioned and mistaken ideas about the kinds of things women can and should do.	60%	72%	72%	55%
—they are less qualified than men for the job.	25	14	11	24
—Neither/Undecided	15	15	17	20
When a pregnant woman wants a leave of absence from her job following the birth of her baby:				
—her employer should be required to give her sick leave with benefits.	49	45	43	41
—she should have to give up her job if asked.	18	16	17	18
—Neither/Undecided	34	39	40	42
In matters concerning family finances such as the sale of property and bank loans:				
—the husband and wife should have an equal say, since marriage is a partnership of equals.	91	93	89	94
—the husband, as head of the household, should have the most say.	7	5	10	4
—Neither/Undecided	3	3	2	2
What would you do if a woman was denied a job or held back because of her sex?				
—I would do nothing since I favor the action.	3	1	1	4
—I would not get involved, since my actions wouldn't matter anyway.	24	12	18	23
—I would contribute money, write letters, have petitions signed.	39	51	43	40
—I would join an organization, protest march, attend rallies.	13	17	12	4
—I'm undecided what I would do.	22	19	26	29

TABLE 5.21 *(continued)*

	OVS	
	Mass Public	**Opinion Leaders**
	(N=938)	**(N=845)**
If an employer is forced to lay off some employees, he should:		
—treat men and women employees exactly the same.	58%	82%
—let the women go first, especially if they are married.	30	8
—Neither/Undecided	12	10

	Chandler*		
	Total Sample	**Men**	**Women**
Do you think it is necessary to pay a man more than a woman for doing the same kind of work?			
—No, would not pay a man more	80%	83%	78%
—Yes, would pay a man more	18	16	21
—No answer	1	1	1

* Chandler 1972; N=1136.

explanation the claim that women are not hired as often as men because they are less qualified. On the contrary, most respondents believe that employers are acting out of prejudice and old-fashioned ideas. They also spurn the suggestion that women should be dismissed first if an employer is forced to lay off some of his employees. Nor is the public indifferent to the complications surrounding the pregnancy of an employed woman. In 1974, the Supreme Court declared it unconstitutional to terminate the employment of pregnant women, on grounds that such an action impeded the protected constitutional liberty to bear children (*Cleveland Board of Education* v. *La Fleur*, 414 U.S. 632, 1974). Public sentiment is apparently in sympathy with this view.

Popular opinion is also unequivocally in favor of paying men and women equally for the same kind of work. As for the income earned from employment and other sources, public sentiment overwhelmingly supports the view that husband and wife should have an equal say about family finances, "since marriage is a partnership of equals." Although, as we have seen, some states continue to discriminate against wives in financial matters, the belief that the husband should have a dominant voice in matters affecting finance has virtually disappeared from the public mind (or at least it is no longer openly professed).

Although popular support for the equal rights of women in both the family and the workplace has grown steadily stronger, there is very little sentiment, either among the mass public or the elites, for so-called affirmative action measures that would give preference to women in such matters as employment or education. In table 5.22, we find that support is minuscule for policies that would rectify past inequalities suffered by women. It should not be assumed, however, that this resistance to affirmative action is directed only at women: data in both our CLS and OVS studies turn up similar responses when the same types of questions are asked about blacks and other minorities. Both the public and the elites, in fact, are even opposed (by ratios of two to one) to inflicting fines or other penalties on employers who refuse to hire qualified senior citizens.

It is worth noting that, as of 1970, there was evidence of *reverse* affirmative action. Thus, a CBS news survey reported that both men and women (by a small margin of 52 percent to 44 percent) would give "preference to men over women in hiring for jobs." Approximately half the population thought an employer is better off to hire a man

TABLE 5.22
Affirmative Action and the Rights of Women (CLS)

	Mass Public	Community Leaders	Legal Elite	Police Officials
	(N=1993)	(N=1157)	(N=488)	(N=224)
Laws requiring employers to give special preference to women when filling jobs:				
—are only fair, considering how often they have been discriminated against in the past.	9%	17%	15%	3%
—are unfair to men who may be more qualified.	77	70	72	87
—Neither/Undecided	13	13	13	10
In setting a policy for admitting students to medical and law schools, a university				
—should set aside a certain number of places for women, to make up for the prejudice they have suffered in the past.	5	12	11	1
—should admit all students on merit alone.	86	78	76	95
—Neither/Undecided	10	10	13	4

"because women don't hold up under pressure as well as men do." Over 60 percent thought it better to hire a man "because a woman will quit if she gets married." One third would consider men for promotion before women (two thirds would not), and nearly the same number would give preference to men over women "in admitting them to universities and professional schools" (Chandler 1972).

Doubtless these figures have been significantly modified in the decade or so since the CBS survey was taken, but it is plain from our own more recent data that the preference pattern that traditionally favored men has by no means turned itself around. To judge from various indirect indicators in our research (such as the data on husbands and wives), what one is most likely to encounter today is a pattern of responses in which neither sex is given preference. The equalitarian norm, in other words, has grown stronger. This, however, is at the level of opinion; practice lags behind. Despite affirmative action programs, men continue to enjoy the advantage in seeking entrance or advancement in most careers.

This disparity between the expressed attitudes toward women's rights and prevailing practices, while continually narrowing as the recognition of their rights becomes stronger, should nevertheless remind us that differences between professed values and practices are by no means unusual in human affairs. We have encountered the phenomenon countless times before. Sometimes practice runs behind the professed norms or the stated law, and sometimes ahead. That the two do not perfectly coincide at any given time is no reason to discount the role of the norms. A certain amount of distance between what is professed by the political culture and what is practiced is inevitable in any complex society involving millions of people at different levels of education, awareness, and political sophistication. They also occupy many different roles which place them at varying distances from the mainstreams of "official" opinion. Social learning does not occur with the same speed or effectiveness for everyone.

Nor are the norms the only element determining behavior. A number of other influences—social, demographic, ideological, cognitive, economic, and so forth—intervene to prevent the norms from being perfectly realized in practice. But the norms are nonetheless vital. They furnish the standards that are frequently translated into law and legally enforced as well. To some extent they are also enforced informally by one's peers and associates, or by the community itself, which acts as a set of forces for rewarding or punishing (and hence for shaping) conduct.

Thus, the beliefs held by the members of the community do matter, even if those beliefs, in an imperfect world, are sometimes ignored, modified, or counteracted in practice. It matters greatly, for example, whether a community predominantly believes in tolerating or in suppressing certain forms of conduct, since a significant proportion of its members will absorb and act on those beliefs and set a standard for others. The norms serve, in addition, to legitimate certain forms of conduct and to declare others out of bounds. The fit between what is professed and what is practiced can never be perfect, but the two will tend, over time, to move toward convergence. The ideas that people hold, and especially the ideas that become institutionalized, written into law, or expressed in the mores, are the magnets toward which conduct will be drawn, even if some members of the community resist their force or gravitate toward them only slowly and protestingly.

It remains only to remind ourselves that the norms also change and that it is practice that sometimes leads the way. Where old laws cease to be enforced and have become, for all practical purposes, "dead letters," one can assume that the emerging norms will reflect the changing practice (as in the matter of sexual freedom, for example). Eventually the laws themselves will also be changed or, at a minimum, fall into disuse, so that the restrictions they once imposed no longer apply and may even be forgotten.

CHAPTER 6

The Learning of Civil Libertarian Norms Among Elites and the Mass Public*

W HO LEARNS civil libertarian norms, how, and why? Evidence from our earlier research and that of others suggests that *social learning*—formal as well as informal—is the most powerful influence on the internalization of such norms. People learn (or embrace) the norms of tolerance, privacy, due process, and other civil liberties much as they learn any other set of social norms, and the conditions which promote such learning are in many respects the same: access to information about public matters, frequency and intensity of exposure to the norms, interest in public affairs, saliency of the norms, and the perceived benefits or costs of upholding the norms.

Although libertarian values may be acquired through such learning devices as imitation and modeling, they are also acquired through one's family, peers, and other reference groups. They are often reinforced by such sources of information and influence as the media, by residence in a sophisticated cosmopolitan environment, and by certain types of social and vocational experiences which train one to make subtle and careful distinctions. Obviously, intelligence and education also play a part.

A tendency toward "intellectuality" may also influence civil liber-

* This chapter was prepared in collaboration with Dennis Chong.

tarian attitudes. Although intellectuality represents one aspect of being educated, it may also be distinguished from ordinary schooling in that the intellectually minded are particularly concerned with ideas and their exploration. Intellectuals are attracted to the work of the imagination and are thereby led to entertain alternative types of discourse. They are also more likely than other people to encounter variety in matters of belief and sensibility. Intellectual life is typically restless and inquiring and by its very nature promotes a readiness to consider alternative opinions and to recognize the legitimacy of disagreement and dissent. (See chapter 9.)

Social learning, insofar as it affects support for civil liberties, is likely to be greater among the influentials (that is, political elites) of the society than among the mass public. In advancing this argument, we are mindful of the earlier work of Stouffer (1955), Key (1961), Dahl (1961), Prothro and Grigg (1960), and McClosky (1964), among others, all of whom inferred from the research evidence then available that democratic norms in general, and those relating to tolerance or civil liberties in particular, enjoyed significantly greater support among the political influentials of American society than among the mass public. Some of the authors (Key, McClosky) were led to wonder whether the defense of liberty and the survival of the democratic system might ultimately depend more on the support accorded them by the influentials of the society than on the backing of the general public.

The reasoning that led to this conjecture grew partly out of the greater consensus on democratic norms exhibited by the elites and partly out of the research finding that while the public often voiced support for libertarian values in the abstract, it was less likely than the opinion leaders to support those values when they were applied to actual situations. Political actives, it seemed, were more consistent in their ability to make appropriate connections between their general libertarian principles and the concrete issues they encountered in everyday life. Some investigators (Key is a notable example) suggested that it was the nation's elites rather than the populace who served as the major repositories of democratic ideas and that a viable democracy could be maintained even if a large proportion of the electorate did not fully comprehend or assimilate libertarian values.

The distinction between political leaders or elites and the mass public—though complicated in various ways by differences in education, social mobility, occupational status, age, gender, residence, ethnicity, and other social factors—focused mainly on their different levels of involvement, awareness, and activity in public affairs. The dominant presumption was that greater involvement in national or even local affairs tended to increase one's exposure to the prevailing norms of the political culture. Since the norms are preponderantly democratic and libertarian, those who are more frequently and intensively exposed to them are also more likely to embrace them. Increases in exposure to political norms, moreover, tend also to increase one's understanding, as well as one's approval, of them, especially when what has to be understood—in this case, a network of civil liberties and a cluster of democratic rules of the game—is intrinsically complicated, and obviously difficult to comprehend and internalize.

Although much has been written and discussed about these findings and interpretations, and about the issues they raise for the maintenance of freedom and the conduct of democracy, little new research has been undertaken to explore questions of elite and mass values as they affect civil liberties, tolerance, and democratic viability. Jackman (1972) reanalyzed Stouffer's data through the use of a multiple regression that controlled for education, region, urban-rural residence, and sex; he claimed that the more democratic and tolerant attitudes exhibited by elites in the research comparing them with the mass public had little to do with their role as a distinctive political stratum and "do not seem to be distinguishable from those of the wider social elite from which they are drawn" (Jackman 1972 p. 759). For Jackman, along with others, the differences in democratic and libertarian belief turned up in the research on elites and masses could be entirely explained by the usual measures of social stratification, especially education. He denied, therefore, any need to assume that political leaders have experienced direct "political effects" that function independently of the social stratification system or that they have been "resocialized" through their more frequent and intensive political activities to a better understanding of the democratic rules of the game. Jackman's findings were challenged on technical grounds by St. Peter et al. (1977), who reanalyzed Stouffer's data once again and concluded that elite-mass differences persisted even after all relevant demographic variables had been controlled.*

Alford and Scoble (1968), however, also found in a Wisconsin study that political leadership had an independent effect on tolerance, although social status, as measured principally by education, appeared

---

*In a rejoinder, Jackman defended his methodology and claimed that the differences turned up by St. Peter et al. were too modest to be taken seriously (Jackman 1977).

to have an even greater effect. A study by Comer and Welch (1975) of a single community reported that elite status has "an effect on ideology and tolerance after removing the effects of education and party identification" (cited by Nunn et al. 1978). Nunn et al. undertook a replication of the Stouffer study in the early 1970s, which confirmed Stouffer's earlier (1954) findings that community elites were substantially more tolerant than the general population. A similar finding was also reported by Davis, who in 1972–1973 conducted a NORC replication of Stouffer (1955). Nunn et al., however, observed that after controlling simultaneously (through a multiple classification analysis) for six demographic variables (including education, city size, and occupation), the differences in the tolerance scores registered by the community elite and the mass "was reduced to nonsignificance" (1978). They concluded that "at least at the community level, a unique political stratum no longer exists in America."

None of the writers, however, to whom Jackman had referred and whom he branded as "pluralists" (Nunn et al. preferred to label them, not altogether disapprovingly apparently, as "democratic elitists"), had ever seriously claimed that the United States possessed a "unique political stratum" whose members had been "resocialized" into a distinctive political elite that exhibited a singular array of political values which set them apart from other Americans.

With the possible exception of Herring (1940) or Berelson et al. (1954), no well-known writer on the matters before us has suggested (as Nunn et al. maintain) *that greater political activity by the people could very well undermine democracy rather than strengthen it"* (1978; original italics). None of the writers whose research is in question asserts, to our knowledge, that it is preferable for the mass electorate not to participate in the political process because it is more inclined than its leaders to hold antidemocratic views. Nor do any of them oppose the wider dissemination of democratic values among the mass public. On the contrary, they tend to express concern about the potential dangers to democratic politics in failing to instruct a large segment of the population about the basic rights and rules of the game that define a democracy. What they *have* said on this score, by way of consolation, is that democrats can take at least some comfort from the fact that if the electorate has a weaker grasp of civil libertarian values than one might hope for, the political influentials and opinion leaders, at any rate, appear to have assimilated democratic norms more thoroughly than the average American. These elites understand more clearly the reasons for embracing libertarian values, and they are likely to apply their libertarian principles more consistently to the problems confronted by a democratic government in its day-to-day activities. Though it would appear to be self-evident, we should remind ourselves, nevertheless, that an investigator who turns up research findings showing differences in outlook between elites and the mass public (or findings of any other sort, for that matter) does not necessarily regard them as desirable social outcomes, just as the messenger who brings unwelcome tidings is not necessarily their advocate.

The Concepts of Elite and Mass Public

One of the difficulties that leads to controversy and misunderstanding about the differences between elite and mass attitudes toward democracy and tolerance arises from confusion about the definition of the key terms. As is well known, the term "elite" in particular is viewed pejoratively in many quarters, infused with value connotations that were never intended by such scholars as Stouffer, Key, Dahl, and others who employed the term (or terms like it) in their analysis of citizen opinions. Our own use of the concept of elite, for example, does not refer to a single, sharply demarcated stratum of the American population. The elite, for our purposes, is not a governing class or a ruling oligarchy in the sense in which European political sociologists such as Mosca, Pareto, and Michels employed the term. It has nothing to do with the Marxist notion of a "ruling class" or with C. Wright Mills's idea of a "power elite." The elite is not comprised of patricians, "blue bloods," Brahmins, the "rich and wellborn," the "Elect," the "upper crust," the "400," or any other term suggesting a privileged class or caste.

The use of the concept in the context of the earlier research on elite and mass attitudes was much more humble, perhaps even pedestrian. It was employed as a shorthand term for such notions as political influentials, political leaders, opinion leaders, community leaders, political actives—all terms that have more to do with leadership, influence, and involvement than with the notions of power, privilege, and control that are appropriate in describing the hegemony of a ruling class in a rigidly stratified society.

In so designating the political elite, we are largely reiterating the meaning attributed to such terms as opinion elite or political influential in an earlier paper on elite and mass attitudes toward democracy (McClosky 1964). It was noted there that these terms are intended

> to refer to those people who occupy themselves with public affairs to an unusual degree, such as government officials, elected office holders, active party members, publicists, officers of voluntary associations, and opinion leaders. The terms do not apply to any definable social class in the usual sense, nor to a particular status group or profession. Although the people they designate can be distinguished from other citizens by their activity and concerns, they are in no sense a community, they do not act as a body, and they do not necessarily possess identical or even harmonious interests. "Articulates" or "influentials" can be found scattered throughout the society, at all income levels, in all classes, occupations, ethnic groups, and communities, although some segments of the population will doubtless yield a higher proportion of them than others. . . . [The] line between the "articulates" and the rest of the population cannot always be sharply drawn, for the qualities that distinguish them vary in form and degree and no single criterion of classification will satisfy every contingency.

To these caveats (which are similar in spirit to those offered by Stouffer, Key, Dahl, Prothro and Grigg, and other investigators of elite and mass politics) one might add that the notion of a political elite, as employed here, is essentially an analytic construct. It refers to those members of society who engage in the kinds and levels of activities that almost any citizen might engage in if he or she chose, but it does not signify that those who *do* participate in these activities are a single, definable group whose members are united, formally or informally, into a unique political stratum. It represents, instead, a classification imposed by political observers and research investigators to enable them to select those individuals or groups in society who have to some appropriate degree marked themselves off from other men and women by their greater involvement and participation in public affairs, their higher levels of political interest and knowledge, and the greater saliency with which they invest public issues.

The elites of the society, moreover, are not only more active than the mass public, but, owing to their experience and familiarity with public affairs, their greater knowledge and investment in political outcomes, and the influence of their leadership roles on their habits of mind, they develop a greater ability than the average citizen to sort things out and to relate their opinions on issues more consistently to their underlying philosophical perspectives. To function as opinion leaders or political influentials, they must seek out information, learn to formulate and defend opinions on public questions, and be able to connect ideas that might easily be lost on most members of the general public. The are aided in these activities, of course, when (as is often the case) they enjoy a high level of education, above-average economic status, and greater access to the groups and institutions that are involved in key decisions—influences that enhance political sophistication.

As these observations suggest, there is nothing mysterious about the process by which the elites of a society come to learn civil liberties and other democratic norms. They are not "resocialized" or transformed; rather, they experience a greater measure of social learning than do individuals who, for whatever reason, have had little opportunity to participate actively in the public affairs of the community or nation. It is our view that whatever contributes to social learning in the United States also contributes to the adoption of libertarian norms, unless offset by some powerful counterforce such as intense ideological conservatism or a vocation (for example, police work) the goals of which are often at odds with civil libertarian values.

A great deal of the social learning most of us experience, of course, derives from education or from other social influences, such as the size and type of community, occupation, degree of exposure to the mass media, membership in an age group or generational cohort, and the like. There are, as it were, many roads to salvation, and it is possible that for some people a good education will carry them as far as they are ever likely to go toward the recognition and adoption of libertarian values. For these people, participation in public life may add little to the store of information and insights they already possess. For many other people, however, active participation and involvement in the public affairs of the community are likely to augment their political sensibilities to a significant degree, thereby increasing the probability that they will approve the libertarian norms of the political culture.

As we shall see, much depends, in addition, on the type of public and vocational activity in which individuals engage. Thus, lawyers, judges, and members of certain types of social reform groups can be expected to be significantly more libertarian than the members of the mass public who enjoy equivalent degrees of, say, education and income, but who are involved in business, engineering, or land management. Although increases in social learning do not inevitably lead to greater support for civil liberties, we expect to find that they will do so most of the time—especially as the norms relating to freedom and control in American society are predominantly libertarian.

As the foregoing suggests, we need to qualify our concept of "the elite." To speak of a single elite obviously misrepresents the realities. In a complex society there are a number of *different* elites. Although they possess certain qualities in common that justify characterizing them as elites, there are, nevertheless, party elites, organizational elites, community elites, national elites, liberal elites, conservative elites, legal elites, and elites devoted to academic affairs, journalism, business, civil rights, and a dozen other major social and economic interests. The point, once stated, seems obvious enough—perhaps too obvious to require statement. But, like may assertions that are virtually self-evident, the observation that we cannot properly speak of "the elite" as though it were a single entity is one we typically tend to overlook. Later in this chapter, we will see not only that there are indeed different elites, but that they vary among themselves in their levels of political sophistication and in the degree to which their members learn and endorse civil libertarian and other democratic values.

Certain of the observations we have made about political elites apply equally to the mass public. Here, too, many of us are inclined (though we obviously know better) to speak as though the mass public were a single homogeneous entity, a clearly defined body of like individuals who respond in the same way to the same norms. Yet all of us will appreciate, upon the slightest reflection, that everyone in the society is for certain purposes part of the mass public and that the members of that public vary among themselves in countless ways. Like the notion of the elite, the term "mass" (or "mass public" or "general public") is an analytic construct, a form of shorthand invented by social observers to simplify communication. As we well know, the mass public, as represented through randomized, cross-section sampling methods, contains some individuals who, by education, status, level of interest, activity, and involvement in public affairs, or other such criteria, could as easily be classified among the political elites as among the mass. For this and related reasons, most studies which compare mass and elite attitudes, including ours, report differences that are smaller than they are in "reality," that is, than they would be if we were able to screen the elites from the mass public more finely. If we were able "to carve

239

nature at its joints" and unequivocally designate some people as belonging to the political elite and others to the mass public, we would doubtless find differences that are even larger than those reported.*

Why should elites be more libertarian than the mass public? Part of the answer is that the norms of the American political culture are predominantly libertarian, and access to those norms is, for various reasons, greater among the elites than among the members of the general public. Freedom and its constituent elements, it seems plain enough, are among the most venerated of all American values. They have been immortalized in the Bill of Rights, the Declaration of Independence, and countless other official documents. They have been lauded by Congressmen, court decisions, newspaper editorials, textbooks, commencement addresses, party platforms, Presidential messages, campaign speeches, advertisements, TV dramas, and, of course, Fourth of July orations—in short, in virtually every form of public communication on almost every type of occasion.

No constitutional provision stands higher in American law than the First Amendment, and, in the twentieth century at least, none has received more attention from judges, lawyers, legal commentators, and professors of law. Civil libertarian rights are guaranteed in every state constitution, written into national and state legislation, inscribed on parchment, and chiseled on monuments throughout the nation. Whether the full implications of these rights are actually understood and embraced by all who pronounce, hear, or read them is another question, and one of the questions to which this chapter is addressed. But few, we believe, would deny that libertarian values have been celebrated throughout the nation with a degree of frequency and ardor unmatched by that of any other set of values, even those relating to equality. The rights contained in the First Amendment and their equivalents in state constitutions also undergird the right to vote, to choose and remove rulers, and to form opposition parties. These and other

---

* As we have indicated in our earlier descriptions of the samples employed in our surveys, our elite samples contain only those respondents who were especially selected because of their role as political leaders, opinion leaders, community influentials, individuals active in public affairs organizations, and the like—in short, individuals who have demonstrated their above-average interest, influence, and involvement in public affairs. Although any cross-section sample of the general population is bound to contain *some* individuals who meet these criteria, no such individuals were incorporated into our elite samples. As these individuals were selected (along with the other individuals in the mass public samples) by a random procedure designed to yield a cross section of the general public, they were kept within the cross-section sample, and for each of the three studies reported are treated as respondents in the mass public sample and not as members of a political elite.

240

rights having to do with the machinery and conduct of a democratic republic presuppose freedom of speech, press, association, and other forms of free expression. Freedom and its insignia, in whose defense we are entreated to be ever vigilant, have been etched into the conscience of sensitive and enlightened Americans. Let anyone who questions the standing of civil liberties as essentially undisputed ideals of American society try to recall the occasions on which American spokesmen have praised not freedom but its opposite, not the liberty to speak or publish or worship, but the desirability of disallowing such activities.

If, however, the values of civil liberties are as widely disseminated and esteemed as we have claimed, how is it that we and other investigators find that these liberties gain their principal support not from the mass public, but from its political elites? Indeed, how is it that a large proportion of the general population, when given a choice, often seem to prefer policy alternatives that would limit or prohibit the exercise of libertarian rights? These are appropriate questions, and they go to the heart of our concerns. The answer, we suggest, lies partly in the fact that, despite their ubiquity and their apparently singular hold on the American public mind, libertarian norms are difficult to learn. Though easily voiced in the abstract, they raise, in principle and practice, complex issues that make extreme demands on our understanding and patience. Some rights (for example, privacy versus freedom of information) clash with each other. Others violate our ideological outlook or sense of moral decency (for example, granting known rapists or child molesters all the benefits of due process in the course of their arrest and trial). Still others deeply offend religious sensibilities (for example, permitting educators to teach evolution, or express atheistic beliefs, to the children of Fundamentalists); while others are affronts to patriotism (for example, permitting radicals to mutilate the flag in a public demonstration against the government). Freedom of speech or press may also be used in ways that outrage our sense of social justice (for example, when bigots are allowed to hold a public meeting in the civic auditorium so that they can hurl racial insults at blacks, Jews, Latinos, or other minorities).

Not all persons in the society are in an equally good position to learn why their presumed belief in freedom obliges them to permit offensive or frightening conduct—especially if they, or their associates, happen to be the victims. Many members of the mass public who are physically or intellectually far removed from the mainstreams of the political culture may never have learned—in the full meaning of the word—why certain forms of conduct they regard as egregious must be permitted, much less protected. To ask loyal Americans, for example, to spend taxpayers' money to allow a community center to be used by some group for the fomenting of seditious activities is to ask them to aid and abet conduct they regard as loathsome and dangerous.

How do ordinary citizens of average education and political experience learn that they are morally and legally required to adhere to a principle such as reciprocity, granting to others the right to exercise all the forms of liberty they claim for themselves? Available data reveal that they are not likely to be familiar with the Bill of Rights, much less the First Amendment (Mack 1956). Nor are they likely to have read or even heard of John Stuart Mill or Justice Black, and they are bound to have little knowledge of the actual opinions expressed on questions of freedom and control by Jefferson, Madison, or Lincoln. It is by no means self-evident to ordinary citizens that their own freedom to speak or publish or join with others in a reasonable cause involves claims that are constitutionally no more worthy than the claims made by outsiders, deviants, nonconformers, criminals, subversives, homosexuals, or the champions of some other type of unorthodoxy.

If we grant due process to criminals and free them on some "legal technicality" so that they can roam the community and rob or assault innocent people, what have we gained? Does society benefit by rewarding marauders and punishing their victims? Have not people who engage in various forms of antisocial conduct placed themselves outside the realm of protections to which Americans are ordinarily entitled? Should we not require citizens to show good faith and solid membership in the community before we grant them the liberties for which they have shown such disrespect?

The answers to these questions are by no means obvious, especially as the governing principles affecting, say, First Amendment rights, as elaborated by the Supreme Court and legal commentaries, are rarely absolute but usually involve an intermingling of liberties and restraints. The Court in any given case may grant freedom up to a point, but not beyond. Almost every Supreme Court decision of note in the area of civil liberties is marked by contingencies and caveats, fine and subtle distinctions, exceptions and limitations, specifications of the conditions under which a given liberty is to be protected or prohibited.

The controlling point here, of course, is that an area of our public life that may appear on the surface to be straightforward—with the dos and don'ts all neatly arranged—turns out upon inspection to be surprisingly knotty and difficult to grasp. For the average individuals in the mass public, the difficulty is exacerbated by their remoteness from the sources of discussion and information which help one to achieve insight and clarification about the norms. However well-intentioned the average citizen may be, it is still necessary to *learn* libertarian principles in order to embrace them. Learning libertarian norms, as they apply to actual (and often puzzling) cases, requires not only motivation but a measure of knowledge, enlightenment, and openness to alternative modes of thought and conduct that are not often found among the mass public (McClosky 1964; Converse 1964). This is not to say, of course, that all (or even most) members of the political elite are adequately equipped to find their way through the labyrinthian byways of constitutional law and the status of rights. We *do* mean to say, however, that compared with the mass public, they are substantially better equipped. If they have not worked their way through the arguments of the Supreme Court justices and constitutional lawyers on questions of due process, speech, or privacy, they have at least been exposed to the conclusions drawn from those arguments. They are, in short, more likely to know what the norms are, even if they do not fully understand the route by which the norms were arrived at.

Findings on Elite-Mass Attitudes Toward Civil Liberties

That the elites are significantly ahead of the general public in their knowledge of what the law requires is borne out by the findings on the Civil Liberties Quiz we included in the CLS questionnaire. (See figure 6.1.) Whereas 25 percent of the general public achieved a high score on this quiz, 50 percent of the community elite scored high—a ratio of two to one. And, as expected, the differences in knowledge about civil liberties between the mass public and the legal elite (lawyers and judges) were larger still. The differences between elites and mass public on a quiz measuring political knowledge and sophistication were even larger.

We should remind ourselves, as we have on a previous occasion (McClosky 1964), that it may be unrealistic to expect the average person in the mass public to be caught up in public affairs, any more than we

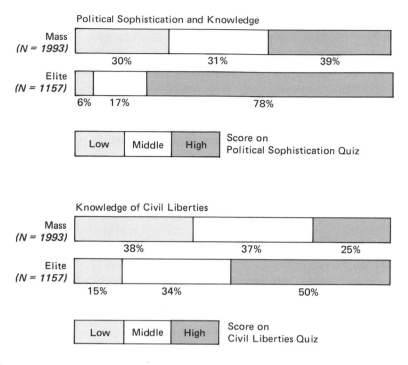

Political Sophistication and Knowledge

Mass
(N = 1993)

30%   31%   39%

Elite
(N = 1157)

6%   17%   78%

| Low | Middle | High |
Score on
Political Sophistication Quiz

Knowledge of Civil Liberties

Mass
(N = 1993)

38%   37%   25%

Elite
(N = 1157)

15%   34%   50%

| Low | Middle | High |
Score on
Civil Liberties Quiz

Notes: Because percentages have been rounded off, occasionally there will be disparities in totals (columns will not add up to 100 percent).

See the Preface to Research Findings in Chapter 1 and Appendix B for an analysis of the components of various categories used in the PAB, CLS, and OVS studies: that is "Political Leaders," "Legal Elite," and so forth.

The CLS was conducted in 1978-1979; the OVS in 1976-1977; and the PAB in 1958.

FIGURE 6.1
Differences in Levels of Political Sophistication and Knowledge of Civil Liberties Between Elites and Mass Public
(CLS)

expect everyone in the society to be interested in gourmet cooking, the ballet, college football, or modern poetry. Public affairs, as we intimated above, is an acquired taste. Although it may be more important than football or ballet, we cannot escape the (perhaps indigestible) fact that approximately half of the adult population do not even bother to vote. There are several reasons for this, of course, but one of them, surely, is lack of interest and knowledge.

We do not, of course, expect the elites to produce perfect scores on tests of support for civil liberties either. Even members of the ACLU will be found to fall away on one test item or another. Social learning, obviously, is not perfect even for the most sophisticated elites. Then, too, many of the civil liberties questions we have put to our samples are extremely difficult for a libertarian to endorse without agonizing conflict. Do Nazis have the right to march into Skokie and frighten half to death the survivors of the Holocaust? Many devout civil libertarians said no to this question. (See also Gibson and Bingham 1979.) Although the principles involved in the defense of civil liberties may in such (actual) cases be difficult for even the most informed elites to decide, they are also, in some instances, unsettled.* Even a brief reading of Supreme Court decisions in crucial civil liberties cases will soon make it plain that there are sometimes as many opinions as there are justices and that more than one principle is at stake.

Apart from these considerations, the several elites may differ among themselves in ideology and in their philosophies of reward and punishment, and they may draw different practical (though equally plausible) inferences from what was thought to be a universal principle or categorical imperative. One wonders, sometimes, which is the more remarkable—that a large number of informed men and women support civil liberties or that they fail to.

Our first task in approaching the data is to ascertain whether differences exist between the mass and elite samples in their orientation toward civil liberties and whether the differences are large enough to lend support to the several hypotheses we have suggested in the preceding pages. For this purpose, we needed to develop a measure of attitudes toward civil liberties for each of the studies, and we have therefore constructed a scale of civil liberties attitudes containing sixty-nine items from the CLS and a similar scale containing thirty-five items from the OVS.† Examples of the CLS items are shown in table 6.1, along with the percentages of the elite and mass samples who scored the items in a libertarian direction.

It is obvious from this table that the community leaders score significantly higher than the mass public on every item in the scale. The differences on most items fall between 15 percent and 20 percent and in some cases go as high as 25 percent or 30 percent. The libertarian scores of the legal elite are, as one might expect, even higher, and by a significant margin. The legal elite, for example, averages 15 percent

*For a full discussion of norms and emerging liberties, see chapter 8 and figure 8.10.

†For a description of the item content of the omnibus civil liberties scale, see Appendices A and B.

TABLE 6.1
Percentage Scoring Libertarian on Omnibus
Civil Liberties Scale (CLS)

| | CLS | | | |
| | Mass Public | Community Leaders | Legal Elite | Police Officials |
Sample Items	(N=1995)	(N=1166)	(N=487)	(N=221)
All systems of justice make mistakes, but which do you think is worse? (A) To convict an innocent person; (B) to let a guilty person to free.	60%	79%	91%	77%
Scientific research that might show women or minorities in a bad light: (B) should be banned because the results might damage their self-respect; (A) should be allowed because the goal of science is to discover the truth, whatever it may be.	59	80	90	77
A humor magazine which ridicules or makes fun of blacks, women, or other minority groups: (B) should lose its mailing privileges; (A) should have the same right as any other magazine to print what it wants.	57	74	92	72
Should demonstrators be allowed to hold a mass protest march for some unpopular cause? (B) No, not if the majority is against it; (A) yes, even if most people in the community don't want it.	41	71	89	54
Forcing people to testify against themselves in court: (B) may be necessary when they are accused of very brutal crimes; (A) is never justified, no matter how terrible the crime.	40	67	93	68
If the majority in a referendum votes to stop publication of newspapers that preach race hatred: (B) such newspapers should be closed down; (A) no one, not even the majority of voters, should have the right to close down a newspaper.	38	62	84	43
If a person is found guilty of a crime by evidence gathered through illegal methods: (A) he should be set free or granted a new trial; (B) he should still be convicted if the evidence is really convincing and strong.	37	54	76	50
The freedom of atheists to make fun of God and religion: (B) should not be allowed in a public place where religious groups gather; (A) should be legally protected no matter who might be offended.	26	53	75	31
A person who publicly burns or spits on the flag: (B) should be fined or punished in some way; (A) may be behaving badly but should not be punished for it by law.	18	29	43	7

NOTES: For comments and procedures regarding the validation of the Omnibus Civil Liberties Scale, see Appendix C. The total number of items in the scale is fifty-two.

Because percentages have been rounded off, occasionally there will be disparities in totals (columns will not add up to 100 percent).

See the Preface to Research Findings (p. 25) and Appendix B for a description of the leader and mass public samples used in the PAB, CLS, and OVS studies: that is "Political Leaders," "Legal Elite," and so forth.

The CLS study was conducted in 1978–1979; the OVS in 1976–1977; and the PAB in 1958.

higher on the individual items than the community leaders and over 35 percent higher than the mass public. Here, as elsewhere in the data, we have a dramatic demonstration of the influence of social learning on civil libertarian scores. The legal elite (consisting of lawyers and judges in a ratio of approximately four to one) obviously has greater familiarity with the norms governing civil liberties and, partly for this reason (we believe), exhibits a stronger inclination to accept their legitimacy. Working, as they do, more closely than any other elite sample (except, perhaps, for the ACLU) with the daily enforcement of human rights, and having greater knowledge of constitutional requirements (as interpreted by the courts), lawyers and judges turn up in great numbers on the side of civil liberties.

It can be safely presumed, we believe, that the legal elite is closer than other elites, and surely closer than the mass public, to the implicit norms of the political culture; that they are more intensely involved with them; and that they respond to those norms with greater consistency. If civil liberties values, as we have argued, are difficult to learn, the legal elite has more occasion to encounter them than other samples, has greater knowledge of them, and is more often compelled to reflect upon their merits and shortcomings. By the very nature of their vocation and activities, the members of the legal elite would also be in the best position to understand the reciprocal obligations that a belief in civil liberties imposes upon individuals who claim them for themselves. It is also possible (though we have no test of it) that at least some of the individuals who choose the legal profession to begin with, do so because they have an above-average concern with libertarian and other human rights.*

It is also worth noting that the content of the items in table 6.1 is varied and encompasses almost the entire range of rights ordinarily incorporated into the broad category of civil liberties. No single substantive domain dominates the items, so that the differences in scores between elites and the mass public cannot be attributed to the influence of an ideological bias. In fact, a deliberate effort was made to vary

---

*We are, of course, mindful of the possibility that, in a society that predominantly endorses libertarian values, some members of the elite will have attained their status as members of the elite partly because they were already favorably disposed toward libertarian norms. In these cases, a degree of social learning of libertarian norms will have preceded their entrance into elite roles. Even so, a fair amount of additional social learning is bound to take place *after* they have begun to participate as members of an elite group. (For a study of the interaction between leadership roles and response to the prevailing norms, see Newcomb 1943.)

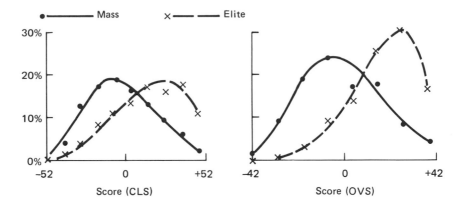

FIGURE 6.2
Distribution of Elites and the Mass Public on the Civil Liberties Scale
(CLS/OVS)

the ideological content of the items so that respondents on the left or the right would not automatically appear to be more tolerant (or less tolerant) because of their respective sympathy or hostility toward certain political groups and causes.

Perhaps a clearer sense of the magnitude of the differences between the elites and the mass can be gained from the frequency distributions for the civil liberties scales in both surveys presented in figure 6.2. While the curves for the general population approach normality, though somewhat skewed toward the lower end of the scales, the curves for the elite samples are strongly skewed toward the higher end. A further indication of the magnitude of the difference can easily be discerned from tables 6.2 and 6.3, where one can observe the cumulative effect of the item responses on scale scores. In the CLS, 33 percent of the mass public score high on the civil liberties scale compared with 60 percent of the community leaders. The percentage high figure for the legal elite is, once again, higher still, reaching an extraordinary 83 percent.

The one group that approximates the general population in its orientation toward the civil liberties are, as we predicted, the police officials. While the reasons for this will be explored more fully later in the chapter, we can note here that the police are likely to be strongly cross-pressured on libertarian values. Although they have more experience with civil libertarian standards and greater knowledge of the law

TABLE 6.2
*Percentage Scoring Libertarian on Omnibus
Civil Liberties Scale (CLS)*

| Civil Libertarian Scores | Total Score | | | |
	Mass Public	Community Leaders	Legal Elite	Police Officials
	(N=1993)	(N=1157)	(N=488)	(N=224)
High	33%	60%	83%	27%
Middle	33	25	14	44
Low	34	15	3	29
	College Graduate and Above (16+ years)			
	(N=467)	(N=838)	(N=475)	(N=56)
High	56%	67%	83%	41%
Middle	26	21	14	43
Low	18	11	3	16
	Some College (13–15 years)			
	(N=404)	(N=201)	(N=1)*	(N=114)
High	45%	50%	—	23%
Middle	32	27	—	45
Low	23	23	—	33
	High School (9–12 years)			
	(N=896)	(N=112)	(N=2)*	(N=53)
High	22%	29%	—	21%
Middle	37	46	—	43
Low	41	26	—	36
	Grade School (0–8 years)			
	(N=186)	(N=4)*	(N=0)*	(N=0)*
High	8%	—	—	—
Middle	35	—	—	—
Low	57	—	—	—

* N is too small to calculate percentages for the column.

than the mass public, they also find that they are frequently caught between their duty to catch lawbreakers and the severe limitations imposed upon them by the laws designed to protect the rights of individuals.

In table 6.3 (which reports the scale results in the OVS) the differences between the mass and the opinion leader samples are again large—33 percent high for the mass sample compared with 76 percent

TABLE 6.3
*Percentage Scoring Libertarian on the
Omnibus Civil Liberties Scale (OVS)*

	Total Score	
	Mass Public	**Opinion Leaders**
Civil Libertarian Scores	(N=930)	(N=838)
High	33%	76%
Middle	35	20
Low	32	4
	College Graduate and Above (16+ years)	
	(N=252)	(N=697)
High	52%	78%
Middle	28	19
Low	20	3
	Some College (13–15 years)	
	(N=217)	(N=109)
High	39%	69%
Middle	32	25
Low	29	6
	High School (9–12 years)	
	(N=379)	(N=29)
High	24%	62%
Middle	41	24
Low	35	14
	Grade School (0–8 years)	
	(N=82)	(N=3)*
High	5%	—
Middle	32	—
Low	63	—

* N is too small to calculate percentages for the column.

for the elite, a difference of 43 percent. Also interesting is the fact that in both tables 6.2 and 6.3 the differences hold up, some of them quite strongly, when education is controlled. While education is obviously a powerful influence and appears to contribute heavily to the learning of libertarian values (by exposing students to democratic ideas and norms, by acquainting them with the nation's history and political institutions, by introducing them to the major documents praising liberty, and so forth), it plainly does not account for the entire variance in the scores on civil liberties registered by our respondents. Especially in the OVS, the differences between the elite samples and the mass public remain impressively large even after the influence of education is, so to speak, neutralized. The nonideological elite, as compared with the community elite in the CLS, contains a larger proportion of respondents who are *actively* engaged in public and/or political affairs.

From the evidence in table 6.4 (see p. 270), moreover, we can safely assume that the differences would be even greater if we were to exclude from the nonideological elite sample the large number of respondents from *Who's Who*, most of whom are persons of eminence and leaders in their field, but many of whom play little or no role in public affairs. They are writers, musicians, engineers, businessmen, and authors of scientific works, but they are not all civic participants and their involvement with public affairs is in many cases only marginal. In any event, the thrust of the evidence concerning the limits of the influence of education is unmistakable: in both surveys, public participation and involvement, political activity, and opinion leadership correlate strongly with the social learning of libertarian norms at all levels of education, including the most highly educated.

Further Tests of Elite-Mass Differences on Civil Liberties

The contingency tables in the previous section showed that the elites (as a whole) were more tolerant than the population-at-large even at the same levels of education. We know from earlier studies, however, that education is just one, although certainly the most significant, in a number of factors which are correlated with tolerance. In addition to education, the age, religiosity, income, sex, and place of residence of respondents are all related to their levels of tolerance. Therefore, a stronger demonstration of elite socialization would have to show the persistence of elite-mass differences even after the appropriate controls are made for all of these social variables.

A "tougher" test of the hypothesis can be made with the use of ordinary least squares multiple regression. By estimating separate equations for the elite and mass samples—with tolerance being the dependent variable, and a number of nominal and interval-level demographic characteristics constituting the independent variables—we can determine whether any difference remains between the tolerance scores of the two groups after they have been matched on the relevant demographic characteristics.*

Although the number of categories and independent variables used in the regression would enable us, if we chose, to make many different comparisons (see table A.1, Appendix C), we have focused our attention on comparisons between typical or average elites and their mass counterparts. The "average" elites are defined as those who possess the modal (in the case of nominal variables) or mean (in the case of interval variables) values of the independent variables used in the multiple regression.

Following this procedure, the "average" elites are between forty and fifty years old, fairly religious, college graduates; have family incomes of between $20,000 and $30,000; live in a small city outside of the South; and participate to a considerable degree in political affairs (mean score of 10.94 on a 14-point participation scale). These elites are compared with members of the mass sample whose tolerance scores are estimated on the basis of the same demographic characteristics, but whose participation score is average for a member of the general population (that is 7.36). In other words, we are comparing elites who partake of more intense forms of political activity with their demographic twins in the mass sample who generally do not venture beyond less time-consuming and costly types of participation such as discussion and voting.

The result of this initial comparison is displayed in figure 6.3. The average elites have a mean score of 16.45 on the civil liberties scale compared with a considerably lower score of 7.67 for their mass counterparts, a controlled difference of 8.78 points. This difference can be put in perspective by considering that the uncontrolled difference in means is 15.75, and the mass sample standard deviation on the civil liberties scale is 19.53. A most interesting datum in figure 6.3 arises from the comparison between the highly participant elites with the demographically paired but nonparticipant members of the society-at-large. The difference in means between these two groups swells to

---

*For the regression used in this analysis and its application to the samples employed in the CLS, see Appendix C.

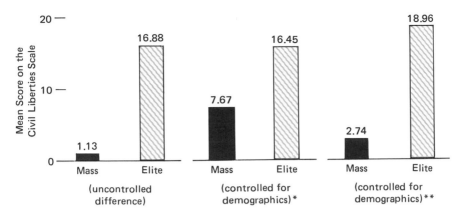

*A comparison between the average elite participant (mean score of 10.94) and the average mass participant (mean score of 7.36) who are otherwise alike demographically.

**A comparison between the highly participant elite (score of 14.00) with the nonparticipant mass (score of 0.00) who are otherwise alike demographically.

FIGURE 6.3
Comparisons of the Mean Scores of Selected Elite and Mass Groups on the
Civil Liberties Scale
(CLS)

16.22, which is even larger than the uncontrolled difference and amounts to almost a full standard deviation.

Thus, whether we match respondents in the elite and mass samples for education only, or for a number of sociological and personal characteristics simultaneously (through a multiple regression procedure), the opinion leaders remain significantly more libertarian than the mass public. Moreover, these differences obviously cannot be traced entirely to the standard influences associated with social stratification, such as education and socioeconomic status. While these influences, of course, contribute to the acquisition of civil libertarian values, participation in the elite roles of the society exerts an influence over and above the influences of education, status, place of residence, and other social characteristics.

Community leadership and activity in public affairs expose one to a wider range of influences that increase social learning and produce greater familiarity with the prevailing values of the political culture. Since, as we have observed, in the United States these values are predominantly libertarian, the elites, who enjoy greater access to the norms and more opportunities to learn them, do in fact embrace them more strongly than do the members of the mass public. In the next section, however, we shall see that not all groups who are classified among the political or community elites of the society have the same characteristics, and not all groups approve the values of civil liberties with the same frequency and enthusiasm.

Although many of us are inclined, for reasons of conceptual and verbal convenience, to speak of the members of a society's elite as though they were a single uniform group, we have noted in the preceding section that the elite (even the political elite) is far from being homogeneous. Elites vary in many different ways: in vocation, politics, ideology, and social role.

In this section, we will examine some of the differences in orientation toward civil liberties that turn up among our elite groups, taking particular note of the manner and degree to which each of them differs from the mass public. In the contingency tables we constructed for comparing subgroups among the legal elite, we found a sharp contrast in attitudes toward civil liberties between the judges and lawyers on the one side and the police and mass public on the other. The police are the major exception to the general description of elite and mass attitudes reported in the preceding chapter. While the judges and lawyers were far more tolerant than a comparably educated subset of the mass public, the police, on the whole, were slightly less tolerant.

In figure 6.4 we have presented elite-mass differences on the civil liberties scale based on separate regression analyses of nine major subgroups within the elite. From the perspective of support for civil liberties, these comparisons between the typical members of each elite subgroup and their demographic counterparts in the mass sample are favorable by and large toward the elite. Six of the nine subgroups are eight or more points ahead of the mass public in their support for civil liberties. The police officials are less tolerant than the comparable members of the mass, while the school administrators and private officials score at about the same level as the general population. Since a more detailed analysis of the elite subgroups will be taken up later in the chapter, we need only to emphasize here that the overall elite-mass difference on the civil liberties scale is not the product of one or two exceptionally libertarian elite groups (such as lawyers and judges), but, on the contrary, tends to prevail to a greater or lesser degree among a variety of elite groups.

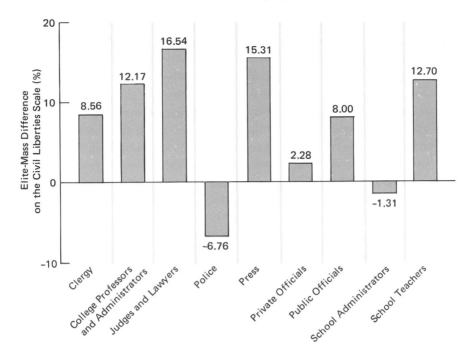

Note: The horizontal line represents the mean scores of the members of the mass public who are demographically matched with each of the elite subgroups named.

FIGURE 6.4

Differences in the Mean Scores of Selected Elite Subgroups and the Mass Public on the Civil Liberties Scale, Controlling for Demographic Characteristics
(CLS)

Nor are the differences in libertarianism between the mass public and the elites a result of differences in ideology. For example, although the elites are slightly more liberal than the mass public on a measure of economic liberalism-conservatism,* it is plain from the data yielded by the regression analysis[†] that at every level of economic liberalism-conservatism, elites score higher on the civil liberties scale than do their demographically matched counterparts in the general public. (See

---

* As measured by a ten-item scale which included attitudes toward government, regulation of the economy, the welfare state, business, labor, the free enterprise system, and so forth.

† For the adjusted equation, see Appendix C.

255

figure 6.5.) The elite-mass differences in mean scores range from 4.27 points among the strong economic conservatives to 11.83 among the strong economic liberals.

Differences in their respective orientations toward civil liberties show up not only for matched samples of elites and the mass public as a whole, but in most cases for their major subgroups as well, even when they share the same economic ideology. The mean differences between the elites and the mass public in their support for civil liberties are, to be sure, reduced (and in a few cases reversed) among the strong economic conservatives, but they tend to grow larger among the moderate economic conservatives, and are still larger among the economic liberals. (See figure 6.6.) Among the latter, in fact, every elite subgroup (except for the police among the moderate liberals) scores higher on the civil liberties scale than does its demographic counterpart in the mass public.

Comparable data from a regression analysis of the OVS study corroborate these findings from the CLS study. In figure 6.7 we have

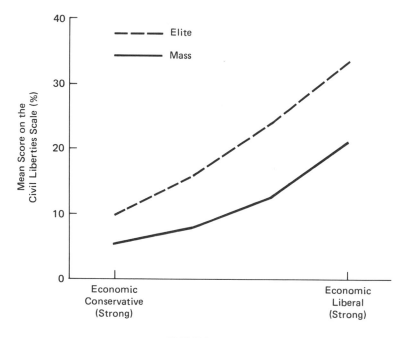

FIGURE 6.5
Comparisons of Elite and Mass Mean Scores on the Civil Liberties Scale,
Controlling for Demographic Characteristics and Economic Attitudes
(CLS)

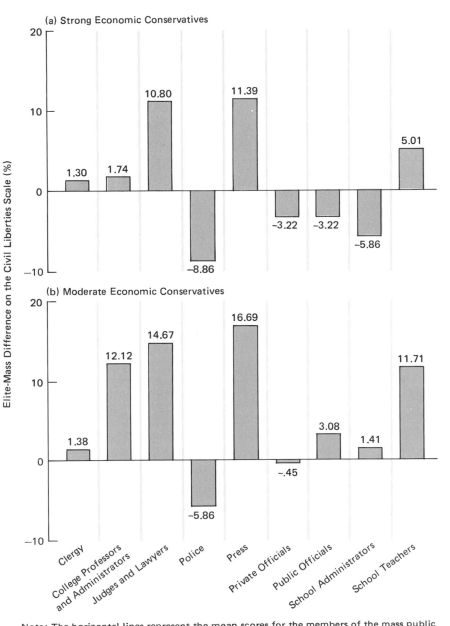

(a) Strong Economic Conservatives

(b) Moderate Economic Conservatives

Note: The horizontal lines represent the mean scores for the members of the mass public who are demographically matched with each of the elite subgroups named.

FIGURE 6.6a-d

Differences in the Mean Scores of Selected Elite Subgroups and the Mass Public on the Civil Liberties Scale, Controlling for Demographic Characteristics and Economic Ideology

(CLS)

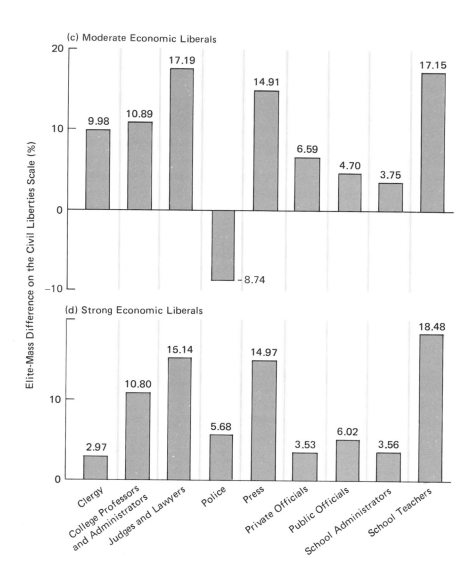

(c) Moderate Economic Liberals

(d) Strong Economic Liberals

Elite-Mass Difference on the Civil Liberties Scale (%)

Clergy
College Professors and Administrators
Judges and Lawyers
Police
Press
Private Officials
Public Officials
School Administrators
School Teachers

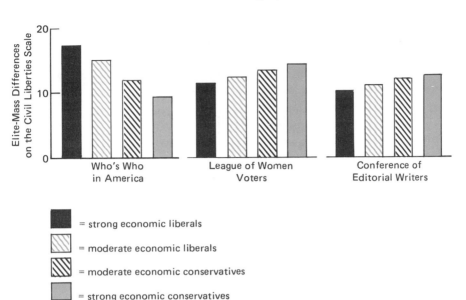

FIGURE 6.7
Comparisons of the Mean Scores of Elite Groups and the Mass Public on the
OVS Civil Liberties Scale After Controlling for Demographic Characteristics
and Economic Ideologies

summarized comparisons from the OVS study between the mass public and elite samples (the elites consisting, in this case, of people selected at random from the rosters of *Who's Who in America*, the League of Women Voters, and the Conference of Editorial Writers). Without exception in twelve comparisons, the elite group registers a significantly higher mean score on the civil liberties scale than does a parallel sample of the mass public, with differences ranging from eight to seventeen points.

Although we have stressed the resilience of the elite-mass differences in tolerance even after we control for economic ideology, it is worth noting that *within* the elite and mass samples, one encounters large differences between the tolerance scores of economic liberals and conservatives. This can be seen, for example, in figure 6.5, where the mean scores of matched samples of elites and the mass public were plotted. Each slope reflects the relationship between economic ideology and civil libertarian attitudes, and both exhibit similar correlations. Among both elites and the mass public, people who strongly support the free enterprise system tend to express less support for civil liberties, and vice versa. Elite economic conservatives are not nearly as tolerant as elite economic liberals, but are nevertheless more tolerant than mass public economic conservatives. Similarly, elite economic liberals are considerably more tolerant than their mass public counterparts.*

As we have had occasion to observe, tolerance often demands considerable foresight, understanding, and self-restraint. Granting the same liberties to people who oppose our beliefs as we grant to our cobelievers requires an appreciation of the theoretical arguments which set forth the long-run virtues of a tolerant society. Since the mass public, as we have contended, is less likely than the elites to have encountered these arguments, they are more prone to want to punish people who violate familiar standards of belief or conduct. They are also more likely than the elites to choose the intolerant response when their own beliefs are challenged.

The greater tendency of the mass public to respond intolerantly to groups and "causes" they dislike is further confirmed in our analysis of the unwillingness of elites and the mass public to "put up with" a variety of controversial groups (atheists, feminists, homosexuals, Nazis, revolutionaries, and student activists) which they view as either "harmful" or "obnoxious." (See figure 6.8.) The data used in this analysis are derived from a set of questions which asked respondents whether they felt a particular group was "harmful," "obnoxious but not harmful," or "mostly beneficial," and whether they were willing to extend the basic rights of assembly and free speech to that group. To give one example, respondents were first asked how they felt about Nazis, and, later, whether they believed the community should allow its "civic auditorium to be used by the American Nazi party to preach race hatred against Jews and other minorities."

Figure 6.8 shows that, among those who perceive a given group as *harmful*, the proportion of tolerant responses is extremely low, but, nevertheless, always higher among the elites than the mass public. In items asking respondents about their willingness to tolerate revolutionaries and student activists, the elite-mass comparisons appear to have been constrained by the presence of so-called floor effects in the data. That is, if the fear of a particular group is of sufficient magnitude,

---

*The relationship between ideology and support for civil liberties is extensively treated in chapter 8.

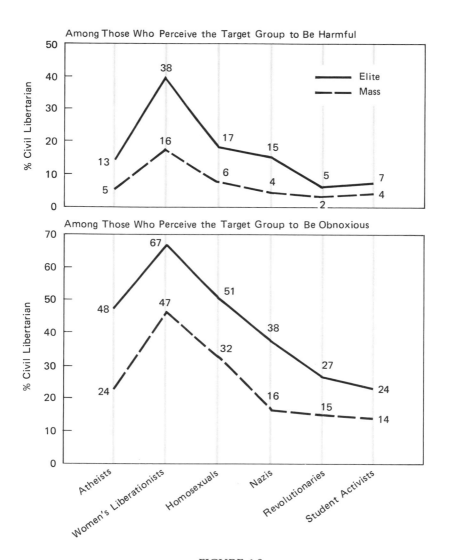

FIGURE 6.8
Levels of Tolerance (% Civil Libertarian) for Controversial Groups among
Elites and the Mass Public, Controlling for Affect Toward the Group
(CLS)

it will tend to overwhelm (or severely diminish) the influence of social learning as it relates to civil libertarian norms.

On the other hand, among people who think the controversial groups are *obnoxious* but not especially harmful, there is a greater latitude of choice between tolerance and intolerance, and it is in this category that the elite-mass differences are consistently large (ranging from 10 percent to 24 percent) and always in the predicted direction. Note, in addition, that the tolerance scores of both elites and the mass public are significantly higher when the controversial groups are perceived as merely obnoxious rather than harmful.

As shown in figures 6.9 and 6.10, elites exceed the mass public's levels of tolerance toward obnoxious or feared groups even when we further match the two samples according to their self-designated ideologies. With a single minor exception, the elite liberals and conservatives are more tolerant of every controversial group than their demographic counterparts in the mass public, despite the comparable levels of apprehension in each sample. Within the elite and mass samples, however, as we have already seen, and for reasons we shall subsequently discuss, the liberals are almost invariably more tolerant than the conservatives.

Our measure of civil libertarian values, as we have indicated, is a composite of diverse topics and ideas that can be subdivided into several domains. To what extent, one might ask, do elites respond uniformly to the various domains of civil liberties? Since our elites are not uniform in composition, but consist of individuals who fulfill different vocational responsibilities, play a number of different roles, and are exposed, to some extent, to different norms, can we expect to find that their responses to civil libertarian values are colored by the differences in their respective vocations and roles?

To investigate this question, we have constructed several additional scales, each designed to measure attitudes toward a different aspect of civil liberties. Three of these scales concern the advocacy of controversial ideas. The first tests the willingness to extend freedom of expression to such groups as revolutionaries, flag burners, and atheists—groups generally identified with the political left. The second tests tolerance toward such right-wing groups as the Nazis and the Ku Klux Kan. The third assesses the willingness to tolerate groups or practices widely held to be offensive, but which are not identified with any ideological tendency (for example, newspapers which "twist the facts and tell lies").

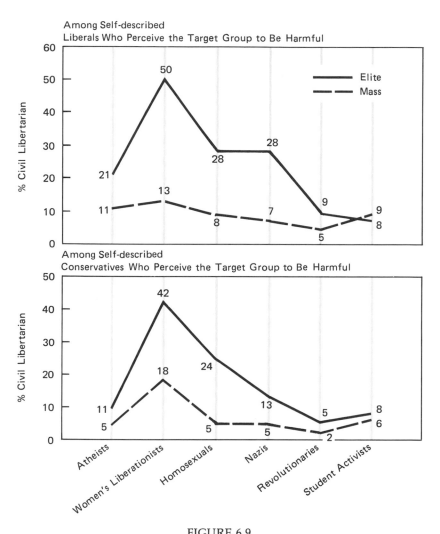

FIGURE 6.9
Levels of Tolerance (% Civil Libertarian) for Controversial Groups among
Liberal and Conservative Elites and the Mass Public Controlling for Affect
Toward the Group
(CLS)

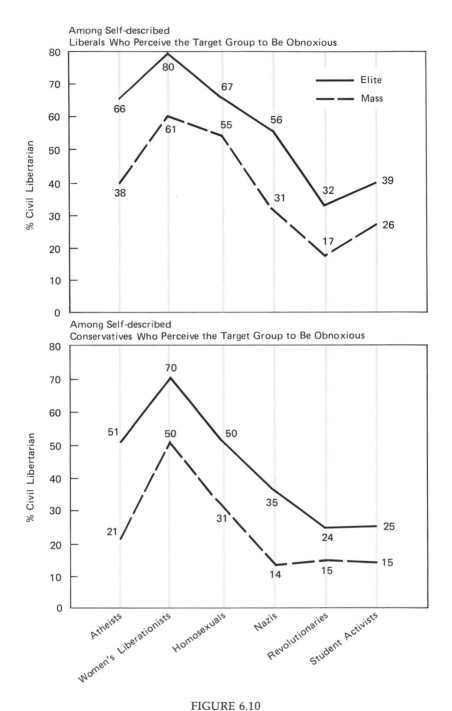

FIGURE 6.10

Levels of Tolerance (% Civil Libertarian) for Controversial Groups among
Liberal and Conservative Elites and the Mass Public Controlling for Affect
Toward the Group

(CLS)

We have also constructed three other subscales that tap attitudes toward a more diverse set of libertarian values. One is concerned with conscientious objection and civil disobedience; another measures attitudes toward nonconforming lifestyles; while the third gauges attitudes toward due process of law and the protection of the rights of the accused. Each of these scales contains at least seven items. We have also included in this analysis the ten-item scale of economic liberalism (previously referred to) that taps attitudes toward the free enterprise system, economic equality, and social welfare programs. In assessing the differences between elite groups and the general public, we have, in this instance, also matched the two sets of groups on education. By way of illustrating the way in which differences between each elite group and the mass were calculated, consider, for example, the attitude of the press toward free speech for left-wing groups: Some 73 percent of the press scored high on our measure of tolerance for left-wing groups, compared with 49 percent of a comparably educated subsection of the general public—a difference of 24 percentage points. (See figure 6.11.)

Calculated in this way, the difference scores reported in figure 6.11 confirm our expectation that the vocational and cultural values of certain elite groups often exert a strong influence on their support for particular dimensions of civil liberties. Although we cannot discuss the results in detail, several observations can be made to highlight the significance of the findings. Consider, for example, the clergy. Although they are slightly more tolerant of political extremism than most college-educated Americans, they are highly intolerant of conduct that violates standards of conventional morality, for example, prostitution, pornography, homosexuality, and the use of drugs. The idea that all persons ought to be free to conduct their private lives according to their own values seems to conflict with the deeply held moral convictions and role responsibilities of the clergy.

At the same time, however, the clergy are more favorably disposed than the mass public or other elite groups toward another form of unconventional behavior, namely, civil disobedience. As can be seen in figure 6.11, they express the strongest support of all groups for conscientious objection to military service, the refusal to obey laws which are regarded as unjust or immoral, and even nonviolent but disruptive protest. The explanation for these unusual attitudes apparently lies in their religious convictions, and, in particular, their strong commitment to the transcendent values of individual conscience. The clergy thus

265

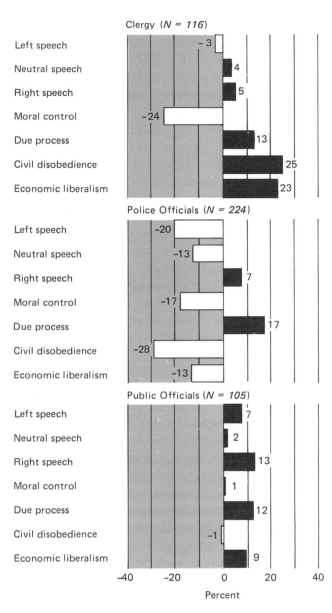

FIGURE 6.11

Effect of Vocation and Role on Elite Support for Selected Libertarian Issues,
Comparing Elites and the Mass Public, Controlling for Education
(CLS)

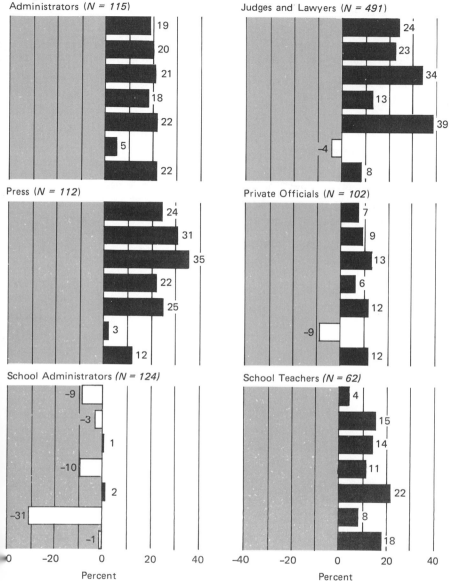

College Professors and
Administrators (*N = 115*)

Judges and Lawyers (*N = 491*)

Press (*N = 112*)

Private Officials (*N = 102*)

School Administrators *(N = 124)*

School Teachers *(N = 62)*

Percent

Percent

he horizontal bars and percentage figures in this graph represent the degree to which each of
ne elite groups scores higher or lower then the mass public on each of the variables listed.

provide an unusual but instructive illustration of the multiple influences that can affect support for libertarian principles.

As our earlier analysis suggests, judges, lawyers, and the press score far ahead of comparably educated members of the general public on most civil libertarian issues. The data reported in figure 6.11, however, add to our earlier understanding of the attitudes of these groups in several ways.

Consider first the matter of ideology. As we know from other findings in our research, the values associated with liberal and conservative ideologies are strongly correlated with attitudes toward libertarian norms. Note, however, that the economic liberalism of judges, lawyers, and the press obviously does not account for their strongly libertarian beliefs. While these elites are only moderately more liberal than comparably educated members of the general public, they are, however, far more libertarian.* (In contrast, the libertarian attitudes of college professors seem to be part of a larger syndrome of consistent support for all liberal values.)

The data also reveal a definite limitation in the commitment of judges, lawyers, and the press to certain kinds of libertarian norms. Despite their high levels of support for most civil liberties, none of these groups exhibit much tolerance for the notion of civil disobedience. The clergy, in fact, are the only elite group to support civil disobedience to any significant degree. One may assume in the case of the legal elites, at least, that their failure to respond to civil disobedience as they do to other libertarian values reflects, in part, their occupational responsibility for enforcing the law and maintaining social stability.

One of the most striking features of figure 6.11 is the marked contrast in attitudes between members of the two occupational groups who are most intimately involved with the protection of citizen rights: namely, judges and lawyers, on the one hand, and police officials, on the other. While the former are among the strongest supporters of libertarian values, the latter are among the least libertarian. What explains these differences?

The major reason, we suggest, can be traced to the occupational duties and responsibilities and subcultural values of the two groups. The police are directly charged with maintenance of social order and

---

*On the three subscales tapping support for freedom of speech, judges, lawyers, and the press were, on the average, 29 percent more likely to score high than comparably educated members of the general public. On our measure of support for economic liberalism, these groups were only ten points ahead of the public.

stability. Their job is to search out suspected lawbreakers and to prevent them from wrongdoing. This occupational responsibility not only attracts individuals with a strong initial concern for order and stability, but encourages the development of a similar concern among those who join the police force. The result is that the police tend to be less committed to the values of individual freedom and more committed to the importance of social control than comparably educated members of the general public.

Although judges and lawyers are also concerned with the maintenance of order, their primary responsibility is to ensure that constitutional rules and due process of law are observed in all cases. That is, they seek to ensure that, in the course of maintaining order, society does not unfairly or unnecessarily violate the rights and protections to which citizens are entitled. Thus, a certain degree of tension between the police and the legal community seems to be woven into the structure of democratic institutions. The result, in part, is the creation of subcultures with markedly different orientations toward civil libertarian norms.

One should also note in figure 6.11 that police officials exhibit stronger commitments to the norms of due process than to those of any other domain of libertarian values. On the five other dimensions of civil liberties, the police scored, on the average, 14 percentage points less libertarian than comparably educated members of the general public. In the single domain of due process, however, they were 17 percentage points more libertarian than the general public. Thus, in matters most directly relevant to their vocational responsibilities, police officials are far more likely to have encountered the norms of democratic doctrine than comparably educated members of the general public.

We should not assume, however, that police acceptance of the norms of due process signifies enthusiasm for all legal niceties. When the law is clear or the norms of proper police conduct are well established, the police generally accept them. When, however, the law is in flux, or when the police are asked to assess the desirability of recent changes in criminal procedure, their underlying concern for order and control asserts itself. A comparison of the items in tables 6.4 and 6.5 makes this point. On matters such as "bending the rules," dispensing with "the usual legal protections," or roughing up suspected criminals, police officials are more civil libertarian than comparably educated members of the general public. The data in table 6.5, however, suggest

TABLE 6.4
Differences Between Police Officials and Mass Public
in Response to Clear Norms of Due Process (CLS)

	Mass Public			Police Officials		
	Non-College	College	Total	Non-College	College	Total
Item	**(N=1082)**	**(N=871)**	**(N=1953)**	**(N=53)**	**(N=170)**	**(N=223)**
When police catch a violent gangster, they should:						
—treat him humanely, just as they should everyone they arrest.	73%	83%	80%	86%	94%	92%
—be allowed to be a bit rough with him if he refuses to give them the information they need to solve a crime.	18	10	15	8	6	6
—Neither/Undecided	8	7	5	6	1	2
Once an arrested person says he wishes to remain silent, the authorities:						
—should stop all further questioning at once.	48	57	52	75	69	70
—should keep asking questions to try to get the suspect to admit his crimes.	25	19	22	20	15	13
—Neither/Undecided	28	25	26	5	16	17
In order for the government to effectively prosecute the leaders of organized crime:						
—it should stick closely to the rules if the government wants other people to respect the law.	64	71	68	65	77	74
—it may sometimes have to bend the rules if there is no other way to convict them.	22	18	20	24	15	17
—Neither/Undecided	14	11	13	12	8	9
If someone is caught red-handed beating and robbing an older person on the street:						
—the suspect should still be entitled to a jury trial and all the usual legal protections.	66	79	72	90	88	88
—it's just a waste of the taxpayers' money to bother with the usual expensive trial.	18	13	16	6	8	5
—Neither/Undecided	17	9	13	4	5	5

TABLE 6.5
Differences Between Police Officials and Mass Public
in Affect Toward Law Enforcement Practices (CLS)

	Mass Public			Police Officials		
	Non-College	College	Total	Non-College	College	Total
Item	(N=1082)	(N=871)	(N=1953)	(N=53)	(N=170)	(N=223)
Police who pose as ordinary citizens and walk down the street with money sticking out of their pockets						
—are unfairly trying to trap people into committing crimes.	38%	36%	37%	20%	11%	13%
—are just doing their duty in trying to catch criminals.	40	40	40	65	70	69
—Neither/Undecided	22	24	23	15	19	18
Giving everyone accused of a crime a qualified lawyer even if the government has to pay for it						
—is absolutely necessary to protect individual rights.	76	86	81	76	72	72
—is wasteful and goes beyond the requirements of justice.	12	7	10	18	19	19
—Neither/Undecided	12	7	9	6	9	9
If a person is acquitted of a crime because the judge made a mistake in legal procedure during the trial						
—it is only fair that a person be set free even if the mistake was a small one.	11	11	11	10	7	8
—setting him free for this reason would be taking legal technicalities too far.	63	68	65	71	83	80
—Neither/Undecided	26	22	24	20	10	13
The "right to remain silent"						
—is needed to protect individuals from the "third degree" and forced confessions.	51	68	58	50	50	50
—has harmed the country by giving criminals too much protection.	31	19	26	33	31	32
—Neither/Undecided	18	13	16	17	19	19

that the police do not endorse some of the required procedures that hamper their effectiveness. For example, while they are more likely than the general public to say that the authorities should stop all further questioning once a suspect invokes his or her right to remain silent, they are less likely than the public to believe that "the right to remain silent" is a desirable legal protection. They are also less likely than the general public to believe that government-provided lawyers are a good idea, that technical legal errors should be grounds for the dismissal of criminal charges, or that the police should be able to use artifice to tempt people to commit crimes.

In sum, the police inhabit a subcultural milieu that makes them less sympathetic than other groups to the problem of protecting individual rights and freedoms. Nevertheless, the police do accept (even if unenthusiastically) due process norms which apply to their particular vocational responsibilities. Thus, the police furnish an especially compelling example of the importance of socialization for the maintenance of libertarian standards.

Emerging and Traditional Civil Liberties

A scanning of the data suggests that elite and mass differences are significantly (though not overwhelmingly) larger on traditional or "well-established" civil liberties than on what we have termed emerging liberties.* Whereas elites and the mass public diverge sharply on the application of such traditional rights as freedom of speech, press, religion, and due process, they differ to a lesser degree on such emerging issues as equal or preferential job opportunities for minorities and women, abortion, homosexual rights, civil disobedience, prisoner rights, open admission to universities, birth control for teenagers, the right to die, crimes without victims, the rights of children and the aged, and freedom of lifestyle.

The explanation for these results, we believe, rests principally on the fact that norms have not yet crystallized around these issues. Public opinion on them is far from settled among the elites or the mass public. The issues, moreover, are still in the process of taking form. To a far

---

* For data relating to established versus emerging norms, see chapters 7 and 8.

greater extent then, say, freedom of the press, they are surrounded by controversy, and not enough time has passed to permit a consensus to emerge. Nor do these issues enjoy the sanction of historical experience and tradition. They are rarely (or never) mentioned in the major historical documents in which our more familiar liberties have been set down, and they are not likely to be the subject of oratory and praise in the speeches of politicians and other community leaders. (If anything, many of them are avoided as vexing and too controversial.) One day, perhaps, some of these issues will be resolved to the point of attaining widely approved status. At present, however, they remain signs of a growing change in attitudes among certain groups in the society, but they cannot be regarded as established libertarian norms.

Although our analysis of elites and the mass public to this point has covered various topics, a few central themes stand out. The most fundamental of them, to which we have returned repeatedly, is the finding that, with occasional exceptions, elites and the mass public differ substantially in the support they exhibit toward civil libertarian norms. These elite-mass differences persist even after we match the two samples on a number of social characteristics, including education. They also persist (although in varying degree) even after we control for economic ideology and affect toward groups perceived as dangerous or obnoxious. We believe that the data, taken as a whole, provide support for the view that the elites have been more exposed to, and have a better understanding of, the libertarian tradition.

We have seen, in addition, that different elite groups vary among themselves in their levels of tolerance. Certain elites were found to support different facets of civil liberties to a greater or lesser degree depending upon their vocation and role. Finally, the differences between elites and the mass public are greater on established, traditional libertarian issues than they are on more recent, emerging issues.

CHAPTER 7

Ideology and Tolerance

Among the attitudes which should relate most strongly to tolerance are those that fall under the heading of political ideology. Indeed, the connections between one's support for civil liberties and one's orientation toward such ideological outlooks as liberalism and conservatism are so intimate that, in analyzing their interrelationship, one must take special precautions to distinguish the two, both analytically and operationally. One must be certain, above all, that in measuring political ideology one is not simultaneously (and unwittingly) measuring tolerance as well; otherwise, any correlations one might turn up between ideology and tolerance would have to be regarded as spurious.

By ideology in the present context we mean that set of attitudes which includes orientations toward equalitarianism; tradition, change, and reform; and such economic forms and practices as private enterprise and the welfare state. In the course of the analysis we shall also consider such ideologically related values as order, authority, identification with business or labor, support for the distinctions arising from class and status, and the intensity of one's commitment to the stabilizing influences of religion, the family, the police, the flag, and the military. Although procedural rights and other civil liberties might for some purposes also be regarded as elements in the ideological distinction between liberals and conservatives, we have separated them as best we can from the nonlibertarian components of ideology, so that we might assess the degree to which tolerance is affected by them.

As we expected, of course, liberals turn out to be more tolerant than conservatives. Indeed, they have higher scores than conservatives on all the dimensions of civil liberties we have been considering—freedom of speech, press, and assembly; symbolic speech, protest, and dissent; freedom of worship; due process; and privacy. The reasons for these expectations can be traced in large measure to the hopes, fears, and values embodied in each of the ideologies. Over the past two centuries, conservatives have repeatedly shown their fear of political and social instability. With rare exceptions, the conservatives have been the party of tradition, stability, duty, respect for authority, and the primacy of "law and order" over all competing values.

Conservatives also place emphasis upon discipline, both internal and external. Far more than liberals they fear human passions and appetites, character weaknesses, and potentialities for lawlessness. Conservatives look to such sources as religion, the family, the community, and the nation for guidance and instruction about the standards of proper conduct. They view human failure, delinquency, and crime as the products of individual deficiencies of character. To reform the criminal one must primarily reform the person, not the society; the same holds for economic and social failure. No amount of tinkering with social or political arrangements will make the weak strong. Nor will any amount of government assistance, such as subventions to the poor, convert the failed into the successful.

Liberals, although sharing some of these values to a degree, differ from conservatives in their willingness to risk a measure of social instability for the sake of promoting certain changes and reforms. Liberals are far more likely than conservatives to view lawbreaking as primarily the fault of society. To bring about institutional changes and needed social and economic reforms, liberals are inclined to go further than conservatives in permitting or even encouraging dissent, protest, and the dissemination of unorthodox opinions—activities that obviously presuppose extensive opportunities for freedom of speech, press, and assembly, as well as other forms of freedom of expression, such as symbolic speech.

The greater tendency among liberals to blame society for what happens to people also inclines them to be less punitive than conservatives toward individuals accused of crime and toward lawbreakers in general. Partly for this reason, liberals exhibit far greater sympathy than conservatives for the rights of the accused and are consistently more willing to honor in full measure their claims to due process. By conservative standards, however, since criminals and felons threaten the order and stability of the society itself, indulgence toward lawbreakers merely undermines the social order. Hence, a conservative system of criminal justice is more concerned to ensure the safety of the community and to convict and punish wrongdoers than to grant malefactors the full benefits of due process.

To the average conservative the security of the social order is threatened by those who promote revolutionary causes by advocating the overthrow of the government by force. That the society should allow freedom of expression to be used for its own destruction strikes most conservatives as short-sighted in the extreme. The same holds for pornography, which may weaken moral values and hence undermine the social order itself.

Liberals are likely to view obscenity and revolutionary advocacy as inescapable by-products (however undesirable) of freedom. They are willing to risk possible injury to the society by permitting unsavory and even "dangerous" opinions to be expressed and broadcast. To them (though not to most conservatives) the society runs a greater risk from the suppression of such opinions than from their dissemination.

The differences between liberals and conservatives in their orientation toward national security also has a bearing on their attitudes and actions regarding civil liberties. Although in this matter the two camps differ once again in degree and emphasis rather than in substance, conservatives are more intensely focused on the safety of the state against all enemies, both internal and external.

Conservatives turn up in our data more frequently than liberals as the promoters of a "hard" line toward individual Americans and organizations thought to be friendly to foreign adversaries. Conservatives, far more than liberals, back policies of surveillance and infiltration in dealing with organizations they regard as sympathetic to hostile foreign nations. While conservatives and the conservative right are not alone in wanting the phones of suspect organizations to be tapped, their quarters "bugged," their mail inspected, and the names of their participants recorded, they are, in light of their preoccupations and patriotic fervor, among the chief advocates of such measures.

Findings on Political Ideology and Attitudes Toward Civil Liberties

Conservatives and liberals may differ in their attitudes toward tolerance partly because of an underlying disagreement about the nature of a *right*. Liberals are, in effect, more inclined than conservatives to believe that rights are *natural* and *inalienable*, that a person possesses

them simply by virtue of being human. No institution has the authority to separate the individual from the rights which are part of his or
her nature; they are ineradicable and endure under all conditions
throughout a person's lifetime. Although some conservatives share this
perspective, many tend to think of rights as contingent upon proper
conduct—as benefits to be earned, won, or merited. Most conservatives
do not appear to regard a right as inextinquishable. An individual who
abuses it, or behaves outrageously, or fails to honor its purposes, may
lose it. Thus one has the right to publish, but not to disseminate materials that advocate the violent overthrow of the government or that portray explicit and lewd sexual conduct.

Support for these observations can be inferred from the data in
table 7.1. As expected, conservatives, significantly more often than liberals, would deny an established right to individuals who do not live
up to certain standards. Thus, among the ideological elites,* 70 percent
of the conservatives and 84 percent of the conservative right (approximately twice the proportion of liberals) believe that a newspaper has a
right to publish its opinions *only* if it doesn't twist the facts and tell
lies. Teachers have a right to express their opinions in class on religion,
morals, and politics *only* if the opinions they express are acceptable to
the community. Although it is well established in American jurispru-
dence that individuals have a right not to be kept in prison without
trial, a substantial majority of the conservatives would withdraw this
right from a person who is considered "dangerous."

Data in table 7.2 from the CLS provide the grounds for similar
inferences. Although the Fifth Amendment unequivocally protects individuals from being forced to testify against themselves in court, more
than four times as many strong conservatives as strong liberals (in the
community leader sample) would deny that right to people accused of
"very brutal crimes." Although the differences are smaller, more conservatives than liberals would deny due process rights to "habitual
criminals," to "rapists" and "child molesters," and to a "violent gangster." (See table 7.3.) Items in table 7.2 on subjects other than crime
reveal a similar tendency for conservatives to regard rights as benefits
to be earned. Thus, a person who is "gay" is considered by 61 percent
of the strong conservatives (compared with 8 percent of the strong

---

* The "ideological elites" (or "criterion groups") are samples of knowledgeable respondents who are active in, or associated with, ideological organizations which range in
their political and philosophical outlooks across the ideological spectrum, from left liberals to the far right.

TABLE 7.1
Liberal-Conservative Differences in Perception
of the Inalienability or Contingency of Rights (OVS)

	Ideological Criterion Groups			
	Liberal Left (N=543)	Liberals (N=875)	Conservatives (N=595)	Conservative Right (N=129)
A newspaper has a right to publish its opinions:				
—no matter how false and twisted its opinions are.	49%	38%	21%	12%
—only if it doesn't twist the facts and tell lies.	38	48	70	84
—Neither/Undecided	14	14	9	4
On issues of religion, morals and politics, high school teachers have the right to express their opinions in class:				
—even if they go against the community's standards.	81	68	16	14
—only if those opinions are acceptable to the community.	3	5	44	56
—Neither/Undecided	16	28	39	29
If minorities aren't receiving equal treatment in jobs or housing:				
—the government should step in to see that they are treated the same as everyone else.	94	92	29	31
—they should try to act better so that they will be accepted.	1	2	38	52
—Neither/Undecided	5	7	33	17
Keeping people in prison without trial:				
—is never justified.	62	56	26	16
—is sometimes necessary when dealing with people who are dangerous.	26	32	63	74
—Neither/Undecided	13	13	11	9
Any American who shows disrespect for the flag:				
—has the right to think what he pleases.	91	78	29	18
—should be turned over to patriots to be taught a lesson.	1	1	19	31
—Neither/Undecided	8	21	52	52

NOTES: The samples in this table consist of criterion group liberals and conservatives. For a description of these samples, see p. 277.

Because percentages have been rounded off, occasionally there will be disparities in totals (columns will not add up to 100 percent).

See the Preface to Research Findings (p. 25) and Appendix B for a description of the leader and mass public samples used in the PAB, CLS, and OVS studies: that is "Political Leaders," "Legal Elite," and so forth.

The CLS study was conducted in 1978–1979; the OVS in 1976–1977; and the PAB in 1958.

TABLE 7.2
*Liberal-Conservative Differences in Perception
of the Inalienability or Contingency of Rights (CLS)*

	Non-libertarian Ideology Scale			
	Community Leaders			
	Strong Liberal	Moderate Liberal	Moderate Conservative	Strong Conservative
	(N=268)	(N=111)	(N=87)	(N=135)
Forcing people to testify against themselves in court:				
—is never justified, no matter how terrible the crime.	78%	56%	66%	49%
—may be necessary when they are accused of very brutal crimes.	7	24	20	33
—Neither/Undecided	15	20	14	18
If a political group known for its violent political activities wants to picket the White House:				
—it should be granted police protection like any other group.	64	46	33	24
—it should be prevented from doing so because it might endanger the President.	22	37	47	59
—Neither/Undecided	15	17	20	17
For the most part, local ordinances that guarantee equal rights to homosexuals in such matters as jobs and housing:				
—uphold the American idea of human rights for all.	85	61	45	24
—damage American moral standards.	8	22	33	61
—Neither/Undecided	7	17	22	16
People with extreme political ideas who want to work as newspaper or TV reporters:				
—should have the same chance as any other Americans to work as reporters.	74	57	61	55
—should not be hired for such jobs because they can't be trusted to report the news fairly.	13	19	20	31
—Neither/Undecided	13	24	20	14
Freedom to worship as one pleases:				
—applies to all religious groups, regardless of how extreme their beliefs are.	86	80	74	68
—was never meant to apply to religious cults that the majority of people consider "strange," "fanatical," or "weird."	6	10	15	19
—Neither/Undecided	8	10	12	13

liberals) to have waived his or her rights to equal jobs or housing. And those who hold extreme political ideas have, according to 31 percent of the strong conservatives, relinquished their right to work as newspaper reporters. The freedom to worship is for many conservatives, also, a contingent right: for example, it can be exercised freely by those who practice conventional forms of worship, but not by those who belong to a "weird" or "fanatical" cult. In the community leader sample, even free speech—surely among the most fundamental rights—is to be enjoyed (according to a disproportionate number of strong conservatives) only by those willing to grant the right of free speech to others. (See table 7.3.) One can also see from table 7.3 (where we have measured ideology by self-designation) that even such elementary and universally recognized democratic liberties as the right to vote and the right to appear on the ballot are more often perceived by conservatives than liberals as contingent, rather than inalienable, rights. Thus, in both the mass public and elite samples, the conservatives are more likely to deny the vote to individuals who are uninformed about the issues. They are also more likely to deny potential candidates the right to be on the ballot if they do not themselves "believe in the ballot."

The differences by ideology, it should be noted, are not uniformly large for all items. Although the scores are in all cases in the predicted direction, there are certain items (such as the right to a trial and to a fair trial) that are so universally recognized that differences between the ideological camps are muted. However, where the norms have not yet fully crystallized and are still in the process of emerging, the public is less constrained by them and the differences between liberals and conservatives are larger. Ideology, in other words, strongly influences the tendency to embrace or reject libertarian values unless those values are so pervasively integrated into the culture that conservatives will subscribe to them (at least verbally) almost as frequently as liberals.

As the data in the preceding tables bear out, the tendency to believe that rights should be denied to people who have shown, by their outrageous or unorthodox behavior, that they do not merit them is not peculiar to conservatives, but is more frequent among them. We take this to mean not that conservatives are opposed to civil liberties, but that they value tolerance and the rights of others less strongly; in effect, they convert rights into privileges to which all are entitled but which some people have lost by their behavior.

Fewer conservatives would take action to protect the rights of individuals or groups whose rights have been denied or invaded. (See table

TABLE 7.3

Perceptions of the Inalienability or Contingency of Rights, by Ideological Self-Designation (CLS)

	Ideological Self-Designation									
	Community Leaders					Mass Public				
	Strong Liberal	Liberal	Middle Road	Conservative	Strong Conservative	Strong Liberal	Liberal	Middle Road	Strong Conservative	Conservative
	(N=99)	(N=272)	(N=338)	(N=375)	(N=54)	(N=82)	(N=270)	(N=562)	(N=646)	(N=80)
Free speech should be granted:										
—to everyone regardless of how intolerant they are of other people's opinions.	86%	80%	72%	74%	70%	67%	67%	61%	57%	56%
—only to people who are willing to grant the same rights of free speech to everyone else.	6	17	21	22	25	23	23	28	29	25
—Neither/Undecided	8	4	7	4	6	10	10	11	15	19
If someone is caught red-handed beating and robbing an older person on the street:										
—the suspect should still be entitled to a jury trial and all the usual legal protections.	96	96	89	86	78	84	82	73	71	75
—it's just a waste of taxpayers' money to bother with the usual expensive trial.	0	2	5	10	15	6	13	17	17	16
—Neither/Undecided	4	3	6	4	7	10	6	10	12	9

TABLE 7.3 (continued)

	Community Leaders					Mass Public				
	Strong Liberal	Liberal	Middle Road	Conservative	Strong Conservative	Strong Liberal	Liberal	Middle Road	Strong Conservative	Conservative
	(N=99)	(N=272)	(N=338)	(N=375)	(N=54)	(N=82)	(N=270)	(N=562)	(N=646)	(N=80)
Should rapists or child molesters be given the same sort of "fair trial" as other criminals?										
—Yes, because the right to a fair trial should not depend on the nature of the crime.	94%	94%	93%	87%	85%	79%	86%	76%	77%	66%
—No, because their crimes are so inhuman that they do not deserve the usual legal protections.	2	4	6	10	11	15	11	20	20	29
—Neither/Undecided	4	2	1	3	4	6	3	4	4	5
When police catch a violent gangster, they should:										
—treat him humanely, just as they should treat everyone else.	94	94	93	87	72	88	88	81	75	62
—be allowed to be a bit rough with him if he refuses to give them the information they need to solve a crime.	2	2	5	9	24	9	8	12	19	27
—Neither/Undecided	4	5	2	3	4	4	4	8	6	11

—All adult citizens, regardless of how ignorant they may be.	90	85	81	77	60	80	77	68	72	56
—Only people who know something about the issues.	4	5	8	9	8	9	5	11	11	25
—Neither/Undecided	6	11	11	14	32	11	19	21	18	19
In a democratic election, which candidates should have a right to be on the ballot?										
—All candidates, no matter what they think about the election system.	90	87	78	68	44	83	76	63	65	69
—Only the candidates who actually believe in the ballot.	4	6	13	23	40	6	13	23	23	22
—Neither/Undecided	6	6	9	9	16	11	11	15	13	9
When two people are arrested, one a habitual criminal and the other a citizen never before in trouble with the law, would the police be justified in treating them differently when arresting them and booking them?										
—No, because everybody is entitled to the same treatment under the law no matter who they are.	65	69	55	56	46	69	68	52	50	44
—Yes, because there is more chance the habitual criminal actually committed the crime, and he may also be dangerous.	22	21	34	34	42	11	25	37	41	50
—Neither/Undecided	12	10	11	11	12	20	7	11	9	6

7.4.) More conservatives than liberals say they would do nothing or would not get involved if the FBI opened their neighbor's mail, if a teacher were fired for being a homosexual, or if blacks were prevented from buying a house in their neighborhood. Conservatives would also be more reluctant to take action if a play were closed because its actors were naked, if a protestor were arrested for calling police a "dirty name," or if a woman were denied a job or held back because of her sex. Conservatives are more willing to act, however, if they are ideologically in sympathy with the individual or group whose rights are being denied, as in the case of the gun club leader whose home was illegally searched or the reporter who was fired from a newspaper or TV station because of his right-wing opinions.

In figure 7.1, the data show how the criterion group samples in the OVS study scored on a thirty-five-item civil liberties scale that encompassed a broad range of libertarian values. As one can see from the figure, the respondents in the liberal samples are, by an overwhelming margin, more favorably disposed toward civil liberties than are the respondents in the conservative criterion groups. Whereas over 90 percent of the active liberals score high on the civil liberties scale, only 20 percent of the conservatives and 10 percent of the conservative right score high. An insignificant number (approximately 1 percent) of those in the liberal camps score low on the civil liberties scale, while those scoring low among the conservative activists range from 48 percent for the conservatives to 65 percent for the conservative right.

Lest it be assumed that the very large differences reported in figure 7.1 are merely a result of the sampling procedure and hence spurious,* we have also attempted to measure the effects of ideology by constructing a fifty-item ideology scale in the OVS study that contains no civil libertarian or tolerance items at all. Instead, the content of the scale is deliberately restricted to items reflecting the three dimensions of ideology to which we referred earlier: attitudes toward equality; toward tradition, change, and reform; and toward issues involving the economy and the welfare state. As can be seen in table 7.5, the relation between ideology (as measured by this scale) and the classification of the ideological criterion groups is a powerful one. Approximately 96 percent of the criterion group liberals and left liberals also score liberal on the ideology scale, while the number of conservatives in the criteri-

* For data showing the intercorrelations among the three subdimensions of the nonlibertarian ideology scale, see Appendix C.

TABLE 7.4

Willingness to Act in Defense of Rights, by Ideological Self-Designation (CLS)

What would you do if:	Ideological Self-Designation									
	Community Leaders					Mass Public				
	Strong Liberal	Liberal	Middle Road	Conservative	Strong Conservative	Strong Liberal	Liberal	Middle Road	Conservative	Strong Conservative
	(N=99)	(N=272)	(N=338)	(N=375)	(N=54)	(N=82)	(N=270)	(N=562)	(N=646)	(N=80)
The FBI opened the mail of one of your neighbors suspected of being a subversive?										
—I would do nothing, since I favor the action.	4%	7%	21%	40%	49%	9%	13%	25%	34%	43%
—I wouldn't get involved, can't help anyway.	1	11	10	11	6	17	24	26	23	23
—I would contribute money, write letters, join organizations, etc., to protest.	77	45	28	17	13	51	34	12	11	11
—I'm undecided.	18	36	41	33	32	23	30	37	32	24
A homosexual teacher was fired because of his or her sexual preference?										
—I would do nothing, since I favor the action.	6	14	32	53	78	5	16	32	49	67
—I wouldn't get involved, can't help anyway.	1	11	8	6	4	23	17	22	15	8
—I would contribute money, write letters, join organizations, etc., to protest.	78	42	21	11	8	51	44	13	10	14
—I'm undecided.	15	33	38	30	11	21	22	32	25	11

TABLE 7.4 *(continued)*

	Ideological Self-Designation									
	Community Leaders					Mass Public				
What would you do if:	Strong Liberal	Liberal	Middle Road	Conserv-ative	Strong Conserv-ative	Strong Liberal	Liberal	Middle Road	Conserv-ative	Strong Conserv-ative
	(N=99)	(N=272)	(N=338)	(N=375)	(N=54)	(N=82)	(N=270)	(N=562)	(N=646)	(N=80)
The police closed a local play because the actors were naked?										
—I would do nothing, since I favor the action.	10%	17%	40%	58%	67%	13%	25%	43%	58%	57%
—I wouldn't get involved, can't help anyway.	8	19	19	13	11	21	24	23	18	17
—I would contribute money, write letters, join organizations, etc., to protest.	50	27	16	10	13	40	32	13	11	10
—I'm undecided.	32	37	25	19	9	26	20	20	13	17
A black couple was prevented from buying a house on your block?										
—I would do nothing, since I favor the action.	1	2	3	7	17	5	7	10	15	24
—I wouldn't get involved, can't help anyway.	2	5	12	15	17	12	16	27	26	25
—I would contribute money, write letters, join organizations, etc., to protest.	90	84	60	41	35	72	55	32	24	24
—I'm undecided.	7	10	25	37	32	11	21	31	36	27

tester for calling them a
dirty name?

—I would do nothing, since I favor the action.	7	21	37	54	69	12	23	41	49	58
—I wouldn't get involved, can't help anyway.	10	17	19	17	15	23	30	28	25	19
—I would contribute money, write letters, join organizations, etc., to protest.	60	31	19	11	6	45	25	9	9	6
—I'm undecided.	23	30	26	18	11	20	22	21	17	17

A black youth, accused of murder, was convicted by a racially prejudiced judge and jury?

—I would do nothing, since I favor the action.	1	1	1	2	2	1	3	1	2	6
—I wouldn't get involved, can't help anyway.	3	4	8	15	7	10	16	21	21	18
—I would contribute money, write letters, join organizations, etc., to protest.	91	84	65	57	58	78	64	47	45	47
—I'm undecided.	5	12	25	27	33	11	17	30	32	29

Local officials denied an unpopular faith-healing religious cult the use of a public park for a meeting?

—I would do nothing, since I favor the action.	11	20	29	44	44	21	30	38	45	43
—I wouldn't get involved, can't help anyway.	6	14	18	16	9	24	22	27	24	27
—I would contribute money, write letters, join organizations, etc., to protest.	43	28	22	13	17	24	19	8	7	10
—I'm undecided.	39	38	31	27	30	31	29	26	24	20

TABLE 7.4 (continued)

	Community Leaders					Mass Public				
What would you do if:	Strong Liberal	Liberal	Middle Road	Conserv- ative	Strong Conserv- ative	Strong Liberal	Liberal	Middle Road	Conserv- ative	Strong Conserv- ative
	(N=99)	(N=272)	(N=338)	(N=375)	(N=54)	(N=82)	(N=270)	(N=562)	(N=646)	(N=80)
A woman was denied a job or held back because of her sex?										
—I would do nothing, since I favor the action.	1%	0%	1%	1%	7%	1%	2%	2%	3%	4%
—I wouldn't get involved, can't help anyway.	3	7	15	15	13	18	18	22	25	30
—I would contribute money, write letters, join organizations, etc., to protest.	90	83	66	57	48	72	69	55	46	48
—I'm undecided.	6	10	19	27	32	9	12	21	26	18
A woman you believed to be innocent was arrested and convicted by false testimony given by the police?										
—I would do nothing, since I favor the action.	1	0	0	0	0	0	0	0	1	0
—I wouldn't get involved, can't help anyway.	0	4	4	7	9	9	10	9	12	5
—I would contribute money, write letters, join organizations, etc., to protest.	95	88	83	80	80	83	77	69	66	82
—I'm undecided.	4	9	13	13	11	9	13	22	21	13

Ideological Self-Designation

A reporter was fired from a TV station or newspaper because of his strong right-wing opinions?

—I would do nothing, since I favor the action.	23	19	16	25	22	26	16	19	20	28
—I wouldn't get involved, can't help anyway.	7	19	28	23	15	21	36	36	34	23
—I would contribute money, write letters, join organizations, etc., to protest.	32	30	22	18	37	26	21	13	11	30
—I'm undecided.	37	32	34	34	26	28	28	32	34	20

A gun club leader was arrested after an illegal search of his home?

—I would do nothing, since I favor the action.	5	4	6	5	4	15	9	9	10	8
—I wouldn't get involved, can't help anyway.	6	15	19	15	22	21	24	28	25	18
—I would contribute money, write letters, join organizations, etc., to protest.	44	45	42	49	57	40	40	31	35	44
—I'm undecided.	44	35	34	31	17	24	28	32	30	30

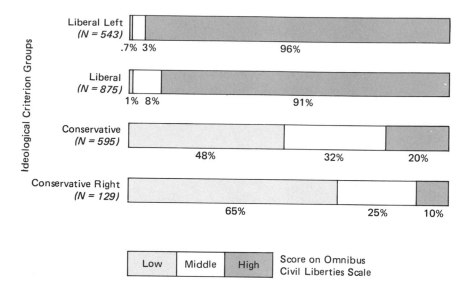

Notes: Because percentages have been rounded off, occasionally there will be disparities in totals (columns will not add up to 100 percent).

See the Preface to Research Findings in Chapter 1 and Appendix B for an analysis of the components of various categories used in the PAB, CLS, and OVS studies: that is "Political Leaders," "Legal Elite," and so forth.

The CLS was conducted in 1978-1979; the OVS in 1976-1977; and the PAB in 1958.

FIGURE 7.1
Attitudes Toward Civil Liberties Among Four Sets of
Ideological Criterion Groups
(OVS)

on group samples who score liberal on the scale is approximately 5 percent.

In light of the magnitude of these correlations, it should come as no surprise that (as can be seen in figure 7.2) the relation between one's ideological orientation and level of tolerance is powerful. The relation holds strongly, moreover, for all three samples in the OVS study, although it is especially strong for the sample of respondents active in ideological organizations. Some 96 percent of the liberals score high on the civil liberties scale, compared with only 17 percent of the conservatives. Among the nonpartisan opinion leaders, the parallel figures are 89 percent for the liberals and 44 percent for the conservatives, while for the mass public the figures are 56 percent for the liberals and 15 percent for the conservatives.

TABLE 7.5

*The Relation Between Ideological Criterion Groups and
the Nonlibertarian Ideology Scale (OVS)*

	Ideological Criterion Groups			
Nonlibertarian Ideology Scale	Liberal Left (N=543)	Liberal (N=875)	Conservative (N=595)	Conservative Right (N=129)
Liberal	96%	85%	4%	6%
Moderate	3	11	9	14
Conservative	1	4	87	80

Whether one measures ideology by membership in criterion groups, by self-designation, or by a carefully validated scale, the results are fundamentally the same, though the *magnitude* of the differences may vary somewhat. Essentially similar results also turn up for the various types of samples employed in the study, although the differences in libertarian attitudes are largest within those samples (for example, the criterion group samples) whose members are most committed to their respective ideologies and best informed about civil liberties and politics in general.

The results showing liberals to be significantly more tolerant than conservatives are not peculiar to the OVS study. As figure 7.3 bears witness, the findings are amply confirmed by the data turned up in the CLS study as well. Even in the general population, 54 percent of the liberals, compared with 19 percent of the conservatives, score at the upper (or tolerant) end of the civil liberties scale. Some 13 percent of the liberals, compared with 48 percent of the conservatives, score at the lower (or intolerant) end of the scale.

The differences between liberals and conservatives is even greater among the community leaders: 79 percent of the liberals, compared with 31 percent of the conservatives, score tolerant on civil liberties. The number of conservatives in this sample who score at the intolerant end of the scale is more than six times as large as the number who score intolerant among the liberals. Impressive differences in the same direction also turn up for the lawyers and judges, even though a large majority of them are favorably disposed toward civil liberties. A comparison of liberals and conservatives among the police officials yields the same basic pattern of differences. While the police officials as a group lean toward conservatism, those among them who score liberal on the ideology scale are clearly more inclined than their conservative col-

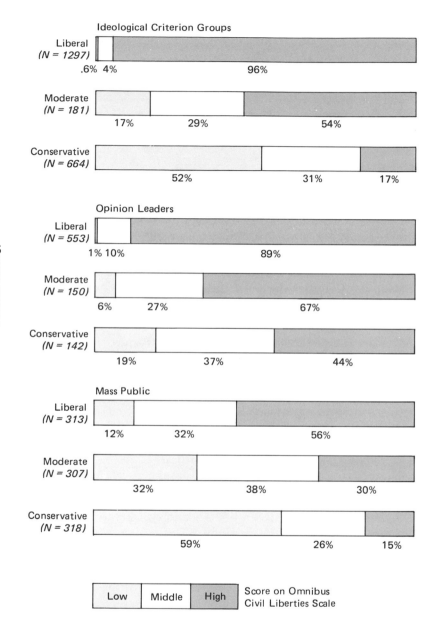

Note: In this table political ideology is measured by the non-libertarian ideology scale. Civil liberties is measured by the 35–item civil liberties scale.

FIGURE 7.2
The Relation Between Political Ideology and Support for Civil Liberties
(OVS)

leagues to respect civil liberties—indeed, by a ratio of almost five to one.

In figure 7.4 we present data from the CLS study based on a procedure in which respondents are classified ideologically according to the 'label' they have chosen as best describing their political beliefs. Although such ideological self-labeling is fraught with dangers (since respondents often misclassify themselves), the data in figure 7.4 are nevertheless consistent with the findings reported in the preceding tables. Even among the members of the mass public (for whom ideological self-labeling is most unreliable) the relation between the respondents' ideological preferences and their scores on our sixty-nine-item civil liberties scale is both strong and in the predicted direction. Some 75 percent of strong liberals score high on the civil liberties scale, and the proportions decline steadily (and sharply) as one moves across the ideological spectrum to the strong conservatives, only 22 percent of whom score high. By the same token, the number scoring *intolerant* on the civil liberties scale increases from 13 percent for the strong liberals to 51 percent for the strong conservatives.

Differences that parallel these results but that are even larger show up for the community leader samples in figure 7.4. An extraordinary 96 percent of the self-described strong liberals score at the tolerant end of the civil liberties scale, compared with 31 percent of the strong conservatives. Only 2 percent of the strong liberals show up as intolerant, and once again the level of intolerance rises steadily as one moves across the ideological spectrum from left to right. The data in figure 7.4 on lawyers and judges and on police officials display a similar pattern. They also parallel closely the findings reported for these samples in figure 7.3.

Thus, in two separate national studies conducted two years apart on various elite and mass samples, in which we employed several different measures of ideological orientation, ideology proved in every case to have a powerful bearing on the attitudes respondents express toward a broad variety of civil liberties issues. With the exception of a small number of issues to which conservatives, by virtue of their ideology, are especially sympathetic, liberals turn up as substantially more tolerant than conservatives on civil liberties questions of many different types.

The differences between the ideological camps are clearly underscored by their responses to the several categories of civil liberties reported in tables 7.6 and 7.7. It is clear from these tables that the differ-

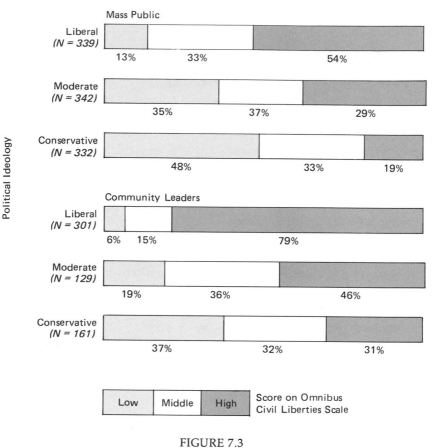

Political Ideology

Mass Public

Liberal
(N = 339)
13%   33%   54%

Moderate
(N = 342)
35%   37%   29%

Conservative
(N = 332)
48%   33%   19%

Community Leaders

Liberal
(N = 301)
6%   15%   79%

Moderate
(N = 129)
19%   36%   46%

Conservative
(N = 161)
37%   32%   31%

| Low | Middle | High | Score on Omnibus
Civil Liberties Scale |

FIGURE 7.3
Nonlibertarian Ideology and Orientation Toward Civil Liberties
(CLS)

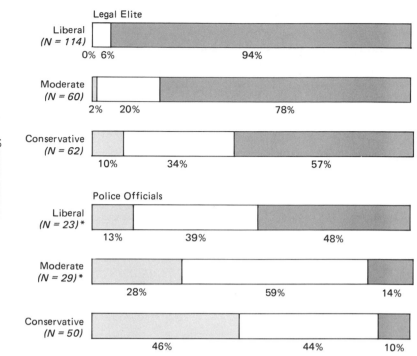

Legal Elite

Liberal
(N = 114)

0% 6%   94%

Moderate
(N = 60)

2%   20%   78%

Conservative
(N = 62)

10%   34%   57%

Police Officials

Liberal
(N = 23)*

13%   39%   48%

Moderate
(N = 29)*

28%   59%   14%

Conservative
(N = 50)

46%   44%   10%

Political Ideology

*The numbers in these categories are so small that the statistics reported may not be reliable.

Note: In this table political ideology is measured by a 26-item scale containing items on
equalitarianism; tradition, change and reform; and the economy and the welfare state. Civil
liberties orientation is measured by a 69-item scale that includes issues from all the domains
of civil liberties.

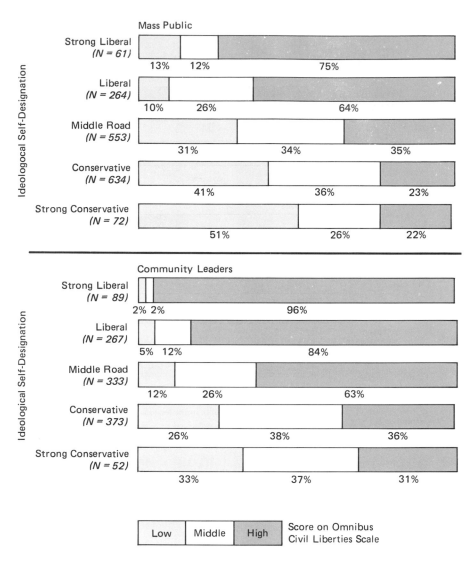

FIGURE 7.4
Ideological Self-Designation and Attitude Toward Civil Liberties
(CLS)

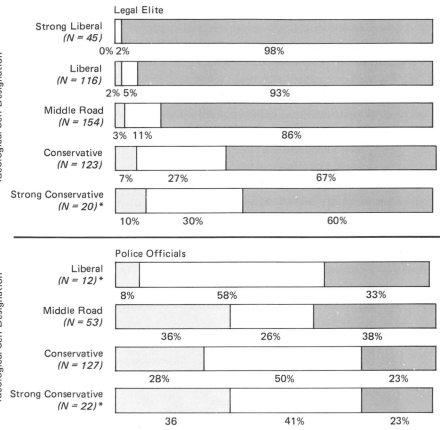

Ideological Self-Designation

Legal Elite

Strong Liberal
(N = 45)
0% 2%   98%

Liberal
(N = 116)
2% 5%   93%

Middle Road
(N = 154)
3% 11%   86%

Conservative
(N = 123)
7%   27%   67%

Strong Conservative
(N = 20)*
10%   30%   60%

Ideological Self-Designation

Police Officials

Liberal
(N = 12)*
8%   58%   33%

Middle Road
(N = 53)
36%   26%   38%

Conservative
(N = 127)
28%   50%   23%

Strong Conservative
(N = 22)*
36   41%   23%

*The original research design included two additional ideological self-descriptions, Far Left and Far Right, but the Ns in these categories were too small to yield reliable statistics.

ences between liberals and conservatives in their levels of support for civil liberties are not confined to certain categories of freedom (press, assembly, due process, privacy, and so forth), but show up strongly for every one of the domains. One can observe this most dramatically in table 7.6, which reports the results for the criterion group samples in the OVS study. Since of all our samples they are the "purest," most active, and most indisputable representatives of the ideological camps under which they have been classified, it should come as no surprise that the differences between the left liberals and the conservative right in their support for freedom of the press is 74 percent; between the liberals and conservatives as such the difference is 47 percent. While the differences are not equally large for all the other domains in table 7.6, they are sizable in every instance.

In any event, one cannot be certain whether the variations in the magnitudes of the differences between one domain and another reflect genuine differences in the way they relate to ideology or differences in the substance of the items that happened to be used. Inspection of the face content of the items in the omnibus civil liberties scales (see be-

TABLE 7.6

Percentage Scoring Libertarian and Antilibertarian for Subcategories of Civil Liberties Scale, by Ideology (OVS Criterion Group)

Category		Left Liberal (N=543)	Liberal (N=875)	Conservative (N=595)	Conservative Right (N=129)
Freedom of Speech	% High	95	88	21	10
	% Low	1	2	37	63
Freedom of Press	% High	91	85	38	17
	% Low	1	3	29	51
Freedom of Assembly	% High	67	68	44	27
	% Low	11	8	14	28
Right of Due Process	% High	90	83	25	19
	% Low	4	5	51	63
Right of Privacy	% High	95	87	12	10
	% Low	2	4	65	71
Freedom of Religion	% High	87	88	64	43
	% Low	2	2	20	43

NOTE: Only those who score *high* and *low* on each subscale (the upper and lower thirds of the distribution on each subscale as determined by the scores of the mass public) are reported in this table. The middle thirds have been omitted to conserve space and simplify the table.

low) suggests that the latter is doubtless at work to some extent, as conservatives are especially prone to choose the intolerant response when an item refers to an activity, group, or value to which they are particularly sensitive (for example, obscenity, subversion, crime). Of course, liberals are subject to a similar type of bias, displaying greater tolerance toward the groups and opinions they like than those they dislike. Nevertheless, as we shall see from the item data in tables 7.8 and 7.9, the liberals are somewhat more likely than conservatives to show up as highly libertarian or tolerant even when they disapprove of the group, activity, or value to which the item refers.

The general tendency of the OVS findings on the subcategories of freedom is clearly confirmed by the results in the CLS study. In table 7.7, we present data from that study on the relation of ideology to the domains of the civil liberties scale. Although the differences between strong liberals and strong conservatives in the mass population are, as predicted, smaller than those reported for the criterion group samples in table 7.6, varying roughly from 20 percent to 40 percent, with an average difference of over 25 percent, they are nevertheless substantial and always in the predicted direction. The differences for the community leaders sample, also presented in table 7.7, offer further testimony for the conclusion that political ideology (as measured by a scale that is itself free of libertarian content) has a significant bearing on the attitudes respondents express both toward tolerance in general and toward every one of the civil liberties subdomains. Among the community leaders, 72 percent of the strong liberals are highly tolerant on issues involving freedom of the press, compared with 36 percent for the strong conservatives. Some 78 percent of the strong liberals, compared with 31 percent of the strong conservatives, are highly tolerant on matters affecting the right of assembly. It should also be noted that the community leaders score more libertarian than the general public in all subdomains.

The differences between ideological camps on particular civil liberties issues are well illustrated by their responses to specific items reported in tables 7.8 and 7.9. In table 7.8, which draws on data from the ideological criterion groups in the OVS study, the percentage scores for the thirty-five civil liberties items included in the survey show liberals to be far more libertarian than conservatives on all but a handful of items. Indeed, on only two items are the scores of liberals and conservatives approximately equal: one item concerns the right to make racial slurs at a public meeting and the other the right to hold

TABLE 7.7

Percentage Scoring High and Low on Subscales of the Omnibus Civil Liberties Scale, by Ideology (CLS)

		Nonlibertarian Ideology Scale							
		Community Leaders				Mass Public			
Civil Liberties Subscales		Strong Liberal	Moderate Liberal	Moderate Conservative	Strong Conservative	Strong Liberal	Moderate Liberal	Moderate Conservative	Strong Conservative
		(N=268)	(N=111)	(N=87)	(N=135)	(N=257)	(N=255)	(N=257)	(N=257)
Freedom of Press	% High	72	54	44	36	52	35	27	22
	% Low	12	20	23	24	23	35	42	51
Freedom of Speech	% High	76	57	53	44	44	25	25	21
	% Low	6	14	20	19	16	26	31	44
Academic Freedom	% High	73	53	38	32	55	42	31	23
	% Low	8	27	29	36	19	31	37	43
Symbolic Speech	% High	72	52	38	31	57	35	31	25
	% Low	15	31	37	47	27	43	49	52
Freedom of Assembly	% High	78	52	39	31	56	35	28	16
	% Low	6	13	30	42	16	33	37	55
Right of Due Process	% High	72	38	41	18	49	29	24	15
	% Low	3	13	20	33	14	27	38	50
Right of Privacy	% High	48	28	29	16	37	32	25	24
	% Low	23	41	45	56	30	40	44	51
Freedom of Religion	% High	70	49	36	26	47	24	22	11
	% Low	11	27	36	44	25	38	47	57

NOTE: Only those who score *high* and *low* on each subscale (the upper and lower thirds of the distribution on each subscale as determined by the scores of the mass public) are reported in this table. The middle thirds have been omitted to conserve space and simplify the table.

meetings that advocate war against enemy nations—items which involve causes toward which conservatives are likely to be initially more sympathetic than liberals. On all other items in table 7.8, the differences between ideological groups of the left and right are not only statistically significant but, in most cases, extremely powerful. Whether the items fall under the rubric of free speech, free press, due process, or one of the other civil liberties categories, the differences between the ideological camps in their responses to many of the items are as large as 50 percent or even 60 percent. The average percentage difference between the left liberals and the conservative right is, for the list of items as a whole, over 50 percent; while for the more moderate liberals and conservatives, it is nearly 40 percent.

Comparable data on the item responses of community leaders and the mass public in the CLS study are presented in table 7.9. Since the number of civil liberties items in this study is very large, we have included only a sample of the items from each subdomain for purposes of illustration. Once again the measure of ideology is the nonlibertarian ideology scale broken into arithmetic quartiles, with the cutting points determined by the frequencies with which the respondents in the mass public distributed themselves across the intervals of that scale.

The results shown in table 7.9 confirm once again that orientation toward specific civil liberties is related to ideological preference. The differences between the ideological camps, though significant in both samples, are a bit larger among the community leaders than among the mass public; principally, in our opinion, it is because the leaders, enjoying a more sophisticated awareness of the nature and implications of the ideologies they respectively embrace, have to a greater degree learned which opinions and values in the civil liberties measure "fit" with their commitment to liberalism or conservatism. Possessing, as they do, a more coherent, informed, and interconnected set of beliefs about public affairs than does the general public, they more often choose responses to the civil liberties items in table 7.9 that reflect the essential ideas in their respective ideologies.

The scores registered by liberals and conservatives in table 7.9 are not, of course, identical for each item. Variations in the scores, and in the size of the differences between liberals and conservatives on the several items, appear to depend to some extent on the *content* of the items. Some forms of freedom are especially favored by liberals and strongly opposed by conservatives, and on items embodying these val-

TABLE 7.8
Responses to Civil Liberties Items, by Ideology (OVS)

	Percentage Choosing the Libertarian and Antilibertarian Response			
	Left Liberal	Liberal	Conservative	Conservative Right
	(N=543)	(N=875)	(N=595)	(N=129)
Freedom of Speech				
For children to be properly educated:				
—they should be free to discuss all ideas, no matter what.	91%	90%	42%	30%
—they should be protected against ideas the community considers wrong or dangerous.	0	2	30	52
When it comes to free speech, extremists:				
—should have the same rights as everyone else.	94	92	69	51
—should not be allowed to spread their propaganda.	1	1	14	29
On issues of religion, morals, and politics, high school teachers have the right to express their opinion in class:				
—even if they go against the community's standards.	81	68	16	14
—only if those opinions are acceptable to the community.	3	5	44	56
Freedom of Press				
The employment of radicals by newspapers and TV:				
—is their right as Americans.	92	85	44	27
—should be forbidden.	1	2	24	46
Which of these comes closer to your own view?				
—Nobody has the right to decide what should or should not be published.	78	70	25	11
—To protect its moral values, a society sometimes has to forbid certain things from being published.	9	17	64	79
Censoring obscene books:				
—is an old-fashioned idea that no longer makes sense.	82	73	17	7
—is necessary to protect community standards.	4	9	62	85

	Percentage Choosing the Libertarian and Antilibertarian Response			
	Left Liberal	Liberal	Conservative	Conservative Right
	(N=543)	(N=875)	(N=595)	(N=129)
Books that preach the overthrow of the government should be:				
—made available by the library, just like any other book.	96%	87%	33%	18%
—banned from the library.	1	6	51	74
How do you feel about movies that use foul language or show nudity and sexual acts on the screen?				
—They have as much right to be shown as other films.	82	74	25	11
—They should be banned.	5	9	61	85
Freedom of Assembly				
Meetings urging America to make war against an enemy nation:				
—have as much right to be held as meetings that support peace.	80	85	82	65
—are so inhuman that we should not allow them to be held.	7	4	5	12
Should a community allow the American Nazi party to use its town hall to hold a public meeting?				
—Yes.	57	56	30	19
—No.	26	28	53	69
If a speaker at a public meeting begins to make racial slurs, the audience should:				
—let him have his say and then answer him.	79	85	80	71
—stop him from speaking.	8	6	7	16
Right of Due Process				
When a criminal refuses to confess his crimes, the authorities:				
—have no right to push him around, no matter what.	77	75	43	30
—are entitled to pressure him until he does.	2	3	16	29
Giving everyone accused of crime the best possible lawyer, even if the government has to pay the legal fees is:				
—necessary to protect individual rights.	86	80	31	40
—wasteful and goes beyond the requirements of justice.	6	9	55	44

TABLE 7.8 *(continued)*

	Percentage Choosing the Libertarian and Antilibertarian Response			
	Left Liberal (N=543)	Liberal (N=875)	Conservative (N=595)	Conservative Right (N=129)
Laws protecting people accused of crime from testifying against themselves should be:				
—strengthened.	58%	45%	17%	19%
—weakened or abolished.	3	4	20	23
When the country is at war, people suspected of disloyalty:				
—should be fully protected in their constitutional rights.	87	72	17	19
—should be watched closely or kept in custody.	5	12	72	72
Right of Privacy				
The use of federal agents to spy on radical organizations:				
—violates their right to political freedom.	83	67	7	6
—is necessary for national security.	5	16	86	85
Tapping telephones of people suspected of planning crimes:				
—should be prohibited as an invasion of privacy.	74	65	18	15
—is necessary to reduce crime.	10	15	64	65
Is it a good idea, or a bad idea for the government to keep a list of people who take part in protest demonstrations?				
—A bad idea.	92	83	17	12
—A good idea.	2	7	60	69
An American citizen:				
—is entitled to have his privacy respected, no matter what he believes.	97	95	50	43
—shouldn't mind having his record checked by patriotic groups.	1	2	35	47
Searching a person's home or car without a search warrant:				
—should never be allowed.	81	77	45	44
—is sometimes justified in order to solve a crime.	12	16	46	47

	Percentage Choosing the Libertarian and Antilibertarian Response			
	Left Liberal	Liberal	Conservative	Conservative Right
	(N=543)	(N=875)	(N=595)	(N=129)
Freedom of Lifestyle				
Our laws should aim to:				
—protect a citizen's right to live by any moral standards he chooses.	56%	48%	18%	9%
—enforce the community's standards of right and wrong.	12	19	63	80
Freedom in sexual conduct between adults should be:				
—left up to the individuals.	96	95	66	45
—regulated by law.	1	1	20	34
The right of a woman to have an abortion during the early weeks of pregnancy should be:				
—left entirely up to her.	92	91	48	35
—severely limited by law.	3	4	39	48
Freedom of Religion				
The freedom of atheists to make fun of God and religion:				
—is a legally protected right.	87	88	64	43
—should not be allowed.	2	2	20	43
Prayers in the public schools should be:				
—forbidden.	64	63	5	1
—permitted.	19	21	87	91

NOTE: For the purposes of this table the order of the items has been rearranged so that the pro-civil liberties response always comes first. Only the percentages libertarian and nonlibertarian are included in the table, the middle category having been omitted to shorten and simplify the table.

ues the differences are usually larger. For example, burning or spitting on the flag (a form of symbolic speech), though obviously distasteful to most Americans, is especially so to conservatives, whose patriotic sensibilities are violated by conduct of this type; 86 percent of the conservative community leaders, compared with 47 percent of the liberals, would punish anyone who engages in such an act. Similarly, conservatives are somewhat less inclined than liberals to permit foreigners to visit or study here if they dislike our government—a denial, of course, of free speech (among other rights).

TABLE 7.9
Responses to Civil Liberties Items, by Ideology (CLS)

	Nonlibertarian Ideology Scale							
	Community Leaders				**Mass Public**			
	Strong Liberal	Moderate Liberal	Moderate Conservative	Strong Conservative	Strong Liberal	Moderate Liberal	Moderate Conservative	Strong Conservative
	(N=262)	(N=111)	(N=87)	(N=135)	(N=257)	(N=255)	(N=257)	(N=257)
Freedom of Press								
Which of these comes closer to your own view?								
—The government has no right to decide what should or should not be published.	56%	47%	38%	32%	38%	24%	26%	23%
—To protect its moral values, a society sometimes has to forbid certain things from being published.	32	41	54	59	48	55	59	66
Novels that describe explicit sex acts:								
—should be permitted in the library if they are worthwhile literature.	75	51	38	34	65	50	33	25
—have no place in a high school library and should be banned.	17	38	51	58	26	38	60	68
Television programs that show people actually making love:								
—should be permitted as long as they are shown in the late evening, during adult viewing hours.	43	30	23	16	45	35	28	24
—should not be allowed on TV at all.	41	51	70	72	41	50	62	68
Freedom of Speech								
Should foreigners who dislike our government and criticize it be allowed to visit or study here?								
—Yes.	82	60	60	47	56	37	35	25
—No.	11	28	31	47	31	46	54	68
Should groups like the Nazis and Ku Klux Klan be allowed to appear on public television to state their views?								
—Yes, should be allowed no matter who is offended.	68	46	41	41	40	23	27	26
—No, because they would offend certain racial or religious groups.	16	20	28	33	36	43	36	48

Symbolic Speech

A person who publicly burns or spits on the flag:

	C1	C2	C3	C4	C5	C6	C7	C8
—may be behaving badly but should not be punished for it by law.	42	29	18	7	32	18	13	9
—should be fined or punished in some way.	47	58	74	86	54	67	74	85

Protesters who mock the President by wearing death masks at one of his public speeches:

	C1	C2	C3	C4	C5	C6	C7	C8
—should have the right to appear in any kind of costume they want.	69	44	39	34	47	29	29	26
—should be removed from the audience by the police.	18	35	33	49	34	50	55	61

Academic Freedom

When a community pays its teacher's salary, it:

	C1	C2	C3	C4	C5	C6	C7	C8
—doesn't buy the right to censor the opinions she expresses in the classroom.	51	35	26	19	45	25	30	18
—has the right to keep her from teaching ideas that go against the community's standards.	31	47	60	71	35	49	52	75

Refusing to hire a professor because of his unusual political beliefs:

	C1	C2	C3	C4	C5	C6	C7	C8
—is never justified.	31	11	11	7	33	21	16	9
—may be necessary if his views are really extreme.	51	71	81	86	48	58	70	84

When inviting guest speakers to a college campus:

	C1	C2	C3	C4	C5	C6	C7	C8
—students should be free to invite anyone they want to hear.	75	56	43	36	65	39	38	30
—the speakers should be screened beforehand to be sure they don't advocate dangerous or extreme ideas.	13	28	40	52	26	42	50	58

Freedom of Assembly

When groups like the Nazis or other extreme groups require police protection at their rallies and marches, the community should:

	C1	C2	C3	C4	C5	C6	C7	C8
—supply and pay for whatever police protection is needed.	56	43	30	19	28	16	16	11
—prohibit such groups from holding rallies because of the costs and dangers involved.	20	32	44	51	47	54	60	70

Should demonstrators be allowed to hold a mass protest march for some unpopular cause?

	C1	C2	C3	C4	C5	C6	C7	C8
—Yes, even if most people in the community don't want it.	83	69	61	51	59	36	40	34
—No, not if the majority is against it.	7	17	21	35	23	33	32	46

TABLE 7.9 *(continued)*

	Nonlibertarian Ideology Scale							
	Community Leaders				Mass Public			
	Strong Liberal	Moderate Liberal	Moderate Conservative	Strong Conservative	Strong Liberal	Moderate Liberal	Moderate Conservative	Strong Conservative
	(N=262)	(N=111)	(N=87)	(N=135)	(N=257)	(N=255)	(N=257)	(N=257)
Right of Due Process								
Once an arrested person says he wishes to remain silent, the authorities:								
—should stop all further questioning at once.	69%	58%	52%	40%	67%	52%	51%	42%
—should keep asking questions to try to get the suspect to admit his crimes.	15	20	24	40	12	18	20	32
If a person is found guilty of a crime by evidence gathered through illegal methods:								
—he should be set free or granted a new trial.	71	45	45	27	53	43	35	24
—he should still be convicted if the evidence is really convincing and strong.	18	41	38	56	29	34	46	64
In dealing with muggings and other serious street crimes, which is more important?								
—to protect the rights of suspects.	27	7	2	4	16	9	7	4
—to stop such crimes and make the streets safe even if we sometimes have to violate the suspect's rights.	40	60	69	79	54	63	72	80
Right of Privacy								
Should government authorities be allowed to open the mail of people suspected of being in contact with fugitives?								
—No, it would violate a person's right to correspond with his friends.	67	49	45	38	63	53	46	45
—Yes, as it may help the police catch criminals they have been looking for.	15	32	40	44	20	23	30	42

If a police officer stops a car for a traffic violation, he should:

—be limited to dealing with the traffic violation and nothing else.	43	24	25	13	42	32	28	25
—be allowed to search the car if he suspects it contains narcotics or stolen goods.	46	66	67	79	46	54	60	69

Freedom of Religion

The freedom of atheists to make fun of God and religion:

—should be legally protected no matter who might be offended.	66	51	40	33	41	24	25	18
—should not be allowed in a public place where religious groups gather.	18	36	36	50	41	52	54	64

When a young woman joins an "offbeat" cult like the Moonies or Hare Krishnas, should her parents have the legal right to force her to leave the group and be "deprogrammed"?

—No, because that would take away her individual freedom to practice any religion she chooses.	38	20	6	9	33	19	14	9
—Yes, because parents have the right and duty to protect their children from influences they consider harmful.	39	53	71	78	42	55	66	79

NOTE: For purposes of this table the order of the items has been rearranged so that the pro-civil liberties response always comes first.

Ideology in this table is measured by the nonlibertarian scale in the CLS study. The civil liberties items in the table were selected as illustrations of the several domains covered by the omnibus civil liberties scale. Only the percentages libertarian and nonlibertarian are included in the table, the middle category having been omitted to shorten and simplify the table.

That conservatives place much greater emphasis than liberals on conformity to community norms, and on the obligation of public servants to adhere to those norms, is illustrated by their far stronger conviction that when a community pays a teacher's salary, it "has the right to keep her from teaching ideas that go against the community's standards." A related item in the OVS study shows approximately three fourths of the liberals and left liberals, but only 15 percent of the conservatives and conservative right, willing to allow high school teachers to express opinions in class on religion, morals, and politics "even if they go against the community's standards"; the majority of the conservative right think that teachers must express only opinions that are "acceptable to the community" (table 7.8). In a similar vein, 91 percent of the left liberals want children in school to "be free to discuss all ideas, no matter what," while the majority of the conservative right reject this notion and want children to be "protected against ideas the community considers wrong or dangerous" (table 7.8). Conservative zeal to protect the community, and especially its young people, from "extreme" or "dangerous" ideas can also be discerned in their responses to the item restricting the right of college students to invite guest speakers of their own choosing; conservatives are inclined to require, instead, that all speakers be screened beforehand "to be sure they don't advocate dangerous or extreme ideas."

The greater tendency among conservatives to disregard or reject certain civil liberties can also be observed in their responses in table 7.8 and 7.9 to the items embodying due process. Concerned as they are with the possible dangers to "law and order," and inclined to take an extremely harsh view of the moral character of lawbreakers, conservatives are prepared to go further than liberals to convict wrongdoers, even if the evidence against them was gathered illegally or if other constitutional improprieties were committed. Conservatives, substantially less sympathetic than liberals to the rights of people accused of crime, are more willing than liberals to compel defendants to testify against themselves in court, more disposed than liberals to "violate [a] suspect's rights" in order to make the streets safe against "muggings" and other street crimes, and far more inclined to keep people in prison without trial if they are considered "dangerous." They also strongly favor placing people suspected of disloyalty under surveillance or in custody when the country is at war. Despite such decisions as *Gideon*, they express far less support for the principle that everyone accused of crime is entitled to be defended by a lawyer, especially if the government has to pay the legal fees.

A similar pattern of conservative skepticism toward various civil liberties can be observed in the OVS data concerning the right of privacy. Conservatives are far more willing than liberals to invade the several domains of individual and organizational privacy for the sake of national security and the preservation of internal order. Among the ideological criterion groups whose responses are reported in table 7.8, over 85 percent of the conservatives but only 12 percent of the liberals approve "the use of federal agents to spy on radical organizations" as necessary to national security. By a ratio of over six to one, they favor the use of wiretapping against persons who are suspected of planning crimes. Some 46 percent of the conservatives, compared with 6 percent of the liberals, would sanction the search of a person's home without a search warrant "in order to solve a crime." And even in their response to the most general statement of a person's right "to have his privacy respected, no matter what he believes"—a right which the liberals affirm almost unanimously— only half of the conservatives are willing to express approval.

Differences that are less striking but nevertheless impressive also turn up on the privacy items in the CLS data (the smaller differences largely reflect the differences in the ideological sophistication of the leader samples in the two studies). Conservatives are more inclined than liberals to permit the government to open the mail of people suspected of being in correspondence with fugitives. They are also, by a significant margin, more sympathetic to the police practice of infiltrating undercover agents into political groups of the far left or the far right. And they are more disposed to permit the police to search automobiles they have stopped for a traffic violation.

The two ideological camps also differ in their attitudes toward freedom of religion. Whether one prefers to think of religion as a privacy right, or as a First Amendment right designed by the Founders to guarantee freedom of thought, conscience, and expression, it is plain from the data in both studies that liberals honor it in significantly greater measure than conservatives. Liberals are far more willing to extend the right to atheists, interpreting religious liberty broadly enough to include the freedom not only to venerate but to reject God and religion. Although liberals prove to be less religious than conservatives on every measure of religiosity used in these studies, they are more inclined to be tolerant of offbeat religious cults "like the Moonies or Hare Krishnas" or other unconventional religious movements. Liberals are also far more receptive than conservatives to the separation of church and state, at least as reflected in the crucial issue of prayer in the public schools. Although the Supreme Court has prohibited such prayers as a violation of the principle of "separation," 88 percent of the conservatives want the public schools to be able to conduct such prayers, while only 20 percent of the liberals would endorse this practice.

Some of the largest differences between the liberal and conservative camps turn up on questions of sexual freedom. Whereas 58 percent of the strong conservatives among the community leaders and 68 percent among the mass public would ban from high school libraries novels that describe "explicit sexual acts," only 17 percent and 26 percent, respectively, of the strong liberals would approve such a ban. Large differences along the same lines occur on the question of permitting television programs to show people "actually making love" (as well as on other questions not included in the figure that involve so-called sexual liberation or the publication of materials alleged to be "obscene").

In the comparisons between the left and right criterion groups in the OVS sample (table 7.8), some three fourths of the liberals would *permit* the showing of films "that use foul language or show nudity and sexual acts on the screen," while 61 percent of the conservatives would prohibit them. On the more general question of "freedom of sexual conduct between adults," 95 percent of the liberals would leave such matters to the individuals, while 66 percent of the conservatives would do so. Data we have collected in these and other studies we have conducted on tolerance of homosexuality, abortion, and other matters affecting sexual freedom and lifestyle bear out repeatedly the differences in the pattern of control we have reported in this chapter. By a wide margin, the conservatives take the lead in opposing a woman's right to choose abortion: almost twice as many liberals (91 percent) as conservatives (48 percent) in the OVS study favor it. The differences are equally large on questions reflecting the rights of homosexuals. Over three fourths of the liberals believe that "complete equality for homosexuals in teaching and other public service jobs should be protected by law," whereas fewer than 10 percent of the conservatives subscribe to this view; over 80 percent of the conservatives admit that it "may sound fair" but they do not believe that it is a "really a good idea."

312

These and a number of related responses furnish evidence widely supported in our data that conservatives have, on the average, a stronger desire than liberals to exert *control* over the social and moral conduct of individuals. They hope to achieve this either by *external* means, through community or institutional enforcement of rules, regulations, standards, and tradition (which often require intervention by the police, the courts, the church, the family, the intelligence agencies, or other stabilizing and enforcement institutions); or by *internal* means, through voluntary conformity to community standards, conventional ideas and values, self-discipline, and strict adherence to established norms.

While some liberals, to be sure, suffer similar fears and share with conservatives some of the values we have just cited, they do so less often and with less intensity. As one can readily discern from the data as well as from intuitive observation of actual political movements, liberals worry far less than conservatives about conformity to approved standards, deference to authority, or adherence to conventional modes of thought and conduct. Take, for example, the responses to the lifestyle item in table 7.8 in which 48 percent of the liberals say they want our laws "to protect a citizen's right to live by any moral standards he chooses," while 63 percent of the conservatives want them "to enforce the community's standards of right and wrong." A similar outlook is expressed in the items listed under freedom of speech in table 7.8, where conservatives, far more frequently than liberals, express their desire to protect children "against ideas the community considers wrong or dangerous" or want to prohibit school teachers from expressing opinions that "go against the community's standards."

Liberals accept nonconformity in opinion and conduct as inescapable by-products of freedom, essential to its vitality. They also welcome certain forms of "deviancy" as challenges to the "stale cake of custom" and as important sources of innovation. Like John Stuart Mill, contemporary liberals tend to perceive the free exchange of divergent views and attempts at social experimentation as potential harbingers of social improvement and progress. They regard the dangers to society from unorthodox beliefs and behavior as minimal compared with their potential benefits—a small price to be paid for social advancement. (Suppressing them is, in any event, far more costly to society than tolerating them.) Unlike conservatives, liberals generally do not fear that society is endangered when individuals are free to say what they please and (within the aforementioned limits) to act as they choose—even in matters considered "sensitive," such as religious worship, national security, or sexual conduct.

Conservative reluctance to guarantee in full measure such liberties as speech, press, and assembly is also related to a fear of change, a preference for the tried and familiar, for institutions, ideas, and practices that have been tested by experience rather than generated and superimposed by reason, doctrine, or programmatic considerations. The ideology scales in both the OVS and the CLS studies (as well as our earlier studies) contain a number of items expressing attitudes toward change, reform, the replacing of traditional policies with untested new ones for the sake of "progress," reliance upon "the practical experience of the past" as against "a plan that tries out new ideas," changes in keeping with "an overall program or theory" versus changes that are allowed "to develop naturally by themselves," and so forth. While it would be an oversimplification to say that conservatives invariably favor the status quo while liberals favor change, one *can* say (as our findings strongly confirm) that conservatives are substantially more resistant than liberals to the *reform* of existing institutions; that they distrust theory, doctrine, and ideas that recommend reforms; and that they continue to believe, along with Edmund Burke and other conservative philosophers that changes in society should evolve slowly and gradually in response to practical experience. Speech and publication become dangerous when they are used to promote reform or to advance programs of change based on theory and doctrine alone.

Most conservatives would claim that they are opposed not to the general principle of freedom of expression as such but to the manner of its application. However much they themselves may honor freedom of speech and press in the abstract, they take a jaundiced view of the use of these liberties by liberals and radicals to promote "subversive" ideas that spring from doctrine—including libertarian doctrine that leads liberals to champion the rights not only of revolutionaries but of atheists, pornographers, criminals, sexual deviates, and other "social misfits." Whereas liberals embrace civil liberties partly because such liberties are needed to correct the defects and injustices of society, in keeping with liberal programs and ideals, conservatives, partly for the same reason, are inclined to shy from them—especially as they strongly distrust visionary theories and programs which purport to map the route to a nobler, more beneficent future. Conservatives, in short, remain profoundly suspicious of the kinds of people Edmund Burke described as "sophisters and calculators," particularly when, by conservative standards, they exploit constitutional liberties to bring about "reforms" that undermine the Constitution and the structure of society itself. (For a modern example of this argument, see Berns 1957.)

Findings on Political and Social Attitudes and Support for Civil Liberties

Until now we have restricted our discussion of ideology to direct measures of liberalism and conservatism, as defined by ideological criterion groups, self-labeling, the attitudes people express toward equality; toward change, reform, and tradition; and toward the economy and the welfare state. In the remainder of this chapter we will examine the connections between support for civil liberties and a number of political and social attitudes which were not included in our definition of ideology but which nevertheless bear a philosophical, political, or intellectual relation to ideology, broadly conceived. We have in mind such variables as orientations toward theory versus practice, the responsibility of individuals for failure or success; support for democratic values; civil rights for minorities, women, homosexuals, and other groups that have suffered discrimination; attitudes toward obedience to law; superpatriotism and international chauvinism; and a number of contemporary lifestyle issues including attitudes toward abortion, sexual freedom, and the counterculture.

That attitudes toward theory and practice as guides to social change relate not only to ideology but also to civil liberties is powerfully demonstrated in our data.* Among the criterion group leaders in the OVS study, 70 percent of those who scored high on tolerance would try "to solve the country's problems" or bring about important social changes by putting their faith in theories, plans, programs, and "thinking" people "who have lots of ideas"—a faith that is shared by only 6 percent of those who score low on tolerance. Some 67 percent of the latter group, compared with 10 percent of the high-tolerance

---

* To measure theory versus practice in the OVS study we constructed a four-item scale that contrasts faith in theories, programs, plans, people with ideas, and so forth as against faith in experience, the "practical experience of the past," practical people "who know how to run things," and changes "that develop naturally by themselves."

group, would prefer to be guided by practical experience rather than theories or programs. They would look to the events of the past as primary guides to change, and they want changes "to develop naturally by themselves" rather than have them follow "an overall program or theory." They also strongly prefer to solve the country's problems by relying upon "practical people who know how to run things" (such as "businessmen"), rather than people who are mainly occupied with ideas (such as "intellectuals" or "professors").

While these results, as we have suggested, partly reflect the connection between ideological outlook and orientation toward theory and practice as sources of inspiration for public policy, they also reflect the stronger commitment of libertarians to the value of ideas and to their power as agents for social change and human improvement.

A more familiar set of correlations that show the connections between political attitudes and support for civil liberties appears in table 7.10, in which respondents who score high on tolerance and those who score low are compared in their orientations toward democratic values other than libertarianism. Our measure of "support for democratic values" is an eight-item scale which focuses on such aspects of democratic government as majority rule, the accountability of governing officials, the legitimacy of opposition parties, the need for free elections, the right of all citizens to run for political office, and the equal right to vote. Although the democracy scale makes no reference to freedom or tolerance, the data in table 7.10 suggest that the stronger one's faith in the principles of democratic government, the greater one's commit-

TABLE 7.10

Relation Between Political and Social Attitudes and Support for Civil Liberties (percentages down): Support for Democratic Values (CLS)

Score on Omnibus Civil Liberties Scale		Support for Democratic Values			Totalitarianism		
		High	Middle	Low	High	Middle	Low
		(N=293)	(N=179)	(N=72)	(N=170)	(N=218)	(N=162)
Community	High	67%	60%	42%	51%	64%	68%
Leaders	Middle	22	22	32	30	19	23
	Low	11	18	26	19	17	9
		(N=319)	(N=360)	(N=260)	(N=307)	(N=377)	(N=258)
Mass	High	49	28	19	25	31	43
Public	Middle	29	36	30	33	36	26
	Low	22	37	51	42	33	31

ment to civil liberties. This finding is buttressed by the data on the totalitarianism scale, which emphasizes the desirability of strong rule by a dedicated oligarchy under a uniform political philosophy.

The results on both scales confirm what is evident from intuitive observation of contemporary politics, namely, that civil libertarian ideas and practices tend to be linked with other values of democracy. The connection, however, while significant, is not overpowering. Just as democratic governments, though universally more tolerant than authoritarian regimes, are not all willing to grant a full measure of civil liberties to their constituents, neither do all individuals who profess to believe in democratic values display a high degree of tolerance across the entire range of civil liberties. As our data show, one can cheerfully support popular suffrage and the holding of free elections (which exact a very small cost, if any) without being willing to allow all groups a virtually unlimited right to speak or publish, or to grant a variety of due process protections to people who commit outrageous crimes. Thus, the correlation between a belief in democracy (as defined in our measures) and support for civil liberties is far from perfect. Some libertarian values are clearly more difficult to absorb than others. Having noted this, we should nevertheless remind ourselves that the correlation between civil liberties and other democratic principles *is* positive and statistically significant.

A much stronger relation is uncovered when we compare the scores of tolerant and intolerant respondents on a large number of questions involving the treatment of people who break the law, either through criminal behavior or acts of civil disobedience. As the data in figure 7.5 strongly demonstrate, the respondents in both the CLS and the OVS studies who score high on the civil liberties scale are far less "hard" in their attitudes toward lawbreakers than are the respondents who score at the intolerant end of the scale. In the CLS study, for example, 81 percent of the community leaders who take a relatively lenient stand toward the treatment of lawbreakers score tolerant on the civil liberties scale—an outlook that is shared by only 30 percent of those who have a tougher attitude toward lawbreakers. The data for the criterion group samples in the OVS study show even larger differences—for example, 94 percent of those who take a "soft" attitude toward lawbreakers score high on libertarianism, compared with only 16 percent of those whose attitudes are "hard." The differences in the mass public samples between those who are primarily committed to law and order and those who place greater emphasis on social justice

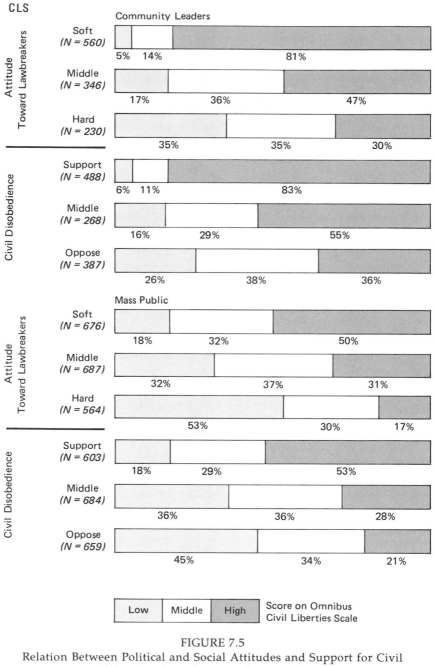

FIGURE 7.5
Relation Between Political and Social Attitudes and Support for Civil
Liberties: Attitude Toward Lawbreakers
(CLS)

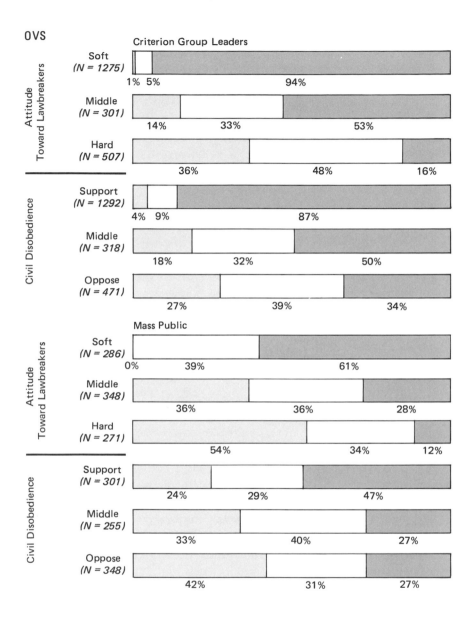

Note: As previously explained, the omnibus civil liberties scales in the CLS study and the OVS study are not identical in item content, although they do have some items in common.

and humanitarianism, while impressive, are, as expected, somewhat smaller than the differences in the elite samples—reflecting once again the greater capacity among the latter for the social learning of an interrelated set of attitudes.

In any event, it is clear that on a host of questions referring to the treatment of prisoners (rehabilitation versus punishment), longer or shorter prison sentences for crimes, the use of the death penalty, improving conditions or using force to stop rioters and looters in the cities, treating criminals as sick or as wrongdoers to be punished, taking a harder or softer line toward demonstrators, requiring the courts to be tougher or easier on lawbreakers, and the like—the respondents who are more benevolent in their attitudes toward those who violate the law are, by every measure in every sample we have tested, substantially more civil libertiarian than are the respondents whose attitude toward lawbreakers is more punitive. Nor do these differences show up only for the type of lawbreaking that would be classified as "criminal." Virtually the same results occur in their respective attitudes toward civil disobedience. Respondents eager to punish those who commit a crime for reasons of conscience score far lower on civil liberties than those with a more sympathetic attitude toward civil disobedience.

As we have said earlier, we expected to find that those most likely to blame society for crime and other human shortcomings would be more civil libertarian than those who trace various forms of dereliction to the faults of individual character. As can be seen in figure 7.6, this expectation is strongly confirmed. Among the OVS criterion group samples, 94 percent of those who tend to blame "the way society is organized" for the "things that go wrong in the world" fall at the tolerant end of the civil liberties scale, compared with only 28 percent of those who blame "human nature." The latter say that one must look to the defects of human character to find the sources of poverty, failure to get ahead, refusal to work hard, and human failure in general. Failure results from laziness and a lack of self-discipline, while success reflects "ability and hard work." Only 1 percent of those who blame society for human failure score intolerant, compared with nearly one third of those who blame the individual. As usual, the differences among tolerant and intolerant respondents in the mass public are smaller, but they are nevertheless substantial.

The intolerant respondents, of course, place far more emphasis on control than do the libertarians and are quicker to punish anyone who

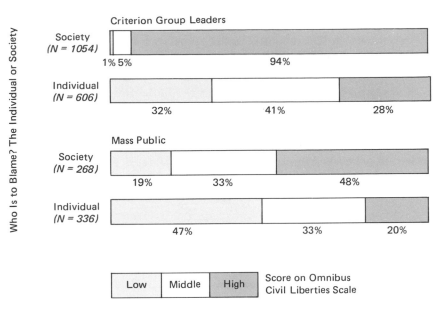

Note: Individual versus society is a six-term scale which tests a respondent's inclination to blame the individual (or human nature) versus society for poverty, "most of the things that go wrong in the world," human failure, failure to work hard, getting ahead, and so forth.

FIGURE 7.6
Relation Between Political and Social Attitudes and Support for Civil
Liberties: Individual Versus Society
(OVS)

breaks the rules, especially since they are inclined to view such deviations as willful. They are also more eager to punish (rather than try to rehabilitate) malefactors, since they believe that a propensity toward crime reflects a wayward nature and inherent character flaws. They also want to reduce the risk of placing criminals and other deviants out on the streets where they would be free once again to commit new crimes and to threaten order and safety. Libertarians, by contrast, being inclined to place major responsibility outside the individual, believe that the rehabilitation of lawbreakers is not only possible but just, and they are far more willing, for the sake of freedom, to risk failure. They, too, are concerned for order and safety, but (as they see it) not at the expense of individual rights. Nor is their concern as urgent and overpowering as it appears to be among the antilibertarians.

In table 7.11, we have compared tolerant and intolerant respondents on a set of measures involving patriotism, superpatriotism, international chauvinism, and "hawk-dove" orientations toward foreign affairs. These differences are as powerful as the ones we have been considering, but harder to explain. As the table demonstrates, persons who score high on scales of patriotism or superpatriotism are far less tolerant in their attitudes toward civil liberties than those who score low. Among the community leaders in the CLS study, for example, nearly 50 percent of the superpatriotic respondents prove to be intolerant on civil liberties, compared with only 5 percent of those who score low on superpatriotism. Similar results turn up for the international

TABLE 7.11

Relation Between Political and Social Attitudes and Support for Civil Liberties: Patriotism

		CLS					
		Patriotism		International Chauvinism		Super-patriotism	
Score on Omnibus Civil Liberties Scale		Low	High	Low	High	Low	High
		(N=174)	(N=194)	(N=193)	(N=197)	(N=357)	(N=96)
Community Leaders	High	81%	38%	81%	39%	79%	14%
	Middle	14	36	13	36	16	40
	Low	5	26	6	25	5	46
		(N=302)	(N=291)	(N=271)	(N=336)	(N=427)	(N=275)
Mass Public	High	56	17	53	20	60	6
	Middle	29	34	28	38	28	34
	Low	15	49	19	42	12	60

		OVS					
		Patriotism		International Chauvinism		"Dove" vs. "Hawk"	
Score on Omnibus Civil Liberties Scale		Low	High	Low	High	Dovish	Hawkish
		(N=1265)	(N=334)	(N=1207)	(N=543)	(N=1033)	(N=617)
Criterion Group Leaders	High	95%	9%	92%	25%	93%	31%
	Middle	4	44	7	42	5	41
	Low	1	47	1	33	2	28
		(N=262)	(N=297)	(N=303)	(N=309)	(N=321)	(N=230)
Mass Public	High	65	8	55	18	46	22
	Middle	28	30	29	30	28	38
	Low	7	62	16	52	26	40

NOTE: Only those who score high and low on each scale are reported in this table. The middle category has been omitted to conserve space and simplify the table.

chauvinism measures used in our two studies (those scoring high on chauvinism being the least tolerant) and for the hawk–dove measure, in which 93 percent of the most "dovish" respondents in the criterion group turn out to be highly tolerant compared with only 31 percent of the most "hawkish" respondents.

Seen from the perspective of the items in these scales, those who score least tolerant on civil liberties are more likely to believe that America is "the last best hope on earth"; that American children should be taught to "love their country more than other countries"; that singing the "Star-Spangled Banner" and pledging allegiance to the flag make people "appreciate America more"; and that "America is still the finest country in the world to live in."* The differences are even larger on the superpatriotism scale in the CLS study (a five-item measure that assesses attitudes toward loyalty oaths for government employees; the treatment of people who show disrespect for the flag and fail "to appreciate America's greatness"; the response to Americans who don't think this is "the best country in the world" and who don't, therefore, "deserve to live here"; and the desirability of keeping America's natural resources at home, to be "used for the benefit of Americans alone").

The international chauvinism scales used in the two studies raise questions about bringing peace and order to the world by making the United States "the one really powerful nation on earth"; and increasing America's military strength rather than working harder for international disarmament. Respondents are asked how they would feel (would it be "tragic and humiliating"?) if the United States "were to lose its role as a leader among nations"; whether the United States should refuse to trade with any nation that is "strongly opposed to our way of life"; and whether we should cut off help to any country that refuses "to follow our lead in foreign affairs." The hawk–dove scale takes these questions a step further and inquires, for example, whether the United States should engage in a preemptive strike against a country threatening to attack it; and whether atomic bombing and germ warfare should be used if necessary to save the United States from defeat.

From the responses to these measures, as summarized in table 7.11,

* These items are representative in content of those in the six-item patriotism scale in the CLS study and the four-item scale in the OVS study. There are five international chauvinism items in the OVS study and four in Form A of the CLS study. The hawk-dove scale has four items.

it is plain that on a variety of questions ranging from simple statements of patriotic preference for America to statements that are "flag-waving," xenophobic, jingoist, or belligerent in flavor, the people who are more chauvinistic or superpatriotic are far less libertarian than people who are less zealous in their patriotism. This set of correlations may strike some observers as baffling, especially as one might reasonably be led to expect that those who regard themselves as the nation's defenders should also be among the leading champions of its constitutional principles and its frequently proclaimed libertarian ideals. In practice, of course, this has not always been the case. On the contrary, as one can easily discern from intuitive obseration alone, the tendency to suppress nonconformers in the name of the flag has been an obvious feature of American political life for generations. Superpatriotic organizations dedicated to the promotion of nationalistic values and the "American way" are typically cool if not hostile to civil liberties. Such organizations—from the "nativist" movements of the nineteenth century to the paramilitary or jingoist movements of our own day—have usually been at the forefront of efforts to narrow the boundaries of free speech and press, to silence radicals, to suppress dissenters, to cut back (or eliminate) certain of the rights of due process, to censor books that are "indecent" or "subversive," and to strengthen efforts to increase surveillance and government control over groups they consider "disloyal," "alien," or "un–American."

Part of the explanation for the connection between patriotic fervor and intolerance has already been suggested. Individuals who are intensely attached to the symbols of flag and country tend to be especially wary that freedom will be used (or misused) to cast doubt on the country's virtues or even to advocate its disruption or overthrow.

Although superpatriots are critical of civil liberties, they rarely express opposition to freedom in the abstract. Instead, they perceive certain applications of civil libertarian rights as misapplications, never intended by the Constitution. Claiming to venerate the nation as they do (again in the abstract), they see themselves as its champions against enemies who misuse the nation's liberties to undermine its institutions and threaten its order and stability. Such enemies, in their view, have clearly placed themselves beyond the protection of the Constitution and the laws.

That most citizens will, in the normal course of events, develop affection and loyalty toward their country is easy to understand. The nation, after all, "is the definitive, norm–giving association, in which there is a confluence of blood ties, law-making, defense and security functions, a common history and tradition, and a set of myths and symbols that together furnish an extraordinary impetus to unity" (McClosky 1969, pp. 98–99). More difficult to understand, however, are the dynamics affecting patriotic loyalties that are so intense that almost all forms of unorthodoxy and nonconformity are considered suspect. However laudable as an attribute of citizenship when expressed in balanced or temperate form, patriotism in its fervent or "superpatriotic" expression veers toward intolerance. When embraced with exceptional passion, patriotism takes on some of the qualities we associate with ethnocentrism, such as irrational antipathy toward people who do not belong to the chosen group.

As our data bear out so strongly, patriots whose sentiments border on chauvinism want to guarantee our national security by making America the one powerful nation on earth. They take great pride in the nation's supremacy, and they cannot abide the thought that it might ever take second place or that it might be forced to relinquish even a small measure of sovereignty by sharing power with other nations. (Superpatriots remain, even today, resentful of American membership in the United Nations.) These attitudes are often transformed into a willingness to use our national power to impose America's will on other nations, a readiness to engage in military adventures and to use the most extreme forms of military attack to ensure the nation's security—and superiority.

It is a mark of patriotism in its more zealous forms that its adherents are hypersensitive to questions of social order and national security. They are inclined to perceive serious dangers both from within and from without, from domestic as well as foreign "enemies." Partly because of these fears, they tend to err on the side of intolerance rather than tolerance, to check dissenters and to forestall or crush assaults (real or imagined) upon the venerated nation and its institutions—or at least the institutions they cherish. They also tend to harbor irrational fears of whoever (or whatever) is thought to be the enemy and to believe that unless fiercely and zealously fought, the enemy will prevail and destroy our integrity.

As we have observed, the arguments for civil liberties in their many complex applications are not easy to learn, and fervent patriots and chauvinists have particular difficulty learning them. Possessed as they are by questions of loyalty and national security, they often equate discussion or criticism of the nation with treason. Nor can they

325

easily understand why anyone should be allowed to use constitutional liberties to jeopardize the country's institutions. In their view, only people with questionable motives would want the right to vilify the "American way." They are so preoccupied with the defense of America that they have difficulty grasping the idea that the liberties set forth in the Constitution were designed to protect individuals against misuses of political authority, and that what is essential to a constitutional democracy is protection not only *for* the nation, but *from* it.

Although the categories of civil liberties and civil rights are sometimes confused, the two can (and should) be distinguished, both analytically and operationally. In keeping with conventional usage, we have reserved the term "civil liberties" for those rights which have mainly to do with the *freedom* of the individual. These include, as we have seen, the freedom to speak, to publish, to assemble, to worship, to be safeguarded against the invasions of one's privacy, to be protected from the arbitrary exercise of state power in the event one is accused of crime (due process), and to be free to live by whatever moral, sexual, and familial standards one prefers.

The concept of "civil rights" is distinguished from civil liberties principally in its emphasis on equality. The NAACP, the Urban League, and CORE are associations which, though largely favorable to civil liberties, are primarily devoted to the cause of racial equality and the elimination of ethnic prejudice. All describe themselves, and are universally known, as *civil rights* organizations. One would also include within the category of associations devoted to the uprooting of prejudice and the achievement of equal rights for their members such organizations as the Anti-Defamation League, the National Organization of Women, and the American Indian Movement. Though these alliances differ from each other in some ways, all have social, political, and economic equality as their principal goals, and all can appropriately be described as civil rights organizations. The American Civil Liberties Union, on the other hand, though it has ventured here and there into the field of civil rights, is primarily devoted to the defense and promotion of the constitutional liberties of all Americans and would usually be described (as its name suggests) as an association mainly devoted to the protection of civil liberties.

Although the efforts to promote civil liberties and civil rights often work to reinforce each other, as we have noted, they are sometimes in conflict. Civil rights organizations have been known, in the name of equality, to propose the censorship of publications (or films or television programs) that preach race hatred or that openly express prejudice against Catholics, Jews, women, homosexuals, or others who have suffered discrimination. By contrast, most strong proponents of civil liberties would maintain that, however unsavory, freedom of expression includes the right to say hateful things even against minorities (or, for that matter, against the majority). The principles of freedom protect the right to express opinions that the community considers outrageous and socially unpalatable, as well as opinions it regards as commendable. Freedom, thus, may be used to deepen the inequalities already suffered by groups that have experienced severe prejudice.

The liberties that are implicit (or explicit) in the American constitutional structure also permit individuals to distinguish themselves from each other, to rise to a higher station in life or to fall to a lower one. Differential or unequal status may, to some extent, be an outgrowth of freedom. Individuals differ in talent to begin with, and the freedom to exercise one's talents as one chooses is bound to sort people out so that some gain advantages while others do not. Some achieve power and fame, and rise to preferred positions in the social structure, while others, equally free to begin with, remain powerless and faceless. Though freedom may thus be served, equality is impeded. In short, the domains of freedom and equality, of civil liberties and civil rights, are not always or in all respects compatible.

Having noted these caveats, we are nevertheless obliged to observe that, more often than not, the advancement of one serves to promote the other. If blacks or Jews or women or Indians are permitted to enjoy the full benefits of their civil rights, many of them will move into higher stations in society in which they will be able to disseminate their views and to protect their rights of privacy and due process with greater effectiveness than before. Even those who do not achieve high standing in the society will nevertheless gain a voice and will be better able to call the community's attention to the disadvantages they suffer.

Viewed from the libertarian perspective, as individuals gain greater command over their civil liberties, they also gain greater access to society's benefits. Possessing freedom, they are in a far stronger position to carry on the struggle for their civil rights. They can publish, organize, assemble, participate in the public debate, lobby legislators and executive officials, defend their rights more effectively in the courts, and, in general, launch a far more demanding and more powerful appeal for the civil rights they have been denied.

Despite the possible conflicts between freedom and equality, it

327

was our belief, and one that the findings strongly confirm, that sensitivity to human rights in one domain (for example, civil liberties) would, in most cases, go hand in hand with sensitivity to human rights in the other. As one can see in table 7.12, those who display high scores on the civil liberties scales also tend to score at the equalitarian end of the several scales we have developed to measure attitudes toward the rights of women, racial minorities, and homosexuals. In the CLS study, for example, 74 percent of the community leaders who are tolerant on civil liberties score highly equalitarian on the five-item scale of women's rights, compared with only 20 percent of those who are intolerant on the civil liberties measure.

Without exception, in the leader and mass samples in both the CLS

TABLE 7.12
*Relation between Political and Social Attitudes and Support
for Civil Liberties: Civil Rights*

		Omnibus Civil Liberties Scale					
		CLS					
		Community Leaders			Mass Public		
		High Tolerance	Middle Tolerance	Low Tolerance	High Tolerance	Middle Tolerance	Low Tolerance
Attitude Scale		(N=689)	(N=284)	(N=170)	(N=648)	(N=647)	(N=652)
Women's Rights	High	74%	40%	20%	65%	39%	18%
	Low	5	25	51	9	26	48
Ethnocentrism	High	16	34	39	19	32	43
	Low	59	27	21	50	34	18
Civil Rights:	High	68	33	26	50	28	17
Minorities	Low	8	23	44	13	33	41
Homosexual	High	68	22	7	65	30	9
Rights	Low	8	42	79	9	35	64
		OVS					
		Criterion Group Leaders			Mass Public		
		(N=619)	(N=150)	(N=29)	(N=302)	(N=302)	(N=301)
Women's Rights	High	79%	21%	5%	68%	32%	15%
	Low	7	45	76	13	39	64
Racial Equality	High	82	21	6	54	35	15
	Low	9	57	80	18	30	58
General Equality	High	58	11	3	43	34	21
	Low	19	70	81	27	36	47

NOTE: Only those who score high and low on each scale are reported in this table. The middle category has been omitted to conserve space and simplify the table.

and the OVS studies, supporters of civil liberties are, by wide margins, more sympathetic to the civil rights of groups that have experienced discrimination. On questions of equal rights for women in employment, home versus career, and the suitability of women for jobs in business and politics, the civil libertarians are invariably more favorably disposed toward women's rights than are the antilibertarians.

The same pattern holds for large numbers of questions affecting the rights of blacks and other minorities. On the questions of equal treatment for minorities in jobs and housing, respondents who score high on civil liberties issues are substantially more equalitarian than those who score low. They are also more equalitarian on questions asking whether minorities fail in business or professions because they lack natural ability or have received insufficient training and opportunity; whether we should strengthen or weaken laws guaranteeing equal opportunities for blacks and other minorities; and whether the nonviolent marches for civil rights in the 1960s were helpful or harmful.

Table 7.12 reveals even stronger differences between civil libertarians and antilibertarians in their responses to various questions involving equality of treatment for homosexuals. Should, for example, the community permit or prohibit the operation of homosexual bars? Should lesbians be given custody of their own children? Should homosexuals enjoy equal rights in jobs and housing? Should the community treat homosexuality as a crime or merely as an alternative sexual preference? Regardless of the question asked, the civil libertarian respondents come out in favor of equality for homosexuals far more often than do the antilibertarians, as one can infer from their scale scores. For example, 68 percent of the libertarian community leaders, compared to only 7 percent of the antilibertarians, scored highly equalitarian on the homosexual rights scale. Conversely, by a ratio of over eleven to one, those who scored low on the civil liberties scale were more likely than those who scored high to be hostile to homosexual equality. The differences in the scores of the respondents in the general population are almost as great.

Thus, we see from table 7.12 and from numerous other subsets of data in the CLS and OVS studies that in the constellations of attitudes held by members of both the mass public and their opinion leaders, the rights associated with freedom are strongly and positively correlated with the rights associated with equality. This observation holds not

329

only for civil rights but for equality as a general value. As our data bear witness, a person who scores high on civil liberties is far more likely than a person who scores low to believe that people would be "about the same" (that is, would be equally virtuous and worthwhile) if they were treated equally; that it is unfair to treat people differently because they differ in ability; that children should be taught that "all people are equally worthy and deserve equal treatment"; that we should increase, rather than decrease, the effort "to make everyone as equal as possible," and so forth. Among the elite samples in particular, the differences on equalitarian items like these, and on the scale of general equality itself, are very large indeed.* Thus, it seems clear from the rather considerable evidence we have turned up that while freedom and equality may at times come into conflict if pressed to their respective limits, an increase in one's commitment to freedom will ordinarily be accompanied by an increase in one's support for general equality and civil rights.

One of the most striking developments of the past two decades has been the rapid change in the styles of personal conduct of a number of Americans. While it is easy to exaggerate the impact of the 1960s and 1970s on the character of American life, it is nevertheless clear that we have witnessed in recent decades some noteworthy modifications in the attitudes and conduct of Americans concerning such matters as sexual freedom, marijuana, abortion, "hippies," the depiction of explicit sex and nudity in films and magazines, and patterns of cohabitation and "communal" living.

Dramatic though some of these developments have been, it would be a mistake to assume that the specific issues that fall under the heading of lifestyle are now "settled." On the contrary, they are vociferously debated and with the election of the Reagan administration and the rise to prominence of other officials and opinion leaders who lean ideologically toward the conservative right, controversy about them has become, if anything, more intensified.

In table 7.13 we have attempted to present the relation between orientation toward civil liberties and a group of variables that embody attitudes associated with the counterculture and the aforementioned

---

*Though economic equality does not fall under the heading of civil rights, and data on this measure have not been included in Table 7.12, those who score high and low on civil liberties also differ sharply on economic equality in the elite samples, though only moderately among the mass public.

TABLE 7.13
*Relation between Political and Social Attitudes and Support
for Civil Liberties: Lifestyle*

		Omnibus Civil Liberties Scale					
		CLS					
		Community Leaders			Mass Public		
		High Tolerance	Middle Tolerance	Low Tolerance	High Tolerance	Middle Tolerance	Low Tolerance
Attitude Scale		(N=689)	(N=284)	(N=170)	(N=648)	(N=647)	(N=652)
Counterculture	High	50%	26%	23%	48%	29%	14%
	Low	26	46	49	27	46	53
Sexual Freedom	High	61	27	12	60	28	11
	Low	12	34	61	12	36	65
Pornography	High	66	16	5	59	32	10
	Low	16	59	90	5	17	59
Abortion	High	73	49	35	59	37	27
	Low	11	24	33	15	32	43
		OVS					
		Criterion Group Leaders			Mass Public		
		(N=619)	(N=150)	(N=29)	(N=302)	(N=302)	(N=301)
Sexual Freedom	High	80%	21%	4%	62%	29%	11%
	Low	4	52	79	7	37	62
Pornography	Permit	85	17	2	71	24	7
	Censor	3	53	85	8	40	78

NOTE: Only those who score high and low on each scale are reported in this table. The middle category has been omitted to conserve space and simplify the table.

changes in lifestyle. We view them as *emerging* issues which have not yet fully achieved the status of acknowledged civil liberties—if indeed they ever will.

In assessing the relation between civil liberties outlooks and attitudes toward lifestyle, we should point out that none of the items in the lifestyle scales have been included in the omnibus civil liberties scales.* Although no overlap exists in the item content of the dependent and independent variables, they do have in common the fact that both sets of variables concern freedom. Therefore, one should keep this fact in mind in assessing the findings reported in table 7.13, since the

*The omnibus civil liberties scales, it should be recalled, include items drawn entirely from the established and widely acknowledged classes of civil liberties such as speech, press, assembly, association, religion, privacy, and due process.

size of the differences between those who score high and low on the civil liberties scales may be somewhat inflated because of the libertarian aspects of the lifestyle variables. We believe, nevertheless, that both conceptually and operationally, the two sets of variables are sufficiently independent of each other to warrant an examination of the relation of one set to the other.

That support for civil liberties is highly correlated with support for lifestyle issues is plain from table 7.13. The higher one scores on the civil liberties scales (in both studies), the more permissive one's attitudes toward sexual freedom, the counterculture, pornography, and abortion. In the community leader sample of the CLS study, for example, 61 percent of those who score at the low end of the civil liberties scale strongly resist the trend toward sexual freedom, compared with 12 percent of the civil libertarians—a ratio of approximately five to one. The differences are even larger for the samples (and scales) in the OVS study. Those who score low on civil liberties, in other words, are opposed to sex education in the schools, want sexual conduct between adults to be "regulated by law" rather than left up to the individual, would not allow birth control devices to be made available to teenagers, and complain that today "there is too much sexual freedom and loose living" in the world. Some civil libertarians, of course, hold these views as well, but far fewer.

Similar patterns of difference between those who score high and low on civil liberties are revealed in the attitudes they express toward the counterculture, pornography, and abortion. Since some of the items in the pornography scale refer to the dissemination of pornographic materials (such as films, books, and magazines—activities which some people believe are, or should be, protected by the right of free press), the correlations between support for civil liberties and attitudes toward pornography are especially (and, to some extent, spuriously) large. Nevertheless, powerful differences exist even when an item does not refer to freedom of expression—as in the question which asks whether laws should be adopted to "stamp out 'sin'—such as prostitution, gambling, pornography, etc."

The items in the abortion scale are much less closely connected to the traditional categories of civil liberties, but the results are clearly consistent with the tendencies we have been describing: civil libertarians are far more willing than those who score low on civil liberties to permit abortions—on demand, or for any other reason. Attitudes toward abortion were measured in the CLS study by a four-item scale which asked, among other questions, whether abortion should be left entirely up to the women; prohibited except in cases of "rape, the risk of a deformed child, or danger to the mother's life"; or "like murder," legally prohibited.

As one can see from figure 7.7, nearly three fourths of the community leaders who score high on civil liberties, compared with only 35 percent of those who score low, favor the right to choose abortion, a difference of two to one. Some 33 percent of those who score intolerant on civil liberties oppose the right to choose abortion, compared with 11 percent of their more tolerant colleagues. The differences on this issue among the general public are of roughly similar magnitude.

Since abortion is generally perceived as a practice that falls outside the purview of civil liberties (although some supporters of abortion would dispute this), what explains the differences on this issue between those who score high and low on civil liberties? Some segments of the population doubtless oppose abortions for sincere religious reasons, as do many Catholics, for example. Others, of course, maintain that they believe in the sanctity of life and that the aborting of a fetus at any stage is akin to murder.

The internal evidence from our research suggests, however, that many who oppose abortion do so for ideological reasons that have little

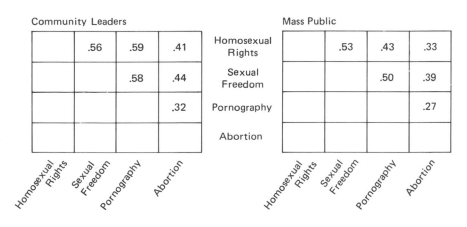

Note: Pearson *r*'s.

FIGURE 7.7
Intercorrelations Among Lifestyle Scales
(CLS)

to do with religion or with philosophical orientations toward the hallowed nature of life. Liberals, for example, are substantially more likely than conservatives to permit abortion—for any reason. They perceive it as part of a woman's right to have control over her own body. Some liberals, and other supporters of abortion, interpret it as an extension of the right of privacy. Many people who oppose abortion, however, especially among conservatives, appear from the data to be motivated less by a concern for the sanctity of life than by their view of abortion as simply another indication of the libertine nature of our society.

That abortion is perceived by many of its opponents as one aspect of a constellation of beliefs that uphold the desirability of sexual liberation and the lowering of moral standards can be inferred from the correlation matrix in figure 7.7. Abortion, pornography, sexual freedom, and homosexual rights are all significantly intercorrelated, especially among the community leaders. Opposition to abortion and resistence to sexual freedom are correlated .44. The correlation between abortion and homosexual rights is .41; and between abortion and tolerance for pornography it is .32. Clearly, the more one is opposed to sexual freedom (or to homosexual rights or pornography) the more one is likely to oppose abortion. (Conversely, of course, those who are tolerant of sexual freedom, homosexual rights and pornography are more likely to favor the right to choose abortion.) As we have seen, those who are cool to civil liberties are predominantly hostile to *all* the values in the lifestyle scales.

If we are correct in our interpretation of the data in figure 7.7 (and of miscellaneous other findings on matters of personal conduct throughout our research), there is a marked tendency for the several lifestyle values to cluster. People who feel the country has gone too far toward sexual liberation also tend to believe that it has become too permissive toward such "deviates" as homosexuals, hippies, marijuana users, pornographers, and prostitutes; that it is too tolerant of "loose living," "sin," and declining moral standards; that we are much too free in allowing abortion, birth control, and sex education in the schools; and that in general we are in danger of becoming a latter-day Sodom and Gomorrah.

In the case of abortion, one has reason to doubt that most anti-abortionists are principally motivated by convictions about the "right to life." For example, 81 percent of the anti-abortionists among the community leaders and 74 percent of those in the general population support capital punishment—larger proportions than those who favor

334

abortion. The major sources for the opposition to abortion (excluding opposition by Catholics and others who are bound by religious precepts) would appear from our data to reflect both a hypersensitivity to debauchery and "sin" and a desire to control human conduct in conformity with conventional standards, as part of an effort to promote order and stability not only in personal conduct but in the society itself.

CHAPTER 8

Social and Psychological Influences on Attitudes Toward Civil Liberties

WE HAVE ARGUED in this book that the willingness to permit others to express offensive or dangerous opinions, or to deviate from community standards in their beliefs or conduct, is not inherently congenial to human beings. Rather, it is a product of social learning. We have further maintained that individuals vary in their capacity for learning social norms. Some people are, by virtue of opportunity, intellectual endowment, or location in the social structure, better equipped than others to learn (that is, to encounter, comprehend, and absorb) the libertarian norms of a society that champions freedom as the cardinal feature of its creed.

Although we do not regard tolerance as innate, we believe, nevertheless, that personality or cognitive characteristics may significantly affect an individual's capacity for learning norms about freedom and control. Certain inner psychological states, in other words, may help to determine whether an individual will be disposed to allow or suppress the exercise of freedom by people whose opinions, conduct, or social characteristics offend him or her. In venturing this belief, we do not posit the existence of some hypothetical "tolerant" or "intolerant" personality. We are merely saying that, other things being equal, variations among individuals in their personality or cognitive characteristics can influence the way in which they respond to the beliefs or activities of others.

Personality may help to shape responses to civil liberties issues in several ways. People, for example, who are easily angered, frightened, or offended by those who express unpopular opinions or who otherwise deviate from community standards are bound to find numerous opportunities among the several domains of civil liberties for registering their anger, fear, contempt, or impulse to punish. While many members of the community will tolerate such forms of nonconforming behavior as legally protected and, in any event, as the inescapable byproducts of freedom of expression, other members who are less sympathetic and more misanthropic toward human frailties may favor their suppression. The behavior to which they object affords them an opportunity to "act out" their fears and antagonisms and satisfies their desire to punish people who offend their values and sensibilities. Their psychological needs, in effect, "spill over" into the political realm, so that a person with strong hostile or misanthropic impulses will register those feelings in a variety of contexts that offer appropriate provocations (McClosky and Schaar 1965).

Whereas (as we shall see) one can expect individuals of more sympathetic disposition to regard the enjoyment of civil liberties as an inviolable right to which all persons, whatever their failings, are entitled, individuals of marked misanthropic bent will be less willing to acknowledge the rights of the "undeserving," more inclined to suppress "outrageous" opinions, and more impelled to strike out against dissenters for their presumed assaults upon established values and institutions. The more misanthropic an individual the more likely he is to direct his aggressive tendencies toward other people who fail to measure up to what he considers appropriate standards (McClosky 1967). Censoring, suppressing, or denying rights to individuals who (in his view) have "abused" their liberties is one way to satisfy his own psychological need to punish people whose actions (by his standards) lie outside the boundaries of acceptable conduct.

Personality also plays a role in the social learning of libertarian norms through its influence on mental performance. Personality disturbances, for example, may affect an individual's cognitive awareness by interfering with effective social interaction, by dulling his sensitivity and impairing his capacity to decipher and absorb the prevailing social norms (di Palma and McClosky 1970). Personality disturbances may also serve to distort judgments by projecting upon others, or upon the society itself, characteristics which are in reality internal to the individual observer. Hence, personality malfunctions may prevent some individuals from fully comprehending that tolerance of free speech or religious freedom or the rights of privacy and due process are among the approved ideals of the American political culture, repeatedly articulated and praised by the nation's notables and opinion leaders.

Findings on Psychological Characteristics

Data gathered in our surveys show (although with some notable exceptions) that a respondent's personality characteristics can have a significant bearing on his or her attitudes toward freedom and control. In figure 8.1 and table 8.1, for example, we have assembled from all three surveys data on various scales that measure one or another facet of a respondent's inclination toward sympathy/misanthropy. Figure 8.1 presents the findings on the relations between civil liberties orientation and the misanthropy scales as such. Although the measures of misanthropy (as well as the civil liberties scales) vary somewhat in content,* it is evident from all three studies that those who score high on misanthropy are less civil libertarian than those who score low. Among the mass public in the PAB study, for example, 54 percent of the highly misanthropic respondents were intolerant, compared with only 13 percent of the least misanthropic. Though varying in magnitude (owing partly to differences in the measures and samples employed) the correlations between misanthropy and distrust for civil liberties are also substantial for all four leader samples in the OVS, CLS and PAB studies. For example, in the OVS opinion leader sample, 85 percent of those who score low on misanthropy score at the high (or tolerant) end of the civil liberties scale, compared with 51 percent of those who score high on misanthropy.

The same general tendency can be discerned in the results turned up by comparing libertarians and nonlibertarians on a variety of other scales which reflect the psychological inclination to express distrust, dislike, or contempt toward other people, especially if they exhibit weaknesses or failings of which the respondents particularly disapprove. The measures in table 8.1—hostility, intolerance of human frail-

---

*They also vary in format. The PAB study used an Agree-Disagree format, while the OVS and CLS studies used the sentence completion format, in which respondents could choose between alternative responses. The misanthropy scale in the OVS study contained twelve items, and the scale used in the CLS study contained six items.

TABLE 8.1
Various Scale Measures of Misanthropy and Support for Civil Liberties
(percentage down)

OVS

Score on Omnibus Civil Liberties Scale	Opinion Leaders			Criterion Group Leaders			Mass Public		
	Hostility			**Hostility**			**Hostility**		
	Low (N=433)	Middle (N=231)	High (N=139)	Low (N=900)	Middle (N=631)	High (N=547)	Low (N=294)	Middle (N=274)	High (N=336)
High	84%	72%	63%	83%	64%	53%	45%	30%	26%
Middle	13	23	29	12	24	26	26	37	37
Low	.2	5	7	5	12	22	30	33	37

PAB

	California F (Authoritarianism)			Intolerance of Human Frailty			Hostility			Paranoid Tendencies		
Political Leaders	Low (N=1450)	Middle (N=1127)	High (N=443)	Low (N=917)	Middle (N=1426)	High (N=677)	Low (N=1108)	Middle (N=1325)	High (N=587)	Low (N=1562)	Middle (N=933)	High (N=525)
Low	88%	55%	28%	85%	68%	40%	81%	65%	45%	76%	63%	45%
Middle	9	28	28	11	19	30	13	21	27	15	21	27
High	3	17	44	4	13	30	6	15	28	9	16	28
Mass Public	Low (N=348)	Middle (N=639)	High (N=497)	Low (N=261)	Middle (N=639)	High (N=584)	Low (N=435)	Middle (N=633)	High (N=416)	Low (N=470)	Middle (N=933)	High (N=569)
Low	11	34	51	17	30	47	22	34	48	47	34	16
Middle	22	38	39	25	35	39	30	37	35	32	34	37
High	67	28	10	58	35	14	48	28	17	21	32	47

NOTES: Because percentages have been rounded off, occasionally there will be disparities in totals (columns will not add up to 100 percent).

See the Preface to Research Findings (p. 25) and Appendix B for a description of the leader and mass public samples used in the PAB, CLS, and OVS studies; that is "Political Leaders," "Legal Elite," and so forth.

The CLS study was conducted in 1978 1979; the OVS in 1976 1977; and the PAB in 1958.

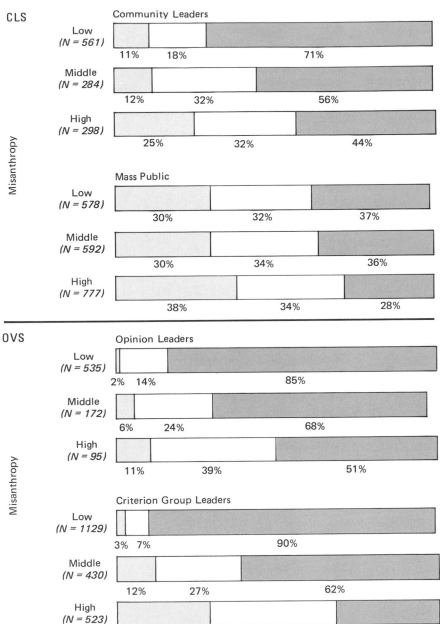

CLS

Misanthropy

Community Leaders

Low
(N = 561)
11%   18%   71%

Middle
(N = 284)
12%   32%   56%

High
(N = 298)
25%   32%   44%

Mass Public

Low
(N = 578)
30%   32%   37%

Middle
(N = 592)
30%   34%   36%

High
(N = 777)
38%   34%   28%

OVS

Misanthropy

Opinion Leaders

Low
(N = 535)
2%   14%   85%

Middle
(N = 172)
6%   24%   68%

High
(N = 95)
11%   39%   51%

Criterion Group Leaders

Low
(N = 1129)
3%   7%   90%

Middle
(N = 430)
12%   27%   62%

High
(N = 523)
29%   40%   32%

FIGURE 8.1
Misanthropy and Support for Civil Liberties
(CLS/OVS/PAB)

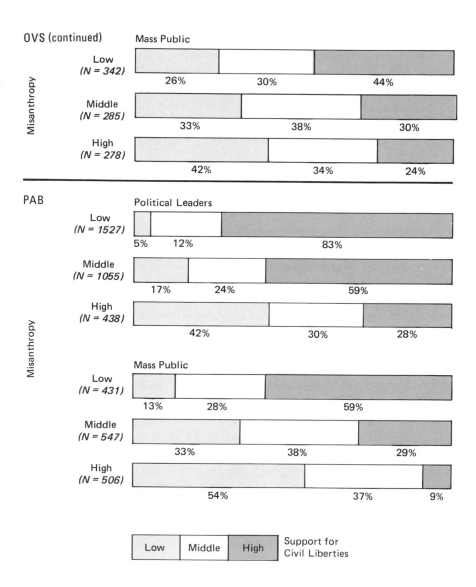

OVS (continued)   Mass Public

Misanthropy

Low
(N = 342)
26%   30%   44%

Middle
(N = 285)
33%   38%   30%

High
(N = 278)
42%   34%   24%

PAB

Misanthropy

Political Leaders

Low
(N = 1527)
5%   12%   83%

Middle
(N = 1055)
17%   24%   59%

High
(N = 438)
42%   30%   28%

Mass Public

Low
(N = 431)
13%   28%   59%

Middle
(N = 547)
33%   38%   29%

High
(N = 506)
54%   37%   9%

| Low | Middle | High | Support for Civil Liberties |

Notes: Because percentages have been rounded off, occasionally there will be disparities in totals (columns will not add up to 100 percent).

See the Preface to Research Findings in Chapter 1 and Appendix B for an analysis of the components of various categories used in the PAB, CLS, and OVS studies: that is "Political Leaders," "Legal Elite," and so forth.

The CLS was conducted in 1978-1979; the OVS in 1976-1977; and the PAB in 1958.

ty, the California F (authoritarian) scale, and paranoid tendencies—express in one form or another an inclination toward misanthropy. We have entered the scores on each of these scales for the mass public and leader samples who score high, middle, or low on civil liberties. In general, the data confirm that there is indeed a connection between one's opposition to civil liberties and one's tendency to express hostility toward people whose characteristics or conduct one views with disfavor.

The percentage scores in figure 8.1 and table 8.1 tell the story: individuals who are particularly impatient with human frailties, who disdain people whom they perceive as having "weak" characters, who are uncommonly suspicious of the motives of others and fear them unrealistically, and who adopt authoritarian, "bullying," or contemptuous attitudes toward outsiders and various minorities are also likely to adopt repressive or punishing attitudes toward people who wish to exercise their civil liberties fully. Their intolerance of human failings, weaknesses, or differences appears to go hand in hand with their reluctance to permit the exercise of the rights of free speech, press, assembly, due process, privacy, and other civil liberties—especially when the persons who wish to enjoy these rights are outside the respondents' approved circles. Though the results are not uniform, one can also detect a tendency for those who are more libertarian to express greater faith in human virtue and to exhibit greater compassion toward human suffering.

Table 8.2 provides a few sample items from the several measures reflecting misanthropy that were particularly effective in accounting for the results we have just reported.* Some of the items focus on the evaluation of human character and weaknesses, while others are of a more social-psychological nature. Some, however, reflect one's atti-

---

*It should be observed, however, that not all the items in the OVS hostility scale show significant differences, partly, we believe, because the "pathological" response in the items was so infrequently chosen by any group. The hostility scale we constructed for the CLS shows no significant differences at all between libertarians and nonlibertarians. Although we are puzzled by this result, we believe the fault may lie in the character of the items, almost all of which refer to anger, vengeance, and violence in *interpersonal* situations, and make no reference to faith in people, antagonism toward the weak, the suffering, the unfortunate, or the deviant. The scale appears to be picking up deep-seated rage responses toward particular individuals rather than misanthropy, and for this reason may be inappropriate for our purposes. Moreover, the distribution of scores for many of the items is strongly skewed toward the "normal" or nonhostile end so that personality differences between groups with different civil libertarian orientations have little opportunity to manifest themselves. Some of the items we developed for assessing personality differences, in other words, do not appear to be up to the task, owing to the almost universal acceptability of one of the response alternatives.

TABLE 8.2

Items Measuring Misanthropy and Support for Civil Liberties

CLS

	Community Leaders			Mass Public		
	High (N=696)	Middle (N=274)	Low (N=178)	High (N=629)	Middle (N=677)	Low (N=651)
If a person has a weak character:						
—he deserves sympathy more than blame.	52%	47%	35%	41%	38%	42%
—he should be treated for what he is, a moral weakling.	15	25	38	15	20	28
—Neither/Undecided	33	29	27	44	42	30
People who have had to work hard for what they have:						
—should know the meaning of poverty and be willing to share what they have.	51	26	30	30	25	21
—should not be expected to share it with those who have not worked as hard.	23	42	52	39	44	55
—Neither/Undecided	26	32	18	30	31	24

OVS

	Opinion Leaders			Criterion Group Leaders			Mass Public		
	High (N=619)	Middle (N=150)	Low (N=29)	High (N=1443)	Middle (N=405)	Low (N=235)	High (N=302)	Middle (N=302)	Low (N=301)
People who want to be liked better:									
—should be given every possible chance to show their worth.	57%	34%	31%	62%	48%	31%	54%	47%	46%
—should first try to get rid of their irritating faults.	20	48	60	19	40	59	27	37	46
—Neither/Undecided	23	18	9	20	13	10	19	16	8

TABLE 8.2 *(continued)*

	OVS								
	Opinion Leaders			Criterion Group Leaders			Mass Public		
	High	Middle	Low	High	Middle	Low	High	Middle	Low
	(N=619)	(N=150)	(N=29)	(N=1443)	(N=405)	(N=235)	(N=302)	(N=302)	(N=301)
Which of these comes closer to what you believe?									
—There is little or nothing to be said in favor of war.	83%	43%	31%	85%	70%	50%	73%	56%	50%
—War is cruel but it does teach people something about honor, loyalty, and courage.	4	25	41	4	12	25	9	22	29
—Neither/Undecided	14	32	29	11	18	25	18	22	21
When I see people who have not been treated well by society:									
—it bothers me a great deal.	87	59	59	88	78	68	78	71	72
—I don't feel it's my responsibility to worry about it.	3	10	9	1	3	11	6	6	8
—Neither/Undecided	11	31	33	11	18	21	16	24	20
Without strong laws and strict moral codes, most people:									
—would learn to control their behavior.	45	14	7	34	11	10	34	15	14
—would give in to every selfish desire.	12	54	74	19	49	69	29	52	66
—Neither/Undecided	43	32	19	47	40	21	37	33	21

Probably the biggest problem in preventing wars is that:

—different countries have different interests.	67	53	44	69	51	46	55	42	46
—human nature is basically aggressive and warlike.	12	28	36	12	25	25	24	31	30
—Neither/Undecided	20	19	21	19	24	29	21	26	24

When it comes to making new friends, a person:

—should be willing to trust people and take a chance.	82	66	52	84	74	61	77	67	63
—has to be pretty choosy to avoid being taken advantage of.	4	14	25	4	10	18	10	16	25
—Neither/Undecided	14	20	22	12	16	21	14	17	12

tudes toward the needs, frailties, or suffering of others. Although the results are not uniformly strong, the items in table 8.2 illustrate the general finding that there is a significant association between opposition to civil liberties and the inclination, when given the option, to choose the more misanthropic (and less sympathetic) response.

The role of personality in helping to fashion one's response to freedom and control, tolerance and intolerance, can also be discerned in the findings on "psychological inflexibility." This personality pattern is characterized by a disposition to polarize issues and to favor dichotomous distinctions. Inflexible people, to an unusual degree, are made uncomfortable by uncertainty or ambiguity in matters of belief. They tend to narrow the number of options in the stimulus field and to display a strong need for tidiness. They cannot bear to leave questions open or unanswered, but are prone to want unequivocal answers to oversimplified questions. Individuals who are inflexible in their psychological needs, motivations, or defense mechanisms are apt to demand (from themselves and others) certain fixed and familiar patterns of conduct and are markedly unreceptive to beliefs or modes of behavior that depart from conventional standards. (See items in table 8.3.) Like the respondents who lean toward misanthropy, those who score high on measures of inflexibility want to regulate and control the behavior of others, and partly for this reason (we believe) will be more inclined than people who score low to punish deviants and silence dissenters.

Personality patterns of the inflexible variety are closely intertwined with the mechanisms of defense (projection, reaction formation, displacement, rationalization, denial, sublimation, and so forth). Through these psychological devices individuals who are unable to handle their own impulses manage to suppress, deny, camouflage, or circumvent them so as to prevent them from reaching consciousness. Defense mechanisms serve to protect fragile egos, and they do so, in part, by censoring or punishing others for conduct individuals fear or dislike in themselves. Not everyone who possesses these characteristics will become politically intolerant, of course, but the probability is strong that rigid and highly "defensive" people will be less sympathetic to civil liberties than people who are less inflexibly defensive.

If this view of inflexibility and the defense mechanisms is correct, we should find that the higher one's score on inflexibility, the weaker one's support for civil liberties. Inflexibility, we believe, functions to dampen enthusiasm for civil liberties not only *directly*, through the relative inability of highly inflexible people to adjust to the diversity of human responses that freedom is likely to generate; but also indirectly, through the play of defense mechanisms that lead one to try to suppress in others certain forms of conduct that one fears in oneself. (The efforts of sexually repressed individuals to prohibit freedom of sexual conduct by others are among the most vivid and familiar examples of these psychological mechanisms at work.)

Figure 8.2 shows some of the effects of psychological inflexibility—specifically intolerance of ambiguity—on one's attitudes toward freedom and control. Although the scales measuring intolerance of ambiguity that we developed for each of the three studies differ somewhat in content and format (which, along with sample differences, affect the magnitude of the scores), they yield essentially parallel results. Among the community leaders in the CLS study, for example, 75 percent of those who score low on intolerance of ambiguity (that is, have a marked capacity for tolerating uncertainty and openendedness in matters of belief) score high on the civil liberties scale, while only 42 percent of the community leaders who score high on intolerance of ambiguity fall into this category. The comparable figures for the mass public are 49 percent and 19 percent, respectively.

In the mass public sample of the OVS study (as in the CLS study), those who score low on inflexibility are twice as likely as those who score high to be strongly libertarian. The highly inflexible are more likely to become impatient or annoyed when opinions are left unresolved. Being intolerant of ambiguity, they are more inclined to believe that most important questions "have a right and a wrong answer." And they are troubled by people who do not decide "the really important questions . . . one way or the other." (See table 8.3.)

In light of these views, one can more easily understand why respondents who are intolerant of ambiguity score low on civil liberties. They are more likely to perceive opinions (and the groups that advocate them) as right or wrong, good or bad, rather than as conditional or qualified. What need is there (in their view) to air all sides of a question; to give all persons their say regardless of the dangerousness of their views; or to encourage the expression of beliefs that are senseless, misleading, odious, and more likely to confound than to clarify? The opportunity to introduce outrageous opinions merely contributes to confusion and hence undermines rather than promotes the truth.

People who are highly intolerant of ambiguity, and the psychologically inflexible in general, are motivated to withhold civil liberties not

347

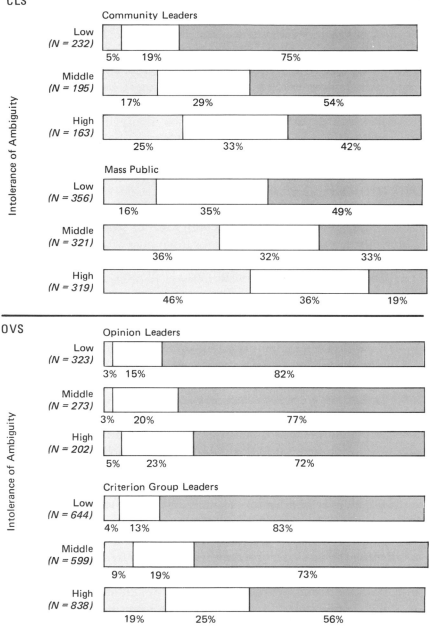

CLS

Intolerance of Ambiguity

Community Leaders

Low
(N = 232)
5% 19% 75%

Middle
(N = 195)
17% 29% 54%

High
(N = 163)
25% 33% 42%

Mass Public

Low
(N = 356)
16% 35% 49%

Middle
(N = 321)
36% 32% 33%

High
(N = 319)
46% 36% 19%

OVS

Intolerance of Ambiguity

Opinion Leaders

Low
(N = 323)
3% 15% 82%

Middle
(N = 273)
3% 20% 77%

High
(N = 202)
5% 23% 72%

Criterion Group Leaders

Low
(N = 644)
4% 13% 83%

Middle
(N = 599)
9% 19% 73%

High
(N = 838)
19% 25% 56%

FIGURE 8.2
Intolerance of Ambiguity and Support for Civil Liberties
(CLS/OVS/PAB)

OVS (continued)

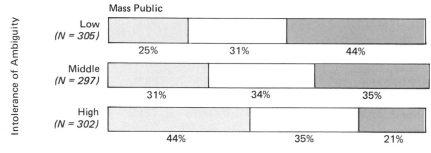

Intolerance of Ambiguity

Mass Public

Low (N = 305)	25%	31%	44%
Middle (N = 297)	31%	34%	35%
High (N = 302)	44%	35%	21%

PAB

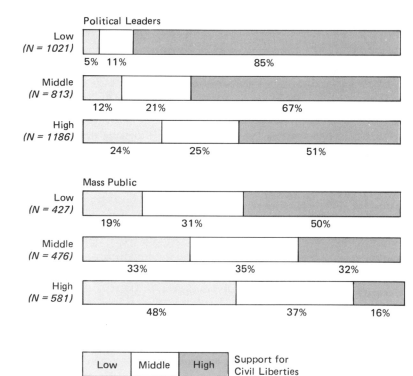

Intolerance of Ambiguity

Political Leaders

Low (N = 1021)	5%	11%	85%
Middle (N = 813)	12%	21%	67%
High (N = 1186)	24%	25%	51%

Mass Public

Low (N = 427)	19%	31%	50%
Middle (N = 476)	33%	35%	32%
High (N = 581)	48%	37%	16%

| Low | Middle | High | Support for Civil Liberties |

only by their views about the adverse effects of tolerance on social stability and the discovery of the truth, but by their tendency to polarize phenomena and to perceive certain beliefs, groups, or forms of conduct as unconditionally worthy or unconditionally unworthy.

As one can observe in figure 8.3 and table 8.3, respondents who are psychologically "rigid"—who, having formed an opinion, doggedly resist having their minds changed and who are perfectionist in the demands they make upon themselves and others—are also likely to adopt severe and judgmental attitudes toward all who exercise their freedom in "unacceptable" ways. They are prone to make sharp distinctions of the "we-they" variety, dividing the world into groups whose character, opinions, or conduct are similar to their own, and hence highly favored, or very different from their own, and hence unacceptable.

While, like other Americans, the strongly inflexible pay lip service to freedom in the abstract, they are obviously made extremely uncomfortable by many instances of its actual exercise. Just as their inflexibility serves to inhibit their own freedom of conduct, so does it also impel them to set narrow limits upon the freedom they are willing to allow others to enjoy. For inflexible individuals, the unhindered exercise by others of certain kinds of liberties is, it seems, psychologically unnerving, as it permits them to engage in conduct that the inflexible deny to themselves—conduct, moreover, that they may perceive as socially or morally deviant.

Some of the psychological tendencies we have been describing also appear to have a bearing on the strong differences in orientation toward civil liberties that turn up when we compare respondents who place great stress on the need for conventionality/conformity and respondents who do not. Just as the psychologically inflexible become uneasy in the presence of diversity, disagreement, uncertainty, or irresolution, those who strongly value conventionality and conformity become greatly troubled by people who diverge from community opinions and standards of conduct, who flout or dissent from established values. They become troubled for example, by the blurring of certain distinctions: political, religious, sexual, and so forth. They are happiest when life is arranged in habitual, dependable, and predictable patterns. As they tell us in table 8.4 they strongly believe "that little girls should play with dolls and little boys with trucks."

The conventionally-minded clearly prefer to be surrounded by behavior and institutions they regard as standard, traditional, and in

TABLE 8.3
Items Measuring Psychological Inflexibility and Support for Civil Liberties

	CLS					
	Community Elite			**Mass Public**		
	High	**Middle**	**Low**	**High**	**Middle**	**Low**
	(N=348)	(N=155)	(N=86)	(N=338)	(N=340)	(N=312)
Most important questions:						
—can usually be answered in more than one way.	90%	85%	72%	89%	78%	75%
—have a right answer and a wrong answer.	7	13	27	7	13	20
—Neither/Undecided.	3	1	1	4	9	5
On an important public issue, I believe:						
—you should always keep in mind that there is more than one side to most issues.	82	75	68	84	79	72
—you should either be for it or against it and not take a middle course.	14	20	31	10	16	26
—Neither/Undecided.	4	5	1	6	5	3
When it comes to the really important questions about religion and philosophy of life:						
—it doesn't really bother me to leave them undecided.	48	24	24	50	30	23
—I feel I have to decide them firmly one way or the other.	37	60	73	34	50	64
—Neither/Undecided.	16	17	3	17	21	13
My opinions on the most important topics:						
—are quite different now from what they were some time ago.	58	40	44	52	44	42
—have never really changed.	23	42	44	28	35	40
—Neither/Undecided.	19	17	11	20	17	17

TABLE 8.3 (continued)

CLS

	Community Elite			Mass Public		
	High (N=348)	Middle (N=155)	Low (N=86)	High (N=338)	Middle (N=340)	Low (N=312)
In my conduct:						
—I realize that nobody's perfect and I try to relax about it.	44%	34%	21%	52%	52%	47%
—I set a high standard for myself and feel others should do the same.	46	57	72	37	37	45
—Neither/Undecided	10	10	8	12	11	8

OVS

	Opinion Leaders			Criterion Group Leaders			Mass Public		
	High (N=619)	Middle (N=150)	Low (N=29)	High (N=1443)	Middle (N=405)	Low (N=235)	High (N=302)	Middle (N=302)	Low (N=301)
In my personal habits:									
—I don't usually follow a strict routine and am not always orderly.	47%	34%	28%	43%	31%	17%	52%	42%	32%
—I try to see that everything is carefully planned and organized.	39	54	64	44	55	76	41	46	55
—Neither/Undecided	14	12	8	12	14	7	7	12	13
In my behavior:									
—I sometimes act impulsively.	62	46	34	58	48	38	59	51	38
—I rarely do things spontaneously, on the spur of the moment.	26	43	56	31	38	52	32	32	44
—Neither/Undecided	12	12	10	11	15	10	9	7	20
In my conduct:									
—I realize that nobody's perfect and I try to relax about it.	39	28	21	37	34	28	46	41	42
—I set a high standard for myself and feel others should do the same.	43	57	69	48	52	62	39	39	46
—Neither/Undecided	19	16	10	15	14	10	15	20	12

Once I've made up my mind on a public question:

—I can often be persuaded to change it if someone has a good argument.	60	47	41	62	58	63	54	45	45
—I'm not likely to change it easily.	27	41	52	26	27	33	32	42	44
—Neither/Undecided	13	13	8	13	15	4	15	13	11

Most important questions:

—can usually be answered in more than one way.	83	63	50	91	85	71	90	72	65
—have a right answer and a wrong answer.	10	30	44	5	8	21	7	18	25
—Neither/Undecided	6	7	6	4	7	7	3	9	10

When it comes to the really important questions about religion and philosophy of life:

—it doesn't especially bother me to leave them undecided.	43	28	15	39	24	32	41	24	21
—a person must decide them one way or the other.	40	63	78	45	58	50	46	60	72
—Neither/Undecided	18	9	8	16	17	18	13	15	6

In trying to accomplish anything in politics you should:

—settle for nothing less than total victory.	3	7	16	2	1	10	2	7	10
—try to achieve the best possible compromise.	87	81	71	92	89	89	88	72	72
—Neither/Undecided	11	12	14	6	10	0	10	22	17

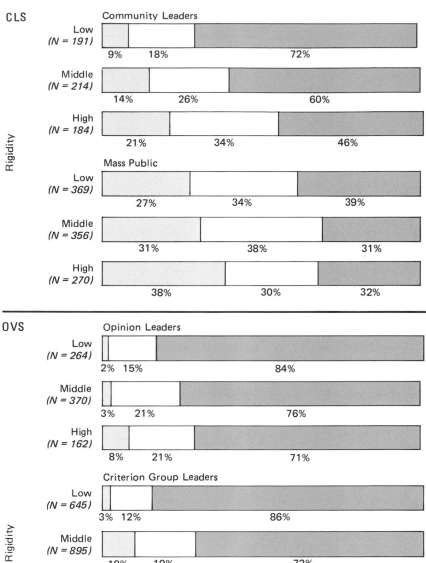

FIGURE 8.3
Psychological Rigidity and Support for Civil Liberties
(CLS/OVS/PAB)

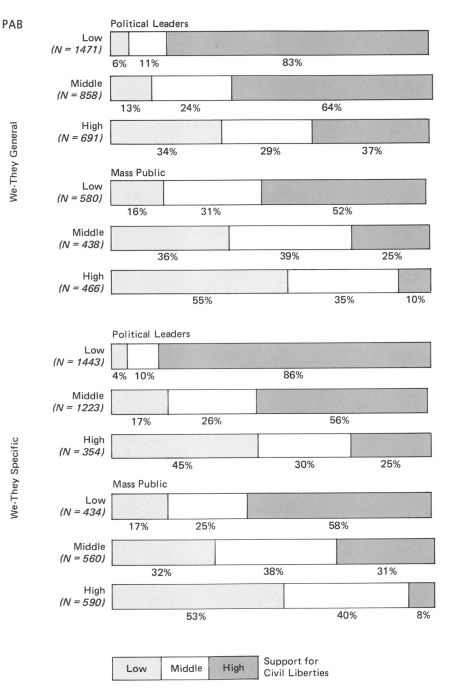

keeping with the known and familiar. They want strict adherence to rules and highly lawful and orderly social arrangements. As one can readily discern in both the scale scores in figure 8.4 and item scores in table 8.4, the more conventional and conforming an individual, the less willing he or she is to support civil liberties. The differences in the scores registered on the conventionality scales in all three studies are, furthermore, rather large, despite variations in content. In the CLS study, for example, 68 percent of the least conventional members of the mass public score high on civil liberties, compared with only 5 percent of the most conventional. Over two thirds of the latter group hold negative views about civil liberties, whereas only 5 percent of the least conventional hold similar views. Scale data from the OVS and PAB studies for both the leader samples and the mass public adhere closely to the same pattern.

Table 8.4 assesses the nature and extent of the connection between one's orientation toward civil liberties and various indicators of conventionality/conformity. Those who score high on the civil liberties scale are dramatically different in their attitudes toward conventionality and the need for conformity than those who score low. Low scorers regard people who try to be "different" as "just a nuisance"; they chiefly admire people who try to "fit in" rather than those "who go their own way without worrying about what others think"; and they strongly prefer children to learn "obedience and respect for authority" rather than "personal independence and the habit of thinking for themselves." By very large margins they want the laws to "enforce the community's standards of right and wrong" rather than to protect the right of citizens to live by their own moral standards. They want children to be brought up "to be like other kids" rather than to be themselves. They believe that society today allows people too much freedom to do as they please rather than impressing them with the importance of "conformity and obedience to the community." The conventionality of their values is also evident in their contempt for "hippies" as lazy, spoiled, and unwilling to work; in their tendency to dismiss people "who get into trouble because of their unusual opinions about politics, religion, or sex"; and in their desire to fire a school teacher who lives with a man to whom she is not married.

The findings in table 8.4 strongly confirm what one might readily have predicted on theoretical grounds; namely, that the strong supporters of civil liberties place much more emphasis on personal independence, individuality, self-expression, being oneself, living by one's

TABLE 8.4

Items Measuring Conventionality/Conformity and Support for Civil Liberties

	CLS					
	Community Leaders			Mass Public		
	High	Middle	Low	High	Middle	Low
	(N=696)	(N=274)	(N=178)	(N=629)	(N=677)	(N=651)
People who usually try to be different from the rest of us:						
—are generally an asset to society.	44%	23%	18%	36%	19%	12%
—are generally just a nuisance.	9	22	38	13	27	43
—Neither/Undecided	47	55	44	51	55	45
The idea that little girls should play with dolls and boys with trucks or trains:						
—is an old-fashioned idea that makes no sense in today's world.	67	34	26	67	43	25
—is still a good idea to help remind boys and girls that they have different roles in life.	15	41	56	17	39	62
—Neither/Undecided	18	25	19	16	18	13
Our laws should aim to:						
—protect a citizen's right to live by any moral standard he chooses.	44	11	5	46	26	11
—enforce the community's standards of right and wrong.	28	68	86	30	53	79
—Neither/Undecided	29	21	9	24	21	10
Whom do you admire more?						
—People who go their own way without worrying about what others think.	54	28	16	49	27	14
—People who learn to fit in and get along with others.	27	55	74	35	59	79
—Neither/Undecided	19	17	10	16	14	7

TABLE 8.4 (continued)

	CLS					
	Community Leaders			Mass Public		
	High	Middle	Low	High	Middle	Low
	(N=696)	(N=274)	(N=178)	(N=629)	(N=677)	(N=651)
If people get into trouble because of their unusual opinions about politics, religion, or sex:						
—it may be our fault for not being more tolerant.	53%	19%	10%	44%	17%	11%
—they have only themselves to blame.	20	51	69	29	46	68
—Neither/Undecided	27	30	21	28	36	21
Most people who "drop out," or become "hippies":						
—are trying to tell us something important about what's wrong with our society.	38	14	14	35	20	14
—are lazy, spoiled, and don't want to work.	18	48	63	26	45	69
—Neither/Undecided	45	38	23	39	35	17
Would it be right to adopt laws which dismiss a school teacher who lives with a man to whom she is not married?						
—Yes.	10	29	58	7	20	49
—No.	74	47	25	82	57	29
—Neither/Undecided	16	24	17	12	23	22

In our society today, too much emphasis is placed on:						
—individual freedom at the expense of the community's interest.	28	60	71	25	36	55
—conformity and obedience to the community.	32	9	8	26	18	9
—Neither/Undecided	40	31	22	49	46	36
The way things are run in America today:						
—people have too much freedom to do as they please.	9	23	49	14	25	48
—people are too restricted in what they are allowed to think and do.	13	11	10	14	13	8
—Neither/Undecided	78	66	41	73	62	44
Which of these values is it more important for our children to learn?						
—personal independence and the habit of thinking for themselves.	76	30	23	65	41	20
—obedience and respect for authority.	9	41	48	18	40	64
—Neither/Undecided	15	30	29	17	20	17

TABLE 8.4 (continued)

	OVS								
	Opinion Leaders			Criterion Group Leaders			Mass Public		
	High	Middle	Low	High	Middle	Low	High	Middle	Low
	(N=619)	(N=150)	(N=29)	(N=1443)	(N=405)	(N=235)	(N=302)	(N=302)	(N=301)
In dealing with their elders, young people:									
—shouldn't have to respect others just because they are older.	48%	10%	3%	34%	19%	4%	32%	10%	6%
—should show more respect than they do now.	27	72	91	40	63	93	44	79	90
—Neither/Undecided	25	18	7	26	18	4	24	10	4
Whom do you admire more:									
—people who go their own way without worrying what others think.	59	39	31	48	29	21	53	24	16
—people who learn to fit in and get along with others.	14	42	52	27	48	69	35	61	77
—Neither/Undecided	27	21	17	25	24	10	12	16	7
Our laws should aim to:									
—protect a citizen's right to live by any moral standards he chooses.	53	13	4	40	9	7	41	18	12
—enforce the community's standards of right and wrong.	16	63	89	25	63	72	32	57	76
—Neither/Undecided	32	24	7	35	28	21	28	25	12
Most young people who "drop out" or become "hippies":									
—are trying to tell us something important about what's wrong with our society.	51	12	11	45	24	28	43	23	12
—are lazy, spoiled, and don't want to work.	10	57	74	13	37	48	21	46	72
—Neither/Undecided	38	31	15	42	40	24	36	31	16

The idea that little girls should play with dolls and little boys with trucks:									
—is too old-fashioned to take seriously.	74	27	10	71	45	35	74	49	36
—makes a lot of sense.	8	45	71	9	28	41	11	27	52
—Neither/Undecided	18	28	19	20	27	24	15	24	13
The most important values children should learn are:									
—independence and self-reliance.	70	35	16	69	40	29	61	34	21
—love and respect for their parents.	5	35	65	7	29	58	16	46	67
—Neither/Undecided	25	30	19	25	31	13	23	20	12
Children should be brought up:									
—to be themselves, even if it makes them different from other kids.	91	77	69	93	81	83	91	85	79
—to be like other kids.	0	3	9	0	5	7	1	4	9
—Neither/Undecided	9	20	23	7	14	10	8	12	12
If people get into trouble because of their unusual opinions about politics, religion, or sex:									
—it means that the people around them are narrow-minded.	47	10	2	29	10	0	34	13	6
—they have only themselves to blame.	8	52	78	12	38	69	19	43	70
—Neither/Undecided	45	39	20	59	52	31	47	44	24

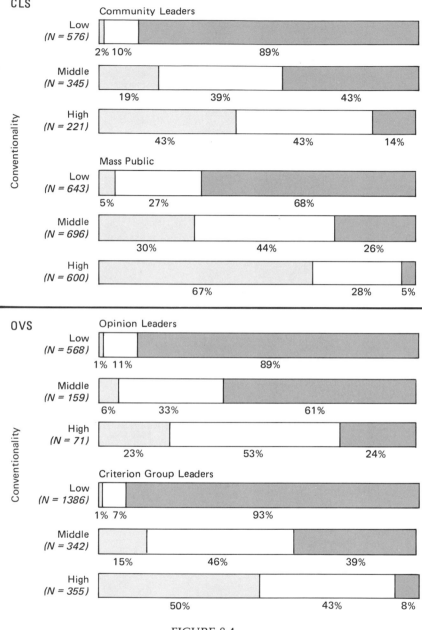

FIGURE 8.4
Conventionality and Support for Civil Liberties
(CLS/OVS/PAB)

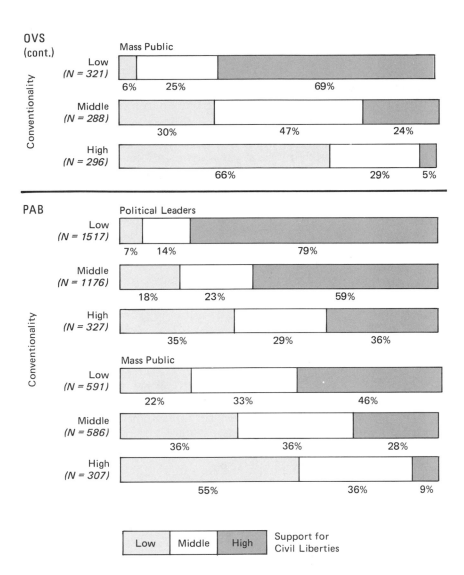

own standards, and developing and holding one's own opinions than they do on obedience, "fitting in," conforming to established codes, and adapting one's ideas and character to whatever standards the community cherishes.

The reasons for the sharp differences shown in figure 8.4 and table 8.4 are not very difficult to fathom. The conventionally minded are critical of various civil liberties partly because they serve to legitimate, and hence to promote, many forms of unconventionality and nonconformity. By protecting nonconformers and enlarging their freedom to think and act as they choose, many civil liberties in effect authorize people to embrace opinions or engage in conduct that society regards as deviant, socially undesirable, or highly damaging to the community's values and stability. (The protections afforded to criminals by the rights of due process serve as a telling example.) Because of civil libertarian guarantees, nonconformers are encouraged to disseminate the most outrageous opinions and to engage in conduct that endangers the integrity of the community itself. Right and wrong become hopelessly confused.

For the conventionally minded, therefore, and for those who place a high value on conformity to established norms, civil liberties, even when honored to some extent, are also perceived as dangerous. If broadly interpreted, they can easily lead to "too much freedom" or to the abuse and misuse of freedom by individuals and groups who do not really share the values of American society.

The psychological needs that lead one to perceive civil liberties in this fashion are not unrelated to the needs that underlie the emphasis on conformity and conventionality. Individuals with these needs aim to achieve an effective measure of control over human thought and conduct. They resist the exercise of freedom that goes beyond clearly designated boundaries. They want not only to have individuals set limits upon themselves, but to have the community prescribe a fairly rigid (and narrow) set of boundaries beyond which individuals must not be allowed to venture. They are impatient with individuals who seek to follow their own course regardless of the community's preference. They fear the uncertainty and disorder which (in their view) might easily be generated by an "excessive" emphasis upon freedom, too great a tolerance of individual desires and idiosyncracies, and an insufficent regard for community rules and standards. In short, the desire to have everyone learn to "fit in" and to adhere closely to the community's standards of right and wrong leads naturally to an effort to narrow the range of civil liberties, since the greater the freedom the more difficult it becomes to achieve conformity and to enforce conventional values.

Evidence from earlier research we have conducted (McClosky and Schaar 1965) suggests that tolerance and support for civil liberties may also be affected to some degree by one's perception of the soundness and stability of the values that underlie the social order. How strongly one is committed to libertarian rights will depend in part on one's feelings about the sturdiness or fragility of the system and one's level of confidence or anxiety about the clarity and vitality of its norms.

The term often used to describe a sense of normlessness, confusion, and uncertainty about prevailing values is "anomie." Anomie is a feeling that "customary restraints and moral limits" have lost their vitality, that society and the individual are "adrift, . . . lacking in clear rules and stable moorings." The anomic individual feels "literally demoralized"; for him the standards that govern behavior in the society are weak or ambiguous (McClosky and Schaar 1965). Anomie, as this suggests (and as we were able to demonstrate), is to a great extent a psychological state of mind as well as a condition characterizing the social order itself. Indeed, it may exist as much in the eye of the beholder as in the society beheld.

As the data bear witness, individuals who are gripped by strong feelings of anomie generally exhibit only weak support for civil liberties. In contrast, respondents who feel confident about the clarity and integrity of society's standards and are fairly secure about their own values tend to be strong supporters of civil liberties.

Both the data from figure 8.5 and other internal evidence from our research confirm that respondents who are more estranged from the dominant values of the political culture are more intolerant of libertarian rights than are respondents who feel more secure about the prevailing norms. Although people who are highly anomic often boast of the nation's superiority (McClosky and Schaar 1965), they nevertheless perceive it as extremely vulnerable and they fear for its safety. Partly because they have not genuinely learned society's norms and are themselves uncertain about the prevailing standards, they are inclined to regard any criticism of the established order (other than their own) as potentially dangerous. They seem to fear that the nation cannot withstand even symbolic insults—to the flag, for example, or to the Constitution or other national insignia. For that matter, they are inclined to view even minor forms of unorthodoxy—in dress, manners, lifestyle,

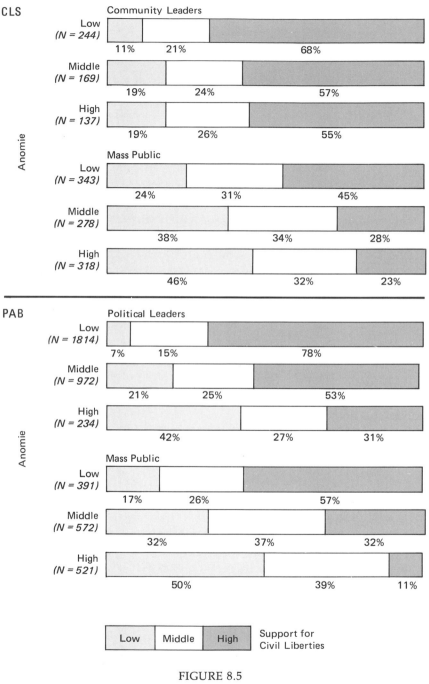

FIGURE 8.5
Anomie and Support for Civil Liberties
(CLS/PAB)

or forms of political participation—as devitalizing, as assaults on a fragile political and social order that hovers precariously at the edge of survival.

One apparent reason for this heightened response, and for the intolerance and denial of due process that go with it, is the failure of anomic respondents to understand or appreciate adequately the values on which the social order rests. They see danger everywhere and hence do not comprehend the case for unlimited and uncensored dialogue or appreciate the importance of such rights as due process for the enforcement of justice. Nor have they effectively grasped the principles of countervailing power and the balance among competing forces that lie at the heart of a free democratic society. Despite their professed veneration of the system, they disapprove (consciously or unconsciously) of many of the key ideas and values upon which it is based (McClosky and Schaar 1965). Because they lack a solid grasp of the pluralistic principles by which democracy functions, they have an inadequate sense of the rights it must protect in order to survive.

Uncertain as they are about the existing norms, unclear about what society regards as right and wrong, alarmed that the nation is drifting into dangerous waters, they seek to limit certain forms of freedom and to avoid the dissemination of certain ideas that might lead to further confusion about the norms and to greater doubt about what they themselves should believe. The anomic individual, in short, is likely to perceive "too much freedom" as contributing further to an already existing state of moral confusion, uncertainty about values, and shifting standards about the proper forms of conduct.

Indecision about norms and a lack of confidence about one's judgments also characterize individuals who are low in self-esteem. While self-esteem is a more elusive, complex, and multifaceted notion than it may seem at first, the term is ordinarily employed to describe people who feel confident about their personal capacities, who respect themselves, and who are generally satisfied with their achievements. People with high self-esteem feel competent in dealing with other people. They feel qualified to manage their own affairs and are sufficiently secure about their appearance and station in life to mingle with others freely and without shame. They tend to be fairly satisfied with their lives, less thwarted by the small defeats to which all of us fall victim at times, and less frustrated about the hand that life has dealt them.

Given these characteristics, persons high in self-esteem have less reason than persons low in self-esteem to seek scapegoats for failure.

Not only are they likely to fail less often, but they experience less of the inner tension and anxiety that drives people with a poor sense of themselves to fear and blame others for their own fate. From previous research we have done on self-esteem (McClosky 1967; McClosky and Schaar 1965), it appears to be far more important for people who lack self-respect and self-confidence to want to surround themselves with a "safer," more secure, and more rewarding social environment. They are, as a result, less able to put up with diversity, with deviation from familiar standards, or with what they tend to regard as "excessive" freedom.

People high in self-esteem possess the inner resources to tolerate unorthodox ideas and conduct without feeling psychologically endangered, whereas individuals seized by self-doubt, insecure about themselves and their ability to manage the world about them, are more likely to be frightened or made anxious by such behavior. Hence one should not be surprised that they want to impose conformity on others and to avert the psychological risk of being confronted by behavior that is unconventional, unfamiliar, or threatening to existing rules.

Individuals who have a strong, positive sense of their own worth also have a greater capacity for social learning and can be expected to have encountered and to have absorbed more thoroughly the libertarian norms of the society. Able to interact more freely with others, possessing the self-assurance to participate effectively in key social roles, and untroubled by the pathological symptoms associated with feelings of failure and rejection, they experience fewer of the psychological impediments to the "correct" learning of society's values than do individuals who are severely wanting in self-esteem.

That self-esteem is correlated with support for civil liberties can be observed in table 8.5. Especially among the mass public, persons who score low on one or another of the several measures of self-esteem included in our studies tend to be more intolerant of civil liberties than those who exhibit high self-esteem.* This holds true whether self-esteem is measured by scales assessing dominance, guilt, need inviolacy (an extreme need to protect one's thoughts and private self against

---

*One reason for the higher correlations among the mass public than among the leaders, we believe, is that the leaders exhibit much higher and more uniform scores on every measure of self-esteem than does the mass public—an outcome that might easily have been anticipated. In all three studies, the proportion of leaders who score high on self-esteem is approximately twice as large as the proportion of high scorers in the mass public. The leaders also have higher, more homogeneous scores on measures of civil liberties, which tends to flatten the correlations even further.

TABLE 8.5
Self-Esteem and Support for Civil Liberties
(percentage down)

CLS

Self-Esteem

Score on Omnibus Civil Liberties Scale	Community Leaders			Mass Public		
	High	Middle	Low	Low	Middle	Low
	(N=392)	(N=156)	(N=45)	(N=348)	(N=321)	(N=332)
High	61%	58%	51%	40%	36%	26%
Middle	26	26	27	35	35	33
Low	13	15	22	25	29	41

OVS

	Opinion Leaders			Mass Public		
	(N=322)	(N=292)	(N=184)	(N=242)	(N=317)	(N=346)
High	78%	76%	78%	38%	33%	30%
Middle	19	19	19	31	36	33
Low	3	5	3	31	31	37

PAB

Score on Omnibus Civil Liberties Scale	Feelings of Personal Unworthiness			Self-Esteem			Psychological Dominance		
				Political Leaders					
	Low	Middle	High	Low	Middle	High	Low	Middle	High
	(N=1434)	(N=1072)	(N=514)	(N=726)	(N=1274)	(N=1020)	(N=137)	(N=472)	(N=2411)
High	78%	62%	47%	48%	67%	80%	41%	51%	71%
Middle	15	21	26	26	20	14	27	24	18
Low	8	17	27	26	14	7	32	25	11

	Mass Public								
	(N=407)	(N=519)	(N=558)	(N=743)	(N=513)	(N=228)	(N=473)	(N=458)	(N=553)
High	51%	33%	15%	18%	39%	56%	17%	26%	47%
Middle	31	34	38	39	32	27	38	40	28
Low	19	33	47	44	29	17	45	34	26

	Status Frustration			Guilt			Need Inviolacy		
				Political Leaders					
	Low	Middle	High	Low	Middle	High	Low	Middle	High
	(N=1709)	(N=977)	(N=334)	(N=1476)	(N=909)	(N=635)	(N=1837)	(N=639)	(N=544)
High	72%	62%	54%	74%	63%	56%	74%	63%	48%
Middle	17	21	24	16	21	23	16	21	26
Low	12	17	22	10	17	21	10	16	26

	Mass Public								
	(N=581)	(N=596)	(N=307)	(N=582)	(N=469)	(N=433)	(N=609)	(N=383)	(N=492)
High	42%	27%	18%	40%	30%	20%	47%	26%	16%
Middle	32	38	34	33	36	35	31	39	36
Low	26	35	48	26	35	45	23	35	48

exposure), status frustration, sense of personal unworthiness, or self-esteem as such.* While each of these scales measures a different facet of the complex psychological state we have described as self-esteem (some reflecting deep-seated inner feelings of confidence or uncertainty and others reflecting social standing and capacity for interaction), the results are essentially parallel, though the differences, as one would expect, vary in magnitude. With some exceptions, then, the lower the self-esteem the weaker is the support for civil liberties.†

Findings on Social Characteristics

So far in this chapter we have seen that certain forces internal to the individual (forces ordinarily classified as "psychological") have a measurable effect on how people view the civil liberties of others. Of course, the motivations that influence individuals' attitudes toward freedom and control are not entirely outgrowths of personality make-up or other psychological influences. They are also the products of social or demographic forces which impinge on individuals in ways that increase or diminish their opportunities, capacities, or motivation for social learning.

The probability that one will encounter and embrace society's ideals about freedom and control, for example, is likely to be strongly affected by one's location in the social structure. Where one's status, education, or vocation place one in relation to the intellectual and moral mainstreams of the society will help determine the nature and frequency of one's access to the prevailing norms and, as a result, one's likelihood of absorbing them. If, as we have maintained, the established norms of the American political culture are predominantly fa-

---

*For an extended and perceptive analysis of the data on self-esteem and political values based on our PAB surveys, see Sniderman 1975.
†It should be noted, however, that the differences reported for self-esteem are substantially larger in the PAB study than in the CLS and OVS studies. Whether this reflects differences in the content and quality of the scales employed or in the format of the questions used, we do not know. In the self-esteem scale in the CLS study, significant differences in the mass sample turn up particularly on items reflecting ability to lead a group, organizing and taking charge of an activity, and participating effectively in the discussions at a public meeting. However, on other items that express feelings of inadequacy and inferiority compared with others, the differences, though in the predicted direction, are small.

vorable to civil liberties, then those members of society who have most access to the norms and the greatest capacity for comprehending them should exhibit the keenest support for freedom and tolerance.

We encountered evidence for this view when we compared elite and mass responses to civil libertarian values. The elites, being more involved in public affairs, better informed, more aware of the principles underlying issues of freedom and control, and more sensitive to the arguments, subtleties, and complexities involved in the application of libertarian rights, exhibited consistently greater support for civil liberties than did the mass public. (See chapter 6.)

We have also seen that the better educated tend to be more tolerant and that differences in education have a strong bearing on the degree to which respondents express support for civil liberties. By exposing individuals repeatedly to the libertarian norms of the political culture, by transmitting the arguments in defense of those norms (as articulated, for example, by the courts and commentators on civil liberties), and by putting students in touch with the ideas and political principles emanating from our most venerated historical figures, education succeeds to a remarkable degree in inculcating attitudes of support for freedom in general and civil liberties in particular.

Further evidence that an increase in awareness and knowledge of public affairs is associated with a rise in social learning, and hence contributes to the acquisition of civil libertarian norms, can be discerned from table 8.6. For both the mass public and the several elite samples in all three of our studies, there is a sizable increase in support for civil liberties as knowledge of political matters rises. The more one knows and understands about public affairs (as measured by our scales of political information and sophistication), the higher the probability that one will respond favorably to the various libertarian rights included in the omnibus civil liberties scales we developed for each study. In the CLS study, for example, almost half of the more informed members of the mass public score high on the civil liberties scale, whereas only 18 percent of the relatively uninformed score high. Even among the community elite, whose members possess, on the average, more political knowledge to begin with, the same pattern of differences emerges: about two thirds of the politically informed score high on the civil liberties scale, compared with only 39 percent of the least politically informed. The same general pattern turns up in both the CLS and OVS studies, even though the items used to construct the two scales differ somewhat in content.

TABLE 8.6
Political Knowledge and Support for
Civil Liberties (percentage down)

Score on Omnibus Civil Liberties Scale	Political Knowledge		
	Community Leaders		
	Low	Middle	High
CLS	(N=889)	(N=188)	(N=66)
High	65%	46%	39%
Middle	23	32	33
Low	12	22	27
	Mass Public		
	(N=576)	(N=601)	(N=770)
High	48	29	18
Middle	27	37	38
Low	25	34	44
	Opinion Leaders		
OVS	(N=31)	(N=208)	(N=606)
High	33%	69%	83%
Middle	47	27	15
Low	20	5	2
	Criterion Group Leaders		
	(N=110)	(N=517)	(N=1515)
High	34	54	77
Middle	30	26	17
Low	35	20	7
	Mass Public		
	(N=292)	(N=374)	(N=272)
High	13	34	53
Middle	38	33	29
Low	48	33	18

If we turn from knowledge of politics in general to knowledge of civil liberties in particular, the differences between the informed and the uninformed in their support for civil liberties are also large. As knowledge of civil liberties increases, so does the level of support. This tendency can clearly be observed in the data in table 8.7 where, for example, the number of respondents in the mass public who score as highly tolerant is approximately three times as great among those who are well-informed about civil liberties as among those who are poorly

TABLE 8.7
Civil Liberties Knowledge and Support for Civil Liberties
(percentage down)

Score on Omnibus Civil Liberties Scale	Level of Civil Liberties Knowledge					
	Mass Public			Community Leaders		
	Low	Middle	High	Low	Middle	High
	(N=626)	(N=669)	(N=698)	(N=115)	(N=319)	(N=723)
High	14%	31%	49%	28%	51%	70%
Middle	35	37	32	33	28	21
Low	51	32	19	39	21	9

informed. The pattern holds for community leaders as well: 70 percent of those who are knowledgeable about civil liberties also prove to be highly tolerant; among the least knowledgeable, the number is only 28 percent.

Essentially similar results turn up when we assess the level of cognitive awareness by measures of "intellectuality." Here we are testing not for actual knowledge or level of education (though both are correlated with intellectuality to some extent), but for one's attitude toward intellectual and artistic matters and the life of the mind. The items in the intellectuality scales refer, among other things, to one's interest in literature, art, and philosophy; to the value of reading books; and to one's attitudes toward intellectuals and intellectual pursuits in general.

Table 8.8 shows that respondents who score high on our measures of intellectuality are substantially more libertarian than those who score low. Among the community leaders in the CLS study, for example, 72 percent of those who are favorably disposed toward intellectual subjects score high on civil liberties, compared with 43 percent of those who express little interest in intellectual matters. In the PAB study, for which we developed a longer and more elaborate intellectuality scale, the differences in orientation toward civil liberties between the intellectuals and the nonintellectuals are even larger. Both studies strongly confirm the popular impression that intellectuals (or their sympathizers) are substantially more likely than other categories of the population to champion civil liberties.

It is a mark of intellectuals, of course, and of those who value intellectuality in general, that they read many more books and magazines, see more plays and films, attend more lectures and participate in many more discussions about ideas than other people; that they are

373

TABLE 8.8
Intellectuality and Support for Civil Liberties
(percentage down)

Score on Omnibus Civil Liberties Union	Intellectuality					
	Mass Public			Community Leaders		
	High	Middle	Low	High	Middle	Low
	(N=303)	(N=240)	(N=399)	(N=294)	(N=129)	(N=127)
CLS						
High	45%	34%	22%	72%	54%	43%
Middle	29	38	31	18	29	32
Low	25	28	48	10	17	26
	Mass Public			Political Leaders		
	(N=534)	(N=556)	(N=394)	(N=1728)	(N=897)	(N=395)
PAB						
High	52%	24%	13%	81%	54%	33%
Middle	29	39	37	13	26	29
Low	20	37	51	6	20	38

keenly interested in the public life of the community; that they participate widely—through writing, speeches, and conversations—in the
public colloquy; and that their activities make highly visible to them
the norms of the political culture. Many intellectuals, moreover, are
unusually sensitive to the values that relate to freedom. Debate and the
exchange of ideas are central to the intellectual vocation, just as the
universities, books, publications, lectures, meetings, and speeches with
which they involve themselves are the props of the intellectual arena
in which they are often the principal players. They regard freedom of
expression as the *sine qua non* of the intellectual vocation, while censorship is the archenemy that stifles criticism, blunts sensibility, and
throttles the life of the mind.

From several perspectives, then, the available data clearly confirm
that the educated, the politically informed, and the intellectually
minded espouse civil liberties more strongly than the less educated
and those uninformed about public affairs. The former, as we have
noted, embrace the constitutional liberties guaranteed, for example, in
the Bill of Rights partly because they have been exposed more frequently to the norms implicit in those guarantees and have had greater
opportunity and motivation to learn them. They are also more likely to
belong to a cohort that prizes libertarian values and rewards its members for promoting them.

Political Interest and Support for Civil Liberties
(PAB) (percentage down)

	Political Interest		
	Mass Public		
Support for	Low	Middle	High
Civil Liberties	(N=472)	(N=582)	(N=43)
High	16%	31%	47%
Middle	39	34	31
Low	45	35	21

These findings and observations serve to reinforce our earlier claim that tolerance of freedom and nonconformity is a response that not only has to be learned but is often difficult to learn. It is especially difficult for people with little knowledge or interest in public affairs. Having little exposure to information and discussions about the meaning of civil liberties, they have had less occasion to ponder such matters as the implications of freedom, the scope of the rights set forth in the Constitution, or the subtle and recondite arguments fashioned by judges and other commentators on human rights about the nature and limits of free speech, press, assembly, religion, privacy, or due process. Nor, as we have observed, is the case for tolerance intuitively obvious. It is by no means self-evident, for example, that the members of a white majority should have a right to make speeches that insult ethnic minorities; that revolutionaries should have a right to advocate the overthrow of the American political system; that the educational system should be forbidden to set aside time and facilities for prayers in the public schools; or that a newspaper cannot be prevented from printing lies. Whether these and other liberties that exact a high price ought to be constitutionally protected raises highly vexing questions, and a fair amount of political sophistication is required to address them and make the case for freedom.

The data in figures 8.6 and 8.7 on the size of the community in which respondents live provides support for the view that the learning of civil libertarian norms bears some relation to a respondent's sophistication, breadth of perspective, and frequency of interaction about public affairs. In these tables we have classified the mass public and leader respondents in our three studies according to the size of the community in which they now reside and the size of the community in which they were raised. These communities range from the smallest, most rural, and presumably most provincial or parochial communities

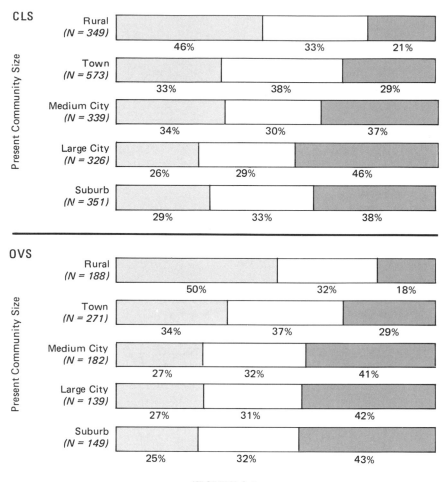

FIGURE 8.6
Support for Civil Liberties by Size of Community in Which Respondents
Now Live (Mass Public)
(CLS/OVS/PAB)

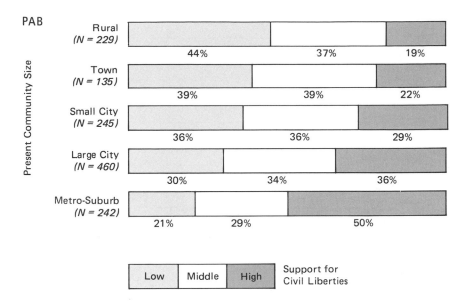

PAB

Present Community Size

Rural (N = 229): Low 44%, Middle 37%, High 19%

Town (N = 135): Low 39%, Middle 39%, High 22%

Small City (N = 245): Low 36%, Middle 36%, High 29%

Large City (N = 460): Low 30%, Middle 34%, High 36%

Metro-Suburb (N = 242): Low 21%, Middle 29%, High 50%

Low | Middle | High   Support for Civil Liberties

Notes: In the CLS and OVS studies: Rural = under 2500; Town = 2500–50,000; Medium City = 50,000– 250,000; Large City = over 250,000; Suburb = suburbs of medium or large cities.

In the PAB study: Town = under 2500; Small City = 2500–10,000; Large City = 10,000– 100,000; Metropolitan Suburban = cities over 100,000 and their suburbs.

Data on the leader samples can be found in Appendix B.

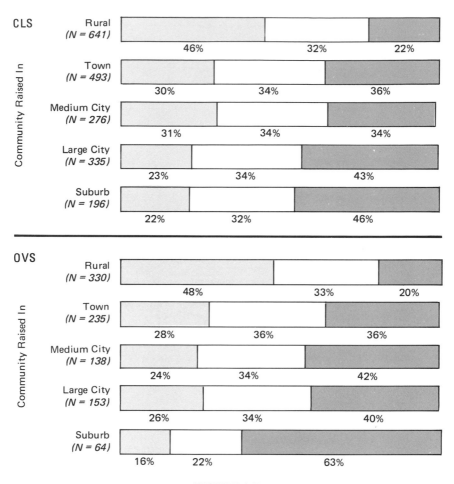

FIGURE 8.7
Support for Civil Liberties by Size of Community in Which Respondents
were Raised (Mass Public)
(CLS/OVS/PAB)

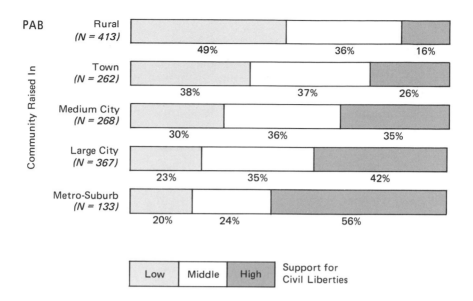

Notes: In the CLS and OVS studies, Rural = under 2500; Town = 2500–50,000; Medium City = 50,000– 250,000; Large City = over 250,000; Suburb = suburbs of medium or large cities.

In the PAB study, Town = under 2500; Small City = 2500-10,000; Large City = 10,000– 100,000; Metropolitan-Suburban = cities over 100,000 and their suburbs.

Data on the leader samples can be found in Appendix B.

to the largest, most urban, and presumably most cosmopolitan communities.

As predicted, the data in figures 8.6 and 8.7 confirm that support for civil liberties increases as the size of the community grows larger and more cosmopolitan. Support is weakest in the farm areas and small towns and strongest in the metropolitan communities. For example, whereas only 21 percent of the rural residents in the CLS study score high on the civil liberties scale, the percentage rises to 46 percent in the large cities—proportionately twice as many. Although the absolute magnitudes vary slightly for the several samples (as one would expect), the same pattern of differences recurs in all three studies. With one exception, the pattern is similar for the leader samples.

Equally striking are the differences that turn up in figure 8.7, where we have classified the respondents in the three studies according to the size of the communities in which they were raised. In every case, the general pattern we have described is repeated: support for civil liberties is lowest in the rural and smaller communities and grows larger as the size and metropolitan character of the community increases. (Cf. comparable findings by Stouffer 1955, Nunn et al. 1978, and Davis 1975.)

Why do we find, in case after case, that the larger, more metropolitan communities and their suburbs contain a substantially greater proportion of people strongly committed to civil liberties than do the rural communities and small towns? What is there about urban life (or for that matter, about rural and small-town life) that produces this striking and consistent result—a result that holds not only for the mass public but for the leaders as well?

At this point, one can only conjecture, but several possible explanations come to mind. The urban areas, of course, are more densely populated, and (despite some striking exceptions) population density ordinarily increases intellectual interaction and a concern with a broader spectrum of public affairs. In the cities and suburbs there are more newspapers, magazines, television stations, and radio newscasts that report national and international affairs and focus on public questions of broad intellectual and political significance. There are also more institutions of higher learning, more public lectures and debates, and a wider range of intellectual and artistic activities. There are more films, plays, bookstores, libraries, museums, and voluntary organizations concerned with public issues—in short, far more facilities and many more occasions for learning about the norms of the national community and about the great issues of state which occupy the minds of thoughtful people. For purposes of social learning, the "locals" of a small, rural community are not only physically but intellectually remote from society's mainstreams.

Although one must be careful not to overdraw the distinctions between the more "cosmopolitan" character of the cities and the more "local" or parochial nature of the small towns and rural areas, the differences between "locals" and "cosmopolitans" have nevertheless been shown to be real. (Cf. Merton 1968.) One encounters in the metropolitan areas a comparatively larger number of people with greater wealth, broader education, and high-status occupations, whose public preoccupations reflect an interest in questions of a more universal nature. The rural areas, by contrast, contain comparatively fewer people of professional standing; fewer managers or executives of large businesses; fewer intellectuals, educators, and students; fewer white collar workers; fewer leaders of large organizations—fewer people in all social strata whose preoccupations are likely to go beyond the immediate boundaries and provincial affairs of their local community.

This is not to say, of course, that all metropolitan communities are tolerant and all rural communities intolerant. Such an assertion would greatly exaggerate the differences. In fact, "locals" and "cosmopolitans" can reside in the same community and even enjoy the same status or roles. It is to say, however, that the urban areas are more likely to produce a comparatively larger number of "cosmopolitans" (who, as Merton describes them, are "oriented significantly to the world outside") while the rural areas contain a larger proportion of "locals" (who, in Merton's language, are "preoccupied with local problems to the virtual exclusion of the national and international scene"). We believe that the differences in support for civil liberties reported in figures 8.6 and 8.7 can in significant measure be explained by the differences between locals and cosmopolitans—between those with far-reaching interests and broader perspectives, who more often reside in the metropolitan centers, and those with more parochial interests and narrower perspectives, who are found in proportionately greater numbers in the rural, more isolated regions of the country. If, as we have argued, it is difficult to learn why one should support the rights of others to think, speak, and even act outrageously, it is (as the evidence suggests) still more difficult to absorb the principles involved in this set of rights if one resides in a community remote from the centers of thought and culture than if one lives within or close to the centers themselves.

The differences in figures 8.6 and 8.7 may also reflect the greater diversity of the populations in the metropolitan centers and the wider variety of life experiences to which their inhabitants are exposed. Diversity, it would appear, promotes, though it does not guarantee, tolerance. As individuals encounter in their daily lives other residents who differ from themselves in religion, race, vocation, wealth, education, political outlook, ideas, lifestyle, and social philosophies, they are more likely to become accustomed to the extraordinary variety of human characteristics as a fact of life, a reality to which they must accommodate if they are to survive in the community. While enclaves of uniformity can be found even in the cities, of course, as like seeks out like and some groups are segregated or segregate themselves by choice from others in the population, the inhabitants of urban areas are, as a rule, more diverse in their social characteristics, intellectual habits, and political encounters than are the residents of the small towns. The greater the uniformity, presumbably, the greater is the emphasis on conformity and standardization, and the stronger is the demand for adherence to local rules and customs.

In figure 8.8 we turn to a different geographic comparison, one that involves the American South and the other regions of the country. In making this comparison, we expected to find that the South would exhibit less support for civil liberties than the other regions of the country. We reasoned that the South, owing partly to historical influences which tended to isolate southerners from the more cosmopolitan residents of the other regions and partly to its social and economic characteristics (for example, more rural, less educated, less industrialized), would be intellectually and politically more distant from the nation's mainstream values and would be slower to adopt libertarian norms than would most of the rest of the country.

Perhaps the most striking finding revealed in figure 8.8, however, is that while the regional differences in orientation toward civil liberties were rather substantial when we conducted our national surveys in 1958, they had become relatively modest by the time we again surveyed the nation in the late 1970s. In 1958, for example, only 18 percent of the general public in the South scored high on the civil liberties scale, compared with 34 percent of the residents of the other regions of the country—a difference of 16 percent. In the CLS study of 1978,

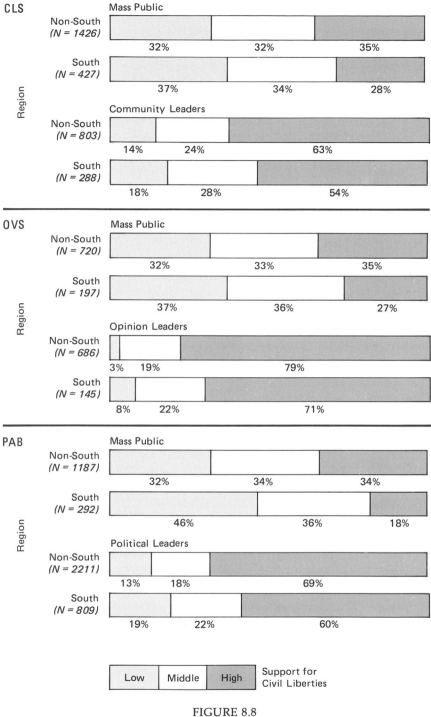

FIGURE 8.8
Support for Civil Liberties by Region
(CLS/OVS/PAB)

however, the difference was only 7 percent (28 percent high for the South and 35 percent high for the other regions). The differences between the southern community leaders and those of other regions was 9 percent in both 1958 and 1978.

The increasing libertarianism of the South doubtless reflects to some extent its changing social and economic patterns. Evidence from various fields of study indicate that the South has come more and more to resemble, in its social characteristics and values, the other regions of the country. One may plausibly assume that as the South continues to change and comes even closer to resembling the other regions in its levels of education, industrialization, urbanization, exposure to mass media, and so forth, the modest differences that still turn up in their respective attitudes toward libertarian rights will gradually disappear.

Small differences in levels of support for civil liberties also show up in the comparisons between men and women. The data in table 8.9 reveal that in the mass public samples of all three studies, males score slightly more libertarian than females—a finding which suggests that, despite, the growing equality of men and women, men, on the average, continue to occupy more of the high-status positions in the society, take more interest in public affairs, hold more positions of public lead-

TABLE 8.9
Support for Civil Liberties by Sex

Score on Omnibus Civil Liberties Scale	Mass Public		Community Leaders	
	Male	Female	Male	Female
CLS	(N=946)	(N=998)	(N=838)	(N=302)
High	35%	32%	58%	67%
Middle	35	32	26	21
Low	30	36	16	13
	Mass Public		Opinion Leaders	
OVS	(N=460)	(N=468)	(N=582)	(N=307)
High	36%	31%	75%	81%
Middle	35	32	21	16
Low	30	37	4	3
	Mass Public		Political Leaders	
PAB	(N=757)	(N=717)	(N=2476)	(N=526)
High	32%	30%	68%	62%
Middle	35	34	19	20
Low	32	36	14	17

ership and influence, and, in general, are more involved in the formulation and dissemination of opinions affecting such matters as freedom and control. As is well known, more women than men are still confined to domestic roles (or to menial roles) and enter the public arena less frequently to engage in the community debate over the values and norms that govern, or *should* govern, the nation. We believe, in short, that the differences we find between men and women in their orientation toward civil liberties are a function of their differential opportunities to learn the prevailing social norms and are in no sense specific to gender.

It is worth noting in this regard that in our two recent surveys of community and opinion leaders (though not in the earlier 1958 survey of political leaders), women exhibit higher scores on the civil liberties scales. While we can only speculate, a possible explanation for this reversal of scores is that the women who rise to roles of leadership or influence in the community, compared with the men in similar roles, are more finely screened. They have had to traverse a more difficult road and to overcome a greater number of obstacles. As a result, the women who succeed in achieving influential roles are likely on the average to exhibit a slightly higher public sensibility and a greater capacity for absorbing the ideals by which the nation is presumably guided. These differences, however, like other small differences in opinion that occasionally show up between men and women, will very likely disappear when equal opportunity between the sexes is more fully realized.

Differences in orientation toward civil liberties of a more substantial nature turn up when we divide our national samples by occupation. (See table 8.10.) For purposes of this analysis we have set out the occupational categories according to the classifications employed by the census bureau; if one assumes that this classification accords even crudely with some hypothetical hierarchy of status, one discovers that the correspondence between occupational status and support for civil liberties, though obviously imperfect, is, for the general population as a whole, significant.*

Table 8.10 shows that there is a general (though somewhat erratic) tendency for tolerance to increase as occupational status rises—a tendency that appears to be related, in part, to the degree to which a given

---

*It should be noted, however, that the occupational categories, as listed by the census bureau are extremely broad and diverse, so that one cannot always be certain who exactly is being compared with whom.

TABLE 8.10

Support for Civil Liberties by Occupation (CLS)

Score on Omnibus Civil Liberties Scale	Occupation							
	Profes-sionals	Mana-gerial	Clerical	Crafts-men	Opera-tives	Farm Workers	Service Workers	House-wives
	(N=344)	(N=247)	(N=525)	(N=203)	(N=244)	(N=58)	(N=154)	(N=83)
Mass Public								
High	53%	34%	33%	26%	30%	9%	25%	19%
Middle	25	38	35	37	37	36	34	21
Low	22	28	32	37	34	55	40	60
	(N=600)	(N=422)	(N=80)	(N=7)*	(N=7)*	(N=8)*	(N=4)*	(N=5)*
Community Leaders								
High	66%	53%	59%	———	———	———	———	———
Middle	22	29	25	———	———	———	———	———
Low	13	19	16	———	———	———	———	———

NOTE: Occupational classifications are those used by the census bureau.

*N is too small to calculate percentages.

occupational category places one in the major communication networks of the society. Thus, civil liberties are most strongly supported by individuals in professional occupations (for example, lawyers, academics, doctors, scientists, journalists, intellectuals, leaders of citizen organizations—occupations whose members are close to the national mainstreams of articulate opinion and who are more likely to exhibit an interest in public affairs than do the members of other occupations. Like some of the other groups we have described, they are among the most cosmopolitan segments of the society—a characteristic which is reinforced by the fact that almost 90 percent of them are also college educated. While the other white collar occupations classified as managerial and clerical are also above average in their support for civil liberties, they do not differ sharply from such blue collar occupations as craftsmen or operatives.

Least favorable to civil liberties are the farmers and housewives, occupational categories whose members tend to be rather parochial in their interests and relatively insulated from the more articulate segments of the culture. They are, on the average, least exposed to the intellectual exchanges and public debates in which the arguments for civil liberties are likely to be set forth. Since, in addition, they are among the least educated of the occupational categories, one can further assume that their opportunities for the social learning of libertar-

TABLE 8.11

Support for Civil Liberties by Occupation, with Education Controlled (CLS Mass Public)

	Occupation							
Score on Omnibus Civil Liberties Scale	Profes- sionals (N=38)	Mana- gerial (N=89)	Clerical (N=307)	Crafts- men (N=145)	Opera- tives (N=192)	Farm Workers (N=47)	Service Workers (N=112)	House- wives (N=61)
Less Than College Education								
High	34%	19%	22%	17%	20%	9%	19%	12%
Middle	40	39	37	43	41	32	36	20
Low	26	42	42	41	39	60	46	69
	(N=305)	(N=157)	(N=217)	(N=58)	(N=52)	(N=11)	(N=41)	(N=22)
Some College Education								
High	55%	43%	48%	48%	64%	9%	44%	41%
Middle	24	38	33	22	21	55	29	23
Low	21	20	19	29	15	36	27	36

NOTE: Occupational classifications are those employed by the Census Bureau.

ian norms are fewer than those enjoyed by the members of most other occupations.

The data in table 8.11 show that within each occupational category, those with more education are more libertarian than those with less education. Indeed, when we take education into account, the differences in libertarianism among the various occupations become even more erratic. The professionals continue to show the strongest support for civil liberties, while the housewives and farmers continue to show the least. But no clear pattern can be discerned among the other occupational categories. Education, it seems plain, helps to account for the relationship between occupational status and support for civil liberties, and controlling for education tends to weaken that relationship.

Findings on Age

Of all the social influences that help to shape the public's attitudes toward civil liberties, none, except for education, appears to have a more powerful effect than age. Warranty for this assertion can be seen in figure 8.9, where, for all the samples employed in the three studies

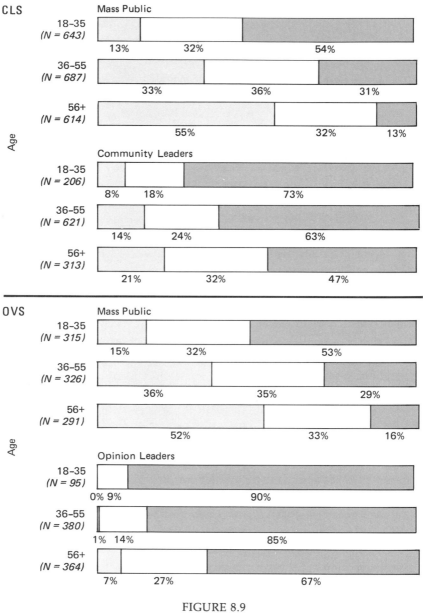

FIGURE 8.9
Age and Support for Civil Liberties
(CLS/OVS)

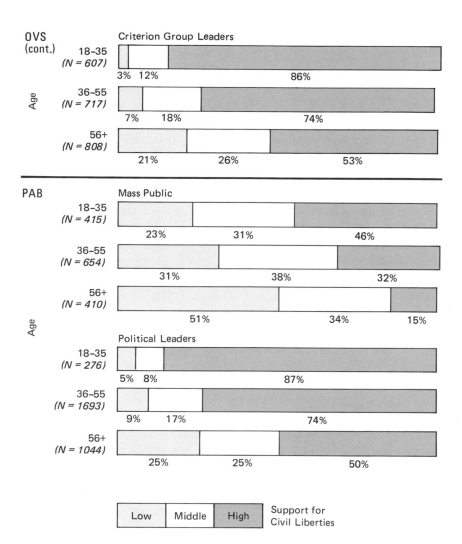

(but, as expected, especially in the mass public samples), the younger age groups register substantially higher scores on the civil liberties scale than do the older age groups.* In every case, as we move from the younger age groups to the older, support for civil liberties declines. (For data from studies by others showing the same trend for 1954 and 1973, see Stouffer 1955, Nunn et al. 1978, and Davis 1975.)

In the CLS study, for example, whereas 54 percent of the younger adults (18–35) score high on the civil liberties scale, only 13 percent of the respondents over 56 years of age score high—a ratio of more than four to one. Similarly, more than half the respondents over 56 years of age score at the low end of the civil liberties scale, compared with only 13 percent of the younger age group.

Among the leader samples, the civil liberties scores are, of course, considerably higher than they are for the general public, but significant differences in orientation toward civil liberties show up even here between the younger and older leaders. Freedom of expression and respect for the rights of due process, privacy, and lifestyle turn out to vary systematically with age: the younger the individual, the less willing he or she is to restrict or prohibit the exercise of these constitutional rights. For example, 73 percent of the community leaders under 36 years of age register high scores on the civil liberties scale, compared with 63 percent of the leaders in the middle age group and 47 percent of those in the older age group.

One can more fully appreciate the meaning of these differences by examining the responses registered by the different age groups on some of the actual items from the civil liberties scale. In table 8.12 we have included items from the several subdomains of the scale that illustrate the nature of the differences between older and younger members of the mass public.†

From the percentage scores on these items, it is obvious that the older the person, the more likely he or she is to choose the more restrictive response on items drawn from every one of the civil liberties

* As we shall see below, this generalization holds strongly even when we control for education, that is, even when we compare younger and older respondents with the same amounts of education.

† The differences for the items shown in table 8.12 were selected to illustrate rather than to represent the differences for all the items in the scale. Some items not included in the table show equally large differences; others smaller. In a few cases, especially those dealing with such due process rights as government respect for the rules, the use of illegal methods to convict a suspect, the right to a jury trial, or the right to a "fair trial, in general, the differences between older and younger respondents tend to be relatively small.

TABLE 8.12

Responses to Civil Liberties Items by Age (CLS Mass Public)

	Age		
	Under 36	36–55	Over 55
	(N=652)	(N=700)	(N=637)
The use of obscene gestures to express anger against a public official:			
—should be considered a constitutionally protected form of free speech.	34%	20%	12%
—is so rude it should be outlawed.	28	45	63
The freedom of atheists to make fun of God and religion:			
—should be legally protected no matter who might be offended.	36	27	15
—should not be allowed in a public place where religious groups gather.	42	48	69
Which of these comes closer to your own view?			
—The government has no right to decide what should or should not be published.	40	28	22
—To protect its moral values, a society sometimes has to forbid certain things from being published.	45	56	64
A group that wants to buy advertising space in a newspaper to advocate war against another country:			
—should have as much right to buy advertising space as a group that favors world peace.	36	26	18
—should be turned down by the newspaper.	44	53	65
A humor magazine which ridicules or makes fun of blacks, women, or other minority groups:			
—should have the same right as any other magazine to print what it wants.	72	57	42
—should lose its mailing privileges.	12	21	36
Protesters who mock the President by wearing death masks at one of his public speeches:			
—should have the right to appear in any kind of costume they want.	50	31	15
—should be removed from the audience by the police.	33	49	72
The "right to remain silent":			
—is needed to protect individuals from the "third degree" and forced confessions.	74	57	44
—has harmed the country by giving criminals too much protection.	13	24	40
If a police officer stops a car for a traffic violation, he should:			
—be limited to dealing with the traffic violation and nothing else.	41	25	24
—be allowed to search the car if he suspects it contains narcotics or stolen goods.	45	63	68

TABLE 8.12 *(continued)*

	Age		
	Under 36	**36–55**	**Over 55**
	(N=652)	**(N=700)**	**(N=637)**
Novels that describe explicit sex acts:			
—should be permitted in the library if they are worthwhile literature.	60%	41%	25%
—have no place in a high school library and should be banned.	30	51	65
The movie industry:			
—should be free to make movies on any subject it chooses.	67	44	26
—should not be permitted to make movies that offend certain minorities or religious groups.	17	25	50
On issues of religion, morals, and politics, high school teachers have the right to express their opinions in class:			
—even if they go against the community's most precious values and beliefs.	37	22	17
—only if those opinions do not offend the community's beliefs.	21	27	44
When inviting guest speakers to a college campus:			
—students should be free to invite anyone they want to hear.	61	37	26
—the speakers should be screened beforehand to be sure they don't advocate dangerous or extreme ideas.	26	45	63
Closing down magazines that print obscene or "dirty" pictures:			
—is a bad idea because it might easily lead to other restrictions on freedom of publication.	52	35	19
—is necessary to protect children from being exposed to unhealthy influences.	26	44	67
If it is discovered that an elementary school teacher is a lesbian:			
—she should be able to go on teaching because sexual preference should not be a ground for dismissal.	64	38	31
—she should not be allowed to continue teaching.	21	37	47
Should demonstrators be allowed to hold a mass protest march for some unpopular cause?			
—Yes, even if most people in the community don't want it.	54	39	30
—No, not if the majority is against it.	22	34	50

NOTE: The items in the table are merely illustrative and do not exhaust the total number of items in the civil liberties scale. Also, we have omitted the Neither and Undecided scores to conserve space.

categories. The differences between the age groups, however, are greater in some issue areas than in others. On the assumption that younger people are less resistant to new or changing norms than older people, we expected to find that the differences between older and younger respondents would be larger on newer, emerging, or unsettled libertarian issues than on more traditional and settled issues. We assumed that the latter would produce smaller differences between older and younger respondents than would issues involving forms of speech, thought, or conduct that were newly emerging, highly controversial, and still unsettled either in the courts or among the informed public.

One difficulty about testing this general hypothesis is that judgments about which issues are settled or unsettled, traditional or emerging, are not always obvious and may largely reflect the subjective opinions of the research investigators. To avoid this, insofar as possible, we decided (somewhat arbitrarily) to consider a liberty settled or established if 60 percent or more of the community leaders took a positive stand on it that was in keeping with the prevailing thrust of judicial decisions. We considered a liberty emerging or unsettled if the courts tended to take a negative or highly equivocal view of it, or if fewer than 60 percent of the community elites support it. Forty-seven items dealing with civil liberties were selected for this analysis and were assigned to either the settled category or the unsettled category.

Using this set of criteria we compared the scores of respondents in the mass public sample of the CLS study who were under 35 years of age with those who were 56 or older. The results, in general, supported our predictions, but not as strongly or uniformly as we had expected. The average difference between the older and younger respondents in their support for the unsettled liberties was 23 percent; whereas the average difference for the settled liberties was 13 percent—an overall difference between the two age groups that was statistically significant and, though not overwhelming, large enough to support the hypothesis. (See figure 8.10.)

When we classified the items into settled and unsettled issues we found that the differences between younger and older age groups were rather striking for some areas, but smaller than expected for others. Among the emerging or unsettled issues, the largest average difference between age groups (35 percent) turned up on items dealing with censorship of obscenity, followed by an average difference of 27 percent for issues involving freedom of lifestyle (for example, homosexuality,

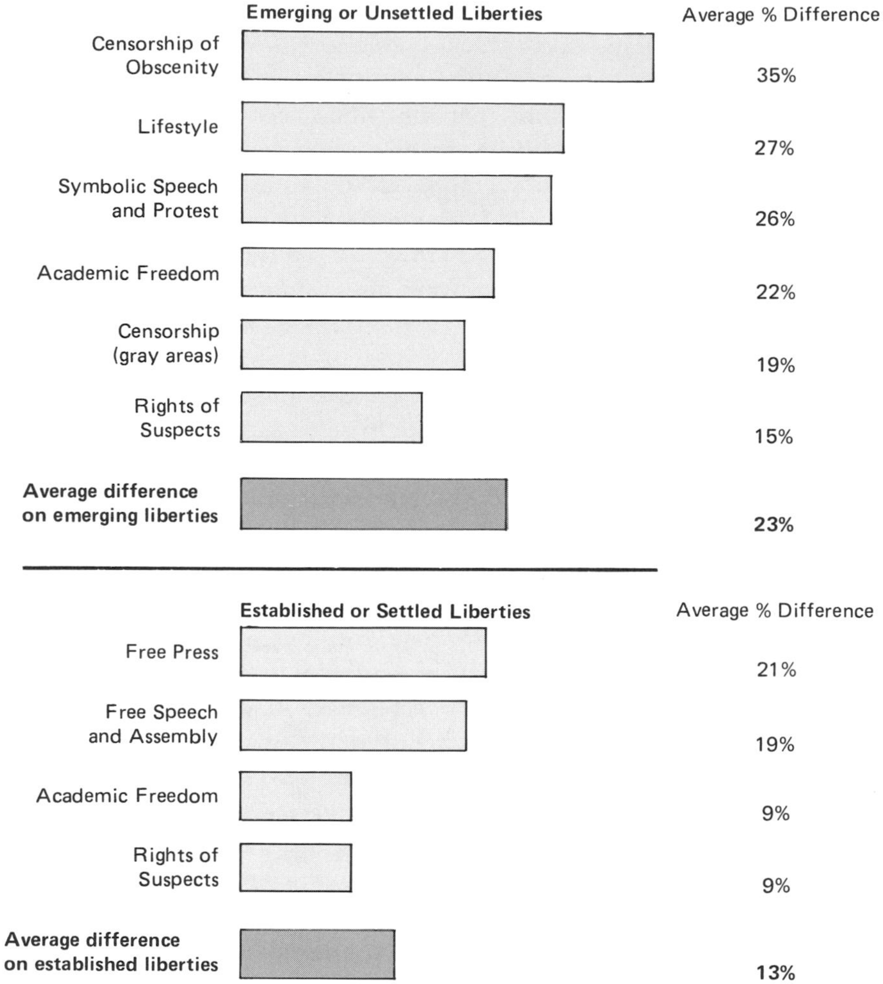

Emerging or Unsettled Liberties   Average % Difference

Censorship of Obscenity — 35%

Lifestyle — 27%

Symbolic Speech and Protest — 26%

Academic Freedom — 22%

Censorship (gray areas) — 19%

Rights of Suspects — 15%

Average difference on emerging liberties — 23%

Established or Settled Liberties   Average % Difference

Free Press — 21%

Free Speech and Assembly — 19%

Academic Freedom — 9%

Rights of Suspects — 9%

Average difference on established liberties — 13%

FIGURE 8.10
Average Differences Between Younger and Older Respondents in Their
Support for Emerging and Settled Civil Liberties
(CLS/Mass Public)

the role of women, abortion) and 26 percent for items involving symbolic speech and protest. On censorship of issues touching on "gray" areas (for example, freedom to publish instructions for building bombs, freedom to run newspaper advertisements advocating war), the average difference between younger and older respondents was 19 percent.

Among the established or settled liberties, the largest average differences between younger and older respondents were 21 percent for issues involving free press and 19 percent for those involving free speech and assembly. These differences, of course, though smaller on the whole than those reported for the emerging liberties in parallel areas, are nevertheless substantial. Significant (though smaller) differences also turn up on emerging versus settled liberties in the area of due process and the rights of suspects.

The findings from our CLS study thus lend at least modest support to the belief that the "rights explosion" of the past two decades—including greater freedom in the more traditional areas of speech, press, and assembly—seems to have struck the younger generations of the society with particular force, though its effects were felt throughout the entire age range. One reason for this, it would seem (others will be discussed later), is that the historical developments that marked the preceding two decades were especially salient to the younger generations: for example, the civil rights movement, resistance to the Vietnam War, student protests in the universities, the "liberation" of women, changing standards about sexual freedom, increases in education, and the striking expansion of the youth cohort itself. While the differences between age groups in their orientation toward civil liberties were most dramatic in the case of the emerging liberties, they also spilled over into the domains of the more traditional liberties, such as free press, speech, and assembly—domains of freedom that were also affected to some extent by the volatile events of the 1960s and 1970s.

It is important to note that the differences between age groups cannot be explained by their differences in education. While the younger age groups are more educated than the older, and education (as we have observed) exerts a powerful influence on one's attitudes toward civil liberties, the differences between generations in their orientation toward freedom and control can only partially be accounted for by the differences in their respective amounts of schooling.

In figure 8.11 we have reported the scores of the several age groups at each of four educational levels, and we have included data from both the CLS and OVS general population samples. While it is

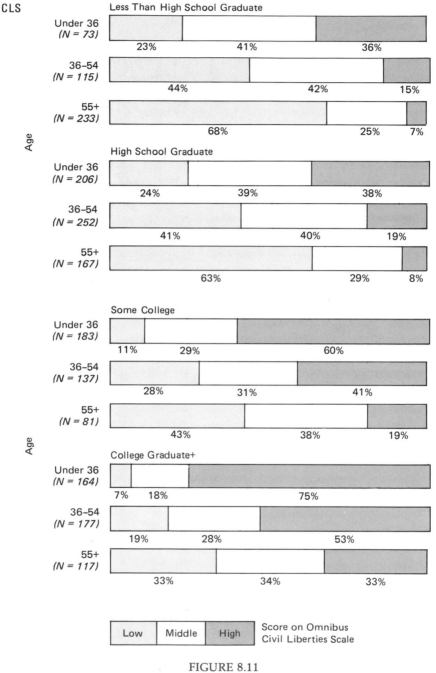

FIGURE 8.11
Age and Support for Civil Liberties, with Education Controlled
(Mass Public)
(CLS/OVS)

OVS

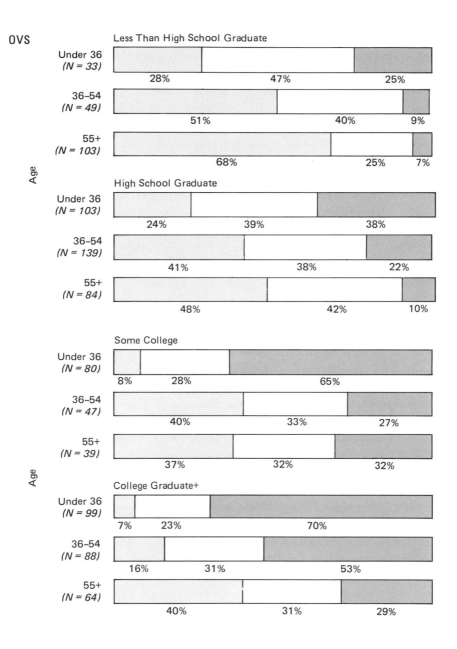

Less Than High School Graduate

Under 36
(N = 33)
28% 47% 25%

36–54
(N = 49)
51% 40% 9%

55+
(N = 103)
68% 25% 7%

High School Graduate

Under 36
(N = 103)
24% 39% 38%

36–54
(N = 139)
41% 38% 22%

55+
(N = 84)
48% 42% 10%

Some College

Under 36
(N = 80)
8% 28% 65%

36–54
(N = 47)
40% 33% 27%

55+
(N = 39)
37% 32% 32%

College Graduate+

Under 36
(N = 99)
7% 23% 70%

36–54
(N = 88)
16% 31% 53%

55+
(N = 64)
40% 31% 29%

Age

Age

obvious from the figure that support for civil liberties increases sharply with each rise in the level of education, it is equally obvious that the differences between younger and older generations remain extremely powerful within each educational group. Among those in the CLS samples who have graduated from college, for example, 75 percent of the younger age group score high on the civil liberties scale, compared with only 33 percent of the older age group. Parallel figures for the respondents who have had "some college" education are 60 percent and 17 percent; for those who have not gone beyond high school the figures are 39 percent and 8 percent. Differences between age groups, with education controlled, are approximately as large for the OVS samples as they are for the mass population samples in the CLS study. Thus, although education exerts a substantial influence on the strength of one's support for civil liberties, age exerts a strong independent influence in its own right.

The relationship between age and support for civil liberties thus appears, from our own data and the research of others (Stouffer 1955; Nunn et al. 1978; Davis 1975; and Jennings and Niemi 1981) to be unmistakable and, in most cases, rather powerful. Far more uncertain, however, is the *meaning* of this relationship. Since we do not have data gathered on the same individuals over an extended period of time, and since we have, in any event, used different scales to measure support for civil liberties in the three studies for which data were shown in figure 8.9, we are unable to demonstrate in a rigorous, scientific way *why* older people express less support for civil liberties than younger people do.

The reasons for this uncertainty have partly to do with the fact that age is not the simple variable it appears to be. Age may be a measure of "lifecycle" or "aging" as such. It may also be a measure of the "generation" in which an individual came to political maturity and acquired his or her political values. (This is sometimes described as referring to the age cohort to which an individual belongs.) Age may also reflect the historical period or *Zeitgeist* through which an individual has lived, the events of which have presumably affected and perhaps significantly altered his or her attitudes toward various social issues, including civil liberties. With cross-section samples surveyed at a single point in time, however, we are unable to disentangle fully the effects of each of these classes of events. (Cf. Palmore 1978.) For example, how can one determine with confidence whether a particular outcome—say, increasing support for civil liberties—is the result of aging or of generational effects?

Despite these vexing considerations, we have reason to believe that all three influences—aging, generational, and *Zeitgeist* effects—are at work and help to account for the variations in attitudes toward civil liberties exhibited by the several age groups in the preceding figures. We rest this judgment, however, largely on intuitive observation and reasoning, as we lack the "panel" or longitudinal data we would need to confirm our assessments empirically.

Take, for example, the influence of aging. While many students of the subject are inclined to discount the view that aging as such affects social attitudes—they tend, for example, to deny that the greater conservatism and intolerance exhibited by older people might result from greater inflexibility—persuasive arguments can be made for believing that aging can (and sometimes does) have an effect on the attitudes people hold about certain public issues. In our view, the explanation for this rests not on the physiological changes that accompany aging, but on the greater inability of older people to relinquish familiar, long-held values and to replace them with new, unfamiliar ones. The norms acquired by individuals over the course of a lifetime tend to resist change and to persist. They do so, in our view, partly because the learning of new norms about a given form of conduct often requires the *unlearning* of old norms. As people grow older, the beliefs that they have acquired at earlier stages of life tend to be reinforced through usage and repeated applications. The old familiar views become habitual, entrenched, and highly serviceable to them. They become important elements in a constellation of beliefs individuals have worked out for themselves in order to function as social beings. These views also serve to connect people with other members of their age cohort who hold similar or related views—the people with whom they most often associate and whose approval they particularly require.

It is obvious, from intuitive observation, that as people grow older they become less willing to experiment and to try out new ideas and lifestyles. They have long become accustomed to seeing and comprehending the world in certain patterns, and they find it extremely difficult to embrace novel standards that depart radically from those with which they are intimately familiar—it is, at any rate, more difficult for them than it is for younger adults, who have had less time or occasion to become habituated to, or dependent upon, firmly settled patterns of thought and behavior. Younger people, moreover, have less to unlearn, fewer incompatible and deeply imprinted standards and values that need to be renounced before newer standards and values can take their place.

Younger people, upon coming of political age, experience fewer conflicts about the newer liberties that have surfaced. Because older people have acquired a more restricted set of standards regarding, for example, such matters as the publication of materials that explicitly describe sexual conduct, many will experience conflict (and repugnance) about the publication of books or magazines that portray such conduct. Younger people, who are more likely to be familiar with such publications as a matter of course, are more likely to take them in stride and to experience less conflict about them. Whereas the older generations may be tempted to suppress films or publications containing such "erotic" materials, the younger generations, having grown up with the newer standards, feel no strain about confronting such materials and see no reason to censor their dissemination. The same principle would hold, of course, for the norms embodied in many of the other civil liberties issues we have been considering.

This does not mean, of course, that the older generations resist change entirely and never learn anything new. As the data from Nunn et al. and Davis bear out, the older generations surveyed in 1972 and 1973 were more libertarian on the same questions than were the older generations surveyed by Stouffer in 1954. Like other age categories in the population, they had grown more tolerant (at least on the Stouffer issues of communism, atheism, and socialism) in the nineteen-year period between the two studies. Older people, in other words, also change their views to some extent as the cultural standards change, but they do not change as much as the younger generations. We are thus led to conclude—from these data and other observations—that while changes in the *Zeitgeist* also affect the attitudes of the older respondents, they ordinarily do not affect them as powerfully as they affect the younger generations, who had fewer (and weaker) conflicts in outlook to overcome and fewer beliefs to unlearn in the first place.

The arguments we have made so far which trace the stronger libertarianism of the younger age groups to their greater ability to learn new norms presuppose that the shifts in the nation's norms have been predominantly in a libertarian direction. While it seems plain enough that this has indeed been the case, we are obliged to point out that if the nation had been drifting in recent decades toward a more repressive set of standards—toward a shrinking rather than an expansion of civil liberties—we might very well have found that the younger age groups would prove no more libertarian (and perhaps even less) than the older age groups. The findings, of course, show the younger age groups to be more libertarian, and both the anecdotal and systematic evidence is strong that the trend of national opinion and practice has been toward an expansion of civil liberties. (For discussion and evidence on this point, see chapter 9.)

While it is obvious from our discussion that what we have called aging is closely intermingled with generational or even *Zeitgeist* effects, we prefer to distinguish the notion of aging from the other terms, since we believe that, despite their interconnections, aging has an independent effect that can be considered separately from generational or *Zeitgeist* explanations.

If aging, or life-cycle, effects refer to the number of years an individual has lived and to the psychological processes by which he or she has become attached to certain values, generational or cohort effects refer to the events, experiences, and beliefs that have presumably fashioned the dominant political and intellectual perspectives of a given generation. The notion of generational effects places primary (though not exclusive) emphasis on the period of political maturation, the formative years during which young adults are most likely to acquire their political and social outlooks and values.

One hears references, for example, to the "New Deal generation," whose members experienced the Great Depression of the 1930s and witnessed first-hand the far-reaching efforts of the Roosevelt administration to alter the character of the society through a program of social legislation. One also encounters references to the "Cold War generation," whose members were politically socialized during the late 1940s and early 1950s, when the United States adopted a posture of "containing" the spread of communism. A more recent example is the "Vietnam generation," men and women who were in their twenties and late teens during the approximately eight-year period in which the United States was engaged in military efforts against the North Vietnamese. Many of the members of this "generation" are alleged to have been embittered, disillusioned, and alienated in their loyalties to the United States by the extraordinary cruelty of the Vietnam War; the enormous human and economic costs it entailed; America's defense, in the name of antitotalitarianism, of a despotic regime; and the eventual defeat and withdrawal of American military forces.

What is implied by the notion of a political generation is not that all of its members come to hold identical views (which, of course, they do not), but that they have been exposed to a more or less common set of experiences which have presumably influenced many or most of them in similar ways. Hence, if they are a generation that was politically socialized during a period in which civil liberties were narrowly conceived and frequently violated without much protest, they will presumably turn out to be less libertarian in their views than succeeding generations who acquired their political norms at a time when civil liberties were more broadly conceived and more actively defended.

Younger generations, as it happens, have also experienced greater education, wider media exposure, a higher level of urbanization and secularization, and other social changes that tend to increase cosmopolitanism and concern for civil liberties.

The generational argument, then, attempts to explain the age differences we have turned up concerning support for civil liberties by claiming, to begin with, that the general trend in the United States during the past half century (if not longer) has been toward the expansion of libertarian rights and rising levels of support for civil liberties, especially by the courts and the nation's opinion leaders, but also among the mass public. As a result, each successive generation over the past decades has acquired, in its formative period, a broader and more tolerant perspective toward rights and liberties than the generations which preceded it.

Although we believe there is merit to the generational interpretation, we have argued that aging and *Zeitgeist* effects also influence civil liberties attitudes.

From our intuitive observation of the rights explosion (see chapter 9) during recent decades and from the available data on the increase in tolerance among all age groups (at least on the Stouffer issues, as reported by NORC and Nunn et al.), it seems fair to say that the events of recent history have markedly altered the *Zeitgeist*. Such developments as the civil rights and women's movements, resistance to the Vietnam War, reaction to the repression and excesses of "McCarthyism," Supreme Court decisions such as *Miranda*, the increasing use of political rallies and mass demonstrations to register political dissent, and the exposure of abuses by the intelligence agencies against individual rights have helped to alter national standards about the scope of civil liberties. While no one can claim to understand fully the reasons for the rights explosion, it is nevertheless clear that its effects have been repeatedly reflected in the national media and felt throughout the population—though principally (we believe) by the younger age groups.

As we have suggested, the changes exhibited by successive generations occur largely because of the impact of exogenous influences, such as those we have cited. If no social changes were to occur in the course of history to alter the *Zeitgeist* and modify society's norms, the several generations would probably remain relatively unchanged in their outlooks and values throughout their respective life cycles. As we have noted, however, sweeping events that affect the enjoyment of libertarian and other rights *have* occurred and have been experienced by people in all age groups. They appear to have made the older generations more responsive to civil liberties, but they have had their greatest impact on younger people.

Findings on Religion and Religiosity

We turn, finally, to one other social influence that appears to affect one's orientation toward civil liberties, namely, religion. Of all the demographic characteristics that influence (or might influence) attitudes toward freedom, religion is among the most controversial. One reason is that religion, more than most other social variables, is defined operationally in different ways by those who have set out to study its influence. Should it refer, for example, to nominal identification or preference, theological content, church attendance, active church affiliation, doctrinal acceptance, strength or intensity of religious conviction, or what? Another reason for controversy is that some religious movements (often those that have suffered persecution) have been in the forefront of the struggle for freedom, while others have led movements for censorship and suppression. Discussions of the influence of religion have also been controversial because of the great sensitivity associated with religious affiliation and belief. Religious differences have, over the centuries, generated some of the fiercest struggles known to the human race. Even today, few issues are so likely to engender rage, conflict, suspicion, defensiveness, and (in some parts of the world) even violence as the issues that surround religious affiliation and conviction.

To what extent does religious identification* as such presently serve as a force to strengthen or weaken respect for civil liberties in the United States? Does it matter for one's attitude toward freedom whether one considers oneself a Catholic, a Jew, a Lutheran, a Baptist, a Methodist, or as having no religious identification at all?

In table 8.13 we present data on those religious denominations on which we were able to collect samples (in a cross-section survey) of sufficient size to permit statistical comparisons to be made. Three groups stand out as scoring higher than average in their support for civil liberties—Jews, Episcopalians, and, most of all, those who claim to have no religious identification at all. Of the denominations listed, Baptists score lowest on the civil liberties scale—a finding that may reflect the high proportion of fundamentalists (and especially southern fundamentalists) among them.

These differences by religious preference also show up clearly among the respondents who have attended college. Among those who have no religious preference, 84 percent have high scores on the civil liberties scale—an extremely large proportion. The percentage scoring high among the Jews who have attended college is 68 percent and among the Episcopalians 61 percent—well above average. By contrast, only 24 percent of the college-educated Baptists express strong support for civil liberties—the lowest score among any of the college-educated groups listed in table 8.13. They are followed by the catch-all category of "Other Protestants," which also contains a higher-than-average proportion of fundamentalists. When all Protestants are combined into a single category and compared with Jews and Catholics, the Jews turn out to be the most libertarian by a significant margin, and Catholics prove on the whole to be more libertarian than Protestants. The Catholic-Protestant differences, however, are not large, and vary, in any event, according to which Protestant denomination is being compared. So far as we can tell from available data on the political attitudes of present-day religious adherents in the United States, the modest differences turned up among them in their orientation toward civil liberties

* As defined by the question: "What is your present religion, if any? Please be specific. For example, are you Catholic, Jewish, Lutheran, Baptist, Mormon, Moslem, or what?"

TABLE 8.13
Religious Preference and Support for Civil Liberties, with Education Controlled (CLS Mass Public)

Score on Omnibus Civil Liberties Scale		No Preference	Jewish	Catholic	Total Protestants	Religious Preference Episcopalian	Lutheran	Methodist	Baptist	Presbyterian	Other Protestant Sects
		(N=261)	(N=44)	(N=488)	(N=1134)	(N=56)	(N=156)	(N=213)	(N=282)	(N=107)	(N=276)
Total Sample	Low	8%	14%	33%	41%	25%	41%	35%	47%	41%	41%
	Middle	23	32	37	34	23	33	38	34	31	37
	High	69	55	30	25	52	26	27	19	28	23
		(N=100)	(N=13)*	(N=280)	(N=645)	(N=15)*	(N=102)	(N=116)	(N=196)	(N=40)	(N=147)
Less than College Educated	Low	.15	—	43	50	—	48	47	49	60	50
	Middle	42	—	40	35	—	38	38	35	25	33
	High	43	—	17	16	—	14	14	16	15	17
		(N=160)	(N=31)	(N=205)	(N=489)	(N=41)	(N=54)	(N=97)	(N=86)	(N=67)	(N=129)
Some College or above	Low	4	7	21	29	12	28	21	44	30	30
	Middle	12	26	32	34	27	24	36	31	34	41
	High	84	68	47	38	61	48	43	24	36	30

*N is too small to calculate percentages for the column.

have less to do with theological doctrine than with their social and political characteristics.

More striking, and certainly more revealing data on the relation between religion and civil liberties are reported in figure 8.12, where we have grouped respondents from the mass public and leader samples in all three studies according to the degree of their "religiosity." The term "religiosity" refers not to religious identity or affiliation, but to the strength of religious conviction—in effect, the degree to which respondents value and rely upon religious beliefs and modes of explanation.

The scales used to assess religiosity vary somewhat in each of the three studies. In the CLS study, we utilized a scale consisting of three questions which asked respondents how religious they considered themselves (deeply, fairly, not very, not at all); whether our best hope for the future rests on "science and human reason" or "faith in God and religion"; and whether religion is "largely old-fashioned and out of date" or "is still useful in answering some of today's problems." In the OVS study, a four-item scale was devised which largely duplicated the items in the CLS study, but also asked whether a person's fate will mostly depend on "mankind's own efforts" or "the will of God." The religiosity measure in the PAB study was a nine-item scale which asked respondents whether they agreed or disagreed with such statements as "I have complete faith in God"; "Everybody needs some strong kind of religion to keep him going"; "I am quite certain the Bible is the word of God"; and "Not until we return to God will we be able to solve our social and political problems." The PAB scale, which also includes an item complaining that "there's so much sin and Godlessness around," contains at least a tinge of fundamentalism in the way several of the items are formulated.

The data in figure 8.12 clearly confirm that as religiosity increases, support for civil liberties declines.* In the CLS study, only 15 percent of the mass public who are deeply religious score high in their support for civil liberties, compared with 55 percent of those who are not reli-

---

* It is essential to keep in mind that the data and inferences considered in this discussion of religion and secularism are meant to apply *only* to the United States and assume a democratic political context. Thus, when we speak of the secular-minded, for example, we are speaking of nonreligious persons who are *democrats*. We are not speaking of religious, secular-minded or nonreligious members of Communist countries, for example, for whom the generalizations presented here would most likely not apply at all. The critics of religion in the USSR might well be among the strongest opponents of civil liberties.

gious. Approximately half of those who are high on religioisity, compared with 20 percent who are low, score at the intolerant, antilibertarian end of the civil liberties scale. The differences between the highly religious and the nonreligious in their support for (or opposition to) civil liberties are at least as large in the OVS and PAB mass public samples. In the OVS study, for example, only 14 percent of the highly religious respondents score high on the civil liberties scale used in that study, while the proportion of nonreligious respondents who are strongly libertarian is 58 percent—a ratio of four to one.

Substantial differences in the same direction also turn up among the elite samples in the three studies—samples whose members share certain key social characteristics, such as a college education. These findings are consistent with those reported in figure 8.13, which show that the differences in support for civil liberties between the highly religious and the nonreligious in the mass public cannot be traced to differences in their education. The two groups differ sharply in their orientation toward civil liberties even when they have similar amounts of schooling.

While the empirical findings on the relation between religiosity and support for civil liberties are clear, the reasons for this relation are more difficult to establish. Several possible explanations, however, can be suggested. One possibility, for example, is that the types of freedom of expression and exchange thought by civil libertarians to be essential to the discovery of truth are less valued by people of strong religious conviction than by the secular-minded. As has often been observed, strong feelings of religiosity go hand in hand with the notion of truth as "received" and "settled," incapable of being resolved by scientific discussion and proof. On the important questions of morals and conduct, the truth is "revealed" to human beings by an Almighty Being who chooses to reveal it and can be neither discovered nor refuted by human debate. Unrestricted freedom of expression is scarcely necessary, therefore, in order for people to learn what is right and wrong.

As the data bear out, many of those with strong religious convictions believe that freedom of expression must not be so broad as to permit individuals to blaspheme the Almighty and undermine moral precepts. Nor can it leave people free to extol sin, to utter obscenities, or to publish pornography. Can God's purposes really be advanced by permitting people to disseminate immoral ideas or to advocate depraved conduct?

Although the devout are not uniformly hostile to civil liberties,

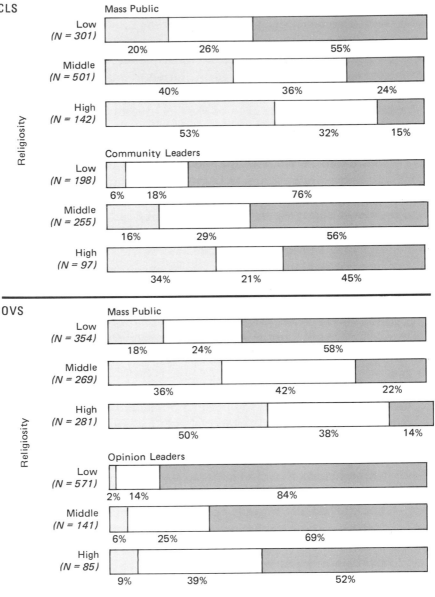

FIGURE 8.12
Religiosity and Support for Civil Liberties
(CLS/OVS/PAB)

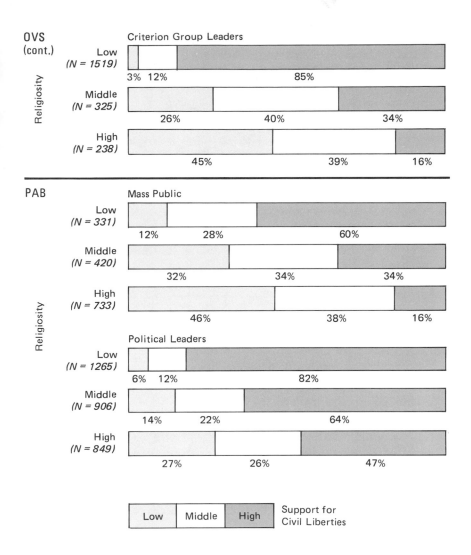

OVS (cont.)

Religiosity

Criterion Group Leaders

Low (N = 1519)
3% 12% 85%

Middle (N = 325)
26% 40% 34%

High (N = 238)
45% 39% 16%

PAB

Religiosity

Mass Public

Low (N = 331)
12% 28% 60%

Middle (N = 420)
32% 34% 34%

High (N = 733)
46% 38% 16%

Political Leaders

Low (N = 1265)
6% 12% 82%

Middle (N = 906)
14% 22% 64%

High (N = 849)
27% 26% 47%

| Low | Middle | High |

Support for
Civil Liberties

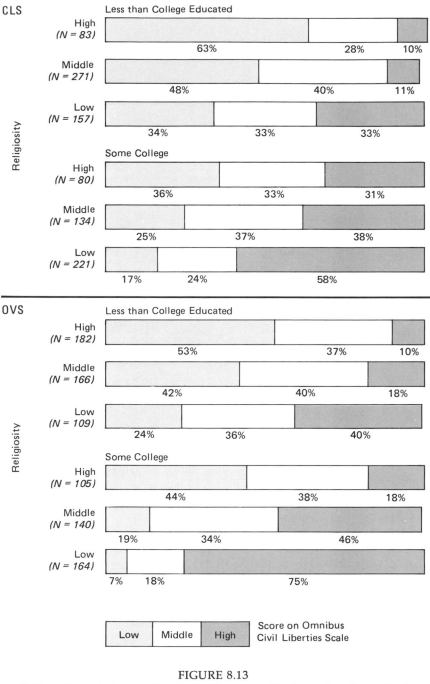

CLS

Religiosity

Less than College Educated

High
(N = 83)
63% 28% 10%

Middle
(N = 271)
48% 40% 11%

Low
(N = 157)
34% 33% 33%

Some College

High
(N = 80)
36% 33% 31%

Middle
(N = 134)
25% 37% 38%

Low
(N = 221)
17% 24% 58%

OVS

Religiosity

Less than College Educated

High
(N = 182)
53% 37% 10%

Middle
(N = 166)
42% 40% 18%

Low
(N = 109)
24% 36% 40%

Some College

High
(N = 105)
44% 38% 18%

Middle
(N = 140)
19% 34% 46%

Low
(N = 164)
7% 18% 75%

| Low | Middle | High |

Score on Omnibus
Civil Liberties Scale

FIGURE 8.13
Religiosity and Support for Civil Liberties, with Education Controlled
(Mass Public)
(CLS)

many of them view certain human frailties and deviations from accepted standards as willful violations of a divinely prescribed moral order that no decent and well-regulated society can (or should) tolerate. The more secular-minded, by contrast, not only regard moral standards as man-made, but consider it inappropriate for the state, as the agent of society, to enforce moral (as distinguished from legal) standards—much less the moral standards of any given religion. The differences between these two perspectives—the highly religious and the secular—produce in practice (as our data confirm) significant differences in the degree to which they are likely to honor many civil liberties.

Because religious "true believers" have embraced a body of received doctrines or dogmas, they have difficulty processing (in Max Weber's phrase) "inconvenient facts." Entertaining facts that do not fit with their theological convictions might shatter their religious belief structure or might require them, at a minimum, to reconcile a number of diverse and incompatible ideas, some of which they could not bear to renounce, even in the face of contradictory evidence. One way to deal with dilemmas of this kind, of course, is to prevent the dissemination of uncongenial facts or ideas, ruling them out as morally unfit and unworthy of consideration by right-minded men and women.

The differences between the devoutly religious and the less religious in their orientation toward civil liberties seem also to reflect to some extent differences in their capacity and opportunity for social learning. Many of the people who remain deeply religious, even though living in a predominantly secular society, are likely to be somewhat circumscribed and parochial in their outlooks, less cosmopolitan and less open to new ideas and experiences. They are likely to be further removed from mainstream opinions than are the more secular-minded, and many will have failed to absorb, as fully as they might, the libertarian norms of the society. Some may be cut off from the dominant values of the political culture by their social circumstances (and especially their memberships in tightly knit religious groups or communities). Others, owing to the intensity and depth of their religious convictions, will have chosen to close themselves off from many of the more temporal sources of opinion. They will have avoided opportunities to encounter the secular, the rational, the scientific, and the naturalistic; and on the occasions when they *have* encountered them, they are likely to have rejected them out of hand as unworthy of serious consideration. The more dogmatic their religious convictions, and the stronger their faith in divine revelation and received truth, the more inclined they will be to avoid learning the arguments that lend credibility to the secular norms. For many of the same reasons, they are less likely to learn that a belief in freedom requires one to tolerate and legally protect an extraordinary variety of opinions, ideas, lifestyles, and practices, even including challenges to religion itself and the preaching of atheism.

Having noted this, we must also observe that the resistance of the devout to certain forms of social learning is not uniform across all civil liberties domains. On some classes of civil liberties they appear to have learned the established norms almost as well as the less-religious. In figure 8.14, where we have rank-ordered the various domains of civil liberties according to the magnitude of the average differences between the devout and the nonreligious, we see that differences in the degree of religiosity have the most striking influence on issues that have to do with personal and sexual morality. On questions relating to sexual freedom, abortion, homosexuality, and the dissemination of "obscene" or "pornographic" materials, the average differences between those who score high and those who score low on religiosity are very large indeed. In every case, the devout take a more antilibertarian stand than the nonreligious.

Differences in the same direction but of slightly smaller magnitude also turn up on questions relating to an increase in freedom for women—reflecting once again the greater traditionalism, conventionality, and emphasis on family values characteristic of the devout. The very religious are also more likely to oppose the withdrawal of life-support measures for prolonging the lives of the terminally ill, and they resist the emerging civil libertarian notion that the hopelessly ill have a right to die if they choose. These attitudes are consistent with a religiously inspired reverence for life, an acceptance of human suffering as unavoidable, and a distrust of human meddling in a realm that is perceived as appropriately God's.

The civil liberties areas that fall toward the middle of the rank order of differences shown in figure 8.14—freedom of speech, press, symbolic speech, assembly, and academic freedom—appear for the most part to be linked to conceptions of the truth. The highly religious, as we have suggested, tend not to believe that knowledge of the truth requires freedom of speech and other forms of free expression. Since in their view the important truths are "received" or "revealed," the unrestricted dissemination of ideas has the potential of leading people away

Civil Liberties Areas

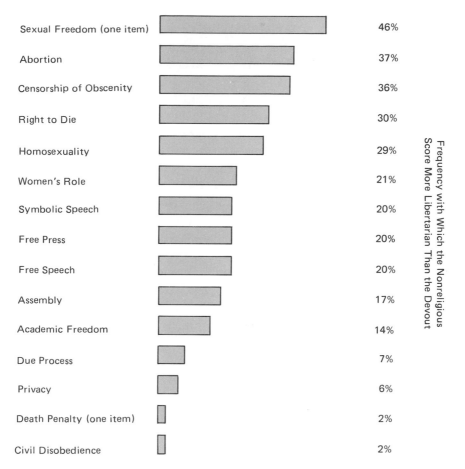

Sexual Freedom (one item)	46%
Abortion	37%
Censorship of Obscenity	36%
Right to Die	30%
Homosexuality	29%
Women's Role	21%
Symbolic Speech	20%
Free Press	20%
Free Speech	20%
Assembly	17%
Academic Freedom	14%
Due Process	7%
Privacy	6%
Death Penalty (one item)	2%
Civil Disobedience	2%

Frequency with Which the Nonreligious
Score More Libertarian Than the Devout

FIGURE 8.14
Civil Liberties Areas: Average Percentage Difference Between the Devout
and the Nonreligious
(CLS Mass Public)

from the truth and toward beliefs that are misleading, perverse, or dangerous.

As for the clusters of civil liberties that fall at the low end of the rank order, and particularly due process and privacy (for example, police surveillance of criminals), the devout appear to be as willing as the nonreligious to leave these matters to the civil authorities. While they are somewhat more restrictive in their attitudes toward these liberties, the average differences are not large. On the issue of the death penalty and the various items on civil disobedience, their scores are no different, on the average, from those of the nonreligious. This finding is surprising, given the assumption that the very religious are, as our data show, somewhat conservative politically, and civil disobedience has mainly been used in the past twenty years to support liberal or radical causes. On the other hand, some (though by no means all) of the very religious place a high value on conscience, higher, perhaps, than they do on legality and conventionality. We suspect that the aggregate scores of the devout on questions of civil disobedience (which match those of the nonreligious) reflect both their concern with traditionalism and order and their reliance on conscience and religiously inspired moral outlooks as the best guides to conduct.

CHAPTER 9

Summary and Conclusions

OUR STUDY of civil liberties and social control has been guided by two related questions: What influences impel some people to honor and protect the liberties of others, even when those liberties are employed for purposes they perceive as hateful? What leads some men and women, even in a democracy, to assail the rights of those with whom they disagree and to honor obedience, orthodoxy, and conformity over freedom?

We began our analysis by observing that the inclination to tolerate beliefs or conduct that one considers offensive or dangerous is not an inborn trait, but is learned behavior. Although one might prefer that it were otherwise, history provides little evidence that men and women are led *by nature* to yearn for freedom, much less to guarantee the liberties of other individuals.

We have further suggested that tolerance may be harder to learn than intolerance. Whereas the impulse to strike down a threatening enemy or an abhorrent idea seems to be a visceral response that depends only minimally on social learning, the willingness to suffer people or ideas that one finds objectionable depends heavily on the learning of appropriate social norms. Individuals can scarcely be expected to protect the rights and liberties of people who disseminate offensive ideas unless they have encountered and absorbed the norms of a libertarian culture (or subculture) which serves as their reference group. Those who become defenders rather than foes of civil liberties need to acquire a greater measure of information and intellectual sophistication about libertarian norms, a sense of relevant principles such as reciprocity, and an ability to understand the rules of the democratic game. Learning the arguments for freedom and tolerance formulated by notables such as Jefferson, Madison, Mill, or the more libertarian justices of the Supreme Court is no simple task. Many of those arguments are subtle, esoteric, and difficult to grasp. Intelligence, awareness, and education are required to appreciate them fully.

Evidence presented throughout this book suggests that social learning is indeed a powerful (perhaps the single most powerful) influence on the adoption of civil libertarian norms. It includes, of course, informal as well as formal education. One learns the norms of tolerance, we believe, much as one learns any other set of norms, and the influences which promote learning are essentially the same: exposure, access, intellectual capacity and comprehension, the removal of social and psychological impediments to effective mental functioning, group pressure and reinforcement, perceived self-interest, and expectations of tangible benefits.

Respect for the freedom of others and for their right to think and act as they choose is also furthered by greater exposure to the media, by residence in a cosmopolitan environment, and by membership in educated and sophisticated subcultures which are among the major repositories and carriers of the ideals of the society. The data suggest that whatever broadens one's perspective tends to generate empathy and promote tolerance by making one aware of the extraordinary variety of standards and forms of social organization under which different people have lived. Narrow social and intellectual perspectives, insularity, distance from the cultural mainstreams, ignorance of the varieties of human experience and subcultures, and an incapacity (whether socially or psychologically induced) to identify with people perceived as "different" tend to beget intolerance. People who cherish the exploration and exchange of ideas, and who are greatly concerned with the pursuit of knowledge, are especially responsive to civil libertarian values. Intellectual life is restless and inquiring; by its very nature, it promotes a readiness to entertain alternative opinions and lifestyles and to recognize the legitimacy of disagreement and dissent.

Why do people who are exposed to civil libertarian norms and who become familiar with them tend to adopt them rather than to reject them? Why doesn't knowledge of the norms lead one to disclaim them? One answer is that in the course of learning the norms one is also likely to learn the reasons behind them and the purposes they serve. As one learns what a given norm provides, one may also encounter the constellation of assumptions, beliefs, supporting arguments, and predicted consequences surrounding the norm. For example, one learns not only that persons accused of crime are entitled to due process, but also that due process is guaranteed by the Constitution and is essential to the safety and fair treatment of anyone who might be charged with having committed a crime. Without due process, an individual might unjustly be deprived of his or her "life, liberty, or property," and would be helpless to prevent or correct the error. To take an example from another civil liberties domain, one who learns that the press ought to be free may also learn that freedom of the press is expressly guaranteed in the Bill of Rights and that without a free press one would be likely to encounter only the views of the people in power. One might also discover that the great leaders in our history—Jefferson, Madison, and Lincoln, among many others—championed freedom of the press and defended it not only as a vital ingredient of the American heritage but as essential both to justice and to other forms of liberty.

Consider also that civil liberties, like other social norms, enjoy a measure of legitimacy and sanction merely because they exist and have received widespread endorsement from the political culture and appropriate subcultures. Social psychological research on the formation and maintenance of norms confirms that groups of people who associate or affiliate with one another tend to develop and reach consensus about common standards. This tendency is related to their effort to achieve common goals (which would be fatally impeded if they did not share many of the same values) and to their need to achieve order out of what would otherwise be social and moral ambiguity. Most individuals exhibit a propensity to respond positively to laws, norms, values, regulations, and any other standards of belief or conduct that are familiar, widely practiced, and, from all appearances, widely approved. By embracing such standards, they are able to avoid uncertainty and chaos and to obtain a degree of order and regularity in their social interactions which is, for most people, reassuring. In the United States, civil liberties norms, once encountered, tend also to be embraced because they bear historical and official warranty. They are precepts in a creed that has repeatedly been endorsed by the most esteemed public figures of the past and present and has been inscribed in official documents and the media.

What is surprising, however, is the frequency with which many Americans, though endorsing civil liberties in the abstract, reject them in their concrete applications. As our data have shown, large groups of American citizens, when offered the opportunity to choose between specific libertarian and antilibertarian responses, often select the latter. Apparently, despite the frequency with which civil libertarian norms are referred to in public discourse, millions of Americans fail to learn them except in their most general form. For reasons we will consider shortly, many people are ill equipped to acquire more than a superficial familiarity with the most general statements about freedom. As we shall see, this outcome results partly from their insufficient motivation or capacity for probing beneath the surface of generalities to the hard core of libertarian values as they are applied in practice, and partly from the difficulties and complexities inherent in the rights themselves.

As we have suggested, a crucial factor affecting the ability to learn society's norms—and hence the inclination to support tolerance and civil liberties—is an individual's location and role in the social structure, and especially his distance from the cultural and opinion mainstreams. The degree of access to the decision points of the society that an individual has and his exposure to its "approved" values and doctrines are obviously affected by education, economic and social status, membership in voluntary organizations (especially organizations concerned with public affairs), and degree of participation in civic and political life. They are also affected by place of residence (urban or rural), type of vocation, age group or generation, and various other influences promoting cosmopolitan or parochial outlooks.

The low level of political interest displayed by vast numbers of the American people—a level of apathy that is strikingly revealed in their low turnout even for presidential elections—also manifests itself in the low level of awareness and sophistication exhibited by the members of the general public when they confront the many vexing issues associated with the enforcement of civil liberties.

Individuals who, through any channel, have greater access to the articulate culture, or who enjoy opportunities to interact with informed, well-educated, and more "worldly" people, are more likely to comprehend the case for tolerance and the arguments against intolerance. They tend to achieve a finer, more discriminating awareness of the costs and benefits associated with the honoring or withholding of civil liberties. Certain vocations—education, the law, journalism, politics—are by their nature more likely than others to encourage tolerance, not only because their members are well educated and more familiar than other groups with the arguments in favor of civil liberties, but because they are compelled to adjust to certain styles of interaction and accommodation that involve a fair amount of give-and-take and the continual assessment of contingencies.

The influence of these and other factors that strongly affect the learning of civil liberties can be discerned throughout our data in the comparisons between the mass public and the opinion leaders, who are better able to learn and incorporate the libertarian norms of the society. On issue after issue, in domain after domain, the leaders appear to have absorbed more thoroughly the specific as well as the general norms of tolerance and civil liberties.

Because they have assumed more active and far-reaching roles, the opinion leaders are likely to exhibit greater sensitivity to public life and the values that govern it. They are more educated, more worldly, better read, and more experienced and informed than the general public. They have greater familiarity than the average citizen with the world's variety of human standards and lifestyles. Their awareness of diversity is reinforced by their greater ability to move about socially, intellectually, and even physically. They are likely to observe the society from a broader perspective, to discern patterns of social organization and conduct, and to evaluate events in a more informed and perceptive fashion. They are also more inclined to embrace coherent belief systems and ideologies and to draw from these beliefs and attitudes appropriate inferences for public policy and civil liberties. Questions of freedom and control, like most other public questions, are generally more salient to them.

The opinion leaders and other influentials in a democratic society are more likely than the average citizen to read about and become aware of the arguments for freedom and tolerance, as well as their limits. If they have not read John Stuart Mill's essay *On Liberty* (or other such documents), they are nevertheless likely to have encountered the case it advances for the defense of freedom. By training and vocational leanings, lawyers are more disposed than any other segment of the population to adjust their beliefs to the rulings of the higher courts. A lawyer's primary orientation, after all, is toward the law, and so long as the law, as interpreted by the courts, is predominantly libertarian, the members of the bar will be strongly motivated to exhibit libertarian preferences as well. However, one must at least consider the possibility that if the courts were to become less libertarian, many lawyers would also move in that direction.

Within the general population, the educated sector most resembles the opinion leaders in ability and opportunity to know and absorb civil libertarian norms. Although the differences in our data between the highly educated and the relatively uneducated are not uniform across all items, they are, on the average, fairly substantial.

We have noted some of the reasons for these differences. Education, though usually treated as a single, unidimensional variable, is in reality an indicator of a complex of variables that includes not only schooling but the nature and style of life. Those who have graduated from college are likely to take a greater interest in political matters than people who have had only a grade school or high school education. At work and in their personal lives, they are more likely to associate with other educated people who are also interested in public questions, who discuss them frequently and may even act on them. Similarly, people who have had the benefit of higher education are more likely than the less educated to read materials, listen to broadcasts, and watch television programs about public affairs. They are more likely to join and participate in voluntary organizations that devote attention to community and national questions. For these and related reasons, they are more exposed to the dominant libertarian norms of the culture and they acquire more cosmopolitan perspectives.

One should not, however, discount the influence of schooling itself on the response to libertarian values. The college educated, compared with the less educated, have had greater exposure in school to the facts and arguments concerning civil liberties. They are more likely to have read the writings of statesmen, judges, commentators, and social philosophers who have made the case for tolerance and human freedom. Through course work, reading, and travel, they will have been in touch with a range of ideas and a diversity of cultures. The general effect of these experiences is to instill a willingness to entertain a variety of opinions and to look with greater tolerance on patterns of thought and conduct that differ from one's own. This does not mean, of course, that every educated person is warmly disposed toward civil liberties, but the data from all three of our studies clearly confirm that support for civil liberties increases markedly as education rises.

The differences between the highly educated and the less educated, however, are not uniform across all civil liberties items. On some items the differences are significant, but on others they are relatively small— or even reversed, as indicated below:

Civil liberties issues that have been:	Average Percentage Difference Between the Highly Educated and the Less Educated
—decided in a libertarian direction by the courts and receive over 60 percent support from the community elites (27 items)	24%
—decided in a libertarian direction by the courts and receive between 50 and 60 percent support from the community elites (21 items)	22
—still somewhat undecided by the courts but a plurality of the community elites support the libertarian position (5 items)	20
—decided in a nonlibertarian direction by the courts, but a plurality of the community elites favor a libertarian stance (3 items)	16
—decided in a nonlibertarian direction by the courts, and a plurality of elite opinion is nonlibertarian (5 items)	8
—decided by the courts in a libertarian direction but opposed by a plurality of the community elites (11 items)	8
—decided by the courts in a nonlibertarian direction, and over 60 percent of elite opinion is also nonlibertarian (14 items)	−6

These figures strongly suggest that the attitudes of the educated toward civil libertarian norms are significantly affected by or at least markedly correlated with, the stands exhibited toward these norms by the opinion elites. When the community leaders are fairly united in their support for a court-approved group of civil liberties, the better-educated members of the mass public follow the elites, and it is here they differ most sharply from the less educated (24 percent). When a plurality of the community elites oppose a *court-approved* set of civil liberties, the average difference between the most and least educated is only 8 percent. On issues that the courts have decided in a nonlibertarian direction, but that nevertheless receive libertarian support from at least a majority of the opinion leaders, the differences between the most educated and least educated members of the mass public are still fairly large (averaging 16 percent). But on those issues on which both the opinion elites and courts take a nonlibertarian stand, the tendency for the educated to score more libertarian than the uneducated is actually reversed (−6 percent on the average).

421

It appears from these findings that the views of the opinion elites have an independent effect on mass opinion, but that the effect varies with education. The better educated take their cues not only from what might be regarded as the "official" (that is, the courts') opinion, but, to an even greater extent, from the views held by opinion leaders. Furthermore, the more united the views of the opinion leaders, the stonger is their influence on the educated public. In addition, elite opinions that correspond with the settled views of the courts have a still greater impact on the beliefs of educated citizens. By contrast, the uneducated public appears to be much less influenced by opinion leaders in its attitudes toward civil liberties than are the members of the educated public; the latter, of course, are closer to the elites not only in schooling, but in their vocations, lifestyles, and greater proximity to the values of the political culture. They are, therefore, particularly susceptible to the attitudes held by the opinion leaders.

One major exception to the greater libertarianism of opinion leaders in America involves certain ideological groups (for example, educated followers of the far right and "hard-core" conservatives).* These groups have been exposed to many of the same processes of social learning as other elite groups, but they differ from the others in that they have also absorbed an alternative set of values which are not always hospitable to civil liberties. The conservatives and the far right, for example, often appear to exhibit less concern for specific civil liberties than for the values and institutions associated with law and order, tradition, social stability, national security, and conventionality. As our data show, solicitude for the latter tends to overpower the sympathy conservatives might feel for the former.

Indeed, many conservatives appear to view civil liberties, especially when pressed to the margin, as conflicting with the values they esteem most. The concern for public safety, for example, is thought by them to be jeopardized by too generous an interpretation of the rights of due process. Social stability, the family, and conventional lifestyles are thought to be endangered by too permissive an attitude toward homosexuality and abortion. Patriotism and national security are thought to be imperiled by permitting radicals to hold demonstrations and advocate revolution. Religion and faith in God are thought to be

---

* From intuitive observation, we have reason to assume that the educated followers of the far left would also score lower on libertarianism than do other educated or elite groups. We were unable, however, to collect an adequate sample of far left supporters and hence do not include them in this analysis.

undermined by the preachings of atheists and by the ban on school prayers. While it would be incorrect to say that conservatives are essentially hostile to civil liberties, the evidence indicates that their support for specific civil liberties (though not for freedom in the abstract) is contingent upon the impact they feel those liberties will have on other values they hold dear. When conflicts arise between civil liberties on the one side and the key values of conservatism on the other, the former often give way.

So far we have dealt with the distinctions between those who have internalized libertarian norms and those who have not. What, however, of those who embrace libertarian values that go beyond current norms, that is, those who support libertarian values that have not been endorsed by the courts or, for that matter, by most of the opinion leaders? What can be said of these individuals who might be described (for want of a better word) as "superlibertarians"?

In the CLS survey we were able to identify twenty-four items that offered respondents a choice between a response implicitly or explicitly sanctioned by the courts and one that is more libertarian than the courts have usually been willing to endorse. These items, which we have combined into a "superlibertarian" scale, vary in content. They refer, for example, to such matters as maintaining the confidentiality of a journalist's sources, the "right" of a radio or TV station to speak one-sidedly for any group it chooses, the authority of undercover police to infiltrate and spy on extreme political groups, government authority to wiretap even with a warrant, the "right" of the members of organized crime to hold a private meeting safe from surveillance, the availability of an individual's prison record and credit rating, federal control of government funded research, the conscientious refusal to obey "unjust" laws, the morality of the death penalty, censorship of television programs "that show people actually making love," the use of dogs at airports to locate narcotics in suitcases or lockers, the "right" to withhold taxes in protest against "the use of tax money to pay for abortions," and an invalid's "right" to choose death in preference to continued medical treatment.

On these and other items in the scale, the courts have tended not to take a libertarian stand; that is, they have emphasized control more than freedom, narrowing rather than enlarging the liberties of the individuals and groups in question. By contrast, superlibertarians have, in most instances, taken the view that emphasizes greater freedom and less control.

423

One question that especially interested us was whether the response of our several samples to superlibertarian values was essentially similar to, or different from, their response to libertarian *norms* (as measured by the omnibus civil liberties scale). Since we have argued throughout this book that social learning usually leads to the internalizaton of libertarian *norms,* the question arises whether it also leads to the internalization of libertarian *values* that have, implicitly or explicitly, been rejected by the courts.

A comparison of those scoring high on libertarianism with those scoring high on our twenty-four item measure of superlibertarianism yields some interesting differences. As can be seen in figure 9.1, whereas the community leaders score substantially higher than the mass public in their response to established libertarian norms (61 percent versus 32 percent), and the legal elite score highest of all (86 percent), neither the community leaders nor the legal elite score very much higher than the mass public on the superlibertarianism scale. In other words, when libertarian values have not been incorporated into the body of institutionalized libertarian norms, even the most informed and sophisticated members of the community, including lawyers and judges, are not inclined to favor them.

It should also be noted in figure 9.1 that while support for libertarian norms among police officials is somewhat higher than that of the mass public, their scores on the scale of superlibertarian values is the lowest of all groups. Only 4 percent of the police score high on this measure, compared with 27 percent of the mass public. The police, who (as we saw in earlier chapters) tend not to be strongly sympathetic to most civil liberties, are even more reluctant to approve any of the forms of freedom that have not received the official blessing of the courts.

Figure 9.2 provides further insight into the differences between the high scorers on libertarianism and the high scorers on superlibertarianism. In this figure we present data on the degree to which education, age, ideology, and political knowledge affect the scores of the different samples on the two scales. Perhaps the most interesting finding in figure 9.2 is that education and political knowledge, which have such a powerful effect on the learning of libertarian norms, function to discourage people from embracing the values which have not received authoritative endorsement. The educated and politically cognizant, in other words, have apparently learned that the values contained in the

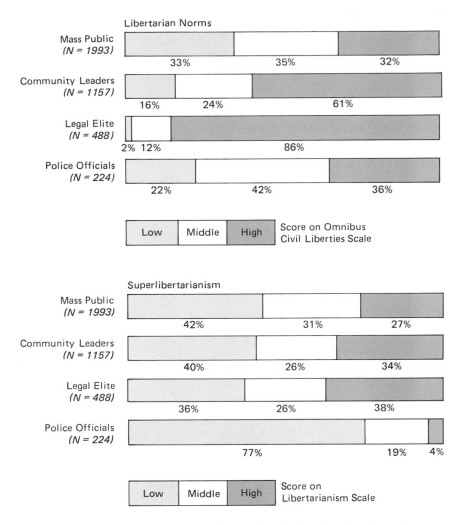

Note: "Libertarian norms" is measured by the omnibus civil liberties scale. The cutting points designating high, middle, and low for this scale and the libertarianism scale have in each case been determined by breaking the distributions for the mass public sample roughly into thirds.

FIGURE 9.1

Distribution on Civil Libertarian Norms and Superlibertarianism
(CLS)

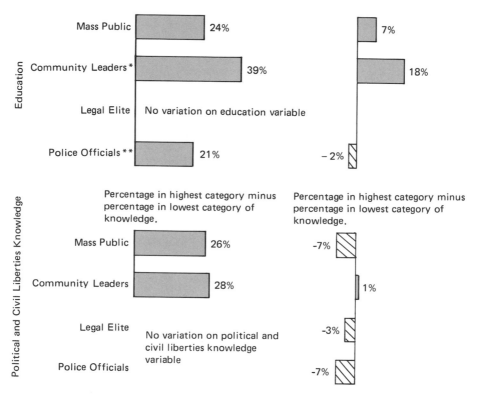

Libertarian Norms

Difference between the percentage of those with 16 or more years of education who score high on libertarian norms and those with 12 or fewer.

Superlibertarianism

Difference between percentage of those with more than 16 years of education who score high on super-libertarianism and those with 12 or fewer.

Education

Mass Public — 24%

Community Leaders* — 39%

Legal Elite | No variation on education variable

Police Officials** — 21%

Mass Public — 7%

Community Leaders* — 18%

Police Officials** — − 2%

Political and Civil Liberties Knowledge

Percentage in highest category minus percentage in lowest category of knowledge.

Percentage in highest category minus percentage in lowest category of knowledge.

Mass Public — 26%

Community Leaders — 28%

Legal Elite | No variation on political and civil liberties knowledge variable

Police Officials

Mass Public — -7%

Community Leaders — 1%

Legal Elite — -3%

Police Officials — -7%

NOTES: The distribution on each scale was broken roughly into thirds so that those who scored relatively high in each category could be compared with those who scored relatively low. It should be noted that meaningful comparisons can be made only between the samples in each scale and not between the scores in the two scales.

*This figure is inflated because almost all of the few members of the community elite in the lower education category are also older.

**We have reported the differences in police scores here in order to be consistent. So few police officials, however, score high on superlibertarianism that the differences reported cannot be considered reliable. In effect, most police officers score low on superlibertarianism regardless of age, education, knowledge, or ideology.

FIGURE 9.2

Comparison of Those Who Score High on Superlibertarianism with Those Who Score High on Libertarian Norms

Libertarian Norms

Superlibertarianism

Difference between percentage of those under 36 years of age who score high on libertarian norms and those over 55.

Difference between percentage of those under 36 years of age who score high on superlibertarianism and those over 55.

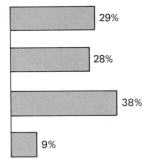

Age

Mass Public — 39%

Community Leaders — 27%

Legal Elite — No variation on age variable

Police Officials

Mass Public — 29%

Community Leaders — 28%

Legal Elite — 38%

Police Officials — 9%

Difference between the percentage of liberals who score high on libertarian norms and the percentage of conservatives who score high.

Difference between the percentage of liberals who score high on superlibertarian norms and the percentage of conservatives who score high.

Nonlibertarian Ideolgy

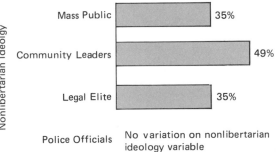

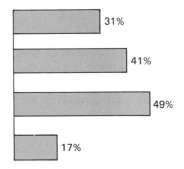

Mass Public — 35%

Community Leaders — 49%

Legal Elite — 35%

Police Officials — No variation on nonlibertarian ideology variable

Mass Public — 31%

Community Leaders — 41%

Legal Elite — 49%

Police Officials — 17%

superlibertarian scale have not been incorporated into the body of accepted norms, and they are inclined, therefore, to reject them.

Also interesting is the finding that both age and ideology, unlike education and political sophistication, correlate strongly with support for superlibertarian values. The marked tendency of younger people and of those who are ideologically liberal to embrace civil libertarian norms carries over, with considerable force, to the approval of superlibertarian values. Both the young and the ideologically liberal seem to be responding to libertarian views as such, and the strength of their motivation in this respect apparently blurs the distinction between institutionalized libertarian *norms* and libertarian *values* that go beyond the current norms. At the same time, the conservatives and the elderly, who tend to score low on the established libertarian norms, are likely, as one might predict, to score toward the lower end of the superlibertarian measure as well. Since they do not warmly embrace the approved norms, one can scarcely expect them to internalize libertarian values that have not been authoritatively sanctioned.

Thus, we see that in approaching questions involving support for civil liberties, one should take into account the status of those liberties in the political culture. The ease with which one learns libertarian values depends not only on the characteristics of the believers and the status of the norms, but on the kinds of civil liberties that are at issue. It is not surprising that one adopts such values more easily if they are clear, familiar, settled, and well established than if they are emerging, still being debated, and not yet cloaked in legitimacy. Moreover, many civil liberties issues are complex and recondite and are not likely to be understood, much less embraced, by people who lack a sophisticated awareness of the principles involved. Our data suggest that large numbers of people find it extremely difficult to understand why, for example, freedom of the press protects a newspaper against prior censorship; or why public libraries should not be able to exclude books that contain sexually explicit materials; or why the state should provide police protection for a Communist or Klan rally; or why radicals should be allowed to desecrate the flag; or why a community should not be able to deny the use of its civic auditorium for meetings of unpopular groups that preach hateful ideas. The exercise of these and various other liberties, in addition, involves conduct that many citizens regard as highly repugnant, threatening, or dangerous. The research findings suggest that the norms which embody such liberties are harder to understand and embrace than the norms which are perceived as less threatening. They are psychologically and socially more costly, and many individuals exhibit an understandable tendency to resist them.

One should keep in mind, too, that freedom, however warmly applauded, is not the only value that people hold dear. Many citizens embrace values that in specific contexts are incompatible with certain civil liberties. Some care more for order and stability than for freedom. Others feel that religion or patriotism should take precedence over civil liberties. Some cannot bear the "excesses" of human conduct which, in their eyes, characterize societies that are too free.

We have also had occasion to remark that while civil liberties are frequently defended as embodying the principles of fairness, not everyone views them in this light. On the contrary, they perceive the exercise of civil liberties in some contexts as distinctly "unfair." The rights of due process, for example, were presumably designed to ensure fair treatment to persons suspected of wrongdoing. Yet to many members of the mass public, and even to some of their opinion leaders, it seems unfair to let guilty persons go free to commit more crimes because of technical errors in the trial procedure or in the way evidence was gathered to convict them. They cannot see why we are obliged to be *fair* to muggers, rapists, kidnappers, or terrorists by letting them out on bail, a practice they view as manifestly *unfair* to their victims or to other innocent members of society who may become their victims.

Questions about fairness can be raised in connection with almost every type of civil liberty. How fair is it to the President of the United States to allow demonstrators to appear in the audience wearing death masks while he is speaking? Is it fair to protect people who use their First Amendment rights to insult minorities while failing to protect the victims against such abuse? Our data suggest that arguments like these are not without force, and many people are persuaded by them. They are likely to be resisted mainly by people who have acquired sufficient knowledge and sophistication to understand that freedom has costs. It is an inescapable feature of a civil libertarian right that not everyone will benefit equally from its exercise in a particular context. Civil liberties are also subject to misuse, as in the case of newspapers that print lies. The sophisticated, however, will understand that the alternative to a free press that sometimes distorts the facts is a controlled press, which would not only have a discouraging effect on the gathering and publication of news, but would report only the official government line.

To the devout it may appear unfair to prohibit prayers in the public schools, but to the more secular-minded who are cognizant of the history of persecution of minority religions by the more powerful and privileged churches, the banning of school prayers seems only a reasonable precaution against the establishment of a state-supported religion. To the opponents of school prayer, fairness lies in treating all religions alike, even if it means excluding them from an official role in the affairs of the state.

One should not assume that all efforts to deny civil liberties are motivated by hostile or malevolent intentions. While our data suggest that personality predispositions influence the hostile stands some people take toward the exercise of freedom by others, many who criticize or object to certain libertarian practices do so out of a conviction that the liberties themselves are being used in ways that are unfair or harmful.

Nor does the denial of civil liberties always signify a failure of social learning. To be sure, many of the individuals who turn out to be intolerant have in fact failed to learn the prevailing norms. Others, however, have learned the norms but reject them in certain instances on grounds that they are too costly, too easily misused, or too often extended beyond the point of what is safe or sensible. Still others, as we have seen, are aware of civil libertarian values and know what society expects them to believe, but they prize other values more highly.

Even people who know and strongly favor the norms of tolerance and freedom are sometimes confronted by occasions so fraught with conflicting values that they eventually choose to deny civil liberties rather than to honor them. A striking example, cited earlier, is offered by the members of the American Civil Liberties Union who resigned because it defended the right of the American Nazi party to assemble and march in Skokie, a community that housed many Jews and victims of the Holocaust. To the ACLU defectors, most of them strong civil libertarians, the right of assembly could not justifiably be extended to include acts of deliberate harassment and provocation against people (many of them elderly and frail) who had suffered the horrors of the Nazi concentration camps. Although claiming a strong belief in civil liberties, many who left the ACLU were unwilling to accept the argument that the rights listed in the First Amendment were meant to be available to everyone, even to the most outrageous and hateful groups among us.

These and other examples bear witness that, in practice, the question of granting or withholding civil liberties rarely confronts us as a simple, isolated issue. Often the question we must face is not whether to grant or to deny freedom, but whether to honor it in a context in which conflicting values and goals are also present. Even strong civil libertarians, for example, might choose to limit or prohibit the right of free speech if its exercise threatened to lead to a confrontation that might become violent.

As we have suggested, one reason civil liberties are difficult to learn is that they are contingent rather than unequivocal or absolute. Although we frequently speak of freedom and control as though they were polarities, it is obvious that freedom cannot be effectively realized in the absence of controls. This need to set limits on liberties while simultaneously protecting them makes for obvious difficulties in settling upon a fixed interpretation of their scope and meaning. As standards shift and social sensitivities are awakened among different segments of the population, conflicts arise which, if or when resolved, move the boundary between what should be permitted and what should be proscribed in one direction or the other.

We have observed that controversies over the balance between freedom and control are bound to erupt in every society in which freedom is recognized and that the problem is made more vexing by the fact that efforts to extend the civil liberties of one group may actually reduce the amount of freedom available to other groups or to the population as a whole. We cited, as an example, the circumstance in which relaxing the laws against loitering might increase the number of "muggers" and criminal marauders, thus inhibiting ordinary people from moving about the community freely. In the area of civil rights, school busing and affirmative action, which aim to rectify imbalances by expanding life chances for certain disadvantaged groups, sometimes increase social tension by angering other groups who feel that their own rights are being diminished. Thus, groups seeking to exercise equally "legitimate" claims confront one another in ways that exacerbate conflict, as one group attempts to enlarge its liberties and opportunities at the expense of the others or as one group tries to limit the exercise by others of claims it considers illegitimate or harmful. The balance shifts as civil liberties, or the rights of the groups that claim them, are narrowed or expanded in practice. Specific civil liberties are subject to the continual play of competing forces which press on the one side to enlarge them and on the other to diminish them. The balance resulting from this ever-present conflict is bound to be a precarious one, as circumstances change and as one or the other of the competing parties gains the advantage.

Many members of the mass public, and some opinion leaders as well, lack the knowledge and sophistication to make fine discriminations about the optimal balance between freedom and control. As we have intimated in our discussion of fairness, it is not always *intuitively* obvious where justice lies in these matters, nor whether the exercise of freedom in a particular context should or should not be tolerated. The problem of learning the "correct" standards is further exacerbated by the shifts that occur in the interpretations of various liberties and the fluctuations in their boundaries as the courts wrestle with cases that continually present new and different situations.

As one might infer from these observations, it is one thing to endorse a given civil liberty in the abstract and quite another to approve it in its specific applications. Abstract ideals involve little cost and are easy to endorse; but the assertion of support for them cannot be taken as a sign that the principles they embody have been adequately learned. While the abstract norm can often be stated and approved in a single, uncomplicated sentence (for example, "I believe in free speech for all, no matter what their views may be") the translation of the norm into its concrete manifestations may assume dozens of complex forms, many of them costly.

The question inevitably arises in practice of how far one is willing to go in translating the abstract rights of free speech and press into support for concrete policies. The application of an abstract right to a concrete situation may so alter its meaning for some individuals that they do not perceive the right and its application as belonging to the same universe. They do not necessarily see that a commitment to free speech grants bigots a right to advocate the deportation of blacks or permits radicals to call for the extermination of the propertied classes. Nor do they believe that the right of due process was ever meant to permit known, dangerous felons to be freed on bail before trial or to refuse to testify when charged with a criminal act.

Many members of the public lack the skill or awareness to perceive that the particular forms of tolerance they oppose are linked to the general rights they claim to favor. Their social learning has, to this extent, been incomplete, so that their judgment about the legitimacy of an applied civil liberty is more influenced by its desirability as a form of social conduct than by its relation to some universal principle of right.

The problem of absorbing the norms of tolerance and other civil liberties is made even more difficult by the fact that the people whose rights most often require protection tend to be among the least acceptable members of the society. As organizations such as the ACLU continually rediscover, the people whose freedom they are called upon to defend are often regarded by their fellow citizens as outcasts, deficient in morals, character, and judgment. Many of the most important civil liberties cases that come before the courts involve the rights of criminals, Klansmen, terrorists, bigots, rioters, cultists, and fanatics. Even if one has learned that, under the rules of the democratic game, everyone is entitled to the same rights, one may be tempted to deny that this principle holds for people whose beliefs or conduct have placed them outside the boundaries of decent society and beyond its protection.

Among citizens who posses only a modest understanding of civil libertarian norms, arguments like these are often appealing. They are not likely to be much impressed by the claim that by protecting the rights of outcasts, they are, in the long run, protecting their own rights. They do not see why one must permit extremists to spew their venom in order to protect the liberties of right-minded citizens whose opinions and conduct are law-abiding and sensitive to the safety and rights of others. To them, the exercise of free speech by, for example, Nazis or revolutionaries is not simply an application at the margin of a constitutional right, but is a cynical abuse of that right by people who have only contempt for it and would deny it to others if they could. Whereas the defenders of civil liberties tend to place more emphasis on the protection of the libertarian right itself than on the nature of the person who claims the right, the opponents of civil liberties reverse the emphasis, focusing less on the rights as such than on the character and personal history of the claimant.

Many members of the public, and especially those who lack a sophisticated awareness of the complexities that attend the distribution and status of rights, apparently find these arguments cogent. For reasons already indicated, they have failed to learn that, under the American Constitution, individuals do not forego their claim to such rights as due process or freedom of speech because they have committed heinous crimes or violated the standards of the culture. This principle of democratic procedure—that rights are in a sense "inalienable"—may be grasped by the more sophisticated defenders of civil liberties, but is by no means obvious.

The findings reported in the early chapters of this book suggest that the impediments to the learning of political norms prevent large numbers of Americans from taking libertarian stands on civil liberties issues. Among the members of the mass public in the CLS, a majority chose the libertarian response only one quarter of the time. On about half the issues, the percentage scoring libertarian ranged from 4 percent to 35 percent. For the entire list of civil liberties items, the average level of support among the mass public was 38 percent. The community leaders, of course, chose libertarian responses more frequently. Within this group, the majority scored libertarian on about half the issues, and the average level of support for the entire set of civil liberties items was over 50 percent. As one can easily infer from the data reported, the broadest support for civil liberties was found among the legal elite sample, a majority of whom embraced the libertarian response on some two thirds of the issues.

While the level of mass public support for civil liberties may be disappointing to many civil libertarians, they may take comfort from the fact, as Stouffer did, that the community leaders, who are more tolerant than the general public, are likely to exercise a disproportionate influence on public policy. Since they occupy positions of prestige and status in society, their role in fashioning decisions that affect civil liberties will be substantially greater than one would expect from their numbers alone. This tendency toward disproportionate influence will be even more pronounced in the case of the legal elite, whose members are engaged in the formulation, interpretation, and enactment of policies which affect civil liberties directly. Effective support for civil liberties, then, is likely to be greater than one might assume from examining data on the mass public alone.

Stouffer also took solace from the age trends found in his data, trends confirmed in our studies as well as in others, which show that the younger generations are significantly more tolerant than the older generations even after accounting for differences in their education. These generational differences reflect a variety of social trends that increase libertarianism and foreshadow future trends. Apart from reflecting differences in education, the stronger libertarianism of the younger generations is a sign of greater freedom in the home and in the schools, greater geographic and social mobility, growing urbanization, a rise in secularism, and increasing social exchange and communication. The higher levels of tolerance exhibited by the incoming generations, in turn, provide reason to believe that, as each new generation matures into adulthood, the general level of freedom and tolerance in the society as a whole rises.

There are other reasons, both empirical and intuitive, to believe that support for civil liberties has been on the rise in recent decades and that the drift of opinion since Stouffer did his research in the early 1950s has been toward greater acceptance of diversity, nonconformity, and dissent. Studies undertaken in 1973 by Nunn et al. (1978) and Davis (1975), essentially replicating the Stouffer survey, confirm that tolerance has increased markedly for all age groups at all education levels on every question employed by Stouffer. Since Stouffer's inquiry was confined almost entirely to questions about tolerance toward Communists, suspected Communists, atheists, and Socialists (that is, people who favor government ownership of railroads and big industries), however, one cannot be certain of the degree to which these findings, striking as they are, can be generalized to other areas of civil liberties.[*] Nevertheless, there is a large body of intuitive and anecdotal evidence which strongly suggests that the rise in tolerance reported by Nunn et al. and Davis with respect to communism, atheism, and socialism has in fact been paralleled by dramatic expansions in other domains of civil liberties as well.

---

[*] The claim that the drift of opinion has been toward greater tolerance since Stouffer's research was conducted has been challenged by Sullivan and his associates (Sullivan et al., 1979). They claim, in effect, that the findings on the rise in tolerance reported by Nunn et al. and Davis have not been adequately demonstrated because, in replicating the Stouffer study, they have (like Stouffer) focused on attitudes toward "left wing groups" (Communists, atheists and Socialists). Sullivan et al. maintain that the public attitude toward these groups has softened since the year Stouffer conducted his survey, and they therefore allege that Nunn et al. and Davis "overstate the amount of real change that has occurred."

To assess changes in the level of tolerance, the Sullivan group introduced an alternative measure in which they first asked respondents to name the group they "liked the least," and followed this with a set of six agree-disagree questions which asked whether the respondent would permit members of the group named to become President of the United States, teach in the public schools, be allowed to make a speech in the city, and so forth.

The Sullivan et al. measure and the conclusions they have drawn from it, however, have become highly controversial, not only because the measure was administered at only one period in the 1970s (1976–78), so that no comparisons can be made with the 1950s or any other earlier periods, but also because inferences based on a comparison between the findings of the Stouffer measures and the very different measures employed by Sullivan et al. are not thought to be valid. An even more serious difficulty, however, is that the Sullivan group, in essence, takes the respondent's attitudes toward a single group (or at most two groups) as the proper indicators of the respondent's general level of tolerance—this despite the obvious fact, demonstrated repeatedly in our studies, that a

The effects of this rights explosion (which has affected both attitudes and practice) can be discerned in dozens of areas and were described in detail in our early chapters on the Bill of Rights and the various domains of civil liberties. The explosion has included not only civil liberties but civil rights. One can cite as examples the far-reaching changes in both the freedom and civil rights of minorities, the expansion of voting rights, and the changes in the status of women and other groups that have previously been disadvantaged in the exercise of their liberties and their claims to a fair share of opportunity. Increasing attention is now being paid to the needs and claims of the elderly, the poor, the disabled, the young, and other groups whose members had previously been essentially voiceless. The nation has witnessed during these years a significant decline in the censorship of books, magazines, films, and other media. Some of the most important developments have involved the strengthening of due process and greater recognition of the rights of the accused.

The expansion of personal liberty is also evident in the recognition by both the courts and the public of the freedom of women to exercise choice in the matter of abortion; in the changes in the public and legal attitudes toward matters affecting freedom of sexual conduct, cohabitation without marriage, and the rights of practicing homosexuals. The 1960s and 1970s in particular saw greater use, and official tolerance, of mass demonstrations and marches for the expression of dissenting opinion and political protest. Court rulings and changes in public sentiment also served to limit the use or soften the character of loyalty oaths and compulsory flag salutes. In addition, the separation of state

---

respondent may be highly tolerant toward a large number of unpopular groups or groups he or she strongly dislikes, but yet feel that a *particular* group (say the Symbionese Liberation Army or the Weathermen) is so dangerous that it should not be permitted to engage in such activities as teaching or holding public rallies in the city.

In addition, an individual might, over the years, grow increasingly more tolerant of many different groups and activities, but might continue to be as repelled by (and as intolerant of) a *particular* group as he or she was at the start. Sullivan and his colleagues would be compelled in this case to classify this individual as no more tolerant at the end of the measuring period than he or she was at the beginning—obviously an incorrect inference.

It seems to us a rather questionable procedure, then, to classify an otherwise highly tolerant person as intolerant because of responses to one or two groups he or she considers particularly alarming. For other critical commentaries on the Sullivan et al. measure and procedures, see communications from Abramson (1980) and Immerwahr (1980). Apart from these technical issues, as we shall see below, there is a considerable body of intuitive evidence pointing to a vast proliferation—indeed, an "explosion"—of civil libertarian rights during the past few decades, at least prior to the Reagan administration.

and church was significantly strengthened by court decisions abolishing prayers in the public schools.

In the same period, greater protections were introduced against illegal wiretaps, unwarranted searches and seizures, and other invasions of privacy. More effective limits were placed on the intelligence and police agencies in their use of surveillance and detention procedures against criminals and radicals. Significant shifts also occurred in the recognition of the right to advocate revolutionary change and in the expansion of prisoner rights in matters of procedure and treatment. Other developments crucial to the expansion of civil liberties included the adoption of "freedom of information" laws and rulings granting greater access to information previously classified as secret; the reaffirmation and strengthening of the protections against prior restraint of publications or other forms of expression; and a greater willingness to permit various forms of symbolic speech. Similar trends were evident in the relaxation of requirements regarding conscientious objection and other forms of civil disobedience. These developments at the level of official policy or governmental action have obviously been accompanied by—and in many cases are clearly the result of—substantial shifts toward greater tolerance among the mass public and its opinion leaders.

From these and other developments too numerous to list, it is plain that the rights explosion that occurred from the mid-1950s to the late 1970s had a significant impact on virtually every domain of civil liberties and civil rights. Its effects have been reflected in the national media and have been experienced, directly or indirectly, by vast numbers of the American people. Indeed, one encounters the response, especially from conservative groups, that the nation has gone "too far" in the recognition of civil liberties—that the society has become too "permissive" and that we are approaching, if we have not already reached, a state of moral erosion and lawlessness that threatens the safety, order, and vitality of the nation itself, as well as such institutions as the family. Reactions of this nature serve to remind us of the fragility of freedom and of the looming presence of sizable and influential subgroups scattered throughout the population who, though praising freedom, find many of its down-to-earth practical applications too frightening or too distasteful to countenance.

We conclude with an observation with which we began—that civil liberties are fragile and susceptible to the political climate of the time. Hard-won civil rights and liberties are not eternally safeguarded, but

437

are highly vulnerable to assaults by strategically placed individuals and groups who find certain rights or liberties morally offensive, dangerous to safety and stability, and devitalizing to the political order. Such assaults become especially threatening when the civil liberties under attack do not enjoy widespread popular support. This, as we have repeatedly seen, is often the case, a result in great part of the failure of large segments of the population to have effectively internalized the libertarian norms to which the American political culture, from the beginning, has been dedicated.

APPENDIX A

PART I

FACTS ABOUT YOURSELF

(Check correct box for each question except where a short answer is called for.)

9/
SEX
1 ☐ Male   2 ☐ Female

10-11/
AGE

01 ☐ Under 18	06 ☐ 36-40	11 ☐ 61-65
02 ☐ 18-21	07 ☐ 41-45	12 ☐ 66-70
03 ☐ 22-24	08 ☐ 46-50	13 ☐ 71-75
04 ☐ 25-31	09 ☐ 51-55	14 ☐ Over 75
05 ☐ 32-35	10 ☐ 56-60	

12/
PRESENT MARITAL STATUS
1 ☐ Never married   4 ☐ Separated
2 ☐ Married   5 ☐ Divorced
3 ☐ Unmarried but   6 ☐ Widowed
living with a mate
7 ☐ Other *(Please Specify)* _____

13-14/
EDUCATION
How far did you go in school? *(Please check the highest level of education you have completed.)*
01 ☐ Some grade school
02 ☐ Completed grade school
03 ☐ Some high school
04 ☐ Graduated from high school
05 ☐ Some college or 2-year degree
06 ☐ Graduated from college
07 ☐ Graduate School
08 ☐ Professional school *(Please specify)*

_____

09 ☐ Vocational school or other *(Please specify)*

_____

15-16/
What was the highest grade your father completed?

_____

17-18/
What was the highest grade your mother completed? _____

19/
RACE
(Check one)
1 ☐ White   3 ☐ Spanish American
2 ☐ Black   4 ☐ Asian American
5 ☐ Other*(please name)* _____

_____

NATIONALITY
In addition to being an American, from which nationality groups (Irish, Italian, German, Japanese, etc.) are you mainly descended?

_____

_____
20-21/   22-23/

RELIGION
What is your present religion, if any? (Please be specific. For example, are you Catholic, Jewish, Lutheran, Baptist, Mormon, Moslem, or what?)

_____
24-25/

☐ No religious preference
In what religion were you raised? *(Please specify)*

_____

_____
26-27/

28/
How religious do you consider yourself?
1 ☐ Deeply religious   3 ☐ Not very religious
2 ☐ Fairly religious   4 ☐ Not religious at all

RESIDENCE
Where do you live? *(Please name state)*

_____
29-30/

31/
What kind of community are you now living in? *(Check one)*
1 ☐ Rural town or farm (under 2,500 population)
2 ☐ Town or small city (under 50,000)
3 ☐ Suburb of a medium or large city
4 ☐ Medium-sized city (50,000-250,000)
5 ☐ Large city (over 250,000)

32/
What kind of community did you **mainly** live in while you were growing up? *(Check one)*
1 ☐ Rural town or farm (under 2,500)
2 ☐ Town or small city (under 50,000)
3 ☐ Suburb of a medium or large city
4 ☐ Medium-sized city (50,000-250,000)
5 ☐ Large city (over 250,000)

Please Be Sure You Have Answered Every Question
1

439

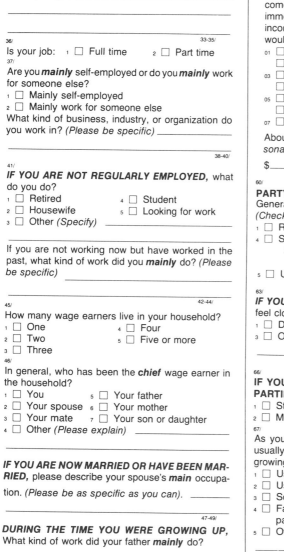

OCCUPATION

IF YOU ARE EMPLOYED AT PRESENT, what is your usual occupation—what kind of work do you *mainly* do? *(In describing your job, please be as specific as you can—for example, what do you actually make or do on your job?)* _____

_____

36/   33-35/

Is your job: 1 ☐ Full time   2 ☐ Part time

37/

Are you *mainly* self-employed or do you *mainly* work for someone else?

1 ☐ Mainly self-employed
2 ☐ Mainly work for someone else

What kind of business, industry, or organization do you work in? *(Please be specific)* _____

_____
                                   38-40/

41/

IF YOU ARE NOT REGULARLY EMPLOYED, what do you do?

1 ☐ Retired   4 ☐ Student
2 ☐ Housewife   5 ☐ Looking for work
3 ☐ Other *(Specify)* _____

If you are not working now but have worked in the past, what kind of work did you *mainly* do? *(Please be specific)* _____

_____

45/   42-44/

How many wage earners live in your household?

1 ☐ One   4 ☐ Four
2 ☐ Two   5 ☐ Five or more
3 ☐ Three

46/

In general, who has been the *chief* wage earner in the household?

1 ☐ You   5 ☐ Your father
2 ☐ Your spouse   6 ☐ Your mother
3 ☐ Your mate   7 ☐ Your son or daughter
4 ☐ Other *(Please explain)* _____

_____

IF YOU ARE NOW MARRIED OR HAVE BEEN MAR-RIED, please describe your spouse's *main* occupation. *(Please be as specific as you can).* _____

_____
                                 47-49/

DURING THE TIME YOU WERE GROWING UP,
What kind of work did your father *mainly* do?

_____
                                 50-52/

What kind of work did your mother *mainly* do?

_____
                                 53-55/

56-57/

INCOME

Check the figure that comes closest to the total income received last year by all the members of your immediate household before taxes. Please include income from all sources. (If you aren't sure, what would be your best guess?)

01 ☐ Under $3,000   8 ☐ $16,001-20,000
    ☐ $ 3,001- 6,000   ☐ $20,001-25,000
03 ☐ $ 6,001- 8,000 10 ☐ $25,001-30,000
    ☐ $ 8,001-10,000   ☐ $30,001-40,000
05 ☐ $10,001-12,000 12 ☐ $40,001-65,000
    ☐ $12,001-14,000   ☐ $65,001-100,000
07 ☐ $14,001-16,000 14 ☐ Over $100,000

About how much of this income, if any, did you *personally* earn? Please write in the approximate figure.

$_____
                                 58-59/

60/

PARTY PREFERENCE

Generally speaking, do you think of yourself as a: *(Check one)*

1 ☐ Republican   2 ☐ Democrat   3 ☐ Independent
4 ☐ Supporter of some other party *(If you support some other party, please name it)*

5 ☐ Undecided   61-62/

63/

IF YOU'RE AN INDEPENDENT, which party do you feel closest to?

1 ☐ Democrats   2 ☐ Republicans
3 ☐ Other *(Please name)* _____

                                 64-65/

66/

IF YOU BELONG TO OR PREFER ONE OF THE PARTIES, how strongly do you favor it?

1 ☐ Strongly   3 ☐ Not very strongly
2 ☐ Moderately   5 ☐ Undecided

67/

As you remember it, which party did your parents usually support in national elections when you were growing up? *(Check one)*

1 ☐ Usually the Republicans
2 ☐ Usually the Democrats
3 ☐ Sometimes one, sometimes the other
4 ☐ Father and mother usually supported different parties
5 ☐ Other *(Please explain)* _____

_____
                                 68-69/
                                 70-71/

Please Be Sure You Have Answered Every Question
2

PLEASE ANSWER BOTH COLUMNS

9/
POLITICAL OUTLOOK AND ACTIVITIES
Many of us don't like to pin political labels on ourselves. Our views are often too complicated to be
described by a single label. Nevertheless, if you **had**
to choose one word or phrase to describe your political beliefs, which of the following would you choose?
(Check one)

1 ☐ Far Left   5 ☐ Conservative
2 ☐ Strong Liberal   6 ☐ Strong Con-
3 ☐ Liberal   servative
4 ☐ Middle-of-the-Road   7 ☐ Far Right
                         8 ☐ Don't know

10-11/
Here is a list of some of the candidates who were
being considered for the presidency in 1972. If you
can remember, which candidate did you personally
prefer most? *(Check one)*

01 ☐ Hubert Humphrey   08 ☐ Nelson Rockefeller
02 ☐ Henry Jackson   09 ☐ John Schmitz
03 ☐ Edward Kennedy   10 ☐ Benjamin Spock
04 ☐ George McGovern   11 ☐ George Wallace
05 ☐ Edmund Muskie   12 ☐ No preference
06 ☐ Richard Nixon   13 ☐ Don't remember

07 ☐ Other *(Please name)* _____

12-13/
Here is a list of some of the candidates who were
being considered for the presidency in 1976. Which
candidate did you personally prefer most? *(Check
one)*

01 ☐ Jerry Brown
02 ☐ Jimmy Carter
03 ☐ Frank Church
04 ☐ Gerald Ford
05 ☐ Ronald Reagan
06 ☐ Morris Udall
07 ☐ No preference
08 ☐ Other *(Please name)* _____
09 ☐ Don't remember

14-15/
If you voted for president in 1976, for whom did you
vote?

01 ☐ Gerald Ford   04 ☐ Don't remember
02 ☐ Jimmy Carter   05 ☐ Didn't or couldn't vote
03 ☐ Other *(Please name)* _____

16-17/

18/
19/

Americans differ in their views about whether certain controversial groups are, or are not, harmful to the
country. How would you describe **your own** feelings about each of the following groups? Do you
consider them **mostly harmful; obnoxious but not really harmful;** or **mostly beneficial** and good for
the country?

GROUPS	(1) Mostly Harmful	(2) Obnoxious but not Harmful	(3) Mostly Beneficial	(5) Undecided
Ku Klux Klan	.20/ ☐	☐	☐	☐
Student Protesters	☐	☐	☐	☐
Women's Liberation (Feminist) Groups	.22/ ☐	☐	☐	☐
Extreme Left-Wing or Communist Groups	☐	☐	☐	☐
Civil Rights Groups	.24/ ☐	☐	☐	☐
Atheist Groups	☐	☐	☐	☐
Organized Crime (The Syndicate)	.26/ ☐	☐	☐	☐
Socialist Groups	☐	☐	☐	☐
American Nazi Party	.28/ ☐	☐	☐	☐
Patriotic Organizations	☐	☐	☐	☐
F.B.I.	.30/ ☐	☐	☐	☐
Black Militant Groups	☐	☐	☐	☐
American Civil Liberties Union	.32/ ☐	☐	☐	☐
Unification Church (Moonies)	☐	☐	☐	☐
Conscientious Objectors	.34/ ☐	☐	☐	☐
Extreme Right Wing Groups	☐	☐	☐	☐
Gay Liberation (Homosexual) Groups	.36/ ☐	☐	☐	☐

37/
38/

Please Be Sure You Have Answered Every Question
3

441

ACTIVITIES

HERE ARE SOME ACTIVITIES IN WHICH SOME PEOPLE PARTICIPATE AND OTHERS DO NOT. FOR EACH ACTIVITY LISTED, PLEASE CHECK THE ANSWER THAT BEST DESCRIBES YOUR OWN PARTICIPATION.

HAVE YOU EVER:	(1) No, never	(2) Yes, once or twice	(3) Yes, often	(4) Don't remember
Voted in national or local elections?	39/ ☐	☐	☐	☐
Helped in a political campaign by wearing a button, contributing time or money, etc.?	☐	☐	☐	☐
Joined a political organization of any kind?	41/ ☐	☐	☐	☐
Discussed candidates or political issues with friends or neighbors?	☐	☐	☐	☐
Visited, called, or written to a public official to get help on a personal problem?	43/ ☐	☐	☐	☐
Followed political news through the press or television?	☐	☐	☐	☐
Tried to solve some community problem by writing letters, attending meetings, joining with others, etc.?	45/ ☐	☐	☐	☐
Taken part in a demonstration, protest march, or sit-in?	46/ ☐	☐	☐	☐

47/
48/

ORGANIZATIONAL MEMBERSHIPS

49/

Have you ever joined or recently been active in any organizations that are mainly concerned with public affairs (such as human rights, tax reform, environmental issues, political reform, civil rights, business affairs, etc.)? ₁ ☐ Yes ₂ ☐ No

IF YES, list the organizations or types of organizations that you consider most important to you.

50-51/
1. _____

54-55/
3. _____

52-53/
2. _____

56-57/
4. _____

THE CONDITION OF THE COUNTRY

In this country, as in others, some people are basically satisfied with certain conditions of the country, while others are dissatisfied. The following table lists a number of such conditions. Please check *in each case* whether you are satisfied or dissatisfied with the way the conditions or problems mentioned are being handled in American today. *(Be sure to check one box for each of the conditions or problems listed.)*

HOW DO YOU FEEL ABOUT THE WAY THESE CONDITIONS OR PROBLEMS ARE BEING HANDLED TODAY?

CONDITION OR PROBLEM	(1) Strongly Satisfied	(2) Mostly Satisfied	(3) Mostly Dissatisfied	(4) Strongly Dissatisfied	(5) Unde- cided
The movement toward racial integration	58/ ☐	☐	☐	☐	☐
The opportunities for a good education	☐	☐	☐	☐	☐
The protection of the environment	60/ ☐	☐	☐	☐	☐
The fairness of our tax system	☐	☐	☐	☐	☐
The effort to provide a good standard of living	62/ ☐	☐	☐	☐	☐
The freedom to live your life as you see fit	☐	☐	☐	☐	☐
The encouragement of goodwill between older and younger people	64/ ☐	☐	☐	☐	☐
Respect for other people's property	☐	☐	☐	☐	☐
Your chance of doing the kind of work you like	66/ ☐	☐	☐	☐	☐
Decent health care for everyone	☐	☐	☐	☐	☐
The willingness to defend people who have been treated unfairly.	68/ ☐	☐	☐	☐	☐
The power of the government to check up on people	☐	☐	☐	☐	☐
The opportunity for people with ability to get ahead	70/ ☐	☐	☐	☐	☐

71/
72/

Please Be Sure You Have Answered Every Question
4

HOW IMPORTANT ARE THESE VALUES?

One way of describing a country is by the values its people hold. Americans share many values, but disagree about how important certain of these values are compared to the others.

In the following table we have listed a number of such values in the column at the left. Across the top of the table we have listed possible answers to the question of how important you believe these values to be.

How would *you* rate each of these values? Which values, in other words, do you consider **extremely important,** which do you consider **important, somewhat important,** or **less important?** *(Please check one box for each value listed.)*

VALUE	(1) Extremely Important	(2) Important	(3) Somewhat Important	(4) Less Important	(5) Undecided
The right to a public trial by jury .9/	□	□	□	□	□
Participating in elections	□	□	□	□	□
Helping a policeman in trouble .11/	□	□	□	□	□
Equal rights for women in all matters	□	□	□	□	□
Freedom to express unpopular and even "dangerous" opinions .13/	□	□	□	□	□
The right to own property and use it as you please	□	□	□	□	□
Serving in the military when called upon by the government .15/	□	□	□	□	□
Respect for law and order	□	□	□	□	□
The right of newspapers to publish freely without censorship of any kind .17/	□	□	□	□	□
Majority rule	□	□	□	□	□
The right to privacy in your correspondence or phone conversations .19/	□	□	□	□	□
Religious toleration for any and all religions	□	□	□	□	□
The right to remain silent if arrested .21/	□	□	□	□	□
The right to hold peaceful protest meetings	□	□	□	□	□
Protection of your home against searches without a warrant .23/	□	□	□	□	□
Serving on a jury when called	□	□	□	□	□
Protecting the environment .25/	□	□	□	□	□
A family's right to live in any neighborhood it can afford	□	□	□	□	□
Equal rights for racial minorities	□	□	□	□	□
Assisting the victims in a national emergency by contributing money and labor .28/	□	□	□	□	□

29/

30/

Please Be Sure You Have Answered Every Question

5

443

WHAT ACTIVITIES SHOULD A COMMUNITY ALLOW?

IN YOUR OPINION, WOULD IT BE RIGHT FOR A COMMUNITY TO ADOPT LAWS WHICH:

	(1) Yes	(2) No	(3) It Depends	(5) Undecided
Tell people where and when they can smoke in public	.31/ ☐	☐	☐	☐
Dismiss a school teacher who lives with a man to whom she is not married	☐	☐	☐	☐
Prohibit the construction of low-cost housing in certain residential neighborhoods	.33/ ☐	☐	☐	☐
Prevent "hippies" and "street people" from moving into the community	☐	☐	☐	☐
Prohibit the operation of bars which cater mainly to homosexuals	.35/ ☐	☐	☐	☐
Try to stamp out "sin"—such as prostitution, gambling, pornography, etc.	☐	☐	☐	☐
Punish people severely for selling or growing marijuana	.37/ ☐	☐	☐	☐
Impose fines for smoking marijuana	.38/ ☐	☐	☐	☐

39/
40/

SHOULD A COMMUNITY ALLOW ITS CIVIC AUDITORIUM TO BE USED BY THE FOLLOWING GROUPS FOR THE FOLLOWING PURPOSES?

	(1) Yes	(2) No	(3) It Depends	(5) Undecided
Foreign radicals who want to express their hatred of America	.41/ ☐	☐	☐	☐
The Jewish Defense League (JDL) to advocate a war against certain Arab countries	☐	☐	☐	☐
Atheists who want to preach against God and religion	.43/ ☐	☐	☐	☐
Feminists to organize a march for the Equal Rights Amendment (ERA)	☐	☐	☐	☐
Protestant groups who want to hold a revival meeting	.45/ ☐	☐	☐	☐
Revolutionaries who advocate the violent overthrow of the American government	☐	☐	☐	☐
Right-to-life groups to preach against abortion	.47/ ☐	☐	☐	☐
The American Nazi party to preach race hatred against Jews and other minorities	☐	☐	☐	☐
Conservationists to protest the construction of a nuclear power plant	.49/ ☐	☐	☐	☐
Gay liberation movements to organize for homosexual rights	☐	☐	☐	☐
Student protesters who call for a sit-in at city hall to shut down the city's offices	.51/ ☐	☐	☐	☐
Patriotic groups to advocate war against some foreign country	☐	☐	☐	☐
The Palestinian Liberation Organization (PLO) to attack Jews and call for the destruction of Israel	.53/ ☐	☐	☐	☐

54/
55/

Please Be Sure You Have Answered Every Question

6

WHAT WOULD YOU DO IF. . . ?

Most people, regardless of how they feel about an issue, rarely become *actively* involved in supporting or opposing the issue. Some people, however, do become active.

In the table below, we have listed, in the column at the left, some public issues that have recently been in the news. Across the top we have listed the kinds of actions people sometimes take on these issues.

For each of the issues listed, would you check the type of action **you feel fairly certain you would take** if any of these issues developed in your community. *(Please check one box for each of the issues listed.)*

WHAT WOULD YOU DO IF THESE THINGS HAPPENED?	(1) I would do nothing, since I favor the action.	(2) I would not get involved, since my actions wouldn't matter anyway.	(3) I would contribute money, write letters, have petitions signed.	(4) I would join an organization, protest march, attend rallies, etc.	(5) I'm undecided what I would do.
The FBI opened the mail of one of your neighbors suspected of being a subversive	56/ ☐	☐	☐	☐	☐
A homosexual teacher was fired because of his or her sexual preference	57/ ☐	☐	☐	☐	☐
A reporter was fired from a TV station or newspaper because of his strong right-wing opinions	58/ ☐	☐	☐	☐	☐
The police closed a local play because the actors were naked	59/ ☐	☐	☐	☐	☐
A black couple was prevented from buying a house on your block	60/ ☐	☐	☐	☐	☐
A woman you believed to be innocent was arrested and convicted by false testimony given by the police	61/ ☐	☐	☐	☐	☐
Local officials denied an unpopular faith-healing religious cult the use of a public park for a meeting	62/ ☐	☐	☐	☐	☐
A woman was denied a job or held back because of her sex	63/ ☐	☐	☐	☐	☐
The police arrested a protestor for calling them a dirty name	64/ ☐	☐	☐	☐	☐
A gun club leader was arrested after an illegal search of his home	65/ ☐	☐	☐	☐	☐
A black youth, accused of murder, was convicted by a racially prejudiced judge and jury	66/ ☐	☐	☐	☐	☐

67/

68/

69-70/

Please Be Sure You Have Answered Every Question

7

445

PART II

YOUR VIEWS ON SOME IMPORTANT PUBLIC QUESTIONS

The following pages contain a number of statements or questions on important public issues about which people often disagree. With a few exceptions (including several questions about yourself), all are matters of opinion rather than fact. To express your own view quickly and easily on each of the questions asked, **all you need to do is to check the answer that completes the sentence in the way that most closely reflects your opinion.**

You will note we have listed only two answers for each question. While this simplifies the choice, we realize that not every issue can be boiled down to only two answers. Some of the answers, therefore, may strike you as overly simple and neither answer may express your view *exactly*. NEVERTHELESS, WE WOULD LIKE YOU TO PICK THE ONE ANSWER THAT COMES CLOSEST TO THE OPINION YOU ACTUALLY HOLD.

We also realize that while some of the answers will seem fair and sensible, others will strike you as extreme or even foolish. Since our purpose is to obtain a description of the beliefs and values of Americans from many different walks of life, we have had to include answers that reflect opinions of *all* shades.

In a few cases you may feel that both answers are so wrong or inappropriate that you can't choose either of them. If this happens, you should check the box labeled NEITHER. If, on the other hand, you agree equally with both answers or if you simply can't decide which answer comes closer to what you believe, check the UNDECIDED box.

Please Be Sure That You Check Only One Box For Each Question And That You Answer Every Question.

7-8/04

9/

Mass student protest demonstrations:
1 ☐ have no place on a college campus and the participating students should be punished.
2 ☐ should be allowed by college officials as long as they are non-violent.
3 ☐ Neither   5 ☐ Undecided

A person who is willing to risk going to jail for breaking the law in the hope of correcting some serious injustice:
☐ is acting foolishly, since he could probably get further by working within the law.
☐ is acting heroically and is more likely to gain his objectives than by obeying the law.
☐ Neither   ☐ Undecided

The courts have ruled that in order to solve a crime, the police can give a suspect a lie detector test:
☐ only if he voluntarily agrees to take one.
☐ whenever they have reason to believe that he is lying.
☐ Neither   ☐ Undecided

12/

The use of obscene gestures to express anger against a public official:
☐ is so rude it should be outlawed.
☐ should be considered a constitutionally protected form of free speech.
☐ Neither   ☐ Undecided

13/

If a news photographer takes pictures of a famous person entering a house of prostitution, publishing the photos should be:
☐ permitted under the guarantees of a free press.
☐ forbidden as an invasion of privacy.
☐ Neither   ☐ Undecided

When people say they really care about others, they are usually:
☐ being honest and sincere.
☐ pretending to care more than they really do.
☐ Neither   ☐ Undecided

In this country, the right to criticize the Constitution:
☐ is itself protected by the Constitution.
☐ can legally be revoked, in times of emergency, by joint action of Congress, the President, and the Supreme Court.
☐ Neither   ☐ Undecided

Novels that describe explicit sex acts:
☐ have no place in a high school library and should be banned.
☐ should be permitted in the library if they are worthwhile literature.
☐ Neither   ☐ Undecided

17/

If a pregnant woman wants an abortion and the father of the child objects, should he have a legal right to prevent it?
☐ Yes, it's his child too, after all.
☐ No, the decision should be entirely the woman's.
☐ Neither   ☐ Undecided

8

18/
A person's credit rating:

1 ☐ should be made available to his creditors, since they stand to lose if he fails to pay his debts.

2 ☐ should not be given to anyone without his consent.

3 ☐ Neither   5 ☐ Undecided

One of the most important liberties the founding fathers included in the Bill of Rights was:

☐ the right of every male citizen to vote in national elections.

☐ the right of citizens to petition the government for correcting grievances or complaints.

☐ Neither   ☐ Undecided

In dealing with prostitution, the government should:

☐ license and regulate it.

☐ arrest or fine the people who have anything to do with it.

☐ Neither   ☐ Undecided

21/
Scientific research that might show women or minorities in a bad light:

☐ should be banned because the results might damage their self-respect.

☐ should be allowed because the goal of science is to discover truth, whatever it may be.

☐ Neither   ☐ Undecided

A student's high school and college records should be released by school officials:

☐ only with the consent of the student.

☐ to any government agencies or potential employers who ask to see them.

☐ Neither   ☐ Undecided

23/
People who usually try to be different from the rest of us:

☐ are generally an asset to society.

☐ are generally just a nuisance.

☐ Neither   ☐ Undecided

If a patient tells his psychiatrist that he is planning to commit a serious crime, the psychiatrist should:

☐ report it to the police.

☐ remain silent because his first duty is to his patient.

☐ Neither   ☐ Undecided

25/
Should rapists or child molesters be given the same sort of "fair trial" as other criminals?

☐ Yes, because the right to a fair trial should not depend on the nature of the crime.

☐ No, because their crimes are so inhuman that they do not deserve the usual legal protections.

☐ Neither   ☐ Undecided

26/
In matters concerning family finances such as the sale of property and bank loans:

☐ the husband and wife should have an equal say since marriage is a partnership of equals.

☐ the husband, as head of the household, should have the most say.

☐ Neither   ☐ Undecided

If the majority in a referendum votes to stop publication of newspapers that preach race hatred:

☐ such newspapers should be closed down.

☐ no one, not even the majority of voters, should have the right to close down a newspaper.

☐ Neither   ☐ Undecided

All systems of justice make mistakes, but which do you think is worse?

☐ To convict an innocent person.

☐ To let a guilty person go free.

☐ Neither   ☐ Undecided

One of the differences between democracies and dictatorships is that democratic governments:

☐ allow private property.

☐ allow citizens to choose their representatives freely.

☐ Neither   ☐ Undecided

30/
Should a judge ever be allowed to ban the press from covering a criminal trial?

☐ Yes, if a really sensational crime such as hijacking or mass murder has been committed.

☐ No, since a trial that is not open to the public is not likely to be a fair one.

☐ Neither   ☐ Undecided

The custom of a woman taking her husband's last name:

☐ should be the woman's personal decision.

☐ should be legally required because it prevents a lot of confusion.

☐ Neither   ☐ Undecided

If a person is acquitted of a crime because the judge made a mistake in legal procedure during the trial:

☐ it is only fair that he be set free, even if the mistake was a small one.

☐ setting him free for this reason would be carrying legal technicalities too far.

☐ Neither   ☐ Undecided

33/
I must admit that when I see a black man dating a white woman:

☐ it makes be somewhat uncomfortable.

☐ it doesn't really bother me.

☐ Neither   ☐ Undecided

Please Be Sure You Have Answered Every Question

34/
If some groups are treated unjustly in our society, do you feel it is your personal responsibility to help them get better treatment?

1 ☐ No, what can one individual do anyway?

2 ☐ Yes, aren't we all supposed to be our "brother's keeper"?

3 ☐ Neither   5 ☐ Undecided

If someone is caught red-handed beating and robbing an older person on the street:

☐ it's just a waste of taxpayers' money to bother with the usual expensive trial.

☐ the suspect should still be entitled to a jury trial and all the usual legal protections.

☐ Neither   ☐ Undecided

Suppose Congress and the President passed a law you considered unjust, immoral, or cruel. Would you still be morally bound to obey it?

☐ Yes, it's out duty to obey any law adopted under proper constitutional procedures.

☐ No, because we each have a higher duty to our own conscience and to what we think is right and wrong.

☐ Neither   ☐ Undecided

37/
Does the government ever have the right to punish someone for a particular speech he made?

☐ No, never.

☐ Yes, if it can be shown that his speech incited a riot.

☐ Neither   ☐ Undecided

A group that wants to buy advertising space in a newspaper to advocate war against another country:

☐ should be turned down by the newspaper.

☐ should have as much right to buy advertising space as a group that favors world peace.

☐ Neither   ☐ Undecided

Using violence to achieve political goals:

☐ is sometimes the only way to get injustices corrected.

☐ is wrong because there are many peaceful ways for people to get their views across.

☐ Neither   ☐ Undecided

40/
If an accident victim suffers hopeless brain damage and the doctors agree she can never again regain consciousness:

☐ the victim's family should have the right to stop any treatment that helps keep her alive.

☐ treatment should be continued because human life is sacred and must be preserved as long as possible.

☐ Neither   ☐ Undecided

41/
Tariffs are usually favored by:

☐ consumer groups who benefit most from them.

☐ producers from both business and labor who want to cut down on foreign competition.

☐ Neither   ☐ Undecided

When a judge forbids attorneys to discuss a highly controversial criminal case with the press, it is usually:

☐ a good idea, because too much publicity can spoil a fair trial.

☐ a bad idea, because freedom of the press is as important as a fair trial.

☐ Neither   ☐ Undecided

The use of dogs in airports to help police locate dangerous narcotics in suitcases or lockers:

☐ violates a traveller's privacy.

☐ is justified in order to catch drug dealers.

☐ Neither   ☐ Undecided

In setting a policy for admitting students to medical and law schools, a university:

☐ should set aside a certain number of places for women, to make up for the prejudice they have suffered in the past.

☐ should admit all students on merit alone.

☐ Neither   ☐ Undecided

45/
Which of these comes closer to what you believe?

☐ Although law is necesssary for an orderly society, some laws are so unjust that people should simply refuse to obey them.

☐ In an orderly country, laws must be obeyed by everyone, even if they are sometimes wrong.

☐ Neither   ☐ Undecided

On issues of religion, morals, and politics, high school teachers have the right to express their opinions in class:

☐ even if they go against the community's most precious values and beliefs.

☐ only if those opinions do not offend the community's beliefs.

☐ Neither   ☐ Undecided

47/
The non-violent marches, boycotts, and sit-ins of black people in the South during the early 1960's:

☐ helped bring about needed reforms that gave blacks their just rights.

☐ merely caused trouble and probably did more harm than good in the long run.

☐ Neither   ☐ Undecided

Please Be Sure You Have Answered Every Question

10

9/
All things considered, I feel I am:
1 ☐ at least as attractive as most people.
2 ☐ not really very attractive.
3 ☐ Neither   5 ☐ Undecided

America's natural resources such as food, coal, metals, and lumber:
☐ should be shared with other countries that are poor and backward.
☐ should be kept here and used for the benefit of Americans alone.
☐ Neither   ☐ Undecided

The laws guaranteeing equal opportunities for blacks and other minorities:
☐ should be made even stronger.
☐ sometimes go too far.
☐ Neither   ☐ Undecided

12
An American who shows disrespect for the flag:
☐ may have his own good reasons for not liking this country.
☐ would do well to attend some lectures on patriotism to learn to appreciate America's greatness.
☐ Neither   ☐ Undecided

When making decisions about public affairs, the majority:
☐ should be able to do whatever it wants to.
☐ has a duty to respect the rights of the minority.
☐ Neither   ☐ Undecided

When comparing myself to others I feel:
☐ I am able to do most things as well as other people.
☐ other people usually do things better than I do.
☐ Neither   ☐ Undecided

15/
It seems to me:
☐ I am rarely given the recognition I deserve.
☐ I receive my fair share of praise when I do a good job.
☐ Neither   ☐ Undecided

To be realistic about it, our elected officials:
☐ know much more than the voters about issues, and should be allowed to make whatever decisions they think best.
☐ would badly misuse their power if they weren't watched and guided by the voters.
☐ Neither   ☐ Undecided

17/
Most important questions:
☐ have a right answer and a wrong answer.
☐ can usually be answered in more than one way.
☐ Neither   ☐ Undecided

18/
When I have to deal with other people:
☐ I usually manage quite well.
☐ I wish I were better at it.
☐ Neither   ☐ Undecided

In my conduct:
☐ I set a high standard for myself and feel others should do the same.
☐ I realize that nobody's perfect and I try to relax about it.
☐ Neither   ☐ Undecided

I have to admit:
☐ I don't always like this country very much.
☐ even if it has faults, I still prefer this country to others.
☐ Neither   ☐ Undecided

21/
Once I've made up my mind on an important question:
☐ I'm not likely to change it easily.
☐ I can often be persuaded to change it if someone has a good argument.
☐ Neither   ☐ Undecided

A minority family that wants to move into a particular neighborhood:
☐ would be well advised to find out whether the neighbors want them or not.
☐ shouldn't have to check with anyone.
☐ Neither   ☐ Undecided

In view of the dangerous world situation, the United States should:
☐ work harder to get all nations, including America, to disarm.
☐ increase its military strength even more.
☐ Neither   ☐ Undecided

24/
To believe that people who differ in ability should be treated differently in certain matters:
☐ is unfair and penalizes people for something that is not their fault.
☐ is only realistic and justified.
☐ Neither   ☐ Undecided

The profits a company or businessman can earn should be:
☐ as large as they can fairly earn.
☐ strictly limited by law to a certain level.
☐ Neither   ☐ Undecided

26/
More minority students should be admitted to our colleges:
☐ even if it means lowering standards of admission.
☐ only if normal standards of admission are met.
☐ Neither   ☐ Undecided

Please Be Sure You Have Answered Every Question
11

27/

An American who doesn't think this is the best country in the world:

₁ ☐ doesn't deserve to live here.

₂ ☐ can still be a good citizen in his own way.

₃ ☐ Neither   ₅ ☐ Undecided

Most of my troubles are:

☐ caused by other people who seem to want to hurt me.

☐ no worse than other people's and some are my own fault.

☐ Neither   ☐ Undecided

Anybody who criticizes the present system in America can expect that others:

☐ will respect his right to express his own opinions.

☐ will avoid him because of his unpopular views.

☐ Neither   ☐ Undecided

Military weapons like atomic bombs and germ warfare:

☐ are so cruel that America should never even think of using them.

☐ may have to be used to save us from losing a war.

☐ Neither   ☐ Undecided

31/

America was for many years regarded abroad as one of the best countries in the world. How would you rank it today?

☐ It's still the finest country in the world to live in.

☐ It's no longer so much better than other countries.

☐ Neither   ☐ Undecided

Loyalty oaths for all government employees:

☐ should be required, to be sure that only patriotic people work for the government.

☐ are unnecessary, since most government employees are loyal Americans anyway.

☐ Neither   ☐ Undecided

People who say they are "open-minded" are:

☐ just looking for an excuse to avoid making up their minds.

☐ simply more willing to consider different points of view.

☐ Neither   ☐ Undecided

34/

My opinions on the most important topics:

☐ have never really changed, even if they seem to.

☐ are quite different now from what they were some time ago.

☐ Neither   ☐ Undecided

35/

When I think of some of the things this country has done:

☐ I am sometimes ashamed to call myself an American.

☐ I am satisfied that the U.S. mostly tries to do the right thing.

☐ Neither   ☐ Undecided

In your opinion, do such rituals as singing the "Star-Spangled Banner" and pledging allegiance to the flag help to increase pride in America?

☐ Yes.

☐ No.

☐ Neither   ☐ Undecided

Our electoral system:

☐ too often elects people who don't know enough to do their job:

☐ has faults, but most of the leaders chosen are competent.

☐ Neither   ☐ Undecided

It seems to me that other people:

☐ often don't take my opinions seriously.

☐ generally pay attention to what I say.

☐ Neither   ☐ Undecided

39/

Scientists who argue that some racial groups are naturally less intelligent than others:

☐ are probably correct.

☐ are clearly wrong.

☐ Neither   ☐ Undecided

In our society today, too much emphasis is placed on:

☐ conformity and obedience to the community.

☐ individual freedom at the expense of the community's interest.

☐ Neither   ☐ Undecided

Teaching children that all people are really equal:

☐ recognizes that all people are equally worthy and deserve equal treatment.

☐ teaches them something that is obviously false.

☐ Neither   ☐ Undecided

42/

In a democracy, must the party that wins the election respect the rights of extreme opposition parties to ridicule and attack the way things are being run?

☐ Yes, because the right of opposition parties, no matter how extreme, can never be abolished.

☐ No, because extremist opposition can prevent the majority party from doing its job.

☐ Neither   ☐ Undecided

Please Be Sure You Have Answered Every Question

12

43/
Whenever I start a new job:
1 ☐ I find it difficult to set it aside even for a short while.
2 ☐ it doesn't bother me to put it aside and shift to something else.
3 ☐ Neither   5 ☐ Undecided

In general, it's better for people of different races:
☐ to keep to themselves as much as possible.
☐ to live and work together so that they can learn to understand each other.
☐ Neither   ☐ Undecided

I find that other people:
☐ often make me feel ashamed of my background and position in life.
☐ usually accept me for who and what I am.
☐ Neither   ☐ Undecided

46/
America has sometimes been described as "the last best hope on earth". Do you share this opinion or not?
☐ Yes, I share it on the whole.
☐ No, I think such an opinion goes too far.
☐ Neither   ☐ Undecided

When I work on something:
☐ I like to take charge.
☐ I prefer to let others organize the tasks.
☐ Neither   ☐ Undecided

48/
People who discriminate against minority groups in such things as jobs and housing:
☐ should be fined or sued for damages.
☐ should have a right in a free country to do as they please in such matters.
☐ Neither   ☐ Undecided

If the majority of employees in a shop vote for a union, the other workers should:
☐ be required to join.
☐ be free nevertheless to stay out of the union if they want to.
☐ Neither   ☐ Undecided

Ordinarily I am:
☐ quite self-confident.
☐ rather unsure of myself.
☐ Neither   ☐ Undecided

51/
The majority of voters:
☐ use their vote wisely most of the time.
☐ are too uninformed and emotional to make sensible choices.
☐ Neither   ☐ Undecided

52/
In your opinion, is the free enterprise system necessary for free government to survive?
☐ Probably not.
☐ For the most part, yes.
☐ Neither   ☐ Undecided

When I am working on something:
☐ I won't consider it done unless it's absolutely perfect.
☐ I do the best I can and try not to worry about it.
☐ Neither   ☐ Undecided

54/
I am often:
☐ blamed for mistakes when I really should be praised for my actions.
☐ given credit when it is due.
☐ Neither   ☐ Undecided

Teaching American children that they should love their own country more than other countries:
☐ is the appropriate thing for parents to do.
☐ is wrong because it goes against the idea of the brotherhood of mankind.
☐ Neither   ☐ Undecided

When it comes to the really important questions about religion and philosophy of life:
☐ I feel I have to decide them firmly one way or the other.
☐ it doesn't really bother me to leave them undecided.
☐ Neither   ☐ Undecided

57/
When people I know get together for a celebration or party:
☐ I often feel that I am left out of their plans.
☐ I am usually included in their plans.
☐ Neither   ☐ Undecided

The way things are run in America today:
☐ people are too restricted in what they are allowed to think and do.
☐ people have too much freedom to do as they please.
☐ Neither   ☐ Undecided

59/
The thought that people are talking about me behind my back:
☐ often haunts me.
☐ is something that doesn't bother me much.
☐ Neither   ☐ Undecided

Please Be Sure You Have Answered Every Question

13

451

^{60/}
When I finish one job:
1 ☐ I can hardly wait to get started on the next one.
2 ☐ I like to take a breather before starting something new.
  3 ☐ Neither   5 ☐ Undecided

Which of these opinions about America comes closer to what you believe?
☐ Americans should count their blessings and not complain so much about the few things that are wrong.

☐ It is every American's duty to criticize the country when it is wrong.
  ☐ Neither   ☐ Undecided

If one of your important freedoms were to be denied either by the government or by other people, how good would your chances be to get your rights restored?
☐ Fairly good
☐ Not very good.
  ☐ Neither   ☐ Undecided

^{63/}
On an important public issue, I believe:
☐ you should either be for it or against it and not take a middle course.
☐ you should always keep in mind that there is more than one side to most issues.
  ☐ Neither   ☐ Undecided

How would you feel if the U.S. were to lose its role as a leader among nations?
☐ I would consider it tragic and humiliating.
☐ I can't be sure, but I don't think it would bother me very much.
  ☐ Neither   ☐ Undecided

^{65/}
Whenever I have been punished it has usually been:
☐ without cause.
☐ because I deserved it.
  ☐ Neither   ☐ Undecided

Our most important aim in dealing with enemy nations should be:
☐ to maintain peace with them.
☐ to achieve victory over them.
  ☐ Neither   ☐ Undecided

^{67/}
At a party or other social gathering:
☐ I enjoy meeting and talking to new people.
☐ I worry that I won't have anything interesting to say to the people I meet.
  ☐ Neither   ☐ Undecided

^{68/}
When funds are scarce, education scholarships should be awarded to young people mostly on the basis of:
☐ academic ability.
☐ financial need.
  ☐ Neither   ☐ Undecided

In a public meeting or class:
☐ I usually enjoy participating in the discussion.
☐ I get very nervous if I think I may have to say something.
  ☐ Neither   ☐ Undecided

Laws requiring employers to give special preference to minorities when filling jobs are:
☐ necessary to make up for a long history of discrimination.
☐ unfair to qualified people who are not members of a minority.
  ☐ Neither   ☐ Undecided

^{71/}
Making decisions and telling others how to carry them out:
☐ is something I find difficult to do.
☐ is something I find easy and even enjoyable.
  ☐ Neither   ☐ Undecided

In the past whenever I've disagreed with someone, it later turned out that:
☐ I was usually right.
☐ I was sometimes right and sometimes wrong.
  ☐ Neither   ☐ Undecided

^{73/}
If I were ever asked to lead a group in some activity:
☐ I believe I would do a satisfactory job.
☐ I doubt I would make a good leader.
  ☐ Neither   ☐ Undecided

People who fit their lives to a rigid schedule:
☐ are the ones who are likely to be most successful.
☐ miss much of the joy of living.
  ☐ Neither   ☐ Undecided

^{75/}
When making new laws, the government should pay most attention to:
☐ the opinions of the people who really know something about the subject.
☐ the opinions of average citizens, regardless of how little they know.
  ☐ Neither   ☐ Undecided

Please Be Sure You Have Answered Every Question
14

9/
Should the government have the authority to ban the sale of certain products that might cause cancer?
1 ☐ Yes, in order to protect citizens from possible harm.
2 ☐ No, because it takes away a person's right to buy what he or she likes.
3 ☐ Neither   5 ☐ Undecided

Giving a federal board of censors the power to decide which TV programs can or cannot be shown:
☐ violates the public's right to watch what it pleases.
☐ is necessary to protect the public against violent or obscene shows.
☐ Neither   ☐ Undecided

When is it appropriate to commit a person to a mental hospital?
☐ If a panel of psychiatrists certifies him as dangerous to himself or others.
☐ Only if he voluntarily consents to being hospitalized.
☐ Neither   ☐ Undecided

12/
In dealing with muggings and other serious street crimes, which is more important?
☐ To protect the rights of the suspects.
☐ To stop such crimes and make the streets safe even if we sometimes have to violate the suspect's rights.
☐ Neither   ☐ Undecided

Closing down magazines that print obscene or "dirty" pictures:
☐ is a bad idea because it might easily lead to other restrictions on freedom of publication.
☐ is necessary to protect children from being exposed to unhealthy influences.
☐ Neither   ☐ Undecided

14/
Can you depend on a man more if he owns property than if he doesn't?
☐ Yes.
☐ No.
☐ Neither   ☐ Undecided

On the whole, the newspapers:
☐ try to do a fair and honest job of reporting the news.
☐ are mainly interested in selling papers and don't care how accurately they report the news.
☐ Neither   ☐ Undecided

16/
Most people on welfare:
☐ would rather live off others than work.
☐ would prefer to support themselves if given the chance.
☐ Neither   ☐ Undecided

17/
Employers who refuse to employ senior citizens who can still do the job competently:
☐ should be fined or denied government contracts.
☐ should be free to decide for themselves what is best for their company.
☐ Neither   ☐ Undecided

In general, people will be honest with you as long as:
☐ you are honest with them.
☐ it is in their own interest.
☐ Neither   ☐ Undecided

Probably the biggest problem in preventing war is that:
☐ different countries have different interests.
☐ human nature is basically aggressive and warlike.
☐ Neither   ☐ Undecided

In order to improve their conditions, the poor:
☐ should help themselves.
☐ should receive special government help.
☐ Neither   ☐ Undecided

21/
Which of these policies do you think would be more effective in reducing crime?
☐ Giving longer and tougher prison sentences to hardened criminals.
☐ Treating prisoners more humanely so they will gain self-respect and become law-abiding citizens.
☐ Neither   ☐ Undecided

A person's diary should be considered:
☐ legal evidence if that person is on trial for a serious crime.
☐ so personal and private a document that no one, not even a judge and jury, is entitled to see it without the person's consent.
☐ Neither   ☐ Undecided

People who keep their yards messy and their houses looking dirty:
☐ owe it to their neighbors to clean them up even if it costs them some financial sacrifice.
☐ should be able to keep them any way they please since this is a free country.
☐ Neither   ☐ Undecided

24/
Police who pose as ordinary citizens and walk down the street with money sticking out of their pockets:
☐ are unfairly trying to trap people into committing crimes.
☐ are just doing their duty in trying to catch criminals.
☐ Neither   ☐ Undecided

Please Be Sure You Have Answered Every Question
15

25/

"Cheating" here and there on your income tax return so as to pay as little as possible:
1 ☐ is like stealing money from the government.
2 ☐ isn't all that wrong since almost everyone does it to some extent.
  3 ☐ Neither   5 ☐ Undecided

Providing medical care for everyone at public expense would:
☐ reduce the general quality of medical care.
☐ greatly improve the health of the nation.
  ☐ Neither   ☐ Undecided

Too much of our tax money is going for:
☐ military defense.
☐ social welfare programs.
  ☐ Neither   ☐ Undecided

28/

Jailing reporters who refuse to reveal their news sources during a trial:
☐ is justified when the names of the sources are necessary for a fair trial.
☐ is wrong because people with important information will then be afraid to tell the truth to reporters.
  ☐ Neither   ☐ Undecided

Pornographic films:
☐ can easily lead unbalanced people to commit violent sex crimes.
☐ are mostly harmless, even if some people find them distasteful.
  ☐ Neither   ☐ Undecided

30/

When a law goes against a person's conscience, he should:
☐ be allowed to disobey it so long as he has good reason and doesn't hurt anyone else.
☐ be required nevertheless to obey it, or else all law will lose its meaning.
  ☐ Neither   ☐ Undecided

Free speech should be granted:
☐ only to people who are willing to grant the same rights of free speech to everyone else.
☐ to everyone regardless of how intolerant they are of other people's opinions.
  ☐ Neither   ☐ Undecided

32/

When a law is particularly unjust, one possible way to change it is:
☐ to call it to the world's attention by refusing to obey it.
☐ to obey it strictly, but try to persuade the lawmakers to change it in the standard way.
  ☐ Neither   ☐ Undecided

33/

Although there have always been poor and hungry people in the world:
☐ we can certainly help by sharing what we have.
☐ we must learn to accept it even though it is tragic.
  ☐ Neither   ☐ Undecided

When groups like the Nazis or other extreme groups require police protection at their rallies and marches, the community should:
☐ supply and pay for whatever police protection is needed.
☐ prohibit such groups from holding rallies because of the costs and dangers involved.
  ☐ Neither   ☐ Undecided

A person who publicly burns or spits on the flag:
☐ should be fined or punished in some way.
☐ may be behaving badly but should not be punished for it by law.
  ☐ Neither   ☐ Undecided

Traditionally in the American political system, the job of interpreting the Constitution is mainly exercised by:
☐ the President.
☐ the Supreme Court.
  ☐ Neither   ☐ Undecided

37/

If a professor is suspected of spreading false ideas in his classes, college officials:
☐ should send someone into his classes to check on him.
☐ should not interfere since it would violate his rights.
  ☐ Neither   ☐ Undecided

A person who has no chance whatever to recover from a painful terminal illness:
☐ should have the right to die when he or she chooses.
☐ unfortunately must wait until life naturally runs out.
  ☐ Neither   ☐ Undecided

If some students at a college want to form a "Campus Nazi Club":
☐ they should be allowed to do so.
☐ college officials should ban such clubs from campus.
  ☐ Neither   ☐ Undecided

40/

When the Supreme Court banned prayers in public schools:
☐ they were simply carrying out the constitutional requirement of separating state and church.
☐ they were denying children their constitutional right to freedom of religion.
  ☐ Neither   ☐ Undecided

Please Be Sure You Have Answered Every Question

41/
A humor magazine which ridicules or makes fun of blacks, women, or other minority groups:
1 ☐ should lose its mailing privileges.
2 ☐ should have the same right as any other magazine to print what it wants.
   3 ☐ Neither   5 ☐ Undecided

Inflation occurs when:
☐ people have more money while there are fewer things to buy.
☐ there is an increase in both unemployment and production.
   ☐ Neither   ☐ Undecided

The stock market goes up and down mainly because:
☐ the confidence of investors changes from time to time.
☐ stock market sales are not sufficiently regulated by the government agencies established to supervise them.
   ☐ Neither   ☐ Undecided

44/
Reporting the events of a trial on television while the trial is in progress should be:
☐ prohibited if there is any danger it might influence the jury's verdict.
☐ allowed because the public has a right to know what is happening in a trial.
   ☐ Neither   ☐ Undecided

The "right to remain silent":
☐ is needed to protect individuals from the "third degree" and forced confessions.
☐ has harmed the country by giving criminals too much protection.
   ☐ Neither   ☐ Undecided

People who are always trying to reform things are usually:
☐ busybodies who do more harm than good.
☐ people who really care about other people.
   ☐ Neither   ☐ Undecided

Having an abortion for *any* reason is:
☐ like murder, and should be legally prohibited.
☐ unfortunate, but sometimes best for all concerned.
   ☐ Neither   ☐ Undecided

48/
The use of primary elections in the U.S. to choose candidates was mainly introduced by:
☐ party "bosses" who can use them to control nominations.
☐ reformers who wanted the voters themselves to choose party candidates.
   ☐ Neither   ☐ Undecided

49/
When I see a homosexual couple embracing or walking hand in hand:
☐ I must admit it bothers me.
☐ it doesn't really upset me.
   ☐ Neither   ☐ Undecided

If a person has a weak character:
☐ he deserves sympathy more than blame.
☐ he should be treated for what he is, a moral weakling.
   ☐ Neither   ☐ Undecided

For the most part, local ordinances that guarantee equal rights to homosexuals in such matters as jobs and housing:
☐ damage American moral standards.
☐ uphold the American idea of human rights for all.
   ☐ Neither   ☐ Undecided

52/
If a person is found guilty of a crime by evidence gathered through illegal methods:
☐ he should be set free or granted a new trial.
☐ he should still be convicted if the evidence is really convincing and strong.
   ☐ Neither   ☐ Undecided

Before a criminal case comes to trial, reporters who have found out certain "facts of the case" should be:
☐ forbidden to publish the information since it might bias the jurors.
☐ allowed to publish the information because no one, not even a judge, should be able to censor the press.
   ☐ Neither   ☐ Undecided

54/
Everyone would be better off if more women:
☐ were satisfied to stay home and have families.
☐ were encouraged to have careers of their own.
   ☐ Neither   ☐ Undecided

The movie industry:
☐ should be free to make movies on any subject it chooses.
☐ should not be permitted to make movies that offend certain minorities or religious groups.
   ☐ Neither   ☐ Undecided

56/
Government regulation of business:
☐ usually does more harm than good.
☐ is necessary to keep industry from becoming too powerful.
   ☐ Neither   ☐ Undecided

Please Be Sure You Have Answered Every Question

57/
The freedom of atheists to make fun of God and religion:

₁☐ should not be allowed in a public place where religious groups gather.

₂☐ should be legally protected no matter who might be offended.

₃☐ Neither   ₅☐ Undecided

Sex education of children:
☐ should be taught in school.
☐ is a matter for the parents to handle.
☐ Neither   ☐ Undecided

People who have had to work hard for what they have:
☐ should not be expected to share it with those who have not worked as hard.
☐ should know the meaning of poverty and be willing to share what they have.
☐ Neither   ☐ Undecided

60/
A person who worries about helping others before helping himself:
☐ will be a much happier person.
☐ will find that he'll not get any thanks for it.
☐ Neither   ☐ Undecided

Freedom to worship as one pleases:
☐ applies to all religious groups, regardless of how extreme their beliefs are.
☐ was never meant to apply to religious cults that the majority of people consider "strange," fanatical, or "weird."
☐ Neither   ☐ Undecided

If there were no laws protecting the rights of accused lawbreakers, most policemen would probably:
☐ push people around more than they do now.
☐ treat people fairly anyway.
☐ Neither   ☐ Undecided

Government regulation of scientific experiments done on human beings:
☐ is necessary to assure that people won't be harmed by the experiments.
☐ interferes with a scientist's freedom to decide what research would benefit mankind most.
☐ Neither   ☐ Undecided

64/
Should groups like the Nazis and Ku Klux Klan be allowed to appear on public television to state their views?
☐ No, because they would offend certain racial or religious groups.
☐ Yes, no matter who is offended.
☐ Neither   ☐ Undecided

65/
Under American law at present:
☐ books can no longer be banned on the grounds that they are obscene.
☐ local communities have the power to ban obscene publications that do not meet community standards.
☐ Neither   ☐ Undecided

If a woman on welfare becomes pregnant and wants an abortion, should the government pay for it?
☐ Yes, she should not be penalized for being poor.
☐ No, it would be an improper use of our federal tax money.
☐ Neither   ☐ Undecided

A homosexual couple who want to get legally married:
☐ should be denied a marriage license because such a marriage would be unnatural.
☐ should have the same rights to marry as anyone else.
☐ Neither   ☐ Undecided

68/
When countries like Chile, Russia, or Uganda clearly violate the human rights of their citizens, which of these policies should the U.S. follow?
☐ Find a way to express American disapproval of such violations.
☐ Keep quiet, since the way foreign governments treat their own citizens is not really our business.
☐ Neither   ☐ Undecided

Television programs that show people actually making love:
☐ should be permitted as long as they are shown in the late evening, during adult viewing hours.
☐ should not be allowed on TV at all.
☐ Neither   ☐ Undecided

Improving the treatment of prisoners:
☐ would probably reduce crime.
☐ would probably increase crime.
☐ Neither   ☐ Undecided

When riots break out, the police:
☐ are usually too easy on the rioters.
☐ often use too much force and cause more violence than might otherwise have occurred.
☐ Neither   ☐ Undecided

72/
These days:
☐ there is too much sexual freedom and loose living.
☐ people have healthier and more relaxed ideas about sex.
☐ Neither   ☐ Undecided

Please Be Sure You Have Answered Every Question

9/
Citizens who refuse to pay their income tax in protest against the use of tax money to pay for abortions:

1 ☐ should be subject to the same penalties as other tax evaders.
2 ☐ should not be forced to pay for something they believe to be morally wrong.
3 ☐ Neither   5 ☐ Undecided

Trying to get around a law without actually breaking it:
☐ is wrong, even though many people do it.
☐ is really O.K., as long as you don't actually break the law.
☐ Neither   ☐ Undecided

Abortion during the early weeks of pregnancy should be:
☐ prohibited except in such extreme cases as rape, the risk of a deformed child, or danger to the mother's life.
☐ left entirely up to the woman.
☐ Neither   ☐ Undecided

12/
If a political group known for its violent activities wants to picket the White House:
☐ it should be granted police protection like any other group.
☐ it should be prevented from doing so because it might endanger the President.
☐ Neither   ☐ Undecided

Once an arrested person says he wishes to remain silent, the authorities:
☐ should stop all further questioning at once.
☐ should keep asking questions to try to get the suspect to admit his crimes.
☐ Neither   ☐ Undecided

If the majority votes in a referendum to ban the public expression of certain opinions, should the majority opinion be followed?
☐ No, because free speech is a more fundamental right than majority rule.
☐ Yes, because no group has a greater right than the majority to decide which opinions can or cannot be expressed.
☐ Neither   ☐ Undecided

15/
If a police officer stops a car for a traffic violation, he should:
☐ be allowed to search the car if he suspects it contains narcotics or stolen goods.
☐ be limited to dealing with the traffic violation and nothing else.
☐ Neither   ☐ Undecided

16/
Replacing traditional policies with new ones that seem attractive but have not been tested by experience is:
☐ often necessary for progress.
☐ usually short-sighted and dangerous.
☐ Neither   ☐ Undecided

According to the U.S. Supreme Court, any person accused of a felony (or major crime) is entitled to have a lawyer defend him:
☐ even if the state has to supply and pay for one.
☐ as long as the accused can find someone to pay his legal fees.
☐ Neither   ☐ Undecided

Under American law, the police can legally hold a suspect in custody without charging him with a crime:
☐ for as long as they find it necessary to gather the evidence they need for a conviction, but no longer than six months.
☐ for only 48 hours, and then they must set him free or formally charge him with a crime.
☐ Neither   ☐ Undecided

Would you say we show too much or too little sympathy toward people who can't manage to succeed at anything?
☐ Too much sympathy.
☐ Too little sympathy.
☐ Neither   ☐ Undecided

20/
Books that could show terrorists how to build bombs should be:
☐ banned from public libraries.
☐ available in the library like any other book.
☐ Neither   ☐ Undecided

When businesses are allowed to make as much money as they can:
☐ everyone profits in the long run.
☐ workers and the poor are bound to get less.
☐ Neither   ☐ Undecided

Heavy press coverage of dramatic crimes like murders or terrorist incidents:
☐ only gives criminals free publicity and may encourage them to commit more crimes.
☐ provides the public with information that it has a right to know.
☐ Neither   ☐ Undecided

23/
When undercover police agents secretly join far right or far left political groups to keep an eye on them:
☐ they are only doing what is necessary to protect our society.
☐ they are violating the rights of the groups' members.
☐ Neither   ☐ Undecided

Please Be Sure You Have Answered Every Question
19

457

24/
Which of these comes closer to your own view?
₁□ The government has no right to decide what should or should not be published.
₂□ To protect its moral values, a society sometimes has to forbid certain things from being published.
₃□ Neither   ₅□ Undecided

When a young woman joins an "offbeat" cult like the Moonies or Hare Krishnas, should her parents have the legal right to force her to leave the group and be "deprogrammed"?
□ No, because that would take away her individual freedom to practice any religion she chooses.
□ Yes, because parents have the right and duty to protect their children from influences they consider harmful.
□ Neither   □ Undecided

26/
Suppose a majority of voters elected a congressman who advocates the use of violence against certain minorities. Should he be allowed to take office?
□ Yes, because we have to stand by what the majority decides.
□ No, because such a person is unfit to hold Congressional office.
□ Neither   □ Undecided

People who demonstrate against laws they consider unjust by lying down in the streets and blocking traffic:
□ deserve credit for being willing to act on their ideals.
□ are just lawbreakers and should be treated as such.
□ Neither   □ Undecided

28/
When authorities have reason to believe that a political demonstration will become violent, they should:
□ seek a court order to stop the demonstration.
□ keep an eye on the demonstration but allow it to be held.
□ Neither   □ Undecided

Giving everyone accused of a crime a qualified lawyer even if the government has to pay for it:
□ is absolutely necessary to protect individual rights.
□ is wasteful and goes beyond the requirements of justice.
□ Neither   □ Undecided

30/
Should a political protest group be granted a permit to hold a parade that blocks midtown traffic for two hours?
□ Yes, and if necessary the city should redirect traffic to protect the group's right to parade.
□ No, because the right to assemble should not keep other people from going about their business.
□ Neither   □ Undecided

31/
Which of these comes closer to your own opinion?
□ Any person who is able to work should not be allowed to receive welfare.
□ No American family should be allowed to live in poverty, even if they don't work.
□ Neither   □ Undecided

The Postmaster General should have:
□ the right to prohibit the mailing of obscene books or magazines.
□ no right to decide what kind of books or magazines can be sent through the mails.
□ Neither   □ Undecided

Most young people who "drop out" or become "hippies":
□ are lazy, spoiled, and don't want to work.
□ are trying to tell us something important about what's wrong with our society.
□ Neither   □ Undecided

34/
Homosexuals should be understood as people who:
□ are sick and need help.
□ have simply chosen a different sexual life style.
□ Neither   □ Undecided

Under American law, if a person is found innocent of a crime, but new evidence is later uncovered which shows he was guilty:
□ he can be retried, and the new evidence introduced.
□ since a person found innocent once cannot be tried again for the same crime, the innocent verdict can never be reversed.
□ Neither   □ Undecided

The Fifth Amendment to the American Constitution mainly guarantees citizens:
□ protection against forced confessions.
□ freedom of speech.
□ Neither   □ Undecided

In dealing with people imprisoned for crime, it is better to:
□ try to rehabilitate them and return them to normal life.
□ punish them for the wrongs they have done.
□ Neither   □ Undecided

38/
Should students have the right to inspect all records and letters of recommendation in their school files?
□ Yes, to make sure the information in them is correct.
□ No, because otherwise the people who write the letters may not say what they really think.
□ Neither   □ Undecided

Please Be Sure You Have Answered Every Question
20

458

39/

If some people can't afford good housing:

1 ☐ they should work harder and save, until they can afford it.

2 ☐ the government should provide it.

3 ☐ Neither   5 ☐ Undecided

Do you think the government should keep a steady watch on people it believes may commit serious crimes, terrorist acts, or hijackings?

☐ Yes, because it may prevent innocent people from being hurt or killed.

☐ No, because it would violate the privacy of individuals who have not yet committed any crime.

☐ Neither   ☐ Undecided

Censoring obscene books:

☐ is necessary to protect community standards.

☐ is an old-fashioned idea that no longer makes sense.

☐ Neither   ☐ Undecided

42/

Should foreigners who dislike our government and criticize it be allowed to visit or study here?

☐ Yes.

☐ No.

☐ Neither   ☐ Undecided

If people get into trouble because of their unusual opinions about politics, religion, or sex:

☐ they have only themselves to blame.

☐ it may be our fault for not being more tolerant.

☐ Neither   ☐ Undecided

Medical research which treats some people with a promising new drug and withholds it from others for the sake of testing the drug is:

☐ unethical.

☐ an acceptable procedure, if the subjects are aware of the risk and consent to the experiment.

☐ Neither   ☐ Undecided

Which do you believe?

☐ All but the most hardened criminals could be rehabilitated if society would only make the effort.

☐ Very few criminals can be turned into good citizens no matter what we do.

☐ Neither   ☐ Undecided

46/

Birth control devices:

☐ should be available to teenagers if they want them.

☐ should be kept from teenagers since they are too young to handle sexual matters sensibly.

☐ Neither   ☐ Undecided

47/

Should lesbian mothers be allowed to have custody of their own children?

☐ Yes, because a child is usually better off with its own mother.

☐ No, because a lesbian household is unnatural and unhealthy for a child.

☐ Neither   ☐ Undecided

The death penalty is:

☐ a proper and necessary punishment for criminals who have committed horrible crimes, such as premeditated murder.

☐ morally wrong, doesn't really prevent crime, and should be abolished.

☐ Neither   ☐ Undecided

When a community pays a teacher's salary, it:

☐ doesn't buy the right to censor the opinions she expresses in the classroom.

☐ has the right to keep her from teaching ideas that go against the community's standards.

☐ Neither   ☐ Undecided

50/

When applying for a job, a person's prison record:

☐ should be made available to potential employers since they are taking a risk.

☐ should be kept confidential since the ex-convict deserves a chance to make a fresh start.

☐ Neither   ☐ Undecided

When women aren't given the same chance as men in job hiring, it is usually because:

☐ they are less qualified than men for the job.

☐ the employers still have old-fashioned and mistaken ideas about the kinds of things women can and should do.

☐ Neither   ☐ Undecided

Protesters who mock the President by wearing death masks at one of his public speeches:

☐ should be removed from the audience by the police.

☐ should have the right to appear in any kind of costume they want.

☐ Neither   ☐ Undecided

53/

If a group wanted to hold a protest demonstration in front of the city jail, would city officials be justified in banning it?

☐ Yes, because it might stir up the prisoners.

☐ No, because the protesters should be able to assemble wherever they believe it would be most effective.

☐ Neither   ☐ Undecided

Please Be Sure You Have Answered Every Question

54/

Suppose the majority gets a law passed making homosexuality a crime. Should homosexuals be fined or arrested?

1 ☐ **No,** because a person's sexual preference is a private matter, beyond the majority's wishes.

2 ☐ **Yes,** because the voting majority has the right to decide the kind of society it wants.

3 ☐ Neither   5 ☐ Undecided

The Bill of Rights in the American Constitution mainly:
☐ protects certain rights and liberties of citizens from being violated by government.
☐ describes the rights of Congress, the President, and the courts.
☐ Neither   ☐ Undecided

When I'm asked to vote on school bonds and other community services which will raise my taxes:
☐ I must admit I'm likely to vote against them if I don't benefit directly from them.
☐ I usually vote for them even if it hurts.
☐ Neither   ☐ Undecided

57/

If it is discovered that an elementary school teacher is a lesbian:
☐ she should not be allowed to continue teaching.
☐ she should be able to go on teaching because sexual preference should not be a ground for dismissal.
☐ Neither   ☐ Undecided

When a product is in short supply or rationed, as gasoline was for a time:
☐ it upsets me when people buy more than they need to keep from running short.
☐ it's only human and sensible for a person to look out for himself and stock up on extras if he can.
☐ Neither   ☐ Undecided

A radio or TV station that always speaks for one political group and against others:
☐ should be required by law to present a more balanced view.
☐ should have the right to support or oppose any group it chooses.
☐ Neither   ☐ Undecided

60/

People with extreme political ideas who want to work as newspaper or TV reporters:
☐ should not be hired for such jobs because they can't be trusted to report the news fairly.
☐ should have the same chance as any other Americans to work as reporters.
☐ Neither   ☐ Undecided

61/

Tapping telephones with a legal warrant:
☐ still violates personal privacy and should be outlawed by Congress.
☐ can be justified when used against known criminals suspected of planning new crimes.
☐ Neither   ☐ Undecided

Selling pornographic films, books, and magazines:
☐ is really a victimless crime and should therefore be left unregulated.
☐ lowers the community's moral standards and therefore victimizes everyone.
☐ Neither   ☐ Undecided

Laws requiring employers to give special preference to women when filling jobs:
☐ are only fair, considering how often they have been discriminated against in the past.
☐ are unfair to men who may be more qualified.
☐ Neither   ☐ Undecided

64/

When inviting guest speakers to a college campus:
☐ students should be free to invite anyone they want to hear.
☐ the speakers should be screened beforehand to be sure they don't advocate dangerous or extreme ideas.
☐ Neither   ☐ Undecided

To gain profit or personal advantage, people:
☐ will often use unfair tactics if they can get away with it.
☐ will usually try to go by the rules and play fair.
☐ Neither   ☐ Undecided

The way property is used should mainly be decided:
☐ by the individuals who own it.
☐ by the community, since the earth belongs to everybody.
☐ Neither   ☐ Undecided

Under the American Constitution:
☐ Congress can make any law it wants to, as long as the President also approves.
☐ Congress can make laws regulating certain things but not others.
☐ Neither   ☐ Undecided

68/

When police catch a violent gangster, they should:
☐ be allowed to be a bit rough with him if he refuses to give them the information they need to solve a crime.
☐ treat him humanely, just as they should treat everyone they arrest.
☐ Neither   ☐ Undecided

Please Be Sure You Have Answered Every Question

22

460

9/
If the leaders of organized crime meet in a private home or office to discuss their criminal activities:
1 ☐ the police should be able to "bug" their meeting place to collect evidence against them.
2 ☐ they should be free to hold such a meeting without interference.
3 ☐ Neither   5 ☐ Undecided

Our laws should aim to:
☐ enforce the community's standards of right and wrong.
☐ protect a citizen's right to live by any moral standard he chooses.
☐ Neither   ☐ Undecided

An individual recently sued a newspaper that reported that he was "gay," a fact he had never wanted to reveal publicly. If you were on the jury, would you favor awarding him monetary damages?
☐ Yes, because the newspaper invaded his privacy, even if its report was accurate.
☐ No, because newspapers should be able to publish any information that is true.
☐ Neither   ☐ Undecided

12/
Most of the things that go wrong in the world can be blamed on:
☐ the way society is organized.
☐ human nature.
☐ Neither   ☐ Undecided

Keeping people in prison for long periods of time before bringing them to trial:
☐ should not be allowed, no matter what the crime.
☐ is sometimes necessary when dealing with people who have long and dangerous criminal records.
☐ Neither   ☐ Undecided

Should government authorities be allowed to open the mail of people suspected of being in contact with fugitives?
☐ Yes, as it may help the police catch criminals they have been looking for.
☐ No, it would violate a person's right to correspond with his friends.
☐ Neither   ☐ Undecided

15/
When a pregnant woman wants a leave of absence from her job following the birth of her baby:
☐ her employer should be required to give her sick leave with benefits.
☐ she should have to give up her job if asked.
☐ Neither   ☐ Undecided

16/
Refusing to hire a professor because of his unusual political beliefs:
☐ is never justified.
☐ may be necessary if his views are really extreme.
☐ Neither   ☐ Undecided

When it comes to pornographic films about sex:
☐ people should be allowed to see anything they want to, no matter how "filthy" it is.
☐ the community should set the standards for what people are allowed to see.
☐ Neither   ☐ Undecided

In trying to help needy people to improve their lives, the government:
☐ has not done enough.
☐ has already done more than it should.
☐ Neither   ☐ Undecided

Forcing people to testify against themselves in court:
☐ may be necessary when they are accused of very brutal crimes.
☐ is never justified, no matter now terrible the crime.
☐ Neither   ☐ Undecided

20/
The U.S. never joined the Common Market because:
☐ it was designed to include European countries only.
☐ the U.S. didn't want to give up its independence.
☐ Neither   ☐ Undecided

A newspaper should be allowed to publish its opinions:
☐ only if it doesn't twist the facts and tell lies.
☐ no matter how false and twisted its facts are.
☐ Neither   ☐ Undecided

22/
Refusing to hire a professor because he believes certain races are inferior:
☐ may be necessary if his views are really extreme.
☐ cannot be justified.
☐ Neither   ☐ Undecided

If a society had to choose between making progress and keeping things stable and orderly, which should it choose?
☐ Making progress.
☐ Keeping things orderly.
☐ Neither   ☐ Undecided

24/
Whom do you admire more?
☐ People who go their own way without worrying about what others think.
☐ People who learn to fit in and get along with others.
☐ Neither   ☐ Undecided

Please Be Sure You Have Answered Every Question
Please Go On To The Last Page
23

25/
If there were a major flood in your area, and you knew your family was safe, what (in all honesty) would your first concern be?

1 ☐ To save your own house and property.
2 ☐ To help other flood victims in any way you could.
3 ☐ Neither   5 ☐ Undecided

In the matter of jobs and standards of living, the government should:
☐ see to it that everyone has a job and a decent standard of living.
☐ let each person get ahead on his own.
☐ Neither   ☐ Undecided

Many employers refuse to hire the handicapped even for jobs they are able to perform well. Should laws be passed that would punish employers who do this?
☐ Yes.
☐ No.
☐ Neither   ☐ Undecided

28/
Regulation or control of government-financed research carried on at universities is:
☐ justified because some of the research may be dangerous.
☐ unjustified because government has no right to meddle in university affairs.
☐ Neither   ☐ Undecided

The "fairness doctrine" of the FCC (Federal Communications Commission) was intended to make sure:
☐ that both sides on controversial political issues can be heard on radio and television.
☐ that newspapers print the truth.
☐ Neither   ☐ Undecided

The idea that little girls should play with dolls and boys with trucks or trains:
☐ is an old-fashioned idea that makes no sense in today's world.
☐ is still a good idea to help remind boys and girls that they have different roles in life.
☐ Neither   ☐ Undecided

31/
The use of computers by the government to maintain central records on the health, employment, housing, and income of private citizens:
☐ is dangerous to individual liberty and privacy and should be forbidden by law.
☐ would help the government fight organized crime and provide emergency assistance and other services to people who need them.
☐ Neither   ☐ Undecided

32/
People who disobey a law they believe to be particularly cruel or unjust:
☐ are disloyal Americans who want to harm this country.
☐ often love America deeply and want it to live up to its ideals.
☐ Neither   ☐ Undecided

The use of prisoners for medical experiments should be:
☐ permitted, as long as the prisoners give their consent.
☐ forbidden, because prisoners might feel they *have* to cooperate in order to be treated better.
☐ Neither   ☐ Undecided

The best way to improve our society is:
☐ to follow an overall program or theory.
☐ to allow changes to develop naturally, by themselves.
☐ Neither   ☐ Undecided

When a TV station reports secret information illegally taken from a government office:
☐ it's just doing its job of informing the public.
☐ the station owners should be fined or punished in some way for reporting such information.
☐ Neither   ☐ Undecided

36/
On the whole, most people:
☐ will act fairly and considerately most of the time.
☐ will show little consideration for the rights of others when it costs them something.
☐ Neither   ☐ Undecided

Should demonstrators be allowed to hold a mass protest march for some unpopular cause?
☐ No, not if the majority is against it.
☐ Yes, even if most people in the community don't want it.
☐ Neither   ☐ Undecided

People who want to be liked better:
☐ should first try to get rid of their irritating faults.
☐ should be given every possible chance to show their worth.
☐ Neither   ☐ Undecided

39/
In order for the government to effectively prosecute the leaders of organized crime:
☐ it may sometimes have to bend the rules if there is no other way to convict them.
☐ it should stick strictly to the rules if the government wants other people to respect the law.
☐ Neither   ☐ Undecided

40-41/
Please Be Sure You Have Answered Every Question
Thank You For Your Cooperation.
24

9/

A person who holds a position of great responsibility such as a doctor, a judge, or an elected official:

₁ ☐ is entitled to be treated with special respect.

₂ ☐ should be treated the same as anyone else.

₃ ☐ Neither   ₅ ☐ Undecided

Democracy is a political system which mostly:

☐ caters to the average person and therefore encourages what is ordinary and second-rate rather than what is excellent.

☐ recognizes the special talents of each individual and tries to bring out his or her best qualities.

☐ Neither   ☐ Undecided

I believe:

☐ that the stars and planets have a definite influence on what happens to us.

☐ that astrology has no foundations in fact.

☐ Neither   ☐ Undecided

12/

In any great struggle to improve human conditions:

☐ we have to expect that some people will unfortunately be hurt.

☐ we must make sure that very few people, if any, will suffer.

☐ Neither   ☐ Undecided

Unskilled workers (such as janitors, dishwashers, and so on) usually receive wages that are:

☐ much too low for the dirty work they do.

☐ about right, considering the amount of skill required.

☐ Neither   ☐ Undecided

14/

The struggle for any great cause requires:

☐ that the decisions of the movement and its leaders be obeyed without question.

☐ that all decisions be made with the free and democratic consent of the rank and file.

☐ Neither   ☐ Undecided

When I'm having a bad argument with someone:

☐ I must admit I sometimes feel like hitting them or throwing something.

☐ I'm rarely angry enough to want to do physical harm to them.

☐ Neither   ☐ Undecided

16/

The major political parties in this country are mainly run for the benefit of:

☐ the majority of the people.

☐ certain special interest groups.

☐ Neither   ☐ Undecided

17/

"Most people from certain backgrounds can't get ahead in this country no matter how hard they try." Do you believe this statement is mostly true or mostly false?

☐ Mostly true.

☐ Mostly false.

☐ Neither   ☐ Undecided

Our system of government:

☐ is about as efficient as we have a right to expect.

☐ is highly inefficient and wasteful.

☐ Neither   ☐ Undecided

The use of federal agents to spy on radical organizations:

☐ is vital to national security and the fight against Communism.

☐ is a waste of time and money, since radicals in this country are too weak to do much harm anyway.

☐ Neither   ☐ Undecided

I must admit, when people take advantage of me:

☐ I try to think of ways to pay them back.

☐ I just try to forget it.

☐ Neither   ☐ Undecided

21/

Most public officials:

☐ sincerely try to serve the people's interests.

☐ are mainly out for themselves.

☐ Neither   ☐ Undecided

The urge to do something mean or hurtful to someone:

☐ comes over me at times.

☐ rarely enters my mind.

☐ Neither   ☐ Undecided

The average person who goes to a government official with a problem:

☐ can expect a fair hearing.

☐ is likely to get the "run around".

☐ Neither   ☐ Undecided

The Americans who put this country down:

☐ forget how well it compares to other countries.

☐ are realists who refuse to kid themselves about its faults.

☐ Neither   ☐ Undecided

25/

Elections:

☐ are mostly a waste of time and money, since the same people run things anyway.

☐ are one of the best ways to keep elected officials on their toes.

☐ Neither   ☐ Undecided

Please Be Sure You Have Answered Every Question

1

26/
"What most people really need, but are ashamed to admit, is a government controlled by a small group of strong and inspired leaders who will give the country order and a clear purpose." Do you think this statement is mostly correct or incorrect?

₁☐ Mostly correct.
₂☐ Mostly incorrect.
    ₃☐ Neither   ₅☐ Undecided

Compared to most other people:
☐ I seem to get angry more often, even if I don't always show it.
☐ I don't get angry very often.
    ☐ Neither   ☐ Undecided

Workers and management:
☐ have conflicting interests and are natural enemies.
☐ share the same basic interests in the long run.
    ☐ Neither   ☐ Undecided

29/
Private ownership of property:
☐ is as important to a good society as freedom.
☐ has often done mankind more harm than good.
    ☐ Neither   ☐ Undecided

Giving everybody about the same income regardless of the type of work they do:
☐ would be a fairer way to distribute the country's wealth than the present system.
☐ would destroy the desire to work hard and do a better job.
    ☐ Neither   ☐ Undecided

The profit system:
☐ often brings out the worst in human nature.
☐ usually teaches people the value of hard work and personal achievement.
    ☐ Neither   ☐ Undecided

32/
The best hope for the future of mankind lies in:
☐ science and human reason.
☐ faith in God and religion.
    ☐ Neither   ☐ Undecided

As a political system, Communism:
☐ is so evil we should go to any lengths to destroy it.
☐ has become so well established that we must learn to get along with it.
    ☐ Neither   ☐ Undecided

34/
In the American court system:
☐ almost every citizen can expect an equally fair trial.
☐ a rich person usually gets treated better than a poor person.
    ☐ Neither   ☐ Undecided

35/
The right to trial by jury:
☐ is overrated because juries can so often be swayed by a clever lawyer.
☐ is still the best way for someone accused of a crime to receive a fair judgment.
    ☐ Neither   ☐ Undecided

Suppose the President and Congress had to violate a constitutional principle to pass an important law the people wanted. Would you support them in this action?
☐ Yes, because the Constitution shouldn't be allowed to stand in the way of what the people need and want.
☐ No, because protecting the Constitution is more important to the national welfare than any law could possibly be.
    ☐ Neither   ☐ Undecided

37/
Do you think you would be better off if you read more books?
☐ Yes, because I would know more.
☐ Probably not, since books don't help you much with real-life problems.
    ☐ Neither   ☐ Undecided

All groups can live in harmony in this country:
☐ only if big changes are made in the system.
☐ without changing the system very much.
    ☐ Neither   ☐ Undecided

Most of the really important decisions in this country are made:
☐ out in the open, where public opinion can judge them.
☐ behind the scenes, by people we've never even heard of.
    ☐ Neither   ☐ Undecided

When I think about the American political system:
☐ I feel pretty much like an outsider.
☐ I feel that I'm really part of it, even if I don't always participate directly.
    ☐ Neither   ☐ Undecided

41/
What kind of people do we need most in positions of government leadership?
☐ Practical people with lots of experience who know how to run things.
☐ People who read books and have lots of ideas and theories.
    ☐ Neither   ☐ Undecided

Please Be Sure You Have Answered Every Question

2

464

42/

The free enterprise system:

1 ☐ survives by keeping the poor down.

2 ☐ gives everyone a fair chance.

3 ☐ Neither   5 ☐ Undecided

The idea that everyone is "created equal" is an important American principle which:

☐ the American people and their government sincerely try to put into practice.

☐ is rarely carried out in practice.

☐ Neither   ☐ Undecided

Which of these opinions about equality comes closer to what you believe?

☐ No matter how we treat everyone, some people will turn out to be better than others.

☐ If we really gave every person an equal chance, almost all of them would turn out to be equally worthwhile.

☐ Neither   ☐ Undecided

45/

When two people are arrested, one a habitual criminal and the other a citizen never before in trouble with the law, would the police be justified in treating them differently when arresting and booking them?

☐ Yes, because there is more chance the habitual criminal actually committed the crime, and he may also be dangerous.

☐ No, because everybody is entitled to the same treatment under the law no matter who they are.

☐ Neither   ☐ Undecided

When a government is in the early stages of creating a new society:

☐ the people must often be ruled with an iron hand for their own good.

☐ it can succeed only if the people themselves can participate in the decisions.

☐ Neither   ☐ Undecided

Whenever our government is slow to respond to the country's needs, it is usually because:

☐ it's hard to know what action would be best to take.

☐ the government isn't really concerned enough about the people's needs.

☐ Neither   ☐ Undecided

48/

Should people with more intelligence and character have greater influence over the country's decisions than other people?

☐ Yes, because they have more to offer and can do more to benefit the society.

☐ No, because every citizen must have an equal right to decide what's best for the country.

☐ Neither   ☐ Undecided

50/

The spread of Communism after World War II:

☐ was the fault of certain liberals and left-wing radicals who sold America out.

☐ was not caused by any American group in particular.

☐ Neither   ☐ Undecided

If adopted here, the main features of Communism:

☐ would greatly benefit the average person.

☐ would make things worse for most Americans.

☐ Neither   ☐ Undecided

When it comes to picking new friends:

☐ I find very few people I can bear to put up with.

☐ I am able to like many different kinds of people.

☐ Neither   ☐ Undecided

52/

In today's fast changing world:

☐ people have trouble deciding what are the right rules to follow.

☐ it's still pretty clear how a decent person is supposed to act.

☐ Neither   ☐ Undecided

The police:

☐ treat some groups unfairly.

☐ treat almost everyone fairly.

☐ Neither   ☐ Undecided

The best way to bring peace and order to the world would be:

☐ to make the U.S. the one really powerful nation on earth.

☐ to cooperate with all other nations to create an effective world peace organization.

☐ Neither   ☐ Undecided

55/

People who mostly talk about literature, art, philosophy, and such topics are:

☐ quite often boring to me.

☐ among the people who interest me most.

☐ Neither   ☐ Undecided

When it comes to friendship:

☐ things were better in the old days, when friendships lasted for a lifetime.

☐ it is just as easy today as it ever was to make friends and keep them.

☐ Neither   ☐ Undecided

57/

Competitive elections:

☐ may not be perfect, but no one has yet invented a better way to choose leaders in a free country.

☐ make little sense when you consider how little most voters really know.

☐ Neither   ☐ Undecided

Please Be Sure You Have Answered Every Question

3

465

58/

I believe that religion:

1 ☐ is still useful in answering some of today's problems.

2 ☐ is largely old-fashioned and out of date.

3 ☐ Neither   5 ☐ Undecided

Which of these comes closer to what you believe?

☐ There is little to be said in favor of war.

☐ War is cruel, but it does teach people something about honor, loyalty, and courage.

☐ Neither   ☐ Undecided

The best way to solve this country's problems and make life better for the American people is to:

☐ overturn the whole society from top to bottom.

☐ work within the system and try to reform it.

☐ Neither   ☐ Undecided

61/

I believe:

☐ there is more to spiritualism than people like to admit.

☐ people who try to contact "spirits" are only being conned.

☐ Neither   ☐ Undecided

Our schools should give more attention to:

☐ patriotic subjects.

☐ the injustices against the poor and the oppressed.

☐ Neither   ☐ Undecided

In the days when everyone knew just exactly how he was expected to act:

☐ people were better off.

☐ people were not as well off as they are today when they are free to live pretty much as they please.

☐ Neither   ☐ Undecided

64/

Who should be allowed to vote?

☐ Only people who know something about the issues.

☐ All adult citizens, regardless of how ignorant they may be.

☐ Neither   ☐ Undecided

The land of this country should be:

☐ turned over to the people.

☐ left in the hands of private owners.

☐ Neither   ☐ Undecided

66/

How often do you trust the government to do the right thing?

☐ Most of the time.

☐ Only occasionally.

☐ Neither   ☐ Undecided

67/

The laws of this country:

☐ favor certain groups much more than others.

☐ try to benefit most Americans equally.

☐ Neither   ☐ Undecided

For the majority to pass taxes that fall most heavily on the few:

☐ is an abuse of the majority's power and should not be allowed.

☐ is an action the majority has a right to take if it wants to.

☐ Neither   ☐ Undecided

People are better off in countries where everyone:

☐ shares the same philosophy and works for the same set of goals.

☐ acts on what his own reason and conscience tell him to believe.

☐ Neither   ☐ Undecided

70/

Which would be fairer—to pay people wages according to:

☐ their economic needs?

☐ how hard they work?

☐ Neither   ☐ Undecided

Which of these values is it more important for our children to learn?

☐ Obedience and respect for authority.

☐ Personal independence and the habit of thinking for themselves.

☐ Neither   ☐ Undecided

Most businessmen:

☐ do important work and deserve high salaries.

☐ receive more income than they deserve.

☐ Neither   ☐ Undecided

In a democratic election, which candidates should have a right to be on the ballot?

☐ Only the candidates who actually believe in the ballot.

☐ All candidates, no matter what they think about the election system.

☐ Neither   ☐ Undecided

74/

Which of these opinions do you think is more correct?

☐ Like fine race horses, some classes of people are just naturally better than others.

☐ All people would be about the same if they were treated equally.

☐ Neither   ☐ Undecided

Please Be Sure You Have Answered Every Question

4

466

APPENDIX B

Civil Liberties Survey: Samples and Sampling Procedures

THE CLS study drew its data from the responses of three different samples. The first was a cross-section sample of the general population of adults from three hundred communities (or sampling units) across the nation; the second was an "elite" sample of community leaders (or "opinion leaders") who lived or worked in the same three hundred sampling units; and the third, also drawn from the same three hundred communities, was an "elite" sample of individuals engaged in certain aspects of law enforcement. All three samples were selected for us by the Gallup Organization, which was also responsible for distributing and explaining the questionnaires to the respondents in the general population sample.

The cross-section sample of the general population is an approximation of the adult civilian population (eighteen years and older) living in the United States at the time of the survey (it excludes persons in institutions such as prisons and hospitals). The sample design is that of a replicated probability sample, down to the block level in urban areas and to segments of townships in rural areas.

The number of adults in the general population selected to participate in the study was 3000, to whom Gallup interviewers distributed our questionnaire during the weeks of May 30 and June 13, 1978, in two surveys of 1500 members each. Since the questionnaires were complicated and lengthy (twenty-four pages each; see Appendix A) and were to be self-administered by the participants, the Gallup interviewers were required not only to deliver the questionnaire to respondents, but to explain to them the nature of the study and the task and to instruct them about the procedures to be followed for the completion and return of the questionnaire.

Each questionnaire was included in a "packet," which also contained a letter from the principal investigator designed to enlist the cooperation of the respondents; a stamped, self-addressed envelope to be used when returning the completed questionnaire; and (since the questionnaires were to be unsigned and anonymous), a signed postcard, to be mailed separately from the questionnaire, informing us that the respondent had completed and returned the questionnaire. The purpose of the postcard was the let us know who, up to then, had failed to respond, so that the nonrespondents might be contacted in a further effort to enlist their participation. (This postcard also provided an opportunity for the respondent to check a box requesting a report on the results of the study.)

Three follow-up procedures were employed to boost the rate of response. The first was a reminder postcard mailed during July and August to those who had not returned the signed postcard (and who were presumed, therefore, to be nonrespondents). The second was a large envelope, mailed to the nonrespondents in September, which contained a duplicate copy of the questionnaire, along with a second explanatory letter soliciting cooperation, another stamped, self-addressed envelope, and a new postcard for the respondent to sign and mail back when he or she had completed and returned the questionnaire. The final follow-up was a new letter from the principal investigator mailed in October and November to those individuals who, from the evidence of the postcard returns, had still not responded. (In some cases, personal letters and phone calls were also employed whenever any of the nonrespondents wrote or called to ask questions or express concern about the survey.)

The effect of having Gallup interviewers personally deliver and explain the questionnaire, and of utilizing the follow-up procedures just described, produced a return of 1993 questionnaires which, after completing our coding and "cleaning" operations, we considered to be completely usable—a response rate of approximately 66 percent.

The follow-up procedures for increasing the returns from the community leader and legal elite samples were largely similar to those utilized for the cross-section general population sample, but the initial procedures for identifying the elite samples and getting the questionnaires to them were somewhat different. In the case of the elite samples, the Gallup Organization, in keeping with our request, asked its interviewers in each of the three hundred sampling units to identify and solicit the (promised) participation of some ten people in the community (or if a small town, the environs of the community) who, by reason of their vocation, role, or public activities, could be regarded either as community leaders (or "opinion leaders") or as members of the law enforcement professions (the so-called legal elite).

In keeping with our request, each interviewer was instructed to supply the "names, addresses, phone numbers, organizational memberships, roles or vocations [of] at least three and preferably four members of the law enforcement professions, [while] the remaining six or seven [were to] be chosen from the other elite roles listed." The instructions also stressed the need for diversifying the elite samples, so that the respondents in each sampling unit would be drawn from a variety of roles, and no more than one person in an area was to be selected from a given category of activities.

The list of groups (or activities) from which the elite respondents were selected were as follows:

Legal Elites
> Criminal attorneys
> District attorneys
> Public defenders/Legal Aid attorneys
> Civil rights attorneys
> Judges (state or federal court preferred, but if unavailable, select local court judges)
> Sheriff or policeman (obtain those above the rank of patrolman, if possible)

Other Community or Opinion Leaders
> Mayor or city council member
> Officer of community service organization (for example, Kiwanis, Lions)
> Officer of fraternal organization (for example, Elks, Shriners, Eastern Star)
> Officer of patriotic or veterans' group (for example, American Legion, Veterans of Foreign Wars [VFW], Daughters of the American Revolution [DAR])

Trade union leaders or officials

Chamber of Commerce officials or other leaders in the business community

Officer of environmental protection group (for example, Sierra Club, Friends of the Earth, recycling groups)

Political party activist or leader from both major parties (for example, county chairman, precinct captain, convention delegate)

Leader, spokesman, or official of civil rights activist group (for example, Friends of the Farm Workers, ACLU, National Organization for Women, gay rights groups, NAACP, Southern Christian Leadership Conference)

Leader or officer of political action organization (for example, Common Cause, John Birch Society, Americans for Democratic Action [ADA], American Conservative Union [ACU], League of Women Voters)

A religious leader (for example, officer of Council of Churches or an influential clergyman of any denomination)

School officials (for example, superintendent, school board members, principal or vice principal)

Leader of a teachers' organization (for example, National Education Association [NEA], American Federation of Teachers [AFT])

An influential college administrator

An influential college professor

Leader of civic improvement organization (for example, neighborhood improvement or beautification organizations)

Leader of PTA and/or other parent action groups

An adult leader of the Scouts, YMCA, YWCA, Boys Club, Campfire Girls, and so forth

A newspaper editor or publisher

An influential working journalist

An especially influential community leader, no matter what his or her organizational affiliation (specify his/her official role and criterion for selection)

Upon receipt of the lists of potential "elite" respondents identified and contacted by the Gallup interviewers, questionnaires identical with those fashioned for the general population survey were mailed to each person listed, along with an explanatory letter (appropriately worded to take account of the activities of the elite respondents and the manner of their selection); a postcard to be signed and mailed back by the respondent upon completing and returning the questionnaire; and a stamped, self-addressed envelope in which to return the questionnaire. The mailing of the questionnaires to the elite respondents, and the three follow-up communications (which essentially paralleled those employed in the cross-section survey of the general public) occurred at approximately the same points in time as the procedures utilized in the cross-section survey.

The number of completed questionnaires returned by elite respondents that were considered (after appropriate screening) as usable was 1157 for the community leaders and 734 for the legal elite—a total of 1891, or a return for the combined elite samples of over 68 percent. We have no way of knowing, of course, the extent of the bias in these returns, especially since there is no known universe of "elites" or "opinion leaders" with whom to compare our respondents, and no economically feasible way of identifying and surveying any such universe of elites. We believe, however, that we have overcome or at least tempered this problem by drawing our samples from so many categories of opinion leaders residing in so many communities of varied characteristics across the country. We consider it reasonable, therefore, to treat them, for research purposes, as an appropriate representation of opinion leaders at the community level throughout the United States.

As for the possible biasing of the results because of the nonrespondents, we have no reason to believe that any such biases, at least in the case of the elite samples, are systematic, or that they seriously distort the results. The questions contained in the survey, as the reader can easily determine by examining the questionnaire, are so varied, cut across so many different topics, and offer so many different points of view, that we have no reason to think that the content of the questionnaire would have systematically turned off certain classes of potential respondents and led them to refuse to fill out the questionnaire. Examination of the questionnaire's contents, in short, provides no reason to expect that the absence of the nonrespondents biases the results in any way that would alter the conclusions of this study.

Furthermore, in a study conducted earlier by the senior investigator that employed a similar set of survey procedures and a lengthy questionnaire similarly varied in content (the PAB survey), a careful comparison was made between the responses of the members of the elite sample who returned their completed questionnaires early (almost immediately after receiving them) and those who returned them months later, only after repeated proddings. The comparison of the answers of the early and late respondents on question after question revealed only negligible differences, leading us to conclude that further heroic efforts to induce the remaining nonrespondents to complete and return their questionnaires would have had no appreciable effect on the results.

There is, however, an element of bias in the configuration of the general population sample, since the proportion of nonrespondents in this case is substantially higher among those segments with less education and lower status than it is among those with more education and higher status—a feature of the sample we fully expected in light of the length and complexity of the questionnaire. The tendency to underrepresent those of little education and low socioeconomic status is, of course, characteristic of most if not all general population surveys, but is no less troublesome for that reason.

Some investigators have tried to correct this deficiency in the representativeness of the sample by weighting the various subsamples so that the demographic characteristics of the total sample appear to resemble the total population as described by the census returns. We have chosen, however, not to employ this procedure, since, *in effect*, it amounts to the invention of respondents who exist only hypothetically but to whom opinions and attitudes are nevertheless attributed because these hypothetical individuals resemble, in their social characteristics, certain individuals already in the sample. While there are doubtless benefits in utilizing a weighting procedure, there are also costs, and investigators do not wholly agree whether the benefits exceed the costs, or the reverse. In any event, we chose, rightly or wrongly, not to use a weighting procedure to correct for the absence of the nonrespondents. However, we might observe that the underrepresentation of those with low education and status, though biasing the results for certain parts of the analysis, does not bias them in a direction that favors the conclusions of the study. On the contrary, the bias in the general population sample works against certain of our hypotheses, especially those relating to the comparisons between the responses of the elite samples and the mass public. We have, in short, reason to believe that a more perfectly representative general population sample would have made a number of our conclusions in the study even stronger.

One final aspect of the procedures relating to the questionnaires and the samples ought to be mentioned, namely, that while we have referred in these methodological comments to a single questionnaire, there were, in reality, two forms of the questionnaire, Form A and Form B, distributed to respondents at random and in equal numbers. The two forms were identical in all respects, except that four pages of Form B contained items that differed to some extent from the items on those pages in Form A. The point of using the two forms was to increase the number of explanatory items and scales that would be available to us for the analysis of the results. The use of the two forms accounts for the fact that the number of respondents reported in the tables of the book is, in some cases, approximately half of the total number of respondents in the study. On the occasions when this occurs, it simply means that the question happened to appear only in Form A or Form B, but not in both. For a list of the items that were substituted in Form B for a like number of items in Form A, see the questionnaire in Appendix A.

NOTE: In the figures throughout the book, the number of respondents (N) shown for a given column indicates the total number of people in the sample who were asked the question; however, the actual N fluctuates slightly from table to table because a few individuals failed for some reason to respond to one question or another. In checking our results, however, we have found that omitting the nonrespondents from the calculation has only a negligible effect on the distribution of responses reported in the tables. It seemed simpler and less confusing, therefore, to report the total sample size in each case.

APPENDIX C

Scale Construction

Multiple Regression Analysis

The multiple regression employed in the analysis of the elite and mass samples (discussed on pages 467–70) employs the following equation to estimate the tolerance scores in the mass sample:

(1) $Y = a + b_1E_1 + \ldots + b_4E_4 + b_5R_5 + b_6S_6 + b_7C_7 + \ldots b_9C_9 + b_{10}Re_{10} + \ldots + b_{12}Re_{12} + b_{13}A_{13} + b_{14}I_{14} + b_{15}P_{15} + e$

where Y is the estimated score on the fifty-two-item civil liberties scale* (which ranges from −52 to +52);

a is the intercept term (the "left out" categories of the nominal or dummy variables in the equation are college graduate, non-South, large city of over 250,000 residents, and "not at all" religious);

E_1 equals 1 if the respondent completed grade school and 0 otherwise;

E_2 equals 1 if the respondent attended but did not complete high school and 0 otherwise;

E_3 equals 1 if the respondent graduated from high school and 0 otherwise;

E_4 equals 1 if the respondent attended vocational school or attended but did not complete college and 0 otherwise;

R_5 equals 1 if the respondent lives in a southern state (Alabama, Arkansas, Delaware, Florida, Georgia, Kentucky, Louisiana, Maryland, Mississippi, North Carolina, Oklahoma, South Carolina, Tennessee, Texas, Virginia, West Virginia) and 0 otherwise;

---

*The regression analysis in Chapter 6 was originally prepared for a paper delivered to the 1980 annual meeting of the Western Political Science Association by Herbert McClosky and Dennis Chong entitled "The Learning of Civil Libertarian Norms Among Elites and the Mass Public." As such, it is based on an earlier, slightly shorter version of the final omnibus civil liberties scale used in the subsequent chapters of this book. A reanalysis of this appendix, using the longer omnibus scale, produced insignificant differences from the results reported here. These data are available upon request to the senior author.

S_6 equals 1 if the respondent is female and 0 otherwise;

C_7 equals 1 if the respondent lives in a rural town or farm (under 2500 residents) and 0 otherwise;

C_8 equals 1 if the respondent lives in a town or small city (under 50,000) and 0 otherwise;

C_9 equals 1 if the respondent lives in a medium-sized city (50,000–250,000) and 0 otherwise;

Re_{10} equals 1 if the respondent is "deeply religious" and 0 otherwise;

Re_{11} equals 1 if the respondent is "fairly religious" and 0 otherwise;

Re_{12} equals 1 if the respondent is "not very religious" and 0 otherwise;

A_{13} is the age of the respondent (fourteen categories);

I_{14} is the family income of the respondent (fifteen categories); and

P_{15} is the political participation score of the respondent (14 points).

The equation specified for the total elite sample is identical except that the terms for "grade school" and "some high school" levels of education (b_1E_1 and b_2E_2) are omitted because there are so few elites having such a background. Such cases as there are have been pooled together with the high school graduates. Both equations, it should be noted, contain a term for political participation, based on a seven-item scale measuring interest, discussion, voting, contacting public officials, working in a campaign, helping out on a community problem, and joining a political organization. The inclusion of this variable will permit comparisons to be made between elites and masses who participate to varying degrees but are otherwise alike demographically.

The results from these two regressions are presented in table A.1. Because of the number of independent variables, and the number of categories (or values) in each of them, potentially hundreds of elite-mass comparisons could be made. One could, for example, choose to compare elites who attended but did not complete college, live in a medium-sized city in the South, are between 30 and 40 years old, are not very religious or wealthy, and participate moderately in political affairs with their demographic counterparts in the general population. By varying the demographic combination each time, comparisons like this could be made repeatedly.

Happily, the analysis can follow a more parsimonious route because many (if not most) of the potential elite-mass comparisons are not substantively interesting, since they involve demographic combinations which are uncommon in the ranks of the elite. We have already noted that there are virtually no elite members in our sample with less than a complete high school education. It is, moreover, very unusual for a member of the elite to not have at least attended college (8%), to live in a rural town (10%), or to profess to being "not at all" religious (7%). On the other hand, the overwhelming majority of elite members are male (72%), have graduated from college (74%), and live outside the southern states (72%). It seems appropriate therefore to eschew elite-mass comparisons which match on obscure demographic combinations in favor of those which pair "typical" elites with their demographic twins among the mass.

The adjusted regression equation, which provided the basis for the data presented in figures 6.5–6.7, is specified as follows:

$$(2)\ Y = a + b_1E_1 + \ldots b_{15}P_{15} + b_{16}D_{16} + b_{17}D_{17} + b_{18}D_{18} + e$$

where Y is the estimated score on the civil liberties scale; a is the intercept term representing the same "left-out" categories as in equation (1) as well as "strong economic conservative"; E_1 to P_{15} are the same independent variables as in equation (1); D_{17} equals 1 if the respondent is a moderate economic conservative and 0 otherwise; D_{18} equals 1 if the respondent is a moderate economic liberal and 0 otherwise; D_{19} equals 1 if the respondent is a strong economic liberal and 0 otherwise; and e is the residual term.

Content and Validity of the Omnibus Civil Liberties Scale

The omnibus civil liberties scale in the CLS study is composed of nine subscales, each representing an analytically distinguishable dimension of civil liberties. The scale contains a total of sixty-nine survey items, all of them initially selected for their face content (or "face validity"). Each item offered the respondent a choice between a civil libertarian response that was for the most part sanctioned by the courts at the time it was asked and a plausible alternative that essentially denied civil liberties. We made every effort to vary the ideological content of the items—that is, to ask about the civil liberties of Nazis as well as Communists, racists as well as black militants, the right as well as the left.

As is usually the case with survey questions, individual items in the omnibus civil liberties scale, though designed to focus exclusively on issues of civil liberties, are inescapably multidimensional in the

TABLE A.1

Results from the Multiple Regression Analysis of the CLS "Combined Elite" and Mass Samples

	Elites		Mass Public	
	b	**Standard Error**	**b**	**Standard Error**
Grade school	——		−11.88	(1.65)
Some high school	——		−13.94	(1.33)
High school graduate	−15.19	(1.53)	−12.77	(1.02)
Vocational school or some college	−12.34	(1.10)	−5.35	(1.07)
Southern state	−2.24	(.90)	−1.47	(.84)
Female	1.91	(1.07)	−2.27	(.74)
Rural town or farm	−3.67	(1.48)	−5.44	(1.06)
Town or small city	−4.16	(.96)	−2.11	(.90)
Medium-sized city	−1.94	(1.18)	−.14	(1.05)
"Deeply religious"	−19.30	(1.76)	−19.97	(1.62)
"Fairly religious"	−15.61	(1.58)	−14.72	(1.45)
"Not very religious"	−6.59	(1.71)	−7.80	(1.58)
Age (14 categories)	−1.45	(.18)	−1.99	(.12)
Family income (15 categories)	.44	(.19)	.02	(.13)
Political participation (14 points)	.82	(.16)	.67	(.13)
Intercept	33.86		35.39	
Y (SD)	16.88	(20.28)	1.13	(19.53)
R	.52		.62	
R^2	.28		.38	
N	1849		1867	

NOTES: Because percentages have been rounded off, occasionally there will be disparities in totals (columns will not add up to 100 percent).

See the Preface to Research Findings (p. 25) and Appendix B for a description of the leader and mass public samples used in the PAB, CLS, and OVS studies: that is "Political Leaders," "Legal Elite," and so forth.

The CLS study was conducted in 1978–1979; the OVS in 1976–1977; and the PAB in 1958.

sense that they tap not only civil libertarian attitudes but other attitudes as well. For example, when respondents are asked whether a group of student protesters should be allowed to use the community auditorium, their response will be affected not only by their attitude toward the right to assemble and express grievances, but also by their attitude toward student protesters, toward order and tranquility, and toward the targets of student protest at the time the question is asked. Nevertheless, questions that are substantively challenging and controversial need to be used in a properly designed libertarian scale because we know from past research that while most Americans endorse many civil liberties in the abstract, they do not always support such liberties when they are applied to concrete situations. When asked if they support free speech, even those who would in practice deny it to many

TABLE A.2
CLS Study

		Equalitarianism	Change and Reform	Welfare State
Community Leaders	Equalitarianism	X	.45	.72
	Change and Reform		X	.46
	Welfare State			X
Legal Elite	Equalitarianism	X	.48	.75
	Change and Reform		X	.51
	Welfare State			X
Mass Public	Equalitarianism	X	.22	.55
	Change and Reform		X	.25
	Welfare State			X

NOTE: Pearson's *r*'s

people with whom they disagree will say that they do. In other words, items of a highly general or abstract nature often do not discriminate very well between respondents who genuinely *do* support civil liberties in most cases and those who do not.

Our method of dealing with the dilemma posed by the need to use items with concrete content was to include in the omnibus civil liberties scale a large number of items that vary widely in content, refer to a variety of target groups, and encompass many different circumstances in which political freedom and control are at issue. We believe that ideological preferences and other elements in the individual responses that are not directly related to attitudes about civil liberties as such will tend to cancel each other out if the number of items is large enough and their content is sufficiently diverse.

To confirm that the omnibus civil liberties scale *primarily* measures attitudes toward civil liberties, even though its individual items may also measure a number of other attitudes, we have factor analyzed the

TABLE A.3
OVS Study

		Equalitarianism	Change and Reform	Welfare State
Ideological Criterion Group	Equalitarianism	X	.80	.88
	Change and Reform		X	.84
	Welfare State			X
Opinion Leaders	Equalitarianism	X	.57	.73
	Change and Reform		X	.67
	Welfare State			X
General Population	Equalitarianism	X	.48	.63
	Change and Reform		X	.50
	Welfare State			X

NOTE: Pearson's *r*'s.

responses of both the opinion leaders and the mass public to the items in the scale. Though factor analysis has fallen into disrepute in many quarters as an exploratory device, it remains an appropriate method for confirming that a large group of questions tap a given attitude domain. Table A.4 contains a list of the subscales and items in the omnibus civil liberties scale and shows their loadings on the unrotated first factor analysis.

As can be seen in the table, all the items as scored by both samples load positively on the first factor, the majority of them with loadings above .4, and many substantially higher. The factor loadings for the subscales, as we had expected, are higher still, most of them in the .7 or .8 range. The eigenvalues (table A.1) demonstrate that the first factor is overwhelmingly the most important, though other factors also make small contributions to the total scores. The results of the factor analysis, in other words, make it plain that the degree of coherence, unity, or "dimensionality" among the many libertarian items in the omnibus civil liberties scale is indeed high and that we can properly speak of those items as constituting a *scale* that yields a valid and trustworthy measure of a respondent's overall support for, or opposition to, civil liberties.

It should be noted that in scoring the omnibus civil liberties scale, we weighted each of the nine subscales equally, so as to neutralize the effects of the differences in the number of items used to construct each subscale. A respondent's score on the omnibus civil liberties scale was thus determined by adding the relative scores he or she received on each weighted subscale. In this way, a high score on, say, the freedom of assembly subscale (which had a large number of items) was given the same weight as a high score on the freedom of speech subscale (which had fewer items). In other words, we saw no reason to weight freedom of assembly more heavily than freedom of speech—in effect, to consider the right of assembly a more "important" civil liberty than the right of free speech—simply because more items happened to be available in the questionnaire to measure freedom of assembly.

A word might also be said about the validation of the omnibus civil liberties scale in the Opinions and Values Survey (OVS). Although the OVS study was not initially designed to focus on attitudes toward civil liberties, the survey questionnaire nevertheless contained a fair number of items that addressed civil liberties issues. From the total pool of 308 attitude items in the OVS questionnaire, we were able to select at least 35 items which, though diverse in content, primarily reflected orientation toward civil liberties and could be used to assess a respondent's overall attitude toward civil liberties.

A factor analysis of these 35 items was also computed for both the mass public and opinion leader samples. As it turned out, nearly two thirds of the factor loadings were above .4 and all but a few items loaded primarily on the first factor. The results, in short, were roughly comparable to those turned up in the analysis of the omnibus scale of the CLS study.

*Factor Loadings on First Factor of Subscales
and Items in the Omnibus Civil Liberties Scale (CLS)*

	Factor Loadings on First Factor	
	Opinion Leaders	Mass Public
	(N=1157)	(N=1993)
Free Speech Subscale	**.75**	**.75**
Should foreigners who dislike our government and criticize it be allowed to visit or study here? Yes/No.	.50	.50
Free speech should be granted: only to people who are willing to grant the same rights of free speech to everyone else/ to everyone regardless of how intolerant they are of other people's opinions.	.36	.29
Should groups like the Nazis and Ku Klux Klan be allowed to appear on public television to state their views? No, because they would offend certain racial or religious groups/ Yes, should be allowed no matter who is offended.	.56	.54
A group that wants to buy advertising space in a newspaper to advocate war against another country: should be turned down by the newspaper/should have as much right to buy advertising space as a group that favors world peace.	.45	.49
If the majority votes in a referendum to ban the public expression of certain opinions, should the majority opinion be followed? No, because free speech is a more fundamental right than majority rule/Yes, because no group has a greater right than the majority to decide which opinions can or cannot be expressed.	.46	.38
Free Press Subscale	**.83**	**.83**
Which of these comes closer to your own view? The government has no right to decide what should or should not be published/To protect its moral values, a society sometimes has to forbid certain things from being published.	.57	.49
A newspaper should be allowed to publish its opinions: only if it doesn't twist the facts and tell lies/no matter how false and twisted its facts are.	.51	.30
People with extreme political ideas who want to work as newspaper or TV reporters: should not be hired for such jobs because they can't be trusted to report the news fairly/ should have the same chance as any other Americans to work as reporters.	.31	.39

	Factor Loadings on First Factor	
	Opinion Leaders	**Mass Public**
	(N=1157)	(N=1993)
When a TV station reports secret information illegally taken from a government office: it's just doing its job of informing the public/the station owners should be fined or punished in some way for reporting such information.	.42	.22
A humor magazine which ridicules or makes fun of blacks, women, or other minority groups: should lose its mailing privileges/should have the same right as any other magazine to print what it wants.	.36	.48
Novels that describe explicit sex acts: have no place in a high school library and should be banned/should be permitted in the library if they are worthwhile literature.	.55	.54
Books that could show terrorists how to build bombs should be: banned from public libraries/available in the library like any other book.	.45	.48
The movie industry: should be free to make movies on any subject it chooses/should not be permitted to make movies that offend certain minorities or religious groups.	.49	.53
Censoring obscene books: is necessary to protect community standards/is an old-fashioned idea that no longer makes sense.	.58	.59
If the majority in a referendum votes to stop publication of newspapers that preach race hatred: such newspapers should be closed down/no one, not even the majority of voters, should have the right to close down a newspaper.	.48	.37
Symbolic Speech Subscale	**.76**	**.72**
A person who publicly burns or spits on the flag: should be fined or punished in some way/may be behaving badly but should not be punished for it by law.	.55	.47
The use of obscene gestures to express anger against a public official: is so rude it should be outlawed/should be considered a constitutionally protected form of free speech.	.57	.49
Protesters who mock the President by wearing death masks at one of his public speeches: should be removed from the audience by the police/should have the right to appear in any kind of costume they want.	.57	.60

	Factor Loadings on First Factor	
	Opinion Leaders (N=1157)	Mass Public (N=1993)
Freedom of Assembly Subscale	**.81**	**.80**
Should a civic auditorium be used by foreign radicals who want to express their hatred of America? Yes/No.	.71	.62
Should a civic auditorium be used by the Jewish Defense League (JDL) to advocate a war against certain Arab countries? Yes/No.	.69	.51
Should a civic auditorium be used by revolutionaries who advocate the violent overthrow of the American government? Yes/No.	.60	.50
Should a civic auditorium be used by right to life groups to preach against abortion? Yes/No.	.28	.20
Should a civic auditorium be used by the American Nazi party to preach race hatred against Jews and other minorities? Yes/No.	.69	.54
Should a civic auditorium be used by conservationists to protest the construction of a nuclear power plant? Yes/No.	.44	.36
Should a civic auditorium be used by student protesters who call for a sit-in at city hall to shut down the city's offices? Yes/No.	.65	.57
Should a civic auditorium be used by patriotic groups to advocate war against some foreign country? Yes/No.	.57	.41
Should a civic auditorium be used by the Palestine Liberation Organization (PLO) to attack Jews and call for the destruction of Israel? Yes/No.	.69	.56
When groups like the Nazis or other extreme groups require police protection at their rallies and marches, the community should: supply and pay for whatever police protection is needed/prohibit such groups from holding rallies because of the costs and dangers involved.	.63	.57
When authorities have reason to believe that a political demonstration will become violent, they should: seek a court order to stop the demonstration/keep an eye on the demonstration but allow it to be held.	.41	.43
If some students at a college want to form a "Campus Nazi Club": they should be allowed to do so/college officials should ban such clubs from campus.	.69	.62

483

	Factor Loadings on First Factor	
	Opinion Leaders	**Mass Public**
	(N=1157)	(N=1993)
If a political group known for its violent political activities wants to picket the White House: it should be granted police protection like any other group/it should be prevented from doing so because it might endanger the President.	.54	.56
Should a political protest group be granted a permit to hold a parade that blocks midtown traffic for two hours? Yes, and if necessary the city should redirect traffic to protect the group's right to parade/No, because the right to assemble should not keep other people from going about their business.	.34	.28
If a group wanted to hold a protest demonstration in front of the city jail, would city officials be justified in banning it? Yes, because it might stir up the prisoners/No, because the protesters should be able to assemble wherever they believe it would be most effective.	.48	.52
Mass student protest demonstrations: have no place on a college campus and the participating students should be punished/should be allowed by college officials as long as they are nonviolent.	.42	.44
Should demonstrators be allowed to hold a mass protest march for some unpopular cause? No, not if the majority is against it/Yes, even if most people in the community don't want it.	.56	.59
Academic Freedom Subscale	**.75**	**.70**
On issues of religion, morals, and politics, high school teachers have the right to express their opinions in class: even if they go against the community's most precious values and beliefs/only if those opinions do not offend the community's beliefs.	.43	.38
If a professor is suspected of spreading false ideas in his class, college officials: should send someone into his classes to check on him/should not interfere since it would violate his rights.	.48	.38
Refusing to hire a professor because he believes certain races are inferior: may be necessary if his views are really extreme/cannot be justified.	.32	.19
Refusing to hire a professor because of his unusual political beliefs: is never justified/may be necessary if his views are really extreme.	.54	.44

484

	Factor Loadings on First Factor	
	Opinion Leaders (N=1157)	**Mass Public** (N=1993)
When inviting guest speakers to a college campus: students should be free to invite anyone they want to hear/the speakers should be screened beforehand to be sure they don't advocate dangerous or extreme ideas.	.62	.62
Scientific research that might show women or minorities in a bad light: should be banned because the results might damage their self-respect/should be allowed because the goal of science is to discover the truth, whatever it may be.	.27	.24
Freedom of Religion Subscale	**.83**	**.77**
Should a civic auditorium be used by atheists who want to preach against God and religion? Yes/No.	.72	.68
The freedom of atheists to make fun of God and religion: should not be allowed in a public place where religious groups gather/should be legally protected no matter who might be offended.	.61	.61
Freedom to worship as one pleases: applies to all religious groups, regardless of how extreme their beliefs are/was never meant to apply to religious cults that the majority of people consider "strange," fanatical, or "weird."	.39	.35
When a young woman joins an "offbeat" cult like the Moonies or Hare Krishnas, should her parents have the legal right to force her to leave the group and be "deprogrammed"? No, because that would take away her individual freedom to practice any religion she chooses/Yes, because parents have the right and duty to protect their children from influences they consider harmful.	.52	.39
Due Process Subscale	**.67**	**.58**
All systems of justice make mistakes, but which do you think is worse? To convict an innocent person/To let a guilty person go free.	.29	.22
Once an arrested person says he wishes to remain silent, the authorities: should stop all further questioning at once/should keep asking questions to try to get the suspect to admit his crimes.	.26	.29
The "right to remain silent": is needed to protect individuals from the "third degree" and forced confessions/has harmed the country by giving criminals too much protection.	.46	.38

	Factor Loadings on First Factor	
	Opinion Leaders	**Mass Public**
	(N=1157)	(N=1993)
If a person is acquitted of a crime because the judge made a mistake in legal procedure during the trial: it is only fair that he be set free, even if the mistake was a small one/setting him free for this reason would be carrying legal technicalities too far.	.39	.14
If a person is found guilty of a crime by evidence gathered through illegal methods: he should be set free or granted a new trial/he should still be convicted if the evidence is really convincing and strong.	.45	.28
Forcing people to testify against themselves in court: may be necessary when they are accused of very brutal crimes/is never justified, no matter how terrible the crime.	.45	.37
In order for the government to effectively prosecute the leaders of organized crime: it may sometimes have to bend the rules if there is no other way to convict them/it should stick strictly to the rules if the government wants other people to respect the law.	.24	.16
In dealing with muggings and other serious street crimes, which is more important? To protect the rights of suspects/To stop such crimes and make the streets safe even if we sometimes have to violate the suspect's rights.	.48	.43
If someone is caught red-handed beating and robbing an older person on the street: it's just a waste of taxpayers' money to bother with the usual expensive trial/the suspect should still be entitled to a jury trial and all the usual legal protections.	.27	.24
Should rapists or child molesters be given the same sort of "fair trial" as other criminals? Yes, because the right to fair trial should not depend on the nature of the crime/No, because their crimes are so inhuman that they do not deserve the usual legal protections.	.25	.33
Keeping people in prison for long periods of time before bringing them to trial: should not be allowed, no matter what the crime/is sometimes necessary when dealing with people who have long and dangerous criminal records.	.24	.26
Giving everyone accused of a crime a qualified lawyer even if the government has to pay for it: is absolutely necessary to protect individual rights/is wasteful and goes beyond the requirements of justice.	.31	.25

	Factor Loadings on First Factor	
	Opinion Leaders (N=1157)	Mass Public (N=1993)
When police catch a violent gangster, they should: be allowed to be a bit rough with him if he refuses to give them the information they need to solve a crime/treat him humanely, just as they should treat everyone they arrest.	.28	.31
Privacy Subscale	**.55**	**.53**
The use of computers by the government to maintain central records on the health, employment, housing, and income of private citizens: is dangerous to individual liberty and privacy and should be forbidden by law/would help the government fight organized crime and provide emergency assistance and other services to people who need them.	.19	.16
Should government authorities be allowed to open the mail of people suspected of being in contact with fugitives? Yes, as it may help the police catch criminals they have been looking for/No, it would violate a person's right to correspond with his friends.	.41	.34
A student's high school and college records should be released by school officials: only with the consent of the student/to any government agencies or potential employers who ask to see them.	.20	.31
If a police officer stops a car for a traffic violation, he should: be allowed to search the car if he suspects it contains narcotics or stolen goods/be limited to dealing with the traffic violation and nothing else.	.42	36
If a patient tells his psychiatrist that he is planning to commit a serious crime, the psychiatrist should: report it to the police/remain silent because his first duty is to his patient.	.30	.23
Lifestyle Subscale	**.71**	**.69**
Should it be right to adopt laws which prevent "hippies" and "street people" from moving into the community? Yes/No.	.55	.51
The custom of a woman taking her husband's last name: should be the woman's personal decision/should be legally required because it prevents a lot of confusion.	.46	.45

	Factor Loadings on First Factor	
	Opinion Leaders	**Mass Public**
	(N=1157)	(N=1993)
Abortion during the early weeks of pregnancy should be: prohibited except in such extreme cases as rape, the risk of a deformed child, or danger to the mother's life/left entirely up to the woman.	.33	.33
For the most part, local ordinances that guarantee equal rights to homosexuals in such matters as jobs and housing: damage American moral standards/uphold the American idea of human rights for all.	.51	.48
Birth Control devices: should be available to teenagers if they want them/should be kept from teenagers since they are too young to handle sexual matters sensibly.	.37	.42
Suppose the majority gets a law passed making homosexuality a crime. Should homosexuals be fined or arrested? No, because a person's sexual preference is a private matter, beyond the majority's wishes/Yes, because the voting majority has the right to decide the kind of society it wants.	.43	.35

NOTE: In computing the factor analysis for the opinion leader sample, we chose to exclude the sample of lawyers and judges. Had we included them, the factor loadings shown in the table would, of course, have been even higher.

Bibliography

Abramson, Paul R. "Comments on Sullivan, Piereson, and Marcus." *American Political Science Review* 74 (September 1980): 780–81.

Alford, Robert R., and Scoble, Harry M. "Community Leadership, Education and Political Behavior." *American Sociological Review* 33 (February 1968): 259–72.

Amnesty International. *Amnesty International Report 1978.* London: Amnesty International Publications, 1979.

Amsterdam, Anthony G. "The Rights of Suspects." In *The Rights of Americans: What They Are—What They Should Be,* edited by Norman Dorsen. New York: Random House, 1970, pp. 433–50.

Appel, Brent. *Legal Memorandum on Due Process.* Personal communication, 1977.

Asch, S. E. "Effects of Group Pressure upon the Modification and Distortion of Judgments." In *Groups, Leadership and Men,* edited by Harold Guetzkow. Pittsburgh: Carnegie Press, 1951.

Barnum, David G. "Decision Making in a Constitutional Democracy: Public Opinion, Elite Behavior, and Public Policy in the Skokie Free Speech Controversy." *Journal of Politics* 44 (May 1982): 480–508.

Becker, Carl. *The Declaration of Independence: A Study in the History of Political Ideas.* New York: Harcourt, Brace, 1922.

Berelson, Bernard; Lazarsfeld, Paul F.; and McFee, William. *Voting.* Chicago: University of Chicago Press, 1954.

Berns, Walter. *Freedom, Virtue, and the First Amendment.* Baton Rouge,LA.: State University Press, 1957.

Bickel, Alexander M. *The Morality of Consent.* New Haven: Yale University Press, 1975.

Bostwick, Gary L. "A Taxonomy of Privacy: Repose, Sanctuary, and Intimate Decision." *California Law Review* 64 (December 1976): 1447–83.

——— . *Legal Memorandum on Privacy and Lifestyle.* Personal communication, 1977.

Bury, J. S. *A History of Freedom of Thought.* New York: Holt, 1913.

Casper, Jonathan. *The Politics of Civil Liberties.* New York: Harper & Row, 1972.

Center for the Study of Democratic Institutions. "The Douglas Convocation on the State of Individual Freedom." *Center Magazine,* March-April, 1979.

Chaffee, Zechariah, Jr. *Free Speech in the United States.* Cambridge, Mass.: Harvard University Press, 1941.

Chandler, Robert. *Public Opinion: Changing Attitudes on Contemporary Political and Social Issues.* CBS News Reference Book. New York: Bowker, 1972.

Comer, John, and Welch, Susan. "A Comparison of Elite and Mass Attitudes in a Local Community: A Test of Two Hypotheses." Paper presented at the annual meeting of the American Political Science Association, San Francisco, 1975.

Converse Philip E. "The Nature of Belief Systems in Mass Publics." In *Ideology and Discontent,* edited by David E. Apter. Glencoe, Ill.: Free Press, 1964.

——— . "Attitudes and Non-Attitudes: Continuation of a Dialogue." In *The Quantitive Analysis of Social Problems,* edited by Edward R. Tufte. Reading, Mass.: Addison-Wesley, 1970.

Cooper, Evelyn Christine. *Legal Memorandum on First Amendment Areas.* Personal communication, 1977.

Bibliography

Cowart, Richard A. *Legal Memorandum on the Restrictions and Qualifications of the Rights of Due Process*. Personal communication, 1977.

Dahl, Robert. *Who Governs?* New Haven: Yale University Press, 1961

Davis, James A. "Tolerance of Atheists and Communists in 1954 and 1972-73." In *A Survey-Metric Model of Social Change*. Unpublished manuscript.

——————. "Communism, Conformity, Cohorts and Categories: American Tolerance in 1954 and 1972-73." *American Journal of Sociology* 81 (November 1975): 491-513.

di Palma, Giuseppe, and McClosky, Herbert. "Personality and Conformity: The Learning of Political Attitudes." *American Political Science Review* 64 (December 1970): 1054-73.

Dorsen, Norman, ed. *The Rights of Americans: What They Are—What They Should Be*. New York: Random House, 1970.

Emerson, Thomas I. "Toward a General Theory of the First Amendment." *Yale Law Journal* 877 (1963):16. Also in *Freedom of Speech*, edited by Franklyn S. Haiman. Skokie, Ill.: National Textbook, 1976.

——————. *Toward a General Theory of the First Amendment*. New York: Vintage Books, 1967.

——————. *The System of Freedom of Expression*. New York: Vintage Books, 1970.

Erskine, Hazel. "The Polls: Freedom of Speech." *Public Opinion Quarterly* 34 (Fall 1970): 483-96.

——————. "The Polls. Government Information Policy." *Public Opinion Quarterly* 35 (Winter 1971-72): 636ff.

Erskine, Hazel, and Siegel, Richard L. "Civil Liberties and the American Public." *Journal of Social Issues* 31 (January 1975): 13-29.

Fellman, David. "Constitutional Rights of Association." In *Free Speech and Association: The Supreme Court and the First Amendment*, edited by Philip B. Kurland. Chicago: University of Chicago Press, 1975. pp. 23-83.

Festinger, Leon. "Social Psychology and Group Processes." In *Annual Review of Psychology, Vol. 6*, edited by C. P. Stone and Quinn McNemar. Stanford, Calif.: Annual Reviews, 1955.

Gaugler, Edward A., and Zalkind, Sheldon S. "Dimensions of Civil Liberties and Personality: Relationships for Measures of Tolerance and Complexity." *Journal of Social Issues* 31 (Spring 1975): 93-110.

Gibson, James L., and Bingham, Richard D. "Conditions of Commitment to Civil Liberties: Libertarian Behavior of American Elites." Paper presented at the annual meeting of the American Political Science Association, Washington, D.C., 1979.

——————. "On the Conceptualization and Measurement of Political Tolerance." *American Political Science Review* 76 (September 1982): 603-20.

Greenawalt, Kent. "The Right of Privacy." In *The Rights of Americans: What They Are—What They Should Be*, edited by Norman Dorsen. New York: Random House, 1971.

Haiman, Franklyn S. *Freedom of Speech*. Skokie, Ill.: National Textbook, 1976.

Harris, Louis, and Westin, Alan F. *The Dimensions of Privacy: A National Opinion Research Survey of Attitudes Toward Privacy*. Stevens Point, Wisc.: Sentry Insurance, 1979.

Hay, George. "An Essay on the Liberty of the Press, Respectfully Inscribed to the Republican Printers Throughout the United States." 1791. In *Freedom of Speech and Press in Early American History: Legacy of Suppression*, edited by Leonard Levy. New York: Harper & Row, 1963.

——————. "An Essay on the Liberty of the Press, Shewing, That the Requisition of Security for Good Behaviour from Libellers, is Perfectly Compatible with the Constitution and Laws of Virginia." 1803. In *Freedom of Speech and Press in Early American History: Legacy of Suppression*, edited by Leonard Levy. New York: Harper & Row, 1963.

Herring, Pendleton. *The Politics of Democracy*. New York: Rinehart, 1940.

Hirschkop, Philip J. "The Rights of Prisoners." In *The Rights of Americans: What They Are—What They Should Be*, edited by Norman Dorsen. New York: Random House, 1970.

Hyman, Herbert H., and Sheatsley, Paul B. "Trends in Public Opinion on Civil Liberties." *Journal of Social Issues* 9 (1953): 6-16.

————— . "The Current Status of American Public Opinion." In *Public Opinion and Propaganda*, edited by D. Katz. New York: Dryden Press, 1954.

Immerwahr, John. Letter to Editor Re: Sullivan, Piereson, and Marcus. *American Political Science Review* 74 (September 1980): 781–83.

Immerwahr, John; Johnson, Jean; and Doble, John. *The Speaker and the Listener: A Public Perspective on Freedom of Expression*. New York: Public Agenda Foundation, 1980.

Jackman, Robert W. "Political Elites, Mass Publics, and Support for Democratic Principles." *Journal of Politics* 34 (February 1972): 753–73.

————— . "Much Ado About Nothing." *Journal of Politics* 39 (February 1977): 185–92.

Jennings, M. Kent, and Niemi, Richard G. *Generations and Politics: A Panel Study of Young Adults and Their Parents*. Princeton: Princeton University Press, 1981.

Jordan, Wilbur Kitcher. *The Development of Religious Toleration in England*. 2 vols. 1932. Gloucester, Mass.: P. Smith, 1965.

Jukam, Thomas O. "Measurement of Political Tolerance and Support for Democratic Liberties." Paper presented at the annual meeting of the American Political Science Association, Washington, D.C., 1979.

Kalven, Harry, Jr. "The Problems of Privacy in the Year 2000." *Daedalus* 96 (Summer 1967): 876.

————— . "The *New York Times* Case: A Note on the Central Meaning of the First Amendment." In *Free Speech and Association: The Supreme Court and The First Amendment*, edited by Philip B. Kurland. Chicago: University of Chicago Press, 1975.

Key, V. O., Jr. "Public Opinion and the Decay of Democracy." *Virginia Quarterly Review* 37 (Autumn 1961a): 481–94.

————— . *Public Opinion and American Democracy*. New York: Knopf; 1961b.

Koller, Douglas B. "Belief in the Right to Question Church Teachings, 1958–71." *Social Forces* 58 (September 1979): 290–304.

Konvitz, Milton R. *A Century of Civil Rights*. New York: Columbia University Press, 1961.

Kurland, Philip B., ed. *Free Speech and Association: The Supreme Court and The First Amendment*. Chicago: University of Chicago Press, 1975.

Ladd, Everett C., and Lipset, Seymour M. *The Divided Academy: Professors and Politics*. New York: McGraw-Hill, 1975.

Lazarsfeld, Paul F., and Thielens, Wagner, Jr., *The Academic Mind*. With a field report by David Riesman. Glencoe, Ill.: Free Press, 1958.

Lerner, Henry, *Legal Memorandum on the Rights of Criminal Defendants*. Personal communication, 1977.

Levy, Leonard, ed. *Freedom of Speech and Press in Early American History: Legacy of Suppression*. New York: Harper & Row, 1963.

Lipset, Seymour M., and Raab, Earl. *The Politics of Unreason: Right-Wing Extremism in America, 1790–1970*. New York: Harper & Row, 1970.

Lister, Charles. "The Right to Control the Use of One's Body." In *The Rights of Americans: What They Are—What They Should Be*, edited by Norman Dorsen. New York: Random House, 1970.

Mack, Raymond W. "Do We Really Believe in the Bill of Rights?" *Social Problems* 3 (April 1956): 264–69.

Majority and Minority Reports on the Repeal of the Sedition Act, February 25, 1799. Text reprinted in *Freedom of Speech and Press in Early American History: Legacy of Suppression*, edited by Leonard Levy. New York: Harper & Row, 1963.

McClosky, Herbert. "The Fallacy of Absolute Majority Rule." *Journal of Politics* 11 (November 1949): 638–54.

————— . "Consensus and Ideology in American Politics." *American Political Science Review* 58 (1964): 361–82.

————— . "Attitude and Personality Correlates of Foreign Policy Orientation." Monograph in *Domestic Sources of Foreign Policy*, edited by James Rosenau, New York: Free Press, 1967.

————— . *Political Inquiry: The Nature and Uses of Survey Research*. New York: Macmillan, 1969.

Bibliography

McClosky, Herbert, and Chong, Dennis. "The Learning of Civil Libertarian Norms Among Elites and the Mass Public." Paper presented at the annual meeting of the Western Political Science Association, San Francisco, 1980.

McClosky, Herbert, and Schaar, John H. "Psychological Dimensions of Anomy." *American Sociological Review* 30 (February 1965): 14–40.

Meiklejohn, Alexander. *Free Speech and Its Relation to Self-Government.* New York: Harper, 1948a.

——————. *Political Freedom: The Constitutional Powers of the People.* New York: Harper, 1948b.

Mendelson, Wallace. *The American Constitution and the Judicial Process.* Homewood, Ill.: Dorsey Press, 1980.

Merton, Robert K. *Social Theory and Social Structure.* Enlarged edition. New York: Free Press, 1968.

Mill, John Stuart. *On Liberty.* New York: Penguin Books, 1974.

Milton, John. *Areopagitica.* Edited by George Sabine. New York: Appleton-Century-Crofts, 1951.

Morgan, Wendy. *Legal Memorandum on Homosexuality, Women, Divorce, and Family Life.* Personal communication, 1977.

Muller, Edward N.; Pesonen, Pertti; and Jukam, Thomas O. "Support for the Freedom of Assembly in Western Democracies." *European Journal of Political Research* 8 (1980): 265–88.

National Opinion Research Center. General Social Surveys. Reprinted in *Public Opinion* 3 (December-January 1980): 19–42.

Naylor, David T. *Dissent and Protest.* Rochelle Park, N.J.: Hayden, 1974.

Newcomb, Theodore M. *Personality and Social Change.* New York: Dryden Press, 1943.

Nunn, Clyde A.; Crockett, Harry J., Jr.; and Williams, J. Allen, Jr. *Tolerance for Noncomformity: A National Survey of Changing Commitment to Civil Liberties.* San Francisco: Jossey-Bass, 1978.

Nye, Russell B. *Fettered Freedom: Civil Liberties and the Slavery Controversy.* East Lansing: Michigan State College Press, 1949.

Ortega y Gasset, José. *The Revolt of The Masses.* New York: Norton, 1932.

Palmore, Erdman. "When Can Age, Period, and Cohort Be Separated?" *Social Forces* 57 (September 1978): 282–95.

Pers, Jessica. *Legal Memorandum on the Rights of Students and Teachers.* Personal communication, 1977.

Pfeffer, Leo. *Religious Freedom.* Skokie, Ill.: National Textbook, 1977.

Piereson, James; Sullivan, John; and Marcus, George. Reply to Paul R. Abramson and John Immerwahr. *American Political Science Review* 74 (1980): 783–84.

Prothro, J. and Grigg, C. "Fundamental Principles of Democracy: Bases of Agreement and Disagreement." *Journal of Politics* 22 (1960): 276–94.

Roche, John Pearson. "American Liberty: An Examination of the 'Tradition' of Freedom." In *Aspects of Liberty,* edited by Milton Konvitz and Clinton L. Rossiter. Ithaca: Cornell University Press, 1958.

Rothman, Rozann. "The First Amendment: Symbolic Import—Ambiguous Prescription." Paper presented at the annual meeting of the American Political Science Association, Chicago, 1976.

Rousseau, Jean Jacques. *The Social Contract.* Harmondsworth, Middlesex, England: Penguin Books, 1968.

Selvin, H. C., and Hagstrom, W. O. "Determinants of Support for Civil Liberties." *British Journal of Sociology* 11 (1960): 51–73.

Shapiro, Martin. *Freedom of Speech: The Supreme Court and Judicial Review.* Englewood Cliffs, N.J.: Prentice-Hall, 1966.

Sherif, Muzafer. "Group Influences upon the Formation of Norms and Attitudes." In *Readings in Social Psychology,* 3rd ed. edited by E. E. Maccoby, T. M. Newcomb, and E. L. Hartley, pp. 220–32. New York: Holt, 1958.

Simon, Rita J. *Public Opinion in America.* Chicago: Rand McNally, 1974.

Simon, Rita J., and Barnum, David. "Public Support for Civil Liberties in Israel and the U.S." *Research Annual* 1 (1978).

Sniderman, Paul. *Personality and Democratic Politics.* Berkeley: University of California Press, 1975.

Spinrad, William. *Civil Liberties.* Chicago: Quadrangle Books, 1970.

St. Peter, Louis; Williams, J. Allen, Jr.; and Johnson, David R. "Comments on Jackman's 'Political Elites, Mass Publics, and Support for Democratic Principles.'" *Journal of Politics,* 39 (1977): 176–84.

Steiber, Steven R. "The Influence of the Religious Factor on Civil and Sacred Tolerance, 1958–71." *Social Forces* 58 (March 1980): 811–32.

Stouffer, Samuel. *Communism, Conformity, and Civil Liberties.* New York: Doubleday, 1955.

Sullivan, John L.; Marcus, George E.; Piereson, James E.; and Feldman, Stanley. "The Development of Political Tolerance: The Impact of Social Class, Personality, and Cognition." *International Journal of Political Education* 2 (1978–79): 115–39.

————. "The Sources of Political Tolerance: A Multivariate Analysis." *American Political Science Review* 75 (1981): 92–105.

Sullivan, John L.; Piereson, James E.; and Marcus, George E. "An Alternative Conceptualization of Political Tolerance: Illusory Increases 1950s–1970s." *American Political Science Review* 73 (September 1979): 781–94.

————. *Political Tolerance and American Democracy.* Chicago: University of Chicago Press, 1982.

Thompson, John. *An Inquiry Concerning the Liberty and Licentiousness of the Press and the Uncontrollable Nature of the Human Mind.* In *Freedom of Speech and Press in Early American History: Legacy of Suppression,* edited by Leonard Levy. New York: Harper & Row, 1963.

Wagner, Arnold. *Legal Memorandum on Freedom of Assembly and Religion.* Personal communication, 1977.

Wasby, Stephen L., ed. *Civil Liberties.* Lexington, Mass: Lexington Books, 1976.

Westin, Alan F. *Privacy and Freedom.* New York: Atheneum, 1967.

Whitt, Hugh P., and Nelsen, Hart M. "Residence, Moral Traditionalism, and Tolerance of Atheists." *Social Forces* 54 (December 1975): 328–40.

Wilson, W. Cody. "Belief in Freedom of Speech and Press." *Journal of Social Issues* 31 (1975): 69–76.

Wortman, Tunis. "A Treatise Concerning Political Enquiry, and the Liberty of the Press." In *Freedom of Speech and Press in Early American History: Legacy of Suppression,* edited by Leonard Levy. New York: Harper & Row, 1963.

Worton, Stanley N. *Freedom of Assembly and Petition.* Rochelle Park, N.J.: Hayden, 1975a.

————. *Freedom of Religion.* Rochelle Park, N.J.: Hayden, 1975b.

————. *Freedom of Speech and Press.* Rochelle Park, N.J.: Hayden, 1975c.

Zalkind, Sheldon S., Gaugler, Edward A.; and Schwartz, Ronald M. "Civil Liberties Attitudes and Personality Measures: Some Exploratory Research." *Journal of Social Issues* 31 (Spring 1975): 77–91.

Zellman, Gail L. "Antidemocratic Beliefs: A Survey and Some Explanations." *Journal of Social Issues* 31 (Spring 1975): 31–54.

Court Cases

Abington School District v. Schempp, 374 U.S. 203 (1963)
Baggett v. Bullitt, 377 U.S. 360 (1964)
Bates v. City of Little Rock, 361 U.S. 516 (1960)
Boyd v. United States, 116 U.S. 616 (1886)
Brady v. Maryland, 373 U.S. 83 (1963)
Brown v. Louisiana, 383 U.S. 131 (1966)
Brown v. Mississippi, 297 U.S. 278 (1936)
Burstyn v. Wilson, 343 U.S. 495 (1952)
Butler v. Michigan, 352 U.S. 380 (1957)
Chaplinsky v. New Hampshire, 315 U.S. 568 (1942)
Cleveland Board of Education v. LaFleur, 414 U.S. 632 (1974)
Communist Party of Indiana v. Whitcomb, 414 U.S. 441 (1974)
Cox v. Louisiana, 379 U.S. 536 (1965)
Cox v. New Hampshire, 312 U.S. 569 (1941)
Dennis v. U.S., 341 U.S. 494 (1951)
Doe v. Bolton, 410 U.S. 179 (1973)
Doe v. Commonwealths Attorney, 403 F. Supp. 1199 (E.D. Va. 1975)
Dusky v. U.S., 362 U.S. 402 (1960)
Elfbrandt v. Russell, 384 U.S. 11 (1966)
Engel v. Vitale, 370 U.S. 421 (1962)
Epperson v. Arkansas, 393 U.S. 97 (1968)
Escobedo v. Illinois, 378 U.S. 478 (1964)
Everson v. Board of Education, 330 U.S. 1 (1947)
"Fanny Hill" v. Attorney General of Massachusetts, 383 U.S. 413 (1966)
Feiner v. New York, 340 U.S. 315 (1951)
Freeman v. Maryland, 380 U.S. 51 (1965)
Frontiero v. Richardson, 411 U.S. 677 (1973)
Gertz v. Robert Welch, Inc., 418 U.S. 323 (1974)
Gideon v. Wainright, 372 U.S. 335 (1963)
Ginzburg v. United States, 383 U.S. 463 (1966)
Gitlow v. New York, 268 U.S. 652 (1925)
Griswold v. Connecticut, 381 U.S. 479 (1965)
Hague v. CIO, 307 U.S. 496 (1939)
Healy v. James, 408 U.S. 169 (1972)
Illinois v. Allen, 397 U.S. 337 (1970)
In Re Winship, 397 U.S. 358 (1970)
James v. Board of Education, 461 F. 2d 566 (1972)
Katz v. United States, 389 U.S. 347 (1967)
Keyishian v. Board of Regents of the University of the State of New York, 385 U.S. 589 (1967)
Kingsley International Pictures Corporation v. Regents of University of the State of New York, 360 U.S. 684 (1959)
Kunz v. New York, 340 U.S. 290 (1951)
Lemon v. Kurtzman, 403 U.S. 602 (1971)

494

Index

NOTE: References to figures and tables are shown in italics.

Index

Index

"Fanny Hill" v. Attorney General of Massachusetts, 181
Federal Bureau of Investigation, 74, 173, 192, *285*, 441, 445
Federal Communications Commission, 462
Federalists, 38, 41
Feiner v. *New York*, 102–03
Fellman, David, 98
felons: rehabilitation of, 165, *166*; rights of, 142, 144–45, 432; *see also* criminals; prisoners
feminists, 123, 124; *see also* Equal Rights Amendment; women; women's movement
Festinger, Leon, 4
Fifteenth Amendment, 10
Fifth Amendment, 136, 137, 140, 142, 144, 157–58, 163, 171, 277, 458; *see also* self-incrimination
films (obscene or pornographic), 18, 58, 290–11; censorship of, 33, *89*, 182–83, 209, *210*, 211, *303*, 326–27, *392*, 400; CLS on, *207*, 209, *210*, *392*; court cases, 182–83, 209; nudity in, *201*, *210*; OVS on, *210*, *303*; prior censorship of, 182–83, 209, 211
First Amendment, 11, 16, 20, 32–92, 136, 171, 172, 174, 178, 180, 182, 183, 203, 240, 242, 311, 429; on assembly, 123; on conduct vs. speech, 93, 94; limitations to, 102, 115; on religion, 103, 104, 105, 105*n*, 106, 107, 134, 135; and symbolic speech, 113; *see also* specific issues
flag, 274; desecration and mockery of, 14, 21, 23–24, 33, 90, 96, 108, *109*, 112, 241, *246*, 262, *278*, 305, *307*, 323, 365, 428; salute of, 33, 96, 107, 108, *109*, 112, 172, 435
food stamps, 180
Ford, Gerald, 441
fornication, 177; *see also* sexual freedom
Founders, 22, 46, 134, 137, 138, 311, 447; *see also* specific names
Fourth Amendment, 144, 171, 174, 189, 195
Fourteenth Amendment, 33, 105*n*, 136, 137, 138
France, 9, 137, 139; *see also* French Revolution
Frankfurter, Felix, 182
Freeman v. *Maryland*, 183
freedom, 356; in abstract, 350; vs. control, 338, 346, 419, 431–32; difficulties in maintaining of, 13–24; early history of, 6–13; as human invention, 5–6; innate vs. artificial nature of, 3, 4, 13, 415; limitations to, 23, 269; OVS on, *78*; reci-procity of, 15–17; and social control, 20; as threat, 4–5; *see also* conventionality and conformity; psychological inflexibility; tolerance
freedom of assembly, 33, 34, 39, 95, 97–103, 274, 275, 299, 301, 314, 326–27, 342, 375; CLS on, 26, *118–19*, *120–21*, *124–25*, *287*, *300*, *307*, 395, 412, *413*; court cases, 100, 101–2; denial of, 100–1, *287*, *303*, *307*; for extremists, 111, *122*, 123, 125, 128; for homosexuals, 178; legal elite on, 126–27; OVS on, 26, *120–21*, *122–23*, *298*, *303*; surveys on, 116–28, 130; and violence, 99–100, 101, 102, 107, 116–17, 123, *125*, *279*, *307*
freedom of association, 34, 39, 88, 97–103, 171, 172, 241; CLS on, 26, *129*; in Constitution, 98; court cases, 98–99; for extremists, 128; for homosexuals, 178; legal elite on, *129*; OVS on, 26, 129; prior restraint of, 100; surveys on, 128–30
freedom of expression, 171, 241, 275, 314, 317, 327, 330–32, 336, 337, 347, 374, 437; CLS on, *282*, 286–87, 311, 390, *392*; vs. freedom of speech, 93–95; for homosexuals, 178; limits to, 80, 314; OVS on, 49, *52–53*, 54, 312–13; vs. privacy of others, 174–75; and symbolic speech, 96–97; *see also* civil disobedience; freedom of speech; symbolic speech
freedom of information, 241, 437
Freedom of Information Act, 192, 195
freedom of religion, 34, 88, 103–7, 130–35, 137, 274, 314, 326, 337–38, 375; CLS on, 26, *131*, *279*, *287*, *300*, *309*, 311, *358*, *361*; court cases, 104–7; denial of, *287*, *309*; exploitation of, 22, 23, 80, *279*, 280; OVS on, 26, *131*, *298*, *305*, 311–12, 314; for prisoners, 143; and separation of church and state, 103–4, 105, 106, *133*, 133–34, *305*, 312, 436–37; surveys on, 130–35; *see also* specific issues
freedom of speech, 20, 33, 34–35, 46, 48, 49–58, 97, 98, 107, 137, 241, 265, 268*n*, 272, 274–75, 299, 301, 305, 313–14, 317, 324, 326, 337–38, 342, 375, 432, 433, 477–78, 480; abstract vs. concrete, 76–77, 78–80, 81–83, 280, 281, 306, 314, 324; CLS on, 26, 49, *50–51*, *84*, *281*, *300*, *306*, *391*, *392*, 395, 412, *413*; for Communists, 74, 76, 77; vs. conduct, 93–95, 317; early history of, 37–42, 46–47; legal elite on, *52*, 86, *87*, 88–92, *89–90*, 126; mass public on, 49, *52–53*, 77, 78–79, 83–85, *84*; OVS on, 26, *52–53*, *56*, *298*, 302–03; PAB on, 49, *50–51*; vs. privacy, 195; in schools, 36–37, *302*, 310, 313; suppression of, 5, 11, 276,

502

Index

human frailty: intolerance of, 275, 320–21, 335, 338, *339*, 342, *343*, *344*, 346, 411
Humphrey, Hubert H., 441
Hyman, Herbert H., 76, 81

Idaho, 222
ideology: and civil liberties support, 255–65, 268, 273, 274, 276, 280, 284, 290, 293, 299, 314, 424, 428; CLS on, *256*, *257–58*, *263*, *264*, *279*, *285–89*, *296*, *300*, *306–09*, 311; OVS on, *259*, *278*, *290*, *291*, *292*, *298*, *302–04*, *311–12*
Illinois: court cases, 102, 139*n*, 140, 141, 142, 178, 182–83
Illinois v. *Allen*, 139*n*
Immerwahr, John, 67*n*
imprisonment, 137, 138; *see also* prisoners; trial
income-tax protesters, *110*, 423
indecent exposure, 177
independence, as American value, 113, 356, *357*, *359*, *360*
India: controlled press in, 8
Indiana: court case, 97*n*
indigents: rights of, 19, 179
individualism, as American value, 113, 115, 356, *357*, *359*
infidelity, 199, *201*
informers, 189, 191; *see also* police: surveillance of groups by
"intellectuality": and civil liberties support, 232–33, 373–74, *374*, 380
intellectuals, 180, 416
intelligence: and civil liberties support, 232, 336; *see also* education
intelligence agencies, 313, 402–03, 437; *see also* specific agencies
Intenal Revenue Service, 191, 192
International Press Institute, 7–8
Iowa: court case, 36, 96*n*
Israel, *125*, 444, *483*

Jackman, Robert W., 234, 234*n*, 235
Jackson, Henry, 441
Jackson, Robert H., 95, 96, 102, 108
James v. *Board of Education*, 96*n*
Japanese-Americans: internment of, 12
Jefferson, Thomas, 37, 38, 41–42, 46, 104, 105, 134, 242, 416, 417; Inauguration Address *(1800)*, 41
Jehovah's Witnesses, 95
Jennings, M. Kent, 398
Jewish Defense League, *124*, 444, *483*

Jews, 79, 80, *125*, 241, 260, 327, 444, *483*; civil liberties support by, 404, *405*; rights of Holocaust survivors, 18, 245, 430
John (king of England), 6
John Birch Society, 470
Jonestown mass suicides and executions, 22
Jordan, Wilbur Kitcher, 7
journalistic privilege, 21, 64–65, 66, *90*, 174, 175, 183, *184*, 423; *see also* freedom of the press
judicial abuses, 139
judicial procedure, 138–41, 146–47, 154, 157, *158*, 165, 167, *168–70*; technical violations of, 163–65, *164*, 242, 271, 428
judicial review, 143, 209
judiciary, 123, *see also* legal elite
juntas, 8
jury, jurors, 22, 139, 142, 144, *162*, 163, 167, *168*; *see also* trial

Kalven, Harry, 39*n*, 43, 46, 97, 112
Kennedy, Edward M., 441
Key, V. O., Jr., 233, 236, 237
Keyishian v. *New York*, 97*n*
Kingsley International Pictures Corporation v. *Regents of University of State of New York*, 182
Kiwanis, 469
Ku Klux Klan, 11, 24, 68, 69, 80, *89*, 99, 130, 262, 428, 433, 441, 456, *481*
Kunz v. *New York*, 95, 101
Kurland, Philip B., 39*n*, 43

labor unions, 34, 97
Latin America: terrorist acts in, 8
Latinos, 241; *see also* Chicanos
law: mockery of, 22
law and order, 165, 167–70, *168–70*, 275, 310, 317, 321, 422; *see also* community standards; police
lawbreaking: lawbreakers, 275, 310; *see also* civil disobedience; criminals; specific crimes
Lady Chatterley's Lover, 182
lawyers, *see* legal elite
League of Women Voters, 259, 470
Legal Aid Society, 469
legal elite (CLS), 25, 419; on academic freedom, 54–58, *55–56*; on censorship, 59; on civil disobedience, 110, 112, *115*, 115–16; on civil liberties issues, 243, 246, 247, *255*, 266–67, 268; on due pro-

Index

Index

U.S. Supreme Court *(continued)*
181, 182; on prayer in schools, 312, 454; on privacy, 185; on racially mixed marriages, 176; on religion, 104–7, 133, 135; on right to counsel, 141–42; on sexual discrimination, 221; on symbolic speech, 26
U.S. Treasury Department, 192
U.S. v. Cruikshank, 98
U.S. v. Edwards, 144

vagrancy, 177
Veterans of Foreign Wars, 469
Vietcong: American demonstrations in support of, 23
"Vietnam generation," 401–02
Vietnam War, 16, 73, 395, 401, 403; pro-Vietcong demonstrations, 23; student protests against, 36, 93, 96
violence, *see* freedom of assembly; revolutionaries; riots
Virginia: court cases, 176, 177
voluntary organizations, 26, 28; *see also* specific organizations
vote: right to, 10, 144, 280, *283,* 317, 436
Voting Rights Act of *1965,* 10

Wagner, Arnold, 100, 100*n*, 104, 105, 106, 107
Walker v. City of Birmingham, 101
Wallace, George, 441
war, 81, *345;* armbands as protest against, 36, 93, 96; right to demonstrate in favor of, 16, 18, 117, 123, *124, 344, 391,* 395
War of Independence, 10; *see also* American Revolution
Warren, Earl, 159, 182–83
wartime: civil liberties restrictions during, 12, 35, *153,* 154, *169*
Washington Post, 73; survey, *197*
Watergate break-in, 21
Weathermen, 436*n, see also* Students for a Democratic Society
Weber, Max, 411
Welch, Susan, 235
welfare, 137, 179, *219,* 265
welfare state, 274, 284, 315
Western Political Science Association, 474*n*

Westin, Alan F., 172; *see also* Harris, Louis, 96, 107
"white primary," 10
Whitney v. California, 94
Who's Who in America, 26, 251, 259
wife-beating, 175
Williams v. New York, 144
Wilson, W. Cody, "Belief in Freedom of Speech and Press," 77*n,* 132*n*
Winship, In Re, 139
wiretapping and electronic surveillance, 20, 21, 74, 171, 172, 174, 185, 187–89, 276, 329, 334, 423, 437; CLS on, *188;* Harris and Westin on, *188,* OVS on, *188,* 311; of organized crime, 187, 423
Wisconsin: court case, 107
witnesses: perjury by, 139; secret, *162,* 163
Wolff v. McDonnell, 143
women: rights of, 19, 21, *55,* 68, 81, *89,* 220–32, 284, 315, 327–28, 395, 436; and careers, 224–30; CLS on, *223, 225, 227, 229, 246, 272, 288, 328;* court cases, 221, 228; legal status of, 222; OVS on *223,* 228, *305,* 312; surveys on, 220–32, 412; *see also* abortion; affirmative action; related subjects
women's movement, 220–21, 260, 395, 402; militancy of, 222, *223,* 224; as part of "rights explosion," 220
work ethic, *198, 343*
World War II, 220, 465; internment of minorities during, 12
Wortman, Tunis, 40*n,* 40–41
Worton, Stanley N., 181, 183, 209
writers: on freedom of the press, 64

Yankelovich, Skelly & White surveys, *198, 201, 225; see also Time/*Yankelovich, Skelly & White surveys
Yates v. U.S., 45
YMCA, 470
YWCA, 470

Zeitgeist, 81, 398–99, 401, 402, 403; *see also* specific issues
Zellman, Gail L., 81
Zenger, John Peter, 37–38